Technical Communication for Readers and Writers

SECOND EDITION

Brenda R. Sims
University of North Texas

Houghton Mifflin Company   Boston   New York

▶ **To my parents, to Patrick, and especially to Bill**

Editor in Chief: Patricia A. Coryell
Sponsoring Editor: Michael Gillespie
Editorial Associate: Bruce Cantley
Senior Project Editor: Tracy Patruno
Senior Manufacturing Coordinator: Marie Barnes
Marketing Manager: Cindy Graff Cohen
Marketing Assistant: Sarah Donelson

Cover photograph: © Tony Stone Imaging

Printed in the U.S.A.

Library of Congress Control Number: 2001133346

ISBN: 0-618-22173-5

1 2 3 4 5 6 7 8 9-DOC-06 05 04 03 02

BRIEF CONTENTS

CONTENTS

PART III

Producing Effective Documents and Presentations for Your Audience

PART IV

Using the Writer's Tools to Correspond with Your Readers

Appendixes

- **Expanded annotations** in the sample documents highlight how the writers have applied the principles and tools presented in the chapters.

New Chapters to Reflect the Changing Workplace

The second edition has three new chapters. These chapters reflect a wider range of the types of documents and presentations that students may produce in the workplace.

- **Chapter 13, "Writing Reader-Oriented Informal Reports,"** presents principles for writing informal reports. The chapter focuses on four commonly written informal reports: progress reports, meeting minutes, field and lab reports, and trip reports. The chapter includes annotated examples of each type of informal report and tip boxes for writing each type of informal report. It also includes charts showing the conventional elements for each report and the questions that readers may ask while reading each element.

- **Chapter 16, "Creating User-Oriented Web Sites,"** presents students with a process for creating user-oriented Web sites. This chapter helps students to focus on designing text, visual aids, and navigational elements to meet the needs of the users and to fulfill the writer's intended purpose. The chapter includes sample Web pages with annotations on how the writers applied the principles and tools presented in the chapter. The chapter gives students advice about designing Web sites for users with disabilities and for global users. It also presents information on copyright and legal issues related to Web sites.

- **Chapter 17, "Creating and Delivering Oral Presentations,"** presents students with principles for planning, rehearsing, and presenting effective oral presentations. The chapter focuses on extemporaneous and scripted presentations and gives students specific advice about the types of media that they can use for presenting visual aids.

Expanded Information to Better Reflect Technical Communication Today

This second edition includes expanded information that reflects the ever-changing world of technical communication and the environment and tools of the workplace.

- **Ethics.** Chapter 3, "Facing Ethical and Legal Challenges," now includes a more in-depth approach to understanding ethics in the workplace. The chapter presents principles that students can apply to ensure that their technical documents are ethical and that the language they use is ethical.

Appendixes

This book has two appendixes. Appendix A, "Documenting Your Sources," presents information on citing sources using APA and MLA style. Appendix B, "Review of Common Sentence Errors, Punctuation, and Mechanics," provides a convenient, brief handbook.

▶ Features to Enhance Learning

Technical Communication for Readers and Writers offers students five recurring features that enhance student learning:

- **Worksheets** at the end of each chapter provide a checklist that students can use as they apply the principles presented in each chapter.

- **Tips** boxes in every chapter summarize key information that students need to create effective documents or to think about critical issues such as ethics. Visually distinguished from the rest of the text and indexed on the inside front cover, students will find it easy to retrieve this information when working on their own assignments.

- **"Taking It into the Workplace"** boxes present up-to-date research in technical communication from the vantage point of the workplace professional. These boxes include quotes from workplace professionals and technical communication scholars, as well as an assignment that requires students to learn about communicating and writing in the workplace.

- **"The Reader's Corner"** boxes present anecdotal information about technical communication—past, present, and future—and suggestions for students to follow when writing.

- **Case studies** at the end of most chapters give students the opportunity to apply the principles of a particular chapter in extended workplace scenarios. Several of the case studies give students the opportunity to practice collaborative writing.

New Design Elements to Make Learning Easier

The second edition's new design makes the book easier for instructors and students to use. The new design models the principles of effective technical communication:

- **Full-color design** uses color for a purpose—not merely as decoration. The color presents information clearly and easily and shows accurate design elements in screen shots, Web pages, and color-printed documents.

- **Marginal comments** direct students to related information in the text or to additional information on the Web.

Part II: Knowing the Tools of the Writer

Part II presents principles students need to create effective, reader-oriented documents. In Chapter 5, "Researching Information Using Primary and Secondary Sources," students learn strategies for formulating research questions and exploring and evaluating primary and secondary sources—including electronic resources. Chapter 6, "Organizing Information for Your Readers," presents techniques for structuring documents that readers can understand and use. In Chapter 7, "Writing Reader-Oriented Sentences and Paragraphs," and Chapter 8, "Using Reader-Oriented Language," students learn and practice style principles at the sentence, paragraph, and word levels. These principles provide students with strategies they can use to write clear, concise, reader-oriented documents. Chapter 9, "Designing Documents for Your Readers," and Chapter 10, "Creating Effective Visual Aids for Your Readers," demonstrate the rhetorical implications of document design and visual aids. These chapters give students "how-to" information that they can easily apply to their own documents and information. Finally, Chapter 11, "Preparing Front and Back Matter," shows students how to prepare the elements required for longer, more formal documents—elements such as covers, title pages, tables of contents, and appendixes.

Part III: Producing Effective Documents and Presentations for Your Audience

Part III applies earlier principles and tools to planning and producing various types of technical documents and presentations. Students learn to apply these principles and tools to proposals (Chapter 12), informal reports (Chapter 13), formal reports (Chapter 14), instructions and manuals (Chapter 15), Web sites (Chapter 16), and oral presentations (Chapter 17). Students examine sample documents written by other students and workplace professionals. These documents include annotations that point out how the documents demonstrate the principles presented in the chapters.

Part IV: Using the Writer's Tools to Correspond with Your Readers

Part IV applies the text's principles and tools to letters, memos, e-mail, and job correspondence. In Chapter 18, "Writing Reader-Oriented Letters, Memos, and E-Mail," students learn rhetorical strategies, principles, and formats for writing correspondence that conveys what they intend and that meets the needs of the readers. In Chapter 19, "Writing Reader-Oriented Job Correspondence," students learn strategies for looking for jobs and for writing résumés, letters of application, and follow-up letters. This chapter also guides students through the electronic job search, including how to effectively use online job boards and how to create electronic and scannable résumés.

PREFACE

Technical Communication for Readers and Writers, Second Edition, has two goals: to prepare students for the many writing tasks they will encounter in the workplace and to provide technical communication instructors with a flexible, comprehensive teaching tool. Beneath these two goals lies the foundation of this book—the belief that writing is more than simply putting words on paper or a computer screen and that students learn best to write by understanding their readers and by writing and revising. This book, therefore, contains samples of student and workplace writing and exercises by which students can apply the principles of technical communication.

Technical communication goes far beyond reporting facts. Technical communication is a series of deliberate problem-solving activities—activities that require critical thinking. Before writers can effectively put words on a computer screen or report facts, they must understand why they are writing, who is reading, and why the readers are reading. Without this information, a document will most likely fail to achieve its desired purpose. When writers understand their purpose and their readers, they can communicate more effectively.

Technical Communication for Readers and Writers presents principles designed to give students the tools and practice they need to respond effectively to varied writing situations. With these principles, students can determine the organization, layout, and content that will best meet the needs of readers.

▶Overview of the Second Edition

In addition to a brief introduction to technical communication in Chapter 1, *Technical Communication for Readers and Writers* contains four major sections and two appendixes.

Part I: Understanding the Role of the Writer

Part I helps students to understand their roles as writers in the workplace. In Chapter 2, "Understanding and Writing for Your Readers," students learn principles for examining workplace writing from several vantage points: that of the writer, the readers, and the workplace. In Chapter 3, "Facing Ethical and Legal Challenges," students learn to consider the ethical dimensions of their communications. In Chapter 4, "Collaborating and the Writing Process," students see how to adapt to the interpersonal challenges and opportunities of collaborative writing. This chapter also suggests ways for students to use electronic media to facilitate collaborative writing.

- **Researching tools.** Chapter 5, "Researching Information Using Primary and Secondary Sources," includes new and updated information on using the primary research tools of interviews and questionnaires. It also includes a greatly expanded section on using electronic resources, particularly the Web, for gathering information. The chapter includes important tips boxes and charts on using search engines and various electronic resources. Using screen shots of Web searches, the chapter focuses on how to effectively use electronic resources to gather information. The chapter ends with a section on helping students evaluate online resources.

- **Formal reports.** Chapter 14, "Writing Reader-Oriented Formal Reports," now gives students a plan for preparing the formal report. This plan focuses on drawing valid conclusions and making recommendations.

- **Electronic job search.** Chapter 19, "Writing Reader-Oriented Job Correspondence," now includes tips for using Internet job boards. The chapter also gives students information on preparing electronic and scannable résumés. This new information provides students with the tools they need to conduct an electronic job search.

- **Documentation styles.** Appendix A includes expanded information on APA and MLA documentation styles. The sections on both styles include models for citing electronic sources.

▶Ancillaries for Students and Instructors

The following ancillaries accompany *Technical Communication for Readers and Writers*:

- **A companion Web site,** which includes resources for students and for instructors. Student resources include online quizzes that reinforce the principles described in each chapter, additional sample documents, and additional case studies and exercises to give students more opportunities to apply what they have learned. Instructor resources include the complete instructor's resource manual that instructors can print, PowerPoint slide presentations to accompany each chapter, and links to additional resources.

- **Instructor's Resource Manual,** which includes guidelines for teaching technical communication, transparency masters, and quizzes.

▶Acknowledgments

The second edition of *Technical Communication for Readers and Writers* has benefited greatly from the insights and suggestions of many colleagues and instructors. I would like to personally thank the following reviewers who have enriched this book with their ideas and enthusiasm: **Thomas Barker,** Texas Tech University; **Ernest Hakanen,** Drexel University; **Penny L. Hirsch,** Northwestern University; **Rebecca Kamm,** Northeast Iowa Community College; **Charles Naccarato,** Ohio University; **C. M. Shehadeh,** Florida Institute of Technology; **Richard Shrubb,** Milwaukee School of Engineering; **Katherine Staples,** Austin Community College; and **John R. Williamson,** University of Kentucky.

Thoughtful reviewers of the first edition include: **Rita J. Bova,** Columbus State University; **Norbert Elliot,** Institute of Technology, Newark, New Jersey; **Joanna Freeman,** Pittsburgh State University; **Peter H. Goodrich,** Northern Michigan University; **D'Wayne Hodgin,** University of Idaho; **Johndan Johnson-Eilola,** Purdue University; **Dan Jones,** University of Central Florida; **Rebecca Kamm,** Northeast Iowa Community College; **Olivia Mason,** Milwaukee School of Engineering; **Mary Massirer,** Baylor University; **Carolyn R. Miller,** North Carolina State University; **Ronald J. Nelson,** James Madison University; **Fiore Pugliano,** University of Pittsburgh; **Mark E. Rollins,** Ohio University; **Scott P. Sanders,** University of New Mexico; **Patrick M. Scanlon,** Rochester Institute of Technology; **Charles R. Stratton,** University of Idaho; **Eva M. Thury,** Drexel University; and **Nirmala Varmha,** Oklahoma City College.

I have also worked with an excellent—and friendly—team at Houghton Mifflin: Bruce Cantley, Tracy Patruno, Cindy Graff Cohen, and Sarah Donelson. They have guided my hand, encouraged me, and shown extraordinary patience. I would especially like to thank my editor, Michael Gillespie, for patiently and intelligently guiding me through this process. Thanks, Michael, for your advice.

At the University of North Texas, I have had the privilege to work with talented graduate students and faculty members who have provided a creative, innovative workplace. Under the supervision of Robert "Bob" Congrove, my technical writing lab staff have patiently and cheerfully answered my questions and solved technical problems. I want to thank all of you.

Most of all, I want to thank my husband, Bill, and my son, Patrick, for their patience, guidance, and—always valued—ideas.

▶ I'd Enjoy Hearing from You

If you have any comments or suggestions for improving this book, I'd enjoy hearing them. Please contact me at the Department of English at the University of North Texas, Denton, TX 76203. My phone numbers are (940) 565-2115 and (940) 565-2050, and my e-mail is sims@unt.edu. I look forward to hearing from you.

Brenda R. Sims

Technical Communication for Readers and Writers

Technical Communication
for Readers and Writers

1

Writing, the Workplace, and This Book

As you begin reading this book, you may be asking: "Why should I take a technical communication course? I came to college to learn about my major, not writing." Indeed, many of you reading this book probably came to college to study engineering, computer science, biology, chemistry, or other technical fields. You probably didn't come to college solely to learn to write. However, in any of these fields, you will communicate your ideas and your progress to your managers, your clients, or your peers primarily through writing. As a professional, you may communicate by writing at the beginning of a project, during a project, and perhaps at the end of a project. You may write during every phase of a project.

Let's consider a mechanical engineer, Ernie Chavez, who works as a piping specialist for an electrical generating company. Ernie spends an average of 40 percent of his time writing. He begins most of his piping analysis projects with a written proposal to a plant manager. If the manager approves the project, Ernie reports his progress and possible changes in written progress reports to the plant manager. Ernie usually closes a project with a final report of his work and the cost of the completed project. Like you, Ernie went to college not to learn to write but to learn his profession; yet writing, he now realizes, is vital to succeeding as a professional engineer.

Let's also consider Jennifer Nowakowski, a computer programmer in the research and development division of a company specializing in software applications for the hotel and restaurant industries. Jennifer and her team have developed a prototype of a software application for inventorying food and supplies in restaurants. Before they can test the prototype, they write a proposal for company executives, introducing the prototype and asking for the funds they need to test it. If they write persuasively, the proposal may convince the executives to fund the test.

In this chapter, you will learn why writing is important to your career and how your workplace may affect your writing. You also will learn how this book will help you prepare to write in your career.

▶How Will Writing Impact Your Career?

Like Ernie and Jennifer, you will have to communicate your ideas effectively to perform your job and succeed in your career. You can't assume that others will see your work and approve it. Instead, you must effectively communicate your work, ideas, and progress to those with the power to implement your ideas or those who supervise you (Barabas). The better able you are to communicate your ideas and your work, the better is your chance of receiving rewards for your ideas and work. Your managers may even evaluate you indirectly and possibly directly on how well you communicate in writing. Your writing skills can even help you to receive promotions (Barnum and Fischer).

If you are like the typical college graduate, writing will fill about 20 to 60 percent of your time as a professional (University of Maryland). For professionals in technical fields, writing will fill at least 40 percent of your time at work (University of Maryland). Most organizations use e-mail and the Web instead of voice communication and other traditional media (Halpern; Perry; Perry and Adam). This percentage also may rise as more organizations trim their work force and professionals follow their written documents through to the production stage rather than relying on clerical staff (Dautermann). Instead of sketching out only a handwritten or printed draft of a document or correspondence for a secretary or administrative assistant, most professionals, especially entry-level employees, now prepare final or nearly final drafts of documents without the aid of clerical staff.

As a professional, you not only will spend much of your time writing; but you will also need to write effectively to succeed in your career. Surveys tell us that 94 percent of college graduates believe that writing well is important for success in their workplace—42 percent believe it is of great importance (Anderson). Although writing well does not solely lead to success in the workplace, it is an important factor. You may find that you can enhance your reputation with your managers, your peers, and your organization through your writing. In a labor force filled with mediocre writers, a professional who writes effectively will stand out and succeed (Hansen and Hansen).

Whether you are writing to propose a new idea to your manager or to record a project's history for the permanent files, clear writing gives you visibility and credibility with your manager, your peers, and, ultimately, your organization. Poor writing, too, gives you visibility—but without credibility. If you write poorly, others may have difficulty understanding your ideas, and your ideas and your work may fail to receive the recognition they deserve.

▶How Does the Workplace Affect What and How You Write?

Several workplace factors will affect you and your writing tasks. These factors include

- Your organization's and your manager's expectations
- Your readers' expectations
- Time and budget limitations
- Ethical considerations
- Collaborative writing

Expectations of Your Organization and Manager

When you become a professional, your organization and your manager may have certain expectations about your documents. They may state or write their expectations explicitly, or they may imply their expectations. Your

THE READER'S CORNER

Are You Ready to Be an Information Broker?

 In the post-industrial age, information is becoming the primary product for many companies. Companies still manufacture and purchase products, but many companies deal primarily in information (Johnson-Eilola 245). For example, traditionally hardware drove the computer industry; software and technical assistance were clearly secondary. Now, software companies, such as Microsoft, drive the computer hardware industry. With this shift to an information-driven age, we will see a new class of service work intertwined with information. Former U.S. Secretary of Labor Robert B. Reich suggests three new classes of this work:

- Routine production: These workers perform repetitive tasks. They might be line managers or clerical supervisors—those who repetitively oversee subordinates' work and ensure that workers follow standard operating procedures (Reich 174).
- In-person service workers: These workers perform the tasks of routine production combined with the ability to work with people. Reich says these workers must be "courteous and helpful, even to the most obnoxious of patrons" (176).
- Symbolic-analytic: These workers identify, rearrange, distribute, abstract, and "broker" information. Their tools are information and symbols, and their products are "reports, plans, and proposals" (Johnson-Eilola 255). Symbolic-analytic workers might be research scientists, engineers, computer programmers, strategic planners, architects, lawyers, or other information brokers.

Post-industrial work inverts the traditional relationship between product and product knowledge: Knowledge and information have attained "primary value" (Johnson-Eilola 256). The more valued workers in this environment will be able to manipulate, revise, and rearrange information (Johnson-Eilola 256): They will be information brokers.

organization or manager may expect the format, organization, or style of a document to meet certain criteria or established guidelines; or a manager may have certain preferences about format and style. For example, many organizations have a standard format for progress or status reports; some even have forms. Some organizations have a standard cover page and a standard layout for letters and memos. Many organizations also have a style sheet that dictates style and grammar rules that the organization expects you to follow when writing documents for internal readers or for readers outside the organization. Find out whether your organization or manager has specific expectations about style and layout, and then meet those expectations to the best of your ability.

This book suggests some general formats and guidelines for many workplace documents. If your organization or manager does not have implicit written guidelines, you can use the example documents and the style guidelines presented here. The examples and style guidelines given in this book will help you to become familiar with the types of documents and style that you may encounter in the workplace. To supplement these examples and guidelines, once you begin your career you can gather samples of effective documents written by your coworkers and then use those documents as models. Your organization and your manager will appreciate that you are trying to create documents that fit with other documents the company produces—that you are being a team player.

Expectations of Your Readers

As a student, you generally know your reader—your instructor—and what he or she expects. In the workplace, however, you may or may not know your readers. They may be your manager or your peers. They may be company executives whom you've never met. They may be clients or potential customers. You may never meet your readers.

The readers for many of your documents may be more than one person or group, and each individual or group may have different expectations of your documents. Your readers may include men and women who live and work in countries and cultures other than yours. Their expectations of you and your document may differ from the expectations of those who work in your own country. As a professional, you will want to account for these differences to write effective, successful documents.

This book will help you learn how to determine what your readers expect and then how to meet those expectations. It also will help you begin to consider what international readers will expect from your documents and then how to write for these readers.

Time and Budget Limitations

As in college, the workplace will limit the amount of time you can spend on writing documents. Your manager and your organization will expect you to write quickly and efficiently. They will expect you to finish documents on time and within the budget. Deadlines and budget limitations may force you to spend extra hours at work or to submit a document before you are ready. For example, your manager may ask you to write the documentation for a new software application that your company is marketing. He or she may require you to have the document ready for user testing within a month even though you normally would need two months. Time and budget limitations may also affect your writing. You may have to adapt an idea or a document to meet budget requirements. Every professional must contend with time and budget limitations; but, like other successful professionals in your field, you can learn to write effective documents despite these constraints. This book suggests ways to streamline your writing process, to prioritize format and design decisions, and to use online resources to help you submit documents on time and within the budget.

Ethical Considerations

As a professional, you may face ethical considerations about the language or the information that you or your coworkers use in workplace documents. For example, how will you report the results of tests on a new airbag design when the testing shows some serious design flaws and redesigning the airbag would delay the production of a new car model? The language you use could affect how your readers perceive the design problem and ultimately how they decide to act. The language you choose could force the company to spend thousands of dollars correcting the design flaws. Your decision could also cause the company to lose sales to a competitor or to install the flawed airbag in automobiles—possibly endangering consumers.

As a professional, you may face similar ethical predicaments. This book will help you to analyze the ethical implications of the language you select for your writing and to understand how language can affect readers' perceptions. It will also give you four ethical frameworks that you can use when facing ethical challenges in the workplace.

Collaborative Writing

When writing in the workplace, you frequently will work with others to produce a document. In fact, 87 percent of the college graduates surveyed by Lisa Ede and Andrea Lunsford said that they sometimes collaborated with others to produce documents (60). In conversations with professionals in various fields, I discovered that they collaborate on most of the documents they write—except short letters, memos, and e-mail. They reported collaborating in these ways:

- Planning a document with others, either in their organization or outside their organization
- Coauthoring or writing as part of a team
- Reviewing and revising documents

Planning Documents with Others

Before a large writing project, most organizations create a team to determine the document's purpose, readers, schedule, and organization. The team may contain only writers; however, in most cases, the team consists of members from different areas of the organization. An organization might select team members according to the function they will perform in the production of the document; the team might have a subject-matter expert, a writer, a graphics expert, and an editor. The organization might select team members according to their knowledge of the product, including members from engineering, computer programming, manufacturing, marketing, or other technical areas.

Collaborative planning can help team members identify global issues early in the document cycle. They can answer important questions about these issues before writing begins. In these planning sessions, team members establish a schedule for producing the document and agree about areas of responsibility. Once the team has planned the document, set the schedule, and assigned areas of responsibility, one or more persons may actually write the document. In some collaborative situations, the team may plan the document but only one person actually writes (Raign and Sims).

Coauthoring or Writing as Part of a Team

In some organizations and writing situations, several people write a document. These people collaborate in one of two ways:

- Each person is responsible for writing a particular section of the document, and then usually one team member serves as a final editor (Raign and Sims).
- Team members write the document together—word by word.

Most teams find the first method of collaborating is more efficient. Regardless of the method, the more successful teams decide on the style, design, and tone of the document early in the writing process.

Reviewing and Revising Documents Collaboratively

Even if you don't work as part of a team to write a document, you probably will collaborate with others when reviewing and revising most documents. You may even collaborate with others by reviewing their documents— documents that you didn't help plan or write. The review can be a formal process in which the writers and other interested parties meet to review the document—often suggesting revisions. These people may meet more than once before formally approving the document. Even if you are not writing as part of a team, you may take part in a formal review of your documents. William Sims, a mechanical engineer, reports that newly hired and unlicensed engineers write under the signature of a licensed engineer; so a senior or licensed engineer must review many documents. Collaboration in this instance does not involve the teamwork mentioned earlier; instead, collaboration takes place at the reviewing or revising stage rather than at the planning or drafting stage.

The review process may be informal. When it is, coauthors and interested parties receive a copy of a document to review. Often, these reviewers make comments and suggestions through e-mail or in a shared file accessible to all reviewers. The authors then use this file for revising. This book will help you to develop techniques for successfully collaborating with others to create effective documents.

▶What Makes Technical Communication Effective?

Technical communication is effective when it successfully conveys your intended message and meets the needs and expectations of your readers. You can best convey your message and meet the needs of your readers when your technical communication has the following characteristics:

- Addresses specific readers
- Uses a clear, concise style
- Uses a professional, accessible design
- Includes complete, accurate information
- Follows the conventions of grammar, punctuation, spelling, and usage

Addresses Specific Readers

Your technical documents can accomplish their purpose only when they

- Meet the needs and expectations of your intended readers
- Convey your intended message in terms that the readers will understand

▶ In Chapter 2, you will learn ways to help you identify your readers so you can meet their needs and expectations (see page 17).

Before you can write documents that will succeed, you will need to identify your readers. This task may be easy when you know your readers. For example, if you are writing instructions for creating a Web page for your coworkers, you will know (or can easily find out) what they know about the task. You can find out if they are familiar with the software you will be using to create the Web page, if they have used the Web, and so on. You can then determine how much detail to include and how to best structure the instructions. However, if you are writing the same instructions for a group of consumers, you will not know the readers. You may not know if they have used the Web or if they have used the software for creating Web pages. In this situation, you can create a profile of your readers. With this profile, you can determine the appropriate level of detail to include.

Uses a Clear, Concise Style

To convey your intended message, your technical documents must be clear. For readers to use your technical documents, the writing must also be concise. Let's look at an example from some instructions to contractors working with electrical transformers:

> The transformers are configured such that operating personnel are exposed to live 12.47kv when any of the enclosure doors are opened.

This instruction doesn't work because it isn't clear or concise; the writer could have more effectively written:

> Danger: To avoid being exposed to live 12.47kv, keep all enclosure doors closed.

TAKING IT INTO THE WORKPLACE

Visiting with a Professional in Your Field

"Writing in the workplace is always situated in a context. . . . Both the organization as a whole and subunits within the organization can affect nearly every aspect of writing."
—Susan Kleimann, Senior Instructional Systems Specialist for the U.S. General Accounting Office (67)

You can best learn about how writing will impact your career by talking with professionals in your current field of study. To help you learn more about writing in your field, locate a professional working in your major field of study. For example, if your major field is computer science, find a computer programmer or systems analyst. If your field is building construction, find a professional who is a project manager for a construction project. You might contact these professionals in person, by telephone, or by e-mail.

Assignment
Once you have located a professional, set up an interview to discuss how these professionals write

and use writing as part of their work. If you aren't able to interview a professional in person, you might suggest a telephone or online interview. At the interview, ask the professional to discuss the following:

- The types of writing that he or she does at work, including the types of documents that he or she writes
- The steps he or she takes when writing a document
- How time and budget limitations affect his or her writing
- The amount of time he or she spends writing
- How and when he or she revises and edits their documents

You may also develop some questions of your own. You may want to ask him or her to give you some samples of documents that he or she writes. After the interview,

- Write a memo to your classmates about what you learned
- Send this memo to your instructor and to your classmates by way of e-mail

---

When technical communication isn't clear and concise,

▶ In Chapters 3, 7, and 8, you will learn to write clear, concise, ethical documents.

- **It can be dangerous.** The original instruction to the contractors does not tell the operators to keep the doors closed. If one of the operators opened the doors, he or she could be severely burned—or, even worse, killed.
- **It can be unethical.** When technical communication is unethical, readers can get hurt and you and your organization can face serious legal charges.
- **It can be expensive.** When technical communication isn't clear and concise, either the writer or the reader spends unnecessary company time; and in the corporate world, time is money. For example, Melissa Brown, a manager of documentation for a marketing company, reports that by including a concise tips supplement in software documentation her

company could reduce the number of calls to technical support (Blain and Lincoln). With the average cost of a call to customer support at $20, her company could substantially save money simply by including these tips sections (Redish 1995).

Uses a Professional, Accessible Design

▶ In Chapter 9, "Designing Documents for Your Readers," you will learn how to design professional documents.

You can use design to make your documents more effective and to achieve your intended purpose. An effectively designed document will do the following:

- **Help readers to locate information and to understand how the writer has organized the document.** For example, in this book you can distinguish the case studies from the exercises so you can easily see where a case study begins. Effectively designed instructions can help readers separate one step from another, so the readers don't skip a step when completing an important task.

- **Represent you and your organization in a professional manner.** When a technical document has an attractive, professional design, readers are more likely to read it. An attractive, professional design can create a positive impression of you, your product, your ideas, and your organization. A sloppy, unprofessional design, likewise, can negatively impress your readers. A professional design can help you to achieve the intended purpose of your document.

Includes Complete, Accurate Information

Even when the design is effective and the language is clear and concise, a technical document can only succeed if the information included is complete and accurate. A successful technical document gives readers all the information they need to understand the problem, to perform the required task, to understand an unfamiliar topic, or to make a decision. When you present complete information, readers have all the information they need to act safely and correctly. You will best know what information to include and not include in your technical documents when you identify and create a profile of your readers. Successful writers don't assume what the reader knows, they find out what the reader knows. Then they can include complete information to help the reader act on the information in the document.

Effective technical documents also give readers accurate information. If your technical document gives readers inaccurate information, you may merely confuse or annoy your readers. However, inaccurate information can be expensive or dangerous. For example, an executive with a U.S. construction company didn't proofread a contract before it was signed. In the contract, the company agreed to complete a project for $200,000 instead of $2,000,000.

The contract writer simply left out a zero. Although the company was able to amend the contract, the company unnecessarily spent thousands of dollars in legal fees and lost much good will with its client.

Follows the Conventions of Grammar, Punctuation, Spelling, and Usage

Effective technical communication follows the conventions of grammar, punctuation, spelling, and usage. When your technical documents—and even your correspondence—don't follow these conventions, readers may misread your communication. Also, when you don't follow these conventions you are sending negative, unprofessional signals to your readers. For example, if you send an e-mail filled with spelling and punctuation errors to a potential client, he or she may assume that you and your organization do sloppy work and then may question whether the technical information is accurate. These errors may also cause readers to focus on your writing rather than on the information you are trying to convey. These same errors may cost you promotions, as your managers may evaluate you on your ability to communicate. In a survey of 402 companies, executives identified writing as the most valued skill in an employee (Hansen and Hansen). Although following the conventions of correctness isn't all that makes up good writing, many managers will evaluate your writing on its correctness.

▶What's Ahead in This Book?

Technical Communication for Readers and Writers will help you to write effectively as a professional. Part I explains your role as a writer in the workplace and introduces some issues that you may face as a technical professional. The chapters in Part I focus on

- Understanding how to analyze and write for readers
- Facing ethical challenges
- Understanding how to collaborate effectively

Part II discusses the "tools" that a writer needs to create effective technical documents. You may have learned how to use some of these tools in other writing courses; some, however, may be new to you. In Part II you will learn about tools for the following tasks:

- Researching information using primary and secondary sources
- Organizing information for your readers
- Writing reader-oriented sentences and paragraphs
- Using reader-oriented language
- Designing reader-oriented pages and documents

- Creating effective visual aids
- Preparing front and end matter

Once you understand the role of the writer and have the tools you need to write effectively, you can begin creating specific technical documents and presentations. In Part III you will learn about the types of documents that you are likely to write in the workplace. You will learn about writing

- Proposals
- Informal reports
- Formal reports
- Instructions and manuals
- Web sites

You will also learn how to deliver effective oral presentations.

In Part IV you will learn how to write effective correspondence. Part IV has two chapters. One presents specific guidelines for writing effective letters, memos, and e-mail. The other explains how to write effective job-hunting correspondence—specifically, résumés, letters of application, and follow-up letters. This chapter also suggests some techniques for conducting an electronic job search and creating electronic and scannable résumés.

Throughout this book, you will see three features:

- **Tips boxes** summarize critical information that will help you to apply the principles presented in the chapter. A list of these boxes appears on the inside of the front cover.
- **"Taking It into the Workplace" boxes** present up-to-date research in technical communication from the vantage point of the workplace professional. These boxes include quotes from workplace professionals and technical communication scholars. Each box includes an assignment where you will learn about communicating and writing in the workplace.
- **"The Reader's Corner" boxes** present anecdotal information about technical communication—past, present, and future—and suggestions for you to follow when writing.

Along with these topics, the book includes examples of student and professional writing. It also includes exercises that will let you practice and improve your writing and editing skills, including some exercises where you will work with a team.

I Understanding the Role of the Writer

2

Understanding and Writing for Your Readers

▶ **OUTLINE**

n Office 1997, Microsoft introduced Clippy (see Figure 2.1). If you use Microsoft Word, you may have seen Clippy—an animated cartoon character with large, winking eyes. Clippy acts as the software user's link to the online help system. Clippy is operated by a type of software called a wizard. Wizards help readers complete various tasks by asking questions. Originally, Clippy offered online help to the user without being asked. Clippy would appear on the screen and ask, "What would you like to do?" Many users of Office 1997 found Clippy annoying. One user complained that "it pops up without warning—even when you don't want it or don't need it" (quoted in Shroyer 238). Another user explained that Clippy "wouldn't be so obnoxious if you could control it. As is, it moves all over the place and gets in the way" (quoted in Shroyer 238). Because so many users reacted negatively to Clippy, *PC World* published articles telling users how to turn off Clippy (Li-Ron). In October 1998, Microsoft gave customers the code to remove Clippy from the systems (Shroyer).

So what went wrong? Why did the users reject Clippy? The users rejected Clippy, in part, because the software designers assumed that the users couldn't work without supervision. In reality, the users found Clippy's help intrusive— the users knew what they were doing, and if they didn't they would ask for help (Shroyer). The software designers assumed that all users knew less than they did and that all users would welcome help from Clippy. These designers' misguided assumptions frustrated many users.

The software designers at Microsoft learned from their users; in Office 2000, Clippy is more user friendly. Clippy sits in one corner of the screen, and the user can turn off Clippy by simply clicking. Like the designers of Clippy in Office 2000, you will want to anticipate how your readers are likely to respond to a document, even to particular words you use. You will want to find out what your readers know about the subject of your document and predict how they will respond to you, to your organization, and to the document.

Figure 2.1

Microsoft's Clippy

Source: Reprinted by permission of Microsoft Corporation.

This information about your readers will influence all aspects of a document—its purpose, organization, design, tone, visual aids, and content. This chapter presents four principles to help you determine the purpose of your documents and to develop a profile of your readers.

▶Principle 1: Determine Your Purpose for Writing

Before you begin writing, think about why you are writing and what you want the document to accomplish. For example, Randy, a mechanical engineer, is writing a feasibility report about repairing a turbine that has been vibrating excessively. The vibration is damaging surrounding equipment and reducing productivity. The purpose of Randy's report is to present three options for repairing the turbine and then to persuade the plant manager and the home office to choose the third option, a million-dollar plan to perform a high-speed balance of the turbine rotor. The first option is to operate the turbine in its current condition and to minimize the vibration damage by increasing the overhaul frequency of the affected equipment. This option will increase maintenance costs and will not permanently solve the problem. The second option is to limit the turbine load to reduce the damage from vibration. This option will cause the company to lose revenue.

Randy will send his report to the home office and to his supervisor. Randy has worked in the home office but has recently been promoted and transferred to the plant where the vibrating turbine is located. He wants to favorably impress his superiors at the home office and his coworkers at the plant. He also wants to establish a good working relationship with his readers and show them that he is capable of solving problems in a timely, reasonable manner. Figure 2.2 shows Randy's summary of this purpose.

You will face writing situations where you will have to ask similar questions to determine the purpose of a document. For some documents, the purpose will be clear from the beginning; but for other documents, the purpose will be apparent only after you have asked questions about your readers and about

▼ **Figure 2.2**

The Purpose of
Randy's Report

The Purpose of My Document

- **What is the purpose of the document?**
  To present three options for repairing the turbine and to persuade readers to fund the third option: performing a high-speed balance of the turbine rotor at a cost of $1 million.

- **Does this document have a long-term goal? If so, what is that goal?**
  To convince the home office and the plant manager that I can solve problems and that I am capable of doing my new job; to establish a good working relationship with the plant manager and with the home office.

the writing situation. Sometimes, the purpose that you identified at the beginning of the writing process changes as you gather information about readers' needs. When this situation happens, you may discover that the document has a long-term goal—such as maintaining the goodwill of the reader or establishing a positive working relationship.

▶Principle 2: Identify Your Readers

As you determine your purpose for writing, you can begin to identify your readers—one of your most important tasks. Documents can accomplish their purpose only when they meet the needs and expectations of intended readers. The time you spend identifying your readers and understanding their purpose for reading may vary from one writing situation to another. For example, if you are writing for readers whom you know well or have worked with before, you will need to spend little time identifying your readers and their purpose for reading. However, if you have never met your readers, plan to spend some time finding out about them and their purpose for reading your document. This section poses three questions to help you identify your readers:

- Are your readers internal or external?
- What do your readers know about the subject?
- Will more than one person or group read your document?

Are Your Readers Internal or External?

Internal readers work for your organization. **External readers** work outside your organization. Whether you are writing to internal or external readers will affect the information, formality, and language that you use. When writing to internal readers, you first may want to determine how they relate to you in the organization's hierarchy—both horizontally and vertically. When you know the horizontal relationship, you have information about the organizational roles of readers on the same level in the hierarchy. These readers may have the same level of authority but perform different duties.

Let's consider the organizational hierarchy at Randy's plant (see Figure 2.3). Below the plant manager, the organization has four areas: environmental staff, production superintendent, support superintendent, and administrative staff. The technical expertise of the people in the production and support groups varies, based on their roles, experience, and educational background. Individuals at the same horizontal level in production have the same level of expertise and similar educational backgrounds. However, the plant operators in this group have a different level of expertise and education. They are technicians who have high-school diplomas and extensive on-the-job experience. They don't have the technical expertise of the engineers and production supervisors, who have engineering degrees.

Your readers' vertical level in the organizational hierarchy will tell you whether the readers have more authority in the organization than you. If you know where they are in the hierarchy, you can better determine the appropriate tone for a document. If you and your readers are at the same level, you probably can use an informal, friendly tone; but if your readers are several levels above you, you may want to use a more formal, less familiar tone. Because these readers may know little about the specific project that you are writing about, you might also provide background information.

External readers may be customers, clients, or other professionals. They probably won't have the information that internal readers have, such as the background of a project or document. When writing for most external readers, use a relatively formal tone and format. For example, organizations generally use informal memos and e-mail when corresponding with internal readers; but when corresponding with external readers, they use a more formal, letter format. This convention, however, is changing as more organizations use e-mail and the Web to communicate with external readers. With e-mail, many writers use a memo format instead of the traditional letter, or they combine parts of the two formats.

▶ To learn more about writing e-mail, see Chapter 18, "Writing Reader-Oriented Letters, Memos, and E-Mail."

When using e-mail to correspond with external readers, remember to use a professional tone. If your working relationship with these readers is new or if your e-mail will serve as a matter of record, use a formal tone. Some organizations will expect you to use a formal tone in any e-mail to external readers.

In traditional paper documents, organizations generally use different formats for internal and external readers. For example, if you are writing a proposal for someone within the company, you might use a one-color memo format with the pages stapled together. However, if you are sending a proposal to a customer outside your company, you might use a two-color layout, a table of contents, tabs between the sections, and an attractive, well-designed cover.

What Do Your Readers Know About the Subject?

Will your readers understand the technical terms that you use? Will they understand the concepts that you present? Readers of technical documents have varying levels of technical expertise. Some of them may have the same level of technical expertise as you; others may know little about your technical field. Your job as a writer is to determine readers' levels of technical expertise and then use terms and concepts that they will understand or to define the terms and concepts that they are likely to find unfamiliar.

Think of expertise as having three levels: high, mid, and low (see Figure 2.4). Readers with a **high level of technical expertise** are generally experts or technicians with a broad and deep knowledge of their field based on many years of practical experience or study. These readers

- Understand technical terms and information in their fields
- Understand and often even expect abbreviations and technical jargon
- Expect few—if any—explanations of technical terms or information

Figure 2.3   Excerpt from an Organizational Chart for a Power Plant

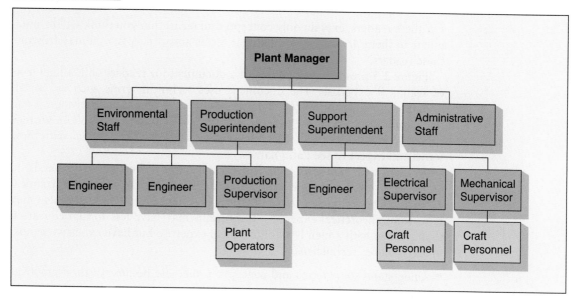

Figure 2.4

Levels of Technical Expertise

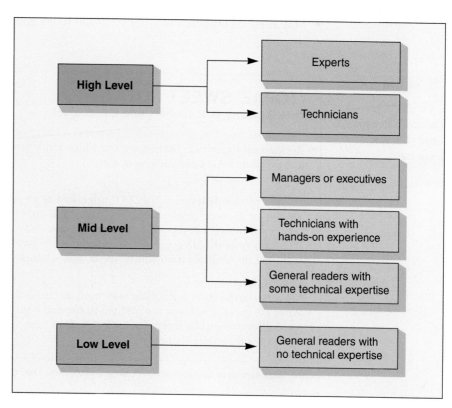

- Want a direct presentation of the information
- Are interested in theory

For these readers, explain only concepts and terms that you think will be unfamiliar to them. If you explain familiar terms and concepts, you may frustrate these readers.

Figure 2.5 presents the opening of a document for readers with a high level of technical expertise. The document uses technical terms such as "open-pollinated seedling of W-26," "polycrossed," and "medium internodes" and the Latin name *(Ipomoea batatas)* for the sweet potato that is the writer's subject. Most readers with a high level of expertise will be familiar with these terms and expect to see Latin names.

Readers with **mid-level technical expertise** are technicians with hands-on experience and managers, executives, and general readers with some technical expertise. The technicians have practical experience in the field and also may have some theoretical expertise. Technicians may have less formal education than readers with a high level of technical expertise but have extensive hands-on experience. Technicians

- Understand some terms and concepts in the field because of their practical experience
- Are interested more in practical, how-to information than in theory
- May need explanations of some technical terms and information

<table>
<tr><td>

▼ Figure 2.5

A Document for Readers with a High Level of Technical Expertise

</td><td>

'TOPAZ' SWEET POTATO
D. R. Paterson, D. R. Earhart, and T. E. Boswell

The 'Topaz' sweet potato [*Ipomoea batatas* (L.) Lam.] developed by the Texas Agricultural Experiment Station combines high yield, good sprout production, and excellent baking and canning quality.

Origin
'Topaz,' previously tested as 8W2641, originated as an open-pollinated seedling of W-26 polycrossed at the U.S. Vegetable Laboratory in 1973 with other parental types developed for multiple disease and soil insect resistances. W-26 was from the 5th generation of mass-selection population I. The authors evaluated the seedlings from which 'Topaz' was selected.

Description
The vines of this entry are trailing with medium internodes. The stems and leaves are green. The leaves are medium in size and heart-shaped. The roots are chunky and slightly tapered at each end. They have an orange flesh color and a smooth, bronze skin color. . . .

</td></tr>
</table>

Source: Texas Agricultural Extension Service, College Station, Texas. Used by permission.

TAKING IT INTO THE WORKPLACE

Readers and the Web

"Think like a reader."
—S. Gayle Bradbury, Technical
Communicator (24)

Let's assume you're looking for information on the Web. What sites do you prefer to read? Which sites do you leave before you find the information that you need? What makes a site reader friendly? Readers on the Web "want to get to their destination quickly without slogging through a lot of verbiage" (Bradbury 24). S. Gayle Bradbury, a technical communicator, explains that if you don't give readers the information they are seeking quickly, you'll lose the readers. As Alice Fugate explains, "far too many Web sites tell you everything except what you want to know" (Fugate 39).

As a Web writer, you will create a more reader-oriented Web site by

- Understanding who's on the Web
- Thinking like a reader

According to Ben Miller, a user interface design specialist with Edward Jones, the demographics of Web users match that of the overall population, with the two fastest-growing groups online being seniors and baby boomers (Fugate 40). Seniors (the over 50 group) comprise the fastest growing group of U.S. Web users. The group grew from 19 percent of all Web users in 1997 to 38 percent of all users in 2000 (The Media Audit). Many of the new users from both groups are new users of technology; these users are "relatively slow to adopt new technologies. . . . They

view computers as tools" not toys (Fugate 40). They want the Web writer to filter out "cyberbells" and whistles. They want pure information that they can access and use efficiently (Fugate 40).

Bradbury suggests that when writing for the Web writers "think like a reader" (Bradbury 24). If 38 percent of your Web site readers are seniors, how do you go about thinking like your readers?

Assignment

To help you think like seniors (the over 50 crowd, not college seniors!), let's assume that you are creating a Web site for your city. You want to learn more about how seniors in your city use the Web and what they like in a Web site. You also want to learn how they navigate a Web site. To gather this information, complete the following assignment:

1. Develop a questionnaire to give to seniors. In the questionnaire, you might ask questions about what Web sites they like to use, what Web sites they find frustrating, and how they navigate a Web site. As you design the questionnaire, think about what you like in a Web site and ask the seniors whether they like similar characteristics. (To learn about writing questionnaires, see Chapter 5, "Researching Information Using Primary and Secondary Sources.")
2. Give the questionnaire to at least five seniors. You might e-mail the questionnaire to some of the seniors.
3. Write a memo to your classmates about what you learned.

For technicians, explain only the most advanced or obscure terms and concepts. Let's consider the instructions for constructing a chase for a woodburning fireplace (see Figure 2.6). The instructions define *chase* but assume that readers have some hands-on construction experience. The instructions recommend to "insulate the chase floor using batt type insulation between the floor joists." The writer assumes that readers know what "batt type insulation" and "floor joists" are even though the readers may have never before constructed a chase.

Managers or executives read technical material to make decisions. They may have backgrounds related to your field, or they may have earned a degree in your field, but their knowledge may not be up-to-date. For example, the vice president of a computer manufacturer might have a degree in business administration and on-the-job knowledge of computers but does not program or design hardware. Generally, managers and executives

- Read to gather information for decision making
- Expect conclusions, recommendations, and implications to appear near the beginning of the document or in an executive summary
- Read selectively or scan documents for the information they need to make decisions
- Need definitions and explanations of most technical terms and information
- Want practical information
- Prefer simple graphics that quickly summarize information

General readers with mid-level expertise (see Figure 2.4) may be interested but not formally educated in your field. They may have degrees in related areas—for example, a reader interested in engineering might have a degree in industrial technology. General readers with mid-level expertise have read widely in your field and understand basic terms and concepts. You might think of them as *sophisticated* general readers.

Readers with a **low level of technical expertise** have little if any knowledge of your field. Examples include a high-school student reading a brochure about the dangers of blood clots, a journalism professor reading a newspaper article about macroeconomics, and a computer programmer reading tax-filing instructions. We are all general readers when we are reading technical information outside our fields of expertise. General readers

- Do not understand basic terms and concepts in your field
- Need simple definitions of most concepts and terms
- Expect examples and analogies
- Expect a simple, direct presentation
- Learn from simple graphics

Writing for general readers with a low level of technical expertise is often difficult because determining what they already know and understand is tricky. Your job as the writer is to gather as much information as possible about these readers. The more you know about their background, education, reading ability, and attitudes, the better you can anticipate what they will understand and the type of vocabulary you can use.

Figure 2.6

A Document for
Readers with Mid-
Level Technical
Expertise

CONSTRUCTING A CHASE

A chase is a vertical box-like enclosure built around the chimney and firebox. You can construct a chase for the fireplace *and* chimney or for the chimney only. The chase is most commonly constructed on an outside wall. In cold climates, insulate the chase floor using batt type insulation between the floor joists.

Three examples of chase applications are shown in Figure 20.

1. Fireplace and chimney enclosed in an exterior chase.
2. Chimney offset through exterior wall and enclosed in chase.
3. Chase constructed on roof.

In constructing the chase, follow these guidelines:

- Maintain a 1/2" minimum air space around the firebox.
- Maintain a 2" air space around the chimney.
- Use a noncombustible material to construct the top chase.
- In cold climates, install a firestop spacer in an insulated false ceiling at the 8-foot level above the firebox assembly. This prevents heat loss through the fireplace.
- In cold climates, insulate the walls of the chase to the level of the false ceiling as shown in Figure 21. This will help prevent heat loss from the home around and through the fireplace.

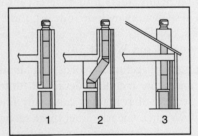

Figure 20
Chase Constructions

Materials for the Chase
To construct the chase, use framing materials much the same as the walls in your home. You can use a variety of materials, including brick, stone, veneer brick, or standard siding materials.

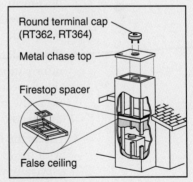

Figure 21
Chase Assembly

Source: Adapted from *E36, E39, E42: Woodburning Fireplace Installation and Operating Instructions for Residential Use* (Mt. Pleasant, Iowa: Heatilator, Inc., n.d.) 18–19. Used by permission of Heatilator, Inc.

Let's look at a document for the owners of a new bicycle (see Figure 2.7). Compare the simple language and friendly tone used in these instructions with the language and tone of the sweet potato document aimed at readers with a high level of technical expertise (see Figure 2.5).

Once you have some sense of your readers' level of technical expertise, you can choose words, concepts, and information that your readers will understand. Once you have determined what your readers know about your subject, don't waste time by giving them information that they already have. If, for example, they are familiar with the background of the project that you are reporting on, give them only a brief summary of the background.

You may have to write a document for readers with different levels of technical expertise. When you do, use the following tips:

▶ **Tips for Writing for Readers with Different Levels of Technical Expertise**

- **Divide the document into distinct sections so that readers can read only the sections that apply to them.** For example, you might have a "Getting Started" section for novice users and an "Advanced Techniques" section for readers with technical expertise.

- **Use devices that help readers find different information in the document.** These devices include indexes, tables of contents, executive summaries, headings, and page tabs that indicate sections (Holland, Charrow, and Wright 38).

- **Put the definitions of technical words, explanations of technical information, and other technical details in footnotes, appendixes, or other special sections that readers can easily find** (Holland, Charrow, and Wright). Clearly label these sections so readers can find them.

- **Direct the language and presentation of a single document to readers with the lowest level of technical expertise.** This technique works especially well for instruction manuals.

- **Write separate documents for each group of readers if you have the time and the budget.** This option will benefit your readers by allowing you to organize and direct the document to one group of readers. However, most organizations rarely have the budget for this option.

- **Put the document online so you can compartmentalize it for readers with various levels of knowledge.** Be sure to include good navigational tools, so readers can easily find the sections they need.

Figure 2.7

A Document for
Readers with a Low
Level of Technical
Expertise

USING THE BRAKES ON YOUR NEW BICYCLE

Your bicycle has caliper brakes. These brakes have brake shoes that are squeezed against a wheel rim much like disc brakes on an automobile. You have a caliper brake for the front and the rear wheels. To operate the brakes, use the brake levers mounted on the handlebars (see the illustration below). The left-hand lever controls the front brake and the right-hand lever operates the rear brake.

To slow your bicycle,

- Squeeze **both** levers to slow your bicycle, beginning with the right-hand lever (or rear brake).

  Be sure to use both brakes. If you use only your front brake, you can lock the front wheel and lose control of the bicycle.

Follow these braking tips for a safe and fun ride:

- When turning, brake slowly to avoid skidding.
- When the ground or pavement is wet, sandy, or covered with gravel, start braking sooner and brake slowly to avoid skidding.
- If the brake shoes or wheel rims are wet, start braking sooner as you will need more distance than normal to stop. As the shoes or rims dry during braking, the efficiency of your brakes may rapidly increase. Be prepared to stop quickly.
- Control your speed going downhill: the faster the speed, the longer the stopping distance.
- Check your brakes and adjust them (if necessary) the first time they don't stop your bicycle quickly and smoothly or don't stop your bicycle as well as they did in the past. (See pages 33-35 to learn how to adjust the brakes or take your bicycle to an authorized dealer.)
- Adjust your brakes when you can squeeze the brake levers to within one inch of your handlebars. (See pages 33-35 to learn how to adjust the brakes or take your bicycle to an authorized dealer.)

CALIPER BRAKES

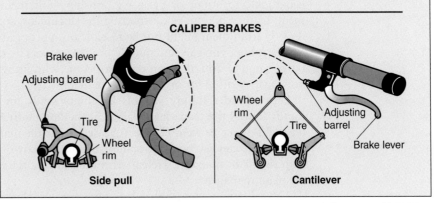

Side pull

Cantilever

Source: Adapted from *Raleigh Owner's Manual* (Kent, Wash: Raleigh USA Bicycle Company, n.d.) 30–31. Courtesy of Raleigh USA Bicycle Company.

Will More Than One Person or Group Read Your Document?

Often more than one person or group will read your documents. **Initial readers,** such as an administrative assistant or even the head of a department, may skim the document to determine who in their organization should receive it. Judging from the summary, cover letter, title, or introduction, the initial reader sends the document to the primary reader. The **primary reader** is the intended reader—that is, the technician who will use the instructions, the executive who will decide to implement the proposal, and so on. The primary reader will use the document to complete a task, to gather information, or to make a decision. Some primary readers may use the document to make a decision but may read only certain sections and then send the document to a **secondary reader,** who has only a minor interest in the document as a whole. The secondary reader might be a technical adviser whose opinion the decision maker is seeking. Such a reader assumes the role of primary reader of the sections that draw on his or her area of expertise. For example, the primary reader of a proposal might be a manager, and the secondary reader might be a technical expert whose view of the "Problems" section the manager requests. The technical expert, however, is the primary reader of the "Problems" section.

▶Principle 3: Determine Your Readers' Purpose, Needs, and Preferences

Just as you have a purpose for writing your document, your readers have a purpose for reading it. They approach your document with specific questions and expectations about the information and perhaps the style of the document. They have specific needs that you can consider when designing your document. How can you determine your readers' expectations and needs? One of the best ways would be to talk to each of your readers. This method, however, may not always be possible because of the number of readers, their geographic location, or your relationship with them. You may not know them, or they may not be expecting the document, so gathering information directly from them might not be feasible or appropriate. If you are writing to a large group, you can find out about your readers by talking with a representative sample. You also can contact people who know your readers or have previously written for or worked with them.

Let's consider Randy and his feasibility study for repairing the turbine. Randy knows the secondary readers at the home office, but he doesn't know the plant manager well. How can he determine the manager's needs and preferences? He can ask both the plant manager and coworkers who have worked with the plant manager. He can also look at reports previously prepared for the plant manager.

The following paragraphs give you some guidelines and questions to help you meet your readers' purpose, needs, and preferences.

Think About Your Readers' Purpose for Reading

Your readers will have one or more of these purposes for reading a technical document:

- To gather information
- To answer a specific question
- To make a decision
- To perform a task or specific action

To determine readers' purposes, you can consider some of the questions that they might ask.

Let's consider Randy's readers. His primary reader is the plant manager; his secondary reader is the vice president of production in the home office. Figure 2.8 lists the questions that Randy thinks these readers will ask. Randy thinks that Thomas, the plant manager (the primary reader), is concerned with three aspects of the recommendation: the cost of the recommended option in time and personnel, whether the recommended option will solve the problem, and why Randy thinks option 3 is the most feasible. Sarah, the vice president (the secondary reader), is most concerned with the financial impact of the solution on the plant and home office budgets, the impact of the shutdown of the turbine on other plants, and the effect of the chosen option on the production of electricity.

Consider Your Readers' Physical Surroundings and Time Constraints

Some readers work in noisy, distracting areas; others work in environments where documents are likely to get dirty and the pages bent and torn. By considering readers' surroundings, you can design and organize the document to meet their needs. For example, if you know your readers will use your instructions in a warehouse, you might put the instructions in a sturdy binding or notebook and laminate the pages so readers can easily clean the pages. If you know your readers will use your reference manual at a small computer workstation, you might use a relatively small page size that will fit next to the computer and put the manual in a three-ring binder that will lie flat. Readers' physical surroundings can influence your choice of cover, binding, headings, page size, line length, paragraph divisions, and type size.

Also consider constraints on your readers' time. Most readers receive many documents each week and have little time to read them all. Organize and design your document to help readers locate information quickly. If, for example, you know your readers are busy executives who receive many proposals, include tabs for each of the major sections, so readers can quickly flip to the sections they are interested in. You could also include an executive summary that briefly states your proposal. If you are presenting your information on the Web, include concise summaries of long passages, so readers can decide whether to read "in more detail" (Fugate 40).

▼ **Figure 2.8**   Excerpt from Randy's Worksheet for Identifying His Readers

---

What Questions Might My Readers Ask While Reading My Document?

Primary Reader: Plant Manager
What are the three options?
What is the cost of each option?
How much time and personnel will each option take?
What are the criteria for evaluating each option?
What are the advantages and disadvantages of each option?
How much downtime, if any, will each option cause?
Which option is most feasible and cost-effective?
Which option is the best long-term solution?
How and why is option 3 better than the other options?
Is option 3 cost-effective?
Is option 3 technically sound? Will it repair the turbine and solve the vibration problem?
Can our plant personnel conduct the high-speed balance, or will we have to hire consultants?

Secondary Reader: Vice President of Production
What impact will option 3 have on the production of electricity in the northern region?
Will the other plants have to pick up the load while the turbine is being repaired? If so, for how long?
How much does option 3 cost?
Is the cost within the plant's budget?
Is option 3 cost-effective?
Has the plant looked at all possible options?
Is option 3 a long-term solution?

▶ You will learn more about using these devices in Part II, "Knowing the Tools of the Writer."

You can use several devices to help busy readers to find information in your document:

- Headings and subheadings
- Tabs that separate the major sections
- Table of contents and index for longer, formal documents
- Page designs with ample white space
- Visual aids that summarize information quickly
- Summaries at the beginning of documents and major sections
- Overviews at the beginning of documents and major sections

When you keep in mind readers' time constraints and physical surroundings, you can better design and organize documents that meet their needs.

Consider Your Readers' Preferences

Your readers will have certain preferences about style, format, design, and media (paper, e-mail, other electronic forms). For example, some people like to receive documents by way of e-mail, and others prefer paper copy. Organizations also have "preferences." Some want their logo to appear on every cover page and in particular colors. Some expect all documents to be printed in a specific typeface. Find out as much as possible about your readers' and your organization's preferences, so you can meet their expectations and make a good impression.

How can you find out about these preferences? You can

- Talk to your readers when possible
- Talk with others who have written for or worked with your readers
- Look at some of the documents that your readers or their organizations have written

As you talk with readers and their coworkers and examine their documents, look for their preferences in style, format, design, and media. You may discover other preferences, but these four areas give you a place to start.

Once you have identified preferences, decide whether you can accommodate them. When possible, try to accommodate them all. Unfortunately, if you are writing to more than one person or group, these preferences may be incompatible. They may contradict your organization's policies for technical documents, or they may be inconsistent in style.

▶ Principle 4: Analyze Your Readers' Attitudes

If you understand your readers' attitudes, you can select the appropriate tone and organization to make your document persuasive or appealing. You can easily determine the attitudes of readers whom you or your coworkers know personally; but when you or your coworkers don't know your readers, analyzing their attitudes is more difficult. You probably won't be able to analyze their attitudes toward you or your organization, so try imagining yourself in their place to determine how interested they may be in the subject or how they may react to your document. The following sections suggest some techniques for analyzing your readers' attitudes about the subject of your document and about you and your organization.

Analyze Your Readers' Attitudes About the Subject

Readers' attitudes about your subject may be negative, positive, neutral, skeptical, or enthusiastic. If their attitudes are positive or enthusiastic, writing your document will be relatively easy because you won't have to entice readers into your document or figure out how to convince them to read or use it. If their attitudes are negative, skeptical, or neutral, your writing task is more difficult because you have to figure out how to motivate them to read your document or how to persuade them to accept your recommendations. For example, if you know readers will resist your recommendations, you might present the benefits or reasons for the recommendations before actually giving the recommendations. When readers have positive attitudes about your subject, you want to reinforce those attitudes. When attitudes are negative, however, you want to change them.

To anticipate readers' attitudes toward a document, think about how they will feel about the topic. For example, a computer software user with a question about how to install that software will need a manual and will be motivated to use the manual. In contrast, a company executive who receives an unsolicited letter from an unknown inventor requesting funding for a new way of measuring ozone in the atmosphere may be skeptical or unenthusiastic. Again, imagine yourself in your readers' place to analyze their attitudes toward your document. You can also

- Ask for help from people who have worked with your readers or who know them
- Talk with your readers about what information to include
- Read background documents and information related to the topic and find out what your readers thought of those documents and information

Let's again consider Randy's writing situation. In analyzing the attitudes of his readers, he begins with the plant manager, Thomas. Thomas is not happy about spending more money on the turbine because less than a year ago the plant spent $750,000 to repair it. Those repairs caused the plant to be offline for more than six weeks. Thomas is nervous about spending more money and losing more production time. Randy works directly with Thomas but is new to the plant and still must prove himself to Thomas. He decides to meet with Thomas to get feedback about the three options. Randy also decides to talk to some friends in the home office who worked with Thomas for several years.

Randy's task with Sarah, the vice president of production, is easier. He reported directly to her for six years, so he decides to e-mail his recommendations to her to get her feedback. He believes that she is likely to agree with his recommended solution but will expect him to analyze all three options and present detailed explanations of their cost.

Analyze Your Readers' Attitudes Toward You and Your Organization

Your readers' attitudes toward you and your organization will influence their reaction to your document. These attitudes may reflect their previous experiences with you or your organization. Readers who have had a good experience working with you or your organization will probably look favorably on your document even before they read it. Readers who have had a negative experience with you or your organization will pose a greater challenge. You will have to use part of your document to gain their confidence. If you don't know your readers, find out whether any of your coworkers have worked with them. If your coworkers have had positive experiences with your readers, you probably can safely assume that those readers will have a favorable attitude toward you

THE READER'S CORNER

How We Read

 Understanding how you read can help how you write. First, your reading eye hops across the page in what are called *saccades*. You pick up information during moments of rest, or *fixations*, when your *fovea centralis* (the point of sharpest vision on the back of your retina) focuses on the page. You then store this sensory information in your *sensory store* for a few hundred milliseconds (if you didn't pick up enough information the first time, you *regress*, or reread). Your short-term memory processes the information in a variety of ways. Do you know the word by sound (*phonemically*) or by sight (*visually*)? Can you verify (or *parse*) the sentence structure and anticipate its direction? Your short-term memory can hold only about seven of these processed *chunks* before turning to your long-term memory for help verifying vocabulary and grammar.

As a writer, you can use these techniques to help your reader:

- Use type that contrasts with its background to facilitate your reader's saccades (rhymes with "what odds").
- Provide your reader with subtle phonemic cues (note the conclusion of the previous sentence): we remember words by sound as much as by sight.
- Use familiar sentence structures to let your reader know where you are going.
- Don't stack several nouns in a row or put too many items in a list; instead categorize the list items. Remember, your reader can hold only about seven such chunks in mind at a time.
- Choose your vocabulary wisely to save your reader's long-term memory some trouble.

and your organization. If the experience has been negative, you may have to design the document to gain the readers' confidence.

Even if your readers don't know you, they may have a preconceived attitude about your organization. Think about your attitude toward the Internal Revenue Service (IRS). Would you be enthusiastic about receiving a letter from the IRS? Most of us would not be because correspondence from the IRS often is unwelcome information about filing tax forms or paying back taxes and penalties. Even though most of us don't know anyone at the IRS, we have a preconceived attitude about the organization and what it does. Likewise, your readers may have a preconceived attitude about your organization because of past experiences with it or because of its reputation.

Let's look at what Randy discovered about the plant manager's attitude toward him and the plant. Since Thomas is an internal reader, Randy knows that he will be interested in the future of the plant and in its reputation with the home office—both issues relate directly to Thomas's credibility and job performance. Randy knows that Thomas respects his abilities but will not accept his recommendation solely because of his abilities. Randy has been working at the plant for only two months, so Thomas will be looking for solid evidence to support Randy's recommendation.

▶**Conclusion**   Think about your readers throughout the writing process, not just at the beginning. They will react to your document section by section, paragraph by paragraph, sentence by sentence, word by word. Readers may not wait until they reach the end of the document to react to it. Instead, they may react to each part as they read it. Statements early in the document may determine a reader's reaction to the entire document, so think about your readers as you write every word, sentence, and paragraph. Spend time identifying your readers and anticipate as well as you can how they will react and respond to your document. After drafting a document, if possible ask one or more of the primary readers to read your draft and tell you unofficially how they would respond. If their response is not what you want, ask them for advice on how to change your document to get the response you want.

WORKSHEET   **for Identifying Your Readers**

▶ **Principle 1: Determine Your Purpose for Writing**
 • What type of document are you writing?
 • What is the purpose of the document?

▶ **Principle 2: Identify Your Readers**
 • Who are your primary readers? Are there secondary readers? If so, who?
 • Are your readers internal or external to the company?
 • What do your readers know about the topic and its related field?

▶ **Principle 3: Determine Your Readers' Purpose, Needs, and Preferences**
 • What questions might your readers ask while reading your document?
 • How and where will your readers use your document?
 • What time constraints are your readers under?
 • What style, format, design, and media do your readers prefer?

▶ **Principle 4: Analyze Your Readers' Attitudes**
 • What are your readers' attitudes toward the subject of your document? How will they react to your document? Why?
 • Have your readers worked with you or your organization? Have the working relationships been positive or negative?
 • What are your readers' attitudes toward you and your organization?

> ## ►EXERCISES

1. Write two paragraphs about one of these topics or about a topic that you select:

   - A car accident that you were involved in
   - A grade that you received
   - A class that you have taken
   - The relationship between body fat and aerobic exercise
   - The relationship between ozone and vehicle emissions
   - The production of cheese
   - Sanitation standards for a meat-processing plant
   - Safety precautions for women walking alone at night
   - The Web and the future of paper communication

   Write each paragraph for a different reader. The readers should have different purposes for reading and different levels of knowledge of the topic. Refer to the "Worksheet for Identifying Your Readers" as you analyze your readers and determine their needs, preferences, and attitudes.

2. Write a memo to your instructor explaining why the following paragraph about market value doesn't adequately respond to readers' needs and level of expertise. Comment on specific language that readers might not understand. This paragraph is from a pamphlet on property tax appraisals written for homeowners. These homeowners have different educational backgrounds and levels of expertise about property tax appraisals. Most of these homeowners have a low level of technical expertise and will read these paragraphs to help them understand their property appraisal, which determines its fair market value.

What Is Fair Market Value?

Section 1.04 of the Texas property tax code defines *market value* as follows:

Market value means the price at which a property would transfer for cash or its equivalent under prevailing market conditions if:

   a. Exposed for sale in the open market with a reasonable time for the seller to find a purchaser;
   b. Both the seller and the purchaser know of all uses and purposes to which the property is adapted and for which it is capable of being used and of the enforceable restrictions on its use; and
   c. Both the seller and the purchaser seek to maximize their gains and neither is in a position to take advantage of the exigencies of the other.

3. Find a short article on a topic related to your major field of study. The article should be for readers at a mid to high level of technical expertise. Make sure that you understand the article; then do the following:

   a. Write a memo to your instructor describing the possible educational background of primary readers of the article, their level of technical expertise, and their purpose for reading the article.
   b. Select a 300- to 400-word passage that you find particularly interesting and rewrite it for readers with a low level of technical expertise.
   c. Attach a copy of the article to your memo and rewritten passage.

> ► **CASE STUDY**

Informing Students About Financial Aid

Background

Although this case is a team project, your instructor may modify it to be an individual assignment. Your team has received the following assignment from the scholarship and financial aid office at your college or university.

> Our school is losing many good students because they cannot afford the cost of tuition, books, and living expenses. Many of these students are unaware of the scholarships and other forms of financial aid that are available. Some scholarships are based on merit only, but others are based on merit as well as need. Some financial aid based solely on need is also available. Scholarships and other financial aid will help students to stay in school. Students, however, may be unaware of these scholarships and financial aid, may think that they don't qualify, or may think that applying for financial aid is too much trouble.

Your assignment is to write two documents:

- A memo to the director of the scholarship and financial aid office suggesting ways to inform students of available scholarships and financial aid.

- A letter to all students informing them that scholarships and financial aid are available to qualifying students. (Your letter should motivate students with financial difficulties to come to the scholarship and financial aid office for information.)

Assignment

Follow these steps to complete the assignment:

1. Answer the questions in the "Worksheet for Identifying Your Readers." Include information about the director of the scholarship and financial aid office and the students who will receive the letter. You may want to visit with the director of the scholarship and financial aid office at your college or university to gather information. If you cannot visit with the director in person, at least go to the office and find out what types of information are available for students.
2. Write a purpose statement for the memo to the director and for the letter to the students.
3. Informally outline the memo and the letter.
4. Write and revise the memo and the letter.

3

Facing Ethical and Legal Challenges

ompanies throughout the United States have published statements about their commitment to ethical conduct. For example, in 2000 the European division of TXU published its code of business conduct to ensure that the company and its employees acted ethically. Dow Chemicals has an 18-page code of ethics that guides employees in many aspects of business conduct. Raytheon has established an office of business ethics and compliance to help employees with ethical dilemmas and to ensure that the company and its employees follow the standards of ethical conduct established by the company.

Ethics involves your ability to act and communicate honestly and fairly and to fulfill your moral obligations and responsibilities to yourself, your fellow employees, your employer, and the public. Ethics, according to Aristotle, is the study of what is involved in doing good (Dombrowski 41). When we say that someone has acted ethically, we usually mean that that person has done the right thing. When you behave ethically, you are acting out of the "intrinsic rightness of the behavior," not just to keep your job or to receive personal or monetary gain (Dombrowski 42).

As a professional in the workplace, you may face ethical dilemmas. You may encounter ethical dilemmas on two levels: how you act in the workplace and how you communicate in the workplace. For example, you may feel pressured to compete at any cost, to sacrifice safety to get a product out on time, or to sidestep environmental regulations to cut costs. The situations that you encounter may involve sacrificing customer or public safety, or they may be more "routine." You also may face ethical decisions when communicating. For example, these dilemmas might include putting incomplete or inaccurate information on a job application to increase your chances of getting a job, or manipulating the language of an annual report to make your company look more profitable. You might be tempted to manipulate statistical data in a report to make the results of a study appear more favorable. This chapter defines three ethical frameworks you can use when examining the ethical implications of your actions and your communications. It also explains laws related to technical communication as well as suggests principles to guide you in ethically communicating technical information.

▶Understanding Ethics

Let's look at an historical incident from the 1940s to the 1970s involving ethical choices. From the 1940s to the 1970s, patients, some terminally ill, were injected with plutonium—mostly without their knowledge or consent—at Oak Ridge Hospital, the University of Rochester, the University of Chicago, and the University of California.[1] In the years following the atomic bombings of the Japanese cities Hiroshima and Nagasaki, the U.S. military and nuclear

---

[1] I gathered information on the human radiation experiments from Judith Braffman-Miller, "When medicine went wrong: How Americans were used illegally as guinea pigs," *USA Today*, and the Department of Energy, "DOE Openness: Human Radiation Experiment."

weapons industry wanted data on the biological effects of plutonium and radioisotopes. To determine these effects, scientists of the Manhattan Project injected 18 unsuspecting patients with plutonium. These patients had all been diagnosed with terminal diseases and weren't expected to live more than 10 years. Some of the patients, according to investigators at the Atomic Energy Commission, had not granted informed consent. The patients that had granted consent did so under false pretenses because the word "plutonium" was classified during World War II. Those patients who survived did not even know that they had been injected with plutonium until 1974.

These experiments continued during the Cold War when the U.S. military wanted to know how much radiation a soldier could endure before becoming disabled. From 1960 to 1971, scientists at the University of Cincinnati performed experiments on 88 cancer patients ranging in age from 9 to 84. These patients were repeatedly exposed to massive doses of radiation, yet medical researchers from the 1930s through the 1950s had determined that whole-body radiation was not effective in treating most cancers. These patients had tumors that would resist radiation—a fact that the doctors already knew (Braffman-Miller, Dept. of Defense). Most of these patients were uneducated, had low IQs, and were poor. These researchers in charge of the experiments wrote in 1969 that "directional radiation will be attempted since this type of exposure is of military interest"(quoted in Braffman-Miller). The doctors did not use this procedure to treat tumors, but instead they used it to study how radiation exposure might effect soldiers. These researchers also denied the patients treatment for the side effects of nausea and vomiting that resulted from the radiation. These researchers instructed the hospital staff to ignore these symptoms: "DO NOT ASK THE PATIENT WHETHER HE HAS THESE SYMPTOMS" (see Figure 3.1). Instead, the staff was to record the time, duration, and severity of these symptoms without treating the patient.

Publicly, the researchers at the University of Cincinnati claimed that the purpose of their research was to study ways to treat cancer. However, in a report to the Department of Defense, they wrote that the purpose of their study was "to understand better the influence of radiation on combat effectiveness of troops and to develop more suitable methods of diagnosis, prognosis, prophylaxis and treatment of radiation injuries" (1 Sept. 1966). What were the ethical responsibilities of the researchers and hospital staff involved? Did they know of the dangers of plutonium? Were they willing to tell the public about their work? As early as January 5, 1944, researchers were aware of the hazards of working with plutonium. In April of 1947, Col. O. G. Baywood, Jr., of the Atomic Energy Commission wrote that "no document be released which refers to experiments with humans and might have adverse effect on public opinion or result in legal suits" (see Figure 3.2).

In the 1960s, the scientists and the government did know of the adverse effects of radiation before they began their tests at the University of Cincinnati. In 1966, we see the first evidence that someone at the University of Cincinnati questioned the ethics of the experiments when Dr. George Shields

INSTRUCTIONS FOR RECORDING OF SYMPTOMS
FOLLOWING IRRADIATION

DEPARTMENT OF RADIOLOGY

GENERAL HOSPITAL

Date: _____

PATIENT _____ NO. _____ WARD _____

TIME OF THERAPY _____

This patient has just received total body radiation for therapeutic purposes. It is possible that the symptoms listed below may develop within the next several days. Please note carefully the time at which these symptoms develop and note their duration and severity.

DO NOT ASK THE PATIENT WHETHER HE HAS THESE SYMPTOMS

	Time of Onset		Duration	Severity
	Date	Hr.		
Anorexia				
Nausea				
Vomiting				
Abdominal Pain				
Diarrhea				
Weakness				
Prostration				
Mental Confusion				

E.L. Saenger, M.D, line 207
H. Perry, M.D., line 200

Daily—Card No. 1

Source: Saenger, E. L. "Research proposal for sub-task in nuclear weapons effect research." Online. Internet. 30 Sept. 2001 Available: http://www.gwu.edu/~nsarchiv/radiation/dir/mstreet/commeet/meet2/brief2/tab_1/br211b.txt.

and Dr. Thomas E. Gaffney put in writing their suspicions. Both doctors ethically pointed out that the researchers deceived patients and were hiding the real purpose of their experiments. Their memos appear in Figures 3.3 and 3.4.

Let's look at two important comments about the actual language Dr. Shields and Dr. Gaffney believe is wrong or at the very least misleading. Shields writes about informed consent:

Figure 3.2

Letter Requesting
That Documents
About Experiments
On Humans Be
Classified as "Secret"
(Reproduced
Verbatim)

UNITED STATES
ATOMIC ENERGY COMMISSION

April 17, 1947

U. S. Atomic Energy Commission
P. O. Box 8
Oak Ridge, Tennessee

Attention: Dr. Fidler

Subject: MEDICAL EXPERIMENTS ON HUMANS

   1. It is desired that no document be released which refers to experiments with humans and might have adverse effect on public opinion or result in legal suits. Documents covering such work field should be classified "secret". Further work in this field in the future has been prohibited by the General Manager. It is understood that three documents in this field have been submitted for declassification and are now classified "restricted". It is desired that these documents be reclassified "secret" and that a check be made to insure that no distribution has inadvertently been made to the Department of Commerce, or other off-Project personnel or agencies.

   2. These instructions do not pertain to documents regarding clinical or therepeutic uses of radioisotopes and similar materials beneficial to human disorders and diseases.

ATOMIC ENERGY COMMISSION

O. G. BAYWOOD, JR.
Colonel, Corps of Engineers.

Source: Department of Energy.

"I believe that the conditions of informed consent will have been observed if the authors change 'all patients are informed that a risk exists, but that all precautions to prevent untoward results will be taken' to the equivalent of 'all patients are informed that a 1 in 4 chance of death within a few weeks due to treatment exists.'" (13 March 1967)

The language that Shields suggests is an ethical treatment of the risk involved in the experiment, whereas the language proposed by the researchers unethically

| ▼ **Figure 3.3** | Memo Suggesting Problems with Human Radiation Experiments (Reproduced Verbatim) |

TO: Dr. Edward A. Gall

FROM: Dr. George Shields

DATE: March 13, 1967

SUBJECT: Protection of Humans with Stored Autologous Marrow

I regret that I must withdraw myself from the subcommittee studying this proposal, for reasons of close professional and personal contact with the investigators and with some of the laboratory phases of this project. The following comments are sent to you in confidence, at your request.

This protocol is difficult to evaluate. The purpose of the study is obscure, as is the relationship of the experimental groups to the purposes. The significance of the study in relation to the health of the patients under study may be considerable if the investigators succeed in prolonging life of these patients with malignant disease, but the risk of treatment may be very high if the authors' hypothesis (that bone marrow transfusions will ameliorate bone marrow depression due to radiation) is incorrect. The radiation proposed has been documented in the author's own series to cause a 25% mortality.

I recommend that this study be disapproved, because of the high risk of this level of radiation. Admittedly it is very difficult, in fact impossible, to balance potential hazard against potential benefit in experiments of this sort. The stakes are high. Our current mandate is that we evaluate the risks on some arbitrary scale. I believe a 25% mortality is too high, (25% of 36 patients is 9 deaths) but this is of course merely an opinion.

If it is the consensus of the investigators and the review committee that a 25% mortality risk is not prohibitive, then the experiment could be reconsidered from the standpoint of informed consent – provided the patient is appraised of the risk in a quantative fashion. I believe that the conditions of informed consent will have been observed if the authors change "all patients are informed that a risk exists, but that all precautions to prevent untoward results will be taken" to the equivalent of "all patients are informed that a 1 in 4 chance of death within a few weeks due to treatment exists, etc."

Finally, although it is not our concern directly, a comment as to experimental design is indicated in this particular protocol. The authors' stated purposes are vague in the first page of the application, but on the last page three purposes are listed since it would require an untreated group and no reference has been made by the authors to such an untreated group of patients.

The second purpose can be fulfilled by this protocol only with the retrospective group (Group 1). The evaluation of bone marrow transfusion in the treatment of bone marrow depression would require a concomitant control group of patients treated only with radiation. It is apparent that the authors feel the radiation risk is too high to re-expose another group to this level of radiation without some effort at radio-protection, and therefore the authors have chosen to use the retrospective group as a control. There is considerable question whether this retrospective group will be entirely similar and therefore whether it will serve the second purpose.

The third purpose, "to determine whether autologous bone marrow therapy may play a role in treatment of bone marrow depression following acute radiation exposure in warfare or occupationally induced accidents", is not the subject of this experiment because normal individuals are not being tested. It is problematic whether the information gained in this study will apply to normal individuals following acute radiation exposure. Therefore it is my definite opinion that the third purpose of this experiment would not justify the risk entailed.

For these several reasons I feel that the experimental design is inadequate, and because of the high risk inherent in this level of radiation, I think experimental design should be a proper subject for our consideration in this instance.

Source: Department of Energy.

| ▼ **Figure 3.4** | Memo Suggesting "Subterfuge" (Reproduced Verbatim) |

UNIVERSITY OF CINCINNATI

(INTERDEPARTMENTAL CORRESPONDENCE SHEET)

TO: Dr. Edward Gall, Chairman

Clinical Research Committee

FROM: Dr. Thomas E. Gaffney

DATE: 4/17/67

I cannot recommend approval of the proposed study entitled "The Therapeutic Effect of Total Body Irradiation Followed by Infusion of Stored Autologous Marrow in Humans" for several reasons.

The stated goal of the study is to test the hypothesis that total body irradiation at a dose of 200 rad followed by infusion of stored autologous marrow is effective, palliative therapy for metastatic malignancy in human beings. I don't understand the rationale for this study. The applicants have apparently already administered 150–200 rad to some 18 patients with a variety of malignancies and to their satisfaction have not found a beneficial effect. In fact, as I understand it, they found considerable morbidity associated with this high dose radiation. Why is it now logical to expand this study?

Even if the study is expanded, its current design will not yield meaningful data. For instance, the applicants indicate their intention to evaluate the influence of 200 rad total body radiation on survival in patients with a variety of neoplasms. This "variety" or heterogeneity will be present in a sample size of only 16 individuals. It will be difficult if not impossible to observe a beneficial effect in such a small sample containing a variety of diseases all of which share only CANCER in common.

This gross deficiency in design will almost certainly prevent making meaningful observations. When this deficiency in experimental method is placed next to their previously observed poor result and high morbidity with this type of treatment in a "variety of neoplasms" I think it is clear that the study as proposed should not be done.

I have the uneasy suspicion, shared up by the revised statement of objective, that this revised protocol is a subterfuge to allow the investigators to achieve the purpose described in their original application; mainly, to test the ability of autologous marrow to "take" in patients who have received high doses of total body radiation. This letter question may be an important one to answer but I can't justify 200 rad total body radiation simply for this purpose, "even in terminal case material" (italics are mine).

I think there is sufficient question as to the propriety of these studies to warrant consideration by the entire Research Committee. I recommend therefore that this protocol and the previous one be circulated to all members of the Committee and that a meeting of the entire Committee be held to review this protocol prior to submitting a recommendation to the Dean.

Sincerely,

Thomas E. Gaffney, M.D.

Source: Department of Energy.

misleads the patients. Now let's look at a statement by Dr. Gaffney. He is writing about the researchers' stated purpose:

> "I have the uneasy suspicion, shared up by the revised statement of objective, that this revised protocol [protocol for the experiments at the University of Cincinnati] is a subterfuge to allow the investigators to achieve the purpose described in their original application" (17 April 1967)

Drs. Shields and Gaffney faced ethical dilemmas and acted ethically. However, the experiment was ultimately approved with some revisions. Drs. Shields and Gaffney, unlike many of their predecessors, acted ethically by pointing out that the scientists at the University of Cincinnati were not honestly stating the purpose of their experiments. The scientists who continued and approved the experiments were not acting in the best interest of the patients or of the staff caring for these patients. These scientists and those who funded the research may have thought that they were acting for the greater good—that they were working to protect soldiers who might be exposed to radiation. They may have believed that they were acting ethically because they might save the lives of thousands of soldiers by sacrificing a few "terminal" cancer patients. However, these scientists deceived the patients by hiding the purpose of their research and by not disclosing the adverse effects of whole-body radiation. They didn't disclose the purpose of their experiments to the patients and the staff, and they used language that misled the readers of their proposals—they didn't act or communicate ethically.

When you face ethical dilemmas in the workplace, you will rarely have clear-cut answers. You will need frameworks to help you weigh the various consequences of your actions while you determine how to respond ethically. You can approach ethical problems from four frameworks:[2]

- The morality of the action
- The consequences of the action
- The rights of the people involved
- The care for relationships

If you look at the **morality of an action**, you consider whether it violates your moral duty. Instead of looking at the consequences of the action, you consider the action itself—to decide whether the action is morally wrong. Some actions are wrong "just for what they are and not because of their bad consequences" (Wicclair and Farkas 16). For example, we consider lying and stealing to be morally wrong even if no one is harmed or if the lying and stealing produce positive consequences.

If you look solely at the **consequences of an action**, you are using what ethical theorists call the *standard of utility*. According to this standard, you select

---

[2] I base these frameworks on the works of Paul Dombrowski; Mark Wicclair and David Farkas; Steven Golen, Celeste Powers, and M. Agnes Titkemeyer; and Tom Beauchamp and Norman Bowie.

the course of action that produces the greatest good for the greatest number of people, or the least amount of harm for the fewest number of people (Wicclair and Farkas 16). Regardless of whether an action is morally right or wrong, the standard of utility "prohibits actions that produce more bad than good" (Wicclair and Farkas 18). Let's consider how the government of Great Britain in 2001 dealt with an outbreak of foot-and-mouth disease. Foot-and-mouth disease is a highly contagious viral disease of cattle, sheep, and other animals. The disease is difficult to control and can devastate herds of livestock. By affecting cattle and sheep, this disease can damage agricultural industries and severely limit the production and marketing of meat and milk. To stop the outbreak of this disease, the government of Great Britain called for the slaughtering of thousands of livestock in areas contaminated by the disease. By slaughtering livestock, it hoped to save thousands of other livestock and family farms. The government was using the standard of utility—it chose the least amount of harm for the fewest livestock and farmers. The government didn't focus solely on whether the action was right or wrong—it considered how it could produce the greatest good for the greatest number of people.

If you look at the impact of the action on others, you consider whether you are violating the **rights of the people involved** in the situation or the communication (Wicclair and Farkas 16). People have the right to be treated fairly, to receive "what is due or owed" and what they deserve or "can legitimately claim"; what they deserve, however, may be a "benefit or a burden" (Beauchamp and Bowie 40). People also have the right to be treated justly. They have the right to expect similar cases to be treated alike—equals to be treated equally and unequals unequally (Beauchamp and Bowie 41). Let's consider the human radiation experiments. Did the scientists violate the rights of the patients and the hospital staff? Did the patients have the right to be treated fairly and justly? Would the scientists have treated more educated or wealthy patients in the same way? The scientists violated the rights of the patients to whom they gave whole-body radiation. They also violated the rights of the staff by not disclosing the purpose of the experiments so that the staff could make informed decisions about the experiments. The scientists violated the ethical framework of considering the rights of the other people involved in the experiments—the patients and the staff.

If you look at the **care for relationships,** you consider how the action affects relationships with others, especially those closest to us—our families, our coworkers, and our community. For example, after the hijacked planes crashed into the World Trade Centers in New York in September 2001, some motion picture companies stopped the release of movies that portrayed hijacking and terrorism. They based their decisions not on whether the movies were good or bad, but instead on their care for those who had lost loved ones in the tragedy.

When facing an ethical problem, you can try to consider the implications from the ethical frameworks above. Some professionals will rely on only one of the frameworks to determine the most ethical course of action. Some professionals use all four frameworks to analyze an ethical dilemma. Many professionals do find that by examining an ethical dilemma through all four frameworks they can better determine the most ethical action or communication. They also can better understand the consequences of their choices.

For example, let's consider Susan, a quality-control engineer for an automobile manufacturer. She is responsible for testing a newly designed side-impact airbag. The company executives are eager to put the airbags into next year's models. Susan's tests of the new design have not been completely successful. In the tests, all the airbags inflated on impact, but 10 airbags out of every 100 tested inflated only 60 percent. The partially inflated airbags would protect passengers from most of a collision impact, but these passengers might receive more injuries than passengers whose airbags inflated fully. If the passengers with partially inflated airbags were small children, the injuries could be especially serious. She asks for more time to further test the airbags—however, the executives tell her that they must get the airbags on the new models.

Susan feels pressured to certify that the airbags are safe. If she looks at the situation from the moral framework, her choice is simple: It is wrong to say the airbags are safe when even one person could be hurt. If she looks at the situation through the standard of utility (the greatest good for the greatest number), her choice is more complex. Will she produce more bad than good if she doesn't certify the airbags? Will more consumers be hurt if she won't certify the airbags and the executives don't put them in the new models? If someone is hurt because the airbag didn't inflate properly, will her company be hurt? Will she lose her job if she doesn't certify the airbags? She can also consider how her actions will affect her relationships with her coworkers, her family members, and the consumer. She can consider whether she is willing to take responsibility for her action publicly and privately.

Using these frameworks, Susan can better recognize her fundamental ethical responsibilities and make an informed decision. Because these ethical frameworks often conflict, this chapter will help you ask the right questions to make ethical decisions and to communicate those decisions ethically.

▶ Making Ethical Decisions

Now that we have defined ethics and considered some ethical frameworks, let's consider three principles that will help you work through ethical dilemmas. Principle 1 will help you ask the right questions. Before you act, you will want to ask questions and seek answers. Then, when you have asked questions, you will be better equipped to make ethical decisions. Principle 2 suggests a decision-making model that you can use in working through ethical dilemmas. Once you have determined the ethical course of action, you will want to present the information ethically. Principle 3 presents guidelines that you can follow for ethical language.

"Uh, Where Are We?"[1]

On December 20, 1998, the two pilots of American Airlines flight 965 grew increasingly confused about instructions from air-traffic controllers. The pilots ultimately lost track of their position before the plane crashed into a mountain near Cali, Columbia. In the crash, 160 people were killed.

The *Washington Post*[2] reported that the crew was distracted by the air-traffic controller's offer to let them land directly from the north rather than circling for a landing from the south. The captain accepted the offer when the first officer told him, "Yeah, we'll have to scramble to get down. We can do it." The captain deployed the 'speed brakes,' flat panels on top of the wing that flip up and assist in rapid descents" (Phillips 1999). The crew was further distracted when the air-traffic controller asked them to report when they passed the ground radio-navigation point called Tulua. The *Washington Post* reported that on the flight-data recorder you could hear the captain flipping through papers in the cockpit looking for the radio codes for Tulua. As the captain was flipping, the plane had already passed Tulua. When the captain finally entered the Tulua code into the flight-management computer, the plane responded and turned to return to Tulua. For 66 seconds, the crew apparently did not notice the gentle turn through the moonless night; and the co-

pilots finally asked, "Uh, where are we?" The captain responded, "Let's go right to, uh, Tulua first of all." The crew then reprogramed the autopilot to begin the right turn—which the crew didn't realize the plane had already started. The crew apparently didn't know where they were in relation to Tulua—they had passed Tulua while they were flipping through papers looking for the Tulua code. The plane was headed directly for a mountain. According to The *Washington Post* and the flight-data recorder, the crew never saw the mountain.

What if the captain could have found the Tulua code more quickly? What if the writer of the manual containing the code had made the code more easily and quickly accessible? To know with certainty that the manual contributed to the crash, we need more information—information lost with the plane. Yet, writers need to consider that the words they write and the documents they design may affect lives. They have an ethical responsibility to write and design accurate, accessible, and clear documents.

---

[1] I want to thank Dr. Sam Dragga of Texas Tech University for telling me about this incident involving American Airlines Flight 965.

[2] Phillips, Don. "'Uh, Where are we?' U.S. Co-pilot asked before Columbia Crash." The *Washington Post* 19 Jan. 1999.

▶Principle 1: Ask the Right Questions

Now that we understand ethics, we can start to determine a process for making ethical decisions. Consider how one company, Raytheon, suggests that its employees face ethical problems. Raytheon has created an Ethics Quick Test for all its employees when making ethical decisions (see Figure 3.5). The test provides employees with a series of questions. These questions may not tell the employees how to act or what to do; however, these questions can guide employees as they examine the options they have when faced with an ethical

Figure 3.5
Raytheon's Ethics Quick Test

> **Raytheon Ethics Quick Test**
>
> When facing an ethical problem, ask yourself these questions:
>
> - Is the action legal?
> - Is it right?
> - Who will be affected?
> - Does it fit Raytheon's values?
> - How will I feel afterwards?
> - How would it look in the newspaper?
> - Will it reflect poorly on the company?
>
> When in doubt, ask. Keep asking until you get an answer.

Source: Raytheon, 2001. Online. Internet. 6 Sept. 2001. Available: http://www.raytheon.com/ethics/qtest.htm. Courtesy of Raytheon.

problem. Now, let's consider some questions that you might use when faced with an ethical dilemma. Like the Raytheon questions, these will help you recognize your fundamental ethical responsibilities.

- Is the action legal?
- Is it honest and truthful? Is it right?
- Are you acting in the best interest of all involved?
- Are you willing to take responsibility for the action or communication publicly and privately?
- Does the action violate anyone's rights?

Is the Action Legal?

As a workplace professional, you must follow all laws that apply to you, your product, and your organization. For example, when you communicate in the workplace, you must follow all laws that relate to ideas and products. If you use a visual aid or graphic from a Web site, you should determine if the information is copyrighted. If it is, you are legally obligated to obtain permission from the owner/creator to use that visual aid or graphic. If you use copyrighted visual aids, ideas, or graphics created and copyrighted by others without permission, you are in essence stealing from the owners.

Follow these guidelines when determining if your communication is legal:

- Get permission for any copyrighted information, graphics, or visual aids.
- If you don't know if the information is copyrighted, don't use it or ask someone who may know.

- Protect yourself and your organization by honoring all trademarks and liability laws.

Along with considering the communication, you will also want to make sure that you and your organization are following the law. For example, a chemical company may financially benefit by dumping harmful elements into our rivers and oceans; however, are their actions legal? Consider also the cigarette companies that in the last century manipulated nicotine levels. These companies, at the time, were acting legally—but were they acting ethically?

Is It Honest and Truthful? Is It Right?

You have a duty to be honest and truthful to your employer and to the public and to report problems and information that might negatively or positively influence your organization, its employees, or its products and services. Likewise, the public expects you to use money, equipment, and supplies honestly and to give accurate, complete information. You will be dishonest and untruthful if you manipulate the language to hide facts, to make data say what you or your managers want, or to leave out unfavorable information. For example, you would be acting unethically to only report the positive results of patients being treated with an experimental drug while hiding or otherwise not reporting negative results.

When facing ethical dilemmas, ask yourself whether the proposed action is right. If it is right, is it right for this particular situation or for all similar situations? If the action is right now, is it right for everyone else in the same situation (Golen, Power, and Titkemeyer 77)? For many situations, this answer will be quite clear. For example, if you manufacture a baby stroller and you know that it can collapse and injure or kill a child, you will clearly see that your company must redesign the product. Other situations may be more complex. For example, suppose you see a coworker use her company credit card to charge personal items. The company has a policy that employees may use the card only for company business. The company policy specifically states that employees may not charge personal items on the card. The coworker conscientiously pays the balance on the credit card each month, so the company doesn't incur any interest charges. Should you tell her supervisor? If you were her supervisor, would you want to know? After all, she is paying the balance each month—the company isn't being hurt. Is it right for her to use the credit card for personal charges?

You can also ask yourself: If it is right in this situation, is it right for everyone else in the same situation? If you can answer "yes," then your action is probably ethical. If you answer "no," then the action is probably unethical. If you are still uncertain, consider your options, ask more questions, or even talk to someone you trust and respect. This person may be able to help you look at the situation (see Principle 2 on p. 51).

TAKING IT INTO THE WORKPLACE

Your Profession and Its Code of Conduct

"Know what's right. Value what's right. Do what's right."

—Quoted from "Ethics at TI," Texas Instruments

Many professional organizations have developed a code of conduct or a code of ethics for their members. For example, the American Society of Civil Engineers has created a code of ethics that its members agree to follow. These codes give members standards for ethical behavior in the profession. While these codes are hard to enforce, they do specifically guide the organization's members in ethical professional behavior. Many businesses have also developed codes of conduct or ethics. Figure 3.6 presents a code of ethics from TXU, a utility company with power plants in the United States, Europe, and Australia. These codes give employees guidelines for ethical behavior, and they tell the public how the company will conduct its business. These codes are more enforceable than are those of professional organizations because companies can dismiss employees who don't follow the code.

Assignment

Assume that you are just graduating from college and that you plan to join a professional organization in your field. You want to find out if it has a code of ethics. Your assignment, then, is to

- Find a professional organization in your field.
- Find out if the organization has a code of ethics. Most professional organizations have a Web site and will post their code on the site. If your organization doesn't have a code of ethics, find another organization that does have a code. (Try to find an organization related to your field.) You might try these online resources:
  - National Institute for Engineering Ethics (http://www.niee.org)
  - Center for the Study of Ethics in Professions (http://csep.iit.edu/codes)
- Bring a copy of the code of ethics to class.
- Answer these questions about your code of ethics. Put your answers in a memo to your instructor:
  - Does the code provide a model for making ethical decisions?
  - Does the code help members to make ethical decisions? If so, how? If not, what would you include in the code?
  - What are the key points in the code?

Are You Acting in the Best Interest of All Involved?

Ideally in any given situation, the best interests of all involved will coincide, making it easy to identify the right action. However, you may face a situation where these interests conflict. If so, you may have an ethical dilemma. Consider how the Red Cross handled donations for the victims of the September 11, 2001, terrorist acts. In radio and television ads across the United States, the Red Cross asked for donations to help the victims. The Red Cross received millions of dollars—more money than it had ever received for disaster relief. Executives with the Red Cross decided that because they had received record amounts of money, they would put some of the money aside

| **Figure 3.6** | Code of Ethics from TXU |

Business Conduct

Our approach to Business Conduct was published following a review of our policy on business ethics in 1999. It is designed to ensure we behave appropriately when doing business and is focused on how we maintain relationships with our stakeholders, including customers, suppliers, contractors and the wider community. Continuing development of our policies on business ethics remains a priority area.

The approach covers certain key standards of behaviour by stating our position as a company and referring to any procedures that are in place to support that position. It is not intended to replace these procedures, but to reinforce them, emphasizing their importance.

The key standards are as follows:

- **our stakeholders.** We will listen to our stakeholders, working with them and for them. We will be creative and innovative in our actions to engage them.
- **part of a wider community.** We will focus on a sustainable future. We will help to understand and protect the environment. We will take social responsibility for our actions. We will respect the cultures of the communities in which we operate.
- **our customers.** We will be fast and flexible in understanding and responding to our customers' needs.
- **our suppliers.** We will work positively with our suppliers in a relationship of trust, mutuality and understanding.
- **our people.** We will treat each other with dignity and respect. We will work safely and with due regard to our health and that of others. We will promote an open and inclusive culture. We will work together, sharing the best of what we do, ensuring and promoting equality, diversity, fairness and respect in the workplace.
- **our decision making and judgement.** We will always work to the highest achievable standard. We will avoid conflicts of interest and all undue influences on our conduct. We will comply with the spirit of laws as well as their letter.
- **our markets and competition.** We will always support and encourage a competitive environment.
- **our information.** We will protect our information and the information provided to us by others.

Source: TXU. "Sustainability Report 2000." Online. Internet. 28 Sept. 2001. Available: http://www.txu.com/eu/uk/environ/sus/policies_organ/policies/bus_conduct.asp. Courtesy of TXU Business Services.

for future disasters. They reasoned that the money would still go to disaster victims, just not to victims of the September 11 tragedies. However, when donors discovered that their money wasn't going to the victims, they felt that the Red Cross was misleading them and was mishandling the money. Was the Red Cross acting in its best interest or the victims' best interests? By earmarking some of the September 11 donations, the Red Cross intended to protect the interests of future victims. However, was it acting in the best interest of the donors and the September 11 victims? By not disclosing to the public what it was doing and by not using the money as the donors expected, the Red Cross lost the trust of many current and potential donors and, in turn, possibly hurt the interests of future victims. When you face ethical problems, think about all the consequences and how these consequences will affect those involved both now and in the future.

Are You Willing to Take Responsibility for the Action or Communication Publicly and Privately?

The "bottom line" for many people is to determine whether they are willing to take responsibility for an action or a piece of communication. Would you want your coworkers, employer, friends, family, or the public to know that you had written a particular document or taken a particular course of action? If you don't want these people to know what you have written or done, then perhaps you are communicating or acting unethically. When faced with an ethical dilemma, consider whether you are willing to take responsibility for your action or communication with your coworkers, employer, friends, family, or the public. You might consider these additional questions when analyzing a possible action or communication:[3]

- Will it reflect poorly on you or your organization?
- How would it look in the local newspaper?
- How will I feel afterward? Will I be pleased with the action?

Does the Action Violate Anyone's Rights?

When faced with ethical dilemmas in the workplace, you may also consider whether the action or communication violates the rights of your organization, other employees, the public, or any others involved with the situation or communication (Wicclair and Farkas 16). These people have a right to be treated fairly and to receive "what is due or owed" and what they deserve or "can legitimately claim." Your organization, your coworkers, and the public also have the right to expect similar situations to be treated similarly, so consider whether you would act or communicate in the same way in similar situations. For example, let's again consider the human radiation experiments. Did the nursing staff at the University of Cincinnati have the right to know the purpose of the research? Did the researchers violate the rights of the nursing staff and the patients by not fully disclosing the purpose of the research and the risks involved in the research?

---

[3] I base these questions on the Raytheon Ethics Quick Test shown in Figure 3.5.

Raytheon Ethics Decision-Making Model

When confronting an ethical problem, consider the following steps:

- **Evaluate** the facts. Does the situation involve potentially illegal or unethical conduct?
- **Identify** the Raytheon values and policies that are relevant to the situation. What is the dilemma?
- **Determine** your responsibility, assess the risks, and consider others who will be impacted by your decision.
- Identify and **proceed** with the best course of action, keeping in mind the relevant values, policies, and interests of others.

Source: Raytheon, 2001. Online. Internet. 6 Sept. 2001. Available: http://www.raytheon.com/ethics/
decmod.htm. Courtesy of Raytheon.

▶Principle 2: Work Through Ethical Decisions

When facing ethical dilemmas, consider using a decision-making model before you act. By using a clear model, you are more likely to select the ethical course of action. Some organizations provide their employees with such models to ensure that their employees make decisions in line with the organization's philosophy. Likewise, professional organizations create models, sometimes called codes of ethics, to prevent members from behaving unethically. For example, a decision-making model for a doctor would guide doctors not to experiment on humans. A clear plan helps take the "guesswork" out of making ethical decisions. Let's look at a possible plan in Figure 3.7. This plan from Raytheon gives its employees four steps to follow when facing an ethical problem.

A plan such as Raytheon's can guide you. The tips in the shaded box below present a plan that you can follow as you work through ethical decisions.

▶ **Tips for Making Ethical Decisions**

- **Gather all the related information.** Make sure that you have all the facts and that your facts are accurate. You don't want to risk losing your job or your reputation by basing an important decision on inaccurate or incomplete information.

(continued on next page)

- **Think first and then communicate.** Once you are satisfied that you have all the facts and that they are accurate, consider all the possible communication choices and the ethical ramifications of those choices before you write. Pursue the course of action that is most ethical.

- **Find out all you can about the people affected by your decision and those who will read your communication.** Then you can determine the best way to approach these people if you want to argue for change or to suggest a course of action that they may not want to consider.

- **Talk to people whom you trust.** They may help you consider alternative yet ethical language choices. If you feel that you cannot trust anyone in your organization, talk to someone whom you trust outside the organization. Don't try to face the situation alone.

- **Aim to establish a reputation as a hardworking, loyal coworker with integrity.** Then, when you do take a stand on an ethical issue, your coworkers and superiors won't take your stand lightly.

▶Principle 3: Communicate Ethically

Once you have decided on an ethical course of action, you will want to communicate that information ethically. You communicate unethically when you leave the readers (and listeners) at a disadvantage or prevent them from making good decisions by manipulating the information or by leaving out information. Through the words and the visuals that you select, you control how readers perceive not only information, but also you and your organization. With this power, you also have an ethical responsibility to use words and visuals honestly and accurately. Let's look at two scenarios.

Scenario 1.   A stereo radio headset comes with a booklet that opens with "Read this important information before using your headset." The booklet warns readers to "use extreme caution or temporarily discontinue use in potentially hazardous situations." However, the booklet never specifically describes any "potentially hazardous situations." For instance, it doesn't warn readers to retract the FM antenna and remove the headset during electrical storms. This imprecise language misleads and, more importantly, endangers readers. The writers may have used the ambiguous phrase deliberately (Shimberg 11) or carelessly. In either situation, their lack of precision could endanger the lives of customers who use the headset.

Scenario 2.   A care booklet for an electric stove says that the burners have an "automatic temperature sensing control" that raises the heat level quickly and then monitors the temperature to keep food from burning. However, the booklet fails to tell readers that only certain models have this temperature sensing control. The booklet misleads readers because it doesn't indicate that only the highest-priced models have the sensing control and includes a visual aid showing the highest price models—not the lower-priced models without the sensing control. The visual aids are in black and white and, therefore, don't clearly show the red sensing control on the burner. Readers who do have the lower-priced models may burn foods or even create fire hazards because they think that their stove has the sensing control.

As the two scenarios illustrate, language and visuals are powerful tools of communication. Through language and visuals, you control how your readers perceive you and the subject of your communication. As you write, think about the meanings underlying the words and visuals that you select. Make sure that the message that readers receive is the message you intend and that you have not distorted or left out any information. To communicate ethically, follow these tips:

> ▶ **Tips for Using Ethical Language**
>
> - Use correct, accurate information.
> - Create honest impressions.
> - Use clear language.
> - Include all the information that readers need or have a right to know.
> - Avoid deemphasizing important information or emphasizing misleading information.
> - Take ownership of your writing.
> - Acknowledge the work of others.

Use Correct, Accurate Information

You have a responsibility to give readers correct and accurate information. For example, a researcher may be tempted to tamper with his or her research data to make it look precise by smoothing out or omitting irregularities so that the data appears statistically significant. The researcher has a responsibility to give readers the actual, untampered data with its irregularities regardless of its statistical significance or insignificance. When you use inaccurate or incorrect information, you can create a false impression.

Create Honest Impressions

Avoid creating false impressions that make readers think that conditions exist when they don't. You can create false impressions with both language and visual aids. Visual aids can mislead readers by including or excluding details. For example, if the particular model of computer that you are including in your company's catalog comes without a compact-disc drive, don't show a computer with a compact-disc drive. Visual aids can also mislead readers by distorting the data. For example, look at the graphic from a cereal box in Figure 3.8. The graphic has very small type and begins at eight rather than zero. The chart implies that Our Brand has one third less sugar than Brands X and Y because the readers don't see the entire chart. Actually, Our Brand has only about 5 percent less sugar than the competing brands.

Whether you are presenting information with words or visuals, give the readers a clear picture. Don't leave out information or cloud the information with vague language or confusing page layout. Consider the paragraphs from information that accompanies a drug used to treat obesity (see Figure 3.9). Does this information leave the readers with a clear impression of the side effects of the drug? Does it directly answer the question about whether the drug damages the heart valves? Does the size of the print make it easy or difficult for people to read?

In contrast, consider the information that accompanies a drug used to treat osteoarthritis (see Figure 3.10). The manufacturer clearly lists the side effects. The manufacturer uses clear, simple language and an accessible page layout to highlight negative information that the reader has a right to know before taking the drug.

While both drug manufacturers include information on side effects and have followed the law, the information in Figure 3.10 creates a more honest impression. The readers can easily see the information. The manufacturer clearly and directly answers the question "What are the possible side effects?" whereas the manufacturer of the other drug doesn't as clearly answer the question it poses: "Will this drug cause damage to heart valves?" Which manufacturer do you think handles the situation more ethically?

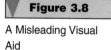

Figure 3.8

A Misleading Visual Aid

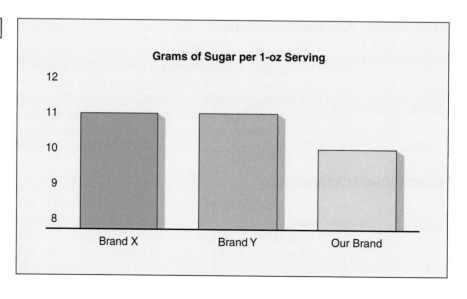

Figure 3.9

Misleading Information

Are there severe side effects associated with taking this drug?

Some weight loss drugs have been associated with pulmonary hypertension, a rare and sometimes fatal disease. In clinical studies of this drug, no cases of pulmonary hypertension have been reported. It is not known whether or not this drug may cause this disease. If you experience new or worsening shortness of breath (the first symptom of this disease) or if you experience chest pain, fainting, or swelling of your feet, ankles, or legs, stop taking this drug and see your physician.

Will this drug cause damage to heart valves?

Some weight loss drugs have been associated with cardiac valve dysfunction (heart valve disease). In two clinical studies, doctors examined patients' heart valve structure using cardiac ultrasound testing. In one study, 30 patients were examined before they took this drug and after they took this drug for three months. None of the patients showed heart valve disease. In the second study, 280 patients participated. One hundred forty patients took this drug, and 140 took a placebo (sugar pill) for 14 months. Four of the 140 (2.9%) who took this drug and five out of the 140 (3.6%) who took the placebo developed heart valve disease. You should discuss this issue further with your physician.

Use Clear Language

Unclear language can mislead or deceive readers. For example, if you are writing an instruction manual for a cordless vacuum cleaner, you might tell readers that the vacuum is "great for unexpected spills and messes and convenient for small, routine cleanup jobs around the house." This information, however, is not precise unless you explain what you mean by "spills and messes." Many readers may consider spills of milk or juice as a job for the vacuum although it is designed to clean up only dry materials such as dirt or cracker crumbs, not liquids. Instead, the instruction manual should say that the vacuum is "great for picking up dry materials such as dust or cracker crumbs. Do not use the vacuum to clean up spills of liquids and other wet materials. If you use the vacuum to pick up wet materials, you could be electrocuted."

You have a responsibility to write clearly to help your readers understand your message. Your intended readers will understand your writing when you write clearly and precisely and when you make the information easy to find. You will learn more about using clear language in Chapter 8, "Using Reader-Oriented Language," and about making information accessible in Chapter 9, "Designing Documents for Your Readers."

Include All the Information That Readers Need or Have a Right to Know

Missing or intentionally omitted information can mislead readers. A memo about the O-rings that lead to the *Challenger* space shuttle disaster in 1986

Figure 3.10

Patient Information for
an Osteoarthritis Drug

What are the possible side effects?

Patients taking this drug and/or related medicines have reported the following
serious but rare side effects:

- **Allergic reactions, such as swelling of the face, lips, tongue, and/or throat.**
  These reactions may cause you to have trouble breathing or swallowing. If
  you have trouble breathing or swallowing, contact your doctor immediately.
- **Stomach and intestinal bleeding.** This bleeding may occur with or without
  warning and, if severe, could lead to death. Although this bleeding happens
  rarely, you should watch for signs. If you see signs of bleeding, contact
  your doctor immediately.
- **Liver problems, including hepatitis and jaundice.** These problems occur
  rarely in patients taking this drug. Contact your doctor if you experience
  the following symptoms of liver problems: nausea, tiredness, itching,
  tenderness in the right upper abdomen, and/or flulike symptoms.
- **Kidney problems, including acute kidney failure and the worsening of
  chronic kidney failure.** If you have chronic kidney failure, speak with your
  doctor before taking this drug. If you experience signs of kidney failure,
  contact your doctor immediately.
- **Hair loss, hallucinations, increased levels of potassium in the blood, low
  blood-cell counts, tingling sensation, unusual headache with stiff neck
  (aseptic meningitis).** If you experience any of these serious side effects,
  contact your doctor.

Some patients have reported the following more common but **less serious side
effects** when taking this drug:

- Back pain
- Diarrhea
- Dizziness
- Headache
- Heartburn and upset stomach
- High blood pressure
- Nausea and/or vomiting
- Urinary tract infection

These side effects, both serious and less serious, appeared in at least 2% of
osteoarthritis patients receiving daily doses of 12.5 mg to 2.5 mg in clinical
studies.

The side effects described above do not include all of the side effects reported.
Your doctor or pharmacist can discuss with you a more complete list of side
effects. If you experience a medical problem that you think may be related to
this drug, talk to your doctor.

contained the following sentence: "The conclusion is that secondary sealing capability in the SRM field joint cannot be guaranteed." This sentence misleads readers because it doesn't give them enough information to correctly assess the potential risks. A more accurate sentence might say: "The conclusion is that the secondary seal is not effective at temperatures below 50 degrees Fahrenheit, so the joint is highly vulnerable to catastrophic failure at such temperatures" (Winsor 15). The first sentence is technically accurate but doesn't give readers enough information to arrive at correct conclusions.

Avoid Deemphasizing Important Information or Emphasizing Misleading Information

Writers can deemphasize information, especially negative information, or emphasize misleading or incorrect information through page layout, type size, or color. For example, the writer of an advertisement for a drug that controls heart rate emphasizes that the drug is safe. The word *safe* appears in a bright red band and in excessively large, 36-point type; yet at the bottom of the page in excessively small, 6-point black type, the advertisement warns that a defibrillator and emergency equipment should be available for the drug user. Clearly, the drug is not completely safe; however, the reader may never see the warning because of the page layout, type size, and color.

Take Ownership of Your Writing

When appropriate, include references to the writer. Your writing will be more effective when you include "I," "we," or an organization's name. Identifying the speaker or actor is a "necessary ingredient for ethical communication" (Rubens 335). Writing that omits references to a speaker or actor is easily manipulated. When a writer says, "Each of the participants was interviewed for 30 minutes," he or she is not taking responsibility for the data; and readers may not know who did the interviewing. Instead, the writer should say, "I interviewed each participant for 30 minutes." The revised sentence does not destroy the factual nature of the information; instead, it identifies the writer as the interviewer and places responsibility for the data from the interviews on the writer.

Acknowledge the Work of Others

If others helped you do the work or if you didn't do all the work, be sure to cite the work of those who helped or worked with you. If you use the work of others, cite your sources accurately. When you don't acknowledge the work of others, your readers assume that you have done all the work. When you take credit for work you have not done, you are acting unethically. If you use someone else's work in your research or writing without proper acknowledgement, you are guilty of plagiarism. Consider how you would feel if one of your coworkers didn't acknowledge your work to your manager or didn't cite your part in a big project.

▶Turning to the Law When Faced with an Ethical Dilemma

If you turn to the law to help you determine how to communicate or act ethically, you may or may not find answers. The law cannot always tell you how to communicate ethically. It can give you clearly defined legal restraints, but it can't give you ethical constraints that come only from the fine-tuning of your own judgment and conscience (Shimberg 11). Legal and ethical considerations can conflict. Paul Dombrowski explains that "ethics cannot be reduced to politics or the law because it must guide us when the law or political rules are silent or in error" (45). Ethics must then fill these gaps or help us know how to act when laws are silent or wrong. The law often sets up only minimal legal restraints for behavior whereas ethics implies "high standards of honest and honorable dealing and of methods used" for professions and businesses (Golen, Powers, and Titkemeyer 76).

By following only the law, you can still act unethically because the law and ethics can give you significantly different viewpoints. Consider the small print on many medicine advertisements. Let's consider the drug advertisement again: It said the drug was safe, yet the small print on the back of the advertisement told the user to have a defibrillator nearby. The advertisement followed the law but not ethical business practices. Think of advertisements you receive through your e-mail or mailbox; for example, just recently I received what looked like a ticket for a cruise. However, the ticket was only valid when the user purchased an airline ticket and hotel room. Unsuspecting readers may have thought they could actually take the ticket and board the ship—without paying. Technically, the unsuspecting readers could have used the boarding document, but only if they purchased something first, such as an airline ticket. This type of advertising may be legal, but is it ethical? As a professional, consider these legal standards as you write and communicate.

Understanding Copyright Laws

▶ For more information on copyright laws, see Chapter 16, "Creating User-Oriented Web Sites."

Copyright laws protect the authors or owners of any document, whether published or unpublished, from unauthorized use of that document by individuals or corporations. If an author sells or gives up his or her ownership of a document, such as to a publisher, copyright laws protect the corporation's ownership of the document. You must follow "fair use" guidelines and avoid using excessive amounts of information from documents written by someone else without getting permission—even if a corporation or other group owns the information. Be wary of using other people's written information and making only cosmetic changes to it. You could be guilty of violating copyright laws, and you certainly would be guilty of violating the author's rights and your moral duty to be honest.

Understanding Trademark Laws

Trademark laws protect the owners of a name or logo used for their products. A trademark is essentially a brand name. "A trademark includes any word, name, symbol, or device, or any combination, used, or intended to be used, in commerce to identify and distinguish the goods of one manufacturer or seller from goods manufactured or sold by others, and to indicate the source of the goods" (United States Patent and Trademark Office). You are responsible for protecting your company's or your client's trademark. To protect a trademark, follow these tips:

▶ **Tips for Protecting a Trademark**

- Use the trademark symbol each time you use the brand name in a document.
- Use a footnote the first time you use the brand name to tell the readers that the name or logo is a registered trademark. You might write: "Kleenex is a registered trademark of Kimberly-Clark Corporation."
- **Don't do anything to hurt the spirit of the trademark. Don't alter the trademark.** For example, Mickey Mouse is a positive symbol synonymous with Disney. Disney employees would alter the spirit of Mickey Mouse by using him in an advertisement for a movie that contains adult language and violence.

Understanding Liability Laws

Liability laws protect the public from inaccurate information from authors, editors, or publishers. These groups are responsible for injury that occurs from defective information even if they gave out the information unknowingly. You can help to protect your organization, your clients, and yourself from possible liability suits by following these tips adapted from Pamela S. Helyar:

▶ **Tips for Following Liability Laws**

- **Use language and visual aids that the users will understand.** For example, if you are writing a manual that children will use, include simple, clear visual aids that the users can easily follow. If you are writing a manual for nonnative speakers of English, use simple

(continued on next page)

language free of **idioms** (expressions whose meaning is different from the standard or literal meaning of the words they contain).

- **Warn the users of potential risks when using the product.** Make sure that users can easily see the warnings and that the warnings are clear and direct. For example, if you are warning users of the risk of cutting their fingers or toes with a lawn mower, put the warning both in the instruction manual and, more importantly, on the mower.

- **Tell the users what the product can do and what it can't or shouldn't do.** Tell users what the product is designed to do and what it isn't designed to do. Put this information not only in the instruction manual that will accompany the product, but also in information that a potential buyer will see. For example, a manual for a gas barbecue grill states: "For outdoor use only. Never operate grill in enclosed areas, as this could lead to gas accumulating from a leak, causing an explosion or a carbon monoxide buildup which could result in injury or death" (Coleman 4). While most users would know that they should operate a barbecue grill only outside, not inside, the manufacturer could be liable if it didn't warn users of the risk of using the grill indoors.

- **Inform users of all aspects of owning the product, from maintaining to disposing of the product.** When purchasing some products or services, the user may have ongoing responsibilities; you must inform the user of these responsibilities. For example, most car manuals provide owners with a maintenance schedule. Along with the schedule, the manual usually includes a statement such as "If your vehicle is damaged because you failed to follow the recommended Maintenance Schedule and/or to use or maintain fluids, fuel, lubricants, or refrigerants recommended in this Owner's Manual, your warranty may be invalid and may not cover the damage."

Understanding Federal Trade Commission Regulations

Federal Trade Commission regulations protect consumers from fraudulent and deceptive advertising. Manufacturers cannot claim or imply that a product or service will do something it can't. Manufacturers can't make false claims about their products. For example, a manufacturer can't claim that a side-impact airbag is completely safe when engineers report that 10 percent of the airbags did not fully inflate.

▶**Conclusion**   As a professional in the workplace, you have a responsibility to create messages that impart clear, truthful, accurate information. Anything less can mislead or even harm you, your organization, or the public. Strive to act ethically in all your dealings with others. Sometimes the decision to act ethically may be difficult and confusing. The principles and suggestions in this chapter will help you as you face ethical challenges and as you try to use ethical language in your communications. The "Worksheet for Ethical Communication" summarizes these principles and suggestions. Refer to it when you have questions or concerns about using ethical language.

| WORKSHEET | ## for Ethical Communication |

▶ **Principle 1: Ask the Right Questions**
- Is the action legal?
- Is it honest and truthful? Is it right?
  Are you acting in the best interest of all involved?
- Are you willing to take responsibility for the action publicly and privately?
- Does the action violate anyone's rights?

▶ **Principle 2: Working Through Ethical Decisions**
- Do you have all the facts?
- Have you found out all that you can about the people involved and about readers of your communication, especially those readers who make the decisions?
- Have you talked to people whom you trust about the situation?
- Are you working to establish a reputation as a hardworking, loyal coworker with integrity?

▶ **Principle 3: Communicate Ethically**
- Have you used correct, accurate information?
  Have you created honest impressions?
- Have you used clear, precise language? Have you avoided misleading language?
- Have you included all the information that readers need or have a right to know, even if that information is negative?
- Have you deemphasized or suppressed important information—information that you should emphasize or highlight?
- Have you avoided highlighting or emphasizing invalid, misleading, or incorrect information?
- Have you or has the organization taken responsibility in the document for the actions and for the communication?
- Have you acknowledged the work of others?

▶ **EXERCISES**

1. This exercise is a team assignment. Your instructor will assign you to a team or allow you to select team members. You and your team will decide on the language to use in a report on the testing of a new battery-powered smoke detector. The situation is as follows:

   Testing revealed that the battery-powered smoke detectors do not always sound when the battery is low. Specifically, 75 percent of the smoke detectors emitted a sound to indicate a low battery, and the sound emitted by 20 percent of the detectors was so weak that a homeowner could not hear it beyond 20 feet. Your supervisor and her manager want to start production of the smoke detectors within two weeks. They are waiting for your test results. Because earlier reports from other employees did not indicate problems with the smoke detectors, your supervisor is assuming that the test results that you report will be insignificant. She and her manager will not be pleased if their division of the company can't begin manufacturing these smoke detectors since the division has not shown a profit in the last three quarters. If the division doesn't begin showing a profit, the company may downsize or eliminate the division.

   Your team should complete the following:

   a. Determine what language choices you have for reporting the test results.
   b. Apply Principles 1 and 3 from the "Worksheet for Ethical Communication" to analyze these language choices. Write a memo to your instructor listing each choice and explaining the consequences of each choice.
   c. Write a memo to your supervisor reporting the test results and recommending a course of action.

2. Working with a team, research an incident that involved ethics, such as the Challenger accident, the collapse of the Kansas City Hyatt Regency walkways, or the Three Mile Island accident. (If you need some ideas, go to the Online Ethics Center for Engineering and Science at http://onlineethics.org or talk to a reference librarian at your college or university library.) In a memo to your classmates,

   • Describe the incident. Tell your classmates what happened.
   • Explain the ethical dilemma involved in the incident. What ethical and unethical decisions were made?
   • Analyze the consequences of the unethical actions. You might use the questions under Principle 1 as you analyze the consequences.
   • Suggest the ethical course of action and the consequences of that action.

   Your instructor may ask you to present your information and analysis in class.

3. Find an advertisement or product information that you believe misleads the reader. You can find advertisements and product information in magazines, in newspapers, on the Web, or in documentation that accompanies consumer products. When you find the advertisement or product information that misleads,

   • Photocopy it so you may bring it to class
   • Write a memorandum to your instructor explaining why the advertisement or product information misleads the reader
   • Attach a copy of the advertisement or

product information to your memorandum

4. Interview a professional in your field who has faced ethical dilemmas when communicating in the workplace. Ask how he or she dealt with these dilemmas. Also ask the professional to give you some sample documents involved in one of these dilemmas or to give you examples of dilemmas that he or she faced. After the interview, write a memo to your classmates. In the memo,

- Introduce the professional and describe his or her job.
- Describe how the professional deals with ethical dilemmas—does he or she have guidelines to follow? Are they his or her guidelines? Are they the employer's guidelines? Are the guidelines from a professional organization?
- If possible, give examples of dilemmas that the professional has faced and attach sample documents involved in these dilemmas.

5. Search newspapers, news magazines, the Web, professional journals, or trade magazines to find a recent public incident that involved an ethical dilemma. Once you have found an incident, write a memo to your instructor

- Describing the incident and explaining how it violated ethical standards
- Describing how the individuals or organizations involved applied unethical standards in their public statements or actions during and after the incident

6. These two scenarios describe ethical dilemmas that you might face in the workplace. Be prepared to discuss them in class.

   a. You are a quality-control engineer for an automobile manufacturer. You are responsible for testing a new design for a side-impact airbag. Company executives are eager to put these new airbags into next year's models because two other major automobile manufacturers have similar airbags in current models. However, your tests of the new design have not been completely successful. In the tests, all the airbags inflated on impact, but 10 airbags out of every 100 tested inflated only 60 percent. The partially inflated airbags would protect passengers from most of a collision impact, but these passengers might receive more injuries than passengers whose airbags inflated fully. If the passengers with partially inflated airbags were small children, the injuries could be especially serious.

   Before reporting the results, you tell your manager that you would like to test the airbags further to make sure that they are reliable and safe. Your manager explains that company executives want to get the airbags on the market as soon as possible—in fact, the marketing department is already working on the promotional material for the new airbags. The executives want the test results by the end of the week, so your manager can't authorize more tests. You now feel pressured to certify that the airbags are safe. Indeed, all the airbags inflated—at least partially. Write a memo to your instructor analyzing the options that you face and the choice that you would make. As you analyze this ethical dilemma, use the "Worksheet for Ethical Communication."

   b. During the summer, you begin work as an intern for Centurian, Inc., a civil engineering company. You got the job on the recommendation of your best friend's dad, Mr. Roger Thomas. You really appreciate the opportunity to work for this company and hope that they may ask you to return during the Christmas break. As part of your responsibilities, you are helping to maintain the company's Web site. As you begin your work on the Web site, you find that the site contains several copyrighted graphics and images. In fact, the image on the homepage is a copyrighted image and the company has apparently not asked for or received permission to use the image. You also find that the company has used passages from product literature without citing sources. Write a memo to your instructor describing the options that you face and the choice that you would make. As you analyze this ethical dilemma, use the "Worksheet for Ethical Communication."

7. Working with a team, research an issue that involves ethics. For example, you might study an issue related to bioethics, such as human stem cell research. If you need some ideas for information on bioethics, go to the National Bioethics Advisory Commission's Publications page (http://www.bioethics.gov) or the Centre for Applied Ethics (http://www.ethics.ubc.ca). If you are interested in a topic related to ethics and engineering, go to the Online Ethics Center for Engineering and Science at http://onlineethics.org. For other issues in ethics, visit with a reference librarian at your college or university library. In a memo to your classmates,

- Describe the issue
- Explain the ethical dilemma involved in the issue
- Analyze the possible actions and consequences of those actions
- Suggest the ethical course of action and the consequences of that action

In a memo to your instructor, present your analysis and suggest the ethical action you would take. Your instructor may ask you to present your information and analysis in class.

A Broken Promise

Background

You are a programmer and software documentation specialist for Custom Programs, Inc., a company that writes software programs for technical applications in the medical field. For over a year, you have been writing software for Custom Programs customers. When you were hired, your manager understood that you knew little about the medical field and thus agreed that medical specialists would examine the software and the documentation to make sure that the information was accurate and complete. Your manager also assured you that a group of users would test the manuals. However, over the past six months, you have been concerned about the feedback that both the medical specialists and the users have been giving you. You have two concerns:

- You fear that the documentation and training materials that you write contain errors and inaccurate information because the medical specialists merely glance at the drafts that you send them. In question-and-answer sessions about the drafts, the specialists seem bothered and evasive about special problems with the drafts and about your questions. You believe that the medical specialists are not reading the drafts for accuracy and completeness but are merely "blindly" approving them.

- You believe that the documentation and training materials don't meet the needs of customers because the user testing is inadequate. The company is not appropriately compensating the individuals who test the drafts, so they don't spend adequate time testing them. In fact, they are annoyed by the tests and resent questions about the

drafts. You have asked the company to allow you to increase the compensation to the testers, but the company says the current compensation is adequate. On the basis of this minimal user testing the company claims that its documentation and training materials are user tested although no legitimate user testing actually occurs. Basically, whatever you write the company prints and gives to its customers in medical clinics, hospitals, and emergency rooms, regardless of its accuracy, correctness, or usefulness to users.

Over the next six months you will be writing documentation for software used in the emergency center of a local hospital. The hospital staff may use this software and the accompanying documentation in life-threatening situations, and you are concerned about possible inaccuracies, errors, and usability.

Assignment

1. Decide what ethical dilemma you face.
2. Apply Principles 1 and 3 from the "Worksheet for Ethical Communication" to analyze the dilemma and to determine what language, if any, you might use to report this dilemma to your manager.
3. Write a brief memo to your instructor explaining this dilemma. If you were to report this dilemma to your manager, list the language choices available to you and the choice that you would select. Explain the consequences of this language and why you would use it.
4. Write the memo to your manager.

4

Collaborating and the Writing Process

As a professional in the workplace, you may work as part of a team to produce various types of documents. The team might collaborate to design a new product, to propose a project, to solve problems, or to write procedures. The type and level of the collaboration will depend on the project, its purpose, and the team's work style. Professionals collaborate because teams often can prepare solutions, products, designs, and written documents better and more efficiently than can individuals working alone. For many professionals, collaborating is frustrating and time-consuming because they don't know how to collaborate effectively and efficiently. Team members can minimize and frequently eliminate these frustrations and time problems by taking certain steps to get started, using current technology to simplify their tasks, and creating an environment favorable for collaborating.

This chapter presents three principles to help you effectively collaborate throughout the writing process. The first principle suggests steps that team members can take to ensure effective and organized collaboration from the start. The second principle suggests using electronic media to collaborate when team members are drafting, revising, and editing; you will learn how technology can simplify and enhance collaboration. The third principle presents guidelines to help you become an effective collaborator.

▶Collaborative Writing in the Workplace

You can write collaboratively in many ways in the workplace: You can collaborate as part of a team where members equally share writing responsibilities or as part of a team where primarily one member's task is writing. You do not have to be on a team, however, to work collaboratively. You also can collaborate by writing for others. Let's begin by discussing that type of collaboration.

Collaborating When Writing for Others

When you collaborate by writing for others, you write all or most of a document while other professionals supply the information you need to write, design, and perhaps publish. A good example of this type of collaboration is Paul's work on a proposal for a new telecommunications system for the Osteopathic Medical Center. Paul is a proposal writer for a telecommunications company. He has a strong background in the telecommunications industry. He understands the hardware used by his company and can communicate effectively with other technical experts and with his company's salespeople. To complete his proposal, Paul discusses the medical center's needs with the center's administrators and with the salespeople who are working with them. He also collaborates with several technical experts and with the salespeople who will present this proposal to the hospital administrators. Paul writes the proposal and then collaborates with graphic designers on the layout. The salespeople, however, will present the proposal to the Osteopathic Medical Center; Paul's name won't appear on the proposal.

You can also write collaboratively by preparing a document for someone else's signature. You might collaborate with that person to determine what he or she wants in the document; and then as you write, you and that person might collaborate to be sure that the document is meeting his or her expectations. In these situations, you will have the ultimate responsibility for gathering and analyzing the information needed for the document. You might collaborate with other professionals to obtain information, but you are responsible for using your expertise to write a document that will carry someone else's signature.

A good example of this type of collaboration occurs in Rhonda's job. Rhonda, an engineer for an architectural engineering company, is responsible for preparing construction specifications. She recently wrote specifications for protecting the underground pipes of a water-pumping station that the company is designing. She researched the protection required for the pipes and wrote the specifications, and the project manager ultimately signed the specifications.

Collaborating as a Team Member

When you collaborate as a team member, you work with one or more people to write a document. For example, a team prepares user manuals for computer hardware. Team members work together to determine the purpose of the manual and the types of information that users will need. Early in the project, the team leader determines each team member's strengths and expertise and uses this information to assign roles and delegate writing assignments. Before writing begins, the team sets a time schedule and creates an outline for the manual. The team creates style guidelines and prototype documents, so that each member knows how to lay out the pages. These early steps help each member to write drafts that the team can easily merge into one document. Individually, team members research and draft specific sections of the manual. They put their sections online in a shared directory where all members can review the sections. Together, team members revise the manual. One team member who serves as editor edits and proofreads the final draft for the team as a whole to approve.

In that collaboration, the team plans and writes the draft; team members are coauthors, equally sharing responsibility for the document. Team members also can collaborate by unequally sharing responsibility for a document: the team plans and outlines the document, but only one or two members write it.

For example, Neil collaborated with coworkers in engineering and management to prepare a proposal. They analyzed the writing situation together, brainstormed about what to include in the proposal, and outlined the proposal, but Neil wrote all sections of the proposal except the plan of action and the budget. The team members did not share the writing responsibility equally, yet each one contributed. Neil wrote most of the proposal because he had worked most closely with the readers and understood their situation. His teammates worked on the plan of action and the budget because he didn't have the expertise to write either of them. In some team writing projects, you may have more or less responsibility because of your job position or technical expertise.

▶ Principle 1: Collaborate to Analyze the Writing Situation and Plan the Document

To collaborate successfully, team members need to move through the stages of the writing process shown in Figure 4.1. Team members should start working together at the beginning of the writing process, not at the drafting stage. This section suggests ways of determining and organizing the team's tasks to analyze the writing situation and plan the document.

At the first team meeting, team members attend to basic housekeeping tasks. These tasks appear in the tips box that follows. Take care of these tasks during the first meeting, to organize the project and to foster effective and efficient communication.

Figure 4.1

The Writing Process
and Collaboration

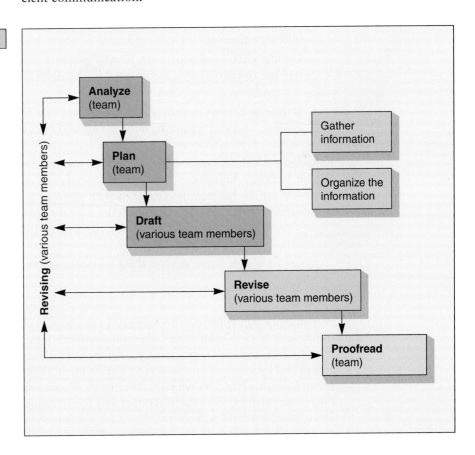

▶ See Chapter 9, "Designing Documents for Your Readers," for more information on style sheets.

▶ **Tips for Conducting the First Team Meeting**

- **Determine your team's assignment.** Before you begin, ask, "What are we supposed to do?" (See the section "Analyzing the Writing Situation as a Team."

- **Trade phone numbers, e-mail addresses, and, if appropriate, fax numbers.** This information is especially important if the team members are geographically separated.

- **Select a project manager or managing editor** (if the team doesn't have one assigned). This person serves as a liaison between the team and management. In a school setting, this person represents the team when contacting the instructor.

- **Decide or assign roles for each team member** (if the roles aren't already assigned). Even though the team is responsible for the final document, each team member will have a primary responsibility for a task that best fits his or her technical expertise and abilities.

- **Determine how the team will communicate**—by means of e-mail, a listserv, a Web site, face-to-face meetings, videoconferences, telephone conferences, or a combination of these media.

- **Decide what word-processing and/or graphics software your team will use to prepare the document.** Make sure that all team members can easily access the software they need.

- **Decide how team members will share computer files of the drafting and revising.** Determine if you will use e-mail, a shared directory, or a Web site.

- **Set a schedule.** Begin with the date the project is due and work backward. For example, if the project is due on April 12, set a date of April 10 for a completed draft with all front and back matter, April 1 for a revised draft, and March 20 for a draft. (See the section "Setting a Schedule and Deciding How the Team Will Communicate.")

- **Create a style sheet.** A style sheet will save you time.

As you and other team members discuss how you will communicate with each other, remember that effective communication need not be face to face. Many teams use electronic media to communicate. For example, a team can use e-mail or a listserv. With a listserv, each team member can send messages to the entire team, and then individual team members can respond or ask questions. Each team member sees the responses and the questions. Team members can even "vote" on certain decisions by means of a listserv or e-mail. Alternatively, many teams choose to set up sites on the Web. Team members can post drafts and other needed information on the Web site. These electronic media allow teams to collaborate with relatively few face-to-face meetings or telephone conversations. With electronic media, you don't have to wait for a meeting or make a phone call to share an idea or ask a question.

Analyzing the Writing Situation as a Team

Before a team can begin determining and organizing its tasks, team members need to look at the writing situation together. But before the team can analyze the writing situation, all team members must understand the project. The team leader, your instructor, or a representative from the organization needs to explain what the team is expected to accomplish. Once the members understand the team's assignment, they can begin analyzing the writing situation. Figure 4.2 suggests some questions that the team might ask. Be sure to allow ample time for analyzing the writing situation, as this step lays the foundation for the rest of the project.

Setting a Schedule and Deciding How the Team Will Communicate

Once the team has analyzed the writing situation and understands its assignment, the team can establish a schedule for gathering information, drafting, revising, and proofreading. A schedule will clarify

- Each member's responsibility
- How each member's work relates to the work of the whole team
- When each member should complete his or her work

The schedule should list specific and reasonable dates for completing individual work and allow for team meetings or other communication to discuss the individual work—especially the drafts written by team members. The schedule also should encourage team members to communicate frequently. Team members need to know how each member's work is progressing, so the team and the project manager can track the project. These meetings and the communication will also help the team to identify and resolve any problems.

▼ **Figure 4.2**	
Questions That Team Members Might Ask When Analyzing the Writing Situation	• Who will read our document? • Have our readers ever worked with individuals on our team or in our organization? If they have, what conflicts or problems, if any, occurred? How can we avoid such conflicts or problems? • How will our readers use our document: to make a decision, to answer specific questions, to gather information, to complete a task? • What do our readers know about the topic of our document? • What are our readers' attitudes about the topic or our organization? • How will our readers react to the topic or to our organization?

If possible, the schedule should allow for the unexpected, such as team members being transferred to other projects or not being available because of illness or other personal situations. At any stage of the writing process, the team may face unexpected problems. For example, the information team members have gathered may turn out to be insufficient, or a draft may fail to meet the needs of readers. Unexpected problems will frustrate even the most organized team; however, a schedule with room for flexibility will alleviate some of the frustration.

Establishing Design and Style Guidelines

▶ For more detailed information about design guidelines, see Chapter 9, "Designing Documents for Your Readers."

The team can also establish design and style guidelines. By deciding on design and style guidelines before writing begins, the team simplifies later revising and proofreading because from the outset all team members use the same style and format when writing individual sections. Your team can write a specification document which describes the readers, outlines the document, provides sample layouts, and establishes style guidelines. When setting up these guidelines, consider the design and style questions listed in Figure 4.3.

▼ **Figure 4.3**

Design and Style Questions That Team Members Might Consider

Possible Design Questions

- What page layout and page size will be most effective for the readers and the purpose?
- What typeface and type size will we use for the text and the headings?
- Where will the headings appear on the page? Will they be indented? If so, how far will they be indented?
- What page margins will we use?
- What bullet style will we use for bulleted lists? Will we indent the bullets? If so, how far?
- What file format will each team member use to submit drafts? What word-processing or desktop publishing format will the team use?
- Will we use color? If so, where? What will our budget allow?

Possible Style Questions

- Will we use any specific abbreviations, terminology, or language?
- Will we use words or numerals for chapter numbers, section numbers, and other enumerations? Will we use Arabic or Roman numerals?
- What terminology will we use when referring to the readers, to the company, or to the team? Will we use second-person pronouns when referring to the readers?
- What conventions, if any, will we use when writing? (For example, if your team is writing software documentation, how will you refer to specific function keys or to the arrow keys on the keyboard? Will you use any icons?)
- How will we refer to figures and tables?

TAKING IT INTO THE WORKPLACE

Collaborating Across Generations

"The office isn't what it used to be. As a result, our working relationships have changed dramatically."
—Ron Zemke, coauthor of *Generations at Work* (quoted in Johnson 72)

During your career, you may report to someone 20 years your senior or 20 years your junior. With these differences, communication and work styles may vary. Ron Zemke reports that people of different generations may have "radically different approaches to their career and the way they relate to their coworkers" (quoted in Johnson 72). For example, consider a 60-year-old born at the dawn of World War II who may value a tradition of office formality versus the eager-to-please recent college graduate born at the end of the Cold War. Both generations have qualities that make them attractive to employers.

The secret to successful workplace collaboration is understanding how your coworkers' "generational framework" affects how they approach work (Johnson 72). Zemke identifies four generations in the workplace and suggests their strengths and some strategies for working with each generation. While these descriptions can help you as you collaborate, realize that each of your coworkers is an individual and despite their generation may have the work styles of other generations. As Kathy Carlisle of Right Management Consultants explains, while nearly all people have certain common generational characteristics, it's a mistake to assess a person's work style solely by their generation. So use these tips merely as guides as you collaborate with various generations.

The Veterans
Born between 1920 and the early 1940s
Their Strengths: experience and knowledge
Tips for Collaborating with Veterans:
- When possible, conduct business face-to-

face. Veterans want to work with "living, breathing humans" (quoted in Johnson 72).
- Treat Veterans with respect. Don't dismiss the value of their abilities or their knowledge.

The Baby Boomers
Born after World War II through the mid-1960s
Their Strengths: working with teams, collaborative decision making
Tips for Collaborating with Boomers:
- Conduct some face-to-face meetings (at least electronically).
- Give them credit for their work and contributions.

Generation Xers
Born in the late 1960s through 1980
Their Strengths: work well independently, but appreciate constructive feedback
Tips for Collaborating with Generation Xers:
- Include time for constructive feedback of their team contribution.
- When possible, avoid the meeting and conduct business by e-mail or groupware.

Generation Nexters
Born after 1980
Their Strengths: enthusiastic, eager to learn, believe in setting goals and working hard
Tips for Collaborating with Nexters:
- Put them on a team with a strong leader. They like supervised, structured environments.
- Put them on teams with Veterans, as their work styles are similar.

Assignment
Prepare a profile of your work style. For example, do you prefer to be the leader or to work with a strong leader? Do you like meetings or using e-mail? After you have prepared your profile, decide if you fit into Zemke's generational profiles.

Gathering Information as a Team

Once the team has analyzed the writing situation, members can begin to decide what information to gather and how to structure that information. Team members might begin by brainstorming to gather ideas from each team member about the important information that the document should include. When setting up a brainstorming session, allow time for all team members to express their ideas. The team can also ask questions like those listed in Figure 4.4 to help determine what information to include.

Organizing the Document

After developing ideas through brainstorming or asking questions, the team can set up clear guidelines for individual work. One method for setting up such guidelines is outlining. Outlining can guide team members as they work individually. In a team situation, members can't assume that each member will keep the same outline in his or her head. Even in the best of teams, oral agreement about what a document will include can create conflicts and misunderstandings. A written outline will help the team to avoid such conflicts and misunderstandings. A written outline also can record what the team intends to include in the document and how the team wants that information organized. This record can help team members to prepare their individual sections as the team intends. (See Chapter 6, "Organizing Information for Your Readers," for more information on outlining.)

▶ Principle 2: Use Electronic Media to Collaborate

Electronic media allow teams to communicate asynchronously. Team members can work at different times and locations and still collaborate. For instance, you might be working on your draft at 7:30 A.M. in New York while your team members are sleeping in California. You e-mail your draft to your team members by 8:00 A.M., so they can work on it when they arrive at work three hours later. Electronic media also allow team members to track and store revisions

Figure 4.4

Questions That Team Members Might Ask When Deciding What Information to Include

- What is the primary purpose of our document?
- What are the objectives?
- What important information should we include?
- What additional information can we include?
- What information can we exclude?
- What types of information will we gather?
- Where can we gather the information, and how will we gather it?

and changes to documents. Without electronic media, teams may lose or forget important ideas.

A team can use any of the following electronic media to make collaborating easier and more efficient:

- Word-processing software to write, revise, and edit drafts
- E-mail, shared directories, or the Internet to exchange drafts and to communicate
- Groupware to collaborate from the same or different location

Using Word-Processing Software

When a team uses word-processing software, team members can exchange drafts by means of e-mail or the Web and can comment on or revise drafts directly on the electronic copies. When you receive a revised draft, you will have a record of those comments and revisions.

Word-processing software has three functions that all teams can use to collaborate effectively:

- The comment function
- The tracking function
- The highlighting function

With the **comment function**, team members can add electronic comments to drafts. The word-processing software will identify each team member's comments so team members can see other members' comments in one draft—not several drafts. When a team member adds comments to a document, the word processor highlights the text. When a team member moves the mouse across the highlighted passage, the comment pops up. The team member can also print the comments. Figure 4.5 shows the comment function from a word processor.

With the **tracking function**, team members can see how the revised version differs from the original draft. Team members can use this function to see marks that differ from the original. This function allows you to show passages that you want to delete (strikeout), to highlight passages that you want to add (highlight), and to revise. Some word processors have a function that will track and highlight any change you make in a draft. Figure 4.5 shows a passage where the word processor has tracked changes. Note that the word processor has used underscoring and red type to highlight this team member's suggested addition and used strikeout to highlight the text that the team member has suggested deleting. This function gives you the option to accept or reject the changes. This function is especially useful to teams whose members aren't working in the same location. Figure 4.5 also shows how a word processor tracks changes and gives readers the option of accepting or rejecting changes. It also shows the tracking box that tells the team members who suggested the change and gives the date of the change. This box also prompts the reader to accept or reject the change. In this passage, the writer recommends inserting "the Executive Committee discussed the funds available" and deleting "discussion by the Executive Committee and on recommendation of the treasurer." The reader recommends accepting the change.

With the **highlighting function,** you can use various colors to highlight text that you want to change, emphasize, or revise. The highlighting function works like an electronic highlighter pen. In Figure 4.5, the reader has used yellow highlighting to draw the writer's attention to a particular passage. Another reader might use blue highlighting for his or her comments. Each team member can use a different color to highlight his or her comments. The writer can then use the mouse to easily delete the highlighting.

Figure 4.5   Word-Processing Functions to Enhance Collaboration

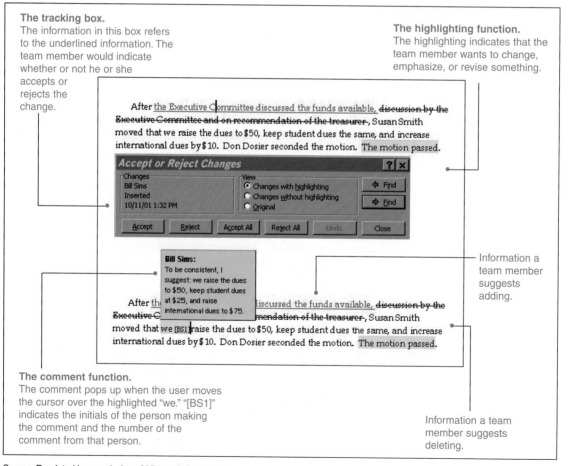

The tracking box.
The information in this box refers to the underlined information. The team member would indicate whether or not he or she accepts or rejects the change.

The highlighting function.
The highlighting indicates that the team member wants to change, emphasize, or revise something.

Information a team member suggests adding.

The comment function.
The comment pops up when the user moves the cursor over the highlighted "we." "[BS1]" indicates the initials of the person making the comment and the number of the comment from that person.

Information a team member suggests deleting.

Using Electronic Tools to Collaborate

Teams can use several electronic tools to exchange drafts and to communicate:

- E-mail and listservs
- The Web and intranets
- FTP (file transfer protocol)
- Videoconferencing
- Groupware

These electronic tools allow team members to share drafts created and to communicate outside of traditional face-to-face meetings. For example, the team might set up on your local area network (LAN) a shared directory where members can exchange or share files. Team members then send their drafts to the assigned directory for other team members to read, comment on, revise, and possibly approve. Everyone on the team can view all documents posted to that directory.

Teams can use e-mail and a listserv to exchange drafts. Team members send their drafts to other members by attaching the file to an e-mail message. With a listserv, all team members receive the draft and see the comments. When using a listserv, a team member can simultaneously send a copy of a draft to everyone on the listserv, so everyone receives the draft and can comment on it. Every member of the listserv can receive all the comments made by other members over the listserv, so a team can simulate a discussion of a draft. By sending drafts via e-mail, teams save time, especially if team members work in different geographic locations. It also can make the revising stage of the team's work easier.

Teams can also use **the Web** and **intranets** to exchange drafts. Team members post drafts and other information to a Web site where team members can post, view, and download drafts. For instance, if you're working with a team on a project in your technical communication class, your instructor may have a class Web site where you can post drafts for your team to download or view. If not, you may be able to create a site on your college's or university's server where your team can house drafts so team members can easily read each other's drafts. In the workplace, most companies have an internal network (intranet) where employees can post drafts for other employees to view and download. This intranet can be especially useful if team members work in different geographic locations.

With **FTP (file transfer protocol) sites,** teams have a common electronic workplace. With FTP, you can upload or download files that are stored on a remote server linked to the Internet. An FTP site can save time because, instead of continually e-mailing drafts, teams can simply upload and download files to a common site.

Videoconferencing provides teams with a means to meet face-to-face without being in the same room. Videocameras can be attached to computers so you can see and hear each other. Many organizations also have videoconferencing facilities where the camera isn't attached to a computer. These facilities accommodate larger groups for videoconferences. For example, your team might want to meet with a client in another country. If both you and your client have access to these facilities, you can easily conduct a meeting.

Groupware is a category of software that helps teams to collaborate and to track revisions to a document. Many groupware programs are currently available, such as Lotus Notes, SiteScape, and Microsoft NetMeeting. Unlike a word processor, groupware allows teams to work on the same document simultaneously. When one team member revises a common document, the revisions appear on everyone's copy of the document. Groupware also allows teams to carry on asynchronous and synchronous discussions. Synchronous discussions are almost simultaneous because they occur in real time. Teams can conduct these synchronous discussions not only with groupware, but also through services such as Instant Messenger on the Internet.

▶Principle 3: Collaborate Effectively

As you collaborate on a writing project, the relationships that develop among team members can affect the project. The collaboration is more likely to go smoothly if team members respect and understand each other. For example, if one member of a writing team likes to correspond by way of e-mail, team members might agree to use e-mail when they want to give information to each other. By encouraging the team to use e-mail, team members show respect for and understanding of one of the team members. If you have never worked with some or all of the members of the team, you and they might spend some time getting to know each other and each team member's expertise. As team members begin to work together, they can frequently share information relevant to the project. Such contact will help all members to feel that they are important and valued members of the team. This section of the chapter presents five guidelines to help team members to collaborate successfully.

Encouraging Team Members to Share Their Ideas

You and the other team members bring unique creativity and expertise to the project. Together, you and the other team members represent a wealth of knowledge and ideas. To best use this knowledge, all members must share their knowledge and ideas. Even when ideas clash, team members can learn and the project may benefit because the exchange of ideas may generate an ingenious solution to a problem or an especially effective way to organize the document. All team members should feel free to express their ideas—even when those ideas differ from the prevailing views expressed by the majority. To encourage this sharing of ideas, team members can

- Listen intently and respectfully to all team members
- Share ideas even when they differ from the views of other team members

Conducting a Successful Teleconference

 As the business world gets smaller, team members may be scattered across the globe. To communicate, team members may need to meet face-to-face yet can't travel to a common location. To solve this communication problem, many teams use teleconferences—meeting by telephone. Unlike the videoconference, the teleconference is a telephone call where all members can talk—they just can't see each other. Aimee Kratts, an information developer for BMC Software, suggests these tips for running a successful teleconference (18–19).

- **Consider each team member's time zone when setting up the teleconference.** If possible, use groupware or your company's calendar booking software (such as Microsoft Outlook) to book the teleconference because this software will automatically convert the conference time to the member's local time zone.
- **Create an agenda.** Send the agenda to the team at least a day before the teleconference.

The agenda will help the team stay on task during the teleconference.

- **Designate a call moderator.** A call moderator will make sure that the team sticks to the agenda and that all team members have an opportunity to speak.
- **During the meeting, repeat questions.** Be sure to repeat questions loudly and clearly to offset possible bad phone connections.
- **Facilitate effective communication.** During the teleconference, make sure that all members have an opportunity to contribute, ask members to clarify ambiguous or confusing comments, and listen for misinterpretations of comments.
- **Take minutes.** You or a designated team member or administrative assistant should take minutes. After the teleconference, distribute the minutes to the team. The minutes are "your last chance to make certain that everyone understands" the decisions made in the teleconference. (See Chapter 13 for information on writing meeting minutes.)

- Disagree and criticize respectfully and politely
- Be open to criticism of their ideas and writing

Listening Intently and Respectfully

Have you ever tried to express your ideas about something that you are truly interested in, but some of your listeners talked to others while you were speaking? Have you ever spoken to a group of people who weren't really listening—who didn't give you their undivided attention? Have you ever talked to listeners who appeared to hear what you were saying, but when you ask for their comments, you discovered that they hadn't really heard you? They looked as though they were listening, but their minds were elsewhere. Such situations are always frustrating, and in a collaborative setting they can discourage members from sharing their ideas. Each team member needs to know that the team will listen and will consider his or her ideas. Team members shouldn't expect the team to accept any or every idea that they present, but they can expect the team to listen and consider each idea.

To encourage other team members to share their ideas, listen intently and respectfully to everyone's ideas. Use both nonverbal and verbal signals to let speakers know that you are paying attention. Such signals help you to be an active listener—a listener who shows that he or she is paying attention. The following tips will help you to be an active listener:

▶ **Tips for Being an Active Listener**

- **Maintain eye contact with the speaker.** You let speakers know that you are actively listening if you maintain eye contact with them. Speakers who receive little eye contact feel that their listeners aren't paying attention.

- **Avoid body language that may distract the speaker or other team members.** To signal that you are listening intently, look at the speaker and avoid gestures that may be distracting.

- **Let the speaker finish his or her statements before you ask questions.** You can encourage all members of a team to speak by letting speakers finish their statements before you ask questions or make comments. If you continually interrupt, speakers may become distracted or assume that you aren't listening. Such interruptions may also discourage team members from sharing their ideas—especially team members who may be shy or timid.

- **Use phrases that indicate that you agree with the speaker.** Use expressions such as "I agree," "good idea," or "I like that" to let the speaker know that you agree.

- **Ask questions when you want something clarified or when you want more information.** By asking questions, you get more information to determine whether you agree or disagree with the speaker. You will also encourage other team members to share their ideas and to ask questions.

- **Occasionally, paraphrase or summarize what the speaker has said.** By paraphrasing, you can make sure that you understand what the speaker has said and give the speaker the opportunity to correct any misunderstanding. If you disagree, try to paraphrase what the speaker has said. You may discover that you actually agree with what the speaker said.

Sharing Information Willingly and Asking Others to Share Their Ideas

You can encourage others to share their ideas if you are willing to share information. If you discover information that may help another team member or that may affect what another team member is doing, share that information with the team in a timely manner. If you share such information, your team members will be more likely to share with you information that may affect your work on the project, and you will develop good working relationships.

Some team members may be shy or quiet and may not feel comfortable expressing their ideas during team meetings. If you see that some team members aren't participating in the team discussions, ask those members to share their ideas. You might ask, "Rob, what do you think of that approach?" or "What are your ideas about the project, Susie?" You might direct the discussion toward the shy or quiet members by saying, "Let's hear what John has to say about this topic" or "We've heard some good ideas from Linda and Patrick. Let's hear what Juan has to say." Ask shy or quiet members to participate, and help the team to include them in the discussions. These members can contribute valuable ideas.

Disagreeing and Criticizing Respectfully

One of the benefits of collaboration is the diversity of ideas and the conflicts that naturally occur. Conflicts are a healthy part of working with others. They can help a team to discover the best way to handle a project or the best way to organize a report. To encourage healthy conflict, team members can follow these tips:

 Tips for Disagreeing and Criticizing with Respect for Others

- **Criticize ideas or writing, not the person.** When you disagree with team members or criticize their writing or ideas, remember that they have feelings. Respect each member's feelings by criticizing his or her ideas or writing—not the person directly. When you want to criticize, avoid comments such as "Jenny, you didn't organize this section correctly." Instead, comment directly about the writing without referring to the writer: "Let's try organizing this section in another way."

- **Criticize objectively rather than subjectively.** You might criticize a specific part of the writing or disagree with a specific part of an idea or draft instead of making broad, subjective comments that you can't back up. For example, when criticizing a team member's writing, comment on specific aspects such as the style, the content, or the organization. You might say, "The draft is free of passive voice, but the style would be friendlier if we included more second-person pronouns," instead of saying, "I don't like the writing in your draft." The first statement objectively comments on the style; the second gives only the speaker's subjective opinion about the style.

(continued on next page)

> • **Include positive comments when you criticize or disagree.** When you criticize a draft written by another team member, at the same time comment on the strengths of his or her writing. For example, you might explain that you are suggesting ways to improve a basically good draft. Focus on the positive qualities of a draft or an idea, and tell the member about those qualities when you suggest changes or when you disagree.

Being Open to Criticism of Your Ideas and Writing

Just as you will criticize and disagree with your team members, they too will criticize and disagree with you. Be prepared to listen and be open to this criticism. Think of your writing and your ideas as belonging to the team and not to you. Then, when team members criticize your writing or your ideas, you won't automatically take the criticism personally. In this way, you will be able to discuss the best way to write the *team's* document or the best ideas for the *team's* project rather than trying to protect and defend *your* document and *your* ideas. When the team begins to evaluate your draft or your ideas, participate in the discussion and be willing to look at your draft or your ideas objectively—even offering suggestions for improving your own work. However, do not hesitate to try to persuade team members to use your idea or a part of your writing if you feel they are overlooking or dismissing it too quickly.

▶Conclusion

Working as part of a team to create a document can be a rewarding and enjoyable experience. When you and other team members listen to and respect each other's ideas, you can exchange ideas and improve your documents. Use the "Worksheet for Successful Collaboration" to help your team work effectively.

WORKSHEET for Successful Collaboration

▶ **At the first meeting,**
- Did you determine the team's assignment or task?
- Did each team member introduce himself or herself?
- Did you trade phone numbers, e-mail addresses, and, if appropriate, fax numbers?
- Did you select a project manager or team leader?
- Did the team assign roles (or tasks) to each member?
- Did you decide how the team would communicate?
- Did you decide what software your team will use?
- Did your team decide what electronic tools you will use to communicate and share documents?
- Did you set a schedule for completing your team's task?

▶ **When communicating with your team in meetings (face-to-face or electronic),**
- Did you listen intently and respectfully to all team members?
- Did you maintain eye contact with the speaker (in face-to-face meetings)?
- Did you let the speaker finish his or her statements?
- Did you avoid body language that would distract the speaker or other team members?
- Did you encourage others to share their ideas?
- Were you open to other team members' ideas?
- Did you willingly share your ideas?
- Did you disagree and criticize respectfully and politely?
- Were you open to criticism of your ideas or writing?

▶ **When critiquing a group member's document,**
- Did you criticize the ideas or the writing, not the person?
- Did you use objective rather than subjective comments?
- Did you begin with positive comments?

▶EXERCISES

1. The city council is trying to get more people to visit your city. The council has hired you and your classmates to write a brochure and prepare a Web site promoting the city. The council wants information about the city's history, attractions, entertainment, shopping, restaurants, and hotels and motels. Your instructor will divide your class into six teams and will select one editor-in-chief for the brochure and another for the Web site. Each editor-in-chief will determine style and design guidelines and will assign each team a section of the brochure or Web site. Once your team has an assignment, team members should conduct an initial meeting. (Be sure to follow the tips on page 70.) At the meeting,

   - Select a managing editor or team leader
   - Analyze the writing situation (remember to determine what information readers will expect)
   - Determine who will research and gather the information that readers will expect (make sure that all team members are responsible for some part of the research)
   - Set a schedule for the research and future meetings

   After team members have completed their research, the team should

   - Organize the information into an outline
   - Determine who will write each section of the outline (your managing editor or team leader may assign sections, or team members may select the sections that they want to write)
   - Set a schedule for completing the drafts of the sections and for revising (remember to use electronic media—such as word processing and e-mail—to draft, revise, and exchange information)

   After your team has completed its assigned sections, your managing editor or team leader will give your sections to the editor-in-chief, who will suggest revisions and then put the entire brochure and Web site together.

2. Keep a record of your work on the brochure or Web site in Exercise 1. You can keep your record on paper or on diskette. Each time that you work on the brochure, do the following:

   - Note the date and the amount of time that you spend working.
   - Note whether you worked alone or with another person.
   - Describe the work that you expected to get done.
   - Describe the work that you accomplished and the problems, if any, that you encountered.

   Record not only the facts but also your experiences collaborating. After you and your team have completed the brochure or Web site, write a memo to your instructor describing how collaboration affected your work and your team's section of the brochure or Web site. Use specific information from your record to support and illustrate the information that you include in the memo.

3. Interview a professional in your chosen field of study to gather information about the kinds of collaboration that you might expect as a professional. For example, if you are majoring in biology, interview a biologist. Before the interview, remember to

   - Call the professional for an appointment
   - Gather some background information on the professional's job

- Prepare questions about collaboration based on the information in this chapter

After the interview, write a memo to your instructor summarizing the information that you gathered about collaboration.

4. Visit your campus computer facilities. Find out what software programs and electronic communication tools a team could use to collaborate. Write a memo to your classmates telling them about these software programs and electronic tools.

> **CASE STUDY**

A Public Relations Problem at Big Lake

Background

This assignment is based on an actual situation that occurred at a power plant owned by a utility company based in Dallas, Texas.[1]

Big Lake Steam Electric Station, a power plant near a small south Texas town, uses steam to produce electricity. The main steam piping system at the plant carries steam to a turbine, which drives a generator that produces electricity. In March of 2001, the manager at Big Lake Steam Electric Station (Big Lake) observed that areas of this main steam piping system were sagging. The main steam system uses constant support hangers (a spring-type hanger) to carry the weight of its pipes and to reduce the effect of the piping system on the plant equipment it serves. Since the late 1960s when the plant was built, engineers have learned that constant support hangers alone cannot support the weight of the pipes over a long period of time. Instead, engineers recommend using a combination of constant support hangers and rigid supports (hangers without springs; see Figure 4.6). Without rigid supports, the sagging worsens, and the weight of the pipes transfers to the plant equipment. This equipment is not designed to carry the weight and will be permanently damaged if the sagging continues.

Knowing the damage that continued sagging could cause, the Big Lake manager asked the Power Engineering Division from the home office of his utility company to study the pipe support problem at his plant. Power Engineering's survey of the plant revealed that the main steam piping system was sagging over six and a half inches. Their survey also indicated that this sagging would become more pronounced in the future and would severely damage plant equipment.

Power Engineering's Solutions for Repairing the Plant

On July 17, 2002, the Power Engineering Division suggested two solutions: the first solution would only stabilize the pipes while the second would stabilize the pipes while correcting the existing sagging in the main steam piping system:

> **Solution 1:** Replace two of the constant support hangers with rigid supports in the area where the main steam piping system was sagging (at a cost of $132,100).

> **Solution 2:** Shorten the piping system by cutting out and removing a short section of the main steam piping system and then adding the rigid supports, thus pulling up the lower portion of the system and eliminating the sag (at a cost of $403,600).

Solution One: Replacing the Constant Support Hangers with Rigid Supports

The first solution would stabilize the pipes but would not eliminate the existing sagging. First, the Power Engineering Division would have to run a computer stress analysis on the pipes to verify that the existing sagging did not result in stresses that would exceed allowable limits. This analysis would require about forty hours; however, the plant would not have to be shut down during that period.

Once the stress analysis was completed and Power Engineering certified that the stress levels were acceptable, the plant personnel could schedule repair for the regular spring maintenance shutdown, so the plant personnel would

[1] This case, written by Brenda R. Sims, is adapted from Richard Louth and Ann Martin Scott, eds., *Collaborative Technical Writing: Theory and Practice* (St. Paul, Minn.: ATTW, 1989). Courtesy of the Association of Teachers of Technical Writing.

| Figure 4.6 | Constant Support Hangers Versus Rigid Supports |

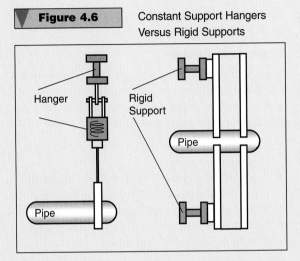

not lose any work time. The Power Engineering Division estimated that a maintenance crew could complete the work in approximately eighty hours.

Although this solution is relatively inexpensive and could occur without an additional, unscheduled plant shutdown, the Power Engineering Division would not recommend it as the best solution because without correcting the existing sag, a permanent low point would be created in the piping system. Low points can trap water and can lead to a serious problem called *water hammer*. Therefore, the plant would have to install a manual drain in the low point; and the plant personnel would have to periodically drain the low point manually. The Power Engineering Division was not convinced that the Big Lake personnel would consistently drain the low point throughout the year.

Solution Two: Shortening the Main Piping System and Adding Rigid Supports

The second solution would stabilize the pipes and eliminate the sagging in the main steam piping system. Unlike the first solution, shortening the main piping system would eliminate the possibility of a low point occurring after the rigid supports were added. Therefore, even though

the second solution costs $271,500 more than the first, it is a long-term solution to the sagging problem. The Power Engineering Division stressed that the plant probably would save money and time in the long run by shortening the piping system along with adding rigid supports because the plant would avoid any possible water hammer damage and additional repairs.

Shortening the piping system would take an additional two weeks beyond the scheduled spring maintenance shutdown. Since this would be an unscheduled shutdown, some of the plant personnel would have to take vacation time or time off without pay.

Discussions About the Solutions

After reviewing these two solutions, the Big Lake manager met with representatives from the Power Engineering Division on July 23 to discuss the feasibility of the solutions and to express his concerns over the cost in time and money posed by both solutions. The Big Lake manager believed that shortening the piping system would cost the plant and the consumer too much money. Since the Big Lake manager was also concerned about the time involved with both solutions, the Power Engineering Division sent a memo to him after the meeting outlining in detail the work needed to shorten and reweld a section of the main steam piping system and to replace the constant support hangers with rigid supports.

An Emergency Plant Shutdown and the Chosen Repair Solution

On August 30, before the plant manager decided how to repair the sagging piping system, the Big Lake plant experienced a boiler tube leak unrelated to the sagging pipes. The plant personnel had to perform an unscheduled plant shutdown to repair the leak. While they were cooling the plant down so that the repair work could begin, one of the constant supports broke, causing the main steam pipe to sag approximately two additional feet. The damaged hanger was temporarily repaired, so that the plant could resume operation and the plant manager could have more time to decide how to deal with the sagging pipe.

Ten days after the unscheduled shutdown, the Big Lake manager rejected the second solution (shortening the main piping system and adding rigid supports) primarily because of its high cost and chose the first solution (replacing the constant support hangers with rigid supports). With this solution, the repair work could occur during the regularly scheduled spring maintenance shutdown, and the plant would avoid an additional unscheduled shutdown and the expense of the second solution.

Citizens' Concern About the Plant Shutdowns and the Sagging Pipes

The August 30 shutdown at the plant greatly concerned the citizens of the surrounding town since the plant employs a large portion of the town's population. When the plant manager first discovered the pipe sagging problem in the main steam piping system, the citizens feared that

- The pipe sagging problem could close the plant permanently
- The steam carried by the sagging pipes could kill plant personnel if the sagging caused the pipes to rupture

Since these fears were unwarranted, the Big Lake manager had bought airtime on the local radio and television stations to explain that Big Lake would remain open and that the plant personnel were safe.

However, the shutdown on August 30 unnecessarily renewed the citizens' fears. They again feared that the plant would possibly close permanently, leaving the plant personnel without jobs. They also feared that if the plant did not close, the personnel would be in danger from the sagging pipes and would be laid off without pay when the pipes were eventually repaired. Now, the Big Lake manager had to convince the citizens that the plant needed only minor repairs that could be handled without an unscheduled

shutdown and that the plant personnel were not in any danger.

Team Assignment

Your team ultimately will write a letter—from the plant manager to the citizens of the small town near Big Lake—to be published in the local newspaper. The purpose of the letter is to

- Convince the citizens that the plant will not close permanently
- Convince the citizens that the sagging of the pipes could not cause a piping rupture that would endanger plant personnel
- Explain the type of repairs the plant manager has planned for the plant

You will interact with the team to

1. Decide what to include in the letter
2. Comment on the individual letters that each team member will write
3. Merge the individual letters into one final draft to turn in to your instructor

Your team will meet during three sessions. The instructions for each session follow below.

Session 1: Deciding What to Include in the Letter

After reading the assignment, your team should discuss the Big Lake situation and complete steps 1 and 2 below.

1. List the characteristics of the audience of the letter, the citizens of the small Texas town near Big Lake. The team can answer the following questions to determine the audience's characteristics:

   - Are the town's citizens interested in the Big Lake situation?
   - What is their current attitude toward the plant?
   - How would a permanent plant shutdown affect the town's citizens?
   - What will the citizens want to know about how sagging pipes will be repaired?

- What rumors have many of the citizens heard about the sagging pipes and how these pipes will affect the plant and its personnel? Are these rumors accurate?

2. Decide specifically what information your team will include in the letter to the citizens of the small town near Big Lake. Put this information in list form and give a copy to your instructor at the end of Session 1.

Before Session 2, each student should write an individual version of the letter and provide

copies for each member of the group and for the instructor.

Sessions 2 and 3: Commenting on the Individual Letters

During Sessions 2 and 3, your team will read and respond to each other's letters by completing the form "Responses to Group Members' Writing" (Figure 4.7) and identify sections from the different letters that the team could include or revise for the final draft of the letter. After reading the letters, each team member will

| ▼ **Figure 4.7** | Responses to Group Members' Writing |

Questions	Member 1	Member 2	Member 3	Member 4
Does the letter convince the citizens that the plant will not close permanently?				
Does the letter convince the citizens that the plant personnel are not in danger?				
Does the letter explain how the plant will be repaired?				
Does the tone of the letter establish empathy between the citizens and the plant personnel?				
Does the opening of the letter get the reader's attention?				
What is the letter's greatest strength?				

1. Write the name of the author under "Member 1" at the top of the second column
2. Answer each of the response questions about Member 1's letter in the appropriate place in the second column of the form
3. Follow steps 1 and 2 for each team member's letter (except your own)

After each team member has completed the response form, your team will

1. Discuss their responses to the different letters
2. Make a list of specific sections from the letters that you could include or revise for the final version of the letter
3. Give a copy of the above list to the instructor at the end of Session 3

Sessions 4 and 5: Merging the Individual Letters into One Final Draft

At the end of Session 5, your team will give one final draft of the letter to your instructor. To produce this draft, your team has several options:

- Write the draft using only sections from the individual letters written by the team members
- Revise sections of the individual letters to create the final draft
- Combine unrevised sections with revised sections of the individual letters to create the final draft
- Write the final draft using only the ideas gained from the individual letters

Regardless of the option chosen, your team should complete the final draft and turn it in to your instructor by the end of Session 5.

II | Knowing the Tools of the Writer

5

Researching Information Using Primary and Secondary Sources

Bill Simmons, a staff engineer for a utility company, must determine why some water pipes in the condensate system of a steam-power plant are vibrating and then write a report recommending a solution. Before making an appointment to go to the plant, Bill thinks about the information he will need to recommend a solution and to write an effective report. He knows he will need to do more than just inspect the system; but with the amount of information available to him, he feels overwhelmed. He's not quite sure where to begin or what sources will best suit his purpose. He needs a research plan and some help selecting appropriate research techniques and sources.

Bill's dilemma is not unusual. Many writers, especially beginners, don't know how to plan the research necessary for a project or what strategies to use for researching information. This chapter presents four principles to help you research and document information.[1]

▶ Principle 1: Plan Your Research

Bill thinks about the purpose of his document. He decides that he is writing primarily to recommend a viable solution to the problem of the vibrating pipes. His solution must be not only cost-effective and feasible but also well supported with research and testing. Bill also recognizes a long-term goal—to establish a reputation as a problem solver and to establish positive relationships with his supervisor and the plant manager.

As a professional, you too may conduct research to complete documents or projects. For some documents you may need only a single fact or figure, while for others you may need to do extensive research using several information-gathering techniques. How can you decide which techniques to use? You might consider using questions like those in Figure 5.1 as you plan your research.

After considering the readers' needs, the purpose, and the subject, develop a detailed plan for your research. Some writers like to draw an informal flow chart listing the steps in the process. Others prefer to list the questions they must answer first and then the steps needed to answer those questions. Let's consider Bill's situation again. After determining the type of information he needs, he decides to interview the plant manager and operations personnel, observe the vibrating pipes, examine company files and archives for instances of similar problems, investigate technical literature on similar problems and their solutions, and test the pipes. Before calling the plant manager, Bill writes these steps down in an informal flow chart (see Figure 5.2). Having planned his research to suit his purpose, Bill is now ready to select the techniques he will use to gather information.

---

[1] I would like to thank Ms. Gayla Byerly, reference librarian at the University of North Texas, for guiding and advising me while writing this chapter.

▼ **Figure 5.1**	

Questions to Consider
When Planning Your
Research

Consider your readers' needs	• Who are the primary readers? Are there secondary readers? If so, who?
	• Do the needs of the primary and secondary readers differ? If so, how?
	• What do your readers' expect from your research? What questions might they ask while reading your document?
	• What do your readers know about the subject? Are they experts, technicians, managers, or general readers?
	• What are your readers' attitudes toward the subject of your document?
	• How will your readers use the findings of your research?
Consider the purpose	• What is the purpose of your research and your document?
	• What do you want to accomplish or find out?
Consider your subject	• What, if anything, do you know about the subject?
	• What information, if any, are you missing? What do you still need to find out?
	• How can you get the information you need?
	• How much time do you need to gather the missing information or to conduct the research? Will the project allow you this much time? Do you need to adjust the scope of the project? Do you need to ask for more time?

▶Principle 2: Select Appropriate Primary Research Techniques

As you plan your research, select research techniques that will give you the information needed to answer your readers' questions. You may often select more than one technique, as did Bill. In this section, you will learn some of the more common primary research techniques:

• Interviews
• Questionnaires
• Observations
• Experiments

Primary research (sometimes called original or firsthand research) is gathering information for the first time—not relying on research previously conducted

Figure 5.2

Bill's Research Plan

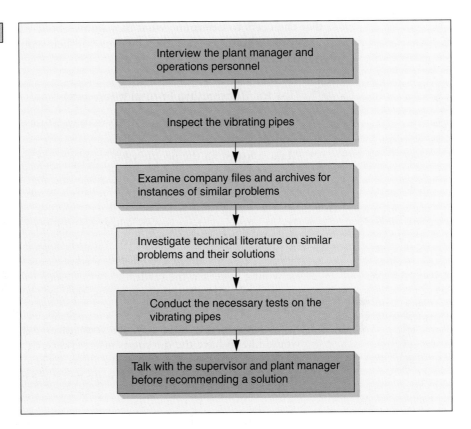

by others. For example, the data collected by the Mars *Pathfinder* is primary research—firsthand information about Mars's composition and climate.

Interview to Gather Information

You can gather valuable firsthand information from informal and formal interviews. Interviews give you the opportunity to get factual information from an expert, to hear firsthand observations of a situation, and to discover the experiences of the interviewee. For example, Bill plans to interview the plant manager and the operations personnel who have observed the vibrating pipes. From these interviews, he hopes to determine the characteristics of the problem, such as how frequently the pipes vibrate or whether the vibration is associated with any particular plant operation.

Informally Interview Coworkers and Colleagues

Interviews may be informal conversations in the office, by telephone, or by e-mail. Informal interviews can be a valuable method for gathering information. For many writing situations, informal interviews are the primary means of gathering information. Bill will informally interview plant managers and other engineers to determine what they know about vibrating pipes and how to stop the vibration. The following tips will help you to conduct successful informal interviews:

> ▶ **Tips for Conducting Formal Interviews**
>
> - **As you plan your research, write down questions that you might ask.**
> - **Make a list of all the people who could answer your questions.** From this list, select people whom you work with or know well to interview informally. (Set up formal interviews with people whom you don't work with or know well.)
> - **Try to interview these people when they are least busy.** When people are less busy, they will more freely share information with you and answer your questions more accurately.
> - **Be willing to return the favor.** If you are open to answering your coworkers' and colleagues' questions, they, in turn, will be more willing to answer yours.
> - **If you use e-mail to interview, ask your interviewee if he or she would like to have the questions inserted directly into the e-mail message or attached in a file.** If the interviewee would like the questions attached, ask what software he or she prefers.

Formally Interview People Whom You Don't Work With or Know Well

Formal interviews are the best choice for gathering accurate and thorough information from people whom you don't work with or know well. Bill will probably set up formal interviews with the plant manager and the operations manager since he doesn't work regularly with them. They will want to gather statistics and data about the vibrating pipes before talking to Bill, and a formally scheduled interview will give them the lead time they need. Use the tips in Figure 5.3 as you prepare for and conduct your formal interviews. Too frequently, beginners go to an interview with only a notepad and pencil—expecting to ad-lib the questions. Although this strategy (or lack of it) may occasionally work for experienced interviewers, most researchers who arrive at an interview without a written list of questions often leave without much of the information they intended to gather.

Gather Information Through Questionnaires

Questionnaires are a research tool for gathering information from a large group spread out over a wide geographic area. You might use a questionnaire to gather information about a group's preferences, attitudes, or beliefs. For example, if you were planning on changing the company's health plan, you

Figure 5.3

Tips for Effective
Interviews

Determine the purpose of the interview	Before you set up the interview, • **Identify the purpose of the interview.** • **Identify the specific information you want to gather.** Let's consider Bill's interview with Richard Hampton, operations manager at the power plant. Bill might identify the purpose of this interview as follows: *The purpose of my interview with Richard Hampton is to identify the frequency of the vibration, the effect of the vibration on the plant's operation, and the operations that seem to trigger the vibration. I also want to know what he believes is causing the vibration.*
Call the interviewee to set up the interview (you may also e-mail the interviewee)	When you call or e-mail, • **State the purpose of your interview** so the interviewee can tell you whether he or she can give you the needed information. If you need the information by a specific date, tell the interviewee. • **Be flexible about the time.** As possible, let the interviewee determine the time and date for the interview. • **Set the interview at the interviewee's office or at a location most convenient for the interviewee.** Make the interview location convenient for the interviewee, even if the location is not convenient for you. • **Ask permission to record** the interview if you plan to use audio or video recording equipment.
Prepare for the interview	Before the interview, find out as much about your subject as possible. • **Gather background information.** Look at secondary sources for the information that you seek. You may look unprepared if you ask questions that the professional literature answers. • **Plan good questions.** Ask specific, open-ended questions (see the section on questionnaires for more information).
Conduct the interview	Before the interview, • Give yourself plenty of time to get the interview. • Arrive on time. • Check your video and audio recording equipment, if you plan to use it. (continued on next page)

Figure 5.3		

(continued)		**At the beginning of the interview,**
		• Thank the interviewee for agreeing to do the interview.
		• State the subject and purpose of the interview.
		• Tell the interviewee how you plan to use the information.
		During the interview,
		• Take notes only when necessary. Be careful to write only important information—don't write so much that you can't maintain some eye contact with the interviewee or that the interviewee has to wait while you complete your notes.
		• Maintain eye contact. Your interviewee will give you more information if you seem sincerely interested.
		• Use your prepared questions.
		• Ask follow-up questions, such as:
		  • Can you give me an example of that?
		  • What additional actions would you suggest?
		• Ask the interviewee to clarify if you don't understand the answer:
		  • Can you give me an example?
		  • Can you simplify?
		  • Would you go over that again?
		• If the interviewee gets off the subject, be prepared to respectfully move the interview back to the intended focus. You might say, "Thank you for that interesting information. I know our time is short, so let's move on to the next question."
		At the end of the interview,
		• Ask the interviewee for final comments:
		  • Would you like to add any other information?
		• Ask permission to quote the interviewee.
		• Offer to send the interviewee a copy of the document where you will use information from the interview (if applicable).
		• Thank the interviewee for his or her time.
		• Leave promptly.

	Follow up	**After the interview,** • Write down the information that you want to remember from the interview. • Write the interviewee a thank-you note within two or three days.

might send a questionnaire to the employees to determine their opinions about the current company health plan. You can also use questionnaires to develop profiles about a group. For example, you might gather demographics about consumers as you ask them about what product brand they prefer or what newspaper they prefer. Questionnaires, however, have three disadvantages:

- The response rate for questionnaires is poor, usually 15 to 20 percent.
- You can't guarantee that the respondents are a representative sample, so you must carefully draw conclusions from the information that you gather from a questionnaire. The respondents who choose to respond to a questionnaire may have a bias about the subject of the questionnaire (Plumb and Spyridakis 626).
- You won't know if respondents misinterpret a question because questionnaires don't allow you to follow up and clarify as you can in an interview (Plumb and Spyridakis 626).

If you decide to send a questionnaire, remember that you are asking the respondents to do you a favor—with little, if any, benefit to them; so make sure that the questionnaire is as efficient and simple as possible.

Determining the Purpose, Sample Group, and Method

Before you begin preparing the questions for your questionnaire, ask yourself these questions:

- What is the purpose of this questionnaire? What do I want to learn?
- What kinds of questions will I ask?
- What will I do with the information that I collect? (Plumb and Spyridakis 627)
- Who is the target group I want to question?
- How will I select the target group (the intended respondents)? Will I select the respondents at random? See Figure 5.4 for questions that you might consider as you select the target group.
- How many questionnaires will I send? Remember that the more questionnaires you send, the more responses you will receive.
- How will you administer the questionnaire—by mail, by e-mail, by phone, or in person? You will receive more responses and quicker responses when you administer the questionnaire by e-mail, by phone, or in person. However, some respondents are uncomfortable, even annoyed, by phone surveys. By phone or in person, respondents may respond with less candor than with mail or e-mail questionnaires. Mailed questionnaires take less time and are inexpensive; however, fewer people will respond.

Preparing Effective Questions

Both closed-ended and open-ended questions are appropriate. **Closed-ended questions** will elicit answers that you can count or quantify. With closed-ended

Figure 5.4

Questions to Consider
When Identifying the
Target Group

Should the target group

- Have a certain level of education? If so, what level?

- Belong to a certain age group? If so, what age?

- Live in a specific geographic area? If so, what area?

- Contain only males, only females, or both?

- Possess a certain level of knowledge about a process or topic? (For example, should the respondents be experts in telecommunications?)

- Know how to use a certain type of tool or software?

- Speak a particular language?

- Have a certain level of income?

Source: Adapted from Carolyn Plumb and Jan H. Spyridakis, "Survey Research in Technical Communication: Designing and Administering Questionnaires." *Technical Communication* 39.4 (1992): 625–638.

questions, you limit respondents' answers. The respondents select only from the answers you provide. With **open-ended questions**, respondents answer with their own words. A questionnaire that uses closed-ended questions might include

- Multiple-choice questions
- Yes/no questions
- Ranking questions that ask respondents to arrange items in order of preference
- Ranking questions that ask respondents to rate items on a scale

Because closed-ended or quantitative questions yield totals and percentages, computer software can read and tabulate the answers. Such questions are particularly valuable when you have a large number of respondents.

Open-ended questions will yield answers that you can't easily tabulate, but they may give you valuable information that you can't gain through closed-ended questions. Open-ended questions tend to elicit more accurate information because they don't limit the respondents to the writer's suggested answers (Anderson). For example, with the question "Why didn't you choose to use the Fleet Assistance Program when you bought your 2002 car?" respondents can list whatever reason may come to mind, whether or not the writer of the questionnaire has considered it as a possibility. Figure 5.5 illustrates open-ended and closed-ended questions that you might include in a questionnaire.

If you personally deliver a written questionnaire, the response rate may be higher, but the geographic area you can survey is greatly reduced. To guarantee

Figure 5.5	Types of Questions Used in Questionnaires

Type of Question	Definition	Sample Question
Multiple choice	Respondents select from one or more alternatives.	What is your household income? $20,000–$40,000 _____ $41,000–$60,000 _____ $61,000–$80,000 _____ $81,000–$100,000 _____ More than $100,000 _____
Yes-no questions	Respondents select "yes" or "no"	Would you use the express rail service to commute to work? Yes _____ No _____
Likert scale	Respondents rank their responses along a scale. Select an even number of choices. Plumb and Spyridakis recommend including no fewer than 3 and no more than 11 choices (633).	The online reporting system has made my job easier. Strongly Agree Agree Disagree Strongly Disagree
Semantic differential scale	Respondents rate their responses along a continuum of opposing concepts. Again, limit the choices to no fewer than 3 and no more than 11. These scales normally measure attitudes and feelings.	Your technical communication class is Easy __ __ __ __ Hard Interesting __ __ __ __ Boring Current __ __ __ __ Out of Date

Formal rating scale	Respondents rate an item or quality on a specific scale, usually 1 to 5 or 1 to 10.	How do you rate the online help for this software? Please circle your rating.
		  1 2 3 4 5 6 7 8 9 10
		  Worst Best

Ranking	Respondents prioritize or rank responses from among selected alternatives.	Please rank the importance of the following factors when you buy a new automobile. Put a 1 next to the most important factor, a 2 next to the second most important factor, and so on. Gas Economy _____ Color _____ Size _____ Side Impact Airbags _____ Dealership _____ Accessories _____
Checklists	Respondents check one response. With an expanded checklist, respondents may check more than one response. (See the sample question.)	Which of the following activities describe tasks that you engage in daily using a personal computer? (Check all that apply.) _____ Sending and receiving e-mail

(continued on next page)

▼ **Figure 5.5**   (continued)

Type of Question	Definition	Sample Question
	Plumb and Spyridakis point out that "to ensure that all respondents interpret the questions similarly, the question instructs respondents to 'Check all that apply.' The 'Other' response option is provided in case the researcher has not considered all possible" activities that the respondent could engage in using a personal computer (633).	_____ Using word processing to write documents _____ Surfing the Web _____ Banking _____ Paying bills _____ Preparing spreadsheets _____ Checking the status of my stocks _____ Checking the news and weather _____ Other (please explain) _____
Short answer/essay or fill in the blank	Respondents write extended text using phrases or sentences, or they fill in blanks.	How well do you think telecommuting will work in your department? _____ _____ What do you believe are the disadvantages of telecommuting? 1. _____ 2. _____ 3. _____

a higher response rate, personally pick up the questionnaires. Figure 5.6 is a questionnaire. It includes both closed- and open-ended questions.

Whether you choose closed-ended questions, open-ended questions, or a combination of both, design your questions carefully. As you write your questionaire, follow these tips:

▶ For more information on ambiguity, see Chapter 8, "Using Reader-Oriented Language."

▶ **Tips for Preparing an Effective Questionnaire**

- **Write unambiguous questions.** If respondents can interpret a question in more than one way, then your results will be meaningless.

- **Use simple, plain language.** Plumb and Spyridakis recommend avoiding "technical terms, acronyms, and abstract or ambiguous words" (631).

- **Avoid questions that influence your respondents' answers or that indicate your opinions.** For example, the following questions unnecessarily influence, or "lead," readers: "Do you think that curbside recycling is an environmentally sound idea?" and "Do

(continued on page 104)

▼ **Figure 5.6**	A Questionnaire

Every semester, we evaluate the quality of service and the software used in the Technical Communication Lab. We would like your help in our evaluation. Please take a few minutes to complete this questionnaire. Your responses will remain anonymous. We appreciate you taking time to respond; our responses will improve how we serve you and other students. Before December 5, please put your questionnaire in the marked boxes near the entrance of the lab.

1. What is your classification?
   Freshman _____ Sophomore _____ Junior _____ Senior _____ Graduate _____

2. Approximately how many hours per week do you spend in the lab?
   0 _____ 1–2 _____ 2–4 _____ 4–6 _____ 6–8 _____ 8–10 _____ More than 10 _____

3. How many class periods, on average, did your class meet in the lab?
   0 period _____ 1 period _____ 2 periods _____ 3 periods _____ Every period _____

4. The lab staff are polite and helpful.
   Strongly Agree _____ Agree _____ Undecided _____ Disagree _____ Strongly Disagree _____

5. Was a staff member especially helpful? If so, which staff member was especially helpful?
   (please explain) _____
   _____

6. Please comment on the facilities in the lab.
   a. The lab has enough space for each student to work.
      Strongly Agree _____ Agree _____ Undecided _____ Disagree _____ Strongly Disagree _____
   b. The computers are adequate for my needs.
      Strongly Agree _____ Agree _____ Undecided _____ Disagree _____ Strongly Disagree _____
   c. The temperature in the lab is just right.
      Strongly Agree _____ Agree _____ Undecided _____ Disagree _____ Strongly Disagree _____

7. Please rank the following software in order of importance for you in completing your technical communication assignments this semester. Put a 1 next to the most important, a 2 next to the second most important, and so on.
   Microsoft Word   _____
   Microsoft PowerPoint   _____
   FrameMaker   _____
   FrontPage   _____
   PhotoShop   _____
   Eagle Mail   _____
   Internet Explorer   _____

8. Would you be willing to pay a higher lab fee for more space in the lab?
   Yes _____ No _____

9. Would you be willing to pay a higher lab fee if the university provided laptop computers for all students?
   Yes _____ No _____

10. On the back of this sheet, please provide any comments that you believe will help us to better serve technical communication students.

Thank you for sharing your opinions.

you think that curbside recycling is a waste of the city's valuable tax dollars?"

- **Test your questions on a small group of respondents to make sure the questions are clear and unambiguous before you finalize the questionnaire.** Correct any problems with the questionnaire. If you have time, test the questionnaire a second time. Remember, once you send out the questionnaire, you can't revise it.

- **Ask only the questions you need.** Respondents often ignore questionnaires that are long or that seem to waste their time.

- **Attach a cover letter.** Clearly and concisely explain the purpose and significance of the questionnaire.

- **Tell the respondents when you will pick up the questionnaire or when they should return it.** Also, include this information in the cover letter or written introduction.

- **Include a self-addressed, postage-paid envelope for returning the questionnaire (if you're using traditional mail).** Your respondents will be more likely to complete the survey and return it to you in a timely manner if they can simply drop it in the nearest mailbox.

- **In the cover letter, thank the respondents for their time.**

Observe People and Situations and Conduct Experiments

Once you have gathered adequate background information, you may decide to look firsthand at the problem or situation. For example, Bill might personally observe the vibrating pipes and then conduct appropriate tests. These direct observations and tests will help Bill to pinpoint solutions. If you directly observe people and situations as part of your research, remember these guidelines:

- **Gather background information.** Before you observe, gather as much background information as possible. Without this information, you may not know what to look for and, therefore, waste your time.

- **Know what to look for.** Do your homework. Find out what you are looking for and where to find it.

- **Take notes as you observe.** Record your observations immediately. Don't rely on your memory. You might forget an important detail. Remember to answer these questions: Who? What? When? Where? Why? How?

An **experiment** is a controlled observation where you test a hypothesis. Learning how to conduct an effective experiment may take months or even years of practice. However, to conduct an effective experiment, follow these tips:

> **Tips for Conducting an Effective Experiment**

- **Establish a hypothesis.** A **hypothesis** is an assumption. For example, to determine the relationship between calcium supplements in preventing bone density loss (or osteoporosis), you might test the following hypothesis: Women will lose less bone density when taking 600 milligrams per day of calcium.

- **Test the hypothesis.** You will need an experimental group and a control group. For example, if we test our hypothesis, we would need an experimental group of women who take 600 milligrams of calcium for one year and a control group who take no calcium supplements for one year. We would conduct bone density tests on each woman in each group before and after the experiment.

- **Analyze the data.** Once you have all the data from the experiment, you have to understand the data so you can determine whether or not your hypothesis is true. You must guard against bias when analyzing the data; you may be tempted to see what you want to see, not what the data actually shows.

- **Report the data.** When you have analyzed the data, you will want to report what you learned. You will learn more about reporting in Chapters 13 and 14.

▶Principle 3: Select Appropriate Secondary Research Strategies

Secondary research is gathering information from previously documented research or studies. For example, if you wanted to research the climate of Mars, you might look at reports written by scientists who analyzed data from the Mars *Pathfinder*. You can find valuable secondary information by searching the Internet or your college or university library. Most college and university libraries have resources to locate information: books, periodicals, trade publications, newspapers, computer data files, maps, films, computer programs, video and sound recordings, indexes, abstracts, and government documents. This list of resources is only a sampling of the many resources available from college and university libraries.

In the workplace, you can also find information in your company or organization's library. Most organizations call this library an information resource center. These centers collect information that is vital to the company or organization's business. For some companies and organizations, the information resource center has a full-time staff who will do the research for you. For example, you might e-mail a question to the staff who does the research for you. You might ask a question such as "How many megawatts of power did

TXU generate between January and March of 2002?" The staff then researches the question and e-mails you the answer. Other companies have staff who provide guidance on where to look for the information, and you do the work.

When you use a library or an information resource center, follow these guidelines:

- **Talk to reference librarians.** Reference librarians are your most valuable library resource. They can help you locate the appropriate resources and teach you how to use them. They are willing to suggest new ways to locate information or to tell you if your library doesn't have the information that you seek. Reference librarians can save you time and frustration.

- **Take detailed notes.** Don't rely on your memory or on haphazard notes. Write down all needed information in a detailed, systematic manner. As you take these notes, include accurate, complete bibliographic information—enough information for your readers to locate the same information.

- **If you are using Internet resources, print a copy of the homepage of the Web site.** Web sites come and go and your paper copy of the home page may be the only proof that the information did exist (Byerly).

The following sections discuss secondary resources and strategies for finding information in those resources.

Understanding the Secondary Resources Available to You

You may better understand the wealth of secondary resources by categorizing them into the following groups: online catalogs, databases, indexes, search engines and subject directories, abstract services, reference works, and discussion groups. You can use these resources to find information in more traditional sources: books, periodicals, reports, trade publications, digital disks, and government documents. You can also use some of these resources to find information on the Web. The following sections briefly describe each of the resources. When you understand the resources available, then we will discuss strategies for effectively and efficiently using these resources.

Online Catalogs

You can use an online catalog to search for library holdings. For most college and university libraries, you can search their holdings from your desktop—you don't have to go to the library building to use the card catalog. With many online catalogs, you can find out if the source you need is checked out by another library patron. If you are looking for information printed before 1975, however, you may want to check the library's card catalog. Most libraries moved to an online catalog in 1975, and they may have missed some

TAKING IT INTO THE WORKPLACE

Copyright Laws and "Fair Use"

"The industry recognizes that creativity thrives when copyrights are strong and an incentive is provided."
—Emery Simon, Business Software Alliance Worldwide Counsel, testifying before the House Judiciary Subcommittee on Courts, the Internet, and Intellectual Property

The Copyright Act of 1976 and the Digital Millennium Copyright Act of 1998 protect the authors of published and unpublished works. The author of a work is entitled to the profits if someone sells or distributes the work except in cases of "fair use." You can use copyright-protected works without the author's permission if you follow the fair use guidelines established by the Copyright Act of 1976. This law protects you if you use a small portion of an author's work to benefit the public. The fair use guidelines allow you to use works for education, research, criticism, and news reporting, or for scholarship purposes that are nonprofit in nature. To determine fair use, consider these factors:

- **The purpose of the use.** Is the use for commercial, nonprofit, or educational purposes? If you are using the work for commercial purposes, you may be violating the copyright law.
- **The nature and purpose of the copyrighted work.** If the information is essential for the good of the public, you may be able to use the copyrighted work without the author's permission.
- **The amount and substantiality of the portion of the work used.** The law doesn't give us strict guidelines, so you must use your judgment to determine how much of a copyrighted work you can use without the author's permission. For example, if you use 400 words of a 1,000-word work, you are not following fair use guidelines. If you use 400 words of a 100,000-word work, you are following fair use guidelines. If you are using even a part of a copyrighted graphic, you must

get permission. You can't use a portion of a copyrighted graphic, so fair use guidelines don't apply to graphics.
- **The effect of the use upon the potential market for or value of the copyrighted work.** If your use of a copyrighted document hurts the author's potential to profit from the work or hurts the potential value of the work, you have violated fair use guidelines.

The copyright acts protect authors even if they haven't registered their work with the U.S. Copyright Office. If you write or create a work for your employer and your employer pays you to write or create the work, that work is the property of your employer. As you write and create documents, ask these questions:

- **Have you relied on large amounts of information from copyrighted works—works that you did not write? If so, do you have permission from the author or authors to use the work?**
- **Have you appropriately cited sources or acknowledged that you have used the work by permission of the author?**
- **Are you unfairly profiting from the copyrighted work of another author?**
- **Have you asked for legal advice?** If you don't know whether you can legally use a portion of work, ask for advice from legal counsel. If you ask for legal advice, you may prevent legal action against you or your employer.

Assignment
Visit one of these Web sites to learn more about copyright laws. Write a memo to your classmates explaining what you've learned.

- The U.S. Copyright Clearance Center Web site: http://www.copyright.com/copyrightresources
- The U.S. Copyright Office Web site: http://www.loc.gov/copyright

print sources when inputting the data into the online catalog (Byerly). Most libraries don't update their card catalogs, so only use one if you are looking for information published prior to 1975 *and* if you didn't find the information in the online catalog. You will learn strategies for searching online catalogs later in this chapter.

Databases

You can use databases to search in journals, newspapers, and government documents. To access databases, you go through commercial or government services that offer a variety of databases. Most college and university and many public libraries pay for access to database services. You can also use databases to gather information from a variety of fields. Although these databases can provide a wealth of information, they can be expensive. Even a simple search can cost more than $50, and a customized search can cost more than $100. If you plan to use a database, carefully plan your search and refine your topic using the strategies that we will discuss later in this chapter. Figure 5.7 lists some of the electronic resources (databases, abstract services, and indexes) that you may access.

Indexes

Indexes are lists of books, newspapers, periodical articles, or other works on a particular subject. Indexes also list the documents available in government documents. We will focus on indexes for searching periodicals, newspapers, and government documents.

Periodical Indexes. Periodical indexes offer you an excellent source of some of the most current information. (**Periodicals** are magazines and journals.) Although periodicals offer excellent information, you may have trouble identifying the many articles related to your topic. Periodical indexes can make this task much easier. These indexes list articles classified according to title, subject, and author. Some indexes are a general index covering multiple fields, such as the *Readers' Guide to Periodical Literature*. Some indexes will also categorize articles by subject. For example, the following indexes list articles in particular fields or list articles by discipline:

- Agricultural Index
- Business and Periodicals Index
- Applied Science and Technology Index
- General Science Index
- Ulrich's International Periodicals Directory
- Engineering Index

Figure 5.7 also lists some indexes that you may want to consider. When you need periodicals, ask your reference librarian which indexes will best help you find the information you need.

Figure 5.7	Partial Listing of Electronic Resources, Including Databases, Abstract Services, and Indexes

Electronic Resource	Description
ABI/Inform Global	Database that covers the full text of more than 1,586 journals in business and management. Search by publication, keyword, and topic. Use a guided search with Boolean operators. Find articles on accounting, taxation, marketing, management, companies, industries, international business, finance, economics, information systems, trends, business conditions, market entry, and technology.
Academic Search Premier	Database that covers the full text of nearly 3,180 scholarly publication abstracts and indexing for nearly 4,150 scholarly journals, with many dating back to 1984. Covers social sciences, humanities, education, computer sciences, engineering, language and linguistics, arts and literature, medical science, and ethnic studies.
Biography Index	Index that contains biographical information from more than 2,700 English-lanugage periodicals for all subject areas covered by H. W. Wilson indexes. Indexes articles and books, autobiographies, bibliographies, biographies, critical studies, collections of letters, book reviews, and interviews.
Business Source Premier	Database that provides full-text articles from approximately 2,260 scholarly business journals. Covers areas such as management, economics, finance, accounting, marketing, international business, industries, information systems, business conditions, and technology.
Congressional Index	Index that covers items related to the U.S. Congress, such as congressional publications, testimonies, bills, laws, and related information.
Criminal Justice Abstracts	Database of citations to resources in criminology and related disciplines.
General Science Abstracts	Abstract service that covers the more theoretical or pure science areas of astronomy, biology, botany, chemistry, geology, environmental studies, medicine and health, and physics. Abstracts come from more than 190 general and specialized journals representing both professional and popular publications, including the science section of the *New York Times*.
Historical Statistics of the United States	Database that reproduces all the data and text contained in the U.S. Census Bureau's *Historical Statistics of the United States: Colonial Times to 1970, Bicentennial Edition,* published in 1975. Topics include all the social, behavioral, humanistic, and natural sciences, including economics, government, finance, sociology, demography, education, law, natural resources, climate, religion, international migration, and trade.

(continued on next page)

Figure 5.7   (continued)

Electronic Resource	Description
INSPEC	One of the largest databases for physics, electrical engineering and electronics, computers, and information technology. Indexes more than 4,200 journals, conference proceedings, books, reports, new product information, and dissertations from 1968 to the present.
Medline-PubMed	Abstract service maintained by the National Library of Medicine. Provides abstracts for journal articles covering biomedical literature in MEDLINE, PreMEDLINE, and HEALTHSTAR. The service is updated daily.
PsycInfo (formerly PsycLit)	Abstract service that provides abstracts for journal articles, books, chapters of books, technical reports, and dissertations on psychology and related disciplines such as psychiatry, education, business, medicine, nursing, pharmacology, law, linguistics, behavior analysis, and social work. Covers more than 1,300 journals representing more than 25 languages.
Social Sciences Abstracts	Index and abstract service that covers more than 350 English-language periodicals in the social sciences.
WorldCat (World Catalog)	Online Catalog produced by FirstSearach OCLC Online Union Catalog. Contains more than 35 million records owned by libraries around the world.

Source: Adapted from Gayla Byerly, "Electronic Resources" (unpublished, 2001).

Once you have gathered a list of periodical articles that may have the information you need, you have to find those articles. Check your library's online catalog or serials holding catalog to find out if your library carries the periodical that you need. Be sure to check the volume number or years of the periodical—sometimes libraries don't carry all the volumes or may be missing volumes. If your library doesn't have the periodical or volume that you need, you may still get a copy of the article that you need by using

- **Interlibrary loan.** Go to the interlibrary loan office at your library. It will help you locate the nearest library that has the article. That library will photocopy the article and mail it to your library. This service can be slow—sometimes it takes two weeks or more to receive an article, and some libraries will charge you for the photocopying.

- **Online document-delivery services.** You access these services on the Web. These services search a database of periodicals. If the service has the article you need, it faxes or e-mails the article to you usually within an hour. These services charge a fee; however, if you're in a hurry, the article may be worth the fee.

Newspaper Indexes.   Newspapers contain all types of information but don't cover most subjects in depth. Newspapers may summarize some topics—especially local issues—and present statistics, trends, and demographic information. Many major newspapers are indexed by subject. Some of the more important newspaper indexes are

- The *New York Times*
- The *Wall Street Journal*

You can access many newspapers on the Web. However, the print and the online versions may vary. If you plan to cite information from a newspaper, use the print version if possible.

▶ To get an idea of the information available from the federal government, go to the Web site titled "Federal Government Information Resources: An Electronic Depository Library," http://www.umr.edu/~library/gov/govintro.html.

Government Document Indexes.   The U.S. government may be the largest publisher in the world. Every year the U.S. government publishes more than 25 million documents for specialized and general offices. You can find documents published by federal agencies and departments such as the Department of Labor, the Department of Housing and Urban Development, the Environmental Protection Agency, and the Internal Revenue Service. You can find these documents through libraries that are registered repositories for U.S. government documents. Many university and some large public libraries are repositories. They usually have a separate reference librarian and staff for the government documents because these documents are cataloged separately. Some libraries also house publications published by state agencies. These publications can provide valuable information on topics such as food, nutrition, agriculture, animal science, natural resources, and state demographics. The federal government also produces many unpublished documents.

Government documents may not be listed in online catalogs at your library. Unlike other documents in the library, government documents are classified according to the Superintendent of Documents system (not the Library of Congress system). You might think of government documents as a separate library within your library. You can also find many government documents on the Internet. To locate information in government documents, you can use the following index:

- **Government Reports Announcements and Index.** This index lists more than one million federally sponsored reports published since 1964. You can only use this index to find documents produced by the federal government or through federally funded research.

- **The Monthly Catalog of the United States Government.** Although this catalog isn't technically an index, it provides a roadmap to locating government documents. You can access the catalog on paper, on CD-ROM, or on the Internet.

- **Fedworld Information Network.** This federal Web site has searchable databases and indexes to locate information produced by the federal government. You can find the Web site at http://www.fedworld.gov.

To effectively and efficiently locate government documents, you might start by talking with a librarian in the government documents section of your library.

Search Engines and Subject Directories

You use search engines to find information on the Internet. **Search engines** index the contents of the Web; using the keywords and phrases that you give them, search engines scan documents searching for these keywords and phrases. If the search engine finds results that match your search request, it presents you with a list of the results, usually ranked from most relevant to least relevant. Search engines are divided into two types:

- **Individual search engines** compile their own database of Web pages.
- **Meta-search engines** query multiple search engines at once. Meta-search engines do not compile their own database of Web documents.

On the surface, you may think that you will get the best results by using a meta-search engine. However, meta-search engines have disadvantages as well as advantages. Meta-searches search wide rather than deep. They respond to a query with results only from the top of each search engine database, while an individual search engine responds to a query with every relevant result available in its database. Since most individual search engines rank results by relevance, the meta-search engine will probably return the most relevant results. Therefore, use a meta-search engine when you are looking for an overview of a topic. To get the best results, try using both types of search engines.

You can also use subject directories to search the Web. A **subject directory** is a database of Web sites that you can search. Unlike search engines, the database of a subject directory is made up of Web sites that a human editor has assigned to a category (such as "Science and Technology" or "Engineering"). Most subject directories differ from search engines. For example, subject directories

- Provide links to the relevant documents rather than storing pages
- Don't compile their own database
- Search only for matches in short written descriptions of the site, not the full text of the document (for example, a subject directory such as Yahoo! scans URLs, titles, and annotations of Web sites)
- Allow you to search deep into the categories until you find what you want, so they are excellent for narrowing your topic

Figure 5.8 lists some useful meta-search engines, individual search engines, and subject directories; the list begins with the meta-search engines. Figure 5.8 does not list every search engine or subject directory available on the Web, but it does list some of the major search engines and subject directories. As you begin your online research, follow these tips when deciding when to use a search engine and when to use a subject directory:

| Figure 5.8 | Search Engines |

Name of Search Engine	Address	Description
Meta-Search Engines		
Ask Jeeves	http://ask.com/index2.asp	Searches its own database, About.com, AltaVista, WebCrawler, and Exite. Allows you to query by natural language. For example, you can query by question such as "How much does a plane ticket to London cost?"
Dogpile	http://www.dogpile.com	Queries 11 separate search engines and directories at once.
Mamma	http://mamma.com	Queries 10 separate search engines at once.
Individual Search Engines		
AltaVista	http://www.altavista.com	Allows you to limit your search by language. One of the most powerful search engines on the Web. Indexes more than 350 million pages.
Google	http://www.google.com	Lists categories of sites grouped by subject or topic. Inserts the text that matches your query in the search results. Partners with the Open Directory Project (see subject directories). Currently, the most used search engine in academic settings (Byerly).
HotBot	http://hotbot.com	Lists categories of sites by subject or topic. Allows you to limit your search by date and type of page. Also allows you to query by natural language.
Lycos	http://www.lycos.com	Lists results by searching the Open Directory Project, DirectHit, and its own search of the Web.
Northern Light	http://www.northernlight.com	Combines a database of more than 250 million Web pages with articles from more than 6,700 full-text sources. Features customizable folders and offers fee-based access to articles. Prioritizes and categorizes results by subject, type of document, source of document, and the language of the document.
WebCrawler	http://www.webcrawler.com	Lists categories of sites by subject or topic. Although it covers fewer sites than other search engines, it is an excellent search engine for computer-related topics.
Subject Directories		
Excite	http://www.excite.com	Lists categories of sites grouped by subject or topic. Use the "more like this" links to lead to other useful sources.
LookSmart	http://www.looksmart.com	Indexes more than 100,000 categories. Has a directory of more than 1.5 million Web sites.
		(continued on next page)

▼ **Figure 5.8** (continued)

Name of Search Engine	Address	Description
Open Directory Project	http://www.dmoz.org	Does not accept advertising, so it is not a commercial site. Staffed by 20,000-plus volunteer editors.
Yahoo!	http://www.yahoo.com	Lists categories of sites by subject. Use this site to begin a search for general topics.

Source: Adapted from Gayla Byerly, "Search Engines with Brief Descriptions" (unpublished, 26 Oct. 2001).

▶ **Tips for Using Search Engines and Subject Directories**

Use search engines when you want to

- **Locate a wide variety of information on your topic.**
- **Find defined information** such as specific terms, facts, figures, quotations, and keywords that may be buried in documents, because search engines scan the full text of documents, not just documents' titles or URLs.

Use subject directories when you want to

- **Find some help locating a topic.**
- **Narrow or refine a topic.**
- **Look for information on a general topic.** For example, if you want to find information on helicopters, you might use a subject directory. However, if you want to find information on Bell Helicopter's tilt-rotor helicopter, you would use a search engine. If you use a search engine for the general category of helicopters, you may find links to thousands of sites—and many of these may be irrelevant. If you use a subject directory, you may receive links to 60 sites that the editors have selected as highly relevant to your topic. After you have narrowed your topic using a subject directory, then go to a search engine.

Reference Works

Any time you look up a word in a dictionary or look up a topic in an encyclopedia, you are using a reference work. Reference works include

- General dictionaries
- Encyclopedias

- Specialized dictionaries, such as *International Who's Who* or *BioTech Life Science Dictionary*
- Almanacs
- Atlases
- Other general research tools

You can access these reference tools in print or online. For example, you might look at the following guide to reference works:

Sheehy, E. P. *Guide to Reference Books.* 11th ed. Chicago: American Library Association, 1996.

Sheehy's guide is not updated frequently, so you may want to search the Web for more current information about reference works. You can also talk to a reference librarian who will be able to direct you to the print or online reference work that you need.

Abstract Services

▶ See Figure 5.8 for a partial listing of abstract services.

Abstract services go one step beyond indexes. Along with bibliographic information, abstract services include a summary of the article. These abstracts can save you time. By reading the abstract before you locate the article, you can decide whether the article contains the kind of information that you are seeking. Some abstract services cover a specific field, such as Computer Abstracts or Chemical Abstracts. Some are broader, such as Dissertation Abstracts International. You can search many abstract services on the Web or on CD-ROM.

Discussion Groups

You can participate in two types of online discussions:

- Newsgroups
- Listservs

Usenet newsgroups publish e-mail messages sent by members of a group. Usenet is a "worldwide style of discussion groups," or newsgroups (Hahn). The discussion groups are called newsgroups because the Usenet was originally designed to carry local news between two universities in North Carolina (Hahn). Usenet consists of thousands of newsgroups organized into basic categories such as business, computers, science and technology, and biology. For example, if you wanted to join a science newsgroup through Google™, you might see a screen like that in Figure 5.9(a). You would select "sci." Google would give you a list of science-related newsgroups (see Figure 5.9[b]). Each group name has two parts separated by a period. The first part, "sci," is the general category or group; the second part is the specific science topic discussed by that group. For example, "sci.aeronautics" is a science newsgroup that discusses science aeronautics.

Figure 5.9(a)

A List of Usenet
Discussion Topics

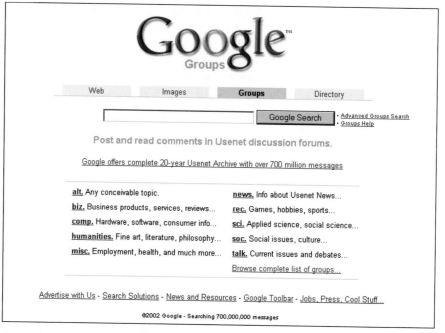

Source: Google. Online. Internet. 5 May 2002. Available: http://www.google.com/grphp?hl=en. Reprinted with permission.

Newsgroups allow members to share information, to discuss issues, to ask questions, and to get answers. Newsgroups may be moderated or unmoderated (most are unmoderated). In a moderated group, any information, or "news," is approved before it is posted. When you send information to a newsgroup, the mail is stored in a database that members access; information isn't sent directly to your computer. Because the information is stored in a database, you can easily search the newsgroup discussions to gather information. For example, if you type in "aeronautics," you might get a screen like that in Figure 5.9(c). From this screen, you can read discussion **threads**—a group of messages on a single topic. The database will sort these messages by relevance or by date (see Figure 5.9[c]). You can also conduct an advanced search by subject, author, message id, or date (see Figure 5.9[d]).

▶ See Principle 4 for information on evaluating sources.

Like newsgroups, **listservs** post e-mail messages sent by members who subscribe to the group. However, listservs send the messages to every person who subscribes to the list. The messages come directly to your computer; you don't have to go get the message. Listservs may be moderated or unmoderated, and members must follow proper Web etiquette and stay on the topic. If you subscribe to a listserv, be wary of information that you receive. If you plan to use the information, know its source.

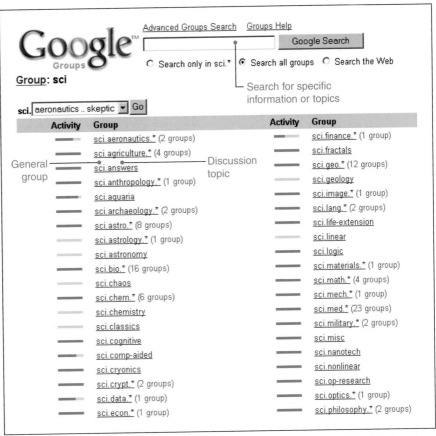

Figure 5.9(b)

Newsgroups

Source: Google. Online. Internet. 5 May 2002. Available: http://groups.google.com/groups?group=sci&hl=en. Reprinted with permission.

Strategies for Finding Information from Secondary Sources

Once you have located possible sources of information, you have to locate the information that you need in those sources. Some librarians use the analogy of mining: You know the general location of the "gold"; now you have to find the specific location and weed out any "fool's gold." In other words, you have to "mine" the information out of the source. In more traditional books and periodical articles the "mining" is relatively easy, even easier if the book has an index. However, with online catalogs, databases, discussion groups, abstract services, and search engines, you have to know how to ask the "right questions" to locate the information that you need. You can use these types of search strategies:

▼ **Figure 5.9(c)**   Search Results from a Newsgroup

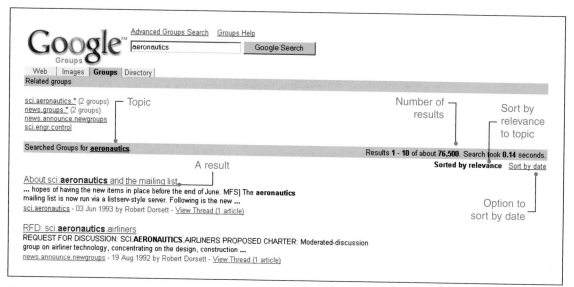

Source: Google. Online. Internet. 5 May 2002. Available: http://groups.google.com/groups?q=aeronautics&hl=en&sa=G. Reprinted with permission.

▼ **Figure 5.9(d)**   Searching a Newsgroup

Google™ Groups **Advanced Groups Search**   Groups Help | All About Google

Find messages   with **all** of the words

                     with the **exact phrase**

                     with **at least one** of the words   10 messages ▾ Sort by relevance ▾   Google Search

                     without the words

Newsgroup   Return only messages from the **newsgroup**

                                                              (Example: rec.games.misc, comp.os.*, *linux*)

Subject   Return only messages where the **subject** contains

Author   Return only messages where the **author** is

Message ID   Find the message with **message ID**

                                                              (Example: moderated-ng-faq-1-983174581@swcp.com)

Language   Return messages written in   any language ▾

Message Dates   ⦿ Return messages posted: anytime ▾

                     ○ Return messages posted between 12 ▾ May ▾ 1981 ▾ and 6 ▾ May ▾ 2002 ▾

Source: Google. Online. Internet. 5 May 2002. Available: http://groups.google.com/advanced_group_search?hl=en. Reprinted with permission.

- Keywords and Boolean operators
- Subject searches

Keywords and Boolean Operators

To locate information in databases with search engines or through abstract services, you may use keywords to search for the information. However, if you use only keywords, you may get hits that don't contain relevant information. You can limit the search by combining keywords with Boolean operators that help you modify your search. **Boolean operators** are words placed between keywords; these words specify how the keywords are related. Boolean operators include *and, or,* and *not.* Using Boolean operators, you can define relationships among various keywords. Each search engine or database may use Boolean operators in slightly different ways, so check the help option, "search tips," or "syntax" section of your database or the search engine. Figure 5.10 suggests some common ways for using Boolean operators to limit or expand your keyword search.

▼ **Figure 5.10**	**To expand your search**	**Examples**
Using Boolean Operators to Limit or Expand a Keyword Search	• Use *or* (finds all entries with either of the words)	Ozone or automobiles (finds all with either *ozone* or *automobiles*)
	• Use a wild card such as an asterisk (finds any entry with the root of the keyword)	Automobiles* (finds any entry that begins with the first four letters of *automobiles*)
	To limit your search	**Examples**
	• Use *and* (finds only entries with the two words combined by *and*)	Ozone and automobiles (finds only entries that contain both words)
	• Use *not* (finds only entries with the first word and excludes entries with the second word)	Ozone not automobiles (finds entries with *ozone* and excludes entries with *automobiles*)
	• Use dates (finds any entry published after a specified date)	Ozone—1998 (finds any entry published in or after 1998)

Subject Searches

If you are searching online catalogs, you may select a subject search. For most online catalogs, a subject search refers only to the Library of Congress or the Dewey subject headings. However, if you select a keyword search, the online catalog will search for not only the subject headings, but also the words within the title and other words in the catalog. So, in general, you should select the keyword search to make sure that you have found all potentially relevant sources (Byerly).

If you're using a directory search engine such as HotBot, you will want to begin with a subject search. Some search engines classify Web sites by subject, as in Figure 5.11. (The search engine may not use the word *subject*; instead, it may use the word *topics, categories,* or *directory.*) For example, if you are looking for information on ozone, you might first select the category or subject "Science & Technology." These search engines also allow you to select subcategories to further refine your search. Figures 5.12 and 5.13 illustrate how you can use the advanced search functions to refine your search.

Figure 5.11

A Subject Directory

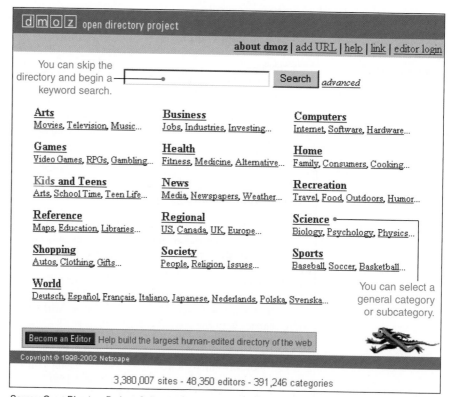

Source: Open Directory Project. Online. Internet. 5 May 2002. Available: http://dmoz.org. Reprinted by permission from http://dmoz.org.becomeaneditor.

Figure 5.12	An Advanced Search

Source: Google. Online. Internet. 5 May 2002. Available: http://www.google.com/advanced_search. Reprinted with permission.

▶Principle 4: Evaluate the Information and Sources

To find all the relevant information on your topic, use a combination of sources: print and online. You will likely find ample information using this combination, but you will want to evaluate the quality of the information. Just because the information is published in print or online doesn't mean that the information is good information. Some information may be out-of-date, incomplete, incorrect, misleading, or biased. Therefore, you will want to evaluate the information that you find. Use these questions as you evaluate information:

- **Is the information unbiased and reliable?** Does the author or source have a vested (or financial) interest in the research? For example, if you were searching for information on the effect of antioxidants on aging, you

Figure 5.13

A Customized Search
with a Meta-Search
Engine

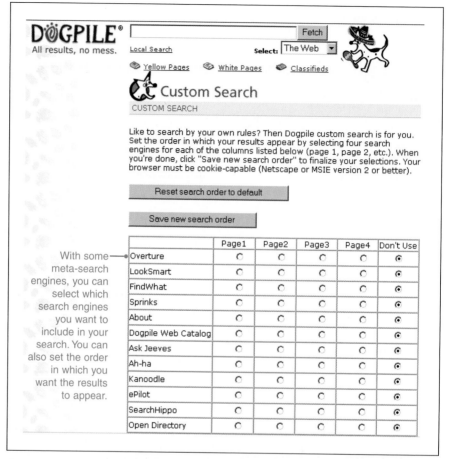

would look for research that was not funded by pharmaceutical companies that manufacture antioxidants or vitamins that contain antioxidants.

- **Is the source credible?** Does the author or source include their credentials? Are the credentials credible, relevant, and reliable? Can you find a section such as "About Us"?

- **Is the information up-to-date?** You want to base your research and your conclusions on the most current information. You can sacrifice your professional reputation by basing your decisions or your research on out-of-date information.

- **Is the information complete?** Does information seem to be missing? Have the researchers or authors covered all areas of the topic?

- **Is the information sufficiently detailed for your research?** Look for information that is sufficiently detailed for your research and for your readers.

Avoid overly simple or overly complex information for you, your readers, and your research.

You may find information from the Web to be the most difficult to evaluate. Any one may publish information on the Web—and the disreputable sources are just as prominent as the most reputable sources. On first glance, disreputable sources may look equally reliable, so you have to learn how to sort the reliable from the unreliable, the reputable from the disreputable sources. Few, if any, standards regulate publications that appear on the Web. No editorial board oversees many Web publications. Currently, no market forces are driving incompetent or unreliable publications off the Web, so carefully research and evaluate any Web sources that you use in your work. As you evaluate Web sources, consider the following limitations of online research and search tools:

- **The Web may not contain all the information available about your topic.** Even in this digital age, not all printed records have been transferred to digital storage; so you may find important information about your topic in traditional print sources such as journals, books, and trade publications. If you are using government documents, understand that many of these documents are not on the Web or catalogued on the Web. The government has only recently mandated that agencies make documents available on the Web, so the documents that you need may only be available at a government repository library. Until all these traditional sources are transferred to digital records, be sure to include traditional library research as part of your search strategy.

- **A search engine indexes no more than 16 percent of the estimated size of the publically indexable Web pages (Lawrence and Giles).** In a 1997 NEC Research Institute study, Steve Lawrence and Lee Giles found that the size of publicaly indexable Web pages had decreased "substantially" since December 1997 (108). Therefore, because no search engine or subject directory indexes every page on the Web, use a combination of directories and search engines.

- **Some Web sources are not up-to-date.** According to Lawrence and Giles, "indexing of new or modified pages by just one of the major search engines can take months" (109).

- **Most search engines and subject directories typically index sites that have many links to them (Lawrence and Giles).** Search results, then, will be populated with results from the more popular sites. A site may be popular not because of the quality or reliability of its information. It may be popular, for example, because the site gives away trips to people who visit the site.

- **Many search engines and subject directories index U.S. sites more than non-U.S. sites—although AltaVista is an exception (Lawrence and Giles).** For some topics, you will want to find information from non-U.S. sites, so try using the advanced search features of the search engine to specify that

The Disadvantages of Web Research

The abundance of information available on the Web doesn't always benefit researchers. The Web offers great breadth but may not always offer depth. For example, periodicals often provide their tables of contents but only rarely offer the actual contents. Abstract services only offer a sampling of their abstracts—not all of the abstracts. To use all the abstracts, you must subscribe to the service for a fee or use the CD-ROM version purchased by libraries. Also, the Web doesn't yet logically tell users what information is or is not available. For example, the U.S. government has made the latest breast cancer research available but currently provides little information on nutritional supplements.

Futher, search engines pass no judgment on their findings. One of the Web's great strengths is that everyone has a voice. For researchers, this leveling of sources has a dark side. Traditionally, publishers have acted as gatekeepers, limiting the amount of material entering the marketplace of ideas. The Web, however, has no such gatekeepers—the homepage of the U.S. Department of Defense is on essentially equal footing with that of suicide cult Heaven's Gate. Serious researchers will make distinctions among such sources, of course, but that is a credit to the researchers, not to the Web itself. As you search the Web, your most important research skills may be skepticism and a willingness to verify sources.

you want results from non-U.S. countries. Be sure to specifiy that you want these results in English—unless you can read other languages.

- **Search engines and subject directories generally index more commercial sites and educational sites (Lawrence and Giles).** Some sites accept payment to have their site appear at the top of some keyword search results—regardless of the relevancy of the site to your search. Try to include some noncommercial search tools such as the Open Directory Project (see Figure 5.8) or some virtual libraries. Look at the domain in the Web address for clues. The **domain** is the suffix at the end of the address; the suffix tells you the nature of the site: educational (.edu), government (.gov), military (.mil), nonprofit (.org), business/commercial (.com), and network (.net). A tilde (~) in the address may indicate that the Web page is a personal page.

- **Document Web sources that you use in your work.** Give your readers accurate and complete bibliographic information, so they can find the source on the the Web. To document any Web source, you will need the author's name, the title, the URL (Web-site address), the publication date, and (for MLA-style citations, discussed in Appendix A) the date you retrieved the source.

Figure 5.14 lists some questions that you may use when evaluating online sources.

▼ **Figure 5.14**   Questions for Evaluating Online Sources

Is the Online Source . . .	Questions to Ask[2]	Comments About the Questions
Written by reliable authors?	• Who created the Web site or the information? • What is the authority or expertise of the author? • If you don't recognize the name of the author, did you find the site through another reliable Web site or source? • Does the Web site contain biographical information on the author? • Can you find other references to the author's credentials or work through other search engines or databases?	Remember that anyone, whether qualified or not, can publish information on the Web—and all voices appear equal. If you are not familiar with an author's name or if you can't verify the information from the author, be wary of using the information in your research. Be wary of Web sites that don't identify site operators.
Published by a reliable group?	• Who is the publisher or producer of the Web site? • Why is the publisher qualified to produce the Web site? • Is the publisher affiliated with a reputable group or organization? • Does the domain give you information about the publisher and its purpose? • Does the Web site include contact information for the publisher or producer?	If the Web site is published from a personal account with an Internet service provider, the site may contain unreliable information. If the information looks interesting or valuable, make sure that you can verify that information from other sources.
Up-to-date?	• When was the Web site or item created? • When was the Web site or item last updated or revised? Has it been updated in the last three months? • Are the links up-to-date? Do the links work? • Is the site still "under construction" or only partially complete?	Be wary of any site that hasn't been updated in the last three months. If the Web site or item is "under construction," you may want to use another Web site or another source. If the links don't work, the site may not contain up-to-date information.
Presented clearly and accurately?	• Is the Web site well constructed? Does it follow good graphic design principles? • Does the site follow basic rules of grammar, spelling, and punctuation?	If a site looks unprofessional, the information that it contains may not be reliable. If the site doesn't follow the basic rules of grammar, spelling, and (continued on next page)

[2] I've adapted some of these questions from "Web Site Evaluation," published by the University of North Texas Libraries.

Figure 5.14   (continued)

Is the Online Source . . .	Questions to Ask	Comments About the Questions
	• Do the authors cite sources? Do they support all claims with appropriate evidence? • Does the information appear biased?	punctuation, you should be wary of the reliability and accuracy of the information. If the authors don't cite sources or support their claims, look for other information to back up their claims or use other sources. A reliable site • Has a professional, well-constructed design • Follows the basic conventions of grammar, punctuation, and spelling • Supports all claims • Documents sources • Presents unbiased information

▶Conclusion

The manner in which you gather information for your documents can make a difference in the success of those documents. Allow ample time to research your topic, so you can effectively anticipate and answer your readers' questions. After you have gathered your information, be sure to accurately cite and document it.

WORKSHEET for Researching Information Using Primary and Secondary Sources

▶ **Principle 1: Plan Your Research**
- Have you considered your readers' needs?
- What do your readers expect from your research? What questions might they ask while reading your document?
- How will your readers use the findings of your research?
- What is the purpose of your research?
- What do you want to accomplish or find out?
- What types of information will you need?
- What do you know about the subject?
- What do you still need to find out? What information is missing?
- How much time do you need to conduct the research?
- Will the project allow this time? Do you need to adjust the scope of the project? Do you need to ask for more time?

▶ See Figure 5.1 for more questions on planning your research.

▶ **Principle 2: Select Appropriate Primary Research Techniques**

Interviewing
- Will the interview be formal or informal?
- What is the purpose of the interview?
- What background information do you need for the interview?
- What questions will you ask?
- Are the questions specific and open ended?

Administering Questionnaires
- What is the purpose of the questionnaire? What do you want to learn?
- What will you do with the information that you collect?

▶ See Figure 5.4 for more questions to consider as you identify the target group.
- What is the target group that you want to question? How will you select the target group?
- How many responses do you need?
- How many questionnaires will you send?
- How will you administer the questionnaire—by mail, by e-mail, by phone, or in person?
- What types of questions will you ask?
- Are your questions clear and unambiguous?
- Is the language simple?
- Do any of the questions influence your respondents' answers or indicate your opinions?
- Have you asked only the questions that you need?
- Have you attached a cover letter? Did you thank the respondents for their time?
- Have you introduced the questionnaire?
- Did you tell the respondents when you will pick up the questionnaire or when they should return it?
- Did you provide self-addressed, postage-paid envelopes for returning the questionnaire?
- Have you tested the questions on a small group of respondents?

Observing People and Situations
- Will observing people or situations help you to answer your questions?
- Do you have the necessary background information to be an informed observer?
- Do you know what you're looking for?

Conducting Experiments
- Have you established a hypothesis?
- Have you set up a reliable method for testing the hypothesis?
- Have you analyzed the data?
- Does your analysis contain any bias?

▶ **Principle 3: Select Appropriate Secondary Research Strategies**
- Have you talked with a reference librarian?

- Have you decided which secondary resources might contain the information you need?
- Have you used a combination of secondary research strategies?
- If you used information from a Web site, did you print of copy of the homepage?
- Did you take detailed notes?
- Did you write down enough information to document your sources?
- Have you used any copyrighted information? Did you seek permission to use the information?

▶ **Principle 4: Evaluate the Information**

- Does the author or organization have a financial interest in the research? Is the author or organization credible?
- Is the information unbiased and reliable?

▶ See Figure 5.14 for specific questions for evaluating online sources.

- Is the information up-to-date?
- Is the information complete?
- Is the information sufficiently detailed for your research?
- Who produced or published the information? Is the producer or publisher qualified to produce or publish the information?

1. For this exercise, your instructor will assign you to a team or ask you to select a team. You and your team are engineering consultants for a city landfill. Managers of the landfill are concerned about the environmental impact of raising the landfill. The city has approved raising it by 10 feet. As the engineering consultants, your team will explain how raising the landfill will affect the local environment and suggest ways to minimize that impact. Your assignment is to list the steps that your team might take to research the environmental impact and then suggest appropriate primary and secondary research strategies that your team might use to gather information.

2. Conduct a formal interview with a professional in your field of study. For example, if you are majoring in chemical engineering, you might interview a chemical engineer who works for an oil company. Before the interview, call the interviewee for an appointment, gather background information on the interviewee, and write down questions that you want to ask. After the interview, write a memo to your instructor summarizing the interview. Include a copy of your interview questions with your memo. Chapter 18 presents information on writing and formatting memos.

3. Use a search engine to find at least five Web sites about a topic in your field. For example, you might look for Web sites about robotics, acid rain, or bioengineering. Visit each site and do the following:

   - Print the homepage of the Web site.
   - Locate the contact information of the producer or publisher of the site.
   - Write a memo to your instructor evaluat-

ing the sites. Use the questions in Figure 5.14 to guide you as you evaluate the sites.

4. Select a topic on which you will write a report for this class. The topic can relate to your major field of study or to your job. Make sure that you have appropriately narrowed the topic. After you have selected a topic, plan a research strategy for using secondary sources:

   - Which reference works contain background information related to your topic? Are any of these reference works available online?
   - Which indexes and abstract services cover your topic?
   - Which discussion groups might contain discussion threads related to your topic?
   - Will government publications contain information related to your topic? If they will, what indexes and catalogs will you use? Which of these tools are available online in your library?
   - Which search engines will you use to search the Web?
   - What periodical indexes will you use?

5. Using the research plan that you developed in Exercise 5, prepare a preliminary bibliography of the sources that you might use for your report. Include at least six print sources, six Web sites, and six periodical articles.

6. Locate one of the sources in the bibliography that you prepared in Exercise 5. Evaluate the information in the source using the guidelines from Principle 4. Write a memo to your instructor explaining your evaluation. Be sure to include complete bibliographic information.

7. Using search engines, answer the following questions related to your major. Be sure to print a copy of the homepage of any Web site that you use and to include complete bibliographic information for each site. Put your answers in a memo to your instructor.

   a. What are two professional organizations in your field?

   b. What publications do each of the professional organizations publish? (For example, do the organizations publish a journal or magazine for their members?)

   c. How often does the publication appear—monthly, quarterly, annually?

   d. Does the organization have a discussion group or a listserv? If so, how do you join? Print a copy of the instructions for joining the discussion group or listserv.

   e. Does the organization have a code of ethics? If so, print a copy of the code and attach it to the memo to your instructor.

8. Working with a team, find a topic for a report for your classmates. You might consider any of the following topics:

   • A problem on your campus, such as parking, crowded classrooms, etc. What is the problem? Why is it a problem? Whom does the problem affect? How would you solve the problem?

   • A problem in your community. You might search the local newspapers to find possible topics. What is the problem? Why is it a problem? Whom does the problem affect? How would you solve the problem?

   • An environmental issue. What is the problem? How does the problem affect the environment? What solutions have been proposed? Which solutions are feasible? What solution would you suggest?

   Once you have decided on a topic, your team should do the following:

   • Plan a research strategy. E-mail a sum-mary of your plan to your instructor.

   • Select at least one primary research technique for gathering information. Decide who will conduct this research.

   • Select appropriate secondary research strategies. Be sure to use a variety of strategies and to take detailed notes.

   • Evaluate the sources using the questions from Principle 4. Send an e-mail to your instructor summarizing your evaluation.

   • Prepare a report for your classmates explaining the problem or issue that you researched and your proposed solution. (See Chapters 13 and 14 for information on reports.) Your instructor may want you to present your report orally, rather than in writing. If so, see Chapter 17.

9. Many universities teach courses by distance—instructors may teach via the Web or via two-way video. You may be taking this course as a distance course. Working either individually or as a team, prepare a questionnaire to evaluate distance learning. Follow the steps below:

   • Plan your questionnaire using these questions:

     a. What is the purpose of the questionnaire?

     b. Who would be the target group?

     c. How many questionnaires would we (I) send?

     d. What would be the best way for administering the questionnaire?

   • Develop a questionnaire. Include a combination of closed-ended and open-ended questions.

   • Administer the questionnaire to a representative group of respondents.

   • Analyze the results.

   • Prepare an oral presentation for your class summarizing the purpose and the results of your questionnaire.

> **CASE STUDY**

Discovering Job Prospects in Your Field

Background

Ann Goodgame is trying to decide whether to continue in her particular field of study. She read that job prospects in her field are not good. However, she won't graduate from college for two years, so she has decided to find out more about job prospects. Ann wants to answer these questions:

- What are the job prospects in her field, nationally and locally?
- What areas of her field seem to have the best prospects for employment?
- What can she do to best prepare for finding a job? What types of skills and knowledge will she need?
- What annual salary should she expect to receive for an entry-level job in her field?
- What local and regional companies are currently hiring in her field?
- What Web sites can she use to look for a job and to post her résumé?

Ann decides to do some research to answer these questions.

Assignment

Assume that Ann's field is the same as your major field of study. Then complete the following steps:

1. Develop a research plan to answer the questions listed above about employment in your field.
2. Find secondary sources giving you employment and salary information. Include two citations from each of the following sources:
   a. Government or state publications
   b. Periodical publications, such as trade journals, research journals, or newspapers
   c. Web sources
3. By using the Web or asking your instructor, find the names of two professionals in your field who can give you information about employment, needed skills, and salaries. If you can't find two professionals, contact a professional organization in your field. You may contact them by e-mail.
4. Write a memo to your instructor explaining your research plan. Be sure to include the sources that you found for step 2 and the names from step 3.

6

Organizing Information for Your Readers

Paul Das sits at his desk looking at the pages of data he has collected for a manual to minimize pollution from waste disposal sites. Paul works in a research laboratory where he and his coworkers develop technology for cities to use in treating and managing wastewater and solid and hazardous waste. They have a contract with the Environmental Protection Agency (EPA) to prepare this manual. After eighteen months, they have completed their research on ways to minimize pollution, and Paul is ready to begin writing the manual. He considers the ways he can structure the information and realizes that structuring it is more than just preparing an outline. It is a process that goes beyond the data he has collected; it involves understanding the readers and the social and cultural forces at work in his company.

In this chapter, you will learn five principles for structuring information. Before thinking about these principles, let's consider how the structure can help readers read and use your documents.

▶Readers and Your Documents

Have you ever tried to read a document where the sentences and paragraphs aren't organized logically? Did you have trouble locating the information you needed in the document? Documents with an illogical organization make readers' tasks difficult—whether that task is to follow a procedure, to make a decision, or to gather information (Felker et al. 9). As an example, consider a section that one of Paul's coworkers prepared for the manual on minimizing pollution (see Figure 6.1).

Let's look at the information in each paragraph of Figure 6.1:

Paragraph 1	Introduction to using chemicals to stabilize or destroy waste
Paragraph 2	More information about using chemicals to stabilize or destroy waste
Paragraph 3	The process of chemical fixation
Paragraph 4	An alternative to applying chemicals to in situ landfills
Paragraph 5	Firms that provide the chemicals to stabilize the waste
Paragraph 6	Problems with chemical fixation in the landfills
Paragraph 7	Problem landfills and chemical fixation

The organization of the document has several problems:

- Information about in situ landfills appears in paragraphs 4 and 6. The writer should have pulled this information together, combining it in one paragraph or presenting it in two successive paragraphs.
- The paragraphs do not follow a logical order.

Chemical Fixation

[1] The application of chemicals to destroy or stabilize hazardous materials and potential pollutants has been a common practice for many years, particularly for industrial wastes. Generally, chemical treatment is quite waste-specific. Thus, an effective system in one case may be ineffective or totally inapplicable in another.

[2] Since the 1970s, several processes involving chemicals have been developed which may be effective on a broader range of wastes. Some of these newer processes are more effective on liquids and thin sludges while others function best with heavier sludges and solids. These processes rely on the reactions of such materials as Portland cement, lime, and common silicates to encapsulate, solidify, or cement waste material.

[3] Each of these processes involves the mixing of a chemical agent such as cement, lime, or silicates with the waste material. With liquid water, the agent absorbs the waste. With solids, the agent coats the surface of the solids to cement them together. With sludges, the agent absorbs and cements the waste. Some of these processes rely mainly on the ability of the chemical system to insulate each particle of pollutant from adjacent leaching fluids; others rely on the formation of a relatively impermeable mass to exclude leaching fluids from passing through the waste.

[4] An alternative to the application of chemical fixation agents to the in situ landfill is to use these agents for stabilizing waste materials. These waste materials can then serve as cover for a problem landfill. After proper processing, these waste materials can be spread, graded, and thereafter cemented into a stable, relatively impermeable cover.

[5] The earliest commercially prominent stabilization system was a process offered by Chemfix for applying to hazardous liquids and sludges. Now, stabilization processes are offered by other firms such as the Environmental Technology Corporation, IU Conversion Systems, Inc., and the Dravo Corporation. The latter two firms primarily offer systems for stabilizing sulfur dioxide scrubber sludge.

[6] We have included information on stabilizing waste materials with chemical agents because, in particular instances, the process is a viable means for controlling potential pollutants. However, this process is not feasible for in situ landfill problems because the success of the system depends on the intimate mixing of the chemical agents and the material to be stabilized; without this mixing, the municipal refuse cannot be coated and encapsulated, and the normal landfill processes of degradation and leaching cannot occur. To ensure the mixing of the chemicals with the refuse would require excavating the entire landfill, which provides little advantage over excavating and relocating the landfill to an environmentally sound site.

[7] An ideal situation would be a problem landfill located near a source of chemically stabilized waste material. The material would be readily available for applying to the landfill as a cap. The chemically stabilized material would then be applied at an approximate compacted thickness of 0.6 m, with appropriate drainage swales to remove surface water.

Source: Adapted from Andrews L. Tolman, Antonio P. Ballestero Jr., William W. Beck Jr., and Grover H. Emrich, *Guidance Manual for Minimizing Pollution from Waste Disposal Sites,* EPA-600/2-78-142 (Washington: GPO, Aug. 1978) 52.

- The document lacks informative headings that identify major topics for readers.
- The document lacks a brief overview describing its organization.

Because the information in Figure 6.1 doesn't have a logical organization, readers can't easily remember it. A more logical organization will help them to remember, understand, and perhaps follow the document (Duin 186).

The information would be easier to follow in a general-to-specific structure as in Figure 6.2:

Paragraph 1	Introduction to using chemicals to stabilize or destroy waste
Paragraph 2	The process of chemical fixation
Paragraph 3	Problems with chemical fixation in the landfills
Paragraph 4	An alternative to applying chemicals to existing (in situ) landfills
Paragraph 5	Use of stabilized waste materials as cover for existing landfills

In this version, the writer has pulled together closely related information into five instead of seven paragraphs. The information on existing landfills now appears in successive paragraphs. The document begins by briefly introducing chemical fixation, moves to more specific information about how chemicals stabilize or destroy hazardous waste, and ends with even more specific information about when chemical fixation is ineffective. The document gives readers a brief overview in paragraph 1 and includes informative headings that allow readers to read only those paragraphs that interest them.

You may be able to use several possible organizational patterns for the documents that you write. The principles that follow will help you to choose appropriately.

▶Principle 1: Decide How to Organize Your Document[1]

Often, you may have two or more options for organizing information. By recognizing these options, you can select the one that will work best for your readers. Ask yourself the following question to determine the most effective structure: Can I group similar information? Pulling together closely related information is "one of the most important organizational principles" in writing (Podis 199). It helps readers to gather the information they need and to receive the intended message of your document. For example, the writer of the document in Figure 6.3 presents all the information about scientific studies

---

[1] Based on a suggested approach to arranging business documents created by Jack Selzer in "Arranging Business Prose."

Figure 6.2

A Document with a Logical, Reader-Oriented Organization

Chemical Fixation in Landfills

[1] The application of chemicals to destroy or stabilize hazardous materials and potential pollutants has been a common practice for many years, particularly for industrial wastes. Generally, chemical treatment is quite waste-specific. Thus, an effective system in one case may be ineffective or totally inapplicable in another. For example, applying chlorine to destroy cyanide and applying lime to precipitate and insolubilize fluorides are standard but waste-specific processes. Since the 1970's, several firms have developed chemical fixation processes that may be effective on a broader range of wastes.[1] In this section, we will discuss how chemical agents destroy or stabilize waste and when chemical agents are ineffective.

How Chemical Agents Destroy or Stabilize Waste

[2] To destroy or stabilize waste, each of these chemical fixation processes mixes a chemical agent such as Portland cement, lime, or silicates with the waste material. With liquids, the chemical agent absorbs the waste. With solids, the agent coats the surface of the solids to cement them together. With sludges, the agent absorbs and cements the waste. Some of these processes rely mainly on the ability of the chemical system to insulate each particle of pollutant from adjacent leaching fluids; others rely on the formation of a relatively impermeable mass to exclude leaching fluids from passing through the waste.

When Chemical Agents Are Ineffective

[3] Although chemical fixation is a viable means for controlling potential pollutants, this process is not feasible for existing landfill problems because the success of the process depends on the intimate mixing of the chemical agents and the material to be stabilized. Without this mixing, the municipal refuse cannot be coated and encapsulated, and the normal landfill processes of degradation and leaching cannot occur. To ensure the mixing of the chemicals with the refuse would require excavating the entire landfill, providing little advantage over excavating and relocating the landfill to an environmentally sound site.

[4] An alternative to applying chemical fixation agents to an existing landfill is to use these agents for stabilizing waste materials not currently in a landfill. These waste materials can then serve as cover for a problem landfill. After proper processing, these waste materials can be spread, graded, and thereafter cemented into a stable, relatively impermeable cover.

[5] When such waste material serves as cover, the problem landfill must be near a source of chemically stabilized waste material. The material would be readily available for applying to the landfill as a cap. The chemically stabilized material could then be applied at an approximate compacted thickness of 0.6 m, with appropriate drainage swales to remove surface water.

1. Chemfix offered the earliest commercially prominent stabilization system for hazardous liquids and sludges. Now, other firms such as the Environmental Technology Corporation, IU Conversion Systems, Inc., and the Dravo Corporation offer stabilization processes. The latter two firms offer systems for stabilizing sulfur dioxide scrubber sludge.

Source: Adapted from Andrews L. Tolman, Antonio P. Ballestero Jr., William W. Beck Jr., and Grover H. Emrich, *Guidance Manual for Minimizing Pollution from Waste Disposal Sites,* EPA-600/2-78-142 (Washington: GPO, Aug. 1978) 52.

Figure 6.3

A Document That
Groups Similar
Information

What About Scientific Studies?

Scientists have been studying a possible link between electric and magnetic fields (EMF) and health effects since the 1960s. Despite a large number of high quality studies, no one knows whether EMF causes health problems. Some studies have not found a link between EMF and health problems, but other studies do in part support the position that exposure to EMF may be harmful.

Scientists have conducted two types of studies of electric and magnetic fields: laboratory studies of cells, organs, animals and people; and epidemiological studies of people.

Laboratory studies have indicated that EMF can have biological effects, such as changes in hormone levels in cell functions and in heart rate. These changes may or may not cause health problems. For example, a single cup of coffee can produce biological changes such as increased heart rate, yet a cup of coffee is generally believed to be harmless.

Epidemiological studies compare two groups of people—those with an illness such as leukemia and a similar but healthy group—to try to identify one or more factors often associated with the illness. All epidemiological studies involve uncertainties such as the possibility that scientists may have overlooked an important cause of an illness or have been unable to accurately identify environmental exposures years after the actual exposures.

While some epidemiological studies have not found a link between EMF and health problems, some studies have found that children who live near powerlines assumed to carry high currents have a greater risk than other children of developing leukemia. Interestingly, most of the studies have not found links between the actual measured fields and increased leukemia risk. All magnetic fields, not electric fields, may be a problem.

Other studies have focused on people who are exposed on their jobs to potentially high EMF levels. These studies have indicated that EMF may cause increased health problems. For example, several studies have indicated a link between increased cancer risk and occupations such as electrician, telephone worker, electric utility worker, and electrical engineer. Most of these studies, however, have not accounted for other possible causes and have not measured the EMF.

The studies conducted do not prove or disprove the theory that EMF exposure is harmful. They do indicate areas that deserve additional research. Further studies will focus on possible occupational risks of EMF and the effects of EMF on cell functions. These studies should provide information in the next three to five years.

Source: Adapted from TXU, *Electric and Magnetic Fields* (Dallas: TXU, n.d.). Courtesy of TXU.

of electric and magnetic fields (EMF) in one section titled "What About Scientific Studies?"

▶ For information on patterns of organization, see Principle 2.

To determine how to group similar information in your documents,

- Consider your readers
- Consider the workplace context—the social and cultural conventions— of your workplace
- Use the standard patterns of organization

Consider Your Readers

Even though your information seems to suggest a particular organizational pattern, that pattern may not work for your readers. Because the readers matter "more than anything" when an effective writer organizes a document (Selzer 44), ask yourself the following questions before you decide how to organize the information in your document:

- **Can I put important information at the beginning of the document?** Readers like to have the important information—or a summary of that information—at the beginning of the document. For instance, readers of proposals like to know at the beginning of the document what you are proposing. They don't want to wait until the middle or the end of the document for the basic proposal. Whenever possible, place the most important information or a summary of it at the beginning of the document.

- **Can I order the information from the simplest to the most complex, the easiest to the most difficult, or the most familiar to the least familiar to clarify it for readers?** If you structure the information so that readers begin with what they already know or understand and move to what they don't know or don't understand, you will help them to read and remember.

- **Will readers scan the document or read it selectively?** Readers rarely read documents from beginning to end. Therefore, choose an organization that allows readers to find the information they need without reading the whole document. Make your organization visible to these readers by using headings.

- **Can I begin with the least controversial or surprising information and move to the most controversial or surprising?** You will usually want to begin with the information that will least surprise or upset readers— especially if you are trying to persuade them to take some action or to adopt your viewpoint. Try to establish common ground with your readers by beginning with information that is not controversial or surprising.

Consider the Workplace Context

The workplace context is the social and cultural conventions of your workplace. Your manager, your organization's policies, and your coworkers may influence how you organize information in documents. You may not be the sole decision maker in determining how you will organize your documents. Before you decide how to organize a document, consider the social and cultural conventions at work in your workplace. The following questions may help you:

- **How will my manager want me to organize the information?** Frequently, your manager will expect you to organize a document in a particular way. If you are in doubt about what he or she expects, discuss your planned organization with your manager or with the person who asked you to write the document.

- **Does my organization have a predetermined organization for similar documents?** For some documents, your organization will determine the organization before you even begin writing, "perhaps because you are responding to another document or because you have been given a strict format from which to work" (Felker et al. 11). In these situations, you may not have much control over the organization of sections or paragraphs in the document. However, within paragraphs, you can organize sentences logically (Felker et al. 11). You can find out whether your workplace has a predetermined organization by looking at similar documents, asking your manager, or reading the organization's style manual.

▶Principle 2: Consider Using the Standard Patterns of Organization

Standard patterns for organizing information include

- Spatial order
- Chronological order
- General-to-specific order
- Classification and division
- Partition
- Comparison/contrast
- Problem and solution
- Cause and effect
- Order of importance

The first two patterns are sequential: the items that you arrange follow each other in physical location (spatial order) or in time (chronological order). The other seven patterns require you to choose the main point and then group the subpoints in a specific way. You can use more than one pattern in a document. For instance, you can use partition to break a whole into parts and then use spatial order to describe the parts. The information you will include in your document determines which pattern(s) to use. Occasionally you may encounter a writing situation where none of the standard patterns is appropriate. In such a situation, try grouping closely related information together.

Spatial Order

When you describe parts by their location—for instance, from left to right— you are using spatial order. You might use spatial organization to describe an object, a mechanism, or a physical location. When you use spatial organization, you begin at one location and end at another—for instance, you might begin describing a screen in a software program from the left and then move to the right as in Figure 6.4. In this figure, the writer begins from the left (as if the reader were actually looking at the screen) with the "Left pane" and moves to "Money Help." The writer could use a similar spatial organization in the text to describe in more detail the functions available on the screen.

> ### ▶ Tips for Using Spatial Order
>
> - **Describe the object, mechanism, or location as if the reader were looking at it.**
> - **Include words that help the reader follow the organization.** Give the reader a "roadmap" to follow. For example, use phrases such as "from the right," "north view," or "left to right."
> - **Use visual aids, when possible, to supplement the text.** If you use a visual aid, be sure to introduce and explain it.

Chronological Order

▶Learn more about chronological order in Chapter 15, "Writing User-Oriented Instructions and Manuals," and in Chapter 19, "Writing Reader-Oriented Job Correspondence."

You read information arranged chronologically almost daily—in recipes, in instructions, in the newspaper. Chronological order occurs most frequently in instructions, process descriptions, and descriptions of events or developments. You will use reverse chronological order when you write a résumé. When you read information arranged in order of occurrence or sequence, you are reading information arranged chronologically. Figure 6.5 illustrates chronological order in two ways. In the first column (as you read the column from top to bottom), the figure moves from the fertilized human egg to the adult. Figure 6.5 also illustrates chronological order from left to right: from obtaining cells to starting a cell culture, and finally to keeping the cell culture growing. This figure demonstrates two types of information that often are best organized chronologically: a procedure (how to do something) and a sequence of events (how something happens).

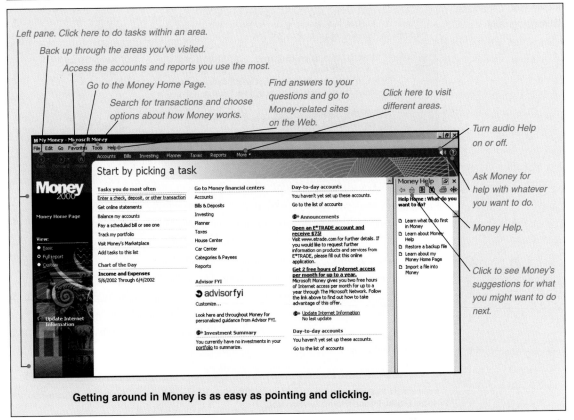

| Figure 6.4 | Spatial Organization |

Left pane. Click here to do tasks within an area.

Back up through the areas you've visited.

Access the accounts and reports you use the most.

Go to the Money Home Page.

Find answers to your questions and go to Money-related sites on the Web.

Click here to visit different areas.

Search for transactions and choose options about how Money works.

Turn audio Help on or off.

Ask Money for help with whatever you want to do.

Money Help.

Click to see Money's suggestions for what you might want to do next.

Getting around in Money is as easy as pointing and clicking.

Source: Microsoft Corporation, *Strategies for Success: 10 Ways to Use Money Effectively* (Microsoft, 1999) 9. Reprinted by permission of Microsoft Corporation.

▶ Tips for Using Chronological Order

- **Use words and phrases that give readers a "mental roadmap" of the chronological sequence.** You might use Step 1, Step 2, etc. You might use an introduction to introduce the sequence—listing the major parts of the sequence. Then use the parts as headings to guide the readers.

- **Use visual aids when appropriate to illustrate the chronology.** If you use a visual aid, be sure to introduce and explain it.

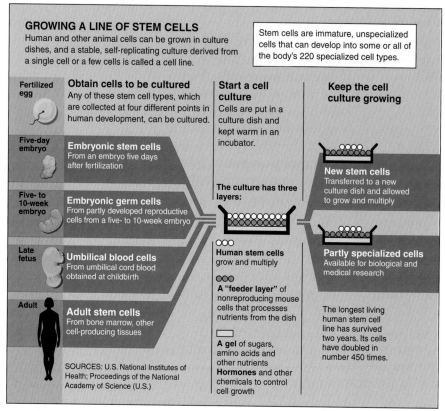

▶ Figure 6.5

Information Organized
Chronologically

Source: KRT Illustration, Lee Hulteng, 11 Aug. 2001, Tribune Media Services. Reprinted with permission of Knight Ridder/Tribune Information Services.

General-to-Specific Order

▶Learn more about
general-to-specific
order in Chapter
14, "Writing
Reader-Oriented
Formal Reports,"
and Chapter 16,
"Creating User-
Oriented Web
Sites."

The general-to-specific order assumes that readers need to understand the general topic before they can understand specific information. For most documents, "write about the 'big picture' before you describe the parts and pieces that make up the whole" (Felker et al. 10). Write first about the general topic and then about the specifics. Most readers also need the conclusion or recommendations first, so they can interpret and understand the specific information in the context of the conclusions or recommendations (Samuels 308). When you solve a problem or make a recommendation, you come to that solution, recommendation, or conclusion last; however, for your readers to understand your work, they need the solution, recommendation, or conclusion first.

Figure 6.6 is an excerpt from an EPA document that uses a general-to-specific organization in the sequencing of paragraphs as well as in individual paragraphs. The writer begins by briefly introducing plume management

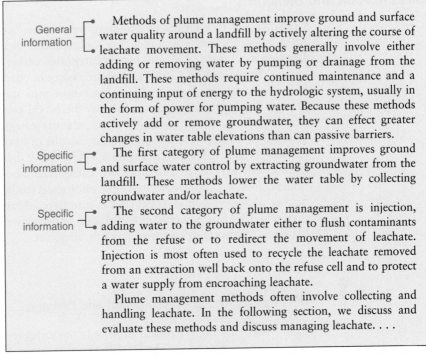

Figure 6.6

A Document That Uses a General-to-Specific Pattern

General information — Methods of plume management improve ground and surface water quality around a landfill by actively altering the course of leachate movement. These methods generally involve either adding or removing water by pumping or drainage from the landfill. These methods require continued maintenance and a continuing input of energy to the hydrologic system, usually in the form of power for pumping water. Because these methods actively add or remove groundwater, they can effect greater changes in water table elevations than can passive barriers.

Specific information — The first category of plume management improves ground and surface water control by extracting groundwater from the landfill. These methods lower the water table by collecting groundwater and/or leachate.

Specific information — The second category of plume management is injection, adding water to the groundwater either to flush contaminants from the refuse or to redirect the movement of leachate. Injection is most often used to recycle the leachate removed from an extraction well back onto the refuse cell and to protect a water supply from encroaching leachate.

Plume management methods often involve collecting and handling leachate. In the following section, we discuss and evaluate these methods and discuss managing leachate. . . .

Source: Adapted from Section 4, "Plume Management," in Andrews L. Tolman, Antonio P. Ballestero Jr., William W. Beck Jr., and Grover H. Emrich, Guidance Manual for Minimizing Pollution from Waste Disposal Sites, EPA-600/2-78-142 (Washington: GPO, Aug. 1978) 68–70.

methods in the first paragraph and then moves to specific categories of plume management in the second and third paragraphs. In the final paragraph, the writer moves to the specific topic of plume management and leachate. Within the third paragraph, the writer uses a general-to-specific organization. The paragraph begins with a definition of injection and then moves to specific ways to apply injection.

▶ To learn more about headings, see page 164 in this chapter as well as Chapter 9, "Designing Documents for Your Readers."

▶ **Tips for Using General-to-Specific Order**

- **State the general information clearly and directly at the beginning of the document, section, or paragraph.** In a longer document, consider putting the general information in a separate section or in a preview that introduces the topic.
- **Use headings to separate the general information from the specific information.** The headings should clearly indicate the general and the specific information, so use informative headings.

Classification and Division

Classification is a means of grouping items into categories. In its simplest form, classification is grouping like items into a broad category or group. **Division** is a means of identifying subcategories within that broad category or group. If you can find items that share common characteristics, you may be able to classify and divide the information into meaningful categories or groups. To classify information, identify the broad group to which that information belongs. To divide information, identify categories within that broad group. For example, look again at the document about exposure to electric and magnetic fields shown in Figure 6.3. The writer divides scientific studies of electric and magnetic fields into two categories: laboratory studies of cells, organs, animals, and people; and epidemiological studies of people. The writer further divides epidemiological studies into two subcategories: studies of children who live near power lines and studies of people exposed to EMF at work. Figure 6.7 shows the categories and subcategories.

> **Tips for Using Classification and Division**
>
> - **Make sure each item will fit in only one category.** Categories should not overlap. The classification shown in Figure 6.7 works because the categories are mutually exclusive.
>
> - **Make sure that each item will fit into a category.** If you have even one item that doesn't fit into a category, you need to add another category or you may have selected a basis for classification that doesn't fit the items. For example, if you are classifying homes, you could classify them by their market value because every home has at least some market value. You could classify homes by the following exterior building materials that cover at least 50 percent of the home: brick, wood, and aluminum siding. However, this classification is incomplete because some homes may have a stucco exterior. You would need to add stucco and other building materials to your possible categories.
>
> - **Classify and divide the items in ways suited to your readers and your purpose.** Choose a principle for classifying and dividing that will fit the information and your purpose. The writer of the document in Figure 6.3 could have divided scientific studies of EMF into two other categories: studies indicating that EMF causes health problems and studies indicating no connection between EMF and health problems. However, such a division would not have fulfilled
>
> (continued on next page)

one of the important purposes of the document: to assure readers that TXU is providing safe electric service to customers at home and a safe working environment for employees on the job.

- **Use visual aids when possible to illustrate the categories and subcategories.** A visual aid my help your readers to understand how you have classified or divided the information.

Partition

Partition is the division of an item into its individual parts. For example, Figure 6.8 illustrates how you might partition the cornea into its three parts: the epithelium, stroma, and endothelium.

Tips for Using Partition

- **Choose a principle for partitioning that will meet your readers' needs and your purpose.** For example, if you want to help a technician understand how the parts of a machine function, you might partition them by their function.

- **Organize the parts in a way that your readers will find helpful.** You can help readers to use and understand your document if you discuss each group of parts in a logical, orderly fashion. For example, if you are discussing the parts of the eye, you might number those parts on a drawing and then discuss them in numerical order as in

(continued on page 147)

Figure 6.7

Classification and Division of Scientific Studies of Electric and Magnetic Fields and Health Effects

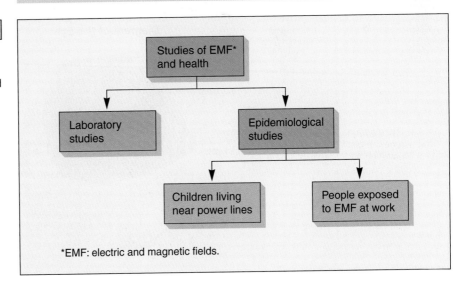

*EMF: electric and magnetic fields.

Structure of the Cornea

Although the cornea is clear and seems to lack substance, it is actually a highly organized group of cells and protein. The cornea receives its nourishment from the tears and aqueous humor that fills the chamber behind it. Unlike most tissues in the body, the cornea contains no blood vessels to nourish or protect it against infection. It must remain transparent to refract light properly, and the presence of even the tiniest capillaries would interfere with this process. The tissue has three main regions, or layers:

The writer partitions the cornea into three parts.

Epithelium: As the cornea's outermost region—comprising about 10 percent of the tissue's thickness—the epithelium functions primarily to block the passage of foreign material (such as dust or water) into the eye and other layers of the cornea, and to provide a smooth surface that absorbs oxygen and other needed cell nutrients that are contained in tears. This layer, which is about five cells deep, is filled with thousands of tiny nerve endings that make the cornea extremely sensitive to pain when rubbed or scratched.

Stroma: Located behind the epithelium, the stroma comprises about 90 percent of the cornea. It consists primarily of water (78 percent); layered protein fibers (16 percent) that give the cornea its strength, elasticity, and form; and cells that nourish it. The unique shape, arrangement, and spacing of the protein fibers are essential in producing the cornea's light-conducting transparency.

Endothelium: This single layer of cells is located between the stroma and the aqueous humor. Because the stroma tends to absorb water, the endothelium's primary task is to pump excess water out of the stroma. Without this pumping action, the stroma would swell with water, become hazy, and ultimately become opaque.

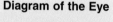

Diagram of the Eye

The diagram reinforces the text by illustrating the parts of the cornea.

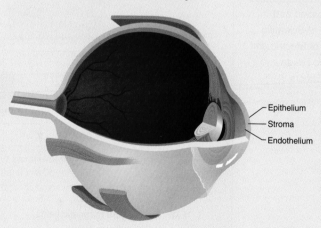

Epithelium
Stroma
Endothelium

Source: Adapted from the National Eye Institute, "The Cornea and Corneal Disease." Online. Internet. 22 Nov. 2001. Available: http://www.mcdhlep.org/gov/cornea.htm.

Figure 6.9. You might also use spatial order, beginning with the parts on the right and moving clockwise to the parts on the left.

- **Use visual aids when possible to illustrate the parts.** A visual aid may help your readers to understand how you have partitioned the information. For example, the diagram of the cornea helps the readers to locate the parts and to understand how they fit in with the rest of the eye.

Comparison/Contrast

You may need to compare or contrast two or more options. When you examine these options, you'll need standards or criteria for comparing. For example, if you were deciding which apartment to rent, you might compare the apartments based on size, cost, amenities, and location. You might even rank these criteria in order of importance to help you select the best apartment for you and your situation.

▶ Learn more about feasibility reports and the comparison pattern in Chapter 14, "Writing Reader-Oriented Formal Reports," page 440.

You may use the comparison and contrast pattern in many documents, but especially in a feasibility report. Feasibility reports compare two or more options. As you report your comparisons, you can organize by options or by the criteria used to compare the options. Figures 6.10 and 6.11 illustrate how you might organize a document comparing Mars and Earth. Figure 6.10 is organized according to the options. Notice that all the information about Mars appears in one section and all the information about Earth appears in another section. This organization has the advantage of presenting the whole picture for each option in one section and emphasizes the options.

▼ **Figure 6.9**

A Diagram with Parts Numbered

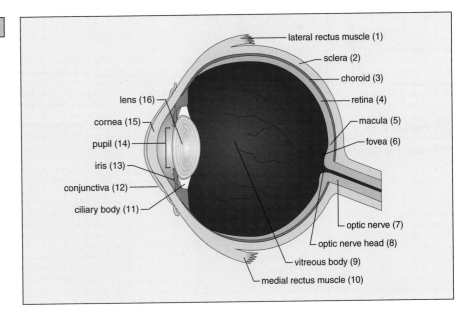

In Figure 6.11, the writer has organized according to the criteria used to compare Mars and Earth. The writer groups the information about the climate of Mars and Earth into the same section, the information about the atmosphere of both planets in another section, and the information about the surface of both planets in another section. This organization emphasizes the criteria and helps the readers to easily compare options based on individual criteria. The advantage of this organization is the point-by-point comparison using the criteria.

Figure 6.12 is a document in which the writer organizes by options to compare three methods for recycling leachate in a landfill. The writer uses the criteria of cost and odor to compare and contrast these methods.

► **Tips for Using Comparison and Contrast**

- **Choose criteria for comparing and contrasting.** For example, if you are going to compare various personal computers, you might use the criteria of cost, reliability, and speed.

- **Evaluate each option using the criteria.** Draw your conclusions only after you have evaluated all options.

(continued on page 150)

Figure 6.10

Comparing by Options

Mars
- Climate
- Atmosphere
- Composition of the Planet's Surface

Earth
- Climate
- Atmosphere
- Composition of the Planet's Surface

Figure 6.11

Comparing by Criteria

Climate
- Mars
- Earth

Atmosphere
- Mars
- Earth

Composition of the Planet's Surface
- Mars
- Earth

| **Figure 6.12** | A Document That Uses Comparison/Contrast |

To eliminate contaminants in landfills, leachate can be collected and then recycled through the landfill. Recycling accelerates the stabilizing of the landfill. The three most widely used recycling methods are

The writers introduce the three options.

- spray irrigation
- overland or at-grade irrigation
- subgrade irrigation.

Spray Irrigation

The writers organize by the three options, using a heading to indicate each option. Under each heading, the writers first define the option and then use the criteria of odor and cost to organize the paragraph. In each paragraph, the writers discuss the criteria in the same order.

Spray irrigation uses nozzles to spray effluent onto the landfill surface. Spray irrigation has one advantage over the other two methods: it effects some leachate treatment during the spraying by aerating and infiltrating the soil surface. However, it does not eliminate odor and is expensive. Spray irrigation has a total cost of $68,900 the first year and $28,000 each subsequent year.

Overland Irrigation

Overland irrigation spreads effluent with trenches, spreading basins, or gaged pipe. During the irrigation, leachate is pumped into the distribution system once or twice a week and allowed to infiltrate into the ground. Overland irrigation does not eliminate odor but costs less than spray irrigation. Overland irrigation costs $7,100 the first year and $2,500 each subsequent year.

Subgrade Irrigation

Subgrade irrigation uses a tile field or well. In the tile field construction, perforated pipe is buried in gravel-lined trenches to spread the leachate. The wells use an injection system. Unlike spray or overland irrigation, subgrade irrigation avoids local odor problems. It also is less expensive than the other two methods. Subgrade irrigation costs $12,350 the first year and $1,550 each subsequent year. Table 1 compares the costs of the three methods.

Table 1. Costs of Leachate Recycling Methods*

The table summarizes information on one of the criteria: cost.

Method	Capital Costs	Annual Operation and Maintenance Costs	Annual Power Costs	Total Cost First Year
Spray Irrigation	$30,900	$3,500	$24,500	$68,900
Overland Irrigation	$ 4,600	$2,500	-0-	$ 7,100
Subgrade Irrigation	$10,800	$1,550	-0-	$12,350

*Source: Pound, C. E., R. W. Crites, and D. A. Griffes, *Costs of Wastewater Treatment by Land Application*. EPA- 430/9-75-003.

Source: Adapted from Section 4, "Plume Management," in Andrews L. Tolman, Antonio P. Ballestero Jr., William W. Beck Jr., and Grover H. Emrich, *Guidance Manual for Minimizing Pollution from Waste Disposal Sites*, EPA-600/2-78-142 (Washington: GPO, Aug. 1978) 48–51. Reprinted by permission of the Texas Agricultural Experiment Station and Bruce Lawhorn.

- **Organize your comparison or contrast in a way that will help your readers and meet your purpose.** In comparing personal computers, you could arrange the document so readers can easily gather the information to decide which computer to purchase. You might organize by criteria to group all the information about the cost (base price, software costs, printer costs) in one section of the document and all the information about reliability (warranty, customer service, previous service records) in another section. You could also organize by options and group the information about one personal computer in one section, the information about the other computer in another section, and so on.

- **Use visual aids, when appropriate, to explain your comparison or contrast information.** Consider using visual aids to summarize when you are comparing or contrasting.

Problem and Solution

▶ To learn more about this pattern in proposals, see Chapter 12, "Writing Reader-Oriented Proposals," and in progress reports, see Chapter 13, "Writing Reader-Oriented Informal Reports."

You can use a problem-and-solution pattern to explain both actual and proposed solutions. The problem-and-solution pattern is frequently used in proposals and progress reports.

Let's again consider the document on electric and magnetic fields (a portion of which appears in Figure 6.3). In the first paragraph, the writers identify the problem: "Scientists have been studying a possible link between electric and magnetic fields (EMF) and health effects since the 1960s." In the final section, "What Are We Doing?" the writers briefly identify the solutions (as shown highlighted in Figure 6.13).

▶ Tips for Using the Problem-and-Solution Pattern

- **Identify the problem early in the document before you begin discussing the solution.** Before your readers can understand and appreciate your solution, they must first know the problem. Emphasize the parts of the problem that your solution addresses and the significance of the problem to your readers.

- **Show how your solution will solve the problem.** Your readers will see the value of your solution only if they understand how it relates to the problem. Give specific details revealing how your solution will eliminate the problem.

- **Group the stages of your solution into meaningful categories.** If your solution has several stages, you can help your readers by grouping the stages into mutually exclusive, nonoverlapping categories.

(continued on next page)

- **Give readers ample evidence that your solution will solve the problem.** If you are trying to persuade readers to adopt a solution that you are recommending, give them the evidence and reasoning they need to accept it. Even if the solution is already in place, you may want to persuade readers that it is worthwhile and effective.
- **Use visual aids when appropriate to illustrate or clarify the problem or the solution.** Visual aids may help you to summarize or clarify the problem or the solution.

Cause and Effect

You can use the cause-and-effect pattern to help readers understand the consequences or the cause of a particular action or series of actions. Depending on your purpose, you can move from the cause to the effect or from the effect to the cause. For example, you can talk about a leak (effect) in a steam-generated electric plant and then explain the cause, sagging pipes. You can also discuss the sagging pipes (cause) and predict the effect, a leak.

Figure 6.14 presents a document with a cause-and-effect organization. The document explains the effects of babesiosis, a tick-transmitted disease of dogs. The writers identify and explain the disease and its cause at the beginning of

Figure 6.13

An Example of a Solution Section (with Solutions Highlighted)

What Are We Doing?

TXU is committed to devoting the resources necessary to address the EMF issue in a responsible manner. TXU formed a task force in January 1987 to keep abreast of any developments regarding EMF, to conduct research, and to coordinate responses to customer EMF inquiries. Through this task force, TXU has become a leader in the industry in addressing the EMF issue.

TXU helps fund the Electric Power Research Institute's EMF reasearch. This institute has spent over $40 million on EMF research in the last 18 years. TXU has also testified before Congress on behalf of the Edison Electric Institute to support increased federal research.

TXU is also conducting its own research into EMF levels produced around its facilities and in customers' homes, and TXU considers the potential for reducing magnetic fields when designing new facilities.

Company employees have participated in two studies monitoring home and work exposure. The company will also participate in a third study, monitoring magnetic fields in the homes of approximately 36 residential customers who volunteer for the project.

TXU shares information with concerned customers and employees. We send printed materials upon request, measure at no charge, and present information to any interested group.

Source: Adapted from TXU, *Electric and Magnetic Fields* (Dallas: TXU, n.d.). Courtesy of TXU.

the document and relate the disease to its specific effects with the sentence beginning "When a dog becomes infected with the Babesia organism . . ."

> ► **Tips for Using the Cause-and-Effect Pattern**
>
> • **Identify either the cause or the effect near the beginning of the document.** Near the beginning of the document, tell your readers what you are trying to do in the document—to explain the causes of a specific effect or the effects of a specific cause. If your readers know how you have organized the information, they can better understand it.
>
> • **Show how the cause directly relates to the effect or how the effect directly relates to the cause.** Make sure that your readers understand the links between the cause and the effect or between the effect and the cause. Don't expect readers to infer the connections; explain them.
>
> (continued on next page)

▼ **Figure 6.14**   An Example of the Cause-and-Effect Pattern

Babesiosis: Its Cause, Effects, and Treatment

The writers introduce the cause of babesiosis.

Babesiosis, also known as Malignant Jaundice, is a tick-transmitted disease of dogs. Babesiosis is caused by a protozoan organism, *Babesia canis,* that enters and destroys the red blood cells. The principal carrier of babesiosis from infected to non-infected dogs is the brown dog tick. The disease can also spread through blood transfusions or in rare cases from an infected female dog to her pups before birth.

The writers explain the effect of babesiosis on dogs.

When a dog becomes infected with the *Babesia* organism, it may become critically sick and die in a few days; or it may become a carrier without showing any signs of the disease. The most specific signs for babesiosis are

• bloody urine
• jaundiced mucous membranes and skin

Other signs include poor appetite, listlessness, fever, weight loss, and pale mucous membranes from anemia; however, these signs also occur with other diseases.

A veterinarian can diagnose babesiosis by finding the microscopic organisms in the red blood cells. If a diagnosis is not possible with this method, the veterinarian must test the blood serum for *Babesia* antibodies. Even if a dog tests positive for babesiosis, the veterinarians cannot treat it because the most effective drugs for treating babesiosis are unavailable in the United States.

Source: Adapted from W. Elmo Crenshaw and Bruce Lawhorn, "Tick-borne Diseases of the Dog," L-22667, rpt. 10M-7-88 (College Station: Texas Agricultural Extension Service, n.d.).

- **Group the causes or effects into logical categories.** Grouping helps readers to understand the relationships among causes and effects.

- **Use visual aids when appropriate to illustrate or clarify the effect or the cause.** Visual aids may help you to summarize or clarify the cause and the effect. Visual aids are especially effective for showing how the cause and the effect relate.

Order of Importance

You can organize information according to its importance. You can use either a descending or an ascending order. You can begin with the most important and move to the least important (**descending**), or you can begin with the least important and move to the most important (**ascending**). With the descending organization, you get the reader's attention with the most important point. You may want to use ascending order when you are trying to persuade a reader who may be hostile or who may disagree with you.

The document shown in Figure 6.15 moves from the most important to the least important question for the readers. The readers of this document are employees of a utility company. If the readers had been customers, the writers probably would have begun with the final question about how customers' bills would change.

▶ Tips for Using the Order of Importance Pattern

- **Give the readers a context for the information.** State the main point or topic at the beginning.

- **Tell the readers how you are organizing the information.** Clearly tell the readers that you are beginning with the most important information or that you are ending with the most important information.

- **Tell the readers why one point is more or less important than another.** Don't assume that your readers will see the information in the same order of importance as you do.

- **Use visual aids when appropriate.** Visual aids may help you to clarify the information.

▶Principle 3: Prepare an Outline

After you have considered your readers' needs and the context for your document, prepare an outline. An outline helps you to see the organization of your document, so you can spot sections that are organized illogically or that lack information. An outline also gives you a plan to follow as you begin writing.

Don't feel bound to write the sections of the outline in sequence. Instead,

| **Figure 6.15** | A Document Organized by Order of Importance (Most Important to Least Important) |

The writers state their organizational pattern: most important to least important.

The writers explain why the first point is most important.

On June 12, 1991, nearly 17 months after we filed the company's rate request, the Public Utility Commission examiners issued their joint recommendations to reduce our rates from 10.2% to 8.2%. Beginning on July 15, the Public Utility Commission will hear our final arguments about the rate request. To help all of you understand the examiner's recommendations and their potential effects on you and the company, the Chairperson of the company answered the following questions. We begin with the question most important to all of us: how the examiners' recommendation will affect the financial stability of the company. Our financial stability is most important because it affects our ability to finance current and future construction and to maintain our current level of operations.

What is the effect of the commission's recommendation to reduce the company's 10.2% requested increase to 8.2%?

We requested the minimum increase necessary to begin restoring our financial integrity. Our rates have been low for many years—25% below the national average. We have not increased rates since early 1984. Since then, our rates have declined 10%; the requested 10.2% increase returns our rates to about where they were in 1984. Under normal circumstances, the company might be able to get by with an order that grants only 80% of the amount requested. However, our financial condition has declined so that we simply do not have any cushion.

Other companies in the state got less rate relief than they requested. Why can't we get by as they have?

The key financial indicator in determining a company's ability to borrow is its coverage ratio, the number of times interest can be paid with earnings. The minimum coverage is generally two times. With the rate increases recently granted two other utility companies, their projected coverage ratios are 2.2 times and 2.9 times. Based on the examiners' report in our rate case, our coverage ratio would be negative this year and would recover to 1.6 times by the end of next year. We would be unable to sell preferred stock or finance with bonds or unsecured debt. This inability to finance would significantly impair current construction.

How have our customers reacted to the proposed 10.2% increase?

With the exception of some orchestrated opposition created by paid solicitors and a few longtime opponents, the customers have had little reaction. Most customers recognize the company's long record of good service at low rates. Our opinion surveys reflect a high level of customer satisfaction at or above that prior to the rate filing.

How will customers' bills differ between the 10.2% increase and the 8.2%?

The difference between the increases is a small amount. With the 10.2% increase, about one-third of our customers' monthly bills are less than $50. The difference on a $50 bill would be about $1.20 per month—again, returning rates to about 1984 levels. We have a remarkable record in maintaining comparatively low rates, particularly since inflation has increased about 30% since 1984.

Source: Adapted from TXU, *Spotlight: Special Rate Case Report* (Dallas: TXU, 1991). Courtesy of TXU.

Organizing Web Sites

When organizing information on paper, you can draw on centuries of tradition. Similar in some ways to the printed page, Web sites nevertheless pose significant new design challenges. Consider how differently we read the printed page and the Web. Reading traditional text is naturally understood as a two-dimensional experience; but people—so far at least—seem to read the Web in three dimensions. Consider how we talk about the Web: "cyberspace" is something through which we "navigate," perhaps hoping to "go to" a specific homepage. We seem to have an extra dimension when presenting ourselves or our organization on the Web.

An advertising copywriter for an organization, for example, seeks to establish that organization's presence in a brochure, using language, design, typography, graphics, and colors. A Web site designer has to consider all of these elements and more. As a three-dimensional experience, a site cannot be the final, palpable product like the brochure. Instead, sites act as gateways to more sites, providing links that allow readers to continue their journey through cyberspace. Unlike traditional print, effective Web sites must be dynamic environments, presenting readers with familiar yet fresh new organizations of information with each visit. Web site organization is maturing rapidly, but we should remember that it took centuries for printers to master their craft. For more information on organizing Web sites, see Chapter 16, "Creating User-Oriented Web Sites."

you might begin with the section that you know the most about or for which you have gathered all the necessary information. Feel free to change the outline as you are writing. An outline is only a plan, not a permanent document. You can use informal or formal outlines.

An Informal Outline

An informal outline may simply be a list of what you plan to include in a document, or it may be a preliminary draft of a more formal outline. Informal outlines don't have to include sentences or parallel structure. Instead, they may be lists of initial thoughts and pieces of information that you write down but don't organize. Informal outlines may be sufficient for short reports, instructions, and correspondence.

Let's look at how a writer expands the discussion of babesiosis (see Figure 6.14) into a document on tick-borne diseases of the dog. The writer begins with an informal outline (see Figure 6.16). You can use informal outlines to create drafts for a formal outline. These drafts help you learn where the information is incomplete or where the organization is illogical.

A Formal Outline

A formal outline differs from an informal outline in two ways: it shows a more detailed structure for the information, and it uses numbers and letters. Because

▼ **Figure 6.16**

An Informal Outline
for a Document on
Tick-borne Diseases
of Dogs

Ehrlichiosis
- ehrlichiosis is a frequently diagnosed tick-borne disease
- the symptoms of ehrlichiosis are depression, poor appetite, weight loss, fever, enlarged lymph nodes, pale mucous membranes, and bleeding tendencies
- ehrlichiosis has either an acute form or a chronic form. Acute form may cause death within a few days of infestation or may last for 3 to 6 weeks. If dog survives acute, the disease may become chronic
- diagnosis ehrlichiosis through finding the rickettsial organism in blood cells or testing of blood serum for ehrlichia antibodies

Babesiosis
- babesiosis is caused by Babesia Canis transmitted by the brown dog tick
- babesiosis is treated with drugs not currently available in US
- babesiosis symptoms: poor appetite, listlessness, fever, weight loss, and pale mucous membranes from anemia, bloody urine, and jaundiced mucous membranes and skin
- diagnose babesiosis by finding Babesia Canis in the blood cells or its antibodies in the blood serum

Borreliosis
- borreliosis or lyme disease first diagnosed in 1975
- borreliosis signs include intermittent lameness in one or more legs from swelling and pain in the joints of the legs and feet, fever
- borreliosis usually occurs in dogs less than 4 years old
- treat borreliosis with antibiotics

Prevention
- most effective prevention is treatment such as dipping, spraying, or using powders to kill ticks before they can cause the anemia or spread disease
- the lawn where the dog lives should also be sprayed to eliminate ticks
- the pet owner should carefully follow the label instructions for any dip, spray, or powder or have a professional treat the dog

▶ For more informa-
tion, see Chapter
11, "Preparing
Front and Back
Matter."

a formal outline establishes a hierarchy among pieces of information, you can easily convert topics and subtopics into headings for a document or into a table of contents for a formal report. As you prepare your outline, determine what format you will use for it, and then use parallel structure for the topics and subtopics.

Selecting an Outline Format

If you are writing an outline that you will not show to others, use any format that you can read, understand, and follow. However, if you will use your outline when collaborating or if your document requires a table of contents, select one of the traditional outline formats:

- Topic outline
- Sentence outline

Organization Makes a Difference

"Outlining does make a difference! Good writers are inclined to prepare written outlines, and these writers spend more time on macrowriting issues (strategy, sequence, etc.). Poor writers spend less time on outlining and more time on microwriting issues (sentence structure, grammar, and spelling)."

—William H. Baker,
Brigham Young University (457)

Researchers have found a positive correlation between outlining or other writing plans and the quality of the subsequent text (Perl; Taylor and Beach; Kellogg; Spivey and King). According to this research, effective writers tend to prepare outlines and to "spend more time on macrowriting issues" such as structure (Baker 457). Less effective writers "spend less time on outlining and more time on microwriting issues (sentence structure, grammar, spelling)" (Baker 457; Hayes and Flower). Researchers have also discovered that readers process information on two levels: microprocessing (focusing on the meaning of individual words and sentences) and macroprocessing (focusing on the relationship of paragraphs and sections) (Lorch and Lorch). Through macroprocessing, readers create a mental road map of a document (Baker).

Readers can more easily remember and process information from documents with an effective macrostructure (or organization) than from documents with an ineffective organization (Lorch and Lorch). An effective organization allows readers to more easily process word- and sentence-level information and to relate this information to the document as a whole. Without an effective organization, readers relate individual sentences and words—local information—only "to the immediately preceding ones"; the readers don't have a clear organization in which to integrate the local information (Baker 457; Kintsch).

What does this research mean for your writing? If you want readers to understand your documents and better recall the information, use a logical, clear organization that gives readers a mental road map (Baker).

Assignment

Let's test Baker's theory that "outlining does make a difference." For your next assignment in your technical communication class,

- Prepare an informal or formal outline.
- Write an e-mail to your instructor answering these questions: Did you spend more time on writing the outline and planning the document or on editing issues? Did you change the outline? Do you think the outline helped you to write a better document?

Be sure to prepare the outline *before* you write the document, not after.

Topic outlines use phrases for the topics and subtopics. For example, a topic outline might use the phrase "signs of ehrlichiosis." Sentence outlines use sentences for the topics and subtopics: "A dog with ehrlichiosis may exhibit any one of seven signs."

Once you have determined which format to use, decide how to number the outline—with a combination of numbers and letters (see Figure 6.17) or with decimals (see Figure 6.18).

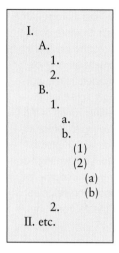

Figure 6.17

Outline Style with Numbers and Letters

```
I.
   A.
      1.
      2.
   B.
      1.
         a.
         b.
            (1)
            (2)
               (a)
               (b)
      2.
II. etc.
```

Figure 6.18

Outline Style with Decimals

```
1.0
   1.1
      1.1.1
      1.1.2
   1.2
      1.2.1
      1.2.2
2.0 etc.
```

Using Parallel Structure

The statements of topics and subtopics in a formal outline should be parallel in structure. In other words, they should have the same grammatical structure. The items in the following numbered list are not grammatically parallel:

> A. Logging on to a computer network
>   1. Find the login prompt
>   2. Typing your login phrase
>   3. Passwords
>   4. What you will see if you login correctly

Items 1, 2, 3, and 4 have different grammatical structures. Item 1 begins with a verb; item 2 begins with a different verb form; item 3 begins with a noun; and item 4 begins with a pronoun. These differences obscure the writer's reason for listing the items in this sequence. The list is clearer when the items are parallel in structure:

> A. Logging on to a computer network
>   1. Find the login prompt
>   2. Type your login phrase
>   3. Type your password
>   4. Look for the message "Welcome to the network"

Now items 1, 2, 3, and 4 have the same grammatical structure—they begin with verbs.

Using an Outline Draft

You can use a draft of a formal outline to analyze the information you have gathered and the organization you plan to use for a document. Let's consider the information for the document on tick-borne diseases of dogs (see Figure 6.16) and put it in a draft for a formal outline (see Figure 6.19). The draft reveals several problems:

- **The information is incomplete and inconsistent.** The sections on the three diseases contain different kinds and amounts of information. The sections on ehrlichiosis and babesiosis each have three subsections, but the subsections are different. The section on borreliosis has only two subsections: signs and treatment. If possible, all three sections should have the same subsections, to create consistent and complete information.

- **The structure of section II is not logical because it has only one subsection.** Each section of an outline should have at least two subsections.

- **The draft lacks parallelism in several places.** (See the parallelism errors marked on Figure 6.19).

Figure 6.19

A Draft of a Formal
Outline

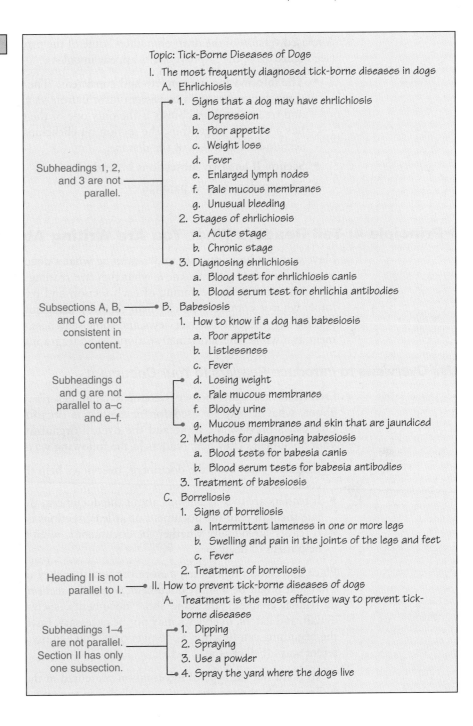

Topic: Tick-Borne Diseases of Dogs
I. The most frequently diagnosed tick-borne diseases in dogs
   A. Ehrlichiosis
      1. Signs that a dog may have ehrlichiosis
         a. Depression
         b. Poor appetite
         c. Weight loss
         d. Fever
         e. Enlarged lymph nodes
         f. Pale mucous membranes
         g. Unusual bleeding
      2. Stages of ehrlichiosis
         a. Acute stage
         b. Chronic stage
      3. Diagnosing ehrlichiosis
         a. Blood test for ehrlichiosis canis
         b. Blood serum test for ehrlichia antibodies
   B. Babesiosis
      1. How to know if a dog has babesiosis
         a. Poor appetite
         b. Listlessness
         c. Fever
         d. Losing weight
         e. Pale mucous membranes
         f. Bloody urine
         g. Mucous membranes and skin that are jaundiced
      2. Methods for diagnosing babesiosis
         a. Blood tests for babesia canis
         b. Blood serum tests for babesia antibodies
      3. Treatment of babesiosis
   C. Borreliosis
      1. Signs of borreliosis
         a. Intermittent lameness in one or more legs
         b. Swelling and pain in the joints of the legs and feet
         c. Fever
      2. Treatment of borreliosis
II. How to prevent tick-borne diseases of dogs
   A. Treatment is the most effective way to prevent tick-
      borne diseases
      1. Dipping
      2. Spraying
      3. Use a powder
      4. Spray the yard where the dogs live

Subheadings 1, 2,
and 3 are not
parallel.

Subsections A, B,
and C are not
consistent in
content.

Subheadings d
and g are not
parallel to a–c
and e–f.

Heading II is not
parallel to I.

Subheadings 1–4
are not parallel.
Section II has only
one subsection.

A revised version of the draft eliminates some of the problems in the first draft (see Figure 6.20; the improvements appear in color):

- **The information is complete and consistent.** The sections on the three diseases contain consistent information on signs, diagnosis, and treatment. Ehrlichiosis is the only one of the three diseases that has a chronic stage; thus, the section on ehrlichiosis contains a subsection on the stages of the disease.
- **Section II has two subsections instead of one.**
- **The wording is now parallel.**

▶Principle 4: Tell Readers What You Are Writing About

Have you ever had difficulty understanding what a document was about? Like you, your readers want to know what they are reading. At the beginning of a document and at the beginning of each section and paragraph, they want to know what is coming. You can help them by using summarizing statements. Specifically, you can use overviews and topic sentences to introduce the document as a whole and individual sections and paragraphs within documents.

Use Overviews to Introduce Readers to Your Document

Overviews are introductory statements that describe what a document is about, what it may be used for, or how it is organized (Felker et al. 13). Overviews preview the topic and the overall organization of information in your document. They help readers in the following ways (Felker et al. 15–16):

- If readers must read the document, overviews help them to understand its contents.
- If readers are merely curious about the document, overviews may stimulate them to read the document or at least sections of it.
- If readers aren't sure whether the document is what they need, overviews help them to decide.

Place overviews immediately before the text that they describe or summarize. That text might be a short document, a specific section of a document, or an individual chapter. For some short documents, such as interoffice memos, e-mail, and letters, overviews may not be necessary. Instead, a topic sentence at the beginning can function as an overview. You can use overviews in three different ways (Felker et al. 13–15):

- To point out the type of information presented in the text
- To identify the specific sections included in the text
- To give instructions about how to use the text

Figure 6.20

The Revised Formal
Outline

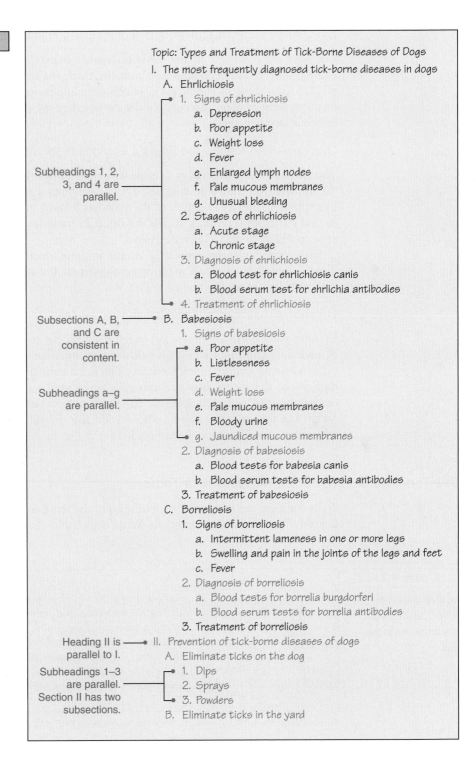

Topic: Types and Treatment of Tick-Borne Diseases of Dogs
I. The most frequently diagnosed tick-borne diseases in dogs
    A. Ehrlichiosis
        1. Signs of ehrlichiosis
            a. Depression
            b. Poor appetite
            c. Weight loss
            d. Fever
            e. Enlarged lymph nodes
            f. Pale mucous membranes
            g. Unusual bleeding
        2. Stages of ehrlichiosis
            a. Acute stage
            b. Chronic stage
        3. Diagnosis of ehrlichiosis
            a. Blood test for ehrlichiosis canis
            b. Blood serum test for ehrlichia antibodies
        4. Treatment of ehrlichiosis
    B. Babesiosis
        1. Signs of babesiosis
            a. Poor appetite
            b. Listlessness
            c. Fever
            d. Weight loss
            e. Pale mucous membranes
            f. Bloody urine
            g. Jaundiced mucous membranes
        2. Diagnosis of babesiosis
            a. Blood tests for babesia canis
            b. Blood serum tests for babesia antibodies
        3. Treatment of babesiosis
    C. Borreliosis
        1. Signs of borreliosis
            a. Intermittent lameness in one or more legs
            b. Swelling and pain in the joints of the legs and feet
            c. Fever
        2. Diagnosis of borreliosis
            a. Blood tests for borrelia burgdorferi
            b. Blood serum tests for borrelia antibodies
        3. Treatment of borreliosis
II. Prevention of tick-borne diseases of dogs
    A. Eliminate ticks on the dog
        1. Dips
        2. Sprays
        3. Powders
    B. Eliminate ticks in the yard

Subheadings 1, 2, 3, and 4 are parallel.

Subsections A, B, and C are consistent in content.

Subheadings a–g are parallel.

Heading II is parallel to I.

Subheadings 1–3 are parallel.
Section II has two subsections.

Overviews That Point Out the Types of Information in the Text

Consider the overview in the TXU document titled "Electric and Magnetic Fields." The writer tells readers about the three major sections in the document, listing them in the order in which they appear (see Figure 6.21). With this overview, readers can quickly decide whether the document contains the information they need.

Overviews That Identify the Specific Sections of the Text

You also can write overviews that identify the sections of the text and describe the information that they contain. These overviews particularly help readers by explaining the organization of the text that follows and providing signposts to that structure (Felker et al. 14). Figure 6.22 includes signposts in the overview to "Electric and Magnetic Fields."

Such overviews are especially useful in long documents, in documents divided into sections, and in documents written for more than one type of reader (Felker et al. 14).

Overviews That Tell Readers How to Use the Text

In some overviews, you may want to tell readers how to use the text. This type of overview combines signposts with instructions for using the text. Figure 6.23 shows an overview with instructions for a software manual. In the first paragraph, the writer lists the manual's three major sections and then tells readers how to use each section. This type of overview clearly tells readers "what the document is about, who should use the different parts of it, and when they should use it" (Felker et al. 14).

Use Topic Sentences to Tell Readers Your Topic

To understand the sentences in a paragraph, readers need a frame of reference. Consider the following paragraph. What is its topic?

Figure 6.21	
An Overview That Points Out the Types of Information in the Text	In the final sentence, the writers list the three types of information that they will discuss in the document. → Reports about possible health effects from exposure to electric and magnetic fields (EMF) continue to concern some employees and TXU customers. The following information will help you to understand this issue. This information describes EMF, existing and planned scientific studies, and TXU and industry efforts to address the EMF issue.

Source: Adapted from TXU, *Electric and Magnetic Fields* (Dallas: TXU, n.d.).

▼ Figure 6.22

An Overview That Identifies the Specific Sections of the Text

Reports about possible health effects from exposure to electric and magnetic fields (EMF) continue to concern some employees and TXU customers. The following sections will help you to understand this issue:

The writier lists the titles of each section to identify the contents of each section.

- The first section, "What Is EMF?" defines and describes electric and magnetic fields.
- The second section, "What About Scientific Studies?" describes existing and planned scientific studies of EMF.
- The third section, "What Are We Doing?" describes what TXU and the industry are doing to address the EMF issue.

Source: Adapted from TXU, Electric and Magnetic Fields (Dallas: TXU, n.d.).

▼ Figure 6.23   An Overview That Tells Readers How to Use the Text

Which Sections Should I Use?

This manual has three major sections: *Getting Started, Learning the Basics*, and *Using the Advanced Features.*

The writer identifies the sections by title.

Getting Started

Getting Started will help you install and start the spreadsheet. Complete this section before moving to the other sections of the manual.

Learning the Basics

If you are new to spreadsheets, try working through the lessons in *Learning the Basics* to learn spreadsheet fundamentals.

The writer tells the reader how to use each section.

Using the Advanced Features

After you are familiar and comfortable with the fundamentals, you can move to *Using the Advanced Features*. This section is appropriate for the more experienced users.

When you compare the heating bills with those of traditional gas furnaces, you can cut your bills by as much as 60%. You can reduce your air conditioning costs from 25% to 50%. Since no outside unit is necessary, you can avoid the noise and visibility problems that you have with traditional air conditioners.

The paragraph is about some type of air conditioner or heater; but if you are like most readers, you can't determine the exact topic. Consider the same paragraph with a topic sentence at the beginning:

> **The geothermal heat pump will save you money on your heating and air conditioning bills.** When you compare the heating bills with those of traditional gas furnaces, you can cut your bills by as much as 60%. You can reduce your air conditioning costs from 25% to 50%. Since no outside unit is necessary, you can avoid the noise and visibility problems that you have with traditional air conditioners.

A **topic sentence** announces what a paragraph is about; it provides the frame of reference that readers need to establish meaning in a paragraph. The topic sentence gives readers a key to unlock the meaning of the sentences that follow.

▶ Principle 5: Use Headings to Show the Organization of Your Document

Headings are subtitles within a document. If you have prepared a formal outline, you can use the entries in the outline as headings and subheadings in your document. Headings help readers in several ways (Felker et al. 17). They

▶ In Chapter 9, "Designing Documents for Your Readers," you will learn how to design and lay out headings that are easy for readers to find.

- Indicate the organization and scope of a document—a service that especially helps readers who want to determine whether a document contains information they need
- Help readers locate specific information
- Give readers cues to the information contained in specific sections

Figures 6.24 and 6.25 show how adding headings can help to reveal content. Effective headings are informative, grammatically parallel, and visible. The following sections will help you to create such headings.

Write Informative Headings

Effective headings inform readers, giving them enough information to decide whether a section contains the information that they need or want. Compare the headings in the left and right columns:

Introduction	How to Use This Manual
Body	Description of the Rheumatoid Arthritis Rehabilitation Clinic
Part 2	What Is the Taxpayer's Role?
Donation Limitations	How Often Can You Give Blood?

Figure 6.24

A Section of a
Document Without
Headings

Soybeans plants are photoperiodic. They grow most of their vegetation during long days and begin flowering as day lengths decrease. Soybean varieties are classified into 11 groups according to their response to different day lengths. For example, Group 00 soybean varieties grow in the northern part of the United States while Group VIII varieties grow in the South. Group IX varieties grow close to the equator. The varieties adapted to the southern parts of the United States have flowering initiated by shorter days than those varieties adapted to the northern parts of the United States. The following sections suggest optimum planting times and insect and disease problems for the southern varieties.

Soybeans are most productive if planted during periods of increasing day lengths when the days are too long to stimulate flowering. Planting at this time will allow the soybean plants to grow taller before they produce flowers and pods. The plants should grow tall enough for mechanical harvest.

Insect damage and disease can commonly reduce soybean yield. In the southern latitudes, stinkbugs and foliar-feeding lepidoptera can damage soybean plants and thus reduce soybean production. Stinkbugs feed on the developing soybean seed; they may infect the seed with a yeast fungus. The fungus results in poor bean quality, lower yields, and poor flavor. Stinkbugs can be controlled with methyl parathion; however, methyl parathion should not be used near livestock or housing because it is highly toxic.

Soybeans are susceptible to phytopathogens such as virus diseases. One such disease is bud blight. Bud blight can infest whole fields, causing the soybean plants not to produce seeds. If this disease becomes severe, it can seriously damage a developing soybean industry.

Source: Adapted from R. A. Creelman and S. A. Reeves, Jr., *Soybean Variety Performance Trials in the Rio Grande Valley of Texas,* 1967–75 (College Station: Texas Agricultural Experiment Station, MP-1287, 1976). Reprinted by permission of the Texas Agricultural Experiment Station.

The headings in the left column don't give any clues about the information in the sections that they introduce. "Body" doesn't give readers any clues to the information they will find if they turn to that section of the document. "Body" could refer to a human body, a body of people, or the body (main part) of the document. Because the headings in the left column don't give any clues about the information contained in a section, they can't help readers locate specific information. In contrast, the headings in the right column describe the information that readers will find in each section.

Write Grammatically Parallel Headings

Use the principles to write parallel headings that you use to write a formal outline. All the main headings in a document have equal rank, so they all should have the same grammatical structure. All the subheads at the same level under a main heading also have equal rank and should have the same grammatical structure.

Figure 6.25

The Document in
Figure 6.24 with
Headings

Growing Soybean Plants in the South

Soybean plants are photoperiodic. They grow most of their vegetation during long days and begin flowering as day lengths decrease. Soybean varieties are classified into 11 groups according to their response to different day lengths. For example, Group 00 soybean varieties grow in the northern part of the United States while Group VIII varieties grow in the South. Group IX varieties grow close to the equator. The varieties adapted to the southern parts of the United States have flowering initiated by shorter days than those varieties adapted to the northern parts of the United States. The following sections suggest optimum planting times and insect and disease problems for the southern varieties.

Optimum Planting Times for Soybean Plants

Soybeans are most productive if planted during periods of increasing day lengths when the days are too long to stimulate flowering. Planting at this time will allow the soybean plants to grow taller before they produce flowers and pods. The plants should grow tall enough for mechanical harvest.

Insect and Disease Problems in Soybean Crops

Insect damage and disease can commonly reduce soybean yield. In the southern latitudes, stinkbugs and foliar-feeding lepidoptera can damage soybean plants and thus reduce soybean production. Stinkbugs feed on the developing soybean seed, they may infect the seed with a yeast fungus. The fungus results in poor bean quality, lower yields, and poor flavor. Stinkbugs can be controlled with methyl parathion; however, methyl parathion should not be used near livestock or housing because it is highly toxic.

Soybeans are susceptible to phytopathogens such as virus diseases. One such disease is bud blight. Bud blight can infest whole fields, causing the soybean plants not to produce seeds. If this disease becomes severe, it can seriously damage a developing soybean industry.

Figure 6.26 shows the various levels that you might have in a document and sample headings that correspond with those levels (the headings are from the revised formal outline presented in Figure 6.20). Notice that both main headings have the same grammatical structure, a noun or noun phrase followed by a prepositional phrase. The three subheadings under the main heading 1, "The most frequently diagnosed tick-borne diseases in dogs," are parallel in grammatical structure with each other but not with the subheadings under the main heading 2, "Prevention of tick-borne diseases of dogs." Subheadings or sub-subheadings in any section of a document must be parallel, or grammatically equal, only with each other, not with all other subheadings or sub-subheadings in the document. Subheadings under main heading 1 need not be parallel with subheadings under main heading 2, and so on. Even if you include the multiple-word sub-subheadings at the beginning of a document, you can still use single-word sub-subheadings at the end.

Figure 6.26

Levels of Headings

Title	Types and Treatment of Tick-Borne Diseases of Dogs
Main Heading 1	The most frequently diagnosed tick-borne diseases in dogs
Subheading 1	Ehrlichiosis
Sub-subheading 1	Signs of ehrlichiosis
Sub-subheading 2	Stages of ehrlichiosis
Sub-subheading 3	Diagnosis of ehrlichiosis
Sub-subheading 4	Treatment of ehrlichiosis
Subheading 2	Babesiosis
Sub-subheading 1	Signs of babesiosis
Sub-subheading 2	Diagnosis of babesiosis
Sub-subheading 3	Treatment of babesiosis
Subheading 3	Borreliosis
Sub-subheading 1	Signs of borreliosis
Sub-subheading 2	Diagnosis of borreliosis
Sub-subheading 3	Treatment of borreliosis
Main Heading 2	Prevention of tick-borne diseases of dogs
Subheading 1	Eliminate ticks on the dog
Sub-subheading 1	Dips
Sub-subheading 2	Sprays
Sub-subheading 3	Powders
Subheading 2	Eliminate ticks in the yard

Source: Adapted from R. A. Creelman and S. A. Reeves, Jr., *Soybean Variety Performance Trials in the Rio Grande Valley of Texas,* 1967–75 (College Station: Texas Agricultural Experiment Station, MP-1287, 1976).

Tips for Creating Effective Headings

- **Identify the primary topic of the section.** Many headings simply state the primary topic or the main point of the section that they introduce. For example, in Figure 6.25, "Optimum Planting Times for Soybean Plants" describes specifically the information that follows.

- **Use questions to tell readers the topic of a section and to create a friendly tone for less formal documents and for less knowledgeable readers (Felker et al. 18).** You can draw the reader into your document and add a friendly tone by using question-style headings. For example, in a document on property taxes, you might use headings like these: "Does My Home Qualify for Tax Exemptions?" or "How Is My Property Valued?" The personal pronoun "my" adds a personal, informal tone to the headings, yet the headings are still clear

(continued on next page)

and informative. You can use "you" in your headings to create a similar effect.

- **Use "how-to" headings for instructions.** Like question-style headings, "how-to" headings help readers to locate the tasks or procedures they need or want.

- **Make sure that the headings are grammatically parallel.** All the headings on the same level should be grammatically parallel (see Figure 6.25).

- **Use key words carefully to tell readers the topic of a section.** Often writers use key words such as "Budget" or "Valuing Property" as headings. In many instances, these short headings adequately inform readers and are appropriate. Instead of "Budget," the writer of a proposal might have written "The Proposed Budget for the Waste Disposal Project." Although the latter heading is more informative, readers would more quickly gather all the information they need from the single-word heading "Budget." However, when using single-word headings, be careful to avoid vagueness.

▶Conclusion

As you consider the information that you have gathered for your documents, select an organization that will help readers to find and use that information. Readers of technical documents have specific goals—to obtain information, to complete a task, to answer a question. Select an organization that will help them to accomplish their goals efficiently and easily. After selecting an appropriate organization, use overviews to preview the document—tell readers what you are writing about. Then use headings to show your approach to the topic. Use the "Worksheet for Organizing Your Documents" to guide you.

WORKSHEET for Organizing Your Documents

▶ **Principle 1: Decide How to Organize Your Document**
- Can you group similar information?
- Can you put important information at the beginning of the document?
- Can you order the information from the simplest to the most complex, the easiest to the most difficult, or the most familiar to the least familiar?
- Will readers scan the document or read it selectively?
- Can you begin with the least controversial or surprising information and move to the most controversial or surprising?
- How will your manager want you to organize the information?
- Does your company have a predetermined organization for similar documents?
- How has your company organized similar documents in the past?

▶ **Principle 2: Consider Using the Standard Patterns of Organization**

The following lists cover the standard patterns of organization presented in this chapter.

Spatial Order
- Did you describe the object, mechanism, or location as if the reader were looking at it?
- Did you include words that help the reader to follow the organization?
- Can you include visual aids to supplement the text?

Chronological Order
- Did you use words and phrases to give readers a "mental road map" of the chronological sequence?
- Can you include visual aids to illustrate the chronology?

General-to-Specific Order
- Did you state the general information clearly and directly at the beginning of the document, section, or paragraph?
- Did you use headings to separate the general information from the specific information?
- Can you include visual aids to supplement the text?

Classification and Division
- Does each item fit into only one category?
- Does each item fit into a category?
- Does your basis for classifying suit your readers and your purpose?
- Can you use visual aids to illustrate the categories and subcategories?

Partition
- Did you choose a principle for partitioning that will meet your readers' needs and your purpose?
- Did you organize the parts in a way that your readers will find helpful?
- Can you use visual aids to illustrate the partitioning?

Comparison/Contrast
- Did you choose criteria for comparing and contrasting?
- Did you evaluate each option using all the criteria?
- Did you evaluate each option using the same criteria?
- Did you organize your comparison or contrast in a way that helps your readers and meets your purpose?
- Can you use visual aids to illustrate your comparison or contrast pattern?

Problem and Solution
- Did you identify the problem early in the document?
- Did you identify the problem before discussing the solution?
- Did you show how your solution will solve the problem?

- Did you group the stages of your solution into meaningful categories?
- Did you give readers ample evidence that your solution will solve the problem?
- Can you use visual aids to illustrate the problem or the solution?

Cause and Effect
- Did you identify either the cause or the effect near the beginning of the document?
- Did you show how the cause directly relates to the effect, or vice versa?
- Did you group the causes or effects into logical categories?
- Can you use visual aids to illustrate the cause or effect?

Order of Importance
- Did you give the readers a context for the information?
- Did you tell the readers how you are organizing the information?
- Did you tell the readers why one point is more or less important than another?
- Can you use visual aids to clarify?

▶ **Principle 3: Prepare an Outline**
- Can you create an informal outline to list what you will include in a short, relatively simple document or to serve as a draft of a formal outline?
- For complex or lengthy documents, which type of formal outline will you select: topic outline or sentence outline?
- Have you used parallel structure in your formal outline?
- Does the outline indicate that the information is incomplete or inconsistent? If so, have you sufficiently revised your outline?

▶ **Principle 4: Tell Readers What You Are Writing About**
- Have you used overviews to introduce readers to your document?
- Do the overviews point out the types of information in the document?
- Do the overviews identify the specific sections of the document?
- Do the overviews tell readers how to use the document?
- Have you used topic sentences?

▶ **Principle 5: Use Headings to Show the Organization of Your Document**
- Did you identify the primary topic of the section in the heading?
- If your document is informal or the readers are less knowledgeable about the topic, can you use question-style headings? Can you use question-style headings to create a friendly tone?
- If you are writing instructions, can you use "how-to" or question-style headings?
- Did you appropriately use key words to tell the readers the topic of the section?
- Did you use grammatically parallel headings?

1. Select an appropriate criterion that you can use to compare or contrast two or more items or groups of items. Some suggested items appear below. Depending on your instructor's instructions, prepare a formal outline or write a brief document in which you compare or contrast the items.

   • Apartment complexes in your town
   • Dormitories on your campus
   • Grocery stores in your town
   • State parks in your home state
   • Internet service providers
   • Planets

2. Partition a single object into its parts. Use one of the items listed below, or choose one of your own. Specify the specific brand or model of the object. In other words, don't partition a generic lawnmower; instead, partition Snapper mulching/recycling mower model 5961. Partition the object into at least two levels of parts—main parts and subparts. For example, you might partition the handle of the mower into the braking controls and the speed controls. Then, depending on your instructor's instructions, diagram your partitioning as in Figures 6.8 and 6.9, or create an informal outline of your partitioning.

   • Lawnmower
   • Electric mixer
   • Refrigerator
   • Printer
   • Auditorium
   • Tools, equipment, or instruments that you use in your major field of study

3. Using the outline or diagram that you created in Exercise 2, write a brief description of the parts of the item you outlined or diagrammed. Use spatial order to describe the parts.

4. Determine the most effective principle of classification or division for a topic and specific readers. Select one of the topic and reader combinations listed below or a combination of your own choosing. Then, depending on your instructor's instructions, prepare a formal outline, a diagram (as in Figure 6.7), or a brief description of your classification or division. Remember that the categories of the classification or division must not overlap.

   • Types of financial aid available to students at your campus
     Readers: students or parents
   • Restaurants
     Readers: visitors to your town or potential restaurant owners in your town
   • Colleges or universities in your state
     Readers: potential students or parents of potential students
   • Types of employment available in your field after graduation
     Readers: graduating seniors or first-year students

5. Prepare a document that explains the cause of some situation, event, or occurrence for a specific reader such as a friend, family member, or classmate. Select one of the topics listed below or one of your own choosing.

   • Thinning of the ozone layer
   • Hurricanes
   • Eclipses of the sun
   • Tornadoes
   • Comets

6. Prepare a document that explains the effects of some situation, event, or occurrence for a specific reader such as a friend, family member, or classmate. Select one of the topics listed below or one of your own choosing.

- Writing skills and your job
- Unemployment in your town or state
- Recycling in your city
- Budget deficit of the U.S. government
- Air pollution
- Lower interest rates on the economy

7. Select a problem in your community, on your campus, or at your workplace, and determine an appropriate solution. Then formally outline the problem and your proposed solution. Your formal outline should have at least two levels. Using the outline, write a letter detailing the problem and solution to the appropriate community leader, to your local or campus newspaper, or to the appropriate person on campus or at your workplace.

8. Assume that a friend has asked you to describe a process or procedure. Using chronological order, write a description of the process or procedure for your friend. You can use one of the processes or procedures listed below or select one of your own.

   - How to create a slide show using software such as Microsoft PowerPoint
   - How to set the security alarm in your apartment or home
   - How to use a tool, machine, software or equipment that professionals in your field regularly use

9. Select a topic below or one of your own choosing and write a memo to your instructor or to your classmates. Use the order-of-importance pattern to organize your memo.

   - The reasons the mail should (or should not) be irradiated
   - The reasons U.S. pilots should (or should not) carry firearms
   - The reasons your college should (or should not) offer more courses online
   - The potential effects of global warming on your lifestyle

10. Decide whether each of the headings listed below is uninformative or informative and explain why. Rewrite the uninformative headings so that they are informative. You may have to add information.

    - Visual Impairment
    - What If My Property Value Rises?
    - Foreword
    - Disabled Employees' Review Committee Findings
    - Guidelines
    - Description
    - The Cost of Extracting Water from Landfills

11. Interview a professional (in person or by e-mail) in your field to find out how his or her workplace and manager influence the way he or she organizes documents. You might ask the following questions:

    - Does your organization have a predetermined organization for some of the documents that you write? If it does, what types of documents are affected, and how does that organization compare with the guidelines you learned in school?
    - How frequently does your manager tell you or expect you to organize a document in a particular way? How flexible is your manager in agreeing to alter that organization? What do you do when you disagree with the organization that your manager expects?
    - Do you ever consider how your organization or your coworkers have organized certain documents such as proposals, feasibility reports, instructions, letters, memos, or progress reports? Where do you find out about the organization of these documents: from a company library, company files, coworkers?

Write a memo to your instructor reporting the information that you gathered from this interview.

Writing Overviews and Headings

The following excerpt, titled "What Is the Taxpayer's Role?" lacks an overview and headings.[2]

- Provide an overview and headings for the document.
- Identify the topic sentence of each paragraph.

As a taxpayer, you have certain rights concerning the appraisal of your property: you have the right to

- equal and uniform tax appraisals. Your property value should be the same as similar properties.
- have your property taxed on its market value or its agricultural value if it qualifies for agricultural appraisal.
- receive all tax exemptions or other tax relief that you are entitled to.
- receive notices of changes in your property value or in your exemptions. Taxing units must tell the public of proposed tax rate increases and give taxpayers time to comment on them.

As a taxpayer, you also have the right to understand what actions you may take if you disagree with the appraisal of your property or with the tax rates. If you believe that your property value is too high or if you were denied an exemption or agricultural appraisal, you can protest to the appraisal review board. If you don't agree with the review board, you can take your case to court. You can speak at public hearings when your elected officials are deciding how to spend your taxes and are setting the tax rate. If you and your fellow taxpayers disagree with the tax rate, you may limit the tax increases by petitioning for an election to roll back or limit the tax rate.

To claim your rights as a property owner, you must fulfill the following responsibilities:

- Make sure that your property appears correctly on the tax records with your correct name and address
- Pay your taxes on time

---

[2] Adapted from John Sharp, "Taxpayers' Rights, Remedies and Responsibilities," Publication #96-295 (Austin, TX: Comptroller of Public Accounts, Tax Division, 1991).

7

Writing Reader-Oriented Sentences and Paragraphs

▶ **O U T L I N E**

You read every day—the mail, newspapers, textbooks, e-mail, Web sites, magazines. Some of the writing that you read is effective, but much is ineffective. Because you read so much ineffective writing, you may be used to verbose, indirect sentences that contain unnecessary words, ineffective verb phrases, and buried actions and actors. Many writers think this type of convoluted writing impresses readers. However, readers of technical documents prefer a simple, direct style that doesn't require them to search for information and meaning.

The following paragraph contains several examples of convoluted writing. Can you spot them?

Convoluted

Let it be known that VISA will send each cardholder a statement at the beginning of the month. Please be aware that VISA will place a charge of $10 on a cardholder's account as a late payment charge each time the "Total Payment Due" is not received before VISA bills the cardholder again. The Company will give reimbursement for this fee only if it was assessed through no fault of the cardholder. Prompt filing of expense accounts after charges are incurred will ensure Company reimbursement to the cardholder in order for the cardholder to make payment to VISA prior to the next billing date.

Notice that the writer buries the action in nouns, writing "place a charge" instead of "charge," "give reimbursement" instead of "reimburse," and "make payment" instead of "pay." Also notice that the writer doesn't make the primary actor the grammatical subject of the sentences that begin "Let it be known" and "Please be aware," although the actor is "VISA"; or of "Prompt filing of expense accounts" although the actor is "you" or "the employee."

Compare the verbose, convoluted example with this revised version:

Revised

At the beginning of the month, VISA will send you a statement. If you don't pay the total amount due before VISA bills you again, VISA will charge your account $10. To avoid this charge, file your expense accounts immediately after using the card, so the company can reimburse you before the total amount is due. If you fail to file your accounts promptly, the company will not reimburse the $10.

The revised version is shorter and concise. The writer uses verbs that express the action of the sentence directly. The writer also focuses on the primary actors—"VISA," "you," and "the company"—making them the grammatical subjects of the sentences.

In this chapter you will learn four principles that will help you write clear, direct sentences. In Chapter 8 you will learn principles that will help you to use language that clearly and concisely conveys what you intend to say in your documents.

►Focus on Actors and Actions[1]

In most of your writing, you will tell a story involving actors and actions. In even the most convoluted writing, you usually can find actors acting. Let's look at a passage in which the writer buries the actors and actions:

Convoluted

It is Sabrina's proposal for the adoption of the spreadsheet software by the accounting department. This software provides assistance in the preparation of the annual budget.

Who are the real actors? In the first sentence, "Sabrina" and "the accounting department" are the actors, although the sentence does not describe their actions. In the second sentence, the actor seems to be "software"; but because of the sentence structure, we can't be sure whether the software or the accounting department is preparing the budget.

What actions does the writer of that passage mention? In the first sentence, the actions appear in the nouns "proposal" and "adoption." Again, in the second sentence, the actions appear in nouns: "assistance" and "preparation." The writer buries the action in nouns instead of using verbs to describe it.

Let's look at a revised version of the passage:

Revised

Sabrina proposed that the accounting department adopt the spreadsheet software. The accounting department can use this software when they prepare the annual budget.

Here, the actors ("Sabrina" and "the accounting department") are the grammatical subjects, and the actions ("proposed," "adopt," "use," and "prepare") appear in verbs. The revised passage illustrates two powerful style principles:

- Make the actors the subjects of your sentences.
- Put the action in verbs.

►Principle 1: Make the Actors the Subjects of Your Sentences

Most readers expect the actor to be the grammatical subject of a sentence. When the actor isn't the subject, readers must stop to search for the actor. In the following example, the writer buries the actor in the pronoun "our." By revising to make the actor the subject of the sentence, the writer creates a more direct statement (the subjects appear in **bold type**; the symbol ≠ means "is different from"; the symbol = means "is the same as").

---

[1] I borrow the concept of actors and actions from Williams (65).

THE READER'S CORNER

Reader-Oriented Poetry

Poetry can teach us a lot about reader-oriented writing. Consider Robert Frost's "Stopping by Woods on a Snowy Evening." In sixteen lines, Frost wanted to convey to his readers how he felt when he stopped in a wintry forest. The first lines read:

Whose woods these are I think I know.
His house is in the village though:
He will not see me stopping here
To watch his woods fill up with snow.

Our first question may be, Why are you stopping in the woods like this? Frost himself sounds uncertain at first. Notice that he almost begins the poem with a question—"Whose woods these are"—and admits he's not sure about who owns the woods ("I think I know"). In the second line, however, Frost appears more confident about his decision to stop. He adds "though" at the end of line 2 to let us know that he's aware that stopping and watching these woods is strange, but that nobody will see him. (The word "village" reinforces our sense of Frost being safely alone in the woods.) Still, even if he's sure nobody will see him, we ask, why watch snow falling in the woods anyway? Consider how the phrase Frost uses in the last line—the "woods fill up with snow"—makes the event sound so new and strange and compelling that his decision to stop suddenly makes sense.

Actor ≠ subject	**Our expectation** was to begin the new uniform policies immediately.
Actor = subject	**We** expected to begin the new uniform policies immediately.

In some sentences, the actor doesn't appear in the sentence. The writer of the first sentence below knew what person or group selected a new organizational plan and adopted a new budget. Less informed readers, however, have no way of learning the identity of this person or group because the writer doesn't include this information. The second sentence lets readers know that the executive committee selected the plan and adopted the budget.

Actor ≠ subject	At the previous meeting, **a new organizational plan** was selected and **a new budget** was adopted.
Actor = subject	At the previous meeting, **the executive committee** selected a new organizational plan and adopted a new budget.

Use People as Subjects Whenever Possible

In your writing, try to make people the subjects of your sentences whenever possible. When you write sentences without people as subjects, your writing will be abstract and often impersonal and bureaucratic. Consider this passage:

People ≠ subjects

As announced earlier, the prescription drug card program will be eliminated effective at the end of the year. Effective January 1, prescriptions that are purchased from local pharmacies may be filed and will be paid at 80% after a $200 deductible. This means that all prescriptions purchased from local pharmacies must be paid for and the receipts saved. A claim form and your receipts should then be mailed in for reimbursement.

Readers of this passage must infer who is purchasing, eliminating, filing, and so on. They could confuse the actions that they are to perform (purchasing, filing, paying, saving, mailing) with the actions that the pharmacy or insurance company will perform (eliminating, paying, reimbursing). Let's look at a revision in which people are the subjects:

People = subjects

As announced earlier, **you** will begin using a new prescription drug program on January 1. Instead of using your prescription drug card, **you** may file with us any prescription that **you** purchase from local pharmacies. **We** will pay 80% of the cost of your prescriptions after **you** meet the $200 deductible. To take advantage of this new program, follow four simple steps:

- Pay for all prescriptions purchased from local pharmacies.
- Save the receipts.
- Complete the attached claim forms.
- Mail the completed form in the envelope provided, so **we** can reimburse you.

Each sentence in the revised version has an actor, and the passage now clearly explains what readers must do and what the company will do. When you use people as actors, you lessen the distance between you and the readers and eliminate ambiguity.

Generally, Use the Active Voice

▶ To learn more about passive voice, see Chapter 3, "Facing Ethical and Legal Challenges," page 57.

Let's look again at some of the sentences in the unrevised prescription passage. The *object* of the action is the grammatical subject of these sentences because the writer uses passive-voice verbs instead of active-voice verbs. In the **passive voice,** the subject is acted upon. In the **active voice,** the subject performs the action.

subject = object of the action

Passive voice   As announced earlier, the <u>prescription drug card program</u> **will be eliminated** effective at the end of the year.

subject = object of the action

Passive voice   Effective January 1, <u>prescriptions</u> that **are purchased** from local pharmacies **may be filed** and **will be paid** at 80% after a $200 deductible.

When writers use the passive voice, readers must search for the actors or infer their identity. When writers use the active voice, the actor is the grammatical subject of the sentence, as readers expect.

Notice how the active voice changes the two passive-voice sentences:

subject = actor

Active voice   As announced earlier, <u>we</u> **will eliminate** the prescription drug card program at the end of the year.

subject = actor

Active voice   Beginning January 1, <u>you</u> **may file** with us any prescriptions that you **purchase** from local pharmacies.

In these active-voice sentences, the actors—"we" and "you"— are in the subject position. Active-voice sentences:

- Tell the readers who is performing the action
- Use fewer words than do passive-voice sentences

Now that you know what effect the passive voice can have, let's find out how to recognize it. A passive-voice sentence has these characteristics:

- The actor and the subject are not the same. The actor may be missing or may appear in a prepositional phrase beginning with *by*.
- The verb consists of a form of the verb *be* plus the past participle of the main verb. (The verb *be* has eight forms: *is, am, are, was, were, be, being,* and *been*.)
- The object of the action is the subject.

Let's look at another passive-voice sentence:

subject

Passive voice   The <u>proper procedures</u> for presenting a guest's check **must**

prepositional phrase

actor

be learned <u>by the front-desk staff</u>.

The subject and the actor aren't the same. The actor appears in a prepositional phrase. The verb consists of *be* plus the past participle of *learn*. Look at the active-voice version of this sentence:

subject = actor   object

Active voice   <u>The front-desk staff</u> **must learn** <u>the proper procedures</u> for presenting a guest's check.

This and other active-voice sentences have these characteristics:

- The actor and the subject are the same.
- The verb does not consist of a form of *be* plus the past participle of the main verb.
- The object appears after the verb.

Use the active voice as much as possible because it generally is stronger, clearer, and more concise. The active voice requires fewer words and makes the actor the subject, so readers can read quickly and understand sentences easily.

To change a sentence from the passive to the active voice, follow these tips:

> ▶ **Tips for Changing a Passive-Voice Sentence into an Active-Voice Sentence**
>
> - Identify the actor.
> - Make the actor the subject of the sentence.
> - Follow the actor with the action (the verb) of the sentence.
> - Follow the action (the verb) with the object or the receiver of the action.

Occasionally, Use the Passive Voice

Sometimes you may have to choose between the active and the passive voice. Let's look at two examples:

Passive voice	Samples **are gathered** every six hours except between 6:00 P.M. and 10:00 P.M.
Passive voice	During the last six months, more than 500,000 bumper stickers were **distributed.**

The writers of these sentences chose the passive voice because the actors either were unknown or were unimportant. Before you decide to use the passive voice, answer these two questions. If you answer "no" to the first question or "yes" to the second question, the passive voice may be appropriate:

1. Do your readers need to know who is acting?
2. Do you want to focus attention on the object rather than on the actor? (We discuss this situation later in this chapter, in the context of Principle 4.)

▶Principle 2: Put the Action in Verbs

Readers expect to find the action of a sentence expressed in verbs. Many writers, however, bury the action in nouns, as in this sentence:

verb

Action in noun   The fire marshal <u>is conducting</u> an **investigation** of the fire that occurred this morning.

Readers must look beyond the verb *is conducting* to find the primary action. The writer names this action in the noun *investigation*, instead of using the verb *investigate*. The verb *is conducting* doesn't give readers the information they need. To improve this sentence, the writer should eliminate the verb *is conducting* and express the "real" action in a different verb:

Action in verb   The fire marshal *is investigating* the fire that occurred this morning.

Readers of this revised version don't have to search for the primary action—it appears in the verb where they expect to find it. The revised sentence is also shorter and more direct.

Identify Sentences in Which the Verb Does Not Express the Action

Most sentences in which the verb is not expressing the action have one or both of these characteristics:

- A noun expresses the primary action of the sentence.
- The verb of the sentence is a form of *be*.

If a noun expresses the primary action, you may be able to identify that noun from its suffix: *-tion, -ment, -ion, -ance, -ence,* or *-ery.* However, the noun may not end in a suffix because some verbs (for example, *hope, result,* and *change*) do not change form when used as nouns.

Let's look at some sentences in which nouns express the primary action; when revised, these sentences are clearer and more concise:

Action in noun   Her **discovery** of the missing bolts happened on Friday while she was cleaning the lab.

Action in verb   She **discovered** the missing bolts on Friday while she was cleaning the lab.

The second sentence of that pair is more direct and reader oriented and has two fewer words than the first.

When the verb is a form of *be*, determine whether a noun is expressing the primary action:

a form of *be*

Action in noun   There <u>was</u> a **discussion** of the zoning ordinances by the city council.

Action in active verb   The city council **discussed** the zoning ordinances.

In the first sentence, the "real" action appears in the noun *discussion*. The effectiveness of the sentence increases when the writer puts the real action in a verb. The original sentence becomes more direct and more concise in the active voice. Using the active voice—making the actor the subject—shortens the original sentence by five words.

Keep the Actor and the Action Together

Once you have successfully expressed the action in a verb, keep that verb and the actor or subject close together in the sentence. If several words separate the subject from the verb, readers may forget what the subject is and have to reread the sentence. Consider this example:

Actor and action separated   **Some managers,** because they have little training in human relations or insufficient managerial experience, **cannot handle** insubordinate employees.

By the time you finally read the action ("cannot handle"), you may have forgotten the actor ("some managers") because fourteen words separate the actor from the action. The sentence is easier to understand when the actor and the action are together:

Actor and action together   Because they have little training in human relations or insufficient managerial experience, **some managers cannot handle** insubordinate employees.

▶ Principle 3: Emphasize the Important Information in Your Sentences

You can convey your intended message and help readers to read your documents quickly if you emphasize the important information in your sentences. Emphasize the most important information by

- Putting it at the end of the sentence
- Putting unfamiliar technical terms at the end of the sentence

Put the Most Important Information at the End

The natural stress point of most sentences is the end. When reading a sentence aloud, you tend to raise the pitch of your voice near the end and stress the last few words (Williams 65). When writing, you can take advantage of this natural stress point to emphasize important information. In the examples that follow, the less important information appears in italics and the more important in bold.

> You have not sent us **your December progress report,** *according to our records.*
> The profits in January **increased by 30 percent,** *for example.*

In both of those sentences, unimportant prepositional phrases appear at the end. By moving those phrases to the beginning of the sentence, the writer emphasizes the more important information about the progress report and the 30 percent increase in profits:

> *According to our records,* you have not mailed us your **December progress report.**
> *For example,* the profits in January **increased by 30 percent.**

The revised sentences flow more smoothly because the natural stress falls on the most important information.

Put Unfamiliar Technical Terms at the End

Readers will better understand unfamiliar technical terms if you put them at the end of sentences (Williams 122). If you put them near the beginning, readers don't have a context for understanding the unfamiliar terms. Consider these sentences:

Unfamiliar technical terms at the beginning	Fast-twitch fibers and slow-twitch fibers are the two basic types of muscle fibers.
Unfamiliar technical terms at the end	Muscles have two types of fibers: fast twitch and slow twitch.

In the first sentence, the unfamiliar terms appear at the beginning and the familiar term "muscle" appears at the end. By putting the familiar "muscles" at the beginning of the sentence, the writer gives the readers a context for the unfamiliar "fast twitch" and "slow twitch."

▶ Principle 4: Tie Your Sentences Together

When you are writing, *you* understand how your sentences relate to each other. However, *your readers* probably don't, so you will want to share your understanding. Order the information in your sentences to guide your readers. This section presents four guidelines to help you tie your sentences together.

Put Old Information Near the Beginning of a Sentence

Old information is information that has previously appeared in a paragraph. **New information** is information that has not yet appeared in a paragraph. In the following paragraph, the writer puts the old information at the beginning of the second through fifth sentences. However, the sixth and seventh sentences begin with new information. The old information appears in boldface.

Muscles have two types of fibers: fast twitch and slow twitch. **Fast-twitch fibers** can develop greater forces and contract faster. **These fibers** also have greater anaerobic capacity. **Slow-twitch fibers** develop force slowly and can maintain contractions longer. **These fibers** have higher aerobic capacity. Training can increase muscle mass, probably by changing the size and number of **muscle fibers** rather than the types of fibers. Some athletes also use performance-enhancing drugs, specifically anabolic steroids, to build **muscle fibers**, although most athletic competitions ban this dangerous practice.[2]

In the first five sentences, we can easily see how the sentences relate and can follow the pattern of the paragraph. However, this pattern breaks down in the final two sentences because the writer introduces new information ("Training" and "Some athletes") at the beginning of the sentences.

In the following paragraph, the old (familiar) information again appears in boldface. The writer consistently places it near the end of a sentence, after presenting new (unfamiliar) information. Therefore, until you reach the end of a sentence, you don't know how the new information relates to the old information in the previous sentence(s).

Old information misplaced

The Blood Center is exploring the possibility of reinstating a recognition program for apheresis donors. One suggestion from a 2002 **apheresis donor** group was to reinstate the plaques with annual updates of **apheresis donation** totals. Below are several styles of **plaques** that have been awarded to **apheresis donors**. Small dated and numbered brass plates indicate the **donation** year and the number of units **donated.**

The writer could clarify the relationship between the old and the new information by moving the old information near the beginning of the sentences:

Revised

The Blood Center is exploring the possibility of reinstating a recognition program for apheresis donors. A 2002 **apheresis donor** group suggested reinstating the plaques with annual updates of apheresis donation totals. Pictures of **plaques** previously awarded appear below. On each **plaque,** small dated and numbered brass plates indicate the donation year and the number of units donated.

---

[2] Adapted from "How Muscles Work." Online. Internet. 11 Nov. 2001. Available: http://www.howstuffworks.com/muscle5.htm.

TAKING IT INTO THE WORKPLACE

How Are Your Editing Skills?

"Some years back I found myself the only technical writer at an instrument manufacturer in southern California. While I enjoyed the crazy challenges the job posed, working as a lone writer had some drawbacks. The biggest of these was the need to serve as my own editor."

—James B. Hansen,
Information Designer (14)

You probably feel relieved when you write the last word of a document. However, when you write that last word, you still aren't finished—that is, you're not finished if you want to ensure that the document is error free. You still need to edit it. If you have time, ask coworkers or friends to help edit your documents. Most writing professionals agree that "editing your own work is not the best way to go" (Hansen 16). However, often you'll write under deadlines or won't be able to find someone to edit your document. When you edit your own documents, James B. Hansen suggests these tips:

- **Use a style sheet or style guide.** If you or your company don't have a style sheet, start creating your own or use style guides such as *The Chicago Manual of Style.*
- **Create a checklist.** Checklists can help you locate your particular writing problems. For example, if you tend to misuse the comma, a checklist can help you to isolate comma errors.
- **Wait a day or two before editing.** Don't edit a document immediately after you write it (Hansen). A waiting period will help you to consider what the document actually says rather than what you intend it to say.
- **Edit the document on paper.** Avoid editing on a computer screen. "Reading speed can drop as much as 30 percent on a computer screen" (Hansen 16; Gomes; Krull and Hurford). You are also more prone to overlooking problems and errors on a screen.
- **Read the document several times.**

Assignment

Using a document that you are writing for your technical communication class or for another class you are currently taking, follow the tips above and edit that document before you give it to your instructor.

In the revised passage, the information flows logically from one sentence to another. The reader doesn't have to figure out how the sentences relate because the writer connects them by putting old information near the beginning of the sentences.

Use Topics to Tie Sentences Together

You can also relate sentences by topic. The first sentence in a paragraph introduces the topic. The second sentence comments on that topic, and the third, fourth, fifth, and subsequent sentences comment further on that topic. In a well-written paragraph, the writer signals the topic by mentioning it in the subject position of each sentence.

In the following passage, the subject of each sentence appears in boldface:

Shifts in topic

Your Personal Identification Number (PIN) should arrive within three days after the card. **VISA** currently does not have the capability to permit cardholders to choose personalized PINs. **The company** selected a four-digit number for your PIN.

▶ Learn more about topic sentences in Chapter 6, "Organizing Information for Your Readers," page 160.

"Your Personal Identification Number (PIN)," the topic of the first sentence, appears as the subject, and the remainder of the sentence provides information about the topic. The second sentence, however, does not comment on that topic but instead introduces a new topic—"VISA"—in the subject position, and that topic does not relate clearly to the topic of the previous sentence. In the third sentence, the writer introduces another new topic—"the company." Because the topic changes, readers may not be sure how the sentences tie together. The writer should signal the common topic in the subject of each sentence:

Revised

Your Personal Identification Number (PIN) should arrive within three days after the card. **Your PIN** is a four-digit number that VISA selected. **Your PIN** cannot be personalized because VISA currently does not have the capability to permit you to personalize your PIN.

In the revised version, the common topic appears as the subject of each sentence, and readers can easily relate the old information to the new information in each sentence. The writer uses the passive voice in the second sentence to place the common topic in the subject position. This writer appropriately uses the passive voice to tie together related information. Sometimes, you can only put a common topic into the subject position by using the passive voice.

In the revised passage discussed above, the topic of each sentence is the same, and the words used to name that topic are nearly the same. In some passages, however, you may want to vary your choice of words to signal a common topic. Consider this paragraph:

Common topic

When rocks erode, **they** break down into sediment—smaller pieces of rock and minerals. **These sediments** may eventually travel in water to new sites such as the sea or river beds. **The water** deposits the sediments in layers that become buried and compacted. In time, **the sediment particles** are cemented together to form new rocks, known as sedimentary rocks. **The layers of sediment** in these rocks are often visible without microscopes.

The subjects (boldfaced) in this passage aren't the same, but each subject relates to a common topic. None of these subjects surprise readers because the subjects contain old information and relate to the common topic: the erosion of rocks.

Figure 7.1		
Commonly Used Transitions	**Time**	before, while, during, after, next, later, first, second, then, subsequently, the next day, meanwhile, now
	Cause and Effect	because, therefore, since, thus, consequently, due to, if . . . then, so
	Place	below, above, inside, outside, behind, at the next level, internally, externally
	Addition	furthermore, in addition, also, moreover, and
	Comparison	likewise, as, like, similarly, not only . . . but also
	Contrast	conversely, on the other hand, unlike, although, however, yet, nevertheless, but

Use Transitions

Transitions are words, phrases, and even sentences that connect one idea or one sentence to another. Transitions indicate relationships of time, cause and effect, space, addition, comparison, and contrast. Figure 7.1 lists common transitions that writers use to connect ideas.

When using transitions to tie your sentences together, put the transition at or near the beginning of the sentence. When you put a transition after the verb or near the end of the sentence, you weaken the effect of the transition and frequently create an awkward sentence, as in this example:

Awkward

The results of the flight tests concerned the company executives. The executives asked the research and development team to retest the new plane, **therefore**.

Putting the transition ("therefore") at the end of the sentence prevents readers from seeing the cause-and-effect relationship until they reach the end of the sentence. With the transition at the end, the sentence fails to stress the most important information. The transition is more effective at the beginning of the sentence:

Revised

The results of the flight tests concerned the company executives. **Therefore,** the executives asked the research and development team to retest the new plane.

Although transition words can help readers to see relationships, use these words in conjunction with the other techniques presented in this chapter to tie your sentences together. Transition words alone aren't enough to tie all your sentences together. If you find that you are using transition words in sentence after sentence, revise your paragraphs to eliminate some of the transition words.

Repeat or Restate Key Words or Phrases

You can tie sentences together by repeating or restating key words or phrases. Repetition and restatement help readers to remember information and to understand the point you are making.

Repeating Words or Phrases   You can repeat key words or phrases to tie sentences together. However, avoid overusing this technique. The following sentences illustrate effective repetition of key words:

> The accident on the space station **depleted** the oxygen **supply.** Because of the **depleted supply,** the crew had to limit its physical activities.

> The city council **recommended** that the city redraw the lines of the districts. This **recommendation** upset many citizens.

The verb *recommend* in the first sentence is echoed in the second sentence by the noun *recommendation.* The repetition allows the writer to put old information at the beginning of the sentence.

Restating with Pronouns   You can use pronouns to refer to nouns that appear in a previous sentence. Pronouns not only help tie your sentences together but also avoid the monotony that results when the same noun appears several times in a sentence or paragraph.

> As the **team** planned the project, **they** created a listserv for sharing information.

Restating with Summary Words   You can tie sentences together by using words that summarize ideas or information presented earlier. Summary words allow you to restate information, usually in just a few words. In the example below, the subject of the second sentence ("this setup") summarizes the equipment mentioned in the first sentence:

> The computer lab purchased **six new laser printers and twelve new personal computers. This setup** will allow the lab to better serve the computer science students.

By using summary words, the writer effectively and concisely restates information from the previous sentence and puts that old information at the beginning of the new sentence.

▶Conclusion

When you follow the principles discussed in this chapter, you will write sentences and paragraphs that readers can read and understand quickly. As you write technical documents, be sure not only to include accurate, useful information, but also to write clear and direct sentences. Use the "Worksheet for Writing Reader-Oriented Sentences and Paragraphs" to check the style of your sentences and paragraphs.

| WORKSHEET | **for Writing Reader-Oriented Sentences and Paragraphs** |

▶ **Principle 1: Make the Actors the Subjects of Your Sentences**
- Did you put the actor(s) in the subject?
- Did you use people as the subject whenever possible?
- Did you use the active voice whenever possible and appropriate?
- If you used the passive voice, do your readers need to know who is acting?
- Do you want to focus attention on the object or the actor?

▶ **Principle 2: Put the Action in Verbs**
- Did you express the action in verbs?
- Are the actor and the action close together in your sentences?

▶ **Principle 3: Emphasize the Important Information in Your Sentences**
- Did you put the most important information at the end of your sentences?
- Did you put unfamiliar technical terms at the end of sentences?

▶ **Principle 4: Tie Your Sentences Together**
- Did you put the old (familiar) information near the beginning of your sentences?
- Did you put the new (unfamiliar) information near the end of your sentences?
- Did you use topics to tie sentences together?
- If you used transitions, did you select the transition that conveys the appropriate relationship?
- Did you overuse transitions? If so, have you revised the sentences and used other techniques to tie the sentences together?
- If you repeated key words or phrases, did you avoid overusing this technique?

► **EXERCISES**

1. Rewrite these sentences to make the actor the subject.

   a. Attempts were made by the engineering staff to assess the project.

   b. The completion of the new building will allow 30 new businesses to relocate to the downtown area.

   c. The cost of the reinspection is to be paid by the insurance company in accordance with the contract.

   d. There have been threats from other landowners nearby due to the trash and mud in the streets caused by unauthorized employees using this lot.

   e. There is no alternative for us except to withdraw the product.

   f. Working together will ultimately finish the new product design on time.

2. Convert these sentences from the passive to the active voice. Follow the procedure described in Principle 1 on page 180.

   a. The annual merit raises were approved by the board of directors.

   b. Employee purchases must be paid for within ninety days or in six payroll deductions by all employees.

   c. Your department's growth figures are being reanalyzed by the accounting department to determine your budget for next year.

   d. Please inform this office as soon as a shipment date is known.

   e. Parking on site is allowed for your superintendent's vehicle.

   f. Reduction of the size of the laser beam has been accomplished.

3. Rewrite these sentences to put the action in the verb.

   a. We must provide support for the three candidates from our district who are running for president, vice president, and secretary.

   b. Our expectation was to begin the new project immediately.

   c. The police are conducting an investigation of the armed robbery that occurred this morning.

   d. Failure to follow the above instructions will be the basis for the rejection of our proposal.

   e. Consideration should be given to an acquisition of the properties.

   f. To ensure the safety of all personnel, we began our sanitation procedure on May 16, 2002, which required the total evacuation of all personnel from the area.

4. Rewrite these sentences to put the more important information and technical terms near the end of the sentence.

   a. The outcome of the election changed because of some unfortunate comments about the city founders, according to the news release.

   b. Several homeowners in the Cottonwood subdivision are suing the developer for faulty foundations and poor building materials, however.

   c. Water pipes in many older homes will freeze and possibly burst under these weather conditions.

   d. Myosin and actin are tiny filaments inside your muscles.

   e. Creatine phosphate is broken down by the muscles.

   f. The cornea copes well with minor injuries. If dirt scratches the cornea, epithelial cells slide over it, patching the injury before infection, for example.

5. For each sentence listed below, do the following:

- Identify the principle or principles that the writer has *not* followed.
- Rewrite the sentences to make them more reader oriented. Follow the guidelines given in Principles 1, 2, and 3.
- After your rewritten sentence, write the number of the principle or principles that you followed while rewriting.

a. Because of the clerk's inability to help us with the equipment, there was a delay in the repairs that we had to do the next day.

b. We reviewed the drawings and found numerous errors upon receipt of the drawings.

c. Because the team did not have sufficient time to complete the project, it was not surprising that it was unable to prepare a satisfactory report.

d. Our intention is to audit the financial records of your company.

e. A reinvestigation of the new employee's travel expenses by the accounting division is necessary before reimbursement from headquarters can be provided.

f. The creation of an international relations committee will increase our budget requirements for the new year, however.

g. Our international sales divisions, which are located in Germany, Japan, Canada, England, Brazil, and Sweden, have increased company profits by 30 percent.

h. There has been a decrease in the number of infants killed because of airbags.

i. Updates about the program can be viewed on the Web site in seven business days.

j. The new computer network for the engineering staff will require six days for installation and training, according to the network operator.

6. These passages do not follow Principle 4. For each passage, do the following:

- Underline the old information in the passage.
- Rewrite the passage so that the old information appears at the beginning of the sentence.
- Make sure that your rewritten passage follows all the principles presented in this chapter.

a. Insect repellents are available in various forms and concentrations. Aerosol and pump-spray products are intended for skin applications as well as for treating clothing. Liquid, cream, lotion, and stick products enable direct skin application. Products with a low concentration of the active ingredient may be appropriate for situations where exposure to insects is minimal. A higher concentration of the active ingredient may be useful in highly infested areas, or with insect species that are more difficult to repel. And where appropriate, consider nonchemical ways to deter biting insects—screens, netting, long sleeves, and slacks.[3]

b. Since its formation in 1968, the North American Electric Reliability Council (NERC) has operated as a voluntary organization. NERC has helped to make the North American electric system the most reliable system in the world. Establishing operating and planning standards to ensure electric system reliability and reviewing the reliability of existing and planned generation and transmission systems is the purpose of NERC. Serving as primary point of contact on issues

---

[3] Adapted from the U.S. Environmental Protection Agency, Office of Pesticide Programs, "Using Insect Repellants Safely." Online. Internet. 25 Nov. 2001. Available: http://www.epa.gov/pesticides/citizens/inspectrp.htm.

relating to national security and terrorism, NERC acts as a liaison between the electric market participants and the federal government. The growth of competition and the structural changes taking place in the industry have significantly altered the incentives and responsibilities of market participants. NERC is in the process of transforming itself into the "one-stop shop" for developing both reliability and commercial standards for the North American bulk electric system. A key part will require federal legislation in the United States to ensure that NERC and its regions have the statutory authority to enforce compliance with reliability standards among all market participants. Under the existing system, compliance with reliability rules is mandatory but it is not enforceable. Legislation will enable NERC to transform itself into an industry-led self-regulatory reliability organization, whose mission will be to develop, promote, and enforce reliability standards.[4]

c. Acid rain looks, feels, and tastes just like clean rain. The harm to people from acid rain is not direct. Walking in acid rain, or even swimming in an acid lake, is immediately no more dangerous than walking or swimming in clean water. However, the pollutants (sulfur dioxide [SO_2] and nitrogen oxides [NOx]) that cause acid rain also damage human health. These gases interact in the atmosphere to form fine sulfate and nitrate particles that can be transported long distances by winds and inhaled deep into people's lungs. Fine particles can also penetrate indoors. Scientific studies have identified a relationship between elevated levels of fine particles and increased illness and premature death from heart and lung disorders, such as asthma and bronchitis.

Based on health concerns, SO_2 and NOx have historically been regulated under the Clean Air Act, including the Acid Rain Program. In the eastern United States, sulfate aerosols make up about 25 percent of fine particles. By lowering SO_2 and NOx emissions from power generation, the Acid Rain Program will reduce the levels of fine sulfate and nitrate particles and so reduce the incidence and the severity of these health problems: asthma and bronchitis. Due to decreased mortality, hospital admissions, and emergency room visits, the public health benefits of the Acid Rain Program are estimated to be valued at $50 billion annually when fully implemented by the year 2010.[5]

d. Bovine spongiform encephalopathy (BSE) is a chronic, degenerative disorder affecting the central nervous system of cattle. It is commonly called Mad Cow Disease. Evidence suggests that certain contaminated cattle-feed ingredients are the source of BSE infection in cattle. The process that leads to the contaminated feed starts when livestock already harboring the BSE agent are slaughtered. After cows and sheep are killed, the edible parts are removed. The inedible remnants are taken to a special plant, where they undergo a process called rendering. Two major products are created:

- fat, which is used in an array of products (such as soap, lipstick, linoleum, and glue)

---

[4] Adapted from North American Electric Reliability Council, "About NERC." Online. Internet. 9 May 2002. Available: http://www.nerc.com/about.

[5] Adapted from U.S. Environmental Protection Agency, Clean Air Market Programs, "Effect of Acid Rain: Human Health." Online. Internet. 25 Nov. 2001. Available: http://www.epa.gov/airmarkets/acidrain/effects/health.html.

- meat-and-bone meal, a powdery, high-protein supplement that is often processed into animal feed

Although the animal remnants are "cooked" at high temperatures during the rendering process, the BSE agent, if present, is able to survive. When this contaminated meat-and-bone meal is fed to cattle as a protein supplement, the BSE agent can be passed on to many new cattle. It is believed that this is how BSE was spread through the U.K. cattle herds. Currently, no test can reliably detect BSE in live cattle. A diagnosis is confirmed by examining brain tissue after death.[6]

7. The following passage is an excerpt from a report written by an engineering and environmental consulting firm. The firm has studied the effects of a planned lignite-powered plant on the environment. This passage is about the location of established residences, schools, hospitals, and other community centers near the site. Rewrite the passage to tie the sentences together. Also, correct any sentences that don't follow Principles 1, 2, or 3.

No schools or hospitals were identified within the site or its one-mile perimeter. Liberty Faith Church and cemetery are located along FM 979 approximately 0.5 mile south of the site. St. Paul's Episcopal Church is located approximately 0.5 mile north of Liberty Faith Church and 0.6 mile south of the site. No future community centers have been planned within one mile of the site.

There will be limited emergency response units located at the site, including a nurses' station, ambulance, fire truck, and fire station. The nearest hospitals off the site are

- Summit County Community Hospital
- U.S. Government Veterans' Hospital
- Brazos Memorial Hospital, Incorporated

Summit County EMS is the nearest emergency medical service located in Frisco approximately 13 miles from the site. Also located in Frisco are the nearest sheriff's station and volunteer fire department unit.

[6] Adapted from Bren, Linda, "Trying to Keep 'Mad Cow Disease' Out of U.S. Herds." FDA Consumer Magazine, U.S. Food and Drug Administration, March–April 2001. Online. Internet. 25 Nov. 2001. Available: http://www.fda.gov/fdac/features/2001/201_cow.html.

8

Using Reader-Oriented Language

In May 1996, SabreTech mechanics loaded five cardboard boxes of old oxygen generators and three tires into the forward cargo hold of ValuJet Flight 592. These oxygen generators had come to the end of their licensed lifetime; they had "expired." ValuJet had provided SabreTech with a seven-step process for removing the generators; the second step of this process instructed the workers as follows: "If generator has not been expended, install shipping cap on firing pins" (Stimpson 1998; Langewiesche 1998). This instruction required 72 SabreTech workers to distinguish between generators that were "expired," meaning most of the ones they were removing, and generators that were not "expended," meaning many of the same ones, loaded and ready to fire. Some of these mechanics were temporary employees. For some of these mechanics, Spanish was their native language. Working under a tight schedule, the mechanics did not clearly distinguish between "expired" and "expended" generators. In reality, many of the generators being removed and then loaded onto ValuJet 592 were expired but were not expended; that is, they could still be fired. Most of the oxygen generators should have been destroyed, or at the very least had the shipping caps placed on the pins. With five boxes filled with generators that could explode, ValuJet 592 took off and within six minutes crashed into Florida's Everglades Holiday Park. Two pilots, three flight attendants, and one hundred five passengers died in the crash.

The engineers who wrote the instructions clearly understood the distinction between "expired" and "expended." This distinction, however, was not clear to all the mechanics. As technical communicators and technical professionals, we have a responsibility to communicate not only objective, accurate information, but also to use language that our readers will understand and that communicates our intended meaning. To ensure that your readers understand your intended meaning, you can use the seven principles discussed in this chapter.

▶ Principle 1: Use Specific and Unambiguous Language

To understand your documents and respond appropriately, readers need specific and unambiguous language. Without such language, they may misunderstand or misinterpret what you write. When you use specific and unambiguous language, you convey your intended meaning precisely.

Using Specific Language

Readers of technical documents expect specific language, not vague language. Specific language is clear and precise; vague language is often unclear and always imprecise. Specific language clarifies the meaning and eliminates questions that readers may ask when the language is vague.

Vague	A computer in one of the labs isn't working properly.
Specific	The monitor on computer 26 in the College of Arts and Sciences lab is flickering erratically.

After reading the vague sentence, a reader might wonder, Which computer? Which lab? What is wrong with the computer? The specific sentence answers all those questions. It identifies the lab where the computer is located, the specific computer, and the problem.

To make your language specific, include examples and details. You can use "such as" or "for example" to introduce the examples:

Vague	For its mission, the relief organization needs food and supplies.
Specific	For its mission to the area damaged by hurricane Carlos, the relief organization needs food and supplies such as

- Canned milk
- Bottled water in one-gallon plastic containers
- Canned meat such as tuna, chicken, or ham spread
- Ready-to-use baby formula and disposable diapers
- Gauze, bandages, and rubbing alcohol

Though grammatically correct, the vague sentence is imprecise. Readers of the vague sentence might not provide the relief organization with the specific food and supplies that it needs. Readers of the specific sentence know exactly what items the organization needs.

Consider another example. Here the vague language occurs because the writer doesn't specify a date.

Vague	KHS&S will replace the masonry frames with the correct metal frames. We must have these frames soon, so we can complete the first floor of both buildings on schedule.
Specific	KHS&S will replace the masonry frames with the correct metal frames. To complete the first floor of both buildings on schedule, KHS&S must deliver the frames by 11/26/2003.

▶ For more information about using the ends of sentences to emphasize information, see Chapter 7, "Writing Reader-Oriented Sentences and Paragraphs," page 182.

In the vague sentence, the writer uses the word *soon* instead of a date. "Soon" could mean, for example, by tomorrow, in a month, or in three months. When writers don't specify a date, readers can insert their own meaning of "soon." To ensure that the readers understand what the writer means by "soon," the writer should use a specific date as in the specific example above. Notice how the writer has placed the date at the end of the sentence to emphasize its importance.

Using Unambiguous Language

In addition to being specific, your language should be unambiguous: it should convey only one meaning. Ambiguity in sentences results from:

- Misplaced modifiers
- Dangling modifiers
- Stacked nouns
- Faulty word choice

Misplaced Modifiers

Misplaced modifiers appear to modify the wrong referent. These misplaced modifiers can cause ambiguity. To eliminate the ambiguity, place the modifier as close as possible to the intended referent. Misplaced modifiers are frequently phrases or clauses:

Ambiguous   Our manager suggested to the vice president that we register for the class **in San Francisco.**

After reading this sentence, can you say for certain whether the class is being held in San Francisco? The meaning is ambiguous because of the placement of the prepositional phrase "in San Francisco." To prevent the ambiguity and possible misreading, either place a prepositional phrase next to the word it modifies or rewrite to clarify your meaning:

Unambiguous   Our manager suggested to the vice president **in San Francisco** that we register for the class.

Unambiguous   Our manger suggested to the vice president that we register **in San Francisco** for the class.

Unambiguous   Our manager suggested to the vice president that we register for the **San Francisco** class.

Let's look at another example. Here the misplaced modifier occurs because the writer has incorrectly placed the modifier "growing in the sterile solution" next to the lab technicians instead of next to "bacteria," which is actually what is growing in the solution—not the lab technicians!

Ambiguous   **Growing in the sterile solution,** the lab technicians observed the bacteria.

Unambiguous   The lab technicians observed the bacteria **growing in the sterile solution.**

Dangling Modifiers

Dangling modifiers have no referent in the sentence:

Dangling   **Trying to put out the fire,** the fire extinguisher broke.

THE READER'S CORNER

Localizing Documents for International Readers

 As you write for international readers, you may want to "localize" a document. Localizing is more than translating words. When writers localize a document, they "adapt it to fit the political, economic, technical, and marketing realities of that country" (Klein 32). Technical documents can change across cultures just as body language, everyday expressions, and forms of greetings change. For example, a U.S. company that produces heart treatment equipment "introduced its products with a cartoon of happily smiling hearts" (Klein 33). Although the graphic worked for U.S. readers, the German readers were offended by this light treatment of heart disease. Likewise, to readers in the United States, the acronyms EPA (for Environmental Protection Agency) and IRS (for Internal Revenue Service) are common; however, these abbreviations don't apply outside the United States (Klein 32). As you write for international readers, remember that readers in various "locales" will have different rules, data, and cultural expectations. For example, the United States is a locale, China is a locale, and India is a locale—each has its own set of rules, data, and cultural expectations.

To localize documents, some companies hire translation/localization agencies. If your company hires one of these companies, make sure the company has ISO 9001 certification covering localization services (Klein 33). You can also consult the following sources to help you localize your documents.

Andrews, Deborah C., ed. *International Dimensions of Technical Communication.* Arlington, VA: Society of Technical Communication, 1996.

Hager, Peter J., and H. J. Scheiber, eds. *Managing Global Communication in Science and Technology.* NY: John Wiley & Sons, Inc., 2000.

Hall, Edward. *Understanding Cultural Differences.* Yarmouth, ME: Intercultural Press, 1990.

Hoft, Nancy L. *International Technical Communication.* New York: John Wiley & Sons, 1995.

Uren, Emmanuel, Robert Howard, and Tiziana Perinotti. *Software Internationalization and Localization—An Introduction.* New York: Van Nostrand Reinhold, 1993.

Varner, Iris, and Linda Beamer. *International Communication in the Global Workplace.* Chicago: Irwin, 1995.

You can also search these Web sites to locate information on a country and its peoples:[1]

- *The U.S. Department of State Electronic Research Collection.* This free Web site allows you to search State Department databases for information on certain countries. As you use this and other sites, be sure to check the publication date as some cultural information about the countries may be out-of-date. To visit this site, go to http://dosfan.lib.uic.edu.

- *The CIA Factbook Online.* This government Web site offers the following information on various countries: population, language, history, cultural information, and so on. You can search this site to locate specific information about a given country. For more information, visit http://www.odci.gov/cia/publications/factbook.

---

[1] Information on the Web sites based in part on St. Amant, Kirk R. "Resources and Strategies for Successful International Communication." *Intercom* (Sept./Oct. 2000) 12–14.

In this sentence, the writer has not identified who is putting out the fire. To eliminate the dangling modifier, rewrite the sentence to add the person in either the main clause or in the modifier:

Correct   **Trying to put out the fire,** I broke the fire extinguisher.

Correct   **As I was trying to put out the fire,** the fire extinguisher broke.

▶ To learn more about passive voice, see Chapter 7, "Writing Reader-Oriented Sentences and Paragraphs," page 178.

You can also create dangling modifiers when switching from the indicative mood (a statement of fact) to the imperative mood (a command or request usually with an understood "you" subject). To identify dangling modifiers in those situations, you can often look for a passive-voice construction following the dangling modifier, as in the following example:

Dangling   **To link to other Web sites and topics,** the green keywords should be clicked on.

Correct   **To link to other Web sites and topics,** click on the green keywords.

To correct the dangling modifier, the writer simply puts the passive voice into active voice with an understood referent—in this case "you."

Stacked Nouns

You can create ambiguity when you use two or more nouns to modify another noun. When you use a stack of nouns as a modifier, you can create hard-to-read and often ambiguous passages. Consider this example:

Stacked nouns   The consultant suggested the manager allow time for a **fitness center member evaluation.**

The sentence is ambiguous because of the stacked nouns: Is the consultant suggesting that the manager evaluate the members or the fitness center? Or is the consultant suggesting that the members evaluate the fitness center? To eliminate the ambiguous language, the writer unstacks the nouns:

Correct   The consultant suggested that the manager allow time to evaluate the members of the fitness center.

Correct   The consultant suggested that the manager allow time for the members to evaluate the fitness center.

You occasionally will use one noun to modify another noun as in *fitness center, space shuttle, software manual,* or *school superintendent.* However, whenever possible, avoid using a noun to modify a noun.

Faulty Word Choice

Let's look at another ambiguous sentence. In this one, the ambiguity occurs because of the word choice:

Ambiguous	We were **held up** at the bank.
Unambiguous	We were **delayed** at the bank.

The ambiguous sentence has two possible meanings: "We" were either delayed or robbed. To eliminate the ambiguity, the writer selects the verb *delay*, which can have only one meaning in the sentence.

Let's look at another example. In this case, the ambiguity occurs because the word *tragedy* refers either to the type of play or to the quality of the children's performance.

Ambiguous	The seventh graders will be presenting Shakespeare's *Hamlet* in the school auditorium on Friday at 7:00 P.M. Parents are invited to attend this tragedy.
Unambiguous	The seventh graders will be presenting Shakespeare's *Hamlet* in the school auditorium on Friday at 7:00 P.M. They invite all parents to attend the performance.

In the unambiguous sentence the writer uses "performance," which can have only one meaning in the sentence. Carefully select the words in your sentences, making sure that readers will understand them in only one way.

▶Principle 2: Use Only the Words Your Readers Need

Readers want to read your documents without wading through unnecessary words. Therefore, use only the words that your readers need to understand what you mean. You can write concisely if you

- Eliminate redundancy
- Eliminate unnecessary words

Eliminating Redundancy

Redundancy occurs when you use words or phrases that unnecessarily repeat the meaning of other words in the sentence:

Redundant	Please give our proposal your **thought and consideration** because the proposed relocation can **help and benefit** the engineering division to better serve the southern region.
Concise	Please consider our proposal because the proposed solution can help the engineering division better serve the southern region.

Each redundant pair ("thought" and "consideration" and "help" and "benefit") uses two words although just one word will do. The words *thought* and *consideration* have the same meaning, and so do *help* and *benefit*. Thus, to be concise, the writer needs to use only one of the words in each pair. Redundancies can occur in pairs. Figure 8.1 lists common redundant pairs. When you see these pairs in your writing, revise to use only one word in the pair and delete the "and."

Redundancy also results from modifiers that repeat all or part of the meaning of other words in a sentence. (**Modifiers** are a word or group of words that describe, limit, or qualify another word.) Examples of redundant modifiers include the following (the redundant words appear in bold type):

Redundant   **end** result, **very** unique, **absolutely** free, **completely** eliminate

For more examples, see Figure 8.2.

The sentences below illustrate the positive effect of eliminating redundant modifiers:

Redundant   The proposed budget cuts will not affect the **final** outcome of our current demographic study or our **future** plans for improving the street drainage.

Concise   The proposed budget cuts will not affect the outcome of our current demographic study or our plans for improving the street drainage.

In the redundant sentence, the modifier "final" is unnecessary because it repeats the meaning of "outcome" (an outcome is always final), and the modifier "future" is unnecessary because it repeats the meaning of "plans" (all plans involve the future). Let's look at another example:

▼ Figure 8.1 Common Redundant Pairs	advice and counsel agreeable and satisfactory aid and assistance any and all assist and help basic and fundamental due and payable each and every fair and equitable fair and reasonable	first and foremost full and complete help and benefit help and cooperation hope and trust null and void opinion and belief prompt and immediate thought and consideration true and accurate

▼ **Figure 8.2**

Redundant Modifiers

Instead of These Redundant Modifiers . . .	Use These Concise Alternatives
absolutely essential	essential
absolutely free	free
anticipate in advance	anticipate
basic fundamentals	fundamentals
circle around	circle
consensus of opinion	consensus
continue on	continue
decrease down	decrease
each individual	individual
end result	result
final outcome	outcome
free gift	gift
future plans	plans
green (purple, red, black, yellow, etc.) in color	green (purple, red, black, yellow, etc.)
human volunteer	volunteer
large (small, medium, etc.) in size	large (small, medium, etc.)
on a weekly (daily, monthly, etc.) basis	weekly (daily, monthly, etc.)
mail out	mail
past history	history
personal opinion	opinion
reduce down	reduce
repeat again	repeat
return back to	return
quite unique	unique
rarely ever	rarely
round (square, oblong, etc.) in shape	round (square, oblong, etc.)
seldom ever	seldom
true facts	facts
twenty (two, thirty, etc.) in number	twenty (two, thirty, etc.)
various different	different
very latest	latest
very unique	unique

Redundant   We asked the research team to analyze a rock that was pink **in color,** cylindrical **in shape,** and 61 pounds **in weight.**

Concise   We asked the research team to analyze a pink, cylindrical rock that weighed 61 pounds.

The prepositional phrases in the redundant sentence repeat the meaning of "pink," "cylindrical," and "61 pounds": pink is a color, cylindrical is a shape, and 61 pounds is a weight.

Eliminating Unnecessary Words

Wordy phrases make documents unnecessarily long. Even when readers understand a wordy phrase, they prefer clear, concise writing. Readers want to read technical documents as quickly as possible, so eliminate any words not absolutely necessary to convey your meaning and purpose. Figure 8.3 lists some wordy phrases and suggests concise alternatives.

Figure 8.3

Revising Wordy Phrases

Instead of These Wordy Phrases . . .	Use These Concise Alternatives
according to our records	we find
a limited number	a few
a majority of	most
a number of	many
at a later time (date)	later
at the conclusion of	after, following
at the same time as	when, as
at this point and time	now, currently
by means of	by
concerning the matter of	about
conduct an investigation	investigate
conduct a study	study
despite the fact that	although, even though
due to the fact that	because
has the ability to	can
has the capability to	can
has the capacity for	can
has the opportunity to	can
in a situation in which	when
in accordance with your request	as you requested
in connection with	about, concerning
in order that	so that
in order to	to
in reference to	about
in regard to	about
in the event that	if

(continued on next page)

▼ **Figure 8.3**	**Instead of These Wordy Phrases . . .**	**Use These Concise Alternatives**
(continued)	in this day and age	today
	in view of the fact that	because
	is able to	can
	is in a position to	can
	it is crucial that	must, should
	it is important that	must, should
	it is incumbent upon	must, should
	it is my (our) understanding that	I (we) understand that
	it is necessary that	must, should
	it is my (our) recommendation that	I (we) recommend
	it is possible that	may, might, can, could
	make reference to	refer to
	Notwithstanding the fact that	although
	prior to	before
	relative to	about
	so as to	to
	subsequent to	after
	take into consideration	consider
	there is a chance that	may, might, can, could
	there is a need for	must
	until such time as	until
	we are not in a position to	we cannot
	will you be kind enough to	please
	with reference to	about
	with regard to	about
	with respect to	about

At first you may not notice the wordy phrases that appear in your writing because you have used them for a long time or have read them in many technical documents. Thus, you may have to make a special effort to spot these phrases and then to replace them with more concise and effective words.

You can also simply eliminate some wordy phrases instead of replacing them with something more concise. Figure 8.4 lists several expressions that you usually can eliminate.

Let's look at the effect of wordy phrases on sentence length and clarity:

Wordy   **As a matter of fact, there is** an old warehouse that the emergency relief groups can use to house the tornado victims **at this point in time.**

Figure 8.4	as a matter of fact
	I believe
Commonly Used	I hope
Phrases That You Can	in my opinion
Usually Delete	in other words

as a matter of fact	it is interesting to note that
I believe	it is significant (important) that
I hope	it should be noted that
in my opinion	it should be pointed out that
in other words	thanking you in advance
I should point out that	the fact that
I think	there are (is)
it is essential	to the extent that
it is evident	

Concise   The emergency relief groups can now use the old warehouse to house the tornado victims.

Wordy   **It should be pointed out that there are** three candidates who our organization **without further delay** will endorse, **despite the fact that we are not in a position** to contribute any money to their campaigns.

Concise   Our organization will now endorse three candidates although we cannot contribute any money to their campaigns.

Wordy   **It should be noted that** mercury levels in the river have increased this year, and **in accordance with your request** our department will **take into consideration** whether **it is essential** to **conduct a study with regard** to possible sources of this pollution.

Concise   Mercury levels in the river have increased this year; and as you requested, our department will consider whether to study possible sources of this pollution.

▶Principle 3: Use Simple Words

When you want to impress your reader, resist the temptation to use words that you don't normally use—words that you rarely use when talking. Many writers believe that they will impress readers by using "fancy," less familiar words such as those listed in Figure 8.5. In technical communication, however, you are more likely to impress readers not with these fancy words but with simple, clear, everyday words.

Your readers will prefer words that are more familiar and words that generally have fewer syllables. Consider these examples:

Less familiar words   Pursuant to our conversation on December 15 . . .
Simple, familiar words   As we discussed on December 15 . . .

Figure 8.5

Fancy and Simple Words

Instead of These Fancy Words . . .	Use These Simpler Words
accompany	go with
accumulate	gather
acquaint	tell
advise	tell
apparent	clear
ascertain	learn, find out
cognizant	know
commence	begin, start
commitment	promise
compensation	pay
contribute	give
demonstrate	show
endeavor	try
equivalent	equal
facilitate	help, ease
furnish	give, provide
herewith is	here is
indebtedness	debt
initiate	begin
initial	first
legislation	law
locality	place
optimum	best, most
prioritize	rank
proceed	go
procure	buy, get
pursuant to	as
subsequent to	after, next, later
sufficient	enough
terminate	end
utilize	use

Less familiar words	Your firm's response purports to explain the source of some of the deviations from the grant guidelines.
Simple, familiar words	Your firm attempts to explain why you deviated from the grant guidelines.
Less familiar words	Our office assistants **will accompany** you to **endeavor** to get our **compensation** checks.

Simple, familiar words	Our office assistants will **go** with you to **try** to get our **pay** checks.

Most readers of technical documents want to gather the information they need as quickly and effortlessly as possible. Documents that contain many fancy, less familiar words take longer to read than documents that include simple, familiar words.

▶Principle 4: Use Positive Language

Whenever possible, tell readers what something is, instead of what it is not. Readers comprehend positive language more easily and quickly than they comprehend negative language. The presence of several negative constructions in a sentence or paragraph slows the pace of reading because readers have to work harder to gather information and meaning from negative language. Figure 8.6 lists some negative phrases and their positive counterparts; you'll discover more as you write.

As the following examples show, using positive rather than negative language leads to clearer and often to more concise sentences:

Negative	**Do not discontinue taking** the medicine until **none** of the medicine is left.
Positive	**Continue taking** the medicine until it is **all** gone.
	or
	Take all the medicine.

Figure 8.6	Instead of Saying What Something Is Not . . .	Say What It Is
Negative Phrases and Their Positive Counterparts	did not succeed	failed
	not many	few
	not all	most
	not on time	late, delayed
	not late, not delayed	on time
	not continue	discontinue
	not discontinue	continue
	not efficient	inefficient
	not sad	happy
	not accurate	inaccurate
	not approve	disapprove
	not disapprove	approve
	not now	later
	not familiar	unfamiliar
	not absent	present

Negative	Fourteen team members were not absent.
Positive	Fourteen team members were present.
Negative	Six of the twenty team members did not attend the meeting.
Positive	Fourteen of the team members were present.
Negative	Because the engineering department was not unaware of the change in scheduling for the project, they could have met the deadline for the beta testing.
Positive	Because the engineering department was aware of the change in scheduling for the project, they could have met the deadline for the beta testing.

▶Principle 5: Use Technical Terminology Consistently and Appropriately

Readers of technical documents expect writers to use consistently the words that refer to technical concepts, instructions, and equipment. For instance, readers of a computer maintenance manual may be confused if the writer uses *screen* and *monitor* interchangeably. The writer should pick one term or the other and use it consistently. Using words consistently is especially important when writing instructions and when describing equipment. For example, if a software manual explains how to select "typefaces" but the software itself uses the word "fonts," readers who don't know that *typefaces* and *fonts* are synonyms may be confused.

▶ For more information on how readers read, see Chapter 9, "Designing Documents for Your Readers," page 221.

Technical terminology—or **jargon**—is the specialized vocabulary of a particular field, profession, or workplace. For instance, professionals in the restaurant business may use the term "back server" for the employees who clear guests' tables during and after meals. Horticulturalists may use the scientific rather than the common name for plants—for example, referring to a pecan tree as *Carya illinoinensis* or a day lily as *Hemerocallis*. Technical terminology offers a concise way to convey technical information. However, readers who are unfamiliar with the technical terms may find them confusing or may misinterpret them. You can solve this problem for some readers by defining technical terms in parentheses the first time you use them or defining them in a glossary. (However, if your readers will not read your document from beginning to end, they may not see your parenthetical definition. If your readers may begin reading anywhere in your document, consider defining the term in a glossary or using a nontechnical term.) Other readers, however, will be uncomfortable with this solution and will prefer that you use nontechnical language whenever possible.

How will you know whether to use technical terminology in your documents? Ask yourself these questions:

- Will all of my readers understand the technical terminology and abbreviations? Will they misunderstand any of the technical terms and abbreviations?

- How can I help readers who don't understand the technical terminology and abbreviations? Will I define terminology and explain abbreviations in parentheses the first time I use them, or will I refer readers to a separate technical-terms glossary?
- Will my readers expect me to use technical terminology and abbreviations?

Follow these tips when using technical terminology:

> ▶ **Tips for Using Technical Terminology**
>
> - **Use technical terminology only if your readers have detailed knowledge of the topic.** You can assume, for example, that an engineer knows what the abbreviation *psi* (pounds per square inch) means; someone without an engineering background may not understand the abbreviation.
> - **Use technical terminology for expert readers.** Expert readers expect technical terminology.
> - **If your readers have casual or scant knowledge of your topic or of your field, avoid using technical terminology that they don't understand.** If you cannot avoid using it, define the terminology that you use.
> - **Consider whether you can use more than one term to refer to a concept, instruction, piece of equipment, and so on.** If so, determine which term you will use.
> - **Use technical terminology consistently.** Once you have selected the term you will use in the document, use that term consistently throughout the document.

▶Principle 6: Use Nonsexist Language

Sexist language can distract or mislead readers, so eliminate all unnecessary references to gender in your writing. This section describes several ways to eliminate sexist language.[1] To use nonsexist language, writers find personal pronouns especially troublesome. Many writers use *he/she* or *s/he* to eliminate gender, but these expressions are awkward, especially when they appear several times in a paragraph. Use the following tips to avoid *he/she* and *s/he* and to avoid associating gender with a person's role or job:

---

[1] Adapted from guidelines developed by the National Council of Teachers of English.

▶ **Tips for Using Nonsexist Language**

- **Avoid gender-specific nouns when referring to job functions or occupations.** Gender-specific nouns, such as *anchorman*, exclude one gender or the other. Figure 8.7 lists nonsexist alternatives to some gender-specific nouns that refer to job functions or occupations.

- **Use plural nouns to eliminate gender-specific pronouns.** The following examples illustrate how using plural nouns results in nonsexist language:

Sexist	**Each employee** should maintain **his** equipment and uniforms.
Nonsexist	**Employees** should maintain **their** equipment and uniforms.
Sexist	**Each teacher** must live in the city where **she** teaches.
Nonsexist	**Teachers** must live in the city where **they** teach.

- **To eliminate gender-specific pronouns, use *you* and *your*.** Often you can avoid sexist language by using second-person pronouns (*you, your*) instead of singular nouns. Use second-person pronouns to address your readers directly. Notice how using second-person pronouns results in nonsexist language:

Sexist	The user should read the troubleshooting section of the manual before **she** calls the help line.
Nonsexist	**You** should read the troubleshooting section of the manual before **you** call the help line.

     or

     Read the troubleshooting section of the manual before **you** call the help line.

- **Avoid using *man* and words that contain *man* to refer to all human beings.** Words such as *mankind* and *man-made* are inaccurate. Instead, you might use *people* or *humankind* for *mankind* and *synthetic* for *man-made*.

- **Use *he or she* or *she or he* when you must use gender-specific pronouns.** Whenever possible, use plural nouns or second-person pronouns to avoid gender-specific pronouns. However, when you can't avoid gender-specific pronouns, use *he or she* or *she or he*. These constructions are clear and inclusive.

Figure 8.7	**Sexist Noun**	**Nonsexist Noun**
Alternatives to Sexist Nouns	chairman, chairwoman	chair, chairperson
	policeman, policewoman	police, police officer
	postman, mailman	postal worker, mail carrier
	fireman	firefighter
	waitress	server
	stewardess	flight attendant

▶Principle 7: Consider Your Readers' Culture and Language

With computer networks and the global marketplace, many companies are doing business with people and companies abroad. When communicating with people from other countries, companies encounter two problems: cultural differences and language interference (Mirshafiei 280). For example, miscommunication often occurs when people in the United States communicate with people whose cultures value "detailed, subjective analyses" and "philosophical argumentation" (Mirshafiei 281). In Middle Eastern cultures, writers often use what people in the United States regard as overstatement and exaggeration; these writers are "highly rhetorical and use a highly complex and decorative language" that people in the United States often find bewildering (Mirshafiei 281). Likewise, many Middle Eastern readers may not understand the tendency for directness and individualism. Such misunderstanding and miscommunication can result when readers and writers don't understand the cultures that drive and dictate communication styles.

Similarly, Japanese writers often use "telepathic communication," an indirect communication style that avoids direct confrontation. Telepathic communication allows writers to imply conflicting opinions and keep the communication smooth (Mirshafiei 281). When the Japanese communicate with people in cultures that expect and value direct, not vague, language, miscommunication may occur. For example, communication problems frequently occur between people in the United States and people in Japan because the telepathic communication style conflicts with the direct style expected by readers in the United States.

As you communicate with international readers, remember that their culture shapes their communication style just as your culture shapes yours. A communication that is unfamiliar to you is not inherently wrong or right; it is only different from the style to which you are accustomed. Your international readers may have as much difficulty with your communication style as you might with theirs. Do your best to minimize this difference and to eliminate possible miscommunication by learning as much as you can about your readers' expectations and culture.

TAKING IT INTO THE WORKPLACE

What Is Simplified English?

The purpose of Simplified English is to "help users of English-language documentation to understand what they read."

—European Association of Aerospace Industries

Developed primarily for nonnative speakers of English, Simplified English gives writers a basic set of grammar rules, style points, and vocabulary words. The purpose of Simplified English is to "help users of English-language documentation to understand what they read" (AECMA 2001). One of the more commonly used versions of Simplified English was developed by the European Association of Aerospace Industries (AECMA). First published in 1986, the *AECMA Simplified English (SE) Guide* sets up the following characteristics for Simplified English:

- Simplified grammar and style rules.
- A limited set of approved vocabulary. Each word has a limited number of clearly defined meanings and a limited number of parts of speech (Boeing).
- Guidelines for adding new technical words to the approved vocabulary.

The AECMA Simplified English also requires writers to[1]

- Use the active voice
- Use articles wherever possible
- Use simple verb tenses

- Use language consistently
- Use relatively short sentences

Although the AECMA version of Simplified English was developed for the aerospace industry, companies in several other industries have modified it or produced their own version. Many industries and companies have adopted a version of Simplified English.

Assignment

Boeing has adopted AECMA Simplified English for its technical documentation and has also modified this version for more general types of technical writing. Boeing has also developed a Boeing Plain Language Checker for more general types of technical writing as well as a Simplified English Checker. You can learn more about Boeing's Simplified English Checker and Plain Language Checker at the Web site: http://www.boeing.com.

Using a search engine, find at least one company (other than Boeing) that uses a version of Simplified English. When you find a company, provide the following information in an e-mail to your instructor:

- Name of the company
- Version of Simplified English the company uses
- Web site address for the information that you gathered

---

[1] Adapted from Boeing, "What Is Simplified English?" Online. Internet. 25 Nov. 2001. Available: http://www.boeing.com/assocproducts/sechecker/se.html.

Consider How Your Language Differs from Your Readers' Language

Along with cultural differences, consider language interference. Your international readers may not understand the idioms and technical or workplace language that you might use with other readers in your country or at your workplace. **Idioms** are expressions whose meaning is different from the literal or standard meaning of the words they contain. Examples of idioms in the

United States include *put up with, turn over a new leaf,* and *know the ropes.* International readers can't understand idioms logically; international readers must memorize what they mean. For example, you might say to your room-mate: "Let's run down to McDonald's and grab a burger." You don't literally mean that the two of you should run to the restaurant and snatch a sandwich from the server. What you mean is "Let's get in the car, drive to McDonald's, and buy something to eat."

When you write for international readers, consider the words and phrases you use, so that your readers will understand what you mean. Even international readers who speak English may not understand some of the expressions you use. For instance, in the United States, people say "line up" outside a theater box office, but people in England say "queue up." In everyday speech, you use many words and phrases that international readers may not under-stand. Likewise, you might use workplace language or technical terminology that is clear to others in your workplace but is baffling to international read-ers—especially to people who have never been to your country or to your workplace. For example, the expression *boot up,* referring to turning on a computer and starting the operating system, may be unclear and even humor-ous to a reader in some countries.

When writing for international readers, try to find out as much as possible about their knowledge of your language and your country and about their lan-guage and customs. Follow these tips to minimize language interference:

> ### ▶ Tips for Writing for International Readers
>
> - **Avoid idioms—expressions whose meaning is different from the standard or literal meaning of the words they contain.** Most U.S. readers, for example, would realize what "dig their heels in" means—that people stubbornly refuse to change their positions. International readers might interpret the expression literally and think that people dig holes in the ground with their feet.
>
> - **Use workplace and technical language that international readers will be familiar or comfortable with.** Avoid using any terminology that is likely to be unfamiliar to your readers. For example, when writing to readers in England and Europe, use metric measurements, such as kilometers rather than miles.
>
> - **Avoid localisms—phrases familiar only to people living in a specific area.** For example, many people in the southern part of the United States use the phrase *fixing to,* as in "I am fixing to go to the store." This phrase sounds odd to people not from the South and certainly would sound odd to an international reader. Brand names are
>
> (continued on next page)

another type of localism. Many people in the United States mistakenly use the brand name "Kleenex" to refer to all facial tissues and the brand name "Coke" to refer to all soft drinks. Such brand names may baffle many international readers.

- **Avoid metaphors and allusions.** Metaphors and allusions may refer to or imply a concept or information that is familiar to readers in the United States but probably is unfamiliar to international readers.

- **If you must use expressions and terminology that international readers may not understand, explain what the language means to avoid misinterpretation or misunderstanding.** Perhaps you also can find and use the corresponding word or phrase in the native language of your readers. You can also have the document you are writing translated into their native language. If you select this option, be sure that the translator knows the readers' language and country well enough to translate idioms and workplace and technical language correctly, not just literally.

- **Write simple, clear, complete sentences.** Divide long sentences into two or more shorter sentences. International readers or readers who aren't native speakers of your language will comprehend information more easily in a short sentence than in a long one.

- **Use a version of Simplified English.** Because nonnative speakers of English will likely read your technical documents, consider using a version of Simplified English. To learn more about Simplified English, see "Taking It into the Workplace."

▶Conclusion

Language is a powerful communication tool when used accurately. You can use this tool to persuade, inform, and instruct. However, to use this tool to your advantage, follow the principles in this chapter to write with clarity, conciseness, and precision. Your words will speak for you. Your readers will not need to ask you to explain what you mean.

WORKSHEET for Using Reader-Oriented Language

▶ **Principle 1: Use Specific and Unambiguous Language**

Specific Language
- Did you use specific language?
- Did you give readers enough examples and details to understand your sentences?

Unambiguous Language
- Did you eliminate all misplaced modifiers?
- Did you eliminate all dangling modifiers?

- Did you eliminate unnecessary noun stacks?
- Did you eliminate all faulty word choices?

▶ **Principle 2: Use Only the Words Your Readers Need**
- Did you eliminate all redundant pairs?
- Did you eliminate all redundant modifiers?
- Did you eliminate any unnecessary words or phrases?

▶ **Principle 3: Use Simple Words**
- Did you use any unfamiliar words that you could replace with simple words?

▶ **Principle 4: Use Positive Language**
- Whenever possible, did you tell readers what something is, instead of what it is not?
- Did you use positive language when possible?

▶ **Principle 5: Use Technical Terminology Consistently and Appropriately**
- Did you use technical terminology consistently?
- Will all readers understand the terminology and abbreviations you have used? If not, have you defined or replaced the terminology or abbreviations they won't understand?
- Did you consider which terms your readers prefer?
- Will your readers expect you to use technical terminology and abbreviations?

▶ **Principle 6: Use Nonsexist Language**
- Did you use any sexist nouns to refer to job functions or occupations?
- Did you use plural nouns to eliminate gender-specific pronouns?
- When possible, did you use *you* and *your* instead of gender-specific pronouns?
- Did you avoid using *man* and words that contain *man* to refer to all people?

▶ **Principle 7: Consider Your Readers' Culture and Language**
- Did you eliminate idoms?
- Did you use workplace or technical language that international readers will understand?
- Did you eliminate localisms?
- Did you avoid metaphors and allusions that may be unfamiliar to your international readers?
- Did you explain any expressions and terminology that your international readers might misunderstand?
- Did you use simple, clear language?
- Did you use short sentences?

► **EXERCISES**

1. Rewrite these sentences, substituting specific language for vague language. Add details and examples to make the language specific.
   a. The dryers in the laundry room are malfunctioning.
   b. The results of the survey will be available soon.
   c. Our analysis of the drinking water revealed a number of items that we can consider.
   d. The profits of our foreign offices decreased significantly.

2. Rewrite these sentences to eliminate misplaced modifiers.
   a. A brochure about the cost-sharing program is enclosed with the application that gives complete details.
   b. The study suggests that we should continue the recycling program to the city and the council.
   c. The technician banged angrily on the flashlight in the laboratory that was dimly lighted.
   d. We watched them perform the final experiment from the room with a one-way mirror.

3. Rewrite these sentences to eliminate dangling modifiers.
   a. After two months as an exchange student in India, the United States was a wonderful sight.
   b. During discussions with Dover Elevator, it was determined that the building needed a new elevator shaft.
   c. After testing the new airbag, the new design was approved for delivery to the auto manufacturers.
   d. The software was upgraded in time for the December meeting by working overtime.

4. Rewrite these sentences to eliminate stacked nouns.
   a. The school district's technology innovation committee meeting will begin at 6:00 P.M. in the district technology center.
   b. NEI-supported scientists recently developed a culturing rabbit cornea tissue method that allows researchers to measure cell movement.
   c. The protocol changes list states that investigation modifications occurred after the study enrollment period.

5. Rewrite these sentences to eliminate faulty word choices.
   a. After the seminar, the citizens were revolting.
   b. The teacher was mad.
   c. The operators were held up in the briefing room.

6. Revise these sentences to eliminate redundant words and phrases.
   a. This important and significant jobs program should help each and every youth dedicated to improving himself or herself.
   b. If and when you complete the programming, we will document the program fully and completely.
   c. To enhance the marketing of our new line of computers, we are offering free gifts to the first 100 customers.
   d. The pipe to the main generator rarely ever leaks.
   e. The decorator plans to paint the auditorium walls green in color and to repeat the color again in the foyer.
   f. We have a very unique opportunity to see the future plans for the space center.

7. Rewrite these sentences, eliminating all unnecessary words and phrases and condensing

wordy phrases. Correct any other style errors that you find in the sentences.

a. There are several scientists who are uneasy about the research results.

b. Preparedness for and response to an attack involving biological agents are complicated by the large number of potential agents (most of which are rarely encountered naturally) and these possible potential agents' sometimes long and lengthy incubation periods.

c. It is important that we turn in our applications by the deadline.

d. As a matter of fact, we will be offering the vaccines again next month.

e. You should check the roof for damage on a monthly basis.

f. The majority of the candidates support the tax rollback but have not taken into consideration the cost to education and social programs.

g. With reference to the revised proposal, it is possible that notwithstanding the fact that we have a good solution, we still should still take into consideration ways to improve it.

h. It is interesting to note that at the conclusion of the council meeting, most of the opponents of the new taxi policy were gone.

i. Until such time as the new health plan goes into effect, all employees should continue to file claims according to the current plan without further delay.

8. Revise these sentences, replacing fancy words with simple words. Correct any other style errors that you find in the sentences.

a. The new health plan will commence on January 1 of next year.

b. During this time of heightened national alert, bomb threats are proliferating nationwide.

c. To obtain optimum performance from your automobile, you should endeavor to follow the maintenance program furnished in the owner's manual.

d. We are cognizant of the fact that you are attempting to facilitate our reimbursement for the incorrect pipe fittings that we purchased from your organization.

9. Change the negative constructions to positive constructions in these sentences.

a. As lab employees, you should not treat any student or faculty member unprofessionally and discourteously.

b. Since the repair team did not know of the crack when they began their work, they could not repair the wall according to their original estimate.

c. Not many of the competitors finished the marathon because of the extreme heat and humidity.

d. Even though the plane was delayed because of fog, we were not late to the conference.

10. These sentences contain sexist language. Revise the sentences, replacing the sexist language with nonsexist language. You may change singular nouns to plural nouns when appropriate.

a. Before the plane made an emergency landing, the stewardess checked the children's seatbelts.

b. Each student should discuss his degree plan with his adviser at least two years before he graduates.

c. The network operator should read all instructions before she updates the network.

d. Many athletic shoes and equipment contain man-made materials.

11. Assume that international readers or non-native speakers of English will read these sentences. Eliminate any language that these readers may not understand.

a. During the debate, the adviser told the candidates to stick to their guns when answering questions about their political views.

b. After the midterm examination, we walked to our apartment and crashed.

c. The victims of the hurricane need medical supplies such as Band-Aids, Kleenex, and alcohol.

► CASE STUDY

Changing Old Habits

Background

Your company has decided to talk to employees about using nonsexist language. In the past, the company has used the pronoun *he* to refer to all employees, except when addressing a female employee by name. The company uses *she* when referring to administrative assistants and clerical staff, although several of the assistants and members of the clerical staff are males. The company also uses the terms *chairman of the board* and *chairman of the committee.*

Several of the employees—male and female—have complained about the sexist language. Other employees, however, don't see a problem with the language. They say that *he* is the universal pronoun and refers to males or females when referring to a group such as the employees of the company. They say that using another pronoun is unnecessary.

Despite resistance from many employees, the vice president, Jon Rowland, wants to make all employees—even the company executives—aware of the importance of nonsexist language. Jon wants employees to use nonsexist language when they speak, write, and refer to other employees and their job functions. He has asked you to write for his signature a memo presenting ways of eliminating sexist language.

Assignment

Your instructor will tell you whether you will write the memo individually or with a team.

1. Write a draft of the memo, remembering to keep the goodwill of all your readers as much as possible while still making the point that sexist language excludes and stating that the company and all employees will use nonsexist language. Be sure to include examples to help your readers understand how sexist and nonsexist language differ. Give the readers some guidelines to help them use nonsexist language.
2. Bring your draft to class for peer evaluation.
3. Revise the draft as necessary, and give it to your instructor.
4. Be prepared to discuss your memo and this case in class.

9

Designing Documents for Your Readers

▶ **OUTLINE**

Readers form an impression of your document before they begin to read it. They draw this impression in part from the design elements—or lack of design elements. These elements help to create a favorable or unfavorable picture of your document and possibly you and your organization. Design elements such as headings, type size, color, page layout, and white space affect the success of a document. These elements also help readers to locate information and motivate readers to read. In this chapter, you will learn four principles to help you design documents that will favorably impress your readers.

▶How Design Makes Documents More Readable

Before we examine those principles, let's compare the presentation of information about canine epilepsy in Figures 9.1 and 9.2. The document shown in Figure 9.1 has no design elements other than the title and paragraph breaks. It doesn't have headings or lists to help readers locate information, so the readers can't read selectively. Readers who are interested in specific information must read until they find that information. For example, someone who wants to know how to medicate and treat an epileptic dog must read six paragraphs before finding that information. In contrast, the document shown in Figure 9.2 contains visual clues to the organization of the text and the information it provides. Readers of that document can, for example, locate specific information about types of canine epilepsy and about treating epilepsy.

Readers process a document from top to bottom unless the writer gives them clues about the organization of the document (Duin). Without these clues, readers may assume that information near the beginning is more important than information near the end, and they may read the information near the beginning of a document especially closely and generally recall it better than they recall information at the end. If readers are likely to need information that appears in the middle or near the end, the writer can give clues through the document design to help readers find that information. The format of the document in Figure 9.2 gives readers clues through headings and lists. The headings visually categorize information so readers don't have to process the document from top to bottom. Instead, readers can scan through the document for the information that interests them. The format of the document in Figure 9.1 gives readers no clues about content and forces readers to process the document in a top-down manner.

▶Principle 1: Consider the Design as You Plan Your Documents

To save yourself time and frustration, consider design elements when you identify your readers and their purpose for reading. If you wait until you have written one or more drafts, you may not have time to incorporate the design elements you want, or you may have to unnecessarily spend time reformatting

Canine Epilepsy

Epilepsy is a disorder characterized by recurrent seizures. Seizures, also known as fits or convulsions, occur when an area of nerve cells in the brain becomes overexcitable. This area is often called a seizure focus. The mechanism responsible for developing this focus is unknown.

A dog can inherit or acquire canine epilepsy. Inherited epilepsy affects about 1% of the canine population. Breeds which may inherit epilepsy include the beagle, Belgian shepherd, German shepherd, dachshund, and keeshond. Researchers also suspect a genetic factor in the following breeds: cocker spaniel, collie, golden retriever, Labrador retriever, Irish setter, miniature schnauzer, poodle, Saint Bernard, Siberian husky, and wire-haired fox terrier.

Acquired epilepsy may occur months to years after an injury or illness that causes brain damage. In many cases, the dog is completely normal except for occasional seizures. Causes of acquired epilepsy include trauma, infection, poisons, hypoxia (lack of oxygen), and low blood sugar concentrations.

A dog with inherited epilepsy has generalized seizures that affect its entire brain and body. The dog usually falls on its side and displays paddling motions with all four limbs. During or immediately after the seizures, the dog may also exhibit loss of consciousness (i.e., the dog will not respond when you call its name), excessive drooling, and urinating or passing of feces. The seizure usually lasts no longer than 1 or 2 minutes. The first seizure of inherited epilepsy usually occurs between the ages of 1 and 3 years. Seizures that occur before 6 months or after 5 years of age probably result from acquired epilepsy.

A dog with acquired epilepsy has partial seizures. A partial seizure affects only one part of the body, and the dog may not lose consciousness. During a partial seizure, the dog may exhibit turning of the head to one side, muscular contractions of one or both legs on the same side of the body, or bending of the body to one side. These signs are localizing because they help to determine the location of the seizure focus in the brain. The localizing sign may occur only briefly, after which the seizure becomes generalized. If the seizure becomes generalized, you or your veterinarian may have difficulty distinguishing between acquired and inherited epilepsy. The first seizure may occur at any age.

You can treat epilepsy by giving anticonvulsant medication orally several times a day. This treatment is effective in 60 to 70% of epileptic dogs. Unfortunately, the medication will not completely eliminate the seizures. Instead, the medication reduces the frequency, severity, and duration of the seizures. Most veterinarians recommend that dogs receive the anticonvulsant medication when the seizures occur more often than once every 6 weeks or when severe clusters of seizures occur more often than once every 2 months. To successfully treat epilepsy, you must consistently give the medication as directed by the veterinarian and continue the medication without interruption. If you discontinue the medication, status epilepticus could occur, resulting in the dog's death. Status epilepticus is a series of seizures without periods of consciousness. If this condition occurs, contact a veterinarian immediately.

Source: Adapted from S. Dru Forrester and Bruce Lawhorn, *Canine Epilepsy* (College Station: Texas Agricultural Extension Service, n.d.). Reprinted by permission.

A Document with Design Elements

Canine Epilepsy

Epilepsy is a disorder characterized by recurrent seizures. Seizures, also known as fits or convulsions, occur when an area of nerve cells in the brain becomes overexcitable. This area is often called a seizure focus. The mechanism responsible for developing this focus is unknown.

Types of Canine Epilepsy

A dog can inherit or acquire canine epilepsy. Inherited epilepsy affects about 1% of the canine population. Breeds which may inherit epilepsy include the beagle, Belgian shepherd, German shepherd, dachshund, and keeshond. Researchers also suspect a genetic factor in the following breeds: cocker spaniel, collie, golden retriever, Labrador retriever, Irish setter, miniature schnauzer, poodle, Saint Bernard, Siberian husky, and wire-haired fox terrier.

Acquired epilepsy may occur months to years after an injury or illness that causes brain damage. In many cases, the dog is completely normal except for occasional seizures. Causes of acquired epilepsy include trauma, infection, poisons, hypoxia (lack of oxygen), and low blood sugar concentrations.

Characteristics of Inherited Epilepsy

A dog with inherited epilepsy has generalized seizures that affect its entire brain and body. The dog usually falls on its side and displays paddling motions with all four limbs. During or immediately after the seizures, the dog may also exhibit some or all of the following signs:

- loss of consciousness (i.e., the dog will not respond when you call its name)
- excessive drooling
- urinating or passing of feces.

The seizure usually lasts no longer than 1 or 2 minutes. The first seizure of inherited epilepsy usually occurs between the ages of 1 and 3 years. Seizures that occur before 6 months or after 5 years of age probably result from acquired epilepsy.

Characteristics of Acquired Epilepsy

A dog with acquired epilepsy has partial seizures. A partial seizure affects only one part of the body, and the dog may not lose consciousness. During a partial seizure, the dog may exhibit one or more of the following localizing signs:

- turning of the head to one side
- muscular contractions of one or both legs on the same side of the body
- bending of the body to one side.

These signs are localizing because they help to determine the location of the seizure focus in the brain. The localizing sign may occur only briefly, after which the seizure becomes generalized. If the seizure becomes generalized, you or your veterinarian may have difficulty distinguishing between acquired and inherited epilepsy. The first seizure may occur at any age.

Treatment of Canine Epilepsy

You can treat epilepsy by giving anticonvulsant medication orally several times a day. This treatment is effective in 60 to 70% of epileptic dogs. Unfortunately, the medication will not completely

(continued on next page)

▼ **Figure 9.2**   (continued)

eliminate the seizures. Instead, the medication reduces the frequency, severity, and duration of the seizures. Most veterinarians recommend that dogs receive the anticonvulsant medication when the seizures occur more often than once every 6 weeks or when severe clusters of seizures occur more often than once every 2 months.

To successfully treat epilepsy, you must
- consistently give the medication as directed by the veterinarian
- continue the medication without interruption.

If you discontinue the medication, status epilepticus could occur, resulting in the dog's death. Status epilepticus is a series of seizures without periods of consciousness. If this condition occurs, contact a veterinarian immediately.

Source: Adapted from S. Dru Forrester and Bruce Lawhorn, *Canine Epilepsy* (College Station: Texas Agricultural Extension Service, n.d.).

the text to fit your design. Before you begin writing, decide on the page size, page layout, typefaces, type sizes, and heading style. By deciding on these elements as you plan, you can format your document as you write; or you can create a template with your word-processing or desktop publishing software to help you create consistent page designs.

As you decide on the design elements, you also can develop thumbnail sketches and a style sheet. **Thumbnail sketches** are rough drawings of possible page layouts (see Figure 9.3). Roger Parker and Patrick Berry recommend sketching your initial page layout ideas: "Try out a variety of ideas. When you finish one sketch, begin another. . . . Don't bother with excessive detail—use thin lines for text, thick lines or block lettering for headlines [headings], and happy faces for art or photographs. Even simple representations such as these will give you a sense of which arrangements work and which don't" (5–6). As you sketch page layouts, you might also consider different types of page layouts and sizes. Figure 9.4 presents some of the common layouts (sometimes called grids).

▶ To learn more about writing with a team, see Chapter 4, "Collaborating and the Writing Process."

A **style sheet** is a tool to help writers and designers maintain consistency throughout a document. A style sheet might include language choices such as those discussed in Chapter 8; it also can serve as a plan for designing a document. Figure 9.5 shows a simple style sheet for the design elements of a software manual written by a team of students. The team put the style sheet in a public directory on the local area network in their computer lab, so each team member could easily access it. A style sheet can help you maintain consistency in several situations. When you are working on a long document, a style sheet can help you remember the design decisions that you made at the start of the project. For example, it can tell you that first-level headings are to be in 14-point green Helvetica type. Style sheets also can help you create a consistent appearance for similar documents or for all of the documents written for a specific organization or company.

Figure 9.3   Thumbnail Sketches

Figure 9.4   Common Page Layouts

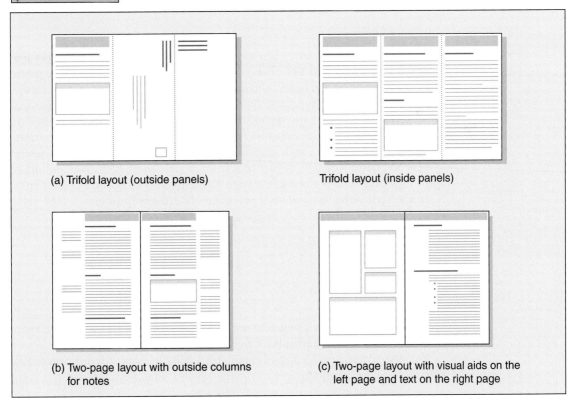

(a) Trifold layout (outside panels)

Trifold layout (inside panels)

(b) Two-page layout with outside columns
    for notes

(c) Two-page layout with visual aids on the
    left page and text on the right page

Team 3
Style Sheet for Software Manual

Page Elements	Page size	9" x 6"
	Margins	$^3/_4$"
	Layout	two uneven columns, the left column for marginal comments and headings left column 1½" right column 3"
	Spacing	single-space for text double-space between paragraphs
	Visual aids	no captions for screen captures placed at point of reference
	Headings	left-hanging
Type Elements	Typeface	Bookman
	Size	12 point for text 14 point for headings 12 point for subheadings
	Style	bold for subheadings
	Color	color 13 for major headings

Many organizations have their own style guides or specific design requirements for their documents. For example, a regional telecommunications company in the southwestern United States requires the company logo always to appear in the same typeface, type size, and color. This company also has specific page layout requirements for business letters and certain types of reports. As you prepare documents for your company, group, or organization, find out whether it has a style sheet or specific design requirements.

When you are working as part of a team, a style sheet helps you and other team members to use the same design elements and to format consistently. Keep the style sheet simple, so team members can easily follow it. The style sheet should list at least these design elements:

- Typefaces
- Type sizes
- Margins
- Heading style
- Line spacing

If team members follow the guidelines spelled out in the style sheet, the team can easily combine each member's section to create one document.

You also can use preformatted templates available in most word-processing software. These templates provide page layouts that you can use for your documents. If you decide to use a preformatted template, you should consider these possible problems: preformatted templates often

- Don't follow good design principles
- Omit key conventional elements required in some documents
- Are commonplace (many writers use these templates, so your document could look like many other documents)
- include inappropriate visual aids or design elements

Therefore, you might consider using the styles function of your word-processing software to create your own templates that you can apply to headings, paragraphs, lists, and so on. By using the styles function, you save time and achieve a consistent look in a document or among several documents. When you create a style for a heading, for example, you don't have to format the headings each time you type one. Instead, you type a heading and then apply the style by putting the cursor in the heading text and selecting the style for that heading using the style box on your toolbar. As you plan the design of your document, follow these tips:

▶ **Tips for Planning the Document Design**

- **Make thumbnail sketches.** Thumbnail sketches will help you to see multiple possibilities for the page design.
- **Create a style sheet or use your organization's style sheet.** A style sheet will help you to create a consistent design. If you're working with a team, a style sheet will save you time.
- **If you're working with a team, create a style sheet and styles before you begin writing.** Make sure each team member has a copy of the style sheets and the styles.
- **Use the styles function of your word-processing software.** Styles can save you time and will help you to use the design elements consistently.
- **If you select a preformatted template, make sure it follows good design principles.** If it doesn't, consider creating your own template.

▶Principle 2: Choose Design Elements to Motivate Readers to Read

As you plan your document, think about design elements that will prompt people to read and use your document. Readers generally notice the design or appearance of your document before they actually read the text, visual aids, or headings. Readers often are first attracted to a document by its packaging:

- The cover
- The binding
- The paper
- The layout

As you consider what will motivate readers to read, you can also consider how and where the readers will use your document. For example, if you know that your readers will use the document in a confined space where they will use liquids, consider laminating the pages and using a smaller page size (such as 6 by 9 inches instead of the standard $8\frac{1}{2}$ by 11 inches). If, for instance, you are designing a document that UPS employees will carry in their delivery vans, the standard $8\frac{1}{2}$-by-11-inch page would be awkward, whereas a $4\frac{1}{2}$-by-5-inch page would better meet the employees' needs. The following sections will give you some tips for designing "packaging" elements that will not only motivate readers to read your documents, but will also work in their environment.

An Engaging, Appropriate Cover

▶ You will learn more about covers in Chapter 11, "Preparing Front and Back Matter."

The **cover** is the part of a document that many readers see first. It could be the first page of a Web site, the first screen of an online document, or the outside of a paper document. An effective cover makes a good first impression and invites readers to read and use the document. It will feature a clear, legible title or opening headline. If, for instance, you use graphics, select ones that do not detract from or overpower the title or headline. If you are creating a cover for a paper document, select a cover material and style that are appropriate for the document and that will enhance your document. If you have the budget, have the cover professionally laminated.

If you are creating a cover or a homepage for a Web site, consider these design tips to motivate readers to stop and read it:

▶ **Tips for Designing Covers for Paper and Web Documents**

- **Use color to draw the readers to the page.** To learn more about color, see page 237 of this chapter.
- **Use ample "white space," or empty space, that highlights and unifies the information you want to highlight.** Be sure to surround the name of the site, document, or organization with ample white space. The white space creates a frame that keeps the related information together.
- **Include information about the contents of the document or Web site.** You might use icons with explanatory phrases that invite readers to read beyond the cover or homepage.

(continued on next page)

- **Avoid using paragraphs of text to describe the document or Web site.** Instead use lists, phrases, and visual aids.
- **Remember that less is more.** A clean, simple cover or homepage can attract more readers than one filled with graphics. When you use too many graphics, the readers don't know what is most important or they may not see the title of the document or the name of your organization.

Appropriate Binding

For long paper documents, several types of binding are available:

- Three-ring binders
- Spiral binding
- Traditional book binding

If readers will use the document to complete a task or to follow instructions, select spiral binding or a three-ring binder; the document will stay open to a specific page. If you will be updating the document frequently, use a three-ring binder; you can then, if necessary, update sections without reprinting the entire document. If you use traditional book binding (often called perfect binding), think of the spine of the book as a locating device: include at least the title of the document and possibly the writer's or the organization's name.

Appropriate Paper

You will want to consider the best type of paper for your readers' purpose and environment. For example, if you know the readers will use your document in a laboratory, use coated paper. Follow these tips when selecting paper:

Tips for Selecting the Appropriate Paper and Page Size

- **Select a 20- or 30-pound bond paper for most documents.** This weight paper gives your document more professionalism. On a more practical note, it doesn't tear as easily. If you select a lighter weight paper, the document may look flimsy and may tear. Also, if you print the document on both sides, the print will bleed through the paper.
- **Select the appropriate page size.** Select a page size that will meet your readers' needs in their environment. For example, if the readers will use your manual in a crowded computer lab, select a smaller

(continued on next page)

page size. If the readers will use your document in an automotive shop, select an 8½-by-11-inch page size.

- **If you will be printing on both sides of the paper, make sure that the printing will not bleed through from one side to the other.** If you select at least 20- or 30-pound bond paper, the printing will not bleed through.

- **Use coated paper to increase the durability of the paper and the resolution of the print.** Coated paper can be more expensive, but print resolution is much higher on coated paper. Coated paper also creates a sharper, more professional look to a document. If you use coated paper, use an off-white or ivory paper to decrease the glare.

- **For formal documents, select a white, ivory, or off-white paper.** Select colored paper (other than the colors above) only when appropriate for the tone, formality, content, and readers. For example, if you are writing a proposal to a client, select a white, ivory, or off-white paper for this kind of a formal document. However, if you are inviting that same client to a Mardi Gras party to celebrate your winning the proposal, you might use light-purple paper with green accents. No matter what color you select, make sure that your readers can easily read the print.

Consistent Page Layout

As readers move beyond the external packaging, they look at the page layout to determine whether and what to read. Page layout can attract readers to your document. A consistent page layout helps readers to locate information. To create consistent page layouts, follow these tips:

 Tips for Creating a Consistent Page Layout

- **Use the same top, bottom, left, and right margins on each page.** For example, if you use 1-inch margins for one section of the document, use 1-inch margins for every section.

- **Use typefaces, type sizes, and type styles for headings and text consistently throughout the document.** For example, if you use a 14-point boldface serif typeface for the first-level headings in the first chapter of the document, use the same 14-point boldface serif typeface for first-level headings in every chapter. Try using the styles function of your word-processing software to ensure that these layout elements remain consistent.

(continued on next page)

- **Put page numbers in the same place on every page.** If you include a header or a footer with the page numbers, include that same style of header or footer on every page (see Figure 9.6). A **header** is a word or phrase that you put at the top of each page to identify a document or specific sections of a document (a **footer** serves the same purpose but appears at the bottom of each page). The wording of the header or footer may change from chapter to chapter or from section to section.

- **Put the page numbers in the outside top or bottom corner of the page.** If you put the page numbers in the center of the page, the readers may not see them as they thumb through your document to locate a specific page.

- **Use consistent paragraph indents and spacing between columns, within lists, and before and after headings.** For example, if you use a 3-space indent for the first paragraph, use the same indent for all paragraphs.

Figure 9.6 Examples of a Header and a Footer

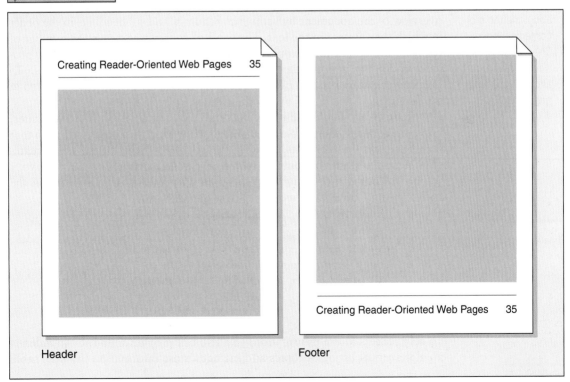

▶Principle 3: Choose Design Elements to Help Readers Locate Information

As you plan page layouts, remember that most readers have a goal when reading your document. They may be reading to

- Answer a question
- Gather information
- Complete a task or procedure
- Learn how to do something

To help readers reach any of these goals, you can include various design elements to help readers locate information. Such locating devices can appear at the document, chapter or division, and page or screen levels.

Document-Level Locating Devices

Document-level locating devices include the following:

- Table of contents
- Navigation tools
- Index

▶To learn more about the table of contents, see Chapter 11, "Preparing Front and Back Matter," page 315.

The **table of contents** appears at the beginning of a document. It offers an overview of the document by listing the headings and subheadings in the order in which they appear in the text. The table of contents also tells the number of the page where a heading appears. Even when writing online documents, provide readers with a table of contents or an overview of the contents. To overview the contents, you can include a menu or a list of the topics covered in the document.

You probably won't find the words "table of contents" on most Web sites; however, you will find a table of contents. Many Web sites have a site map that serves as a table of contents. A **site map** lists the contents of the site by category. An online table of contents won't have page numbers but can help your readers to locate information and to know what information appears on the site. Figure 9.7 illustrates two tables of contents:

- A list of contents for the FDA (U.S. Food and Drug Administration) site. When you click on any of these categories, you go to a page that includes a list of subcategories (as in a table of contents for a paper document).
- The contents of the CBER (Center for Biologics Evaluation and Research) area of the FDA site. When you click on these categories, such as "Reading Room," you see the subcategories for that category (see Figure 9.8).

To help readers locate information, you also can provide an index. An **index** is an alphabetical listing of topics and includes more information than the table

| Figure 9.7 | Online Table of Contents |

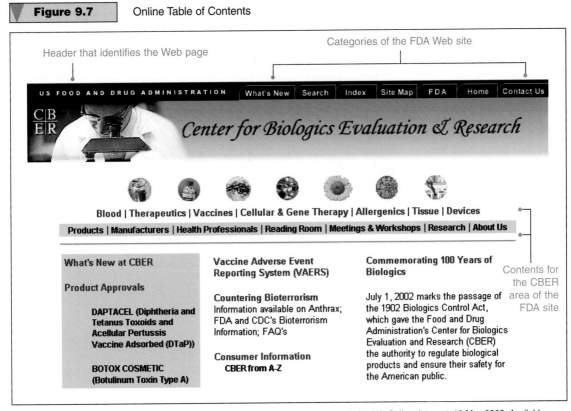

Source: Food and Drug Administration, Center for Biologics Evaluation and Research (2002). Online. Internet. 13 May 2002. Available: http://www.fda.gov/cber.

of contents. In a paper document, the index goes at the end of a document. You can find an example of an index at the end of this book. Online documents may also have indexes. (To see an example of an online index, refer to page 521 in Chapter 16.)

Chapter- or Division-Level Locating Devices

You might break a long document into chapters, divisions, or parts. For example, you might group the chapters of a long document into divisions. When you use chapters or divisions, indicate where each chapter or division begins by using

- Tabs
- Divider Pages

| **Figure 9.8** | Online Table of Contents |

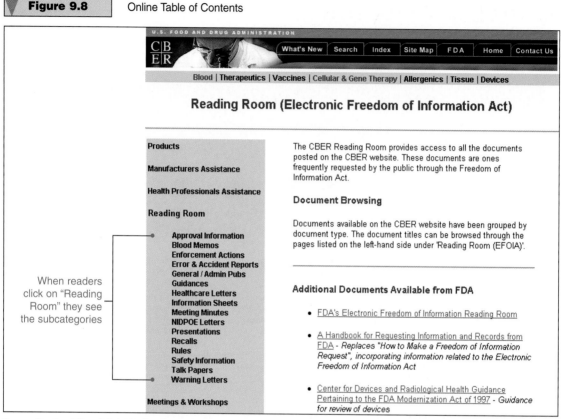

When readers click on "Reading Room" they see the subcategories

Source: Food and Drug Administration, Center for Biologics Evaluation and Research (2002). Online. Internet. 13 May 2002. Available: http://www.fda.gov/cber/reading.htm.

Tabs

Tabs—frequently used in manuals, procedures, and proposals—allow readers to quickly and easily locate chapters and divisions. If you decide to use tabs in your documents, select tabs with a professional appearance, and print a shortened version of the chapter or division title on the tab.

Divider Pages

Divider pages help readers to locate chapters and major divisions. Divider pages appear before chapters, divisions, or chapter groupings. In this book, for example, divider pages appear at the beginning of Parts I, II, and so on. These pages list the title of the part and the chapters included in that part. Each divider page that appears before a chapter usually lists a brief table of contents for that chapter.

Page- and Screen-Level Locating Devices

Page- and screen-level devices that you can use to help readers locate information include:

- Headers and footers
- Headings
- Color
- White space
- Navigation tools

Headers and Footers

Headers and footers help readers locate specific pages; they also may tell readers the chapter title and the division or part title. (Figure 9.6 on page 231 illustrates a header and a footer.) Headers and footers can contain page numbers, chapter titles, chapter subtitles, division titles, and book titles. You can also use a header or footer on a screen or Web page. An effective screen or Web page will include an "identifying graphic banner" such as a header with the title of the Web site or the grouping of pages (Yeo 13–14). This information helps readers to navigate through the pages and locate information. For example, Figure 9.7 has a header that identifies the Web site and includes tools for navigating the site.

Headings

▶For more information on headings, see Chapter 6, "Organizing Information for Your Readers," page 164.

Look again at Figures 9.1 and 9.2 (see pages 222–224). When information is grouped, or "chunked"—as it is in Figure 9.2—readers can easily locate the information they need. In the absence of chunking—as in Figure 9.1—readers read down from the top of a page or a screen until they find the information they want.

To chunk information, you can use headings. Headings help readers locate information on a page or screen and show the organization of information. Figure 9.9 shows three ways of positioning headings.

As you create headings, follow these tips:

▶ **Tips for Designing Headings**

- **Put the headings flush with the left margin.** Readers can more easily locate a heading if you place it flush against the left margin. Avoid centering headings because readers can't locate centered headings as quickly as flush-left headings.
- **Generally, use no more than four levels of headings in one document.** Too many levels can clutter a document and confuse readers.

(continued on next page)

- **Use more lines of space above your headings than after your headings.** For instance, in a double-spaced document, use three lines of space above the heading and two lines of space after. In a single-spaced document, use two lines of space above and one line after.
- **Always put a heading with at least two lines of text below it. Don't leave a heading without at least two lines of text at the bottom of a page.** Headings without these lines appear to float at the bottom of a page (see Figure 9.10).
- **Use different type sizes—and possibly type styles—to indicate levels of headings.** Readers associate size of type with importance—the larger the type, the more important the information (White 95). (See page 243 of this chapter for information about type size and headings.)

Figure 9.9   Three Positions for Headings

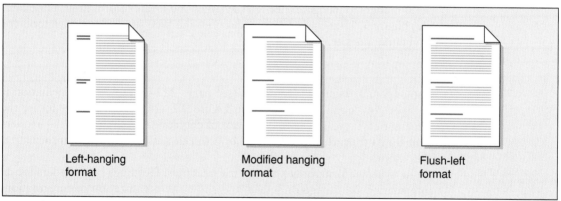

Left-hanging format

Modified hanging format

Flush-left format

Figure 9.10

A Floating Heading

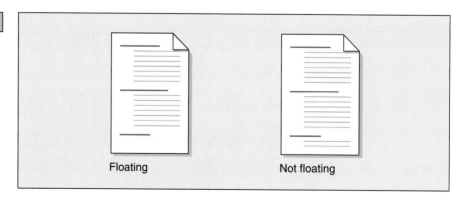

Floating

Not floating

TAKING IT INTO THE WORKPLACE

Using Color to Structure Information

"While design should be an integral part of communicating a message, care should be taken that the document is not over-designed—that is, the design should enhance and clarify the writing, but not overshadow the message. Design should aid readability and understanding. The best designed pieces are those where the reader does not notice the design. . . . If it is seamless with the message, the design has done its job."

—Gina Wilson, GW Designs, Austin, Texas

Color has become an important design tool, yet writers often think primarily about what and how much color to use, rather than how color can "enhance and clarify the writing" (Wilson).

When used as a key to information structure, color can help readers to handle more information and process it more efficiently (Horton). When studying how color interacts with the structure of documents, researchers have discovered that

- Color can help readers group objects, "taking precedence over other visual" cues (Keyes 647). Readers group by color before they group by shape, size, or other visual attributes (Keyes; Horton; Martinez and Block). Readers see color as taking precedence over size, shape, or location.
- Color grabs a "reader's attention first *before* the reader has understood the surrounding informa-

tional context—where it is in the hierarchy, what type of information it is, or its relation to other text" (Keyes 647). Readers, then, perceive a color element independently of its surrounding text.
- Color creates a separate "visual plane" that differentiates and consolidates visual information (Keyes 649). For example, readers might separate color type from noncolor type. This separation helps readers to scan documents.
- Multiple colors distract readers because each color group forms a separate category that competes for the reader's attention (Krull and Rubens). Therefore, when selecting color, "less is definitely more" (Keyes 648).

When selecting color for your documents,

- Think carefully about what you want to highlight with color. Regardless of the information that you select, the readers will perceive that information first.
- Use different shades of one color rather than several different colors.

Assignment

Find a document that uses color effectively to structure information. Write a memo to your instructor explaining why the document effectively uses color. Be sure to attach the original document so your instructor can see the color.

Color

Color can guide readers through your document. Figure 9.11 illustrates ways you can use color to help readers locate information and to guide them. You can use color with locating devices at the document as well as the page level. You can use color for the following locating devices:

- Headings
- Tabs
- Divider pages
- Headers and footers
- Navigational tools in online documents

Because color attracts readers' attention, use color to emphasize and highlight information, as shown in Figure 9.12. For example, you can

- Use colored bullets to highlight a list
- Put key words in color to indicate links in online documents
- Use horizontal rules to highlight blocks of text or sections of a document
- Use shading within or colored rules around boxes that highlight a warning or a special note

Figure 9.11 Using Color to Help Readers Locate Information

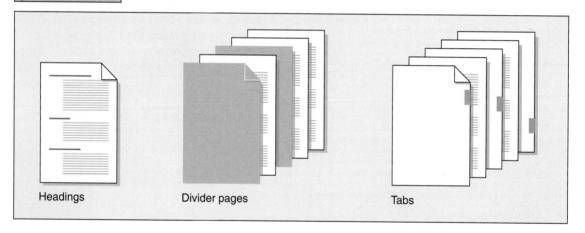

Headings   Divider pages   Tabs

Figure 9.12 Using Color to Emphasize and Highlight

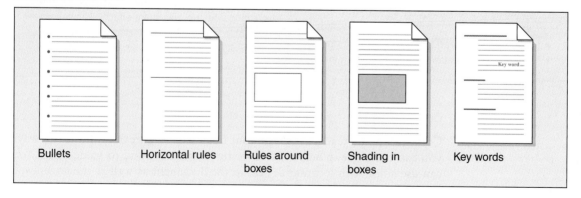

Bullets   Horizontal rules   Rules around boxes   Shading in boxes   Key words

When you use color, follow these tips:

▶ Tips for Using Color

- **Use the same color throughout the document for the same type of information.** For example, if you use green for the first-level headings in the first chapter, use green for the first-level headings in all chapters. If you use different colors for the same type of information, the colors will serve merely to decorate rather than to help readers locate information.

- **Use color along with other devices, such as white space, boldface, or type size.** Colorblind readers need clues other than color to help them locate information. If you indicate a locating device with color only, some readers may not be able to use that device.

- **Use colors primarily to communicate, not to decorate.** With relatively inexpensive printers, you can now easily add color to any document. Color attracts readers' eyes. If the color merely decorates, it may distract readers from the information you are trying to communicate. Color that is only decorative may overpower the information.

- **Consider readers when selecting colors.** Some colors have different meanings in different contexts (Horton; White). For example, when many U.S. readers see instructions printed in red, they associate the red with danger. However, when they see the color red while driving, they know to stop. In business, red is often associated with power. In the United States and other Western cultures, people associate black with death and mourning. In some contexts, black connotes formality and power. However, people in China associate white with death. As you select colors for your document, consider what the color may indicate for your readers, especially those readers from other cultures.

- **Use color to unify a document or a series of documents.** Used consistently, color can unify a document or a series of documents. Throughout one document or a series, use the same color for the same types of information or visuals. For example, if you use blue for the headers, footers, and bullets of the first document in a series, use the same shade of blue in all other documents in the series.

White Space

Readers look for relationships among the elements on a page—text, visual aids, headings. Those elements should look as though they belong together;

otherwise, readers may be confused. To create a unified layout, frame the page or screen elements with white space, or blank space (Lay; Yeo). To use white space effectively, follow these tips:

▶ **Tips for Using White Space**

- **Push related elements together with white space.** White space "pushes" page elements together (Lay 73–75), helping readers to see what elements belong together. For example, leave more white space before a heading than you leave after it, so readers can see clearly what text the heading describes.

- **Surround with white space any elements that you want to emphasize.** By simply surrounding elements with white space, you will emphasize them. For example, notice that white space surrounds the bullets in this textbook. The text aligns to the right of the bullet, not under the bullet; and the white space highlights the bullet. If the text aligned under the bullet (see Figure 9.13), the displayed list would be less visible on the page or screen.

- **Set off elements such as headings, bullets, and graphics with white space.** The white space will increase their visibility and allow readers to locate them easily.

▶For more information on designing online documents, see Chapter 16, "Creating User-Oriented Web Sites."

Navigation Tools

For online documents, include navigation tools to help readers move from page to page and to locate information and pages. The most commonly used navigation tools are buttons, icons, and text. As you design navigational tools, follow these tips:

▶ **Tips for Designing Navigation Tools**

- **Place navigation tools at the top or bottom of the screen.** These tools should provide relevant, descriptive links to other places in the document (Yeo 13).

- **Include a button that brings readers back to the homepage or the main menu page.**

- **Place all navigation tools in the same position on each screen.**

- **Use the same design for the tools throughout the document.**

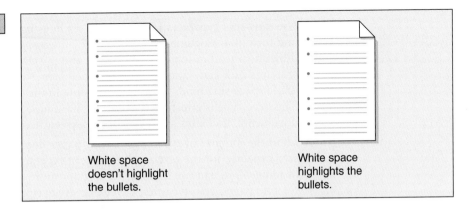

Figure 9.13

Using White Space in Bulleted Lists

White space doesn't highlight the bullets.

White space highlights the bullets.

▶Principle 4: Choose Design Elements to Help Readers Read Your Documents

As you plan, consider design elements that will make your document easy for readers to read. When you select the type in which your text will appear, consider the typeface, type size, and type style of each text element. The type that you select can "help or hinder" the readability of your document (Parker 47).

Appropriate Typefaces

When selecting the appropriate type for your documents, you can select from two different groupings of typefaces: serif and sans-serif (see Figure 9.14). A **serif** is a short stroke or line at the top or bottom of a letter. In serif type, the thickness of some of the strokes of a letter may vary, helping readers to distinguish the shapes of letters. In sans-serif type—type without serifs (*sans* means "without" in French)—no small strokes project from the top or bottom of the letters, and, generally, the thickness of the lines of a letter is uniform.

Follow these tips to select the appropriate serif or sans-serif typeface:

▶ **Tips for Selecting Serif and Sans-serif Typefaces**

- **Use serif typefaces for paper text.** Use serif type for most paper text because the serifs guide readers' eyes from letter to letter; the serifs help readers to see the text "in terms of words and sentences instead of as individual letters" (Parker 60). Serifs and the variations in stroke thickness help readers to distinguish between letters with similar shapes (*l* and *I* for example) and to recognize the shapes of all letters.

(continued on next page)

- **Use sans-serif typefaces for titles and headings in paper documents and for online documents.** In paper documents, sans-serif type is difficult to read in long blocks of text and in small sizes, but small amounts of it can "add impact to a document," especially when white space surrounds the elements printed in it (Parker 61–62). Sans-serif type is effective for the text, headings, and titles of online documents. It creates a more readable screen than does serif type.

- **Limit the number of typefaces in your paper documents to two:** a serif typeface for the text and a sans-serif typeface for the titles and headings. You can use a different, perhaps more decorative typeface for title pages, chapter titles, covers, or divider pages. Otherwise, use no more than two typefaces in a paper document.

- **Select a typeface that is easy to read.** Your word-processing or desktop publishing software may offer decorative or script typefaces. You can use them for logos, title pages, chapter titles, divider pages, and covers. However, text set in these typefaces is uninviting and hard to read (see Figure 9.15).

Figure 9.14

Examples of Serif and Sans-serif Typefaces

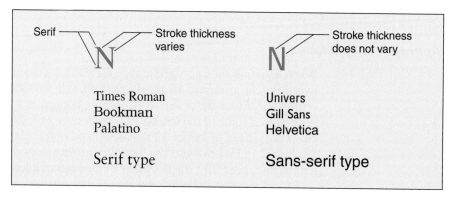

Figure 9.15

An Example of Text Set in a Hard-to-Read Typeface

What is your procedure if someone is out sick, and do you have a substitute list? The school has a skeleton list of substitutes. Since good substitutes are hard to find, we see how the other classrooms look as far as ratios go. The younger the child the higher the priority—the younger the child the lower the ratio. We also would like to have a permanent floater who goes from classroom to classroom on an as-needed basis. We can also call the Springfield school to see how the situation looks over there. If necessary, we can bring someone over from Springfield.

Appropriate Type Sizes for Text and Headings

Type size is measured in points; 72 points equal one inch. Most word-processing and desktop publishing programs allow you to adjust the type size up to 72 points. When deciding what sizes of type to use in your documents, follow these tips:

> ▶ **Tips for Selecting the Appropriate Type Size**
>
> - **For text,** use 10- or 12-point type.
> - **For headings and most titles,** use a larger type size. Generally use a type size 20 percent larger than the text type size. For example, if the text type size is 12 points, use a 14-point type for the headings. The title can be in a slightly larger type size.
> - **For footnotes,** use 8- or 10-point type.
> - **For slides,** use 24- to 36-point type. (For more information on slides, see Chapter 17.)

Appropriate Type Styles and Case

With word processing and desktop publishing programs, you can modify the appearance of the type to create different looks in your document. With most word-processing software, you can use boldface, italics, underlining, shadowing, outlining, and reversed type. Change type style with discretion and consistency. These styles can improve your documents' appearance by providing "visual relief in an otherwise uniform page of text" (Felker et al. 72). However, if overused, these type styles can clutter the page or screen, confuse readers, and fail to focus readers' attention on what you intended to communicate. To use type styles and case effectively, follow these tips:

> ▶ **Tips for Selecting Type Styles and Case**
>
> - **Use boldface type to add emphasis.** Boldface type increases the visibility of headings and individual words and phrases. In paper documents, use boldface for headings and, sparingly, to emphasize isolated words in blocks of text; do not use it for entire paragraphs or more than two or three lines of type. In online documents, designers recommend that you reserve boldface type for headings (Yeo 14).
> - **Use italics to add emphasis.** Italics also increase the visibility of isolated words and short phrases, though less dramatically than
>
> (continued on next page)

boldface. Avoid overusing italic type. Use it for isolated words and short phrases, such as for non-English words, not for entire paragraphs or large blocks of text.

- **Use shadowed, outlined, and reversed type sparingly.** These type styles can "seriously hinder legibility" and are especially hard to read in small sizes and in uppercase letters (Parker 67). If you use reversed type, use a sans-serif typeface in a relatively large size.

- **Avoid underlining.** Underlining interferes with readers' ability to recognize the shapes of some letters. It can distort letters with descenders—*y, j, p, q, g*—and marks of punctuation such as commas and semicolons. Instead of underlining, use boldface, italics, or color.

- **Avoid text in uppercase (capital) letters.** Text in upper- and lowercase letters is easier to read than text printed in uppercase letters. Lowercase letters take up less space, so readers can "take in more words as they scan a line of text"; and lowercase letters give each word a distinct shape, which helps readers to recognize and recall (Benson 41). Shape helps readers distinguish letters and identify words (Felker et al. 87). As Figure 9.16 shows, all words set in uppercase letters have the same basic shape or outline, but words set in lowercase or in both upper- and lowercase letters have different shapes. The uniform shape of words set in uppercase letters slows readers' ability to recognize each word.

Unjustified Right Margin

When lines of text are of different lengths and do not align on the right, the text is **unjustified** or **ragged**. When lines of text are equal in length, the text is said to be **justified**, and the right margin *even* (see Figure 9.17). Readers find text with unjustified right margins easier to read (Benson 41). When line lengths vary, readers' eyes can move more easily from one line to the next. When text is justified, the lines all look the same, and readers can't easily distinguish one line from the next and may find their eyes moving to the wrong line as they read down a page or screen. You will see justified type in many books and formal documents.

The space between words in justified text is inconsistent. From one line to the next, the space between words may vary so that all lines will align evenly on the right side of the page or screen. This inconsistent spacing can slow reading and make readers wonder whether a word is missing. In the justified example in Figure 9.17, notice the inconsistent spacing between words and the uniformity in line lengths. In the unjustified example in the figure, notice the uniform spacing between words that results when the right margin is unjustified.

THE READER'S CORNER

Typography

Typography—the design and selection of letter forms—began with the ability to print from movable type around 1450. The three major type families—gothic, roman, and italic—were all based on the Latin script used by calligraphers. During the Middle Ages, scribes throughout Europe had developed a convenient single-stroke approach. Dominant when the first printing presses emerged in Germany, this major calligraphic form served as the basis of the typeface known as gothic. In Italy, however, where the humanist movement celebrated the ancient classical writers and their emphasis on individual dignity, the dark, imposing gothic letters seemed inappropriate for new editions of classical authors such as Cicero. Admiring the rounded calligraphy used by the classical authors themselves, Italian printers developed a type they called "antiqua" to distinguish it from the "modern" gothic. Known today as "roman," this typeface spread with humanist thought throughout western Europe; Germany alone continued to favor the gothic typeface. The third major type family, italic, replicated the fast, informal cursive used by chancellery clerks; when it debuted early in the 1500s, printers used it, like gothic and roman, for entire texts. Within a few decades, however, printers judged italic more appropriate for specific situations (such as non-English words), a judgment with which most contemporary typographers would agree.

Figure 9.16   Text Set in Uppercase Letters and in Upper- and Lowercase Letters

> Because readers recognize words by their shape, text in
>
> UPPERCASE LETTERS IS HARDER TO RECOGNIZE.

Figure 9.17   A Comparison of Justified and Unjustified Right Margins

Justified Text

Spacing between words is inconsistent —

Lines are the same length —

Justified text gives documents a formal look; but it is harder to read than unjustified text, and the inconsistent spacing between words may bother your readers. Unjustified text gives documents a more open look. The unequal line lengths of unjustified text help readers to move smoothly from line to line and eliminate the inconsistent spacing associated with justified text.

Unjustified Right Margin

Spacing between words is consistent —

Line length varies —

Justified text gives documents a formal look; but it is harder to read than unjustified text, and the inconsistent spacing between words may bother your readers. Unjustified text gives documents a more open look. The unequal line lengths of unjustified text help readers to move smoothly from line to line and eliminate the inconsistent spacing associated with justified text.

▶Conclusion

With the tremendous options available for designing documents with word-processing and desktop publishing software, you may want to use a wide assortment of design options such as various page layouts, heading styles, typefaces, type appearances, and type sizes in one document. However, if you use too many of these options or overuse any one of them, you will weaken your document and perhaps even cause your document not to achieve its intended purpose.

Good design does not call attention to itself; it is invisible to readers. You want readers to notice what you are trying to communicate. If readers primarily notice your design, then your design may not be simple enough. To create simple, effective designs, consistently use a carefully selected page layout with appropriate white space and select effective and appropriate heading styles, typefaces, and type sizes. Figures 9.18 and 9.19 (see pages 248 and 249) illustrate many of the principles of good design. For the document in Figure 9.19, the company required the designers to put all the information on one 8½-by-11 inch page (front and back). The designers have effectively designed the document to include much information in a small space.

WORKSHEET for Designing Documents for Your Readers

▶ **Principle 1: Consider the Design as You Plan Your Documents**
- Did you use thumbnail sketches to help you consider possible page layouts?
- If you used a preformatted template, did it follow good design principles?
- Did you use the styles function of your word-processing software?
- If you're working with a team, did you create a style sheet and styles or use your company's style sheet?

▶ **Principle 2: Choose Design Elements to Motivate Readers to Read**
- Did you select an engaging, appropriate cover for a paper document, opening page for a Web site, or first screen for an online document?
- Did you select an appropriate binding for long paper documents?
- Did you use the appropriate paper for the readers and the purpose?
- Did you use a page size that meets the needs of the readers' environment?
- Did you select a paper color appropriate for the formality of the document?
- Did you use typefaces, type sizes, and type styles for headings and text consistently throughout the document?
- Did you put page numbers in the same place on every page?
- Did you put the page numbers in the outside top or bottom corner?
- Did you use the same paragraph indents and spacing between columns, within lists, and before and after headings?

▶ **Principle 3: Choose Design Elements to Help Readers Locate Information**

Document Level
- In long paper documents and Web sites, did you use document-level locating devices such as a table of contents, an index, or a main menu?

Chapter or Division Level
- Did you use chapter- or division-level locating devices such as tabs or divider pages?
- Did you use page- or screen-level locating devices such as headers, footers, headings, color, white space, or navigation tools?

Page and Screen Level
- Did you put more space above the headings than after the headings?
- Did you use a different type size (and possibly color) to indicate heading levels?
- Did you put the headings flush with the left margin?
- Did you use the same color throughout the document for the same type of information?
- Did you use color along with other devices, such as white space, boldface, or type size, so colorblind readers can locate information in your document?
- Did you use white space to surround elements that you want to emphasize?
- Did you place navigation tools at the top or bottom of the screen?
- Did you include a button that brings readers back the homepage or to the main menu?
- Did you use the same design for the navigation tools throughout the site or online document?

▶ **Principle 4: Choose Design Elements to Help Readers Read Your Documents**

Type Size
- Did you use a serif typeface for the text of paper documents?
- Did you use a sans-serif typeface for online documents?
- Did you use no more than two typefaces in paper documents?
- Did you select a typeface that is easy to read?
- Did you use 10- or 12-point type for the text?
- Did you use a larger type size for first-level headings and titles?

Type Style and Case
- Did you use type styles, such as boldface and italics, effectively and consistently?
- Did you avoid underlining?
- Did you use upper- and lowercase letters instead of all uppercase letters?
- Did you use unjustified text (ragged right margins)?

Figure 9.18   A Quick Reference Card from Centex Construction Group

All headings are in the same color. The designers have used only two colors for the type.

The designers have used a sans-serif typeface for the headings and a serif typeface for the text.

Color, italics, and white space emphasize the tips.

The designers have put more space before the headings and less space after.

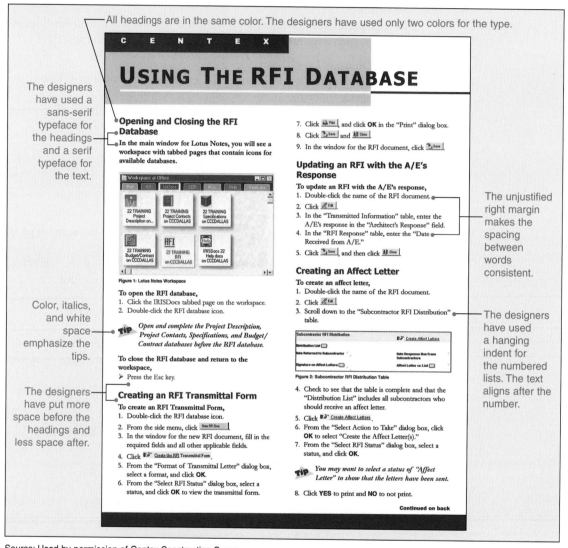

The unjustified right margin makes the spacing between words consistent.

The designers have used a hanging indent for the numbered lists. The text aligns after the number.

Source: Used by permission of Centex Construction Group.

Figure 9.19 A Page from an Internal Training Manual at Centex Construction Group

Chapter 3
Keeping the Participants Interested

Modified hanging headings help readers to locate information.

Once you have your equipment in place and you have planned and rehearsed your presentation, you're almost ready. However, you can improve your chances for a successful presentation by understanding ways to keep your participants interested (and awake). In other words, put yourself in your participants' seat! This chapter will present some strategies to help you keep participants interested:

- Give participants only the information they need.
- Anticipate participants' needs and questions.
- Provide participants with a "road map" and examples.
- Help participants enjoy your presentation.

The designers effectively use color to emphasize the headings. Notice that a colorblind reader could still easily locate the headings because they appear in boldface type as well as color.

Strategy 1: Give Participants Only the Information They Need

Keep your presentation short and simple. Participants want to hear only the information they need and no more. As you prepare for your presentation, consider the following:

- **Listening to information takes twice as long as reading that same information.** Thus, if you can read 10 pages in 8 minutes, your participants can comprehend the same information in about 16 minutes.
- **Condense your presentation into a few points.** Don't try to give participants every bit of information you have about a topic or all the tiny details. Instead, select the key points and present those. If necessary, you can refer your participants to the quick reference cards or to other printed handouts.
- **Plan the presentation to take slightly less then the allotted time.** Look for ways to tighten your presentation, so you have time for the participants to ask questions. Your participants will prefer a presentation that is a couple of minutes short rather than a presentation that exceeds the allotted time.

The designers have used a hanging indent for the bulleted lists. The text aligns after the bullets.

The designers have used a sans-serif typeface for the headings and a serif typeface for the text.

Strategy 2: Anticipate Participants' Needs and Questions

As you are preparing and even as you are speaking, think about what participants already know and what they will want to know about the topic.

- **Customize your presentation according to what you know about your participants.** You will always begin your presentation with the same four databases: Project Description, Project Contacts, Specifications, and

Source: Used by permission of Centex Construction Group.

► **EXERCISES**

1. Find a paper or online document that has an *ineffective* design. Look for such documents on the Web, on campus, at home, or at work. Write a memo to your instructor explaining the problems with the design. With your memo, include a photocopy or printout of the document.

2. Redesign two pages or screens of the ineffective document that you found for Exercise 1. Be sure to correct the design problems that you identified in your memo for Exercise 1.

3. Write a memo to your instructor evaluating the design of the report "What You Can Do About Lyme Disease" in Figure 9.20.

4. Revise the page design of "What You Can Do About Lyme Disease." Rewrite any passages necessary to improve the report. Be sure to correct the problems that you identified in your memo for Exercise 3 and any style errors. You will find an electronic copy of this report on the Web site for this book.

5. Write a memo to your classmates telling them how to create a template in the word-processing software that you use on your campus. Give your classmates the information they need to create a template.

6. Working with a team assigned by your instructor, find and redesign two documents. Follow these steps to complete this exercise.

   • **Step 1: Organize your team.**

      a. Select a team leader to serve as managing editor of the project. The managing editor is responsible for communicating with your instructor, handing in the final documents, assigning tasks when necessary, and proofreading the final documents.

      b. Exchange telephone numbers and/or e-mail addresses.

   • **Step 2: Locate the documents.**

      a. Find two documents that are poorly designed or have an outdated design. These documents should be part of a series of documents or should be from the same organization. Each document should be no longer than two pages (or one page front and back). You want to create a unified look for the two documents.

      b. Ask your instructor to approve the documents.

      c. When your instructor approves the documents, make copies for each team member.

      d. If you have access to a scanner, scan the documents so the team will have access to an electronic copy.

   • **Step 3: Plan the design of the documents.**

      a. Make a list of the design problems that you need to solve.

      b. Create a style sheet for redesigning the documents.

      c. Create thumbnail sketches for possible page designs.

      d. When you have decided on a sketch for your design, determine the page size that will work best for your design.

      e. Create a template for your design.

   • **Step 4: Using the style sheet and template, rewrite and redesign the documents.**

      a. Correct any style errors in the original documents. See Chapters 7 and 8.

      b. Hand in your documents to your instructor. Attach copies of the original documents.

Figure 9.20   The Document for Exercises 3 and 4

WHAT YOU CAN DO ABOUT LYME DISEASE

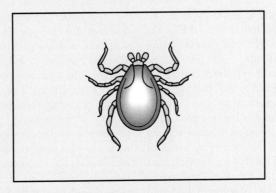

Figure 1. *Ixodes scapularis, the black-legged tick, is a suspected vector of Lyme disease in Texas.*

Like buckling up when you enter a car, there are certain positive safety measures you can take to reduce the probability of being exposed to ticks and the new summertime disease known as Lyme disease. Use of repellents, wearing proper clothing, and knowing how to spot and remove ticks before they become firmly attached, are all effective methods of reducing the possibility of being exposed to Lyme disease.

Lyme disease, so named because it was first identified near the town of Lyme, Connecticut, causes symptoms that often include a circular rash and accompanying flu-like symptoms. If left untreated, symptoms can include painfully stiff joints and other neurological complications.

Lyme disease is transmitted primarily, if not exclusively, by ticks. Ticks are small arachnids, related to insects, and can be identified by having eight legs and a flattened, leathery body (Fig. 1).

Ticks feed on blood from a variety of animals such as birds, reptiles, raccoons, deer, dogs, cattle, and man. Unfortunately, in the process of feeding on more than one host during its lifetime,

ticks can act as carriers of disease organisms, carrying germs from infected to healthy animals. In the northeastern states, Lyme disease is transmitted by the deer tick, *Ixodes dammini*, from mice, deer, and other wild and domestic animals. Little is yet known about the wild carriers of the disease in Texas.

Although the number of cases in Texas is on the rise, the Lyme disease problem hasn't become as serious as in the Northeast and Great Lakes regions. Eighty-two confirmed cases of Lyme disease were reported by the Texas Department of Health, with the majority of these cases being reported from the eastern and northeastern portions of the state.

The best way to deal with this disease is to take measures to avoid being bitten by ticks. This means wearing appropriate protective clothing outdoors, avoiding tick-infested sites, and using tick repellents. When in wooded areas it is best to wear long pants with the cuffs tucked into the socks.

(continued on next page)

▼ **Figure 9.20**   (Continued)

Ticks typically hitch rides on humans from their perches on grass blades or low brush. Once picked up on a shoe, sock, or pants leg they climb upwards until they find a suitable place to attach. Tucking pants legs into the sock eliminates one of the most popular sites for ticks to gain access to the skin. Use of repellents such as diethyl toluamide (DEET), the active ingredient in OFF® and most other commercial insect repellents, will give some protection from ticks. Newer repellents containing permethrin, which are applied to the clothing, both repel and kill ticks before they can attach.

You should carefully examine yourself and other family members following an outdoor activity in potentially tick-infested sites. Carrying a roll of masking tape on outings is handy for removing ticks that have not yet attached to the skin. Pressing the sticky side of the tape on the crawling tick should easily remove it from the skin.

Should you find a tick attached to the skin, the following procedures should be used for removal:

Use blunt tweezers or disposable gloves to handle the tick. If fingers must be used, shield them with a tissue or paper towel. Infectious agents may be picked up through mucous membranes or breaks in the skin by handling infected ticks. This is especially important for people who "detick" pets or other domestic animals, as ticks infesting dogs and other domestic animals can carry Lyme disease or several other diseases capable of infecting humans.

Grasp the tick as close to the skin surface as possible. This reduces the possibility of the head detaching from the body upon removal.

Pull the tick straight out with a steady, even pressure. Do not twist or jerk the tick as this may cause the mouthparts to break off and remain in the skin, increasing the chances of infection. Continue the steady pressure even if the tick does not release immediately—it may take a minute or so of pulling to cause the tick to release.

After removing the tick, thoroughly disinfect the bite site and wash your hands with soap and water. Home remedies such as applying Vaseline®, grease, or a hot match to the rear of the tick are not recommended. These practices cause the tick to salivate and can actually increase the chance of getting the disease.

After removing the tick, you may wish to preserve it in alcohol—plain old rubbing alcohol will do. Be sure to label the container with information about the time and place where the tick bite occurred. This activity will help you to remember details of the incident if the rash or other symptoms associated with Lyme disease appear later. This information will also be of help to a physician in diagnosing the illness.

Fortunately, prompt treatment with antibiotics is very effective in curing Lyme and other tick-borne diseases, but most people agree that protecting yourself from tick bites in the first place is the best approach.

Note: The information given herein is for educational purposes only. Reference to commercial products or trade names is made with the understanding that no discrimination is intended and no endorsement by the Cooperative Extension Service is implied.
D4 Misc. Leaflet D4001   4-92

Source: Michael Merchant, *What You Can Do About Lyme Disease* (College Station: Texas Agricultural Extension Service, n.d.). Used by permission of the author.

A "Disastrous" Design

Background

You are the manager of a large computing facility at a university. The facility employs 150 employees spread over several buildings on campus and has equipment worth millions of dollars. You are responsible for the safety of the employees and the equipment. Recently, the facility lost some important equipment because of flooding after spring rains. During the flooding, some employees were injured and taken to a local hospital.

You want to prevent such damage and injury in the future, not only when flooding occurs but also when other emergencies—fires, tornadoes, bomb threats—arise. You decide to review and revise the "emergency situations" instructions that all your employees receive. As you read these instructions, you notice some design and style problems:

- Readers can't easily scan and locate information.
- The instructions contain unnecessary information.
- The instructions contain many sentence and language problems.
- The layout of the instructions are in a format that readers won't use in an emergency. Readers need a layout that will allow them to quickly see and follow emergency instructions.

Assignment

The "emergency situation" instructions for your computing facility appear in Figure 9.21. You can find an electronic copy of these instructions on the Web site for *Technical Communication for Readers and Writers*. For this assignment, revise and redesign the instructions, creating a layout appropriate for the readers who will use the instructions in emergency situations. As you revise and redesign, consider the following:

- Use any size page or any page layout that is appropriate for the readers and your purpose.
- Include only information that readers will need in an emergency. Remember that in an emergency readers may have only minutes, or perhaps even seconds, to get out of the building or to decide how to proceed. You may eliminate any information that is unnecessary for the readers.
- Correct any style errors.
- Select a layout that will allow readers to quickly see and follow the emergency instructions.

| **Figure 9.21** | The Document for the Case Study "A 'Disastrous' Design" |

EMERGENCY SITUATIONS

Emergency situations can occur from natural or man created circumstances. Prior consideration of actions to be taken during emergencies can help reduce the confusion caused by such disruptions. It is not possible to attempt to cover all potential disaster situations. The situations that will be addressed by this procedure are fire, flood, tornado, and bomb threats. This procedure is only intended to be a guide. Each person will be expected to use common sense in addition to this procedure to insure their own personal safety, and the safety of other personnel in the Computing Center as well.

ASSISTANCE NOTIFICATION

During any emergency situation, Computing Center personnel will probably need assistance from some other group in dealing with contingency problems. In order to ease personnel tension and help avoid confusion for all departments on campus, the Police Department has been designated to be the initial contact for all emergency services. Therefore, any time an emergency situation occurs (fire, flood, tornado, bomb threat, etc.), the first thing to do will be to notify the Police. In order to expedite a request for assistance, the Police Department suggests that the following procedure be used:

(1) Call Emergency Number 113
(2) State the situation. Example: "We have a fire."
(3) State the location of the emergency. Example: "In room 617 of the Administration Building."
(4) Reaffirm your desire for assistance. Example: "Please send help."
(5) Stay on phone as long as possible to give additional information.

EVACUATION RALLY POINT

Whenever it may be necessary or advantageous to evacuate a building, the problem of determining whether or not everyone gets safely out of the building arises. In order to verify that everyone does evacuate, Rally Points have been established for Computing Center personnel. When you evacuate a building because of an emergency situation, please go to the Rally Point as quickly as possible and check in so you can be accounted for. If you fail to follow this procedure, a decision may be made for someone to reenter the building to make a search for you. Needless to say, if you have evacuated the building safely, your failure to check in may cause injury or loss of life to the personnel trying to find you.

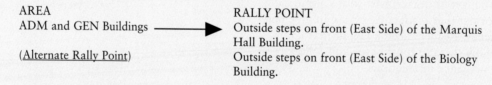

AREA	RALLY POINT
ADM and GEN Buildings ⟶	Outside steps on front (East Side) of the Marquis Hall Building.
(Alternate Rally Point)	Outside steps on front (East Side) of the Biology Building.

If you are at work but plan to be away from your work-station for an extended period, you should notify a coworker to that effect. That way, your absence may be accounted for at the Rally Point. Additionally, if you are at some other location on campus and hear of an emergency at the Computing Center, you should go to your designated Rally Point and check in.

(continued on next page)

Figure 9.21	(continued)

FIRE CONTROL

In all probability, a fire from either accident or civil disturbance is the most likely emergency situation to occur. Most buildings on campus should have fire and smoke detection systems installed. These systems are tied in with the buildings' electrical system with battery backup for operation during power outages. In addition to fire and smoke sensors located throughout a building, fire alarms can be signaled by activating the emergency pull switches located in strategic places such as main entrance ways and designated exits. The alarm system should provide for automatic notification of a fire to the Police Department. However, for safety measures, a fire in the Computing Center should be reported by phone (113) to the Police Department, who will in turn notify the fire department. The Fire Department estimates a response time within seven (7) minutes from time of notification.

PERSONNEL SAFETY

The most important resource the Computing Center has is the people that work here. Some of the activities listed below have employees taking action against a fire. The employees involved are expected to exercise individual discretion when making decisions on the proper course of action to take against a fire. The rule to live by should be, "When in Doubt, Shout, and Get Out" (i.e., evacuate to the designated Rally Point).

CONTROLLING SMALL FIRES

Small fires usually do not need the expertise of professional firefighters to put them out. For our purpose, a small fire is defined as a fire that has not spread beyond its point of origin. When possible, an attempt should be made to control small fires by utilizing the portable hand held fire extinguishers, which are located in strategic areas of the Computing Center. Usually, a small fire can be controlled in less than sixty (60) seconds. The hand held fire extinguisher will usually be empty after one (1) minute of continuous usage.

In the Computing Building, there are three (3) portable fire extinguishers strategically located in the Input/Output Area in Room 633B. One is kept on the wall in the Forms Storage Area immediate adjacent to the main entrance door to the Input/Output Area. A second one is kept in the wall cabinet opposite the electrical panels that are installed beside the main entrance hall to the Input/Output Area. A third portable fire extinguisher is kept on the South wall adjacent to the East end of the Air Conditioning Unit in the Input/Output Area.

In Control Center, there are seven (7) portable fire extinguishers strategically located in the High Security Computer Room. One is kept in the wall cabinet on the South wall, adjacent to the HALON Fire Control Panel. One is kept on the outside corner wall of the Communications Room, across from the UPS Electrical Closet. One is kept on the East wall in the Lounge Area, adjacent to the Microwave Oven. One is kept on the North wall, adjacent to the West wall of the Forms Storage Room. One is kept on the North wall, adjacent to the East wall of the Disk Room. One is kept midway on the West wall in the Disk Room. Another is kept midway on the East wall in the Disk Room.

In order to keep confusion to a minimum in the event of a fire, each individual must routinely practice fire prevention when on the job, keep informed of fire extinguisher locations and operation,

(continued on next page)

know both primary and alternate evacuation routes, and always give top priority to personnel safety when taking action against any fire. If and when a fire occurs, the person first noticing the fire should take the responsibility to obtain the closest extinguisher and attempt to control the fire. Simultaneously, this person should ask another coworker for assistance in either controlling the fire, sounding a fire alarm, notifying the Police, and/or assisting in evacuating the building.

FIRE CONTROL PROCEDURE FOR COMPUTING BUILDING PERSONNEL

The senior (I/O) operator will be the person expected to determine the appropriate action to take against a fire. If the senior operator decides not to fight the fire, or if an attempt to control a fire fails:

(1) Notify the Police Department (Phone 113).
(2) Sound building fire alarm.
(3) Evacuate the building.
(4) Wait at Rally Point for further instructions.

FIRE CONTROL PROCEDURE FOR CONTROL CENTER PERSONNEL

The Console Operator will be the person expected to determine the appropriate action to take against a fire. However, even if the operator does decide to try controlling a fire with a portable fire extinguisher, this action must be taken within the guidelines of the Official Fire Plan for the Control Center, due to the HALON 1301 Fire Detection and Suppression System that is installed. The Official Fire Plan for the HALON 1301 protected zones follows:

OFFICIAL CONTROL CENTER FIRE PLAN (For the HALON 1301 Protected Zones)

In the event that the HALON 1301 Fire Extinguishing Agent has been released, the following steps are to be followed:

1. Personnel should not re-enter an area where the HALON 1301 has been discharged until the Police or Physical Plant personnel has given permission, even though the HALON 1301 is considered to be a non-toxic gas.
2. When notifying the Police Department, please be specific and state, "There has been a fire in the Control Center, Room ____, and the HALON Fire Extinguishing Agent has been discharged."
3. Notify the Physical Plant or Stand-by Maintenance to alert the Electrical and Heating/Air Conditioning Shops that the HALON 1301 has been discharged. Personnel at these shops have been advised that a HALON 1301 discharge is a priority item.
4. DO NOT ATTEMPT TO RESET THE BREAKER PANELS. The breakers on several electrical panels MUST be reset only by Electrical Shop employees.
5. DO NOT ATTEMPT TO RESET THE FIRE DAMPERS. The fire dampers MUST be reset by Electrical Shop and/or HVAC employees to restore air conditioning and return air to the affected HALON Zone(s).
6. DO NOT ATTEMPT TO RESTART ANY COMPUTER SYSTEM. All computer equipment MUST be checked for damage before restoring electrical power.

Source: Adapted from Computing Center, *Emergency Situations* (Denton: University of North Texas, n.d.). Reprinted courtesy of the University of North Texas Computing Center.

10

Creating Effective Visual Aids for Your Readers

▶ **OUTLINE**

Y ou've heard the expression "A picture is worth a thousand words." Indeed, you can often convey information in technical documents more effectively and efficiently with pictures than with words. You can often use "pictures"—visual aids—to explain abstract concepts; those same concepts described with words alone may be difficult for readers to understand. How can visual aids help readers?

- Visual aids can support and supplement the text. Visual aids especially help readers who are unfamiliar with concepts or who want to gather information at a glance.
- Visual aids can summarize the information in the text and present the information in a different way to help readers understand it.
- Visual aids can present some types of information more quickly and efficiently than words. For instance, using a map to show the locations of coral reefs is more efficient than using words for conveying the locations.

Visual aids can support the words and purpose of your documents. For instance, if your purpose is to show readers how to exit a building during a fire, diagrams of the building with arrows marking the exits will be much more effective than a paragraph describing the location of the exits. Many readers expect visual aids. Many expert readers, for example, expect tables and graphs summarizing the results of testing. Tables help readers to see relationships among test results or to spot trends.

Your readers are bombarded with visual information through television, advertising in all media, video games, movies, and the Web. Because readers are so accustomed to receiving information visually, they will often respond best to technical documents that use not only words but also visuals to convey information. Many of your readers may demand a visual as well as verbal presentation of some concepts and data. Without the visuals, many readers may abandon a document or miss important information because they may not read page after page of text.

However, in most documents, you can't rely solely on visual aids to communicate information. For example, in Figure 10.1, the writers rely primarily on pictures to tell the readers how to open the window exits and the airstair door exit. The readers neither need nor want a detailed verbal explanation of these procedures. Nevertheless, the writers do include brief step-by-step instructions for these procedures. The visual aids alone convey the message, but the written instructions serve to clarify if a reader needs more information.

To balance the visual and verbal elements, consider the needs of your readers and what you want to communicate. This chapter will help you to choose the most appropriate visual aids for readers and to strike the proper balance between visual and verbal elements.

| Figure 10.1 | Effective Drawings with Few Words |

Emergency and General Information

Window exits

Airstair door exit

To open the window exit:

1. Pull the red handle down.
2. Pull the window toward you.
3. Throw the window out of the exit.

To open the airstair door exit:

1. Pull the red handle.
2. Turn the handle in the direction indicated by the arrow.
3. Push away from you to open the door.

▶Principle 1: Look for Areas Where Visual Aids Will Help You Communicate

Think about the documents that you have read or that you might write at work. Many of them probably contain visual aids. Effective visual aids can help you convey part or all of a message. Before you select a visual aid, consider what readers expect from your document and what they know about the topic. Then follow these tips:

> ▶ **Tips for Planning Your Visual Aids**
>
> - **Plan the visual aids early in the writing process.** Think about the visual aids as you decide what information to include in the document. If you wait too long, you may not have the time or resources to create the visual aids that you need, or you may find that to add visual aids you will need to reformat the document. Begin planning the visual aids before you write the rough draft.
> - **Consider the different ways in which you can present information visually.** As you learned in Chapter 9, you can use design elements, such as headings, lists, and page layout, to present information visually.

Visual aids help you to

- Show how to follow instructions or explain a process
- Show what something looks like
- Show and summarize relationships among data
- Emphasize and reinforce information
- Show how something is organized
- Simplify complex concepts, discussions, processes, or data
- Add interest to your document

Show How to Follow Instructions or Explain a Process

▶ To learn more about using visual aids with instructions, see Chapter 15, "Writing User-Oriented Instructions and Manuals."

Visual aids are excellent tools for giving readers instructions or for explaining a process. Many instructions without visual aids are hard to follow. For example, imagine trying to learn how to do a partial curl-up (sometimes called a crunch) for the first time without a visual demonstration or pictures. Without a demonstration or pictures, these curl-ups—for most of us—would be difficult to do correctly. With pictures, you can easily learn how to do a curl-up (see Figure 10.2). Many readers could follow most of the instructions without referring to the written instructions.

Visual aids also help readers to visualize processes. Figure 10.3 illustrates the launch sequence of the *Centaur* shuttle. This diagram helps readers to visualize events that they cannot see from Earth.

▼ **Figure 10.2**

Drawings That Help
Readers Follow
Instructions

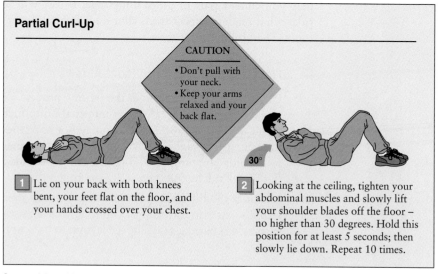

Source: Adapted from *The Fit Back Workout* (Daly City, CA: Krames Communications, 1990) 10.

Show What Something Looks Like

Visual aids such as photographs and drawings are excellent techniques for helping readers to see what something looks like. Often, you can only help readers to visualize a concept, theory, or object by including a visual aid. For example, Figure 10.4 is a digitized color photograph of an erupting volcano on Io, one of Jupiter's moons. This photograph helps scientists to study the amount of gas and dust in the eruption. The photograph easily illustrates differences for the amateur. Figure 10.5 shows a photograph of Whip coral. The photograph helps readers to visualize the coral. Each of these visual aids helps readers to quickly grasp a concept or to visualize something.

Show and Summarize Relationships Among Data

In some documents, you may want to display numerical data or show how one set of data relates to another. Perhaps you want to show the results of a laboratory test, a survey, or a trend or other changes over time. Visual aids permit readers to quickly see the relationships among the data.

Figure 10.3 A Diagram That Shows a Process

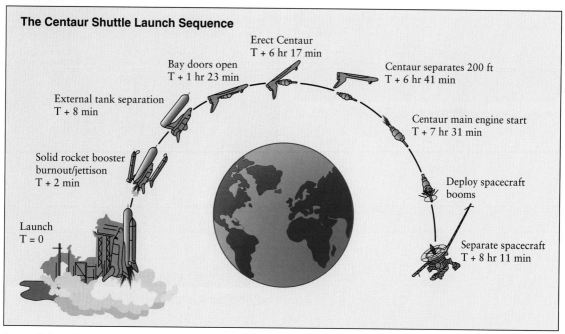

The Centaur Shuttle Launch Sequence

Erect Centaur
T + 6 hr 17 min

Bay doors open
T + 1 hr 23 min

Centaur separates 200 ft
T + 6 hr 41 min

External tank separation
T + 8 min

Centaur main engine start
T + 7 hr 31 min

Solid rocket booster
burnout/jettison
T + 2 min

Deploy spacecraft
booms

Launch
T = 0

Separate spacecraft
T + 8 hr 11 min

Source: National Aeronautics and Space Administration, *Galileo: Exploration of Jupiter's System* (Washington: GPO, 1985) 8.

You can use several types of visual aids to show relationships among numerical data. Figure 10.6 is a line graph that illustrates the dramatic change in enrollment at Baylor University after the signing of the GI Bill in 1944. The same numbers presented in a paragraph would not adequately convey the scope of the change. Figure 10.7 is a table that shows a relationship between acres mined and acres reclaimed. The table also summarizes by including the total acres mined and reclaimed.

 Figure 10.4 An Illustration That Shows What Something Looks Like

 Figure 10.5 A Photograph That Shows What Something Looks Like

Volcano Erupting on Io *(Photri-Microstock)*

Red Whip Coral *(Stefania Lamberti)*

Figure 10.6

A Line Graph That
Shows Relationships
Among Numerical
Data

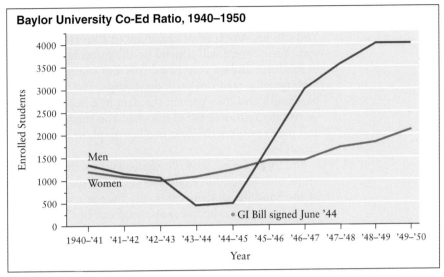

Baylor University Co-Ed Ratio, 1940–1950

Source: Judy Henderson Prather, "The G.I. Bill," *The Baylor Line* 57.1 (1995) 36. Reprinted by permission of *The Baylor Line*.

Figure 10.7

A Table Summarizing
Numerical Data

MINING & RECLAMATION				
Land Mined and Reclaimed	**Oh My Mine**	**Darling Mine**	**Clemintine Mine**	**Total (in acres)**
Mined in 2002	210	745	643	1,598
Mined Since 1990	13,465	20,442	13,456	47,363
Reclaimed in 2002	268	1,875	897	3,040
Reclaimed Since 1990	15,601	21,465	14,575	51,641

Emphasize and Reinforce Information

You can use any type of visual aid to emphasize information presented in the text. Your choice will depend on the information that you want to emphasize or reinforce and on your objectives. For example, if you want to emphasize the findings of a series of tests on airbags, you might first discuss the data in a paragraph and then present the data in a horizontal bar graph or a line graph to visually reinforce the discussion. You might also display the data in a table and then reinforce the data in a bar graph or line graph. Let's look at a specific example.

In *Drugs, Crime, and the Justice System,* the Bureau of Justice Statistics uses visual aids to reinforce and to emphasize the text discussion. In its discussion of the handling of drug cases, the Bureau uses bar graphs showing that drug cases, like other criminal cases, drop out of the criminal justice system at various stages (see Figure 10.8). These bar graphs compare drug cases with other types of criminal offenses.

Show How Something Is Organized

Often, readers need to know how something is organized; but they may have trouble understanding textual descriptions of an organizational structure.

▼ **Figure 10.8**

Bar Graphs That
Emphasize and
Reinforce Text
Information

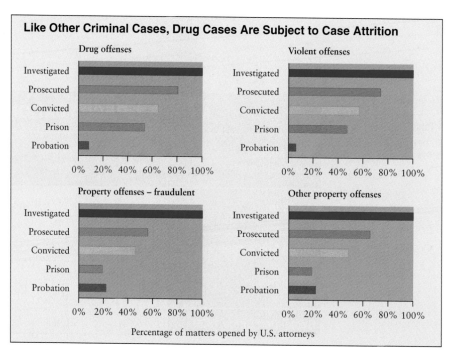

Source: Dept. of Justice, Bureau of Justice Statistics, *Drugs, Crime, and the Justice System* (Washington: GPO, Dec. 1992) 65.

Visual aids can make the organization clear. For example, the Web site for the National Credit Union Administration includes a chart showing how the administration is organized (see Figure 10.9). This chart quickly identifies the three offices that the board and chair oversee: the Office of Inspector General, the Executive Director, and the General Counsel. The chart also shows that the Office of the Executive Director oversees two types of offices: central and regional. Under regional offices, the chart includes a U.S. map showing the regions. Without the visual aid, readers of the Web site would have difficulty following a paragraph describing this organization. Notice also how the chart is designed to fit on the screen of a small as well as a large monitor. The chart uses color to show that all the central offices belong in the same group and are equal in the hierarchy. Traditional organizational charts use a horizontal

Figure 10.9

A Chart That Shows How Something Is Organized

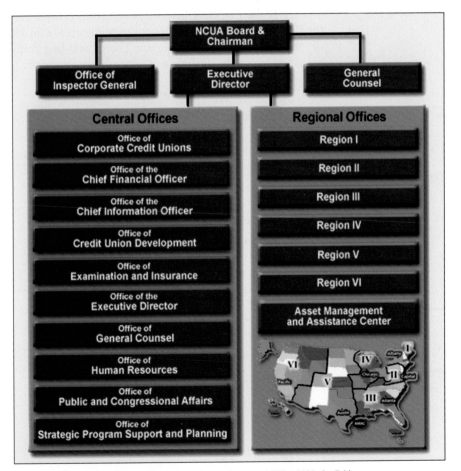

Source: National Credit Union Administration. Online. Internet. 15 May 2002. Available: http://www.ncua.gov/org/orgchart.html.

layout to show equal rank; however, the chart wouldn't fit on a screen if the central offices appeared horizontally rather than vertically.

Simplify Complex Concepts, Discussions, Processes, or Data

Complex information presented in prose is often difficult for readers to understand and analyze. The same information presented in a visual aid may be much easier to understand and analyze. For example, the scientists working on the Galileo mission wanted to show the stages of a probe's descent into Jupiter's atmosphere after being launched from the Galileo satellite. They used a graph to plot and briefly describe the probe's descent (see Figure 10.10). Even though the visual aid is complex, it still simplifies information that would be difficult to follow without a visual aid.

Figure 10.11 is another example of a visual aid that simplifies information. Writers at the National Science Foundation created these graphs to compare the U.S. research and development expenditures from 1982 to 1996 with those of other G-7 countries and Japan. The second line graph separates the nondefense research and development expenditures from the total expenditures. The

Figure 10.10   A Graph That Simplifies Complex Information

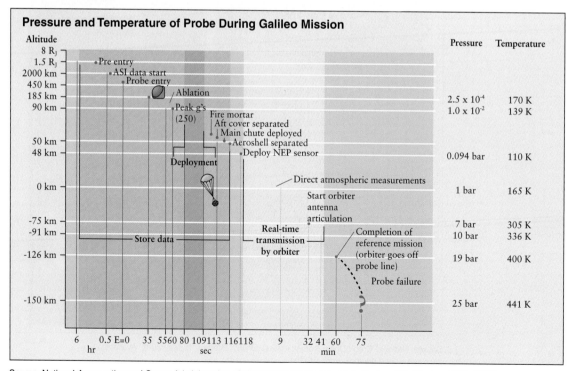

Source: National Aeronautics and Space Administration, *Galileo: Exploration of Jupiter's System* (Washington: GPO, 1985) 87.

Figure 10.11

Line Graphs That
Simplify Complex
Data

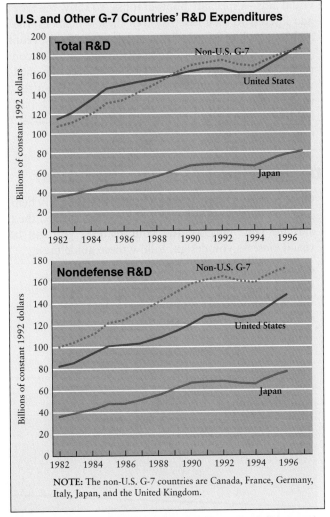

Source: National Science Foundation, National Science Board, *Science and Engineering Indicators* (Washington: GPO, 2000). Online. Internet. 17 Dec. 2001. Available: http://www.nsf.gov/sbe/srs/seind00/c2/fig02-27.htm.

information displayed in Figure 10.11 would be cumbersome to present and hard to follow in a paragraph. The graphs clearly compare the countries' expenditures and make the information easier to understand.

Add Interest to a Document

When used appropriately, visual aids such as photographs, pictographs, and decorative graphics can make your document more interesting and visually appealing. For example, when scientists discuss volcanic eruptions, they use visual aids—especially photographs—to show the eruptions and lava flows. To add interest to their discussion of these volcanoes, the scientists might include a photograph of Mount Etna, a volcano in Sicily, erupting (see Figure 10.12).

Some visual aids not only add interest but also convey important information. For example, Figure 10.13 compares the media that adults say they watch, read, or listen to for the daily news. The artist used bars proportioned to show the percentages for each media. On each bar, the artist added a hand holding a coin. This pictograph clearly adds interest to the document, but it also informs.

▶Principle 2: Design Visual Aids That Are Clear

Once you have found places where visual aids will help you to achieve the purpose of your document and you have determined the most appropriate visual aids for your purpose and your readers, you can begin to design effective visual aids. As you design, follow these guidelines:

- Use simple, uncluttered visual aids.
- Give each visual aid a number and a specific title.
- Consider whether international readers will read the visual aids.
- Use color to enhance and clarify visual aids.

Figure 10.12

A Photograph That
Adds Interest

Eruption of Mount Etna, Sicily *(Giampiccolo Images/FPG/Getty Images)*

Figure 10.13

A Pictograph That
Adds Interest and
Informs

Figure 10.13

The daily news
Media that adults say they watch, read or
listen to **every day** to get their news:

Local TV news	54%
Local newspapers	52%
Radio	49%
Network TV news	39%
National newspaper	9%
Internet/ on line	7%
Political talk radio	6%

Source: Copyright 1997, *USA Today*. Reprinted with permission.

Use Simple, Uncluttered Visual Aids

Your visual aids will be effective if your readers can quickly and easily
understand them. Readers will quickly and easily understand your visual aids
when the aids are simple and uncluttered. To create simple, uncluttered visual
aids, follow these tips:

> **Tips for Creating Simple, Uncluttered Visual Aids**
>
> - **Include only the information your readers need.** Avoid including too
>   much information.
> - **Try creating two or more visual aids to avoid overwhelming readers
>   with too much information in one visual aid.** If you have too much
>   information for one visual aid, you can either eliminate some of the
>   information or create two visual aids. If you use two visual aids,
>   make sure that each one clearly serves a purpose and enhances your
>   document.
> - **Try using diagrams and drawings to eliminate unnecessary detail.**
>   Photographs often have too much detail and clutter. Figure 10.14
>   compares a photograph and a drawing of the Mir space station.
>   The drawing more clearly shows the parts of the space station.
>
> (continued on next page)

Figure 10.14   A Comparison of a Photograph and Drawing of the Same Equipment

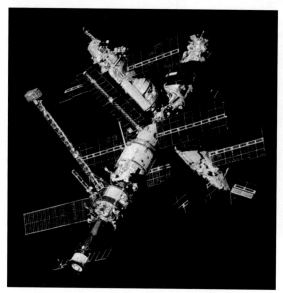

Mir Space Station *(Photo: NASA/SPL/Photo Researchers, Inc.)*

> • **Exclude distracting visual information in photographs.** Compare the photographs reproduced in Figure 10.15. The photograph on the left is ineffective because it includes distracting information. In the photograph on the right, the photographer has clarified the visual aid by eliminating the distracting information.

Give Each Visual Aid a Number and a Specific Title

Include a number (such as "Table 16" or "Figure 2.6") and a title with your visual aids. Numbers help readers locate the aids. Titles, or captions, identify the information in the visual aid. The titles should be brief yet informative phrases describing the content of the visual aid. Compare these examples:

Vague title   Figure 6. A figure showing inflation
Specific title   Figure 6. A comparison of inflation rates from 1984 to 1994

The vague title needlessly repeats "figure." The writer of the specific title uses "comparison" to indicate what the visual aid shows about inflation. The specific title also identifies the years that the visual aid covers, and it gives readers the information they need to locate a specific visual aid and to identify the information in it. To number visual aids, follow these tips:

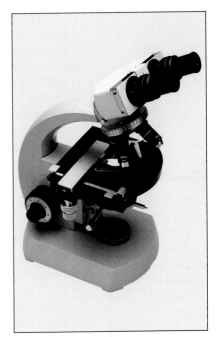

Figure 10.15

A Comparison of
Backgrounds in
Photographs

Cluttered Background   Simple Background

(left: Jay Freis/Image Bank/Getty Images; right: Eyewire Collection/Getty Images)

> **Tips for Numbering Visual Aids**
>
> - **Number the visual aids consecutively within each document.** If you don't divide your document into chapters, number the visual aids consecutively from the beginning to the end of the document.
> - **If you divide your document into chapters, number the visual aids in each chapter separately, starting with 1.** The numbering of visual aids starts over with each new chapter.
> - **Include the chapter number with the visual aid number.** For example, you would number the visual aids in Chapter 2 as 2.1, 2.2, 2.3, and so on, and those in Chapter 3 as 3.1, 3.2, 3.3, and so on.
> - **For some documents, use Arabic numerals (1, 2, 3, etc.) for figures and Roman numerals (I, II, III, etc.) for tables.** For some technical documents, readers may prefer or even expect separate numbering sequences for figures and tables. Figures are all visual aids that aren't tables. If you are unsure of what your readers expect, look at similar documents written by your coworkers or by others in your field. If you don't see a separate numbering sequence, use Arabic numerals for all visual aids, including tables.

You have several options for the location of the numbers and titles. In the past when writers prepared documents with a typewriter, figure numbers and titles always appeared below the figure, and table numbers and titles always appeared above the table. However, with the use of graphics software, the ground rules for placement are changing. Now, the placement of numbers and titles may vary from document to document. Decide where your readers are likely to look for the numbers and titles, or follow the conventions of your organization. Once you decide where to put the numbers and titles in a document, *consistently* put them in the same place throughout the document.

Consider Whether International Readers Will Use the Visual Aids

▶ For more information about writing for international readers, see Chapter 8, "Using Reader-Oriented Language," page 211.

Visual language, like verbal language, differs from nation to nation and culture to culture. A visual aid, for example, that is effective for your U.S. coworkers may not be appropriate for international workers. Consider these examples:

- British software designers used the wise old owl as an icon for the help file. The designers assumed that this image would work in the international community. However, in Hispanic countries, the owl symbolizes evil. In India, if someone calls you an owl, it means you are crazy (Bathon 24).
- People in Africa expect the label on a food product to have a picture of exactly what is in the jar or can: "WYSIWYG—'What you see is what you get' to eat." A baby food manufacturer should have used a picture of carrots—not a picture of a baby (Bathon 24).

In both examples, the writers and designers assumed that the international readers would interpret the pictures as most U.S. readers would interpret them. Differences among international readers make drawings, photographs, and symbols especially problematic.

Before you put visual aids into a final document, consider how readers in other countries and cultures will "read" them. When feasible, ask people of the same nationality as your readers to look at the visual aids you plan to use. These people can help you predict the success of a visual aid or can suggest ways to change it so international readers will read it as you intend. As you design visual aids for international readers, follow the guidelines in "Taking It into the Workplace."

Use Color to Enhance and Clarify Visual Aids

Color can be a powerful tool. However, according to Roger Parker and Patrick Berry, "the first question to ask yourself when considering color is not *how* to use it but *whether* to use it at all" (n.p.). As Parker and Berry explain, most documents can benefit from color if it's applied correctly. As you consider whether or not to use color, ask yourself these questions:

TAKING IT INTO THE WORKPLACE

The International Language of Graphics

"Always, always keep the audience in mind so that you use a medium, format, and colors that convey your message in the most effective manner possible to the targeted audience. Simplicity often works best no matter who your audience may be. Otherwise, the message can be lost in the delivery mechanism."

—Christine Clarke, Affiliation Manager, Alex Sheshunoff Management Services

Companies are increasingly using graphics due to the globalization of markets and of more widely used graphical user interfaces (Bosley). Graphics have several advantages for communicating with international readers:

- Graphics can "fit into space too small for text" (Bosley 5) and can "reduce the size and number of editions of documents" (Horton 682–683).
- Graphics can help a reader learn because they are less ambiguous. Readers find it "easier to see and understand than to see, translate, and then understand" (Horton 683).
- Graphics can improve reader comprehension (Horton).
- Graphics can replace some technical terms that writers can't easily translate (Bosley).

William Horton and Deborah Bosley suggest some guidelines for creating graphics for international readers:

- **Give graphics a neutral look** (Horton). For example, use a simple line drawing of a hand; the hand shouldn't appear to be masculine or feminine. Use outlines or neutral drawings such as stick figures to represent people (Bosley).
- **Use simple graphics.** Eliminate any unnecessary details (Bosley; Horton).
- **Use color only where the chosen color** doesn't cause readers to interpret the graphic incorrectly. The symbolic meaning of color varies among cultures. For example, in Japan, blue symbolizes "villainy," whereas in Arabic countries blue symbolizes virtue, faith, and truth. Bosley suggests using black and white or gray and white for international graphics, but Horton suggests that "color can prove especially valuable" if the writer carefully considers symbolic meanings (687).
- **Use graphics that don't have religious or English/North American connotations** (Bosley; Horton). For example, avoid light bulbs to indicate ideas or red, octagonal shapes to indicate "stop" (Bosley 7).
- **Consider the reading direction of the readers** (Horton). North American readers usually read graphics from left to right and clockwise; however, Middle Eastern readers read graphics from right-to-left in a counterclockwise direction (Bosley). Horton suggests designing international graphics that readers can read from top to bottom; the graphic might also include an arrow to direct the reader.

Assignment

Find a visual aid that an international company has used for its readers. The company must market its products or services internationally. After you find the visual aid, answer these questions in a memo to your instructor:

- Does the visual aid have a neutral look? Explain your answer.
- Does the visual aid use simple graphics with few, if any, words?
- Does the visual aid make the product or service easier to understand? If so, how? If not, how would you improve the visual aid?

- **Can you afford to use color?** Color printing costs are higher than costs for black-and-white printing. If color will enhance your visual aids, make sure that you have money in your budget for color.

- **Will color enhance the visual aid or add to its impact?** Certain visual aids are bland by nature and probably won't lose much impact if you use black and white. For example, the drawings of the *Galileo* in Figures 10.24 and 10.26 (see pages 281 and 283) don't need color.

- **Will my document compete with color documents?** (Parker and Berry n.p.) If your readers expect color visual aids, their absence could become a liability (Parker and Berry n.p.). However, color does not compensate for a poorly designed, inaccurate, or unclear visual aid.

If you decide that color will enhance your visual aids, follow these tips:

▶ **Tips for Using Color to Enhance and Clarify Visual Aids**

- **Don't overuse color.** (Parker and Berry n.p.) If you use too many colors in a document or even on one page, you probably won't impress your readers, and you may even confuse them. They may not know what you are trying to emphasize with the colors or if each color has a distinct meaning.

- **Choose colors that will give your documents a unified look.** You can use the color wheel (see Figure 10.16). When selecting colors for a document, pick analogous colors—three or four adjacent colors on

(continued on next page)

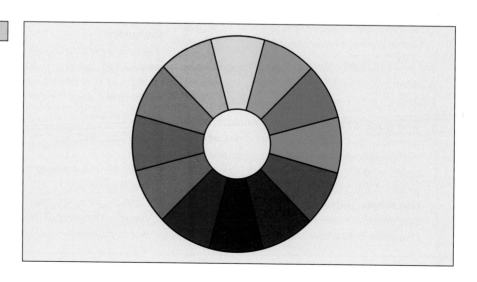

the color wheel (Parker and Berry n.p.). For example, you might select blue, green, and yellow.

- **Choose a triad of colors to create contrast in your visual aids.** A triad of colors is three colors that are relatively equidistant from each other on the color wheel—such as red, blue, and yellow (Parker and Berry n.p.).

- **Choose colors that stand out against the background to create effective contrast.** For example, don't use a shade of orange on an orange background; the readers can't easily see the shade of orange (see Figure 10.17). However, do use contrasting colors such as black and orange.

- **If your readers associate a color with a particular meaning, use that color as the readers expect.** For example, U.S. readers associate red with danger or warning and yellow with caution. However, for readers outside the United States these colors have different meanings.

- **If you want words or objects to look larger, use light colors.** Dark colors make objects look smaller. For example, look at the triangles in Figure 10.18. The triangles are the same size; however, the light green triangle looks larger than the purple triangle.

▶Principle 3: Select the Appropriate Visual Aid

Some visual aids are more appropriate for certain types of information and data than are others. Line graphs, for example, are more appropriate than pie charts for showing trends. You can use visual aids to achieve any of these purposes:

▾ **Figure 10.17**

Using Color to Create Contrast

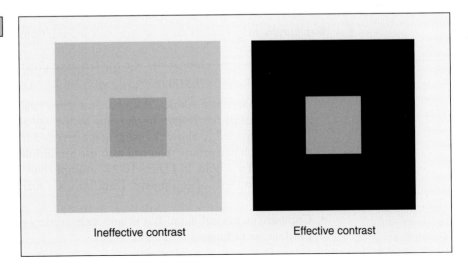

Ineffective contrast   Effective contrast

Figure 10.18

Light Colors Make
Objects Look Larger

- Showing what something looks like (drawings, photographs)
- Showing how to follow instructions (drawings, photographs)
- Explaining a process (flow charts, diagrams)
- Showing or summarizing relationships among data (tables, bar graphs, line graphs, pie charts, pictographs)
- Showing how something is organized (organizational charts)

You also can use visual aids to emphasize and reinforce information; to simplify concepts, discussions, processes, or data; and to add interest to a document. For these uses, you can select any type of visual aid appropriate to the information and to your readers.

In this section, you will learn about ten types of visual aids and the uses most appropriate for each one. Figure 10.19 summarizes the most appropriate uses for each of the visual aids discussed in this section.

Bar Graphs

Bar graphs help readers to compare and see relationships among numerical data. **Bar graphs** use horizontal or vertical rectangles—bars—to show numerical data. The taller or longer the bar, the larger or greater is the quantity of the numerical data. Use bar graphs when you want to do any of the following:

- **Show the parts of a whole.** Each bar in Figure 10.20 shows preferences among types of retirement investments by the age of the investor. Each bar is subdivided to show the percentage invested in stocks, bonds, and cash by each age group. You can also use a multiple-bar graph to show the parts of a whole. In Figure 10.21, multiple bars show industry spending on types of equipment. Data for each year appear in four bars.

- **Compare numerical data.** Bar graphs help readers to compare numerical data, as in Figures 10.20 and 10.21.

Figure 10.19

Uses of Visual Aids

Type of Visual Aid	Uses
Bar graph	Showing relationships among data Summarizing relationships among data
Diagram	Explaining a process
Drawing	Showing what something looks like Showing how to follow instructions
Flow chart	Explaining a process
Line graph	Showing relationships among data Summarizing relationships among data
Organizational chart	Showing how something is organized
Photograph	Showing what something looks like Showing how to follow instructions
Pictograph	Showing relationships among data Summarizing relationships among data
Pie chart	Showing relationships among data Summarizing relationships among data
Table	Showing relationships among data Summarizing relationships among data

Figure 10.20   A Divided Bar Graph

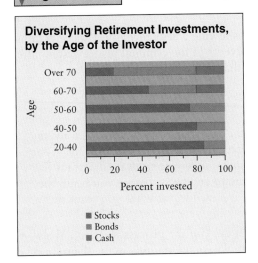

Figure 10.21   A Multiple-Bar Graph

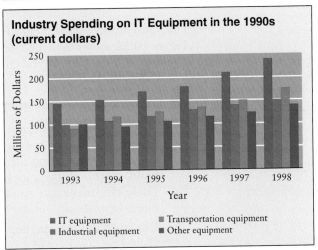

Source: National Science Foundation, National Science Board. *Science and Engineering Indicators* (Washington: GPO, 2000). Online. Internet. 17 Dec. 2001. Available: http://www.nsf.gov/sbe/srs/seind00/c9/fig09-06.htm.

- **Show trends.** Bar graphs can show trends over time. For example, Figure 10.21 shows how U.S. industries have spent money on information technology in relation to other types of equipment from 1993 to 1998. (Although bar graphs can show trends, line graphs generally are more effective for showing changes over time. See page 285.)

> ▶ **Tips for Creating Bar Graphs**
>
> - **Begin by creating the horizontal and vertical axes for the graph.** If you are using graphics software, the software will automatically prompt for information for creating these axes.
> - **Put tick (or hash) marks at regular intervals on the appropriate axis.** The tick marks should indicate quantities, such as percentages or amounts of money. Most graphics programs will automatically position the tick marks.
> - **Use an appropriate scale.** As a rule of thumb, extend the longest bar nearly to the end of its parallel axis, as in Figure 10.21 (see the 1998 IT technology bar).
> - **Label the bars appropriately.** Most readers prefer the labels at the beginning of the bar next to the appropriate axis. You can place the labels in a separate key (as in Figures 10.20 and 10.21), but this arrangement takes more time to read. If you decide to use a separate key, make the key easy to understand.

Diagrams

Diagrams are an excellent choice for showing a sequence of events or actions. Figure 10.22 shows the sequence of events in the criminal justice system after a felony has occurred. As you create diagrams, follow these tips:

> ▶ **Tips for Creating Diagrams**
>
> - **Sketch several rough drafts of the diagram.** You may need to make several preliminary drafts to determine exactly what you want in the diagram. Whether you use computer software or draw diagrams by hand, diagrams take a lot of time to create; so before you begin the final draft, make sure you have a clear idea of what you want the diagram to show.
> - **Use labels and explanations that explain the process clearly.** Labels should be easy to read. You can place explanations in the diagram if they won't interfere or cause clutter. If the explanations will be more confusing than helpful, you can explain the diagram in a paragraph that precedes or follows it.

Figure 10.22   A Diagram That Shows a Sequence of Events

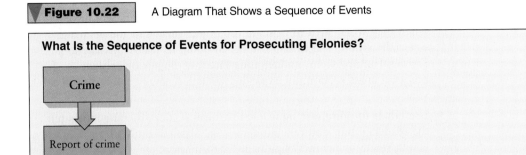

Drawings

Drawings are excellent visual aids for showing readers what something looks like and for instructing. Many writers select drawings instead of photographs to help readers see how something is put together. Drawings can emphasize important details or parts that are not apparent in a photograph. Drawings also allow you to explode (make larger) a particular detail. Figures 10.23, 24, 25, and 26 present drawings that help readers to see details. As you create drawings, follow these tips:

Tips for Creating Drawings

- **Give your drawings a professional look.** Try using computer software to create your drawings. Learning how to use most of the drawing software takes time and training, especially if you are creating complex drawings like those in Figures 10.23, 24, 25, and 26. If you plan to use computer software, allow time to learn how to use it. If you plan on creating drawings by hand, make sure that you have the tools and training to create drawings with a professional appearance.

(continued on next page)

- **Render your drawing from the same angle that readers will have when they work with or observe the object shown in the drawing, especially when readers will use the drawing to follow instructions.** Figures 10.23, 24, 25, and 26 illustrate four angles or vantage points: a cross section, an exploded view, a cutaway, and an external view.

- **Use labels to point out significant features or details.** The labels tell the readers what features and details are significant. Without the labels, readers may miss significant information.

- **When appropriate, make the feature or detail that you want to emphasize larger than it really is.** The large size will emphasize the feature or detail.

▼ **Figure 10.23**

A Drawing That
Shows a Cross
Section

Cross Section of a Tooth with an Abscess

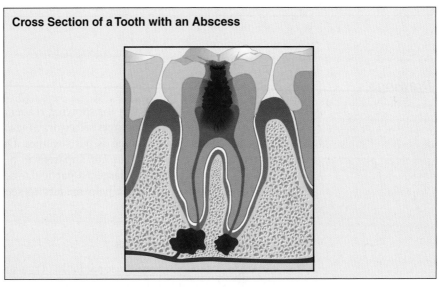

Source: "Tooth Repair" (n.p.: Whittle Communications, 1993) 2.

| **Figure 10.24** | A Drawing That Shows an Exploded View |

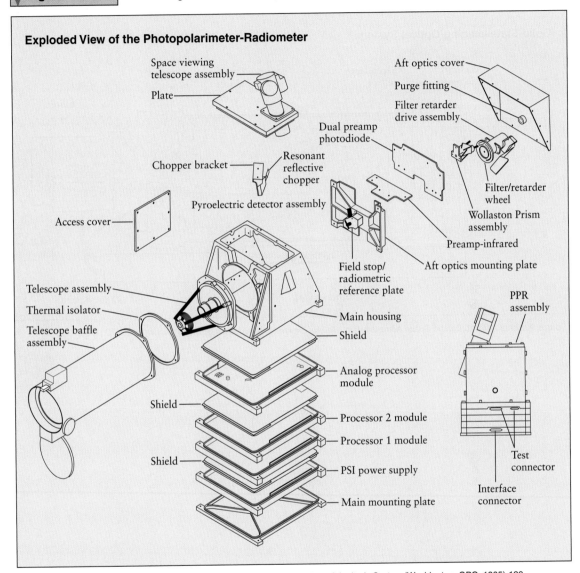

Exploded View of the Photopolarimeter-Radiometer

Source: National Aeronautics and Space Administration, *Galileo: Exploration of Jupiter's System* (Washington: GPO, 1985) 129.

Figure 10.25 A Drawing That Shows a Cutaway

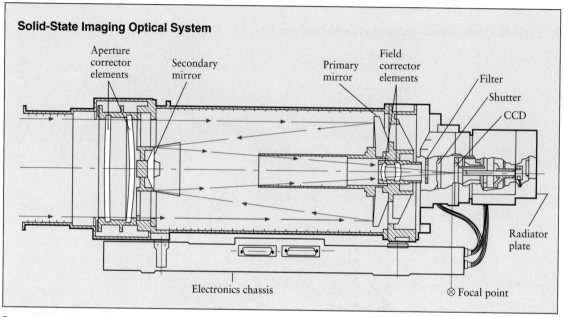

Solid-State Imaging Optical System

Aperture corrector elements

Secondary mirror

Primary mirror

Field corrector elements

Filter

Shutter

CCD

Radiator plate

Electronics chassis

⊗ Focal point

Source: National Aeronautics and Space Administration, *Galileo: Exploration of Jupiter's System* (Washington: GPO, 1985) 122.

| Figure 10.26 | A Drawing That Shows an External View |

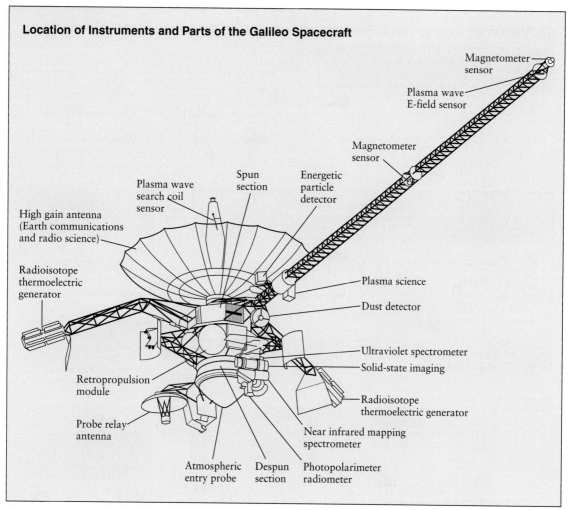

Location of Instruments and Parts of the Galileo Spacecraft

Source: National Aeronautics and Space Administration, *Galileo: Exploration of Jupiter's System* (Washington: GPO, 1985) 120.

Flow Charts

You can use **flow charts** to explain a process or to show a sequence of steps or events. Flow charts are especially useful for explaining a complex process that has conditional (if/then) steps. Flow charts generally work best for processes that have a definite beginning and a definite end (diagrams often work well for ongoing processes, such as recycling).

Flow charts usually consist of circles, rectangles, diamonds, and other geometric shapes that indicate the steps of a process. In some fields, various

▼ **Figure 10.27**   A Flow Chart That Illustrates a Process

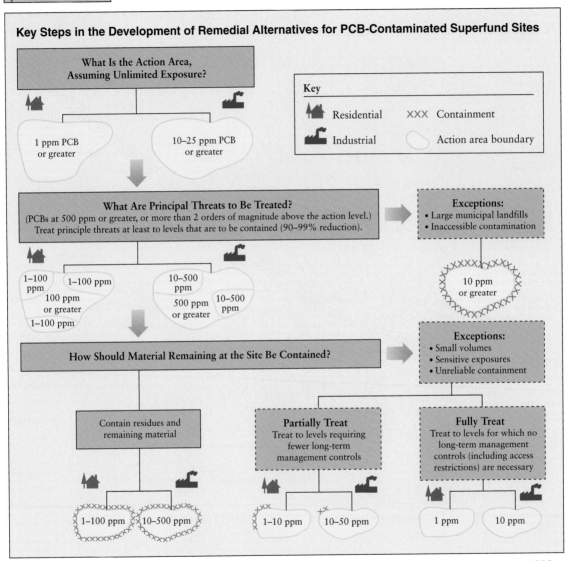

Key Steps in the Development of Remedial Alternatives for PCB-Contaminated Superfund Sites

Source: Environmental Protection Agency, *A Guide on Remedial Actions at Superfund Sites with PCB Contamination* (Washington: GPO, Aug. 1990).

geometric shapes have specific meanings, and people in those fields understand that certain shapes represent specific outcomes and events. If the shapes that you use in your flow chart have specific meanings, make sure your readers will know what the shapes represent, or use a key (see Figure 10.27). As you create flow charts, follow these tips:

THE READER'S CORNER

Visual Aids in Space

Launched in 1972 and 1973, Pioneer 10 and Pioneer 11 were unmanned space satellites designed to explore Jupiter and Saturn—missions they completed successfully. In 1986, Pioneer 10 became the first man-made object to travel beyond the solar system; it will reach the nearest star in 100,000 years or so. Would Pioneer 10 encounter intelligent life during its voyage; and, if so, just what message should Earth send?

Together, Frank Drake, Carl Sagan, and Linda Salzan Sagan designed a plaque carried aboard the Pioneer spacecraft. Etched into a 6-inch-by-9-inch gold-anodized aluminum plate, the plaque tells of human life—where and when the species lived and its biological form. The top left of the plaque depicts a schematic of a universal "yardstick"; it serves as the primary code for two of the three major representations: one of the solar system and another of the Sun in relation to fourteen pulsars and the center of the galaxy. The third representation is of a man and a woman alongside the silhouette of the satellite (to provide readers with a sense of scale). The man is waving, a friendly gesture for humans that also clearly displays our all-important opposable thumb. The designers carefully drew the figures and physiognomy of the man and woman to be ethnically neutral, yet they didn't attempt to explain what may be a very mysterious difference between the two physical types shown on the plaque.

Tips for Creating Flow Charts

- **Sketch a rough draft of the flow chart.** By making a rough draft, you can make sure that the labels will fit inside the geometric shapes and that you have included all the steps. You may have to sketch several drafts to make sure that the flow chart is accurate and that the shapes are the right size.

- **Put all labels identifying a step inside the geometric shapes.** The labels will distract and possibly confuse the reader if you place them outside the shapes. Make sure that the shapes are large enough to contain the labels, as in Figure 10.27.

- **Sequence the shapes so that the action flows from left to right or from top to bottom.** When the action flows from left to right and takes more than one line, begin the next line at the left margin.

Line Graphs

Line graphs show relationships among data with more precision than bar graphs. Like bar graphs, line graphs use a horizontal and a vertical axis; but line graphs use lines instead of bars to indicate relationships. Line graphs are especially effective when you want to do either of the following:

Figure 10.28   A Line Graph That Shows a Trend

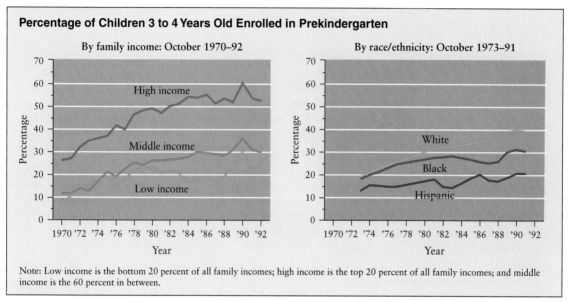

Percentage of Children 3 to 4 Years Old Enrolled in Prekindergarten

By family income: October 1970–92   By race/ethnicity: October 1973–91

Note: Low income is the bottom 20 percent of all family incomes; high income is the top 20 percent of all family incomes; and middle income is the 60 percent in between.

Source: Dept. of Education, Office of Educational Research and Improvement, *The Condition of Education*, NCES 94-149 (Washington: GPO, 1994) 27.

- **Show or compare trends.** Line graphs show patterns of change over time. Figure 10.28 shows enrollment in pre-kindergarten over about a twenty-year period. Tables can present the same numerical data as line graphs; but, as Figure 10.29 shows, readers can identify trends from a line graph more easily than from a table of numbers. The table in Figure 10.29 contains the same numerical data as the line graph in the figure, but the trends are much easier to spot in the line graph.

- **Compare variables.** Line graphs can show readers how two or more variables compare under similar situations. For example, the line graph in Figure 10.30 compares the rocks at various depths in the Piedmont in Virginia.

Line graphs generally show how changes in one variable (the independent variable) affect changes in another variable (the dependent variable). For example, Figure 10.30 shows how three dependent variables are affected when the percentage of mass loss (the independent variable) varies. The independent variable always appears on the horizontal axis. Once you have determined the dependent and independent variables, follow these tips when creating line graphs:

Figure 10.29   A Comparison of a Table and a Line Graph Based on the Same Numerical Data

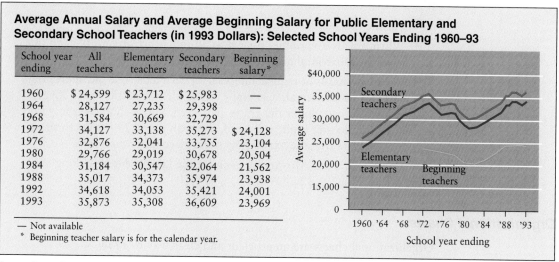

Average Annual Salary and Average Beginning Salary for Public Elementary and Secondary School Teachers (in 1993 Dollars): Selected School Years Ending 1960–93

School year ending	All teachers	Elementary teachers	Secondary teachers	Beginning salary*
1960	$ 24,599	$ 23,712	$ 25,983	—
1964	28,127	27,235	29,398	—
1968	31,584	30,669	32,729	—
1972	34,127	33,138	35,273	$ 24,128
1976	32,876	32,041	33,755	23,104
1980	29,766	29,019	30,678	20,504
1984	31,184	30,547	32,064	21,562
1988	35,017	34,373	35,974	23,938
1992	34,618	34,053	35,421	24,001
1993	35,873	35,308	36,609	23,969

— Not available
* Beginning teacher salary is for the calendar year.

Source: Dept. of Education, *The Condition of Education 1994*, NCES 94-149 (Washington: GPO, 1994) 154, 155.

Figure 10.30

A Line Graph That Compares Variables

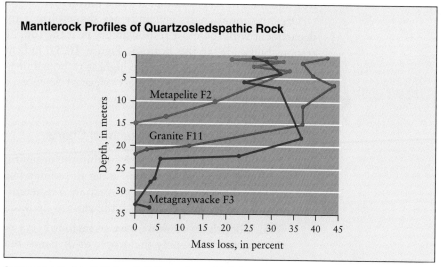

Source: M. J. Pavich, G. W. Leo, S. F. Obermeier, and J. R. Estabrook, *Investigations of the Characteristics, Origin, and Residence Time of the Upland Residual Mantle of the Piedmont of Fairfax County, Virginia*, U.S. Geological Survey Professional Paper 1352 (Reston: U.S. Geological Survey, 1989) 27.

> ▶ **Tips for Creating Line Graphs**
>
> - Put the independent variable on the horizontal axis.
> - When time is a variable, treat it as an independent variable and put it on the horizontal axis.
> - Place tick marks at regular intervals on each axis. Use the appropriate scale for each interval. Generally, make the tick marks short; longer tick marks can clutter the graph. The vertical axis should begin with zero. If it doesn't begin with zero, use hash marks or breaks to show your readers that the axis begins some place other than zero.
> - Label each axis. Most readers prefer the labels centered along each axis.

Organizational Charts

Organizational charts are an efficient and clear way to show

- The hierarchy of people and departments in an organization
- The lines of responsibility in an organization

The same relationships explained only with words may be difficult for readers to grasp. Without a visual organizational chart, readers may misunderstand the relationships. The chart reproduced in Figure 10.31 shows the organization and lines of responsibility for one university.

Organizational charts generally are shaped like a pyramid. The person or department with the most responsibility is at the top, and those with the least responsibility are at the bottom. Figure 10.31 indicates that the Board of Regents and Chancellor have the highest responsibility and that the heads of Payroll, Public Relations, and the College of Sciences, for example, have less responsibility.

> ▶ **Tips for Creating Organizational Charts**
>
> - **Use color to indicate divisions within the organization.** For example, in Figure 10.31, the divisions under the comptroller are one color and the divisions under the provost are a different color. The colors help the readers to distinguish the various divisions of the university.
> - **Remember that you don't have to include every person or division in the organization—only the people or divisions that the readers need to see.** The chart in Figure 10.31, for example, does not show people and divisions of the College of Sciences or the College of Engineering. The chart might include the dean, the associate dean, and the various departments in the colleges.

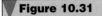 **Figure 10.31**   An Organizational Chart

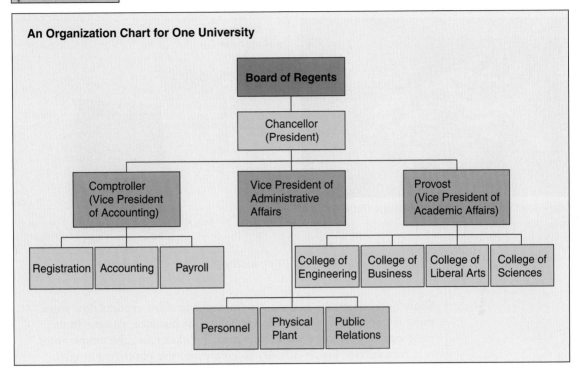

Photographs

Photographs are excellent visual aids when you want to do any of the following:

- **Show what something looks like.** Often words are not enough to help readers know what something looks like, especially if they have never seen what you are describing. For example, if you are describing a piece of equipment that readers may need for an experiment, a photograph is an effective tool. If you are cataloging various types of sea life, you might use photographs (see Figure 10.32). Guides to various types of sea life in oceans around the world contain pictures of each type of sea life discussed. Photographs are the only practical means of helping readers to recognize the sea life.

- **Show where something is located.** You may want to show readers where something is located on a machine, a piece of equipment, and so on. A computer company used a photograph with labels to help readers locate and identify the parts of a personal computer (see Figure 10.33).

Figure 10.32   A Photograph That Shows
What Something Looks Like

Leafy Sea Dragon *(Darryl Torckler/Stone/Getty Images)*

Figure 10.33   A Photograph That Helps
Readers Locate Something

CPU (central processing unit)
CD drive
Floppy disk drive
Monitor
Zip drive
Keyboard
Wireless mouse

(Ryan McVay/PhotoDisc/Getty Images)

- **Show how something is done.** If you want to show readers how something is done, photographs are excellent. For instance, you might use photographs to show readers how a steelworker takes the temperature of a furnace (see Figure 10.34). To create and use photographs effectively, follow these tips:

> **Tips for Taking and Using Photographs**
>
> - **Eliminate as much unnecessary detail as possible.** Show only the necessary parts and details.
> - **Use an appropriate angle.** Take the photograph from the angle at which readers will actually view the object.
> - **Use scanners and digital cameras to reproduce photographs or drawings for your documents.** With a scanner and its software, you can size photographs, eliminate distracting details that you were unable to avoid when taking the photograph, and integrate the photographs into your document.

Pictographs

Pictographs are similar to bar graphs but use pictures or drawings instead of bars. For example, in Figure 10.35, lines of writing on a legal document serve the same purpose as the bars in a bar graph. As in bar graphs, the measurements in

Figure 10.34	A Photograph That Shows How Something Is Done

Steelworker Taking Temperature of Furnace *(Charles Thatcher)*

Figure 10.35	A Pictograph

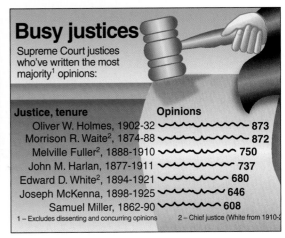

Source: Copyright 1997, *USA Today.* Reprinted with permission.

pictographs may not be as exact as those in a line graph. In fact, many pictographs don't have a visible vertical or horizontal axis or tick marks. Some pictographs are similar to divided bar graphs, but a picture or drawing replaces the bars. For example, the pictograph shown in Figure 10.36 uses a pyramid shape instead of bars.

Pictographs make your document visually interesting. They are especially helpful to nontechnical readers or when projected onto a screen during an oral presentation. As you create pictographs, follow these tips:

▶ Tips for Creating Pictographs

- **Use pictures and drawings that are meaningful and appropriate to the readers, the tone, and your purpose.** Create pictographs that fit your purpose and your readers. Pictographs should fit the tone of your document. For example, if you are preparing a multimillion-dollar proposal to the U.S. Department of Defense for building a new aircraft carrier, a pictograph would be inappropriate not only for the purpose, but also for the formal tone of the document.

- **Use drawings rather than photographs.** Photographs contain too much detail and are too realistic for most pictographs.

- **Use color to enhance pictographs.** Color makes pictographs more visually interesting.

(continued on next page)

- **Label pictographs.** Even though pictographs are less exact than some other visual aids, they are not merely decorative. Pictographs need appropriate, readable labels.
- **Use pictographs primarily for nontechnical readers—readers who are less knowledgeable of your field.** If you want to use pictographs for more knowledgeable readers, use them only in oral presentations. Pictographs, for example, might be appropriate for an oral presentation that supports a written proposal, but not in the written document itself. However, make sure that the pictograph is appropriate for the occasion of the oral presentation.

Pie Charts

Pie charts are circles divided into wedges—like pieces of pie. Each wedge represents a part of the whole. The pie chart shown in Figure 10.37 demonstrates how a county spends tax dollars. You can effectively use pie charts during oral presentations and with nontechnical readers.

▼ **Figure 10.36**

A Pictograph Similar to a Divided Bar Graph

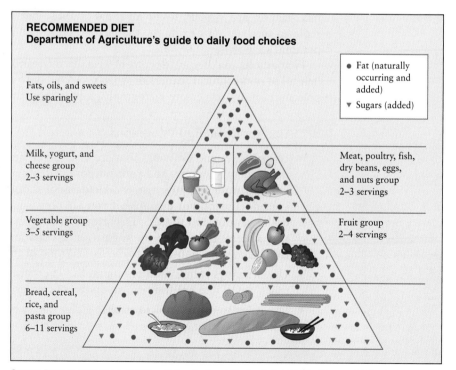

Source: Dept. of Agriculture, *Nutrition: Eating for Good Health,* Bull. 685 (Washington: GPO, 1994) 3.

▶For more information about using visual aids in oral presentations, see Chapter 17, "Creating and Delivering Oral Presentations."

You can easily create pie charts with computer software. You can make them three-dimensional, or you can rotate them for a professional look. As you create pie charts, follow these tips:

> ### Tips for Creating Pie Charts
>
> - **Label each wedge of the "pie."** Place the labels inside the wedges. If the labels won't fit, use **callouts**—lines drawn out to each label. Depending on your computer software, you may be able to pull out or explode some of the small wedges so that the labels will fit inside them.
> - **Sequence the wedges from the largest to the smallest.** Place the largest wedge in the 12-o'clock position, and move to the smallest wedge as you work around the "clock."
> - **Use color to make pie charts visually interesting.**

Tables

Tables present detailed information arranged in vertical columns and horizontal rows. You can find tables in many types of technical and consumer writing. For example, the labels of most food products have a table describing their nutritional value. Many manuals use tables to present troubleshooting information, and many technical reports include tables.

Although writers most frequently use tables to display numerical data, tables are also effective for presenting information in words (see Figure 10.38).

Figure 10.37

A Pie Chart

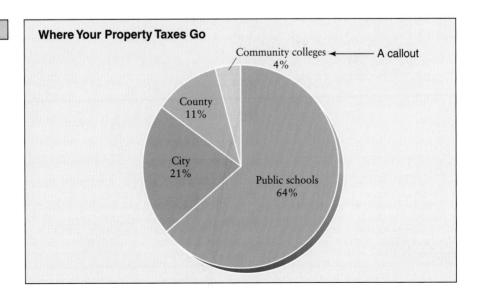

| Figure 10.38 | A Table Consisting of Words Rather Than Numerical Data |

What Are Some of the Effects of Illegal Drugs?

| Drug type | Short-term effects | | Duration of acute effects | Risk of dependence |
	Desired	Other		
Heroin	• euphoria • pain reduction	• respiratory depression • nausea • drowsiness	• 3 to 6 hours	• physical-high • psychological-high
Cocaine	• excitement • euphoria • increased alertness, wakefulness	• increased blood pressure • increased respiratory rate • nausea • cold sweats • twitching • headache	• 1 to 2 hours	• physical-possible • psychological-high
Crack cocaine	• same as cocaine • more rapid high than cocaine	• same as cocaine	• about 5 minutes	• same as cocaine
Marijuana	• euphoria • relaxation	• accelerated heartbeat • impairment of perception, judgment, fine motor skills, and memory	• 2 to 4 hours	• physical-unknown • psychological-moderate
Amphetamines	• euphoria • excitement • increased alertness	• increased blood pressure • increased pulse rate • insomnia • loss of appetite	• 2 to 4 hours	• physical-possible • psychological-high
LSD	• illusions and hallucinations • excitement • euphoria	• poor perception of time and distance • acute anxiety, restlessness, sleeplessness • sometimes depression	• 8 to 12 hours	• physical-none • psychological-unknown

Sources: NIDA, "Heroin," *NIDA capsules,* August 1986: DEA, *Drugs of abuse,* 1989: G. R. Gay, "Clinical management of acute and chronic cocaine poisoning: Concepts, components and configuration," *Annals of emergency medicine,* (1982) 11(10): 562–572 as cited in NIDA. Dale D. Chitwood, "Patterns and consequences of cocaine use," in *Cocaine use in America: Epidemiologic and clinical perspectives,* Nicholas J. Kozel and Edgar H. Adams, eds., NIDA research monograph 61, 1985; NIDA, James A. Inciardi, "Crack-cocaine in Miami," in *The epidemiology of cocaine use and abuse,* Susan Schober and Charles Schade, eds., NIDA research monograph 110, 1991; and NIDA, "Marijuana," *NIDA capsules,* August 1986.

Source: Dept. of Justice, Bureau of Justice Statistics, *Drugs, Crime, and the Justice System* (Washington: GPO, Dec. 1992) 20.

Whether your tables consist of words or numbers, they are likely to be effective when you want to do either of the following:

- **Present detailed information in a concise, readable format.** With tables, you can present dense information in a format that readers can quickly read and understand.
- **Help readers locate information.** When you want to help readers locate information quickly and easily, you often can use a table. Confronted with paragraphs of prose, readers have to keep on reading until they find the information they need; in contrast, a table lets readers locate key words and information quickly.

To create a table, put the information into vertical columns topped with appropriate headings, as in the table shown in Figure 10.38. Figure 10.39 shows a common structure for a table. Some of the items in Figure 10.39 will not appear in all tables. As you create tables, follow these tips:

▶ Tips for Creating Tables

- **Use computer software to create tables.** Whether you use specialized graphics software or word-processing software, you can easily create tables with computer software. The software will generally ask you for the number of rows and columns you need. You simply insert the information into the rows and columns, and the software automatically formats the table.
- **Label all units in a table containing numerical data.** For example, if you use percentages, dollars, pounds, kilometers, and so on, identify these units in the appropriate column head or in the table title.

(continued on next page)

Figure 10.39

The Structure of a Table

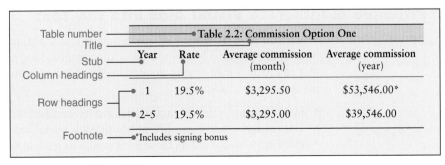

Source: Courtesy of Tonya McKinney.

- **Use letters rather than numbers for table footnotes if numbers may confuse readers.** In tables of numerical data, readers can mistake footnote numbers for mathematical notation. For example, 14^2 could mean "14 squared" rather than "footnote 2." If you think readers might misinterpret a footnote number, use letters: 14^b instead of 14^2.

- **Use rules to separate the column heads from the table number and title and from the data in the body of the table.** The rules help readers to locate the column heads. For more information, see Principle 2.

- **Use rules to help readers to read across a table to find specific information.** For example, you might place rules after each grouping of information or after every five rows of information.

- **Use shading to help readers distinguish columns or rows.** For example, you might shade the first, third, and fifth columns in a table that has six columns. Or you might shade every other row in a table. Some graphics and word-processing software give you the option of selecting shading or color for columns and rows.

- **Align the numbers and words correctly.** Vertically align columns of numerical data at the right or on the decimal points if the numbers are decimals:

Right-aligned column	7
	11,890
	789
	8,900
Decimal-aligned column	0.23
	203.78
	33.90
	3.00

If the table contains words rather than numbers, align the words at the left.

▶Principle 4: Integrate Visual Aids into the Text

When you have designed and created your visual aid, integrate it into the text of your document. Think about how the visual aid supports and reinforces the text to create a meaningful document. To effectively integrate visual aids into the text, do the following:

- Introduce and refer to each visual aid by number.
- Tell readers what is important about each visual aid.
- Place each visual aid as close as possible to its text discussion.

Introduce and Refer to Each Visual Aid by Number

When you want readers to look at a visual aid, introduce and refer to it by number. Many readers will only know that you want them to look at a visual aid or what you expect them to learn from the visual aid if you refer them to it. You can introduce and refer to visual aids in one or two sentences or in a parenthetical reference:

One-sentence introduction	As Figure 17 illustrates, heart disease kills more U.S. women than the next four causes of death combined.
Two-sentence introduction	Heart disease kills more U.S. women than the next four causes of death combined. Figure 17 shows the five leading causes of death among U.S. women.
Parenthetical reference	Heart disease kills more U.S. women than the next four causes of death combined (see Figure 17).

In each example, the writer introduces the figure by number and by content. Readers need both types of reference.

Sometimes you will want to tell readers how to use or read a visual aid or give them information they need to understand a visual aid. The following introduction tells the reader when and how to use a table:

> If you receive an error message when installing the software, use Table 16. Read down the first column of Table 16 until you find the error message that you received. When you find the message, go to the second column, labeled "What to do when you receive this message."

Tell Readers What Is Important About Each Visual Aid

Briefly explain the purpose of each visual aid, or tell readers what they should notice in each one. Readers may not draw the same conclusions that you drew, so state those conclusions to make sure that the readers understand the purpose and meaning of the visual aid.

For example, the writers of a scientific paper on women and cardiovascular diseases wanted readers to understand the urgency of studying these diseases specifically in women; so they wrote the following explanation of two bar graphs, one showing the causes of death among U.S. women and another the causes among U.S. men:

> Once a neglected field of research, cardiovascular diseases in women have rapidly become a major topic of scientific investigation. In 1994, cardiovascular disease

killed more U.S. women than U.S. men and was the leading cause of death among women. Cardiovascular disease kills more U.S. women than the next four causes of death combined.[1]

The writers clearly state two important pieces of information that they want readers to understand after reading the bar graphs: cardiovascular diseases kill more U.S. women than men, and the diseases kill more U.S. women than the next four causes of death combined.

Place Each Visual Aid As Close As Possible to Its Text Discussion

Visual aids are most effective when they appear either on the same page as the text that refers to them or on a facing page. Readers may ignore a visual aid if they have to flip from the discussion to hunt for the visual aid elsewhere in the document. If you cannot avoid placing a visual aid at some distance away from its text discussion, be sure to refer to the visual aid and tell readers where to find it. For example, if a visual aid appears in an appendix, you might write the following:

A large-scale map of the Bobwhite Quail habitat in Texas appears in Figure 26 in Appendix C (see page 51).

If you want readers to take another look at a visual aid that you discussed earlier in your document, you might write the following:

The nonspinning portion of the *Galileo* orbiter, discussed earlier, provides a stable base for four remote sensing instruments (see Figure 3.2, page 120, for a diagram of the orbiter).

▶Principle 5: Use Computer Software to Create Professional-Looking Visual Aids

Several types of computer software let you create professional-looking visual aids: spreadsheets, graphics, and drawing software. With spreadsheet software, you can input data to a spreadsheet and then use the spreadsheet to create various tables and graphs. You then can import these tables and graphs into word-processing software. With graphics software you can create visual aids such as bar graphs, line graphs, flow charts, organizational charts, and pie charts. These software programs make your job easy and your visual aids as professional-looking as those created by a graphic artist. You can easily import visual aids created with most graphics software into documents created with word-processing software. With drawing software you can create pictograms and drawings. This type of software tends to be more difficult and time-consuming to use and learn than are spreadsheet and graphics packages, but it

---

[1] Beil, Laura. "Change of Heart: New Insights Gained as Cardiovascular Research Shifts More to Women." Dallas Morning News 6 Feb. 1995: 6D.

allows you to create drawings and pictograms much like those done by a graphic artist or draftsperson.

You can use scanners to reproduce both photographs and text. Scanners take photographs and text and save these images onto a floppy or hard disk. Then with appropriate software you can manipulate these images. For example, you can make scanned photographs or other images larger or smaller, and you can delete background objects from a photograph. You also can take two different photographs and combine them to create a new image.

Computer software allows you to try out several versions of a visual aid before you decide on the final version. When you select the final version and pull it into your document, you can move the visual aid around on a page or within the document until you find the most appropriate location for it.

Although graphics software and scanners can help you to create professional-looking visual aids, they raise some practical issues for you to consider. Because graphics software and scanners are becoming increasingly easier to use, you may be tempted to create more visual aids than your readers need. Resist the temptation: unnecessary visual aids will clutter the document and take up valuable space. Many writers create "busy" visual aids that actually confuse readers or deemphasize important information; many writers inappropriately use the preset templates for visual aids such as pie charts, bar graphs, and line graphs. These preset templates are not effective for some data—for example, they may distort some trends in a line graph or bar graph by using an inappropriate scale.

▶Conclusion: **Ethics and Visual Aids**

▶For more information on ethics, see Chapter 3, "Facing Ethical and Legal Challenges."

Graphics software and scanners allow writers to manipulate data, pictures, and images in ways that were not easily possible before this technology became available. You may face ethical choices when using this technology. Your readers will expect your visual aids to be ethical, accurate, and honest.

One type of manipulation results from **airbrushing**—deleting images or objects from a photograph. A common use of airbrushing is to eliminate blemishes and wrinkles from close-up photographs of people's faces. Airbrushing is ethical and legitimate when used to highlight essential or important information in a picture; airbrushing becomes unethical when it removes information from a photograph to deceive or mislead the viewers.

Bar graphs, line graphs, and pictograms require you to create a scale on the horizontal or vertical axis. The scale you select will affect how your readers perceive your data. Be sure that the scales you create present data honestly. If you use inappropriate scales, you will exaggerate the differences in data when differences are minor, or you will make differences in data look small even though they really are great. Let's look at an example.

Figure 10.40 shows the most recommended home builders. The difference between Burgert, the most recommended, and Raign is only 1.34 percent. The bar graph, however, makes the difference between Burgert and Raign look

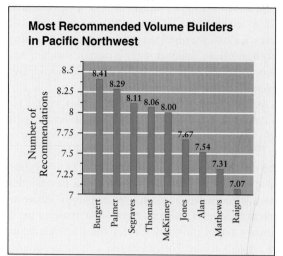

Figure 10.40   A Bar Graph with an Inappropriate Scale

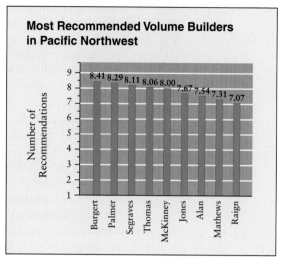

Figure 10.41   A Bar Graph with an Appropriate Scale

quite dramatic—certainly more than 1.34 percent. The scale that determines the length of the bars could mislead readers to believe that the percentage of people recommending Burgert over Raign is much greater than it really is. The graph needs a smaller scale and size to more accurately represent the difference between Burgert and the other builders (see Figure 10.41). As you create visual aids requiring scales, make sure that the visual aid accurately and honestly presents the data and the differences among the data.

WORKSHEET

for Creating Effective Visual Aids for Your Readers

▶ **Principle 1: Look for Areas Where Visual Aids Will Help You Communicate**
- Did you consider visual aids early in the writing process?
- Can you use visual aids to show readers how to follow instructions or explain a process?
- Can you use visual aids to show readers what something looks like?
- Can you use visual aids to show and summarize relationships among data?
- Can you use visual aids to emphasize or reinforce information?
- Can you use visual aids to show how something is organized?
- Can you use visual aids to simplify complicated concepts, discussions, processes, or data?
- Can you use visual aids to add interest to your document?

► **Principle 2: Design Visual Aids That Are Clear**
- Are the visual aids simple and uncluttered? Do they emphasize or show the information that you intend?
- Did you include only the information your readers need?
- Did you exclude distracting visual information in photographs?
- Does each visual aid have a number and a descriptive title?
- Did you consistently position the titles of the visual aids throughout the document?
- If international readers will read your document,
  - Can they read and understand the visual aids?
  - Did you use simple graphics?
  - Did you use appropriate colors?
  - Did you avoid graphics with religious or English/American connotations?
  - Did you consider the reading direction of the readers?
- Did you overuse color?
- Did you use colors that unify your document?
- Do your visual aids have appropriate contrast?

► **Principle 3: Select the Appropriate Visual Aid**
- When you wanted to show what something looked like, did you use drawings or photographs?
- When you wanted to show how to follow instructions, did you use drawings or photographs?
- When you wanted to explain a process, did you use flow charts or diagrams?
- When you wanted to show or summarize relationships among data, did you use tables, bar graphs, line graphs, pie charts, or pictographs?
- When you wanted to show how something was organized, did you use organizational charts?

► **Principle 4: Integrate Visual Aids into the Text**
- Did you introduce each visual aid appropriately?
- Did you refer to each visual aid by number?
- Did you explain the purpose of the visual aid?
- Did you tell the readers what to notice in the visual aid?
- Did you place each visual aid as close as possible to its text discussion?

► **Principle 5: Use Computer Software to Create Professional-Looking Visual Aids**
- When possible and appropriate, did you use computer software or scanners to create visual aids?
- Did you exclude unnecessary or ineffective visual aids?
- Did you manipulate data, pictures, or images appropriately and ethically?
- Do your visual aids create ethical, accurate, and honest impressions?

►**E X E R C I S E S**

1. Visit the computer labs available to you on campus. Find out the following:

   a. What graphics software is available to students, and what types of visual aids can you create using the software?

   b. What drawing software is available to students, and what visual aids can you create using the software?

   If your campus doesn't have labs or graphics and drawing software, visit a computer software store or office supply store to gather information. After you have gathered information on software,

   • Create a table summarizing the information that you gathered.

   • Write a memo to your instructor reporting what you found out about available graphics and drawing software.

   • Include the table that you created with your memo. Be sure to number your table, label it, and integrate it into your memo.

2. Figure 10.42 indicates the number of tax returns filed electronically to the ten IRS service centers. Use the information in this figure to create the following visual aids. For each visual aid, include a number and a descriptive title. When possible, use computer software to prepare the visual aids.

   a. A line graph showing trends in filing individual tax returns electronically to the following service centers from 1986 to 1990: Memphis, Ogden, Kansas City, and Philadelphia.

   b. Two pie charts showing the proportions of total returns filed electronically to the cities serviced by the Memphis service center in 1986 and 1990. You will need to determine the percentage of the total

number of individual returns filed electronically for each city.

   c. A bar graph comparing the total number of individual returns filed electronically to the Austin, Ogden, and Philadelphia service centers from 1986 to 1990. Remember that time is an independent variable.

   d. A pictograph showing the number of individual tax returns filed electronically from 1986 to 1990 in the United States.

3. Examine several technical publications or journals in your field.

   • Select examples of effective and ineffective photographs, diagrams, and drawings.

   • Write a memo to your instructor analyzing the photographs, diagrams, and drawings that you selected.

   • Include a copy of the visual aids at the appropriate place in the memo. Number the visual aids and give them titles.

4. Create a drawing that you might use in a set of instructions or operating manual for a piece of equipment. You might select a household appliance, equipment used in your field, or equipment for which you are writing instructions in your technical communication class. Label the appropriate parts of the equipment, and give your drawing a number and a descriptive title. You can create the drawing by freehand, with drawing software, or with a scanner. If you scan a drawing, then use appropriate computer software to create labels for each part.

5. Create an organizational chart for an organization that has at least four levels of managers or departments. Use one of these organizations:

   • A civic organization such as the local Boy Scouts or Girl Scouts

▼ **Figure 10.42**   The Table for Exercise 2

Number of Returns Filed Electronically

Individual Returns

Service centers & districts	1986	1987	1988	1989	1990
United States	24,814	77,612	683,462	4,160,516	4,193,242
Andover	0	172	16,631	74,672	291,168
Albany	—	172	6,327	10,692	34,677
Augusta	—	—	—	2,448	16,660
Boston	—	—	—	11,151	55,334
Buffalo	—	—	13,304	66,016	95,491
Burlington	—	—	—	1,546	6,583
Hartford	—	—	—	5,446	47,764
Portsmouth	—	—	—	2,744	23,550
Providence	—	—	—	4,629	12,109
Brookhaven	0	0	0	14,404	186,433
Brooklyn	—	—	—	11,193	58,864
Manhattan	—	—	—	3,211	42,670
Newark	—	—	—	—	84,899
Philadelphia	0	8,913	58,508	69,198	319,449
Baltimore	—	—	—	8,559	61,903
Philadelphia	—	—	—	—	85,103
Pittsburgh	—	—	—	—	42,603
Richmond	—	8,913	58,508	60,639	120,166
Wilmington	—	—	—	—	9,674
A/C International	—	—	—	—	—
Atlanta	0	0	0	92,897	520,871
Altanta	—	—	—	—	187,501
Columbia	—	—	—	35,081	106,655
Fort Lauderdale	—	—	—	9,096	69,092
Jacksonville	—	—	—	48,720	157,623
Memphis	1,953	16,376	152,199	238,122	699,407
Birmingham	—	—	28,813	47,150	110,585
Greensboro	1,953	16,376	123,386	142,943	251,058
Jackson	—	—	—	—	45,758
Little Rock	—	—	—	—	67,352
Nashville	—	—	—	48,029	143,207
New Orleans	—	—	—	—	81,447
Cincinnati	9,157	25,976	153,492	267,458	612,306
Cincinnati	9,157	25,976	60,558	61,288	105,062
Cleveland	—	—	—	20,882	82,192
Detroit	—	—	—	51,582	136,678
Indianapolis	—	—	62,036	82,482	161,324
Louisville	—	—	30,898	43,902	91,466
Parkersburg	—	—	—	7,322	35,584
Kansas City	0	440	5,450	42,776	474,214
Chicago	—	—	—	12,471	166,019
Des Moines	—	—	—	—	35,181

Figure 10.42 (continued)

Milwaukee	—	440	5,450	14,001	64,880
Springfield	—	—	—	16,304	67,840
St. Louis	—	—	—	—	96,540
St. Paul	—	—	—	—	43,754
Austin	**0**	**0**	**70,832**	**141,766**	**474,204**
Albuquerque	—	—	—	—	35,424
Austin	—	—	—	26,623	88,593
Dallas	—	—	70,832	97,565	203,411
Houston	—	—	—	47,578	61,496
Oklahoma City	—	—	—	—	60,128
Wichita	—	—	—	—	45,152
Fresno	**0**	**0**	**10,592**	**43,342**	**225,048**
Honolulu	—	—	—	—	10,926
Laguna Niguel	—	—	—	10,536	120,148
Los Angeles	—	—	—	5,462	38,816
San Francisco	—	—	—	9,460	17,110
San Jose	—	—	10,592	17,884	38,048
Ogden	**13,704**	**25,735**	**96,880**	**175,777**	**390,142**
Aberdeen	—	—	—	1,404	8,873
Anchorage	—	—	—	883	6,222
Boise	—	—	—	7,296	14,336
Cheyenne	—	—	—	4,721	10,365
Denver	—	—	—	22,018	52,863
Fargo	—	—	—	408	6,647
Helena	—	—	—	3,192	11,162
Las Vegas	—	—	—	3,618	14,885
Omaha	—	—	2,343	12,491	30,447
Phoenix	13,704	19,142	47,998	45,702	66,509
Portland	—	—	—	19,087	31,311
Sacramento	—	6,593	12,312	14,759	30,062
Salt Lake City	—	—	16,657	12,391	33,582
Seattle	—	—	17,570	27,807	72,878

Source: Dept. of the Treasury, Internal Revenue Service, *1990 Annual Report from the Commissioner of Internal Revenue,* Publ. 55 (Washington: GPO, 1990) 27.

- The company you work for
- A campus or student organization such as a fraternity or sorority or a service organization
- A city department such as the fire or police department
- Applying for a passport
- Applying for financial aid at your college or university
- Explaining a process or procedure common in your field or at your place of employment
- Applying for graduation at your college or university

6. Prepare a flow chart illustrating one of these processes. Include readable labels, a descriptive title, and a number.

7. Evaluate the visual aid in Figure 10.43. As you evaluate, consider these questions:

- Is it simple or cluttered? If cluttered, how would you improve the visual aid?
- Is the drawing clear? If not, what would you do to clarify the visual aid?
- Does the color enhance the visual aid? If so, has the designer used the appropriate colors?

- Has the designer selected the appropriate type of visual aid? If not, what type would you select?

Be prepared to discuss your evaluation in class. Your instructor may ask you to relate your evaluation in a memo or an e-mail addressed to him or her.

Figure 10.43

The Visual Aid for Exercise 7

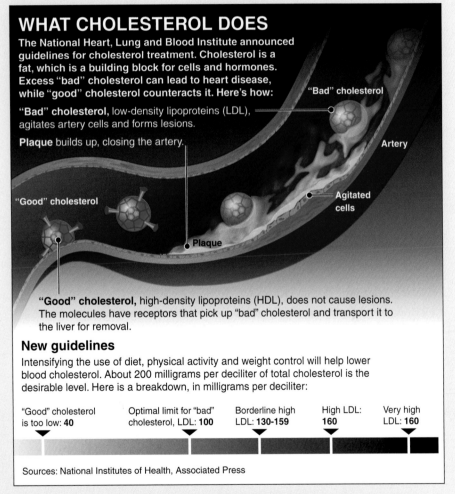

WHAT CHOLESTEROL DOES

The National Heart, Lung and Blood Institute announced guidelines for cholesterol treatment. Cholesterol is a fat, which is a building block for cells and hormones. Excess "bad" cholesterol can lead to heart disease, while "good" cholesterol counteracts it. Here's how:

"Bad" cholesterol

"Bad" cholesterol, low-density lipoproteins (LDL), agitates artery cells and forms lesions.

Plaque builds up, closing the artery.

Artery

"Good" cholesterol

Agitated cells

Plaque

"Good" cholesterol, high-density lipoproteins (HDL), does not cause lesions. The molecules have receptors that pick up "bad" cholesterol and transport it to the liver for removal.

New guidelines

Intensifying the use of diet, physical activity and weight control will help lower blood cholesterol. About 200 milligrams per deciliter of total cholesterol is the desirable level. Here is a breakdown, in milligrams per deciliter:

"Good" cholesterol is too low: **40**

Optimal limit for "bad" cholesterol, LDL: **100**

Borderline high LDL: **130-159**

High LDL: **160**

Very high LDL: **160**

Sources: National Institutes of Health, Associated Press

Source: *Dallas Morning News* 16 May 2001: 14A. Reprinted by permission of the *Dallas Morning News*.

11

Preparing Front and Back Matter

While at work, you will write many different documents. These documents might include a progress report for your manager, a proposal for revising the plant design, or a feasibility report recommending new hardware for the manufacturing division. For many of these documents, you'll want to include reference aids, often called front and back matter. **Front matter** consists of the reference aids that come before the body of the document. **Back matter** consists of reference aids that come after the body of the document. Front and back matter have purposes such as

- **To help readers locate information in the document.** The table of contents, list of illustrations, and index help readers to find information.
- **To help readers decide whether they want to read the document.** The abstract, executive summary, and the table of contents give readers the information they need to decide whether they will read the document.
- **To summarize the document when readers may not have time to read the entire document.** The executive summary may replace the document for executives and managers.
- **To help readers to understand the document.** The glossary, list of symbols, and the appendix may help readers to understand or may support information in the document.

Few documents have all varieties of front and back matter discussed in this chapter. As the writer of a document, you'll determine the type of front and back matter that best meets your purpose and your readers' needs. You might decide to sequence the front and back matter differently in some documents; or your organization may have standard formats and style guidelines, or even printed forms, for some front and back matter. Before writing a document, check to see whether your organization has such guidelines for the type of document that you are writing. If it does, follow them. If it doesn't, find copies of successful documents written by others in the organization. These documents will show you how other employees formatted the front and back matter of similar documents and perhaps reveal some of your organization's unwritten preferences for front and back matter. If your organization doesn't have guidelines for front and back matter, you can decide what format to use. This chapter presents three principles to help you prepare effective front and back matter.

▶Principle 1: Prepare the Front Matter

Many documents contain one or more of these items of front matter:

- Letter of transmittal
- Cover
- Title page
- Table of contents

- List of illustrations
- Abstract and executive summary

These elements identify or give an overview of a document and help readers to locate information and illustrations. We will examine each one in this section.

Letter of Transmittal

▶ For information on letter formats, see Chapter 18, "Writing Reader-Oriented Letters, Memos, and E-Mail," page 573.

The letter of transmittal, or cover letter, has the following objectives:

- To summarize the subject and purpose of the document
- To identify the occasion—the reason for preparing the document
- To emphasize any information in the document that is likely to especially interest the readers—information such as methods, conclusions, recommendations, or changes from the proposal or original plan for the document

As you write your letter of transmittal, follow the organization presented in these tips:

> ### ▶ Tips for Writing the Letter of Transmittal
>
> **In the First Paragraph . . .**
> - State the title or subject of the document.
> - State the occasion of the document—the reason for preparing it, such as to complete a class assignment, to complete a request from a manager or client, or to respond to a request for proposal.
>
> **In the Middle Paragraph(s) . . .**
> - State the purpose of the document. (Some writers include the purpose in the first paragraph.)
> - Mention any specific information from the document that may especially interest readers.
> - Summarize your conclusions and recommendations (unnecessary for instructions and manuals).
> - *Optional:* Include and possibly explain any changes to your work since the proposal or to the document since you last corresponded with the readers.
>
> **In the Final Paragraph . . .**
> - Offer to answer any questions that readers may have about the document or its contents.
> - *Optional:* Mention and possibly thank any person, group, or organization that helped you prepare the document.

You can either attach the letter of transmittal to the cover of the document, place it inside the cover before the title page, or send it separately. If you decide to send the letter separately, be sure that it tells readers when you or your organization plans to send the document itself.

The First "Covers"

The history of writing formats is logically inseparable from the history of writing systems themselves. Historians believe that two written systems, developed independently of one another, are the source of all the major writing systems. The Chinese developed a writing system that influenced all Eastern writing; the Sumerians developed a system that influenced all Western writing. The Sumerian script, eventually known as cuneiform, first appeared on small tokens for simple bookkeeping purposes. As the Sumerian civilization developed from a hunter-gatherer to an agricultural society (around 8000 B.C.), the number of tokens increased. Markings on distinctively shaped tokens, some in the form of animals, stood for the real thing. By 3500 B.C., the Sumerians were building cities, and their lives were increasingly dedicated to commercial growth. To conduct commercial transactions, they constantly needed more tokens. Perhaps the Sumerians developed clay envelopes, in which archaeologists have found tokens stored, to protect the tokens during transactions. The Sumerians duplicated the markings on the tokens on the envelopes, and eventually the Sumerians realized that the tokens themselves were no longer necessary: all the information they needed was on the envelopes. Some historians argue that this moment—when written characters were finally detached from their small clay embodiments—marks the beginning of abstract, alphabet-based writing.

The letter of transmittal is the first part of your document that readers will see. Therefore, it should give a good impression of you and your organization. Figure 11.1 shows a letter of transmittal written by a technical communication student. She prepared the report mentioned in the letter for the Louisiana Parks and Wildlife Department.

Cover

The cover of a formal report serves three basic purposes:

- To protect the pages
- To identify the document
- To create a positive impression of your document (and your organization)

Before you design a cover, check to see whether your organization has a standard cover design to appear on all documents. If it does, use that design. If it does not, and if you are responsible for designing covers, remember that the cover may help to spark readers' interest or establish a certain tone. For example, if you're preparing a cover for a proposal to customize telecommunications functions for a corporation, you might customize the cover by using the client corporation's colors or displaying a picture of the client's headquarters.

For the cover of most documents, use heavy yet flexible paper or card stock. Most photocopy shops carry heavy paper and card stock in various weights and colors.

Figure 11.1   A Letter of Transmittal

Louisiana State University
Department of Environmental Studies
Baton Rouge, Louisiana 85004

April 23, 2001

Dr. Sam Woods
Director
Department of Parks and Wildlife
P. O. Box 13726
New Orleans, LA 85007

Dear Dr. Woods:

We are pleased to submit the accompanying report, "Black-Bellied Plover ————— Title of document
Habitat in Louisiana," in response to your request. The report examines ————— Occasion of document
Black-Bellied Plover habitat in Louisiana as part of a program to save this ——— Purpose of document
species from becoming endangered.

For this report, we examined the literature about previous sightings of ——— Specific information that especially interests the reader
Black-Bellied Plover in Louisiana and analyzed satellite images of those
sighting locations. Based on this information, we concluded that Black- ——— Conclusion
Bellied Plovers prefer pasture/shrub land. To protect any remaining Black-
Bellied Plovers, we must conserve and monitor the locations where the bird ——— Recommendation
has been most frequently sighted.

If you have any questions, please call me at (504) 555-2161. ——— Offer to answer questions

Sincerely,

Danielle Brown

Danielle Brown
Research Assistant

Use any of these methods to print the cover and attach it to the document:

- **Use a laser printer to print the cover on ordinary paper; then photocopy the cover onto heavier paper such as card stock.** Heavy paper can damage some laser printers. Therefore, you may need to print the cover on printer paper and then copy it onto heavier stock.
- **Laminate the cover for durability and a more professional-looking appearance.**
- **Bind the document with spiral binding or three-ring binding.**
- **Use a binder that has a clear pocket on the front to hold the cover that you have printed.** For this type of binder, you can use printer paper.

These printing and binding options are inexpensive and give reports a professional appearance. Spiral or three-ring binding secures the pages of the document much better than a paper clip or a file folder. Most photocopy shops have the machinery to bind documents.

Most covers include some or all of this information:

- Document title
- Your name and position (optional, especially when writing for an organization)
- Your organization's name or logo
- Name of the organization or client for whom you prepared the document—unless the document is for the general public
- Date of submission

Figure 11.2 shows the cover of a proposal issued by a telecommunications company. The cover mentions the title of the report, the name of the issuing company (World Networks, Inc.), and the identity of the intended readers (officials in Courtney County); but it does not give the writers' names. Figure 11.3, in contrast, shows the cover of a document prepared for the general public. This cover identifies the issuing organization (Centex Corporation) but does not mention its intended readers.

Title Page

Some title pages look exactly like the cover; some repeat only certain parts of the cover; and some are completely different from the cover, having few if any graphics and no color. Title pages contain some or all of this information:

- Document title
- Name of the organization or group for whom you prepared the document
- Your name and position
- Your organization's name or logo
- Date that you submit the document to its intended readers

Figure 11.4 presents the title page from a student document.

| **Figure 11.2** | A Cover That Identifies the Intended Readers and the Issuing Organization |

Title of the
document

Telecommunications for the Prison System

Proposal for Courtney County ←— Name of the
RFP 96-025   organization
                                   for whom the
                                   writer prepared
                                   the document

World Networks, Inc. ←— Name and logo
                        of the writer's company

Figure 11.3	A Cover for a Document Written for the General Public

Source: Courtesy of Centex Corporation, Dallas, Texas.

Black-Bellied Plover Habitat in Louisiana: A Recommendation

A title that indicates the subject and purpose of this document

Name of intended readers ——————————————————• **Prepared for Louisiana Department of Parks and Wildlife**

Writer's name ——————————————• **By Danielle Brown**

Writer's organization ——————————• **Louisiana State University**

Date submitted ——————————————• **April 2002**

Many companies have a specific format for title pages. Some standardized formats call for much more information than generally appears on a title page. Figure 11.5 illustrates a title page from a user's manual. This title page differs from the typical title page for many reports. This title page lists the title of the manual, the writer's company name and logo, and information that identifies the intended readers: the specific printer model and the language used to write the manual. Many documents written for consumers don't identify the name of the writer, the name of the intended readers, or a date.

Table of Contents

▶ For information on outlining, see Chapter 6, "Organizing Information for Your Readers," page 153.

The table of contents is a sort of road map. It indicates what a document is about and helps readers to locate specific sections or to read selectively. The most effective tables of contents list more than just the first-level headings in a document. (If your document has only one level of headings, consider subdividing some sections to help readers locate information. Be sure to follow the guidelines for outlining presented in Chapter 6.) Figure 11.6 shows a table of contents that contains only first-level headings that convey no information about the subject of the document. Readers curious about the "Discussion" section, for example, would have to search more than fifteen pages to find a particular subsection or topic.

To prepare an effective table of contents, follow these tips:

▶ **Tips for Preparing a Table of Contents**

- **Use the exact wording that appears in the headings and subheadings in the body of the document.** If the heading in the body of the text is "Habitat of Black-Bellied Plover," the wording in the table of contents should be the same, not a shortened version such as "Habitat."

- **Show the heading levels by varying the type style and indenting** (see Figure 11.7). By consistently varying the type style and indenting, you help readers to locate first-level headings (or major sections). Then the readers can locate appropriate subheads.

- **List only the first three levels of headings if your document has more than three levels.** Including four or more levels will make the table of contents hard to read.

- **Use guide dots (. . . . .) to connect the headings and the page numbers** (see Figure 11.8).

- **Include the list of illustrations, abstract or executive summary, and any other front matter except the cover, title page, and letter of transmittal.** Use lowercase Roman numerals (i, ii, iii, etc.) for the page numbers of the list of illustrations, abstract, executive summary, and any other front matter (see Principle 3 on page numbering later in this chapter).

Figure 11.5 A Title Page from a User's Manual

Title of manual also identifies the intended readers: the users

HP DeskJet Printer User's Guide for Windows

Identifies the model of the printer and the language used in the manual; these items help to identify the intended readers: users who can speak English and have a 970C series printer

970C Series

English

Name and logo of the writer's company

HEWLETT® PACKARD

Expanding Possibilities

Source: Copyright 1999 Hewlett-Packard Company. Reproduced with permission.

Some word-processing software has functions for generating a table of contents after you have typed your document. These functions can save you time and help you to use in the table of contents the exact wording that appears in the body of the document. Check the user's manual or online help of your word-processing software to see whether it has a function for generating a table of contents. You can also use this same function to generate the list of illustrations, discussed in the next section.

The most commonly used style for the table of contents appears in Figure 11.7. Many writers and organizations, especially in the sciences, prefer a decimal system, which adds decimal numbers to the headings and subheadings in the table of contents (see Figure 11.8). Since neither of these styles is better than another, select the style that your readers or organization expects. If your readers and your organization have no expectations, look at similar documents to see how others in your organization or field have prepared tables of contents; then pattern your table of contents accordingly.

List of Illustrations

If you use any visual aids in your document, list the numbers and titles of these visual aids in a list of illustrations (see Figure 11.9). The list of illustrations appears on a separate page after the table of contents. The list of illustrations is sometimes titled "List of Tables and Figures." To prepare a list of illustrations, follow these tips:

Figure 11.7 An Effective Table of Contents

Contents

Abstract ii
List of Illustrations iv
Introduction 1
Black-Bellied Plover and Its Habitat 2
  Description of Black-Bellied Plover 2
  Habitat of Black-Bellied Plover 5
  Migration of Black-Bellied Plover 7
  Status of Black-Bellied Plover 11
Methods for Identifying Black-Bellied Plover Habitat 13
  Historical Sightings of Black-Bellied Plover 14
  Satellite Imagery of the Habitat 20
    Rectifying the Images 23
    Classifying the Landuse 27
  Remote Sensing of the Habitat 28
Results from the Sightings Information, Satellite Imagery, and Remote Sensing 29
  List of Historical Sightings of Black-Bellied Plover in Louisiana . . 30
  Landuse Classes in the Satellite Imagery 32
  Landuse Class of Black-Bellied Plover Habitat 35
Recommendation for Protecting Black-Bellied Plover in Louisiana . . 37
  Landuse in the Black-Bellied Plover Habitat 38
  Habitat Areas in Louisiana 39
Works Cited 41
Appendixes 42
  A. Satellite Imagery of Similar Habitats along the Gulf Coast 43
  B. Remote Sensing of Similar Habitats along the Gulf Coast 49

Show heading levels by indenting

Vary the type style to indicate heading levels

Use the exact wording that appears in the body of the document

Line up all numbers, Arabic and Roman, on right-hand digits

Use guide dots

| **Figure 11.8** | A Decimal-Style Table of Contents |

Contents

"1" indicates the chapter or section—in this reference, Chapter 1

"3" indicates the third subsection of Chapter 1

This number indicates the first sub-subsection of Subsection 2 in Chapter 2

Figure 11.9

A List of Illustrations

Illustrations

Guide dots

Figures

Tables

Tips for Preparing a List of Illustrations

▶ For more information on tables and figures, see Chapter 10, "Creating Effective Visual Aids for Your Readers," page 270.

- **If you used separate numbering sequences for tables and figures, separate the tables from the figures in the list of illustrations.** You can title the entire list "List of Illustrations" or "Illustrations."
- **If you used only one numbering sequence, title the list "Illustrations" or "List of Illustrations."** If your document contains only tables, you can use the title "List or Tables" or simply "Tables." If your document contains only figures, you can title the list "List of Figures" or simply "Figures."
- **Use the exact wording and number that appears with the illustration.** If the illustration number and title is "Figure 3.1. Migration Path of Black-Bellied Plover," the wording in the list of illustrations should be the same, not a shortened version such as "Figure 3.1. Migration Path" or "Migration Path."
- **Use guide dots (. . . .) to connect the illustration and the page number.** See Figure 11.9.

Abstract and Executive Summary

The abstract and executive summary give an overview of the facts, results, conclusions, and recommendations of a document. They present the information that readers need to act or make a decision without reading the entire document or to decide whether they want to read the entire document or just parts of it.

The abstract and executive summary usually appear near the beginning of a document. In this section, you will learn how to write informative abstracts, descriptive abstracts, and executive summaries.

Writing Informative Abstracts

Informative abstracts are primarily for readers knowledgeable about the topic of the document. These abstracts must be able to stand independently from the document. When writing an informative abstract, follow these tips:

> ### ▶ Tips for Writing Informative Abstracts
>
> - **Identify the document.** Because an informative abstract must stand independently from the document, just writing "Abstract" above the text of the abstract will not give potential readers enough information. Instead, also include the document title, your name, and perhaps the name of your organization or department.
> - **State the objectives or problem addressed in the document.** Don't assume that readers know the objectives or the problem that your document addresses. Instead, state the objectives or the problem. With this information, readers can decide whether your document contains information that they need or want to read.
> - **Conclude with the key results, conclusions, or recommendations.** Because an informative abstract must be able to stand alone, include the key results, conclusions, or recommendations of your research or document, excluding all examples and details. This information will be the largest part of the abstract. If the methods used to conduct the research are new, unique, or vital to understanding your results, conclusions, or recommendations, include them too.

Generally, abstracts are one paragraph long. Figure 11.10 presents an informative abstract of a report on the habitat of the Black-Bellied Plover. The abstract identifies the report's title and writer. The writer also states the objective of her report in the first two sentences and then concludes with the key results of her research and a recommendation. You can also find good examples of informative abstracts in some professional journals. Many journals limit abstracts to 200 words.

Writing Descriptive Abstracts

A descriptive abstract, unlike an informative abstract, is not a substitute for the document itself. Instead of reporting key results, conclusions, and recommendations, a descriptive abstract mentions the major topics of the document. Its purpose is to help readers decide whether they want to read the document. Figure 11.11 presents a descriptive abstract of a report on the habitat of the Black-Bellied Plover.

Figure 11.10 An Informative Abstract

Abstract
Black-Bellied Plover Habitat in Louisiana ———————————————————— Title of the document

By Danielle Brown ———————————————————————————— Name of the writer

The Black-Bellied Plover *(Pluvialis squatarola)* is a shorebird species threatened with becoming endangered because of the loss of habitat through
twentieth-century urbanization. As a step toward preventing this species from
becoming endangered, this report identifies the Black-Bellied Plover habitat in ———— Problem
Louisiana. To identify the habitat, I examined information about Black-Bellied   addressed in
Plover sightings in Louisiana over the last 50 years and the landuse categories   the document
derived from satellite imagery of the sighting locations. These examinations
indicate that Black-Bellied Plover habitat in Louisiana is generally pasture ———— Conclusion
and shrubland. To protect this species, the Louisiana Department of Parks and ———— Recommendation
Wildlife or the private sector should conserve and monitor this habitat, especially in the areas where the most frequent sightings have occurred on Grand
Isle and around Calliou Bay.

Figure 11.11 A Descriptive Abstract

Abstract
Black-Bellied Plover Habitat in Louisiana ———————————————————— Title of the document

By Danielle Brown ———————————————————————————— Name of the writer

The Black-Bellied Plover *(Pluvialis squatarola)* is a shorebird species threatened
with becoming endangered because of the loss of habitat through twentieth-
century urbanization. This report identifies Black-Bellied Plover habitat in
Louisiana based on previous sightings over the last 50 years and on landuse   Major topics of the
categories derived from satellite imagery of some of these sighting locations.   report
The report also recommends conservation techniques to protect this species.

Writing Executive Summaries

▶ To learn more
about summaries,
see Chapter 12,
"Writing Reader-
Oriented
Proposals,"
page 359.

Executive summaries present the conclusions and recommendations of a document (see Figure 11.12). An executive summary provides the information
that its readers need to act or to make a decision. The readers of an executive
summary are not necessarily the primary readers of the document itself. Let's
consider an example in which the primary readers of the executive summary
and of the body of the document are different people.

Engineers write a report on pipe stress problems at an electricity-generating
plant. The primary readers of the report are other engineers and the plant
operations manager—all experts in engineering and electricity-generating

plants. In the report, the writers discuss the methods they used to examine the problem, the specifications of the testing of the pipes, and the detailed results of those tests. They use technical language, knowing that their professional colleagues will understand it. However, many of the people who will decide whether or not to fund the solution that the engineers propose aren't engineers. For these readers, the engineers write an executive summary in which they use nontechnical language and include only the information that these readers will likely need to knowledgeably decide about the proposed solution.

In your executive summaries, use nontechnical language, and give readers only the information they will need to determine whether they should read your document. Readers of executive summaries don't want or need detailed information about the methods; for many of these readers, detailed information about your methods or about the theories behind your project may be confusing or frustrating. Instead, these readers want the following:

- **A general overview of the topic of the document or research.** In this overview, succinctly state the topic of your document—such as the problem addressed, the procedure or situation analyzed, and so on. Also briefly state the objective of your document or research. In some instances, you may need to provide some background information to help readers understand the topic.
- **A concise statement of the key results, conclusions, and recommendations without excessive detail.** Readers want to know the "bottom line."

Put yourself in the readers' shoes and try to anticipate the questions that they may ask as they read the summary:

- **What problem or situation does the document address?** Specifically identify the problem or situation that your document addresses. Readers will be especially interested in how the problem or situation directly affects them, their employees, their department, or their organization. They also will be interested in the cost of the problem or situation to their department or organization.
- **How will the results, conclusions, and recommendations affect the department, employees, organization, and others?** Readers will be especially interested in costs and savings. Readers of executive summaries are less interested in details and evidence that supports the findings and more interested in information that will help them to make a decision or implement recommendations.
- **What are the key results, conclusions, or recommendations?** If you know that readers will understand the subject of your document, include your key results. Such readers may expect you to summarize the significant data concerning the results. Briefly summarize your results and significant data, keeping in mind that these readers will use

this data to make decisions, not to conduct further studies. Some readers, in contrast, may not understand your subject or may not want to read about your results. For these readers, leave out the results and present only conclusions and recommendations. Such readers are interested in what action you recommend based on your analysis or research—even if your recommendation is simply to study a situation or problem further or to "wait and see."

For most documents, place the executive summary at the front of the document. In some organizations, the executive summary circulates separately—it is not bound with the document. In other organizations, the executive summary is bound with the document and appears prominently before the document. The executive summary presented in Figure 11.12 focuses effectively on the conclusions and recommendations. As you write your executive summary, follow these tips:

▶ Tips for Writing Executive Summaries

- **Include the title of your document.** Some writers in the workplace also include the words "Executive Summary" with the title. You might consider identifying the summary in this way if your executive summary will circulate separately from the document or if you will not bind the summary with your document.

- **Identify the problem or situation that your document addresses.** Include how the problem or situation directly affects the readers, their employees, their department, or their organization.

- **Focus on the conclusions and recommendations, not on the details of your findings.** Avoid including details and evidence that support your conclusions. In the summary, include only information that will help readers to make a decision or to implement the recommendations.

- **Include the information that readers need to make decisions or to implement the recommendations.** Include only the information they need—exclude examples, details, or supporting information.

- **Use nontechnical language.** Many readers of executive summaries may not be experts in your field. Even if the document is for technical readers, write the summary for decision makers who may not know the technical language of your field.

- **Give readers only the information they will need to determine whether they should read your document or to make a decision.** Eliminate, for example, any information about your methods or about the theories behind your project.

Figure 11.12	An Executive Summary

Title of the → **Recommendations for Improving the Technical Communication**
document **Computer Lab**

The Technical Communication Computer Lab has outdated equipment. Specifically, the lab has sixty outdated personal computers with dual floppy disk drives. The personal computers have 14-inch, low-resolution monitors. These computers cannot support the latest Windows software applications and desktop publishing. Although the lab does have twelve personal computers capable of running the latest versions of Windows, faculty members cannot conduct classroom activities with only twelve computers. Also, with only twelve up-to-date computers, many students get little if any experience on the type of computer technology they will use in the workplace. Because of our outdated computer equipment, many faculty members are not requiring their students to use computers to create their technical communication documents and are, therefore, not adequately preparing their students for the workplace.

Overview · We have considered three ways to deal with this problem:

- Close the lab and force students to use their own personal computers and the open-access labs in the library.
- Request that the College of Arts and Sciences provide $400,000 during the next fiscal year to upgrade all the personal computers and to buy current versions of Windows and desktop publishing software. With this request, the student fees would remain at the current level of $70 per student per technical communication class.
- Raise the student fees to $98 per student in the next three fiscal years. With this fee, we can update twenty computers and buy Windows and desktop publishing software for these computers the first year, and do the same for the remaining twenty computers the second year, and the final twenty computers the third year.

Conclusions and
recommendations

We recommend the second solution. However, if the College of Arts and Sciences will not provide the $400,000, then we recommend the third solution. We do not recommend the first solution because the technical communication faculty and students need a lab where they can hold class—the open-access labs are not set up for faculty members to conduct class sessions. The second and third solutions would provide faculty with a place to conduct class sessions and students with up-to-date computers and software that they will encounter in the workplace.

▶Principle 2: Prepare the Back Matter

▶Learn about indexes in Chapter 15, "Writing User-Oriented Instructions and Manuals."

Back matter appears after the body of a document. However, some traditional back-matter elements, such as the glossary and list of symbols, may appear before the body, in which case they are part of the front matter. Some of the most common types of back matter in technical documents include the following:

- Works cited list or list of references
- Glossary
- List of abbreviations or symbols
- Appendixes
- Index

Works Cited List or List of References

If you cite the works of others in your document, include a works cited list or a list of references after the body of your document. You might use MLA, APA, or a company-approved style of documentation. For specific information about documenting sources, see Appendix A, "Documenting Your Sources."

Glossary

▶For more information on readers and their levels of expertise, see Chapter 2, "Understanding and Writing for Your Readers."

A **glossary** is an alphabetical list of specialized words and their definitions (see Figure 11.13). A glossary provides definitions of terms unfamiliar to some readers, without slowing the flow of the document. Effective glossaries allow you to meet the needs of readers with different levels of technological expertise. Figure 11.13 shows part of a glossary from a document on computer networking products. To write an effective glossary, follow these tips:

▶ Tips for Creating a Glossary

- **In the body of the document, identify all words that appear in the glossary.** Put these terms in italic or boldface type, or place an asterisk next to each one. Use the same system of marking throughout the document, and be sure to explain to readers what you are doing—perhaps in the letter of transmittal or in a footnote accompanying the first glossary word in the text. This footnote will explain that terms defined in the glossary appear in the body of the text in, for example, boldface italic type: "This and all other terms appearing in boldface italic type are defined in the Glossary, which begins on page 77."

- **Carefully define all terms that readers may not understand.** In the definition, use words that readers are likely to understand, and

(continued on next page)

include cross-references to other closely related terms defined in the glossary (see Figure 11.13).

- **List the words in alphabetical order.** Alphabetical order helps readers to locate the words.

- **Use phrases or clauses, not sentences, for the primary definitions.** After the primary definition, you can use sentences for secondary definitions or explanations. If you use words defined in the glossary, cross-reference those words. For example, look at the definition of *gateway* in Figure 11.13. In this definition, the writer uses *host,* which is also in the glossary; so the writer tells the reader to "See host."

- **Include the glossary and its first page number in the table of contents.**

Figure 11.13

A Partial Glossary

Glossary

American Standard Code for Information Interchange (ASCII)
A seven-bit code intended as a U.S. standard for interchanging information among communication devices.

asynchronous
A method for transmitting data in which each character is sent one bit at a time. Each character has a start and stop bit to synchronize signals between the sending device and the receiving device. See **bit**.

bit
A binary digit, either 0 or 1.

byte
The amount of space in computer memory or on disk occupied by a single character. A byte can be 6, 8, or 9 bits. See **bit**.

gateway
A hardware/software package that allows incompatible protocols to communicate. Usually connects personal computers to a host machine. See **host**.

host
A computer attached to a network that provides services to another computer beyond simply storing and forwarding information. See **network**.

local area network (LAN)
A system that links computers to form a network, usually with a wiring-based cabling scheme. LANs connect personal computers to allow users to communicate, share resources, and gain access to remote hosts or other networks. See **host**.

network
A system that sends and receives data and messages, typically via a cable. A network allows a group of computers to communicate, share peripherals (such as printers), and gain access to remote hosts and other networks.

List of Abbreviations or Symbols

If your document contains many abbreviations or symbols, include a list explaining what they mean (see Figure 11.14). This list usually appears at the end of a document before the appendix, although some writers put it in the front matter after the table of contents and list of illustrations. Follow these tips as you prepare a list of abbreviations or symbols:

Tips for Creating a List of Abbreviations or Symbols

- **List the abbreviations in alphabetical order.** Alphabetical order helps readers to locate abbreviations.
- **Use phrases or clauses for explaining what the abbreviations or symbols mean.** You can simply write the words that an abbreviation or symbol represents; you can also include other information that readers may need to understand the abbreviation or symbol.

Appendixes

Appendixes generally contain information that is *not essential* for readers to understand the main points, conclusions, and recommendations. Appendixes contain information that may interest only a few readers or that would interrupt the flow of the document. An appendix might include maps, details of a survey or experiment, a sample questionnaire, an interview, large charts, computer printouts, or supporting documents. Any of these items should supplement the body of the document. Material in appendixes supports information in the body of the document, offering further reading or sources where readers can learn more. To prepare an effective appendix, follow these tips:

Tips for Preparing an Appendix

- **At the appropriate place in the body of the document, refer to each appendix.** For instance, if you summarize survey results in the body of the document and include the survey instrument and tabulated results in an appendix, tell readers: "Sixty-five percent of the respondents reported that they used electronic mail more frequently than voice mail (see Appendix B for the tabulated results)."
- **Put each major item into a separate appendix.** Identify each appendix with a letter or a title: Appendix A, Appendix B, and so on.
- **List each appendix in the table of contents.** If you've titled an appendix, include the complete title.
- **Put *essential* items in an appendix only when these items are so long or so large that putting them in the body of the document would severely interrupt the flow of information.** Otherwise, include only nonessential information.

Figure 11.14

A Partial List of
Abbreviations

Abbreviations

ESS	Electronic Still Store. The graphics box over the anchor's shoulder.
NC	News Conference.
PREPS	Preparations. Used in story descriptions.
REAX	Reactions. Used in story descriptions.
SOT	Sound On Tape. Used in a script to tell the editor where to place the sound on tape.
VO	Video Only.

▶ Principle 3: Number the Pages

As you prepare your front and back matter, follow these standards for numbering the pages:

- Use lowercase Roman numerals (i, ii, iii, etc.) for the front matter.
- Use Arabic numerals (1, 2, 3, etc.) for the body and back matter.
- Put the odd numbers on right-hand pages and the even numbers on left-hand pages.
- Begin the body of the document on a right-hand page even if doing so means that the facing left-hand page will be blank.
- Leave the title page and any blank pages unnumbered even though you will include them in your page count.

▶ For more information on page numbers and headers and footers, see Chapter 9, "Designing Documents for Your Readers."

Figure 11.15 shows the page numbering of a formal document. The writer leaves the title page, page i, unnumbered. The writer uses lowercase Roman numerals for all the front-matter elements. The first page of the body is a right-hand page. Page vi, the left-hand page that faces the first page of the body, is blank because the list of figures fits on page v.

You can put page numbers in two effective places on a page: the top or bottom outside corners (see Figure 11.16).

- On left-hand pages, place the page number in the top or bottom left-hand corner.
- On right-hand pages, place the page number in the top or bottom right-hand corner.

Page numbers in the outside corners are easier for readers to see as they flip through a document than are page numbers in the center of the top or bottom margins or in the inside corners. You also can help readers locate information by including a header or a footer with the page numbers.

| Figure 11.15 | Sample Page Numbering of a Formal Document |

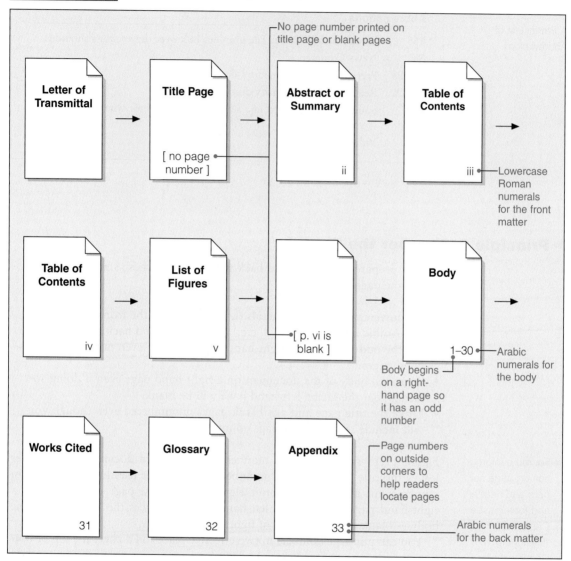

No page number printed on title page or blank pages

Letter of Transmittal

Title Page

[no page number]

Abstract or Summary

ii

Table of Contents

iii —Lowercase Roman numerals for the front matter

Table of Contents

iv

List of Figures

v

[p. vi is blank]

Body

1–30 —Arabic numerals for the body

Body begins on a right-hand page so it has an odd number

Works Cited

31

Glossary

32

Appendix

33

Page numbers on outside corners to help readers locate pages

Arabic numerals for the back matter

▶**Conclusion** When you know the readers and purpose of your document, you can select the appropriate front and back matter. Front and back matter help readers to locate information, to understand the information, and to decide whether they will read a document. Some front matter can even substitute for a document when readers don't have time to read the entire document or can help readers to make decisions. From the front and back matter, readers often draw their first impressions of a document. If, for example, the cover has an unprofessional

Figure 11.16	The Position of Page Numbers and Headers or Footers on Facing Pages

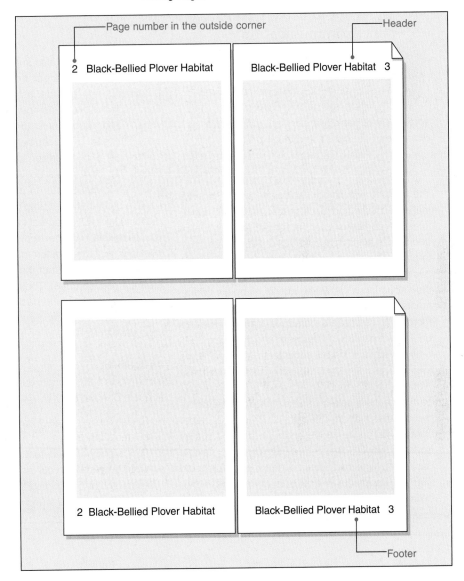

or uninteresting appearance, readers may decide to ignore the document. If the table of contents doesn't help readers to locate information, readers may not find the information they need and may use another company's product. If a manual lacks an effective index, readers may ignore the manual and instead call you or your company for help; such help can be time-consuming and unnecessarily expensive.

TAKING IT INTO THE WORKPLACE

Moving Front and Back Matter into the World of Online Communication

"Writing for the Internet requires multilayered thinking, i.e., you are constantly having to sculpt a three-dimensional, linked world. For someone who has spent her life writing in two dimensions, the transition can be difficult."

—Althea Caces, M.A., Professional Writer, Atlanta, Georgia

The Web is redefining traditional notions of what makes up front and back matter and what constitutes the appropriate format for documents. Online documents aren't mirror images of their paper counterparts. Gary Beason explains that when a certain computer company put its documents on the Web, the "boundaries between individual books [documents] began to disappear"; the books became more of a searchable database than a traditional book with chapters, a title page, and an index (339). Unlike traditional paper documents, documents on the Web are dynamic. Beason reports that these Web documents multiply into a set of documents in part because a series of files makes up the documents—files that are often in flux. Traditional paper documents, on the other hand, are static once they appear in print. However, does this dynamic, flexible nature of online documents suggest that we should put all documents online or that readers prefer online documents?

Online and paper documents each have distinct advantages. Online documents cost less than paper documents and provide instant access to information, especially with computer software and hardware. Paper documents, on the other hand, are easier to read; if a document is "more than a few sentences, print is easier to read than a monitor" (Bellis 21). How, then, do you decide what to put online and what to put on paper? Jack Bellis suggests a combination of both online and paper documents to take advantage of the strengths of each. As you seek this balance between online and paper, consider that the written product will change as technology changes; but the change should not be arbitrary (Beason 348). Thus, will documents in the future have the front and back matter of today's documents? That decision may just be up to you and your coworkers.

Assignment

Using one of the search engines that you learned about in Chapter 5,

- Find an online letter of transmittal, cover, table of contents, and index
- Print a copy of each item
- Write an e-mail to your instructor describing each item and including the address (URL) of each item that you found

The principles you've learned in this chapter will help you to prepare effective front and back matter. In the workplace, remember to look at documents prepared by your coworkers or find out if your organization has a style manual to help you determine your organization's preferences and guidelines for preparing front and back matter.

WORKSHEET	**for Preparing Front and Back Matter**

▶ **Principle 1: Prepare the Front Matter**

- Does the letter of transmittal
  - State the title of your document?
  - Identify the occasion and purpose of your document?
  - Summarize your conclusions and recommendations?
  - Include any changes to your work since you last corresponded with the readers?
  - Offer to answer any of the readers' questions?
- Does the cover
  - Include the document title?
  - Include the name of the organization, group, or person for whom you prepared the document? (optional)
  - Include the name and/or logo of your organization? (optional for student documents)
  - Include your name? (optional)
  - Create a positive impression of you, your document, and/or your organization?
- Does the title page
  - Include the document title?
  - Include your name? (optional)
  - Include the name of the organization, group, or person for whom you prepared the document? (optional)
  - Include the name and/or logo of your organization? (optional for student documents)
  - Include the date that you submitted the document?
- Does the table of contents
  - Create an effective road map of the document?
  - Include the exact wording that appears in the headings and subheadings in the body of the document?
  - Include the first-, second-, and third-level headings?
  - Show the heading levels with varied type styles and indenting?
  - Include the list of illustrations, abstract or executive summary, and other front matter except the cover, title page, and letter of transmittal, when applicable?
  - Use guide dots to connect the headings and the page numbers?
- If you have used visual aids, did you include a list of illustrations? If so, does the list of illustrations
  - Include all visual aids?
  - Include the number and title of each visual aid?
  - Use guide dots to connect the title of the visual aid to the page number?
- Does your document need an informative abstract? If so, does the informative abstract
  - Include the document title?

- State the objectives of or problem addressed in the document?
- Conclude with the key results, conclusions, or recommendations?
- Does your document need a descriptive abstract? If so, does the descriptive abstract
  - Include the document title?
  - Describe the major topics of the document?
  - Exclude the key results, conclusions, and recommendations?
- Does your document need an executive summary? If so, does the executive summary
  - Include the document title?
  - Identify the problem or situation that the document addresses?
  - Focus on the conclusions and recommendations, not on the details of your findings?
  - Include the information that readers need to make decisions or to implement the recommendations?

▶ **Principle 2: Prepare the Back Matter**
- Does your document need a works cited list or a list of references?
- Do your readers need a glossary? If so, did you
  - Identify in the text all words that appear in the glossary?
  - Define all terms that readers may not understand?
  - List the words in alphabetical order?
  - Use phrases or clauses, not sentences, for the primary definitions?
- Do your readers need a list of abbreviations or symbols? If so, did you
  - List the abbreviations in alphabetical order?
  - Use phrases or clauses, not sentences, to explain what the abbreviations or symbols mean?
- Does your document require that you include an appendix? If so, did you
  - Refer to the appendix at the appropriate place in the body of the document?
  - Put each major topic in a separate appendix?
  - Identify each appendix with a letter or a title?
  - List each appendix in the table of contents?

▶ **Principle 3: Number the Pages**
- Did you use lowercase Roman numerals (i, ii, iii, etc.) for the front matter?
- Did you use Arabic numerals (1, 2, 3, etc.) for the body and the back matter?
- Did you use odd numbers for the right-hand pages and even numbers for left-hand pages?
- Did you begin the body on a right-hand page?
- Did you leave the title page and any blank pages unnumbered—even though you included them in your page count?
- Did you put the page numbers in either the top or bottom corner of the page?
- Did you include a header or footer?

1. Write a letter of transmittal for a document that you are writing. Follow the paragraph-by-paragraph outline in "Tips for Writing the Letter of Transmittal" on page 308.

2. Prepare a tentative table of contents for a document that you are writing. Include all first-, second-, and third-level headings that you intend to use.

3. Design a cover and title page for a document that you are writing. Use word-processing, graphics, or desktop publishing software. As you design the cover, decide what materials and binding style you will use. When you complete the cover and title page, turn in the following to your instructor:

   - A memo explaining the material you will use for the cover and justifying your design of the cover and title page—why you selected the graphical elements, what the graphical elements represent, whether the design is the organization's standard design (if applicable), and so on
   - The cover printed on plain paper (indicate in the memo how you will present the final version of the cover: type of paper, type of binding, and so on)
   - The title page

4. Decide whether any material for a document that you are writing should appear in an appendix. Then write a memo to your instructor explaining your decision. If you decide to include material in an appendix, answer these questions in your memo:

   - Why is the material better placed in an appendix than in the body of the document?
   - What readers are likely to be interested or to need the information presented in the appendix?

   - What is the purpose of the material that will appear in the appendix?

5. Decide whether a document that you are writing should have an informative abstract or an executive summary. Then write the abstract or the executive summary for your document.

6. Write a memo to your instructor evaluating the letters of transmittal that appear in Figures 11.17 and 11.18. In your memo, comment on whether the letters are clear and contain all the elements listed on page 308.

7. Write a memo to your instructor evaluating the executive summary shown in Figure 11.19. Comment on how well it gives a general overview of the document and concisely states key results, conclusions, and recommendations. Also consider whether the writer has answered the questions that readers might ask.

8. Figure 11.20 presents the body of the report "Prescribed Range Burning in Texas." Readers of this report know little about prescribed range burning. Using the information presented in this report, prepare the following elements:

   - Letter of transmittal addressed to the readers
   - Title page
   - Table of contents
   - Executive summary
   - Informative abstract

9. Figure 11.20 contains style, design, and visual aid problems. Write a memo to your instructor identifying the types of style and design problems. Include examples of the problems in Figure 11.20. Be prepared to discuss your memo in class.

10. Rewrite a passage from Figure 11.20. The passage must have some of the style prob-lems that you identified in Exercise 9. The passage must be at least three paragraphs.

Figure 11.17

The Letter of
Transmittal for
Exercise 6

Dear Dr. Raign:

I submit the accompanying report entitled "Dentistry in the North Carrollton Area" as the final project for ENGL 301, Technical Writing.

The report presents information from a demographic study of the north Carrollton area and from interviews with area dentists. This information will help dentists in this area better understand their market and its opportunities. My study indicates that the north Carrollton market is quickly being saturated with dentists. For new and established dentists in the area to be competitive, I recommend that they create a positive, innovative environment, establish good relationships with patients and other dentists, establish and justify reasonable and competitive fees, add a personal touch to their practice, and develop a marketing plan.

I especially want to thank all the area dentists who have willingly assisted and encouraged me during this study. If you have questions about the accompanying report, please call me at 696-4122.

Sincerely,

Jennifer T. Valentine
Attachment

Figure 11.18

The Letter of
Transmittal for
Exercise 6

Dear Michael,

Attached is the project report for the last six months for engineering and design activities for the Oakmont Station. To date, we have spent a total of 466,726 hours on these activities. The attached report is self-explanatory and provides information on the project schedule, project cost, specific engineering and design activities, and our recommendations for the remainder of the project.

If you have questions about the report, you may contact me at my office.

Sincerely,

Jim Anderson
Project Manager
Enclosure

▼ **Figure 11.19**

The Executive
Summary for
Exercise 7

Executive Summary

In the first part of this report, I define typical technical communication jobs such as those in the public and private sectors. I then use these categories to organize the types of jobs uncovered in a seven-week survey. The remainder of the paper offers possibilities for students to enhance their degrees by gaining knowledge about software that employers required in the advertisements found in the survey.

According to the survey, most job openings for technical communicators require the following:

- at least two years of related work experience
- working knowledge of a broad range of computer software
- specialization in technical fields

According to the survey, most of the job opportunities were in the area of user documentation. Of the employers requiring academic degrees, 30.3% specified a technical writing degree along with the two years of related work experience.

Based on the survey, the employers most frequently requested knowledge of one or more of the following software:

- Word
- Ventura
- FrameMaker
- Windows

Based on the survey, the employers most frequently requested a specialization or background knowledge in the following areas:

- telecommunications
- public relations
- online documentation
- project management
- technical editing
- Web page design

Source: Courtesy of John P. Ramsey.

▼ **Figure 11.20**   The Report for Exercises 8, 9, and 10

Prescribed Range Burning in Texas

Larry D. White and C. Wayne Hanselka

Introduction

Fire was a natural ecological factor on most Texas rangelands before European settlement; therefore, native vegetation is well adapted to burning. Fire effectively suppresses most woody plants while encouraging grass and forb growth. However, sound range, livestock and wildlife management must accompany the use of fire if benefits are to be realized.

Prescribed range burning follows guidelines that establish the conditions and manner under which fire will be applied on a specific area to accomplish specific management and ecological objectives. This contrasts with wildfires that can occur any time fuels will burn, often under extremely hazardous conditions. The conditions selected for a prescribed burn (season, vegetational growth stage and weather factors) must be conducive to *safe* and *effective* burning. Management objectives determine the fire characteristics needed to maximize benefits, minimize damage and conduct a safe burn.

The most commonly recognized management objectives that can be accomplished by using prescribed fire include:

- Improved pasture accessibility
- Increased production of forage and browse
- Suppression of most brush and cacti species
- Control of selected forbs and/or grass species
- Improved herbaceous composition
- Improved grazing distribution of livestock and wildlife

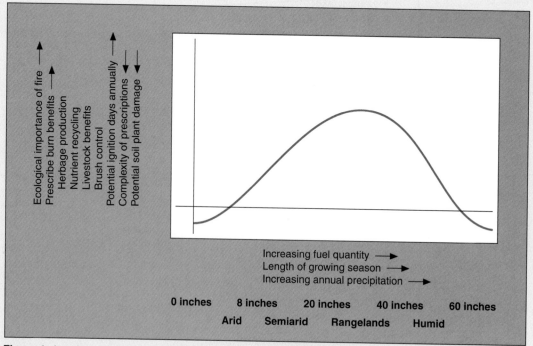

Figure 1. A variety of factors influence the impact of prescribed burning.

▼ **Figure 11.20**   (continued)

- Increased available forage and browse
- Improved forage quality and/or palatability
- Increased animal production
- Removal of excessive mulch and debris
- Control of certain parasites and pests
- Improved nutrient cycling

Each management objective requires a particular set of conditions for burning and a specific type of fire to achieve the desired response. Therefore, carefully evaluate objectives before a fire plan is developed.

Different Fires—Different Responses

Plant response after a fire is influenced by the intensity of the fire, condition of plants at the time of the burn and weather conditions and grazing management decisions following the fire. However, fire effects differ depending on rainfall, fuel quantity and length of growing season (figure 1).

Several factors that determine a fire's intensity are fuel quantity and continuity, air temperature, humidity, wind speed, soil moisture and direction of the flame front movement relative to the wind. Generally, the intensity of a fire increases with greater quantity and continuity of fuel, higher temperature and wind speed and lower humidity and soil moisture. A fire set to move in the same direction as the wind (headfire) tends to be more intense than a flame moving against the wind (backfire). Controlling the fire's intensity through correct firing techniques under appropriate conditions is a key factor in achieving the desired responses from a prescribed burn.

An equally important factor to consider when planning a burn to accomplish specific objectives is the stage and type of growth of desirable and target species. For example, the growth stage of forbs at the time of the burn greatly affects the current and following year's production. Forbs are prolific seed producers, but an untimely fire can destroy forb reproduction and wildlife food. Forb seedlings are highly susceptible to fire; therefore, a late winter burn after many annuals have germinated reduces their population. Burns conducted during early to mid-winter with good soil moisture result in late winter annuals and allow rapid recovery of perennials.

Non-sprouting shrubs are easily killed by fires even though the foliage is not consumed (for example, Ashe juniper). Most shrubs sprout from a bud zone at or below the soil surface. These plants are difficult to kill after the seedling stage. However, top kill is often achievable and greatly reduces competition with perennial grasses and forbs for several years. Because of the extensive root system on mature brush plants, sprouts often grow rapidly and produce canopies similar to pre-burn conditions in 3 to 5 years depending on species.

Perennial grasses are better adapted to burning than woody plants and forbs because of differences in location of growing points. For most grasses (during dormancy), the growing points are located near or below the soil surface. Annual grasses may be killed by fire after they germinate but may be promoted if burning occurs before germination. Fires that consume annual grasses before seed drop greatly reduce next year's seedling production and affect food supplies for some wildlife, such as quail.

The differences in growth cycles between warm and cool season grasses allow timing a burn to enhance one class over the other. Early greenup grasses, such as threeawn, can be harmed by an early spring burn with little damage to deep-rooted perennial grasses. However, cool and wet soil conditions can reduce heat penetration to the sprout zone of shrubs resulting in less damage. Usually, late winter burns improve forage quality, provide rapid grass recovery for earlier grazing, control winter annuals and reduce shrub competition by top removal and seedling kill.

Winter dormant plants recover faster than drought-stressed plants burned during the spring, summer or fall. Also, summer fires are extremely hot and more damaging to vegetation than winter burns. The vegetation is drought stressed and highly flammable at this time of year. High soil temperatures and low humidity combined with flammable fuels contribute to summer burn intensity. Use summer burns only after careful evaluation and planning. If the burned area remains bare for long periods, the potential for soil erosion is greatly increased.

▼ **Figure 11.20** (continued)

In summary, much of the prescribed range burning involves the correct combination of firing techniques, seasonal timing and appropriate weather and range conditions on the day of the burn.

However, these are not the only factors that influence plant response after a burn. Precipitation amounts and season received have a significant effect on range recovery following a burn. Grazing management practices are also important in affecting the recovery rate and level of recovery.

Principles for Using Prescribed Fire

A successful burning program involves three basic steps: (1) thorough planning which includes total range evaluation, pasture selection, management goals, training for conducting a safe burn and preparations for the burn; (2) safe and effective execution of the burn on the specified area(s); and (3) sound range, livestock and wildlife management before, during and after the burn(s).

The Fire Plan

The fire plan identifies the recommended guidelines, procedures, preparations and resources needed for conducting a burn. The plan should describe ignition procedures, location of control crews and location of firelines. Have a contingency plan for control if the fire should escape. Discuss this with your volunteer fire chief in advance of the burn. Volunteer fire departments should be notified of the burn date(s) and burn plan. Regulations for prescribed burning are controlled by the Texas Air Control Board. Obtain and follow current regulations.

Several points to remember in planning a burn are:

- Preburn grazing management (including wildlife population control) is necessary to allow adequate fuel build-up and improved desirable plant vigor.
- Prescribed burns require adequate preparation, equipment and experienced personnel.
- Fire plans and prescriptions are only guidelines.

- Fire behavior must be predictable for effective containment.
- Fire intensity is determined by weather, fuel conditions and type of fire.
- The greater the intensity of the fire, the greater the risk of escape.
- Fire primarily topkills perennial plants.
- Vegetation recovery rate is dependent on species, their vigor, fire temperature, weather conditions and management before and after the burn.
- Postburn management of livestock and wildlife is critical to recovery and improvement of desirable plant species.
- Repeated fires are usually necessary to meet objectives.

Prescribed fire can be used alone or in combination with other range improvement practices (table 1). If sufficient grass fuel cannot be produced, use more intensive practices combined with proper grazing management to promote range improvement. Using fire in combination with other practices often extends longevity and improves the economic rate of return.

Executing the Burn

Consider the day of the burn as judgment day. The first priority is to insure that preparations are complete and check local weather forecasts. The National Weather Service can provide an estimate of conditions during and following the burn. Also measurements of on-site wind speed, wind direction, air temperature and relative humidity are recommended before and during the burn for timely adjustments in procedures.

Only one person (the fire boss) should be in charge of the burn. Identify who the fire boss is to prevent false alarms and unnecessary expense to the fire departments. This person must decide whether to burn and constantly re-evaluate fire behavior, ignition and control during the fire. Even after years of experience, there is always a need for concern and constant alertness. No prescription can be followed to the letter but must be adapted each moment before and during the burning.

▼ **Figure 11.20**   (continued)

Range Condition	Percent of potential	Brush management practice
Excellent	100 to 75	Prescribed burn Individual plant treatment Biological control
Good	74 to 50	Roller chop Individual plant treatment Prescribed burn Biological control
Fair	49 to 25	Roller chop and burn Shred and burn Chain and burn Broadcast herbicide Broadcast herbicide and burn Biological control
Poor	24 to 0	Root plow and seed Disk and seed Tandem roller chop, seed and burn

Table 1. Relationship between range condition and optimum use of brush management practices.

Before beginning the burn give final notification to volunteer fire departments, sheriff's departments and neighbors. This cannot be overemphasized.

Use small test fires to evaluate fire behavior each time conditions change and adjust the plan as needed. The test fire allows better evaluation of existing conditions and potential outcome of the larger burn before a commitment is made. Changes may be necessary to maintain control or to alter intensity of the fire to accomplish specific management objectives. Once the fuel is burned, the opportunity for that season is gone.

Ignition crews must be constantly aware of fire behavior. The potential for escape is greatest during ignition if current factors are not fully appreciated. Make adjustments immediately for any changes in wind direction, velocity, fuel flammability and relative humidity.

The person igniting the fire must be careful never to allow a heat build-up that can escape. Do not get in a hurry; allow the fire to do its job. Flame heights become dangerous when they reach more than halfway across the fireline. Avoid conditions that carry ignited leaves and ash outside the burn area.

Maintain two-way communication between all personnel. Accurate and rapid communication allows proper decisions and immediate action.

Keep sprayers, along with an accessible water source, readily available for controlling small fires. The need for other equipment such as a dozer, chain saws, handtools and graders will depend on conditions. Everyone on the fire should understand their responsibilities and the burn plan. Only the fire boss should direct the actions on the burn, including control of any escaped fires.

Predicting Fire Behavior

Weather conditions and firing techniques significantly influence fire behavior. The variables most affecting fire behavior are topography, fuels, weather and firing techniques. These factors may be counteractive, additive or dominant.

Topography

Topography affects wind behavior and heat build-up which in turn affects flame front movement over

▼ **Figure 11.20**   (continued)

the area. Prediction of wind patterns is necessary so that prefire control measures are taken and appropriate firing procedures are used. A fire moves faster upslope and slower downslope when compared to level terrain. Wind is channeled up canyons with increasing speed. In addition, wind in valleys and on slopes moves upward during the day because of surface heating and downward at night because of surface cooling unless prevailing winds are strong enough to overcome local conditions. Eddy currents over the crest of a hill and around objects create different fire intensities, rates of spread and direction of fire front movement. Sometimes these conditions create fire whirlwinds that can carry sparks, burning debris or flames across a normally safe fireline. Firewhirls are small, tornadic winds, like a dust-devil, created from intense hot spots and rapid rising air at a concentration point.

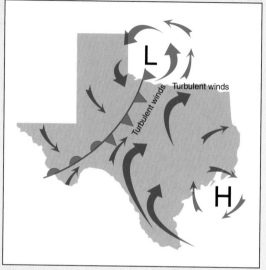

Figure 2. Prevailing wind direction depends on the location of fronts and high and low pressure cells.

Fuel

Fuel moisture content directly affects ignition and flammability. Green, living tissue is more difficult to ignite than dead material, which ordinarily promotes the spread of fire. Temperature, humidity, wind, precipitation and dew, season, time of day, topographic location and microclimate determine fuel moisture. Completely dried grass crackles and breaks easily into pieces when crushed in the hand, while dry twigs snap. In general, grass fuels are relatively safe to burn, whereas plants with high oil content are explosive and can create serious firebrand problems. Moisture content of dead grass, leaves and small branches changes quickly with atmospheric moisture; hence they are considered fast burning fuels. Logs, stumps and large branches, by contrast, take up moisture more slowly. Longer periods of atmospheric drying (several days) are required for prescribed burns to consume logs. Once these fuels have been ignited they may burn for several days. Do not concentrate these fuels near firelines.

The quantity of fuel that burns determines the amount of heat developed during a fire. Generally, 1,500 to 2,000 pounds of grass per acre are required for an effective broadcast burn. The heat

generated affects fire characteristics and results. A good grazing management program allows for development of necessary fuel, especially in above-average rainfall years.

Weather

Weather conditions before, during and after the burn have a major influence on fuels, conditions, procedures and recovery. Predicting wind speed and direction is necessary so that the fire burns in a predetermined manner. Wind movement can be predicted if burning is conducted with a knowledge of weather systems and the effect of high and low pressure cells. Winds associated with frontal weather systems will shift in a clockwise direction as the front approaches and passes over (figure 2). Wind direction changes quickly as a front moves through an area. The wind in South Texas will be from the southeast shifting to the southwest as a front approaches. In North and West Texas, winds are usually from the southwest shifting to the west. Wind speed increases and is often gusty and turbulent just before the front passes. After passage of the front, the wind direction is usually from the north and may be

Figure 11.20 (continued)

unstable for some time. After a day or two, the winds will be from the northeast or east. The shape of the front and rate of movement are important. Generally, movement of fronts during the winter causes constantly changing conditions in Texas.

Wind speed greatly affects the flame height, rate of spread and uplift of embers and burning material. Speed must be sufficient to carry fire easily through the fuels but not high enough to cause the fire to jump the downwind firelines. Wind speed should be between 5 and 15 miles per hour for effective burning.

Low wind movement is dangerous because of possible whirlwind development and unpredictable direction of spread. High wind speeds may reduce fuel consumption and increase chances of escape. Wind direction must be consistent throughout the burn to avoid unpredicted fire behavior. Usually, large fires create their own wind around the convection column of smoke, heat and flame front. Two fires moving toward each other can create an intense hot spot or firewhirl.

The height and density of plants affect wind velocity. Unless sufficient fuel occurs within a brush stand, wind velocities may be insufficient to move flames properly and damage the brush. Also fuel should be uniformly distributed and in sufficient quantity to carry the fire under the canopy of a shrub or tree to generate the necessary heat to kill plant tissue. Mechanically cleared firelines and roads in brush or trees create openings that produce unusual wind movements.

Relative humidity affects fuel moisture, fire intensity and rate of spread. The lower the relative humidity, the hotter the fire and the greater the risk. Fine fuels such as grass burn with the same intensity when relative humidity is between 25 to 45 percent. Cooler fires result when the relative humidity is 45 to 60 percent. Less uniform and intense fires occur when relative humidities are above 60 percent. Do not attempt to burn when relative humidities are below 20 percent.

Day to night changes in air temperature and relative humidity create different fire behavior potentials. Fires of different intensities can be executed by selecting different times of day or night and different weather conditions. The density of a brush stand and the amount of shade created by the vegetation affect the relative humidity near the soil surface. Except under extremely dry conditions, brush stands burn slower and less intensely than open grassland areas.

Firing Techniques

Proper ignition procedures are needed to effectively contain a fire and accomplish management objectives. Ignition procedures greatly influence fire behavior and spread. Fires either move in the same direction as wind (headfire), in an opposite direction of wind (backfire) or at a right angle to the wind (flankfire)(figure 3). The headfire is the most intense because of its faster rate of spread, wider burning zone and greater flame heights. The flankfire is of intermediate intensity.

Backfires require higher fuel quantities and a more continuous fuel distribution than headfires. Since backfires move slower and have a less intense flame front, they are easier to control. Also, in heavy fuels, a backfire may consume more fuel and provide greater plant basal damage to brush than fast moving headfires by keeping heat closer to the soil surface. Set backfires as close to the fireline as possible to prevent high flames and embers from crossing the fireline.

Headfires are effective at top killing shrubs and trees with intense heat several feet above the soil surface. Headfires burn under a wider range of weather and fuel conditions than backfires but are more dangerous. Headfires may be required to burn large acreages in a reasonable amount of time. However, a series of firelines across a pasture can be used to set a number of backfires in a short period. Costs of fireline construction are higher.

A combination of the head and backfiring technique is the stripfire. This is simply a line of fire set within the pasture at right angles to the wind direction. The result is a headfire across the strip and backing fire into the wind. This technique is used to speed up the widening of firelines. The ignition crew should regulate the width of the strip so that the

▼ **Figure 11.20**   (continued)

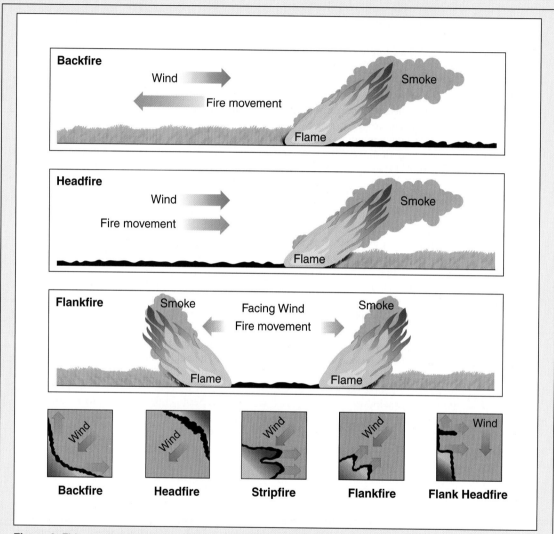

Figure 3. Firing techniques commonly used for prescribed burning.

flame front does not leap the fireline or burned-out area. Changes in fuel quantity and continuity require appropriate changes in width of the stripfired area.

Once a headfire moves 50 to 100 feet, its major flame front characteristics have developed. A 50- to 100-foot wide stripfire can be set to confirm the necessary width of the fireline before setting the major headfire. Properly station all control crews for this test burn. Do not set a second stripfire or the headfire until the flame-front from the strip has calmed.

Backfiring from a fireline, followed by headfiring, has been successfully used throughout Texas (figures 4 and 5). The backfire plus stripfiring is used to sufficiently widen the downwind fireline before the

Figure 11.20 (continued)

headfire is ignited. This allows flexibility in wind direction and potentially more suitable burn days during a season than when a plan requires a specific wind direction. Also, adjustments in firing can compensate for shifts in wind direction. Observing backfires and stripfires improves judgment on fireline width, potential escape conditions and flammability before setting the headfire.

Fire Containment Practices

Containing a fire to the specified area requires use of natural or man-made breaks in fuel continuity and burning under conditions that minimize chances of escape. Improperly set fires could escape across any fireline. Exercise constant vigilance by personnel throughout all burns. The key to containment is immediate response to any potential escape.

Usually, firelines are constructed using mechanical equipment to expose the mineral soil or by applying fire retardant compounds or water on the fuel. Always plow firelines away from the area to be burned to prevent burying fuel that can smoulder and create sparks for long periods. Usually a fireline 1 or 2 blades wide is adequate, depending on conditions and firing techniques.

Generally, adapt the firing procedure to the kind of firelines and natural barriers available. Use a 1- or 2-foot retardant fireline if care is taken to backfire precisely along the chemical line and not promote flames that can reach flammable fuels. Thus,

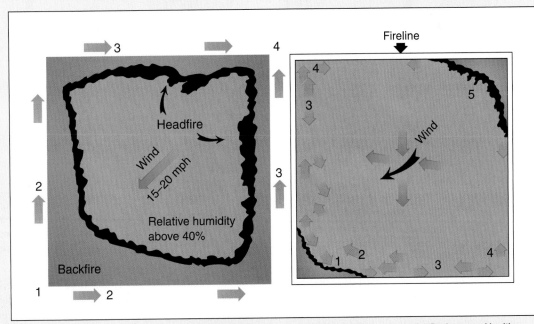

Figure 4. Using combinations of backfiring, stripfiring, flank headfiring and headfiring allows the fire boss and ignition crews to conduct successful burns with fire to help contain the burn. One procedure (left) utilizes a backfire (1) lit simultaneously in each direction. (2) After the backfire has burned 50 to 100 feet on the downwind sides, ignite the remainder of the area (3) and burn as a headfire (4). (From publications by Dr. Henry Wright, Texas Tech Univ.) By using all combinations of firing techniques (right), more difficult burns can be accomplished. The backfire plus narrow stripfires (1) are used to widen the firelines on downwind sides. A wider stripfire is used to increase fireline width and test burnout for containment of the headfire (2 and 3). A flank headfire is used to widen burnout of corners (4). The headfire is set using two torches to the burnout corners (5).

▼ **Figure 11.20**   (continued)

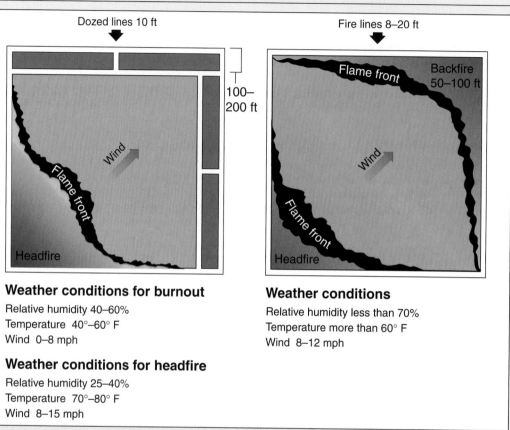

Weather conditions for burnout

Relative humidity 40–60%
Temperature 40°–60° F
Wind 0–8 mph

Weather conditions for headfire

Relative humidity 25–40%
Temperature 70°–80° F
Wind 8–15 mph

Weather conditions

Relative humidity less than 70%
Temperature more than 60° F
Wind 8–12 mph

Figure 5. Fire plans and prescriptions differ with objectives, vegetation, personnel training, etc. Fixed wind direction (left) requires burnout of upwind firelines in January and February and ignition of the headfire in February or March. A fire plan using "simultaneous" backfiring and headfiring (right) requires greater coordination and on-the-ground judgment but does not require a fixed wind direction in the prescription. (From publications by Dr. Henry Wright, Texas Tech Univ.)

fire is used under carefully controlled conditions to widen and create a sufficient fireline. Disking is satisfactory if mineral soil is well exposed and flammable fuel is eliminated in the disk strip. Often disking does not adequately destroy the fuel continuity, and use of hand tools or retardants is required to prevent fire from skipping through patches of fuel. Also, disking may reduce accessibility for trucks and sprayers to move quickly along the fireline.

Drip torches (using a diesel-gasoline mixture) are recommended to set uniform, narrow fires without considerable resetting. Burning tires, pear burners and matches are less reliable and create a wider initial flame front. Erratically set fires result in stringers of fire proceeding at different rates drawing each other and creating erratic behavior.

Use special care when burning volatile fuels to prevent embers from crossing firelines. For example, burn juniper piles within 500 feet of the perimeter during the growing season or under high moisture conditions when the surrounding grass is not flammable (figure 6). Use this same practice for any

▼ **Figure 11.20**   (continued)

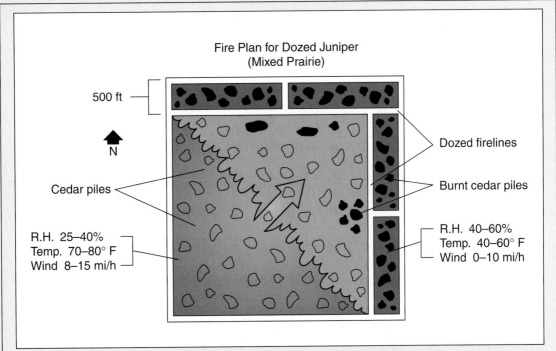

Figure 6. When the grass is green, juniper piles in the 500-foot strip (black splotches) on the downwind sides (north and east) are burned with wind velocities less than 10 miles per hour and relative humidity above 45 percent. Eight months later (when grass is dormant), the grass in the 500-foot strip is burned (strip-headfire technique) when the wind speed is less than 10 miles per hour and relative humidity is between 40 to 60 percent. Lower relative humidities may be used if the grass fuel is less than 2,000 pounds/acre. All large concentrations of piles are backfired on the downwind sides of main area to be burned, and then the entire area is burned into the prepared firelines with a wind speed of 8 to 15 miles per hour and a relative humidity of 25 to 40 percent. (From publications by Dr. Henry Wright, Texas Tech Univ.)

brush pile or concentration of dead fuel that poses a threat to containment. Hot fires under piles will destroy existing vegetation, especially if burned during the growing season. Hand seeding in the ash may be a valuable practice for more rapid recovery.

Safety is the Key

If it cannot be done safely, do not burn. Escaped fires can damage property, life, equipment, animals and vegetation that negate the beneficial effects achieved with the planned burn.

The fire boss is responsible for executing the burn safely and effectively. Burn plans provide realistic guidelines for when, where and how to conduct the burn. However, actual burn conditions seldom perfectly match the desired guidelines. Apply techniques that best match the current and expected conditions and use experienced personnel to provide leadership. Do not wear clothing that is highly flammable or melts easily; cotton is recommended.

The landowner using prescribed fire is legally responsible. Arrange for liability insurance and involve neighbors in planning and executing the burn(s). Inform fire and sheriff's departments. Proof of planning and use of accepted burning practices may be invaluable in negating charges of negligence if a fire escapes, resulting in a lawsuit. The Texas Air

▼ **Figure 11.20**   (continued)

Control Board in Austin has specific regulations on when and under what weather conditions prescribed burns can be legally conducted. Obtain a copy of the regulations. It is the manager's responsibility to have flagmen on highways to slow traffic if smoke obscures visibility. Generally, fires should move away from highways or houses with a good uplift of smoke. Do not burn when temperature inversions can occur. Ask your weather service if such conditions are likely during the burn and following night.

The bottom line in safety is to have a good plan, executed under appropriate conditions with adequate equipment, personnel and preparations. This includes a plan for containing any fire that escapes from the specified area.

Burn Prescriptions

Generally, the prescription for a successful burn includes wind speeds of 5 to 15 miles per hour, steady wind direction, air temperature 40° to 80°F., relative humidity 25 to 60 percent and uniform fuel continuity of 1,500 pounds per acre or more. Generally, fire intensity and rate of spread increase with drier fuel, lower RH and higher air temperature, wind speed and fuel quantity.

Costs of Prescribed Burns

The cost of a prescribed burn differs for each ranch, pasture and time of year. Each ranch must develop a budget and keep records of actual expenditures for future analysis. In some counties cost-share assistance is available for fireline construction, labor and equipment rental. Costs range from 50 cents per acre to $8 to $10 per acre or more depending on fireline construction and manner of calculation. Costs of follow-up burns should be lower, however.

Summary

Prescribed burning is a viable improvement practice for most Texas rangelands. When integrated with other practices, fire can be used to maintain desired vegetation composition and structure. Many man-agers are not able to effectively use fire until they achieve better range conditions. Good grazing management programs complement prescribed burning.

The basic principles affecting fire behavior are considered by the manager for developing a realistic fire plan. The fire plan identifies the overall objectives for the ranch as well as for each pasture and range site to be burned. Ideally, burn entire management units to avoid overconcentration of livestock and wildlife. Base the stocking rate on actual acreage burned and adjust for recovery rate. Control white-tailed deer and exotic game populations to prevent overuse of key browse and forb species.

Burning when brush regrowth is young and when fine fuel loads are near maximum can more effectively maintain high production ranges. Brush stands require two to three burns before most objectives are realized. Select the better sites for burning; hence, the net return per dollar invested should be higher.

Described techniques, prescriptions and guidelines provide a basis for using prescribed fire. Consider local experience when adapting prescriptions and plans. Emphasize safety [and] avoid over-optimism. Use fire where benefits can realistically be achieved and integrated with the ranch operation. Take advantage of high forage production years, using excess forage as fuel for a burn. Careful grazing management is an important part of any prescribed burning program.

Assistance and training are available for developing your prescribed burn program. Agencies currently involved are the Texas Agricultural Extension Service, Soil Conservation Service, Texas Forest Service and Texas Parks and Wildlife.

Acknowledgments

Cover photos supplied by J.F. Cadenhead, W.A. McGinty, R.Q. Landers and L.D. White. The authors wish to thank Tommy Welch, R.Q. Landers and Calvin Richardson for their in-depth review of the manuscript.

Source: Larry D. White and C. Wayne Hanselka, *Prescribed Range Burning in Texas,* 5M-8-91 (College Station: Texas Agricultural Extension Service, 1991). Reprinted by permission of the authors.

III Producing Effective Documents and Presentations for Your Audience

12

Writing Reader-Oriented Proposals

▶ **OUTLINE**

Proposals are documents designed to persuade someone to follow or accept a specific course of action. Proposals usually offer to solve a problem or to provide a service or product, and then they suggest a specific plan for solving the problem or for providing the service or product. Some proposals also lay out a specific timetable and budget. An effective proposal is persuasive; it convinces readers to accept and possibly to pay for the work that it proposes. If you propose a project for a fee, you will want to persuade your readers that you can carry out the project within a reasonable time and at a reasonable cost. A proposal, then, is a "sales" document: it sells a proposed action and your services or the services of your organization to carry out that action. A proposal may have these elements:

- Description of the problem or need
- Description of, and justification for, the proposed service, product, or solution
- Specific plan for providing the proposed service or product or for solving the identified problem
- Timetable for carrying out the plan
- Budget (if the project is for a fee)
- Description of the people who will carry out the plan and, if applicable, of the organization that employs them

You might write a proposal in response to several scenarios. Let's look at five scenarios and how the writers responded:

Scenario 1   Bill Martinez works for a large construction company. His company is building a new manufacturing plant. The manufacturing process will create large amounts of ash. According to EPA guidelines, the company must dispose of the ash properly. Bill is responsible for hiring a company to develop recommendations for disposing of the ash. Therefore, he sends out requests to several environmental service companies, inviting them to submit their qualifications to develop the recommendations. (The sample proposal in Figure 12.10 is a proposal from one of the environmental service companies.)

Scenario 2   A government agency in Wisconsin decides that it should renovate its office building. The building is fifty years old and has several problems: it doesn't meet current fire code regulations; the windows and outside doors provide little insulation from the weather; the bathrooms have plumbing problems; and the offices are not appropriately wired for current telecommunications and fiber optic technology. The agency wants to find a qualified construction company to renovate the building at a reasonable price. The agency advertises the proposed work in newspapers across Wisconsin. Any companies interested in submitting bids can then request the specifications of the project.

Scenario 3 The United States Army solicited proposals for manufacturing night vision sight for the M24 Sniper Weapon System. The army put an RFP (request for proposals) in *Commerce Business Daily* (see Figure 12.1). The RFP describes the specifications for the night vision sight, gives the due date for the proposal, and provides information about obtaining specifics about the request.

Scenario 4 Susan Rowland writes software documentation. In recent months, her workload—as well as that of the other documentation writers—has dramatically increased. Susan knows that her company currently has a hiring freeze, so she can't hire another writer. She believes that the only way to help with the increased workload is to update the computer software and hardware used to write and produce the documentation. Therefore, she writes a proposal to her regional supervisor requesting updated software and hardware for her department.

Scenario 5 Leanne Gong wants to research whether or not the concentrations of mercury and lead allowed by the government are safe. She wants to determine whether people living in areas with allowable concentrations of mercury or lead have a history of health problems. To conduct this research, Leanne needs funds. She looks for RFPs in the *Federal Registry* and other sources. She can't find an RFP that matches her proposed research, so she prepares a proposal to send to various private and public agencies, hoping these agencies will fund her research.

These five scenarios illustrate the two primary types of proposal situations: solicited and unsolicited. Scenarios 1 through 3 illustrate situations requiring solicited proposals. **Solicited proposals** originate when a person, an organization, or a government agency requests qualified organizations and individuals to submit their qualifications to do work (Scenario 1), to submit bids to complete proposed work (Scenario 2), or to submit proposals for manufacturing equipment or other items according to specifications (Scenario 3). In each of these scenarios, the organizations and individuals write proposals based on the requests and specifications of another organization, individual, or government agency.

Scenarios 4 and 5 illustrate situations requiring **unsolicited proposals**—proposals *not* requested by the organization, individual, or government agency that receives them. Unlike solicited proposals, unsolicited proposals must

Figure 12.1

A Request for Proposals from *Commerce Business Daily*

Specifications —

Due date for proposal —

Information for obtaining specific information about the request —

US Army CECOM, Command, Control, Communications and Intelligence (C31) Acquisition, Fort Monmouth, New Jersey 07703-5008
59–59 • NIGHT VISION SIGHT FOR M24 SNIPER WEAPON SYSTEM SOL DAAB07•93-R-K533 DUE 122293 POC Contact Michael L. Lang, Contract Specialist, (908) 532-4042. Matthew Meinert, Contracting Officer, (908) 532-4043. The US Government intends to issue a solicitation to interested sources who have the capability to manufacture a Night Vision Sight for the M24 Sniper Weapon System (SWS). The sight must incorporate third generation image intensifier technology and appropriate magnification power and maximum possible field of view thus enabling the SWS to meet the requirements of paragraph 3 below. The night vision sight: 1. Shall be either (a) a module that connects with and uses the current M24 Leupold day optics, OR (b) an integrated system that contains both day and night optics. 2. Shall have a maximum weight of 6.3 required, 4.5 lbs desired. Weight includes day sight and mounts for clip-on configuration night sight, or total system weight for integrated day/night configuration. 3. When mounted to the M24 SWS, the M24 SWS must achieve a daytime probability of hit (PH) between 0.95 and 0.85 on an averaged basis, over a course of fire with stationary known distance targets out to 800 meters. The M24 SWS must also achieve a minimum nighttime PH of 0.70 on an averaged basis, over a course of fire with stationary known distance targets out to 600 meters under clean air, starlight to quarter moonlight conditions. 4. Shall demonstrate the following performance characteristics: (a) image tube center resolution:)55 lp/mm, (b) magnification:)7X, (c) field of view:)2 degrees, (d) elevation and windage adjustment: One minute of arc per click. The zero position of the reticle shall not move more than 0.55 minutes of angle (MOA) from the optical axis when each knob (both elevation and windage) is cycled from 0 to the extreme adjustments and returned, for 10 cycles. The Government is interested in obtaining comments from industry who have the capability to provide a device meeting the above requirements as part of a category B (Adaptation) Non-Developmental Item (NDI) procurement. Two hardware samples will be required and are to be delivered concurrent with submission of the proposal. Proposals are due 30 days after the date of solicitation which is tentatively scheduled for 22 Nov 93. Any deviations from the requirements of the solicitation must be addressed in the offeror's written proposal, and will be considered in the Government's proposal evaluation. Specific information regarding the Government's test procedure and evaluation criteria for the hardware samples will be included in the forthcoming solicitation. The Government provides this data without assuming responsibility for its accuracy or for any conclusion/interpretation which may be drawn from the data which is provided solely for information purposes and should not be relied upon as a basis for interpretation of a bid. The solicitation may include more detailed information concerning price history. Therefore, telephone or other requests for price history will not be accepted. Respond in writing only to AMSEL-ACCC-C-CR (LAN). No Phone calls will be accepted. A solicitation will be provided to all interested bidders on or about 22 Nov 93. The solicitation will include Government requirements for a two-year multi-year procurement. A pre-proposal conference will be held approximately 15 days after issuance of the solicitation. All responsible sources may submit a bid/quote/proposal which shall be considered by this agency. Only written requests will be accepted. (0307)

Source: *Commerce Business Daily,* PSA-0967, 5 Nov. 1993: 21.

convince readers that a specific need or problem exists before explaining a plan, cost, or qualifications. You can write unsolicited proposals to people in your own organization as in Scenario 4, or you can write them to people outside your organization as in Scenario 5. In Scenario 5, Leanne Gong decides to send unsolicited proposals because she can't find any RFPs that request the kind of research that she wants to conduct. Therefore, she targets a group of agencies that fund research and sends them her proposal.

Susan Rowland's and Leanne Gong's task—writing an unsolicited proposal—can be more difficult than writing a proposal in response to a specific request. Susan and Leanne not only have to convince readers that they have good projects and can carry out those projects at a reasonable cost, but they also have to persuade readers that their projects are worthwhile and will fulfill a need. Susan wants to convince her readers that her department has an increased workload and that the computer software and hardware used by the documentation writers is preventing the department from completing that workload in a reasonable time and with the quality the company expects. Leanne wants to persuade her readers that the allowable levels of mercury and lead may be too high and that a scientific study can determine whether or not the levels actually are too high.

The five scenarios illustrate how proposals originate and the possible locations of the readers. Readers of proposals can work within or outside your organization. If the readers work within your organization, as in Susan's scenario (Scenario 4), the proposal is *internal,* written to someone within the writer's company or organization. If the readers work outside your organization, as in Scenarios 1, 2, 3, and 5, the proposal is *external.* The following principles will help you to write effective proposals whether they are solicited or unsolicited, internal or external.

▶Principle 1: Find Out About the Readers of Your Proposals

Before writing any proposal, find out about the people who are most likely to read it. You can write an effective proposal only if you understand your readers and have some idea about how they will respond to the problem and to the work that you propose. To find out about your readers, ask yourself these questions, which will help you to customize your proposal:

- **What positions do your readers hold in the organization? If the readers work in the organization that employs you, where are their positions in relation to yours in the organizational hierarchy?** If you know readers' positions in the hierarchy, you can more accurately determine who will approve or disapprove your proposal, who will understand the topic and the background of your proposal, and who will be your primary and secondary readers. Are your readers above you, below you, or at the same level as you in your organization? If they outrank you, you may want to use a more formal approach or to have your immediate supervisor read a draft of your proposal before you send it to your primary readers. If you and your readers are at the same level in the organization, or if you outrank them, they may expect a less formal approach.

- **Will more than one group read the proposal? If so, what sections of the proposal will each group read?** Often, several groups of readers may read a proposal. For example, managers or executives may read the summary to determine whether the proposal has potential merit. If they decide that it has merit, they may send the proposal to the accountants to look at the budget and to technical experts to look at the solution and the plan of work.

- **What do your readers know about the problem or need that prompted your proposal?** If your proposal is unsolicited, readers probably will know little about the problem or need addressed in your proposal. If your proposal is solicited, readers will understand the problem.

- **What do your readers know about you or your organization? Have their previous experiences with your organization or with you been positive? If not, why?** Find out whether your readers have had previous experiences with your organization. Was the experience extended or brief, positive or negative? What impression are the readers likely to have of you or your organization? When you know the answers to these questions, you can write the qualifications section of the proposal and lessen any negative concerns your readers may have about you or your organization.

If you are aware of the answers to all these questions, you can write a proposal that meets your readers' needs and expectations. Once you have found out about your readers, you can determine what they may ask about your proposal.

▶Principle 2: Prepare to Answer Readers' Questions

The success of your proposal depends on how

- Persuasively and logically you argue for your proposed solution, product, or service
- Convincingly you argue that you or your organization is best qualified to carry out the plan
- Persuasively you argue that you or your organization can complete the work within a reasonable time and at a reasonable cost

How can you provide readers with the information they need, without overstating what your organization can provide? First determine what your readers expect and what questions they will seek answers to as they read your proposal, and then decide what you or your organization can reasonably propose. You have a responsibility to explain specifically and accurately the work that you or your organization can provide, so readers will not expect more or less than you intend to deliver and will not hold you or your organization responsible for more or less work than you propose. In your eagerness to get a proposal accepted, don't exaggerate or overestimate the work that you can perform.

A series of questions relating to three areas will help you to anticipate what readers expect from your proposal and what they may ask as they read it: the problem or need addressed in the proposal; the proposed solution, product, or service; and the plan of work. You will find these questions in Figure 12.2. Figure 12.2 relates the questions to the conventional elements of proposals discussed in Principle 3.

To answer the readers' questions, you need to research the readers and their organization. You might find out about the organization's history, its financial standing and goals, and its organizational hierarchy. You also can research the organization's corporate culture to see how it might affect your readers' perspectives and ideas. With this information, you can better anticipate your readers' questions and provide persuasive answers.

In addition to anticipating readers' questions, consider what you and your organization can realistically propose and the strengths and weaknesses of your proposal. Figure 12.2 lists questions that you can consider as you evaluate what you are proposing. You want to make sure that your proposal will appeal to readers without compromising what you and your organization can actually do.

| **Figure 12.2** | Writers' and Readers' Questions About the Conventional Elements of Proposals |

Element	Writers' Questions	Readers' Questions
Introduction and problem definition	How can the proposal demonstrate that you understand the problem or need? Should you restate the problem or need to show readers that you understand it?	*If the proposal is solicited:* What do readers expect from your proposal? *If the proposal is unsolicited:* Why should readers be interested in your proposal? What problem or need does your proposal address? Why is the problem or need important to readers?

(continued on next page)

▼ **Figure 12.2**   (continued)

Element	Writers' Questions	Readers' Questions
Proposed solution, product, or service	How can you reasonably solve the problem or meet readers' needs? What are the strengths of your solution, product, or service? How can you emphasize those strengths? What are the weaknesses of your solution, product, or service? How can you counter those weaknesses and readers' objections to them? How does your solution, product, or service meet readers' needs? Can you and your organization reasonably carry out the solution, product, or service? How can you make the solution, product, or service attractive to readers without compromising what you and your organization can actually do?	How will you solve the problem or satisfy the need? Specifically, what do you propose to make or to do? Are other solutions, products, or services possible? If so, why have you chosen the solution, product, or service presented in the proposal? How does your choice compare with the other possibilities? How will readers view the solution, product, or service you've selected?
Plan of work	What are the strengths of your plan? What are the weaknesses of your plan? How can you counter those weaknesses and the readers' possible objections to them? Is the plan one that you and your organization can reasonably carry out? How can you make your plan attractive to readers without overstating what you and your organization can do?	What will you do? How long will the plan take? Is the plan reasonable?
Qualifications	How can you demonstrate that you and your organization are qualified and that the readers can depend on you to do what you propose?	Why should readers believe that you can do what you propose? Why should readers believe that they can depend on you or your organization to do what you propose?
Budget	Does the budget reflect the actual cost of the plan? Have you justified your budget and anticipated readers' possible objections to it?	How much will the proposed solution cost? Is the proposed solution worth that cost to readers?

►Principle 3: Use the Conventional Elements of Proposals

►See Chapter 11, "Preparing Front and Back Matter," for information on preparing the front and back matter of a formal document, and Chapter 18, "Writing Reader-Oriented Letters, Memos, and E-Mail," for information on letters and memos.

As the five scenarios presented earlier illustrate, you may write proposals in response to many different situations. The formats for the proposals may vary with the situations. If your proposal is formal, you might choose to include a letter of transmittal, title page, table of contents, and executive summary. If your proposal is informal, you might select a letter or memo format. Whether you use a format with front matter or a letter or memo format, your proposal will have some or all of the conventional elements discussed in this chapter. From one organization to another, these elements may have different names; but their purpose remains the same. For example, instead of *problem definition* your organization may use the phrase "scope of work," and instead of *budget* your organization may use "cost estimates." If your organization prefers certain names for the elements or requires particular elements to appear in its proposals, use those names and include those elements. If you are responding to an RFP or a request for a bid, the request may specify the elements and the format that you should follow. Follow the specifications of the requesters; otherwise, they may reject your proposal or bid.

Most readers want a description of the project—including a statement of the problem; the proposed solution, product, or service; your plan for solving the problem or providing the proposed product or service; and the cost. Many readers also will want to know whether you and your organization are qualified to do what you propose. Most proposals contain these conventional elements:

Summary

Description of the proposed project

    Introduction

    Problem definition

    Proposed solution

    Work plan

Qualifications

    Personnel

    Resources

Budget

Conclusion

For some proposals, you may not need some of these elements—especially the qualifications and budget. These two elements may not be necessary based on your relationship with the readers and on the purpose of your proposal. For example, if you are writing an informal proposal to your manager, you wouldn't include a qualifications section because your manager knows your qualifications. However, if you are writing a more formal proposal to external readers, you would probably include a qualifications section.

The following sections describe these conventional elements. They correspond to the questions that readers may ask and questions that you should ask (see Figure 12.2).

Summary

▶ For more information on summaries, see Chapter 11, "Preparing Front and Back Matter," page 320.

The **summary** is a condensed version of your proposal. Because readers will look at the summary first, it is often crucial to the success of a proposal. Based on the summary, many readers may decide whether or not to consider a proposal. Many readers may read only the summary. Readers who have received many proposals in response to one RFP may use the summaries to determine which proposals to consider seriously.

The summary contains essential information about the proposed solution, product, or service; the plan of work; and the cost of the proposal. To write an effective summary, follow these tips:

▶ **Tips for Writing an Effective Summary**

- **Concisely state the problem or need addressed in the proposal.** Include only the information necessary for readers to understand the problem or need. Exclude supporting information and details.

- **Summarize the proposed solution, product, or service.** Be sure to show how it meets the readers' needs and requirements.

- **Describe your plan for carrying out the proposed solution, product, or service.** Exclude details about the plan as you are summarizing—that is, present only the basics of the plan.

- **Summarize your qualifications or those of your team and/or your organization (if your proposal includes a qualifications section).** Some proposal writers only include the qualifications of the organization in the summary.

- **Summarize the budget (if your proposal includes a budget section).** You may summarize by simply stating the total cost of the proposed solution, product, or service. For some sales proposals, many companies leave the budget information out of the summary; they want to "sell" the proposed product or service before giving the reader the financial data. As Neil Cobb, a regional director for SBC (an international telecommunications company), explains, if your product isn't the lowest priced on the market, you want to tell the readers about the product and the company before you give them the "bottom line." In this way, you can, hopefully, persuade your readers of the value of your product so they will see its value in relation to its cost.

Presidential Proposals

As one of three equal branches of the federal government, the office of the president of the United States often has exerted executive power only by persuading the other branches, especially the legislature, to act in concert. Many famous presidential addresses to Congress were essentially proposals, and some were more successful than others. One notable failure occurred in January 1918 when President Woodrow Wilson proposed that his "Fourteen Points" were the "only possible" program for world peace after the end of the Great War—World War I. A fierce moralist, Wilson struck many members of Congress as too overbearing when he presented his principle of universal justice as the only solution, without which "no part of the structure of international justice can stand. The people of the United States could act upon no other principle." His Fourteen Points did in fact become the basis for the League of Nations, but—to Wilson's deep disappointment—Congress refused to allow America to join. Would the result have differed if Wilson's proposal had been more diplomatic—more "reader oriented"?

President Franklin Delano Roosevelt was a more canny politician, as his proposal of war against Japan, after the attack on Pearl Harbor, shows. Even though Congress was almost certain to approve his proposal, Roosevelt was noticeably more diplomatic—more "reader oriented"—than Wilson in his presentation: "I believe I interpret the will of the Congress and of the people when I assert that we will . . . make very certain that this form of treachery shall never endanger us again. . . . I ask that the Congress declare [a state of war]."

The summary is a powerful tool. An effective summary persuades readers to read more about your proposed project. Figure 12.3 presents the summary from an unsolicited proposal for a training and reference manual for a university Office of Disability Accommodation.

Description of the Proposed Project

The **description of the proposed project** is the heart of the proposal. It presents detailed information about the problem or need; the solution, product, or service; and the plan. The description may include an introduction, problem description, proposed solution, and work plan.

Introduction

The introduction briefly describes the product or service that you are proposing and tells why you are proposing it. For example, you might state that you are writing in response to a request from readers or to a specific request for proposals. In the introduction, you also can tell readers what follows in the proposal. The writers of the example shown in Figure 12.4 combine the introduction and the summary; this combination is common in

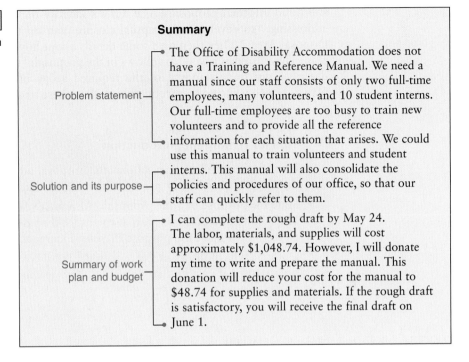

Figure 12.3

The Summary from an Unsolicited Proposal

Summary

Problem statement —
The Office of Disability Accommodation does not have a Training and Reference Manual. We need a manual since our staff consists of only two full-time employees, many volunteers, and 10 student interns. Our full-time employees are too busy to train new volunteers and to provide all the reference information for each situation that arises. We could use this manual to train volunteers and student interns. This manual will also consolidate the

Solution and its purpose —
policies and procedures of our office, so that our staff can quickly refer to them.

Summary of work plan and budget —
I can complete the rough draft by May 24. The labor, materials, and supplies will cost approximately $1,048.74. However, I will donate my time to write and prepare the manual. This donation will reduce your cost for the manual to $48.74 for supplies and materials. If the rough draft is satisfactory, you will receive the final draft on June 1.

Figure 12.4

The Introduction to a Solicited Proposal

Purpose of the proposal —
As you requested, Nowakowski and Associates, Inc., is pleased to provide this work plan and cost estimate to develop a conceptual closure plan for the Caney Branch ash disposal facility. We understand that Hill

Problem the proposal addresses —
Manufacturing has decided to mine around the ash area. In November of 2001, we provided, as you requested, preliminary cost estimates for three capping scenarios that could potentially be part of an overall closure plan for Caney Branch. However, these closure scenarios and perhaps others require a more detailed analysis of the hydrology and geochemistry of the system before you select an appropriate closure

Description of what follows in the proposal —
scenario. On the basis of our recent discussion, the following proposal describes our understanding of the required scope of work and our work plan.

short and informal proposals. The writers identify the problem that they are addressing: "to develop a conceptual closure plan for the Caney Branch Ash Disposal Area." They then give some details about how they will develop the plan. They also describe what follows in the proposal: "the following proposal describes our understanding of the required scope of work and our work plan." As you write your introduction, follow these tips:

> **Tips for Writing the Introduction**

- **Identify the problem or need that the proposal addresses.** Briefly describe the problem or need that the proposal addresses.
- **State the purpose of your proposal.** Although your readers will likely know the purpose, state it to ensure that you and the readers clearly understand the purpose of your document.
- **Describe what follows in the proposal.** Tell the readers the organizational pattern that you will follow in the proposal.

Problem Definition

Once you have told readers what you are proposing, convince them that you understand the work that you are proposing and that you designed your solution and work plan after studying their needs. If the proposal is unsolicited, convince readers that the proposal addresses a significant problem or need and demonstrate how that problem or need affects them. Persuade them first that a problem or need truly exits and then that it is important to them.

Anticipate and answer any questions that readers may have, so they know that you clearly understand their situation. (Figure 12.2 lists questions that readers might ask as they read any problem description. Your readers may have other questions about the specific subject addressed in your proposal.) Depending on whether the proposal is solicited or unsolicited, the problem definition may

- Define the problem—in detail for an unsolicited proposal and with less detail for a solicited proposal.
- Give the background of the problem or situation or explain how it developed (primarily for unsolicited proposals). The background may help readers to understand that a significant problem exists or that you understand their needs.
- Explain why the product or service that you propose is necessary (for unsolicited proposals). For instance, if you are proposing a research project, explain why the research is important.

As you prepare the problem definition, follow these tips:

> **Tips for Writing the Problem Definition**

- **Define the problem or need.** If you are writing an unsolicited proposal, give the readers the details they require to understand the problem or need and why they should then consider your proposed solution or plan. If you are writing a solicited proposal, include fewer details. Instead, give the readers only enough details to know that you understand the problem. This definition is important since proposals often result in some deliverable, and you want a written record of your understanding of the problem or need.

- **Present the necessary background for the readers to understand the problem or need and the proposed solution or plan.** If you conducted library research, briefly summarize your research. If you examined company reports or interviewed people affected by the problem or need, use the information that you gathered to give readers the information they require to understand the context of your proposal.

- **Give the readers the information they require to understand why they should accept your product or service.** Explain why the proposed product or service is necessary to the readers or their organization.

Figure 12.5 presents the problem-definition section (called "Scope of Work") of a solicited proposal. The readers know what their needs are, so the primary purpose of this problem-definition section is to show that the writers

Figure 12.5
The Problem-Definition Section of a Solicited Proposal

Scope of Work

To define the problem, the writers restate the work that the readers expect.

> We understand that our scope of work will include the following:
>
> - developing a set of recommendations for capping and closing the ash area at the Caney Branch ash disposal facility
> - compiling a conceptual design document that describes and illustrates the recommended approach for capping and closing the ash area

The writers state the work their work plan does *not* include.

After developing the conceptual design document, we will, if desired by Hill Manufacturing, present the technical merits of the plan at a meeting with Hill and then with the state water commission. As you requested, the conceptual document will not include any final design specifications or detailed estimates of the costs required to implement the recommended closure plan. However, we propose to develop preliminary cost estimates as necessary to evaluate various closure alternatives.

understand the readers' needs. Thus, the writers restate the work that the readers expect of them as well as what the readers do not expect of them.

Figure 12.6 shows the problem-definition section of an unsolicited proposal for a university Office of Disability Accommodation. Using examples and terms the readers will understand, the writer specifically explains the problems

Figure 12.6   The Problem-Definition Section of an Unsolicited Proposal

Current Problems at the Office of Disability Accommodation

The writer presents the background.

The Office of Disability Accommodation uses many volunteers and student interns. These volunteers and interns may work in the office for only a semester, creating a large turnover. They may work as few as 5 or as many as 20 hours per week. With the number of these volunteers and interns and the high turnover, the office frequently has workers who do not understand how to do the various tasks assigned to them. To complete their assigned tasks, the volunteers and interns frequently must interrupt you and your administrative assistant or other workers. These frequent interruptions slow the work of the office. The volunteers and interns have to interrupt others because they do not understand how to

- handle most student and faculty problems independently
- operate the various office computers and equipment correctly
- administer basic office policies and procedures.

Frequently, the volunteers and interns will decide to handle a faculty or student problem independently even though they do not completely understand how to handle that problem. Such actions can create other problems that you or your administrative assistant must then handle. For example, a new volunteer might tell a faculty member that the office will be happy to monitor an exam for any student with a disability when in fact we only monitor exams for students who must use the technology in the computer lab for disability accommodation. Such mishandling is frustrating

The writer defines the problem.

for you, your assistant, students, and faculty members. The volunteers and interns frequently must also ask questions about simple tasks such as running the copy machine or processing a student or faculty request because they have not received any training and do not have any written source of information about office machinery or policies and procedures.

The writer explains why the problem is significant.

The purpose of this office is to help students with disabilities by informing faculty and students about appropriate and necessary accommodation and also to help faculty to understand how to accommodate. When this office runs inefficiently and makes mistakes because of uninformed and untrained volunteers and interns, we don't create the positive image that the students and the faculty need.

resulting from the turnover of volunteers and students. This problem-definition section (called "Current Problems") points out why the problems are significant. The writer explains, for example, that these problems prevent the office from creating "the positive image that the students and the faculty need" and "slow the work of the office."

Proposed Solution and Work Plan

After you describe the problem or need, your readers will want to know how you plan to solve the problem or meet their needs. They will especially want to see a clear link between your proposed solution and their problem or needs. Readers will also expect you to present a detailed plan for carrying out the work. As you present this plan, consider the questions that the readers might ask. For example, they might ask: "How does your plan compare with other possible solutions? Why should we adopt your plan instead of another plan? Why is this plan better than the others?" (for more questions, see Figure 12.2). You must persuade your readers that you have not only crafted a detailed plan that will solve the problem, but also that your plan is the best way to solve the problem.

▶ For more information on ethics, see Chapter 3, "Facing Ethical and Legal Challenges."

In some work plans, you may want to explain not only what you and your organization will do, but also what you will not do. Your readers have a legal and ethical right to understand what you and your organization are proposing and also what you are not proposing. If you do not tell readers what you will and will not do, they may expect more than you intend. You can prevent such miscommunication by spelling out exactly what you are and what you are not proposing.

The proposed solution and work plan in the proposal for Hill Manufacturing appear in the sections titled "Work Plan" and "Schedule" in Figure 12.10 (see page 371). (Proposal writers and companies use different titles to refer to the proposed solution and work plan sections. Use the titles that the RFP requires or that your organization prefers. If they don't have requirements, select the most appropriate titles for your readers.) In this proposal, the writer links the proposed solution and work plan to the problem. Figure 12.7 shows how the writer (Nowakowski) links the solution and work plan directly to the reader's (Hill's) problems and needs. In the problem-definition section (called "Scope of Work" in Figure 12.10), the writer mentions three areas of work: "developing a set of recommendations for capping and closing the ash area," "compiling a conceptual design document," and "a meeting with Hill and then with the state water commission." In the "Work Plan" section, the writer mentions these three areas in the list of tasks and explains how the tasks will fulfill the work requested by Hill. The proposal writer lists and describes the tasks necessary to carry out the work and then presents a schedule.

As you prepare the proposed solution and work plan, consider the questions in Figure 12.2 and the following tips:

Figure 12.7

The Link Between the Problems of Hill Manufacturing and the Work Proposed by Nowakowski and Associates

Hill's Problems/Needs	Nowakowski's Solution/Work Plan to Solve the Problems/Needs
Set of recommendations for capping and closing the ash area at the Caney Branch Ash Disposal Area	Task 1. Review data and develop preliminary closure options Task 2. Collect and analyze additional data Task 3 (partial). Evaluate closure alternatives
Conceptual design document that describes and illustrates the recommended approach for capping and closing the ash area	Task 3 (partial). Develop a conceptual closure plan
Presentation of the technical merits of the plan at meetings with Hill and the state water commission	Task 4. Attend strategic planning meetings

▶ **Tips for Preparing the Proposed Solution and Work Plan**

- **Link the proposed solution to the problem by explaining how the solution will solve the problem and/or meet the needs of the readers.** Tell your readers specifically how your proposed solution will solve the problem that you described in the problem-definition section. Don't assume that the readers will see the link; instead, directly state the link—even in a solicited proposal.

- **Explain, in detail, how you plan to do the proposed work.** You want the readers to understand the scope of the work that you are proposing.

- **Present a detailed, step-by-step plan for carrying out the work.** Be sure to justify your plan and to anticipate the readers' possible questions.

- **If necessary, explain specifically what you are and are not proposing to do.** You want the readers to clearly understand not only what you and your organization will do, but also what you will not do.

- **Consider including a visual aid to illustrate the schedule.** Many proposal writers include a visual aid, such as a time line or chart,

(continued on next page)

illustrating the schedule (see the table in Figure 12.8 and the Gantt chart in Figure 12.10 on page 374).

- **Create a realistic schedule.** Be careful not to create an overly optimistic schedule in your eagerness to get your proposal accepted. Allow ample time to complete each phase of the work plan. Your readers and your organization want a realistic schedule, not one that is impossible to meet.

Qualifications

The **qualifications section,** sometimes called project team, facilities, or personnel, is important for readers who want to know whether you and your organization are capable of carrying out the work that you propose. This section includes some or all of the following information:

- **Qualifications of the people (including yourself, if necessary) who will carry out the work plan.** You can include a paragraph summarizing each person's qualifications for the project, or you can attach résumés in an appendix. If you attach résumés, use the qualifications section to introduce the project personnel and refer readers to the appendix, or summarize each person's qualifications and then refer readers to the appendix.

- **Qualifications of the organization.** For some proposals, you may need to "sell" your organization's qualifications. You can demonstrate to readers that the organization has carried out similar work and has the facilities and knowledge to successfully and efficiently complete the work. In this section, you might give readers a brief background of your organization and projects that it has completed successfully. You also can include information on specific facilities that the organization will use to complete the work—especially if those facilities compare favorably with industry standards or your competitors.

▼ **Figure 12.8**
A Table Showing a Schedule

Task	Beginning Date	Ending Date
Upgrade the system	March 4, 2002	March 30, 2002
Configure the network	March 30, 2002	June 1, 2002
Configure and install routers	June 1, 2002	June 15, 2002
Test the system	June 15, 2002	June 17, 2002

TAKING IT INTO THE WORKPLACE

The Future of Proposals

"We're expecting proposals to go truly online via extranets and auction houses (some bids are handled that way today). Solution generators are interactively letting us adapt solutions on the fly."
—Neil Cobb, Executive Director, SBC Proposal Centers

With the explosion of software and of electronic communication via the Web, the process of creating proposals is changing, especially in companies whose business depends in part on proposals (Cobb; Fry). Neil Cobb has been writing proposals since the early 1990s. In the early 1990s, his teams for the most part wrote each proposal "from scratch," occasionally using pieces from previously written proposals. In the mid 1990s, his teams began to use electronic "libraries" and software to create some types of proposals. His teams created an online library of product descriptions, solutions, plans of action, budgets, and so on from successful proposals. Proposal writers and coworkers throughout the company could access this library to create "cut and paste" proposals. His teams also created software that would create small-business proposals for some of the company's services. Other companies are also using proposal software to help their employees create proposals (Fry).

As Cobb and his teams move toward 2010, they are developing an online proposal center that employees and customers can access by way of extranets and auction houses. Cobb expects his team will launch online solution generators that can allow employees to adapt solutions in the field as they are working with customers. This online trend is certainly changing the process of writing proposals and will perhaps change the medium for delivering proposals.

Assignment

Interview a professional who works for an organization related to your major to find out how that organization prepares proposals. If possible, try to interview a professional who writes proposals, who is an account manager selling a large product or service, or who manages professionals who write proposals. You might ask how he or she and their organization prepare proposals: Do employees use the Web for preparing or sending proposals? If so, how? Do they have an online library where they can cut and paste information for proposals? If so, how much do they usually have to revise information to use it in a proposal? How has proposal writing changed since he or she began writing proposals? Write a summary of your interview for your instructor.

Figure 12.9 shows the qualifications section from the Hill Manufacturing proposal. The writers summarize the qualifications of the people who will carry out the proposed work. The writers also include specific information about each person's responsibilities on the project and explain why each person is uniquely qualified to work on the project. The writers don't present résumés in an appendix because their organization has previously worked with Hill Manufacturing.

Qualifications

Bob Congrove, P.E., Senior Engineer, will serve as project manager and
will provide much of the technical analysis and input for developing the
conceptual closure plan. Mr. Congrove served as project manager for the
Caney Branch Phase II Investigation and knows the conditions and water
commission permitting processes and requirements.

Alejandro Martinez, P.E., Senior Civil Engineer, will provide conceptual
design input on engineered components of the closure plan, such as capping
specifications, and will assess the technical and financial feasibility of various
closure options. Mr. Martinez has over 22 years of applied engineering
experience, including designing landfill caps, liner systems, and slurry walls,
and developing landfill closure plans.

Brandon McCarroll, Principal Hydrogeologist, will provide input about
geochemical processes affecting the mobility of ash leachate constituents. In
addition, Donna Camp, Ben Armstrong, and Terry Huey (support staff) have
recently worked on ash disposal projects and associated water commission
permitting. As necessary, they will provide technical input and review. They
will also participate in meetings with Hill Manufacturing and the water
commission.

Budget

The **budget**, sometimes called a cost estimate or cost proposal, is an itemized
list of the estimated costs of the work plan. For some proposals, readers will
expect a justification along with the budget. The budget justification explains
each budgeted item and its purpose for the proposed solution. As you prepare
your budget, follow these tips:

> **Tips for Preparing the Budget**
>
> - **Carefully estimate the cost of labor, equipment, and any materials
>   needed to carry out the work plan.** To ensure that you have
>   included all costs, look at the budgets for similar projects or propos-
>   als or ask an experienced coworker to look at your budget.
>
> - **Estimate as accurately as possible.** If you underestimate your costs
>   in trying to get a proposal accepted, you may be bound by your esti-
>   mate. If your estimate is too low, your organization could lose the
>   good will of your client if you have to charge more money for the
>   services. Or if you have contracted for a specific amount, you may
>   not be able to ask the client for additional money; your organization
>   will have to fund the additional expenses and could lose money.

The budget for the Hill Manufacturing proposal (see Figure 12.10) is in a section titled "Cost Estimate." There, the writers present a total estimate for the project and separate estimates for each task.

Conclusion

In most proposals, the conclusion briefly restates the problem or need and the proposed solution. The conclusion also restates

- What the proposal offers readers
- How the proposal will benefit readers
- Why readers should accept the proposal
- Why readers should accept you and your organization to carry out the proposed solution

For short proposals in memo or letter format, the conclusion is likely to be a brief statement of whom readers should call if they have questions.

▶Two Sample Proposals

The two sample proposals in Figures 12.10 and 12.11 illustrate conventional proposal elements. In Figure 12.10, an environmental sciences and engineering firm is responding to an RFP. The writers propose to prepare a plan for capping and closing an ash area at a lignite mine owned by Hill Manufacturing. In Figure 12.11, a student proposes a manual for the Office of Disability Accommodation at her university. This office helps students with disabilities receive appropriate accommodation from the university and helps faculty members who have these students in their classes. The readers of her proposal are the director and assistant director of that office.

Figure 12.10 A Solicited Proposal Prepared by Nowakowski and Associates for Hill Manufacturing

Nowakowski & Associates, Inc.
243 26th Street, Suite 808
Montrose, Colorado 80303-2317
303/555-1823 Fax: 303/555-1836

March 24, 2002

The writer uses the letter format for the proposal.

Ms. Ginny Thompson
Hill Manufacturing
400 North Vintage Street
St. Louis, Missouri 75201

The writer identifies the document as a proposal.

Re: Work Plan and Cost Estimate to Develop a Conceptual Closure Plan for the Caney Branch Ash Disposal Facility, Martin Lake

Dear Ms. Thompson:

The writer combines the summary and introduction. Here, the writer describes the problem, the proposed work, and the organization of the proposal.

As you requested, Nowakowski and Associates, Inc., is pleased to provide this work plan and cost estimate to develop a conceptual closure plan for the Caney Branch ash disposal facility. We understand that Hill Manufacturing has decided to mine around the ash area. In November of 2001, we provided, as you requested, preliminary cost estimates for three capping scenarios that could potentially be part of an overall closure plan for Caney Branch. However, these closure scenarios and perhaps others require a more detailed analysis of the hydrology and geochemistry of the system before you select an appropriate closure scenario. On the basis of our recent discussion, the following proposal describes our understanding of the required scope of work and our work plan.

Scope of Work

We understand that our scope of work will include the following:

Because the proposal is solicited, the writer uses "Scope of Work" to identify the problem definition and only briefly states the scope of work. The writer also states the work that the project will not include.

- developing a set of recommendations for capping and closing the ash area at the Caney Branch ash disposal facility (Caney Branch)
- compiling a conceptual design document that describes and illustrates the recommended approach for capping and closing the ash area

After developing the conceptual design document, we will, if desired by Hill Manufacturing, present the technical merits of the plan at a meeting with Hill and then with the state water commission. As you requested, the conceptual document will not include any final design specifications or detailed estimates of the costs required to implement the recommended closure plan. However, we propose to develop preliminary cost estimates as necessary to evaluate various closure alternatives.

| ▼ **Figure 12.10** | (continued) |

Work Plan

The writer provides an overview of the work plan.

To develop the conceptual closure plan, we will balance the level of effort and associated costs for preparing the plan with the requirements to provide sufficient documentation and justification for addressing possible questions from the state water commission. We will work closely with Hill to ensure that the level of effort and work are consistent with Hill objectives. We will complete four tasks to complete the work that Hill requires.

The writer describes in detail each task in the work plan.

Task 1. Reviewing Data and Developing Preliminary Closure Options
We request that Hill Manufacturing provide any water level data, sump discharge volume data, and sump water quality data obtained at Caney Branch since the Phase II Investigation (2000–2001). We will review these data, along with the historical data provided in the Phase II Report, to further develop possible closure options. In developing a preliminary list of closure options, we will review correspondence from the state water commission and registration papers regarding Caney Branch. We will also examine the water commission's precedents for closure of ash disposal facilities at other lignite mines in the state. We will also use these reviews to further evaluate possible data gaps in the various closure options.

Task 2. Collecting and Analyzing Additional Data
During Task 2, we will evaluate the need for collecting additional data; we currently envision two specific needs. The latest water-level readings, taken in selected ash and overburden wells at Caney Branch, were measured in early May of 2001. The last complete set of readings for all wells occurred in October of 2001. Historically, water levels in the ash have generally exhibited an upward trend but may be approaching a quasi-static condition. The quasi-static water level in the ash under present stratigraphic conditions is important because it serves as a "baseline" when estimating the long-term water-level conditions in a post-mining scenario. Therefore, we propose to obtain another set of water-level measurements in wells within and near Caney Branch to evaluate the baseline condition.

We also foresee the need for new data on the ground-water chemistry for ash and overburden wells. Because attenuation of ash leachate constituents will likely be a critical basis for limiting the scope of closure activities, we will collect samples from selected wells to confirm that ash leachate constituents are continuing to attenuate. We presently anticipate that collecting and analyzing the samples from six monitoring wells will be sufficient to document that attenuation.

We will collect and analyze the samples in the same manner as in the Phase II investigation. Field analyses would include Ph, Eh, specific conductance, and temperature. However, we will analyze the samples in the lab for a shorter list of constituents than those evaluated during the Phase II investigation. The proposed list of constituents includes calcium (dissolved), magnesium (dissolved), sodium (dissolved), potassium (dissolved), chloride, sulfate, alkalinity, boron (dissolved), and selenium (dissolved). We will be most interested in the key parameters of sulfate, boron, and selenium. To estimate cost, we have assumed that Core Laboratories, which analyzed the water samples for Phase II, will analyze the samples. However, if desired, the Hill Manufacturing lab could analyze the samples.

Task 3. Evaluating Closure Alternatives and Developing a Conceptual Closure Plan

The current mine plan calls for mining within 400 feet of Caney Branch. This plan will have substantial effects on both the short- and long-term hydrogeologic conditions near the ash area. Therefore, we will consider these effects when evaluating the closure options:

- effects of mining on the rate of ash water leaching
- extent of ash area dewatering caused by adjacent mining and the possible effects on induration of the ash
- time required to resaturate the spoil and ash material after mining
- post-mining hydrologic conditions (effects of spoil characteristics, ponds, etc., on post-mining hydrology)
- historical and future attenuation of ash water constituents
- hydrologic effects of constructing a flow barrier between the ash area and Barrier Lake (A slurry wall is currently not a preferred option, but we will review it to address possible questions from the water commission or to provide an alternative.)
- cost-feasibility of construction options
- applicability of the water commission's Draft Risk Reduction Rules to Caney Branch
- potential post-closure care requirements and costs.

Although we don't anticipate substantial modeling efforts associated with developing the conceptual plan, the existing model developed during the Phase II investigation will help us to address some of the hydrologic issues. In some cases, we can use previous model simulations to assess an issue; and in other cases, we anticipate performing additional simulations. We anticipate using the HELP (Hydrologic Evaluation of Landfill Performance) model to evaluate the hydrology of various capping scenarios. In other cases, we will draw on experience at the Barrier Lake Mine and perhaps simple hydraulic calculations of water balance to develop estimates. The actual level of effort and list of critical issues will depend upon which closure options we evaluate.

We will develop a narrative to justify and describe the conceptual closure plan and simple conceptual design drawings to illustrate the closure concept. We will present the draft closure plan to Hill Manufacturing at a meeting (Task 4).

G. Thompson, March 24, 2002, p. 4

| | Figure 12.10 | (continued)

The report to Hill will not include complete documentation of model results and analytical analyses as part of the conceptual planning.

Task 4. Attend Strategic Planning Meetings

We will estimate the time and material expenses required to prepare for and present the technical merits of the proposed conceptual closure plan in meetings with Hill Manufacturing and the water commission. Our cost estimate assumes two meetings, one with Hill Manufacturing and one with the water commission.

Schedule

The writer describes the schedule for completing the work.

We estimate eight weeks for drafting the conceptual closure plan. We assume that Hill Manufacturing can provide during the first week of the project any additional data that they have collected since 2001 (see Task 1). We anticipate performing the field work associated with Task 2 within the first two weeks of the project. We will proceed with Tasks 1 and 3 while the lab analyzes the additional water samples (two- to three-week turnaround). After we receive the sample results, we estimate that we can finalize the conceptual closure plan in approximately three weeks. Table I summarizes the tentative schedule.

Table I: Schedule of Tasks

The writer includes a Gantt chart to illustrate the schedule.

Task	In weeks, beginning April 1, 2002							
	1	2	3	4	5	6	7	8
Review data and develop preliminary closing options	4/1 ▼		4/21 ▼					
Collect data in the field	4/1 ▼	4/15 ▼						
Analyze collected data			4/15 ▼		5/7 ▼			
Evaluate closure alternatives and develop a closure plan					5/1 ▼		5/21 ▼	
Present closure plan to Hill and to the water commission								5/21 5/30 ▼▼

| Figure 12.10 | (continued) |

Cost Estimate

The writer introduces the budget.

We propose to execute the work plan on a time and materials basis according to our 2002 Schedule of Charges. We will provide periodic reports to the Hill Manufacturing Project Manager detailing the progress of the project and will work closely with Hill Manufacturing personnel to streamline the work effort and ensure that the project deliverables are consistent with Hill Manufacturing expectations. We will not exceed the following total cost estimate without authorization from Hill Manufacturing. If the project requires less effort, the invoiced amount will be less than the estimated budget. The itemized cost estimate appears in Table II.

Table II: Itemized Cost Estimate

The writer presents a detailed budget for each task.

Task 1: Labor

Principal	4 hrs. @ $110/hr.	$ 440
Senior	24 hrs. @ $90/hr.	2,160
Staff	4 hrs. @ $55/hr.	220
Support Staff	3 hrs. @ $30/hr.	90
		$2,910

Task 1: Expenses

Communication/Shipping		$ 75
Photocopies		25
		$ 100

TASK 1 TOTAL $3,010

Task 2: Labor

Principal	2 hrs. @ $110/hr.	$ 220
Senior	16 hrs. @ $90/ hr.	1,440
Staff	30 hrs. @ $55/hr.	1,650
Support Staff	2 hrs. @ $30/hr.	60
		$3,370

Task 2: Expenses

Vehicle		$ 250
Per Diem	2.5 days @ $70/day	175
Sampling Equipment		100
Communication/Shipping		200
Photocopies		25
		$ 750

Task 2: Outside Services

Lab Analyses	6 samples @ $108/sample	$ 648
10% Handling		65
		$ 713

TASK 2 TOTAL $4,833

▼ **Figure 12.10**   (continued)

Task 3: Labor

Principal	32 hrs. @ $100/hr.	$ 3,200
Senior	140 hrs. @ $90/hr.	12,600
Project	16 hrs. @ $75/hr.	1,200
Staff	40 hrs. @ $55/hr.	2,200
Drafting	24 hrs. @ $40/hr.	960
Support	12 hrs. @ $30/hr.	360
		$20,520

Task 3: Expenses

Communication/Shipping	$ 200
Photocopies/Reproducing	200
	$ 400

TASK 3 TOTAL $20,920

Task 4: Labor

Principal	20 hrs. @ $100/hr.	$2,000
Senior	20 hrs. @ $90/hr.	1,800
Support Staff	4 hrs. @ $30/hr.	120
		$3,920

Task 4: Expenses

Travel	$ 200
Communication/Shipping	150
Photocopies/Reproducing	25
	$ 375

TASK 4 TOTAL $4,295

ESTIMATED PROJECT TOTAL $33,058

Qualifications

The writer describes the qualifications of all the people who will complete the tasks.

Bob Congrove, P.E., Senior Engineer, will serve as project manager and will provide much of the technical analysis and input for developing the conceptual closure plan. Mr. Congrove served as project manager for the Caney Branch Phase II Investigation and knows the conditions and water commission permitting processes and requirements.

Alejandro Martinez, P.E., Senior Civil Engineer, will provide conceptual design input on engineered components of the closure plan, such as capping specifications, and will assess the technical and financial feasibility of various closure options. Mr. Martinez has over 22 years of applied engineering experience, including designing landfill caps, liner systems, and slurry walls, and developing landfill closure plans.

Figure 12.10 (continued)

G. Thompson, March 24, 2002, p. 7

Brandon McCarroll, Principal Hydrogeologist, will provide input about geochemical processes affecting the mobility of ash leachate constituents. In addition, Donna Camp, Ben Armstrong, and Terry Huey (support staff) have recently worked on ash disposal projects and associated water commission permitting. As necessary, they will provide technical input and review. They will also participate in meetings with Hill Manufacturing and the water commission.

The writer concludes by offering to answer questions.

If you have any questions about our recommended approach for developing the conceptual plan or about any other aspect of this proposal, please call me at (303) 555-1823.

Sincerely,

Tom J. Nowakowski
Senior Engineer
Project Manager

Figure 12.11   An Unsolicited Proposal Written by a Student

Proposal to Create a Training and Reference Manual for the Office of Disability Accommodation

Summary

The writer summarizes the problem, solution, schedule, and budget.

The Office of Disability Accommodation does not have a Training and Reference Manual. We need a manual since our staff consists of only two full-time employees, many volunteers, and 10 student interns. Our full-time employees are too busy to train new volunteers and to provide all the reference information for each situation that arises. We could use this manual to train volunteers and student interns. This manual will also consolidate the policies and procedures of our office, so that our staff can quickly refer to them.

I can complete the rough draft by May 24. The labor, materials, and supplies will cost approximately $1,048.74. However, I will donate my time to write and prepare the manual. This donation will reduce your cost for the manual to $48.74 for supplies and materials. If the rough draft is satisfactory, you will receive the final draft on June 1.

The writer uses informative headings.

Current Problems at the Office of Disability Accommodation

The writer describes the nature of the problems.

The Office of Disability Accommodation uses many volunteers and student interns. These volunteers and interns may work in the office for only a semester, creating a large turnover. They may work as few as 5 or as many as 20 hours per week. With the number of these volunteers and interns and the high turnover, the office frequently has workers who do not understand how to do the various tasks assigned to them. To complete their assigned tasks, the volunteers and interns frequently must interrupt you and your administrative assistant or other workers. These interruptions slow the work of the office. The volunteers and interns have to interrupt others because they do not understand how to

- handle most student and faculty problems independently
- operate the various office computers and equipment correctly
- administer basic office policies and procedures

The writer cites specific examples of the problem.

Frequently, the volunteers and interns will handle a faculty or student problem independently even though they do not completely understand how to handle that problem. Such actions can create other problems that you or your administrative assistant must then handle. For example, a new volunteer might tell a faculty member that the office will be happy to monitor an exam for any student with a disability, when in fact we only monitor exams for students who must use the technology in the computer lab for disability accommodation. Such mishandling is frustrating for you, your assistant, students, and faculty members. The volunteers and interns frequently must also ask questions about simple tasks such as running the copy machine or

| **Figure 12.11** | (continued) |

processing a student or faculty request because they have not received any training and do not have any written source of information about office machinery or policies and procedures.

The purpose of this office is to help students with disabilities by informing faculty and students about appropriate and necessary accommodation and also to help faculty to understand how to accommodate. When this office runs inefficiently and makes mistakes because of uninformed and untrained volunteers and interns, we don't create the positive image that the students and the faculty need.

Proposed Solution: A Training and Reference Manual

The proposed Training and Reference Manual will provide new volunteers and student interns with the training and information to

The writer links the solution to the problems listed in "Current Problems."

- handle most student and faculty problems independently
- operate the various office computers and equipment correctly
- quickly learn the basic policies and procedures.

I will write the Training and Reference Manual from my experience and will consult with your administrative assistant for technical information. The Training and Reference Manual will include the following sections.

Answering Student Inquiries
- Telephone Inquiries
- In-House Visits

Working with New Students
- Necessary Forms and Procedures
- Campus Offices of Assistance

Working with Faculty Members
- Pre-Semester Notification Packets
- Faculty Guide

The writer presents a detailed outline to show how the proposed manual will solve the problem.

Using Office Equipment and Computers
- Equipment and Furniture
- Computers

Understanding Procedures
- Registering Students
  Early Registration
  Regular Registration

- Testing
  Regular Semester Exams
  Final Exam Procedures

▼ **Figure 12.11**   (continued)

- Filing
  Confidentiality
  Location of Different Files

- Issuing Elevator Keys
  Assigning Keys
  Returning Keys

Working with Various Groups with Disabilities
- Hearing Disabilities
- Visual Disabilities
- Motor/Mobility Disabilities
- Learning Disabilities
- Head-Injury Disabilities
- Hidden Disabilities
- Speech Disabilities

Working with Volunteers
- Applications
- On-Campus Service Groups

The writer includes a schedule.

I can complete the Training and Reference Manual during the next seven weeks. During the week of May 17, the office volunteers and students will use the rough draft and give me their comments. I will then submit the draft to you on May 24. If the draft is satisfactory, you will receive the completed manual on June 1.

My Qualifications for Writing the Proposed Manual

The writer describes her experience.

I have worked in the Office of Disability Accommodation and in the computer lab for disability accommodation for three years as a student volunteer. I have seen and experienced first-hand the problems and frustrations of not understanding how to handle a student or faculty problem. I have worked in all phases of the office and am able to write the proposed manual. In addition, I am a senior majoring in rehabilitation therapy, so I understand the legal and ethical issues involved in working with students with disabilities.

Budget

The following table reflects the estimated cost of writing and printing the manual:

4

Items	Time and Supplies	Cost (dollars)
Writing and Editing the Manual	100 hours @ $10.00 per hour	1,000.00
Binding Costs	Vinyl Front and Back Spiral Binding	5.18
Colored Illustrations	10 pages @ $2.50 per page	25.00
Tab Inserts	$.89 for 5 pages x 4 packets	3.56
Copying Costs	300 pages @ $.05 a page	15.00
Total Cost		**$1,048.74**

The writer uses a table to present the budget.

I will donate my time in return for a receipt for my donation. Your cost for materials and supplies will be $48.74.

Conclusion

I am excited about the possibility of preparing this much-needed manual for our office. This manual will resolve our ongoing problem with training volunteers and student interns. I look forward to the possibility of working with you on this manual.

WORKSHEET **for Writing Reader-Oriented Proposals**

▶ **Principle 1: Find Out About the Readers of Your Proposals**
- Is the proposal solicited or unsolicited?
- Are your readers internal or external?
- If your readers are external, what positions do they hold in their organization? What do they know about you or your organization? Have their previous experiences with you or your organization been positive? If not, why?
- If your readers are internal, where are their positions in relation to yours in the organizational hierarchy?
- Will more than one group of readers read the proposal? If so, what sections will each group read?
- What do your readers know about the problem or need that prompted the proposal?

▶ **Principle 2: Prepare to Answer Readers' Questions**
- Did you answer all the relevant writers' questions in Figure 12.2?
- Did you answer all the relevant readers' questions in Figure 12.2?

▶ **Principle 3: Use the Conventional Elements of Proposals**
- Does the summary
  - Concisely state the problem or need addressed in the proposal?
  - Summarize the proposed solution, product, or service?
  - Describe your plan for carrying out the proposed solution, product, or service?
  - Summarize your qualifications and these of your team and/or your organization (if appropriate)?
  - State the total cost of the proposed solution, product, or service (if appropriate)?
- Does the description of the proposed project include an introduction that
  - Identifies the problem or need that the proposal addresses?
  - States the purpose of your proposal?
  - Tells the readers the organizational pattern that you will follow in the proposal?
- Does the problem definition
  - For an unsolicited proposal define the problem or need with sufficient detail for the readers to understand the problem or need and why they should then consider your proposed solution or plan?
  - For a solicited proposal briefly define the problem with enough detail for the readers to know that you understand the problem or need?
  - Present the necessary background for the readers to understand the problem or need and the proposed solution or plan?
  - Present the information readers need to understand why they should accept your solution, product, or service?

- Does the proposed solution and work plan
  - Link the proposed solution, product, or service to the problem?
  - Explain how that solution, product, or service will solve the problem or meet the readers' needs?
  - Present a detailed, step-by-step plan for carrying out the work?
  - Explain, if necessary, what you are and are not proposing to do?
  - Present a realistic schedule that allows you and/or your organization to complete each phase of the work plan on time?
- Does the qualifications section
  - Include your relevant skills and experience and those of your team and/or your organization?
  - Include, if necessary, information on your organization's equipment and facilities?
- Does the budget section
  - Include an accurate estimate of the cost of labor, equipment, and any materials needed to carry out the work plan?
  - Include, if necessary, a justification for each budget item?

▶ **E X E R C I S E S**

1. For your technical communication class, you will prepare a report. Follow these steps to select a topic and write a proposal for that report.

   • Make a list of possible topics, and gather some information about each one. You might select topics related to your major or to your current job. As you gather information, you might use some of the tools (such as search engines, interviews, and so on) that you learned about in Chapter 5, "Researching Information Using Primary and Secondary Sources."

   • Brainstorm about the feasibility of each topic. As you brainstorm, you might list the pros and cons of each topic and consider the amount of time you will have to complete the project and the importance of the topic to you, your career, and your field or workplace.

   • After you've thought about the pros and cons of each possible topic, select a topic and write a memo asking your instructor to approve your choice. In your memo, give your instructor enough information to understand and evaluate the topic.

   • Include a list of possible sources of information in your memo to your instructor. Be sure to follow either MLA or APA style as you list your sources. (See Appendix A for information on MLA or APA style.)

   • After your instructor approves your topic, write a proposal to your instructor. Include all the conventional elements relevant to your proposal. (Your instructor may prefer that you write your proposal for a reader other than him or her. For instance, if you are proposing to research a problem at work, you might address the proposal to your manager.)

2. Evaluate your proposal using the questions listed in the "Worksheet for Writing Reader-Oriented Proposals." After you have evaluated your proposal, revise it based on your answers to the questions.

3. To complete this exercise, bring three copies of the proposal that you revised in Exercise 2. Using the copies of your proposal, three of your classmates will read and evaluate your proposal based on questions under Principle 3 in the "Worksheet for Writing Reader-Oriented Proposals." Your instructor may ask you to post your proposal on a public drive where up to three classmates will use the comment function of a word-processing program to comment on your proposal (see Chapter 4, "Collaborating and the Writing Process," page 75).

4. Based on your classmates' answers to the questions in Exercise 3, revise your proposal if necessary. Then prepare a final draft for your instructor.

► **C A S E   S T U D Y**

Working for the Community

Background

You probably are aware of many problems and needs on your college campus or in the surrounding community. For instance, your campus may have a shortage of parking places for commuter students, or the computer labs may close too early in the evening. In the surrounding community, some children may not receive new toys at Christmas, or some families may not have enough food to eat. These are only a few of the possible problems and needs that you might encounter.

Assignment

You or your team will write a proposal to solve a problem on your campus or in the surrounding community. To write this proposal, complete these steps:

1. Select a problem on campus or in the surrounding community. Make sure that you and all members of your team are familiar with the problem and that team members can gather the needed information about the problem to propose a solution in the allotted time.

2. Gather information about the problem and about readers of the proposal. Develop possible solutions to the problem.

3. Discuss the advantages, disadvantages, and feasibility of each solution. Then determine the most effective solution for the readers.

4. Write the proposal.

13

Writing Reader-Oriented Informal Reports

You will give many reports during the course of your career. These reports will be both oral and written. You've been giving reports during much of your school life—for example, in grade school, you probably wrote or presented a report on a book that you had read. In middle school, you might have reported on a historical figure; and in high school, you may have written a lab report in your biology class. If you have a job, your manager may have asked you to complete a project and you reported the status of the project. Even though each of these reports may have a different format and a different subject matter, they are all reports. **Reports** are oral or written communications that present information that helps people to understand, to analyze, to act, or to make a decision. Reports can be formal or informal. In this chapter, we will discuss informal reports. In Chapter 14, we will discuss formal reports.

An **informal report** communicates information about routine, everyday business. Informal reports can cover any number of topics, from what you thought about the new restaurant in town to a memo requesting that your manager approve $3,500 to buy a laptop computer. You might present an informal report in a paper memo, in an e-mail, or in an oral presentation. Even though we use the word *informal,* this word doesn't indicate that the information or purpose of the report is insignificant. For example, an informal report informing the architect of a problem in a bridge design could save lives.

How do you know if a report is formal or informal? Your readers and your organization may give you some clues. Your readers may require that the report be formal or informal. In some organizations a report might be formal, while in another organization the same report might be informal. For instance, a field report in most companies is an informal report; yet at TXU, an energy company, these reports generally are formal reports. To determine if a report is formal or informal, find out what your organization and your readers expect. You might also look at similar reports written by your coworkers. After you analyze these expectations and look at similar reports, you may still be uncertain about whether to treat your report as formal or informal; but generally, you will use informal reports to communicate information about everyday business. But remember that this everyday business may be essential to you, your career, your organization, or the public.

In this chapter, you will first learn three basic principles that you can apply to any informal report. You can use these principles as a problem-solving framework for any informal report. After we've discussed these basic principles, we'll consider the formats that you might use for these reports and then apply principles to four commonly used informal reports: progress reports, meeting minutes, field and lab reports, and trip reports.

►Principle 1: Find Out About the Readers

Before you can decide on the format (or perhaps even whether the report is formal or informal), you need to find out about your readers. This task may be easy for some reports. For example, if you are writing a progress report for your manager on your monthly activities, you will know what your reader expects. You will probably even know the report format that he or she prefers because you routinely present information to him or her. However, if you are reporting progress on a project for external readers, you may be writing to more than one person and you may know little about their needs and expectations. Because you don't routinely write for these external readers, your task is a little more difficult.

As you analyze the readers of your report, you might consider these questions:

- What do your readers know about the topic of your report?
- Why are they reading your report—to gather information? to complete a task? to make a decision?
- What questions will they ask as they read the report?
- Are the readers internal or external?
- What positions do your readers hold in the organization? If they are internal readers, where are their positions in relation to yours in the organizational hierarchy?
- Will more than one group read the report?
- What do your readers know about you or your organization? Have their previous experiences with you or your organization been positive? If not, why?

Once you know your purpose for presenting the report and the needs of the readers, you can better prepare an effective report. Whether you're writing a report that presents the progress of your work or the minutes from a meeting, begin your task by finding out about the readers because your report will succeed only if you meet their needs and expectations.

►Principle 2: Prepare to Answer Readers' Questions

►For more information on analyzing your readers, see Chapter 2, "Understanding and Writing for Your Readers."

To help your readers understand your report, you will want to gather the information necessary to answer their questions. This task may be as simple as printing a spreadsheet or as complex as using primary and secondary research techniques to gather the information. For some reports, once you have gathered the information you will need to analyze that information and then make appropriate recommendations or draw conclusions.

Although the specific questions will vary with the topic and purpose, your readers will want you to answer these basic questions:

- What is the purpose of your report?
- Why are they receiving the report?
- How does the report affect them or their organization?

For each of the informal reports described in this chapter, you will find a figure that lists specific questions that the readers may ask as they read your report. These questions will help you as you prepare your informal reports.

▶Principle 3: Determine the Appropriate Format and Conventional Elements for the Report

Once you find out about your readers, you can determine the most appropriate format. You can use any of the following formats for your informal reports:

▶ To learn more about memos, letters, and e-mail, see Chapter 18, "Writing Reader-Oriented Letters, Memos, and E-Mail."

- **Memos.** You will use the memo format for most informal reports. Some organizations call informal reports "memo reports." You use memos for informal, internal correspondence. In other words, you send memos to people within your organization. For example, you would send a memo about the status of your project to your manager; however, you would send a letter to report that status to your client—who is external to your organization.

- **Letters.** Letters are more formal than memos. Most organizations expect you to use letters when corresponding with people outside the organization. However, if you are sending your informal report to someone several levels above you in your organization, you might consider using the letter format. Check with your coworkers to determine what level of formality your organization prefers in this situation.

- **E-mail.** Many organizations send informal reports via e-mail because of its speed and convenience. Also, with e-mail readers and writers can easily adapt the reports. For example, if you are writing meeting minutes for your construction team, you can send a draft of the minutes to all the meeting participants. They can examine the draft, insert comments, and e-mail the revised draft to you. You, then, can revise the minutes and save time at the next meeting because the participants have already seen a draft.

- **Preprinted forms and templates.** Some organizations have preprinted forms and templates for some informal reports. The form or template may simply be a cover sheet for the report, or it may be a format for the entire report. For example, Centex Construction Company has templates for meeting minutes in its company database. Employees use this template to create and archive the minutes. The template prompts the writer for the project name, project number, date, and so on. TXU uses an "Examination

Action Item List" template to accompany field reports. This template includes sections for the observation, the recommendation, and the engineer's comments. Other organizations have preprinted forms for progress reports. Before you select the format for your informal reports, find out if your organization has preprinted forms and templates for these reports. These preprinted forms and templates may save you time.

▶ For more information on organizing, see Chapter 6, "Organizing Information for Your Readers," and Chapter 18, "Writing Reader-Oriented Letters, Memos, and E-Mail."

When you have determined the appropriate format for your readers and your organization, you are ready to draft your report using the conventional elements. Because the conventional elements vary for informal reports, this chapter presents the conventional elements for four common informal reports:

- Progress reports
- Meeting minutes
- Field and lab reports
- Trip reports

If you are writing an informal report other than one of these, follow one of the standard patterns of organization in Chapter 6 or the direct approach for correspondence in Chapter 18.

▶Writing Progress Reports

Progress reports describe the current status of a project. Readers of progress reports may be managers, clients, coworkers, or sponsors of a project. These reports have three primary purposes:

- To describe progress on one or more projects so readers can monitor the work
- To provide a written record of progress
- To document problems with, and changes to, a project

You may write progress reports in two types of contexts: when reporting your progress on one project or on several projects assigned to you. For example, Tom is an engineer for an architectural engineering firm. He spends 60 percent of his time working as the lead engineer on a plant design project for a power-generating company and 40 percent assisting on three other design projects. Once a month, Tom submits a progress report to the lead mechanical engineer of the power-generating company. In addition to this monthly progress report, Tom writes a biweekly progress report where he reports not only on the plant project, but also on the other three design projects.

Besides helping readers to monitor Tom's progress, these reports provide a written record of that progress. This record gives readers evidence of Tom's work and a history of his work on the projects. Suppose Tom's company decides to postpone work on the power plant for one year. The monthly progress reports that he wrote before the delay will provide a record of the work previously done; so when the project starts up again, Tom or other engineers can refer to the reports to determine where to resume work. The reports could prevent Tom or others from duplicating work completed before the company postponed the project.

Whether you write a progress report on one project or on several projects, consider your readers. Why will they read your report? How will they use it? What questions will they want it to answer? Whether you are reporting on one project or several, readers will ask questions about the project or work that the report covers, your progress, future work, and the overall status of the project.

To help readers understand your progress report, mention the time period and the specific project or projects that the report covers. Readers also want to know the objectives or purpose of the project, so they can determine how it relates to their responsibilities and to their organization. This information helps readers to put your report in context.

Readers are interested in your specific accomplishments during the reporting period to see whether your work is progressing as planned. Readers will want to know your schedule and possibly your budget for the next reporting period or for the remainder of the project if you will not be writing any other progress reports. They also may want to know what kinds of results they can expect during the next reporting period. To describe your progress and to report work planned, consider these questions:

- What work have you accomplished since the beginning of the project or since the last progress report?
- Is the project progressing as planned?
- What work have you planned for the next reporting period or for the remainder of the project?

Readers also want to know the overall status of the project. If the project is not progressing as planned, they want to know what specific problems you have encountered, the effect of these problems on the project, and your recommendations for handling these problems. Some readers also will want to know the results of your work. This information may help readers to determine the future work on your project and others. If you have recommendations for improving the project—regardless of whether it is progressing as planned or you have encountered problems—your readers may want to know your ideas. Readers may use the information about the overall status and your recommendations to determine whether to adjust the project, budget, schedule, or personnel. To report the overall status of your project, consider these questions:

- What are the results of the work?
- What problems, if any, have you encountered?
- What changes, if any, do you recommend?
- How will these changes affect the project?

Using the Conventional Elements of Progress Reports

Most progress reports contain these conventional elements: introduction, discussion of the progress, and conclusions. This section describes how to include these elements in a reader-oriented progress report. Figure 13.1 presents questions that readers may ask and relates those questions to the conventional elements of a progress report.

Introduction

The introduction identifies your project and the purpose of your report. Specifically, in the introduction you will

- Identify the project or projects that the report covers
- State the time period that the report covers
- State the objectives of the project or projects (if readers need this information)

Figure 13.1

Readers' Questions About the Conventional Elements of a Progress Report

Element	Readers' Questions
Introduction	What project does the report cover? What time period does the report cover? What are the objectives of the project?
Discussion of the progress	What work have you accomplished since the beginning of the project or since the last progress report? Is the project progressing as planned? What work have you planned for the next reporting period or for the remainder of the project? What are the results of the work? What problems, if any, have you encountered?
Conclusions	What changes, if any, do you recommend? How will these changes affect the project? What is the overall status of the project?

TAKING IT INTO THE WORKPLACE

Progress Reports and Telecommuting

"Keeping in contact with team members is vital—your coworkers need to know what you are doing."

—Jean H. Weber, Senior Member, the Society for Technical Communication (23)

Does working at home and saving hours of driving sound appealing? Some companies are finding that their employees are more productive when they work at home—that is, when they telecommute (Weber). However, telecommuting is not without its pitfalls. To improve productivity, employees and their managers need to set some guidelines. One of the most important of these guidelines is to have open lines of communication—before and during a project. At the beginning of the project, the team might follow these guidelines:

- Define the working relationship and role of each team member—if possible in a face-to-face meeting (Tumminello and Carlshamre; Weber).
- Make sure that each team member has explicit goals and weekly assignments (Weber).

Once a team has defined roles and set goals and assignments, the telecommuters can "go to work." To ensure that the project is successful, your team can follow these guidelines to keep the lines of communication open.

- Report your progress (or lack of progress) to your team and your manager. "Keeping in contact with team members is vital—your coworkers need to know what you are doing and that you are keeping up your share of work" (Weber 23).

- Honor checkpoints and deadlines. These become even more important when team members are working in different locations (Weber).
- Inform your team members and your manager "of where you are," how they can contact you, and when you will be available during the working day (Weber 23).

During your career, you may be a telecommuter. Remember that communicating—especially your progress—will be key to your success.

Assignment

Interview a workplace professional about telecommuting (sometimes called off-site work) at their organization. You might ask the following questions about telecommuting:

- Does your organization allow employees to telecommute (or to work off site)? Do you telecommute or work with employees who do?
- If so, what system do you use to report on work? Does the organization have a formal system for or policy on reporting work completed by telecommuters?
- If the professional doesn't telecommute or work with someone who does, ask, "Does your company have a formal policy on telecommuting?" If so, what is the policy? If not, what person in the company might visit with you about telecommuting?

Write an informal report to your instructor communicating what you have learned.

Frequently, you can identify a project and its time period in one sentence, such as "This report covers progress on the Midwest Relocation project from January 1 through March 31." You would explain the objectives of your project to help readers put your report in context or to remind them of its purpose. For example, you might explain the problem you are trying to solve or the situation you are studying. You also can state the objectives as you defined them in the project proposal. Figure 13.2 shows a paragraph in which the writer states the objectives of a project and also identifies the project and the time period that the progress report covers.

Discussion of the Progress

The discussion of the progress answers readers' questions about how the project is proceeding and about what work you've planned for the next reporting period or for the remainder of the project (see Figure 13.1). Readers will be especially interested in

- How your progress compares with what you planned to accomplish during the reporting period
- Any problems that you have encountered
- The results of your work

Whether your progress report covers one project or several projects, you can organize the discussion of the progress in two ways:

- By the progress made during the reporting period and the progress expected during the next reporting period (see Figure 13.3)
- By the tasks or projects to be completed (see Figure 13.4)

▶See Chapter 6, "Organizing Information for Your Readers," page 147, for more information on using a comparison and contrast organization.

Using the *progress-made/progress-expected pattern,* shown in Figure 13.3, you can organize the discussion around the progress made on one or several tasks or projects during the reporting period and the progress expected during the next reporting period. Using the *task/project pattern,* shown in Figure 13.4, you can organize the discussion around one or several tasks or projects, discussing the progress made and expected on task or project 1, then moving to task or project 2, and so on.

▼ **Figure 13.2**

The Introduction to a Progress Report

Project information → This letter describes the current status of, and progress on, the lignite-handling system for the Old Eagles plant. The
Objective of project → purpose of this project is to renovate the current lignite-handling system at the plant. This letter covers our work on the obsolescence study, the mechanical engineering, the structural engineering, and the electrical engineering from
Time period of → July 1, 2001, to August 30, 2001.
project

Figure 13.3

The Progress-
Made/Progress-
Expected Pattern

I. Progress made during the current reporting period (the work that you accomplished during the time period covered by the progress report)

   A. Task 1 (or Project 1)
   B. Task 2 (or Project 2)
   C. Task 3* (or Project 3)

II. Progress expected during the next reporting period (the work that you expect to complete during the next reporting period)

   A. Task 1 (or Project 1)
   B. Task 2 (or Project 2)
   C. Task 3 (or Project 3)

* Your project may have more or fewer than three tasks.

Figure 13.4

The Task/Project
Pattern

I. Task 1 (or Project 1)

   A. Progress made during the current reporting period (the work that you accomplished during the time period covered by the progress report)
   B. Progress expected during the next reporting period (the work that you expect to complete during the next reporting period)

II. Task 2 (or Project 2)

   A. Progress made during the current reporting period
   B. Progress expected during the next reporting period

III. Task 3 (or Project 3)

   A. Progress made during the current reporting period
   B. Progress expected during the next reporting period

As you write the discussion of your progress, follow these tips:

> ### Tips for Writing the Discussion of the Progress
>
> - **Explain how your progress compares with what you planned to accomplish during the reporting period.** Readers want to know if your project is on schedule.
> - **Report any problems that you have encountered.** Explain how these problems affected your progress and the status of your project. Will
>
> (continued on next page)

these changes affect the budget, the schedule, or the personnel?

- **Include the major results of your work, if applicable.** Readers need information about results and problems so they can approve or change the project, budget, schedule, or personnel. By including information about problems, you document those problems and possibly lay the foundation for changes later in the project.

- **Use either the progress-made/progress-expected pattern or the task/project pattern.** The progress-made/progress-expected pattern emphasizes the total amount of progress you have made as well as the work you expect to do during the next reporting period. The task/project pattern emphasizes the task or the project, not the amount of progress made or not made.

- **If your progress report is long, consider putting the results and problems in a separate section.** You can title that section "Results and Problems" or "Evaluation of the Progress."

Conclusions

The conclusion summarizes the overall progress made on the project and, if necessary, recommends changes. In this section, you might recommend ways to overcome problems that you are experiencing, or you might suggest ways to alter the project to get better results. You also can briefly mention these recommendations in the introduction or at the beginning of the discussion of the progress.

In the conclusion,

- Summarize the progress made on the project
- Summarize any problems experienced during the reporting period
- Evaluate the overall progress made on the project
- Recommend ways to improve or change the project or future work, if necessary

The two sample progress reports presented in this chapter illustrate the conventional elements. In Figure 13.5, a student reports on her progress on a manual for the Double Oaks Golf Shop; she uses the progress-made/progress-expected pattern. In Figure 13.6, an engineering company reports on its progress on a lignite-handling system; it uses the task/project pattern.

▶Writing Meeting Minutes

Minutes are the official record of a meeting. The meeting could be as informal as a meeting of your product-development team or as formal as a meeting of a city council. You may read or write minutes from meetings within your organization or meetings between representatives of your organization and

| **Figure 13.5** | A Progress Report Written by a Student |

The writer uses the memo format for her internal readers

MEMO

March 5, 2002

To: Professor Patricia McCullough
From: Nicole Sanders
Subject: Progress report on the employee manual for Double
            Oaks Golf Shop

Introduction

This report covers my progress on an employees' manual for the Double Oaks Golf Shop since February 15. This manual will include up-to-date procedures for opening, maintaining, and closing the shop and for maintaining the inventory; it will also include the current policies for the employees. Although my work is progressing satisfactorily, I have experienced some problems in gathering information from the management of the shop.

●—Project
●—Time period

My Progress During the Past Three Weeks

The writer uses the progress-made/progress-expected pattern

During the past three weeks, I had planned to interview the sales staff and the manager of the shop and to update and revise the procedures and policies for the shop. I have completed the interviews; and based on the information gathered in these interviews, I have updated the procedures currently in writing. However, I have not updated and revised all the procedures and policies because from the interviews, I learned that many of the procedures are not in writing. To write the remaining procedures, I need information from the manager and from the managers of other small golf shops.

Description of progress

Interviews with the Sales Staff and the Manager

I interviewed five members of the sales staff—Bart Thompson, Stella Smith, Melissa Connors, Dan Sandstedt, and Bradley Davis. Bart and Melissa explained that few of the current procedures and policies appear in writing. Before the interview, I assumed that the current employees' manual contained most of the procedures and policies but that the procedures and policies were out of date. However, Bart and Melissa explained that the manual did not contain any inventory procedures—a major responsibility for the sales staff.

Progress made

I also interviewed the manager of the club, Donna Shoopman. She explained how the manual differed from the current policies of the shop. She also confirmed that the procedures for maintaining the inventory and closing the shop were not in writing.

Updating and Revising the Policies and Procedures

I have updated and revised the policies on employee dress, customer satisfaction, substance abuse, disciplinary issues, and work

Figure 13.5   (continued)

P. McCullough   2   March 5, 2002

schedules. I updated and revised these policies based on information from Donna, the shop manager. I have also up-dated and revised the opening procedures for the shop. These were the only procedures in writing.

Problems encountered

Problems with Updating and Revising the Procedures

Progress made

I cannot completely update the procedures for maintaining the inventory and for maintaining and closing the shop because they are not in writing. Donna plans to give me the procedures for maintaining the inventory, closing the shop, and maintaining the shop by March 12. These procedures will serve as a foundation for the procedures section of the manual. I cannot finish the procedures section of the manual without the information from Donna.

Progress Expected During the Next Three Weeks

Description of progress

During the next three weeks, I will
- interview managers of other small golf shops
- finish updating and revising the procedures
- prepare a completed draft of the manual

Interviewing Managers of Other Golf Shops

Future work

I will interview Don Price, manager of Briarwood Golf Shop, and Bonnie Barger, manager of Brentwood Golf Shop. These interviews will help me appropriately revise the procedures for maintaining the inventory and the shop.

Completing the Updating and Revising of the Procedures

I will update and revise the procedures for maintaining inventory and for maintaining and closing the shop after receiving the procedures from Donna. I will also use the information from the interviews with the managers of Brentwood and Briarwood Golf Shops to help me appropriately revise these procedures.

Conclusion

Conclusions

Overall status

My interviews with the sales staff and with the manager gave me valuable information and guidelines for writing the manual. Even though I am behind schedule, I can complete the draft of the manual by March 30 if Donna gives me the procedures by March 12.

| **Figure 13.6** | A Progress Report from an Engineering Company |

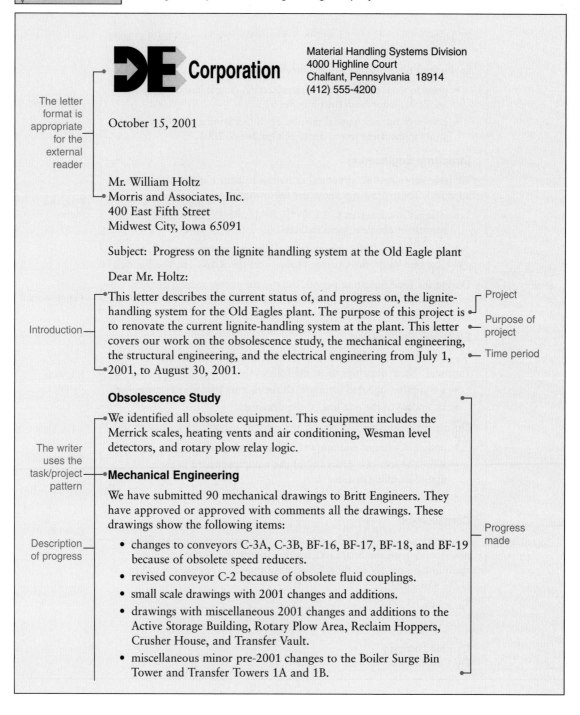

D E Corporation

Material Handling Systems Division
4000 Highline Court
Chalfant, Pennsylvania 18914
(412) 555-4200

The letter format is appropriate for the external reader

October 15, 2001

Mr. William Holtz
Morris and Associates, Inc.
400 East Fifth Street
Midwest City, Iowa 65091

Subject: Progress on the lignite handling system at the Old Eagle plant

Dear Mr. Holtz:

Introduction

This letter describes the current status of, and progress on, the lignite-handling system for the Old Eagles plant. The purpose of this project is to renovate the current lignite-handling system at the plant. This letter covers our work on the obsolescence study, the mechanical engineering, the structural engineering, and the electrical engineering from July 1, 2001, to August 30, 2001.

Project

Purpose of project

Time period

Obsolescence Study

We identified all obsolete equipment. This equipment includes the Merrick scales, heating vents and air conditioning, Wesman level detectors, and rotary plow relay logic.

The writer uses the task/project pattern

Mechanical Engineering

We have submitted 90 mechanical drawings to Britt Engineers. They have approved or approved with comments all the drawings. These drawings show the following items:

Description of progress

- changes to conveyors C-3A, C-3B, BF-16, BF-17, BF-18, and BF-19 because of obsolete speed reducers.
- revised conveyor C-2 because of obsolete fluid couplings.
- small scale drawings with 2001 changes and additions.
- drawings with miscellaneous 2001 changes and additions to the Active Storage Building, Rotary Plow Area, Reclaim Hoppers, Crusher House, and Transfer Vault.
- miscellaneous minor pre-2001 changes to the Boiler Surge Bin Tower and Transfer Towers 1A and 1B.

Progress made

▼ **Figure 13.6**   (continued)

W. Holtz   2   Oct. 15, 2001

In the final reporting period, the mechanical engineering division will
- provide a quotation for the fire protection system based on the June 14, 2001, letter from Britt Engineers.
- complete the mechanical portion of the remaining obsolescence study items listed in our letter of October 6, 2001.

—Future work

Structural Engineering

We have submitted 82 structural drawings to Britt Engineers for their approval. These drawings show the following items:

- changes to conveyors C-3A, C-3B, BF-16, BF-17, BF-18, and BF-19 because of obsolete speed reducers.
- miscellaneous 2001 changes and additions to conveyor C-2, the Transfer Vault, the Crusher House, and the Active Storage Building.

Progress made

During the final reporting period, the structural engineering division will complete the structural portion of the remaining obsolescence study items listed in our letter of October 6, 2001.

—Future work

Electrical Engineering

We have submitted sixteen drawings to Britt Engineers for their approval. These drawings show the following:
- a complete, updated listing of all the motors that we have supplied.
- an update of the one-line power drawing.

Progress made

During the final reporting period, the electrical engineering division will

- design I/O (input and output) rack arrangements.
- write the software program for the equipment used in the lignite-handling system.
- simulate and document the program.

—Future work

Conclusions

Our work on the Old Eagles project is progressing as planned. We are now working on the final tasks for the project and plan to complete them in the next six months. If you have questions, please contact me at (123) 456-7890.

Overall status

Sincerely,

Cynthia Dempsey
DE Corporation

Margin annotations: Description of progress · Conclusion

THE READER'S CORNER

Dramatizing Progress Reports

The progress report has surprising dramatic qualities. In Joseph Conrad's novella *The Heart of Darkness* (1902), Charlie Marlow recounts his work as skipper of a river steamboat on the Congo River. Part adventure story, part detective story, the novella is also part progress report: The skipper reports his meetings with the bookkeeper and the manager, the repairs he made to the steamboat, and finally his progress in shipping goods upriver. The real progress, though, is the narrator's gradual psychological awakening to the horrifying emptiness of life (the "heart of darkness"), symbolized by his predecessor, Kurtz. Having severed all contact with his employers, Kurtz has become a brutal and insane god to an African tribe deep in the Congo; Kurtz's own progress report concludes, "Exterminate all the brutes."

A powerful critique of heartless bureaucratic imperialism, Conrad's novella was revived to serve a similar purpose in the 1979 film *Apocalypse Now.* Criticizing America's imperialism in Vietnam, the film portrays a U.S. military captain sent on a clandestine mission to "terminate" a renegade "Colonel Kurtz" holed up in a remote Cambodian compound. In the captain's voice-over, we can still hear elements of the progress report: dutiful reports of an efficient but senseless village bombing so an officer can go surfing, the endless "securing" of Do Lung Bridge, and of course the voyage upriver. Colonel Kurtz's own progress report concludes with an echo of his namesake's: "Drop the bomb."

representatives of external organizations. For example, a construction company may meet with the owners of a project they are handling; the company will keep minutes of meetings with the owner to provide a record of what occurred at the meeting. Meeting minutes are sent to those who belong to the group or organization represented at the meeting; these minutes also may be made public—as in the minutes from a city council. For these meetings, the minutes may be published in a newspaper or made available online for anyone to read.

Using the Conventional Elements of Meeting Minutes

As the writer of minutes, you will make an accurate record of the actions taken (or not taken) at the meeting. Your job is to record this information, not to interpret. Effective and accurate meeting minutes have these conventional elements:

- Information about the meeting and attendees
- Old business
- New business

The following sections present information for using these conventional elements. Figure 13.7 presents the conventional elements along with the questions that readers may ask as they read each element.

Element	Readers' Questions
Information about the meeting and the attendees	• What is (are) the name(s) of the group(s) involved in the meeting? • Where did you meet? • What was the date and time of the meeting? • What type of meeting occurred? • Who attended and didn't attend the meeting? • What time did the meeting adjourn? • Who recorded the minutes?
Old business	• Did you approve the minutes of the previous meeting? • Did you amend the minutes before you approved them? • Did you act on business discussed at a previous meeting? If so, what did you do or discuss? • What motions, if any, were introduced? Who introduced and seconded them? Did the group pass, fail, or table the motions?
New business	• What major topics did the group discuss? • What motions, if any, were introduced? Who introduced and seconded them? Did the group pass, fail, or table the motions? • Who read reports, introduced action items, and so on?

Information About the Meeting and Attendees

Since the minutes serve as the official record of a meeting, they should include the following information that identifies the meeting:

- **The name(s) of the group(s) involved in the meeting.**
- **The location, date, and time of the meeting.** Only include the beginning time, not the ending time, here.
- **The type of meeting.** Is the meeting a regularly scheduled meeting? Or is it a called, or special, meeting?
- **The attendees.** List the first and last names of those people who attended the meeting, those who were absent from the meeting, and any guests who attended the meeting. At a large public meeting, such as a city council meeting, you may have an auditorium filled with guests. For these situations, you only need to list the guests who spoke or participated directly in the meeting.

- **The time the meeting adjourned.**
- **Name and title of the person who writes the minutes.**

The first three pieces of the above information appear in a heading for the minutes. The list of attendees generally appears in a sentence or paragraph immediately after the heading, and the time the meeting adjourned appears as the last item of business in the minutes. If you want further information on including these introductory elements, see these sources: *Robert's Rules of Order* and *The Gregg Reference Manual.*

Old Business

If the meeting is not the first one of your group or committee, you will have old business. For most meetings, the old business is simply to approve the minutes of the previous meeting. In some meetings, however, the attendees may discuss and update or amend items introduced at previous meetings. For example, at the previous meeting, a member of the group may have introduced installing and getting approval from the Department of Transportation for traffic lights near a commercial development. At the next meeting, the group may want to discuss whether or not they received approval or when the lights would be installed. This business would be "old business." The group would put these items on the agenda before new business.

You will simply record what action is taken on the minutes or on a previously introduced item of business. For example, you might write, "Johnson moved to approve the minutes of the last meeting. Smith seconded the motion. The motion passed by a vote of 6 to 0." (Or you could write, "the motion carried by a vote of 6 to 0.")

New Business

To record new business, you record the major topics discussed and any action taken at the meeting. In a perfect meeting, the group will discuss the items as they are listed on the agenda. However, because meetings often deviate from the agenda, you may find it difficult to take accurate minutes. Your goal is to create a "snapshot" of items discussed in the meeting. As you write meeting minutes, try following these tips:

▶ **Tips for Writing Accurate Meeting Minutes**

- **Include each major topic discussed.** For most meetings, especially formal ones, you will have a list of these topics on the agenda. If the meeting is less formal, include the major topics or items discussed.
- **Record any motions made, who made the motion, and the outcome of the motion.** Include whether the motion was passed, defeated, or

(continued on next page)

tabled. Also, include the vote count—"the motion carried by a vote of 7 to 2." If the group amended the motion, record specifically how the motion was amended.

- **Record the names of people who read reports, introduced action items, and so on.** As part of the minutes, include the names of people who, for example, make motions and read reports. Exclude the names of people who simply take part in the discussions—you will include the names of these people when you list the attendees in the first part of the minutes.

- **Summarize the discussions.** Effective meeting minutes summarize the discussions. Minutes aren't transcripts, so you want to include enough information to create an accurate record and to omit information that readers will not need.

- **Make sure that the minutes accurately and positively reflect on you, the organization, and those who attended and participated in the meeting.** Because minutes aren't a transcript, you should separate the actions from the emotional exchanges. For example, if the group argues, don't write, "The motion to paint the new office space taupe with hunter-green accents passed 6 to 1 after Garcia and McCarroll argued about the color. At one point, McCarroll said that 'the organization had no taste when it comes to interior decorating.'" Instead, simply write, "After discussion, the motion to paint the new office space taupe with hunter-green accents passed 6 to 1."

- **If the discussion moves too quickly or you didn't hear or understand something, interrupt the discussion and ask the group to clarify.** Your job is to create an accurate record; so if you don't understand something or need someone to repeat a motion, for example, ask the group to clarify.

- **Consider using a laptop computer to record the minutes.** The laptop may help you to take the notes more quickly. It also may help you to provide a more accurate record of the meeting—you will have to rely less on your memory.

Figure 13.8 illustrates effective meeting minutes. Notice how the writer has included all of the conventional elements and used a format to help readers locate information.

▶ Writing Field and Lab Reports

You may write a field or lab report after you complete an experiment or after you inspect some machinery or other equipment. You might also write a field or lab report after you examine a site. For example, your company may be

Figure 13.8	Meeting Minutes

The writer identifies the group, date, time, and attendees.

Monthly Regional Directors' Meeting

Wednesday, March 14, 2002

Attendees: Jo Bernhardt, Director; Anne Constanides; Marj Smith; Stuart Irby; James Bell; and Patrick Sims. Stan Audrain was not present because he is on leave.

Jo Bernhardt called the meeting to order at 3:30 P.M. in the conference room.

Old Business

The writer uses headings to help readers locate information.

1. The minutes of the February 13 meeting were approved by a unanimous vote.
2. Jo Bernhardt distributed information on the progress of the United Way campaign. She reported that we have two weeks left in the campaign and that the southwest region had reached its goal.

New Business

1. Jo Bernhardt distributed the following information and asked the directors to be ready to discuss the information at the April meeting:

   a. Sales figures for the first quarter

   b. Suggested revisions to the online proposal center

The writer numbers each major topic discussed and each act of business to help readers identify these items.

2. After a discussion of the new engineer training, Patrick Sims moved that we extend the training to a whole day instead of a half-day session and that we ask some engineers to join the training staff in planning the training. Anne Constanides seconded the motion. The motion carried by a vote of 4 to 2.

The writer identifies the persons introducing and seconding motions.

3. Stuart Irby introduced information on the new dam project. He requested that the engineers receive a briefing on the project. After discussion by the managers, Stuart changed his request into a motion. Marj Smith seconded the motion. The motion passed unanimously. Stuart will set up a date, time, and location for the briefing.

The writer identifies the persons introducing new business.

4. Jo Bernhardt adjourned the meeting at 4:45 P.M.

The writer identifies the recorder of the minutes.

Respectfully submitted by Anne Constanides, project engineer.

considering buying a manufacturing plant. Your managers send you to the plant to inspect the equipment. When you return, you might write an informal report recording what you found during your inspections and what you recommend.

Using the Conventional Elements of Field and Lab Reports

A field or lab report has the following conventional elements:

- **Introduction.** State the purpose of your report and the problem addressed in the report.
- **Methods.** Describe the methods you used. Because this report is informal, you only need to briefly describe the methods. In field and trip reports, most writers deemphasize the methods.
- **Results.** State the results of your experiment, inspection, and so on. These results may be preliminary. If so, be sure to state that they are only preliminary.
- **Conclusions.** Tell the readers what you learned from the results.
- **Recommendations.** If your reader expects recommendations, include them in the report.

In many field and lab reports, you may not have a heading for all of the conventional elements. Figure 13.9 presents questions that readers might ask as they read the conventional elements of a field or lab report. The field report in Figure 13.10 illustrates how a writer used the conventional elements to report on his inspection of a chimney at a power plant.

▶Writing Trip Reports

You may write trip reports after you return from business trips. You might, for example, attend a seminar on new software for tracking construction projects. When you return to the office, your manager may want you to report on the seminar. Your manager will want to know what you learned and what you recommend. Your manager will not, however, be interested in a minute-by-minute itinerary of what you did and what occurred at the seminar. You may also write trip reports after you visit with clients. After these trips, you will want to tell your manager how the organization can follow up with these customers and how the organization can better serve them. You might also report on whether the customers are receiving the service, information, and so on that they need or expect. You might also write trip reports after you visit with employees who work away from the home or regional office. For example, you might supervise field representatives who work in regional offices. You may visit them to find out about their work. After such a trip, you might write a report about how their work is proceeding or about any problems they are having.

Element	Readers' Questions
Introduction	• What is the purpose of your report? • Why did you conduct the inspection, experiment, etc.? What led to the inspection, experiment, etc.?
Methods	• What method did you use for your inspection, experiment, etc.?
Results	• What were the results? • What did you learn? • What problems, if any, did you observe?
Conclusions	• What do the results mean? • Are the results conclusive? • If you observed problems, are these problems major or minor?
Recommendations (optional)	• What do you recommend? • If you observed problems, how do you recommend solving the problems?

▼ Figure 13.9

Readers' Questions About the Conventional Elements of Field and Lab Reports

Using the Conventional Elements of Trip Reports

When you write trip reports, consider using these conventional elements:

- **Introduction.** Include the following: the place, the date, and the purpose of your trip.
- **Summary.** Summarize for the readers what you observed, learned, and recommend.
- **Discussion.** Present the details of the important information that you gathered during the trip. Remember, the readers aren't interested in reading "first, I did this; then, I did that." Instead, the readers want to know what you learned and why that information is important to them and to the organization.
- **Recommendations.** State and explain your recommendations.

Because you will usually write a trip report to an internal reader, most trip reports take the form of a memo. Figure 13.11 presents the questions that your readers might ask as they read the conventional elements of a trip report. Figure 13.12 presents a trip report written after an employee attended demonstrations of hands-free cell phones.

Figure 13.10   A Field Report

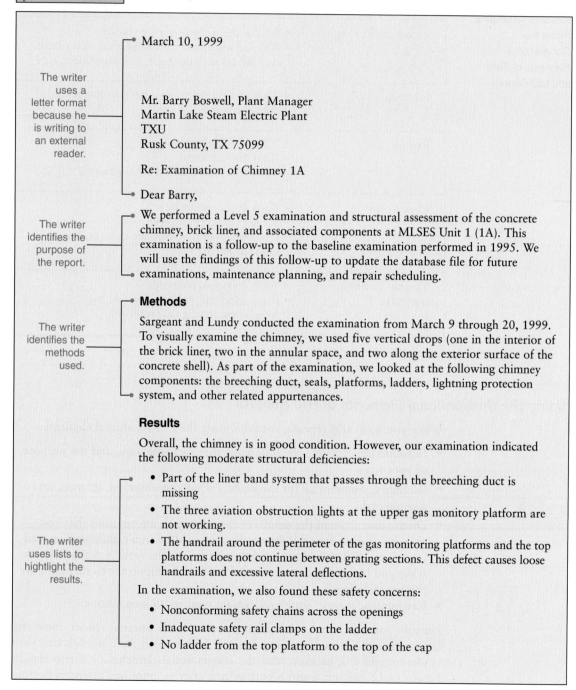

The writer uses a letter format because he is writing to an external reader.

March 10, 1999

Mr. Barry Boswell, Plant Manager
Martin Lake Steam Electric Plant
TXU
Rusk County, TX 75099

Re: Examination of Chimney 1A

Dear Barry,

The writer identifies the purpose of the report.

We performed a Level 5 examination and structural assessment of the concrete chimney, brick liner, and associated components at MLSES Unit 1 (1A). This examination is a follow-up to the baseline examination performed in 1995. We will use the findings of this follow-up to update the database file for future examinations, maintenance planning, and repair scheduling.

Methods

The writer identifies the methods used.

Sargeant and Lundy conducted the examination from March 9 through 20, 1999. To visually examine the chimney, we used five vertical drops (one in the interior of the brick liner, two in the annular space, and two along the exterior surface of the concrete shell). As part of the examination, we looked at the following chimney components: the breeching duct, seals, platforms, ladders, lightning protection system, and other related appurtenances.

Results

Overall, the chimney is in good condition. However, our examination indicated the following moderate structural deficiencies:

The writer uses lists to hightlight the results.

- Part of the liner band system that passes through the breeching duct is missing
- The three aviation obstruction lights at the upper gas monitory platform are not working.
- The handrail around the perimeter of the gas monitoring platforms and the top platforms does not continue between grating sections. This defect causes loose handrails and excessive lateral deflections.

In the examination, we also found these safety concerns:

- Nonconforming safety chains across the openings
- Inadequate safety rail clamps on the ladder
- No ladder from the top platform to the top of the cap

Figure 13.10 (continued)

Conclusions and Recommendations

Except for the safety items and the missing liner bands in the breeching duct, the findings are not an immediate concern. However, we recommend repairing the following items to minimize the potential for significant structural problems:

The writer combines the conclusions and recommendations into one section.

- Replace the missing liner bands in the breeching duct. The severe environment requires that the replacement rods be coated with coal tar epoxy and encased in 316L stainless steel pipe.
- Restore the aviation obstruction lights.
- Make the discontinuous handrail section continuous to minimize excessive lateral deflections per OSHA guidelines.
- Correct all safety items noted in this report.

The writer politely closes by offering to answer questions.

If you have questions, please call Ken at (123) 456-7891 or me at (123) 456-9123.

Sincerely,

Aaron Neuman
Structural Engineer

Source: Adapted from Ken Mixer and Aaron Neuman, "Martin Lake Steam Electric Station Chimney No. 1A Examination" (TXU: 10 March 1999).

Figure 13.11

Readers' Questions
About the
Conventional
Elements of Trip
Reports

Element	Readers' Questions
Introduction	• Where did you go? • When did you go? • What was the purpose of your trip?
Summary	• What did you observe or do? • What, briefly, did you learn? • What, briefly, do you recommend?
Discussion	• What did you learn? • Why is the information important to the organization?
Recommendations	• What do you recommend? • Why?

▶ Sample Informal Reports

Throughout this chapter, you have read samples of the following types of informal reports:

- Progress reports (Figure 13.5 on page 397 and Figure 13.6 on page 399)
- Meeting minutes (Figure 13.8 on page 405)
- Field reports (Figure 13.10 on page 408)
- Trip reports (Figure 13.12 on page 411)

Your organization or your manager may have a specific format or perhaps a template for these informal reports. Ask your coworkers or your manager if your organization has a preferred or an expected format for these reports. If so, use that format or template. If not, use these sample reports to guide you.

| **Figure 13.12** | A Trip Report |

Memorandum

Date: September 21, 2002

To: Robert Congrove, Director of Safety

From: Eric Hacker

Subject: Trip to IT Dynamics

The writer identifies the destination, date, and purpose of the trip.

This memo summarizes the information I gathered from a trip to IT Dynamics in Madison, Wisconsin, on September 18, 2002. The purpose of my trip was to attend demonstrations of several hands-free cell phones.

The writer summarizes what he observed and what he recommends.

Summary

IT Dynamics demonstrated three hands-free cell phones. I recommend Nokia's CARK-91 for employees who have a company vehicle and Motorola's Timeport 270c for vehicles in the company fleet.

Discussion

IT Dynamics offers three hands-free cell phones:

- Nokia's CARK-91 for $175 plus installation
- Sharper Image's speaker/microphone cradle for $129
- Motorola's Timeport 270c for $349

The writer presents detailed information about what he learned. He selects only the information that is important to his reader.

The Nokia cell phone can be retrofitted into any vehicle; with this integrated setup, the cell phone uses the vehicle's antenna to boost reception. This cell phone had the best reception of the three models. However, the phone is not portable.

The Sharper Image cell phone has a cradle to hold the phone; however, with this model the reception was poor. I had trouble hearing the speaker and tended to lean into the phone when talking. As I leaned, I took my eyes off the road.

The Motorola cell phone was easy to use and to transport. This cell phone has voice activation and speakerphone capabilities. Users simply clip the cell phone to the sun visor. The reception was excellent. However, the cost of this phone is double that of the Nokia model.

Recommendations

The writer presents and explains his recommendations.

I recommend that we purchase the Nokia CARK-91 and have them installed into 200 fleet vehicles. Because of the cost of the Motorola model, I recommend that we purchase the Motorola Timport 270c only for the employees who have a company-issued vehicle. By purchasing both models, we will have a hands-free option in 60 percent of the company vehicles. I would like to talk with you and Gene about these recommendations. Call me at x7980 to set up a time to talk.

| WORKSHEET | **for Writing Reader-Oriented Informal Reports** |

▶ **Principle 1: Find Out About the Readers**
- What do the readers know about the topic of your report?
- Why are they reading your report—to gather information? to complete a task? to make a decision?
- Are the readers internal or external?
- What positions do your readers hold in the organization? If they are internal readers, where are their positions in relation to yours in the organizational hierarchy?
- Will more than one group read the report?
- What do your readers know about you or your organization? Have their previous experiences with you or your organization been positive? If not, why?

▶ **Principle 2: Prepare to Answer the Readers' Questions**
- What is the purpose of your report?
- Why are the readers receiving the report?
- How does the report affect them or their organization?

▶ **Principle 3: Determine the Appropriate Format and Conventional Elements for the Report**
- What format will your readers expect: memo, letter, e-mail, or preprinted form or template?
- Does your organization require or prefer that you use a particular format for the report? If so, which format?

▶ **Progress Reports**
- Does the introduction
  - Identify the project(s) the report covers?
  - Identify the time period the report covers?
  - State the objectives of the project?
- Does the discussion of the progress section
  - Describe the work that you have accomplished since the beginning of the project or since the last progress report?
  - Tell the readers if the work is progressing as planned? If it is not progressing as planned, did you explain why?
  - Follow either the progress-made/progress-expected or the task/project organizational pattern?
  - Tell the readers the work you have planned for the next reporting period or the remainder of the project?
  - Include the results of your work?
  - Identify any problems you have encountered?

- Does the conclusions section
  - Recommend changes, if necessary? Did you explain how the changes may affect the project?
  - Summarize the overall status of the project?

▶ **Meeting Minutes**
- Does the information about the meeting and the attendees
  - Include the names of the group(s) involved?
  - Identify the location, date, and time of the meeting?
  - Identify the meeting's type?
  - Identify who attended the meeting and who was absent?
  - Record the time the meeting adjourned?
  - Identify who recorded the minutes?
- Does the old-business section
  - Record whether or not the group approved or amended the minutes of the previous meeting (if applicable)?
  - Record any motions made, who made the motion, and the outcome of the motion?
  - Record any actions or discussions of business from previous meetings?
- Does the new-business section
  - Record each major topic the group discussed?
  - Record any motions made, who made the motion, and the outcome of the motion?
  - Identify the people who read reports, introduced action items, and so on?
  - Do the minutes accurately and positively reflect on you, the organization, and those who attended and participated in the meeting?

▶ **Field and Lab Reports**
- Does the introduction
  - Identify the purpose of your report?
  - Explain why you conducted the inspection, experiment, etc.?
- Does the methods section
  - Identify the methods you used for the inspection, experiment, etc.?
- Does the results section
  - State the results of the inspection, experiment, etc.?
  - Identify any problems that you observed?
- Does the conclusions section
  - Explain what the results mean?
  - Evaluate any problems that you observed?
- Does the recommendations section
  - State what you recommend?
  - Recommend how to solve any problems that you observed?

▶ **Trip Reports**
- Does the introduction
  - Identify the place, time, and date of the trip?
  - Identify the purpose of the trip?
- Does the summary section
  - Identify what you observed or did?
  - Summarize what you learned?
  - Summarize what you recommend (if applicable)?
- Does the discussion section
  - Explain what you learned?
  - Explain why this information is important to the reader and/or the organization?
- Does the recommendations section
  - State what you recommend?
  - Justify or explain your recommendations

1. With a team, list the strengths and the weaknesses of the progress report shown in Figure 13.13. The writer of this report is a college student who works part-time as a trainer for Magic Computers, a computer repair service. The owners of the service asked the writer to prepare a manual for their repair teams and managers. They want to have the manual by May 15, when they will begin training two new teams.

2. Recommend ways to improve the progress report shown in Figure 13.13. The readers are busy owners who also work full-time at other jobs. In your recommendations, comment on the organization of information, the style, and the page design.

3. Revise the progress report shown in Figure 13.13, incorporating your team's recommendations from Exercise 2.

4. Write a progress report for the project that you proposed in Exercises 1, 2, and 3 in Chapter 12.

5. If you are working on a collaborative project in one of your classes, write the minutes of one of your meetings. E-mail the minutes to each member of the team and to your instructor. Be sure to follow the conventional elements and to answer the readers' questions in Figure 13.7.

6. Like many college campuses and communities, your campus or community certainly has an inconvenient situation. For example, the city may have an intersection where many accidents occur. For this exercise,

   - Identify an inconvenient situation on your campus or in your community.
   - Observe the situation or inspect the area on two or three consecutive days. (Be sure to observe during peak times—for example, don't observe the intersection at 2:00 A.M.)
   - Write a field report to the appropriate school administrators or city officials. Be sure to use the conventional elements and to answer the readers' questions in Figure 13.9.
   - Include a specific recommendation in your report.

7. Visit a business in your community to learn about the products or services that it offers. After your visit, write a trip report for your instructor. Be sure to follow the conventional elements and to answer the readers' questions in Figure 13.11

| **Figure 13.13** | The Progress Report for Exercises 1, 2, and 3 |

Memo

Date: March 19, 2001
To: Barbara and Don Simpson, Owners of Magic Computers
From: Carol Arnold
Subject: Progress report on my manual for Magic Computers

During the last three weeks, I have worked on a managers' and repair teams' manual for Magic Computers. I began by looking for other similar residential computer repair services in other cities. I found four such services: Computer Doc in Flower Mound, 24-Hour Computer Repairs in Carson City, Computer FixIt in Desoto, and Boswell's Computer Repair in Estes. I called these four services to set up appointments to visit with their owners and managers. I was able to set up appointments with only three services; Boswell's cannot set up an appointment with me until the owner returns from vacation on March 30.

My interview with Jim Smith, owner of Computer Doc, was quite helpful. Jim showed me the office space and the equipment that Computer Doc uses. They use a wide variety of equipment. The most helpful part of my interview with Jim was the information he gave me for the procedures for the repair teams. He helped me to determine a list of the major procedures that the repair teams must know to repair a personal computer.

My interview with Jane Price, manager of 24-Hour Computer Repairs, was also quite helpful. Jane also showed me her office and the equipment that her repair teams use. They also use a wide variety of diagnostic software. The most helpful part of my interview with Jane was the information that she gave me about the manager's duties. She helped me to define and to list the daily, weekly, and monthly duties of the manager.

I also interviewed Jim and Alice Wilson, owners of Computer FixIt. My interview with the Wilsons was a little disappointing because they only had 30 minutes to spend with me. They did not have time to discuss the specific procedures followed by their repair teams or their managers.

Along with the interviews, I also accompanied two repair teams from Magic Computers. I accompanied each team for one day. I followed the team members as they took repair calls, entered the customers' business or home, listened to the customers, diagnosed the problems either by examining the computer or by using diagnostic software, and then made repairs on site. I asked them questions about their responsibilities and procedures. I made notes as I watched and questioned them. Accompanying these teams was quite helpful. I learned some specific procedures for questioning the computer owner and for creating a checklist for the owners to fill out. I also learned where the teams seem to work differently when diagnosing problems, working with the customers, and billing the customer. For example, one team bills customers for an entire hour even if the team works for only 15 minutes while the other team prorates the hourly fee. I will talk to you about what you expect and then write the procedures accordingly.

During the next three weeks, I will set up an appointment with the owner of Boswell's Computer Repair. I will also draft a set of procedures for the repair teams and then have the teams test these procedures. I will also visit with the manager of Magic Computers to determine her responsibilities before I begin writing the manager's section of the manual. Overall, I am pleased with the progress I am making. I am a little behind schedule because I could not meet with the owner of Boswell's and because I spent an extra day with the repair teams. However, I don't think these delays will prevent me from completing the manual before May 15, when our new teams come on board.

Relocating an Office

Background

Charles Patterson works part-time at the Global Travel agency. The agency experienced rapid growth during the past year, and its current location—one large office and a small storage area—is too small. The office originally housed only three employees but now houses six. These employees cannot work easily with clients because of noise and insufficient space.

The owners of Global Travel asked Charles to investigate possible new locations for the agency and then to recommend the best of these locations. Charles began work on this project two weeks ago. Since that time, he has interviewed the owners and the manager; they want the new location to have these characteristics:

• An outer office for a receptionist.
• A waiting area and six small offices for the travel agents and the manager. Each office should accommodate two chairs for clients, one desk, and a computer table.
• A large walk-in closet for storage.
• An area where employees can eat lunch and take their breaks.

After interviewing the owners and the manager, Charles contacted the managers of three office buildings: the Kirby Building, the Cumberland Building, and San Jacinto Tower.

He met with Nathaniel Ross, manager of the San Jacinto Tower on February 10. Mr. Ross showed Charles office space that would meet Global Travel's needs and gave him the rental and deposit information for that office space. Charles made appointments with Diana Alcorn, manager of the Kirby Building, and with Dianne McCarroll, manager of the Cumberland Building, for the week of February 23.

Charles also contacted three moving companies—AM/PM Vanlines, Cross-Country Moving and Storage, and Johnson Vanlines. He asked each company to bid on moving Global Travel to each of these three buildings. He expects to receive these bids by February 25.

Once Charles meets with the managers of the Kirby Building and the Cumberland Building and receives the bids from the moving companies, he will study the office space available in each of the three office building and the cost involved in moving to these buildings. He then will decide on the best location for the company and write his findings and recommendations in a report to the owners of Global Travel.

Assignment

Write a progress report in memo form to the owners and manager of Global Travel. Use the questions in Figure 13.1 to plan this report.

14

Writing Reader-Oriented Formal Reports

Cassie and Jon are technical writers employed by an engineering firm that works with companies to renovate and rebuild manufacturing plants. Cassie's group is working with a company to find out why a tower collapsed at one of its plants. Cassie will write a report explaining possible reasons for the collapse. Jon is working with another group to prepare a report recommending various ways to repair the tower. Cassie and Jon are working on the same project but are preparing two different types of reports. Both Cassie and Jon will prepare a formal report, but their purposes for writing are different. Cassie will present the results of her research and draw conclusions based on those results. Jon will present results, draw conclusions, and make recommendations based on those conclusions.

Like Cassie and Jon, you may write formal reports. A **formal report** communicates less routine business than an informal report. Like an informal report, a formal report can cover any number of topics. However, unlike an informal report, a formal report may have front and back matter. A formal report might be the final step in a series of documents. This series might begin with a proposal, continue with progress reports, and end with a formal report. This final report may have titles such as project report or completion report. Or you might write a formal report that isn't preceded by a proposal or a progress report. For example, your manager might ask you to evaluate telecommuting: you might examine whether telecommuting improves employee productivity. For this project, you would research telecommuting using both primary and secondary sources and write a report presenting the results of your research, possibly making recommendations as well.

In this chapter, you will learn four principles that will give you a plan for writing reader-oriented formal reports. This chapter also specifically discusses a common formal report: the feasibility report. It is a type of research report (sometimes called a recommendation report) that workplace professionals frequently write. The chapter ends with two sample formal reports.

►The Types of Formal Reports

You've heard the word *report* since you were in grade school. When you enter the workplace, you will be asked to write reports. What exactly do we mean by report? **Report** is an "umbrella" term for a group of documents that inform, analyze, or recommend. To meaningfully discuss reports, we need standard terminology. However, the workplace and many fields don't have standard terminology for referring to reports. For example, some terms refer to the report topic, such as meeting minutes, lab reports, or field reports. Other terms refer to the phase of the research or project, such as progress reports or completion reports. Still other terms refer to the purpose of the report, such as recommendation reports.

If you are new to your company and your manager asks you to write a report, spend some time talking with your manager to determine what type of

THE READER'S CORNER

Reports and the Free Press

 Early reports played a significant role in the development of the modern newspaper. Before the printing press, when literacy rates were low, newspapers did not exist. Instead, ancient emperors (including the rulers of the Romans and the Chinese) dictated news that was to be read aloud, posted, or read throughout their empire. An independent free press—so crucial to modern democracies—began to develop during the late Middle Ages when elite European trading families began to exchange information among themselves. One family, the Fuggers, owned an important financial house in the German city of Augsburg. Their regular newsletters mostly provided commercial reports on the availability and prices of goods and services, but they also occa-sionally reported political developments that might affect commerce. Such commercial newsletters became regularly printed newspapers in Dutch hands during the early 1600s. Their *corantos* ("current news") helped this geographically central nation to dominate European commerce. English and French translations of the *corantos* quickly became available, and national papers soon followed in England and France. The history of press censor-ship begins shortly thereafter. No longer able to control the press as earlier autocrats could, European monarchs began to repress these first free presses, sometimes replacing the papers with their own official "news" publications. In 1766, Sweden established the first law to guarantee the freedom of the press.

report and format he or she expects. You might ask: "What is the purpose of the report?" "Do you have a preferred format for the report?" You can also look at similar reports written by coworkers.

For this chapter, we will use the purpose of the report to categorize formal reports into

- Informational reports
- Analytical reports
- Recommendation reports

Informational Reports

Informational reports present results so readers can understand a particular problem or situation (see Figure 14.1). For example, the manager of a city's Web site might prepare an informational report for the city council; the report would provide statistics on the number of people who visit the site, the number of people who pay their city water and sewage bills online, the number of links to other city-related Web sites, and the number of city departments that use the site to provide information to city residents. The purpose of this type of report is to present facts—often called results—not to analyze the facts or to draw conclusions.

▶ To learn more about informal reports, see Chapter 13, "Writing Reader-Oriented Informal Reports."

As you learned in Chapter 13, a report can be formal or informal. When you determine the formality of the report, you know what format to use and whether to include front and end matter. *Formal* and *informal* refer to the format of the report, not to the purpose or significance of the report or to the organization of the report's body. To determine if an informational report should be formal or informal, determine whether the report is routine. For example, consider the Web site manager we discussed earlier. He or she might write an informational report to the city's public information officer providing statistics on the site for the month. This report is routine and would be informal. The report to the city council, however, is not routine because the Web manager doesn't routinely present reports to the city council. The council might request such a report because it wants to know if the city is using too many or too few city resources on the Web site and if it is improving communications to city residents. Because it is not routine, this report would be formal.

Informational reports might

- **Present information on the status of current research or of a project.** For example, you might report on the status of a project to construct a new runway at an airport.

- **Present an update of the operations in your division.** For example, the Web site report for the city council presents an update of work done by the city's public information division.

- **Explain how your organization or division does something.** For example, you might report on how your division tracks the work of subcontractors.

- **Present the results of a questionnaire or research.** For example, you might present the results of a questionnaire sent to employees to gather information on their commutes to work: How far do they drive to get to work? Do they carpool? Do they or would they use public transportation? and so on.

These are only examples of the kind of information that you might present in an informational report.

Figure 14.1

Types of Reports Categorized by Their Purpose

Type of Report	Presents Results	Draws Conclusions	Makes Recommendations
Informational	✔		
Analytical	✔	✔	
Recommendation	✔	✔	✔

Analytical Reports

▶ You might want to use a cause-and-effect pattern to organize part of an analytical report. See Chapter 6, "Organizing Information for Your Readers," page 151.

Analytical reports go a step beyond presenting results. Analytical reports present results, analyze those results, and draw conclusions based on those results (see Figure 14.1). In other words, analytical reports analyze and interpret the information or data in the results. They answer the question "What do the results mean?" These reports attempt to describe why or how something happened and then to explain what it means. For example, let's again consider the Web manager's report to the city council. Along with presenting the results, the manager might analyze those results and present conclusions. Based on the low percentage of city residents who use the site to pay their water and sewage bills, he or she might conclude that either the residents don't know the service is available or that the residents can't easily find the service on the Web site. Note that the manager's purpose in the report is only to draw conclusions based on the results, not to make recommendations.

Like informational reports, analytical reports can be formal or informal and can present and analyze a variety of results. They can:

- **Explain what caused a problem or situation.** For example, you might present the results of a traffic study at an intersection where many accidents have occurred. In the report, you would explain why the accidents occurred—based on the results of the traffic study.

- **Explain the potential results of a particular course of action.** For example, based on the results of your research, you might conclude whether or not opening a new office branch will increase business for your organization. You might present conclusions on whether the potential income will offset the cost of running the new office.

- **Suggest which option, action, or procedure is best.** For example, you might present options for treating people with diabetes and report which treatment has the best outcome.

These are only a few examples of the conclusions that you might present in an analytical report.

Recommendation Reports

Recommendation reports advocate a particular course of action. Recommendation reports usually present the results and conclusions that support the recommendations. These reports may seem to be the same as analytical reports, so how do you differentiate between the two? Think of it this way. You might conclude that treatment X is more effective than treatments Y and Z. This statement is your conclusion, but it is not necessarily a recommendation to use treatment X—although it might seem that way. You might, for example, recommend using treatment Z because of cost; or you might recommend not using any treatment at all. Consider the Web manager's report. Even though the percentage of city residents using the site to pay their water and sewage bills is low, the manager might recommend that the city council not do anything to increase the activity on the site because the public information division doesn't have the money to increase publicity.

Like informational and analytical reports, recommendation reports may be formal or informal. Recommendation reports might address any of the following situations and advocate a specific course of action. These, again, are only examples; you may encounter other situations for writing recommendation reports.

- **What should we do about a problem?** You might recommend a course of action for dealing with a problem. For example, you might answer the questions: "What should we do about the problem of excessive absences in the manufacturing division?" "What should we do about overcrowding in the school?"

- **Should we or can we do something?** You might look at whether your organization can or should do something. For example, you might answer the question: "Even though we currently have two engineers working on runway projects for the airport, should we hire another project engineer to work on the new runway construction project that we will begin next year?"

- **Should we change the method or technology we use to do something?** You might examine whether a change would benefit your organization. For example, your organization currently sends all printing to an outside vendor. Should you continue to use the vendor or move all printing in house?

Although the categories of reports—informational, analytical, and recommendation—make report writing seem easily defined, you may find that the categories blur as you are writing in the workplace. As you write reports, be flexible and ask questions. Seek help from people senior to you in the organizational hierarchy.

▶Principle 1: Identify the Readers and Purpose of Your Reports

Before you begin writing your report, you need to identify the readers and purpose of your report (see Figure 14.2). If possible, begin by talking with the readers or with the person who asked you to write the report. With most reports, you will know the purpose; with some reports—especially types of reports that you're writing for the first time or that someone asked you to write—you may need to spend a little time defining the purpose. These questions may help you as you define the purpose:

- What do you want readers to know, do, or learn from the report?
- Do you only want to present results, not to draw conclusions or make recommendations?
- Do you want to draw conclusions?
- Do you want to make recommendations based on conclusions?
- Is the report routine?

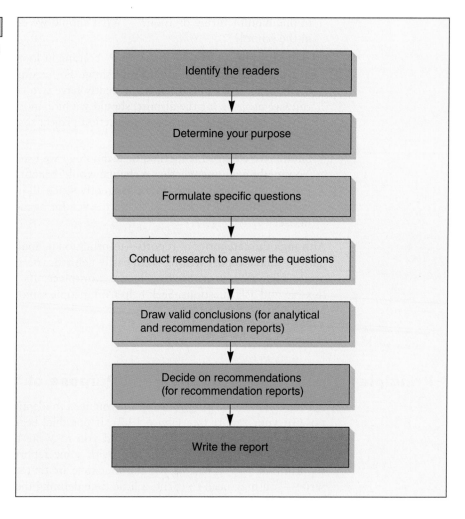

Figure 14.2

A Plan for Preparing a
Formal Report

▶ For more information on analyzing your readers, see Chapter 2, "Understanding and Writing for Your Readers."

As with informal reports, you want to find out as much as possible about your readers. To help you analyze the readers of your reports, consider these questions:

- What do your readers know about your field or the topic of your report?
- Why are they reading your report—to gather information? to complete a task? to make a decision?
- How much detail will readers need or expect? Does this need or expectation differ among the various readers? If so, how?
- Do your readers expect an informal or formal report?
- Are the readers internal or external?
- What positions do your readers hold in the organization? If they are internal readers, where are their positions in relation to yours in the organizational hierarchy?
- Will more than one group read the report?
- What do your readers know about you or your organization? Have their previous experiences with you or your organization been positive? If not, why?

Once you know your purpose and understand your readers and what they expect, you can prepare to meet their needs and to ensure that your report achieves its intended purpose.

Pay particular attention to two important factors that will help you to discover what readers need or expect: readers' familiarity with the topic and their purpose for reading (Holland, Charrow, and Wright). Readers who are familiar with the topic of your report will "find it easier to grasp new material about the topic than readers" who are not familiar with it (Holland, Charrow, and Wright 30). If readers are not familiar with, or do not understand, your field, include adequate detail and explain technical terms and concepts. If you know that the knowledge level will vary among your readers, consider these three options:

- Writing separate reports
- Directing the language and detail to readers with the lowest level of knowledge
- Compartmentalizing the report (Holland, Charrow, and Wright 37–38)

Writing separate reports is rarely an option because it would be time-consuming and expensive. If you direct the language and details to readers with the lowest level of knowledge, readers highly familiar with the topic may become bored by or impatient with what they see as simplistic and tedious explanations. Thus, compartmentalizing the report is the most efficient and effective method for writing for varied readers. When you compartmentalize, you create a separate section for each group of readers. You can compartmentalize by simply using headings, tables of contents, summaries, and indexes to help readers find the sections that will interest them (Holland, Charrow, and Wright 38). You also can place definitions and explanations of technical terminology and concepts in footnotes, glossaries, appendixes, or other special sections within the report (Holland, Charrow, and Wright 38).

After you have a sense of what your readers know about the topic and what they expect, consider these basic questions that the readers will ask when they receive your report:

- What is the purpose of this report—to present results? to draw conclusions? or to make recommendations?
- Why are we receiving the report?
- How does this report affect us and our organization?

Make sure that you consider these basic questions.

▶Principle 2: Formulate Questions and Research When Needed

▶ For more information on researching information, see Chapter 5, "Researching Information Using Primary and Secondary Sources."

Have you ever asked a question and gotten the wrong response? Have you ever been asked a question and you didn't know what the reader was asking? If you ask vague questions, you may not receive the answer you need or expect. Likewise, if you use vague questions when preparing to research your topic, you may not find the answers you are seeking or you may use the wrong research techniques or sources to find information. When you ask clear, specific questions, you can more effectively research your topic and then meet the expectations of your readers and achieve your purpose. In some cases, these questions may be defined for you, especially if someone asks you to write a report. If the questions aren't defined, you will want to spend some time formulating specific questions.

As we learned in Chapter 6, good writers tend to spend more time on macrowriting issues (Baker). As part of macrowriting for most reports, you need to formulate specific questions that help you to determine the kinds of research needed for your report. Consider these questions for an analytical report on the health risks of electric and magnetic fields:

Vague	Do electric and magnetic fields cause health problems?
Specific	What are the health risks of exposure to low-strength, low frequency electric and magnetic fields produced by power lines and electric appliances?

The first question is vague because it does not specify the strength, frequency, and origin of the electric and magnetic fields. The second question gives the researcher specific information to use when researching the topic.

When you have formulated specific questions, you're ready to determine what primary research techniques and secondary research strategies are appropriate for answering your questions. Once you have a plan, try to spend as much time as possible researching your topic.

▶Principle 3: Make Conclusions and Recommendations Based on Sound Research

▶For more information on ethics, see Chapter 3, "Facing Ethical and Legal Challenges."

After you have formulated specific questions and researched your topic, you're ready to draw conclusions and make recommendations. For many reports, drawing valid conclusions is relatively simple if you have thoroughly researched your topic and gathered sufficient information or data. If you've not done adequate research, you may have a difficult time drawing sound conclusions or you may draw invalid conclusions. Depending on the topic of your report, these invalid conclusions could put you, your organization, or your readers at risk. You have an ethical responsibility to conduct sufficient research to draw valid conclusions.

To draw valid conclusions, follow these tips:

> ### ▶ Tips for Drawing Valid Conclusions
>
> - **When examining the results of your research, look for any cause-and-effect relationships.** When you find these relationships, you may be able to draw valid conclusions.
>
> - **Look for any results that seem to point to the same conclusion.** In most projects, you want more than one or two results that point to the same conclusion. You typically need more evidence than just one or two results to draw a valid conclusion.
>
> - **Watch for areas where you have used illogical or unsupported arguments.** For example, new menu items at a restaurant may not necessarily have caused a decrease in revenue. This decrease may have been caused by other factors. Before you argue that the new items caused the decreased revenue, you would need to examine other factors, such as the opening of a new restaurant nearby or the economic situation in the area.

If you have thoroughly carried out the research plan up to this point, you will easily see the recommendations that the conclusions suggest. For example, if your conclusions indicate that customers are bringing in their cars for service because of faulty ignition systems, the clear course of action will be to send a recall notice to each customer who purchased that model car. The company would then repair, at no charge to the customer, the ignition systems. Of course, this recommendation is not one that you would have liked to choose, but the results of your research should dictate your recommendations, not your desires for a particular outcome or recommendation. Even if you don't like it, this recommendation is ethical and in the long run will protect you, the company, and—most importantly—the customers who are driving the cars.

►Principle 4: Use the Conventional Elements When Writing Your Reports

►For more information on front and back matter, see Chapter 11, "Preparing Front and Back Matter."

When you have drawn your conclusions and determined the recommendations you will make (if necessary), you're ready to write the report. You will want to use the conventional elements we will discuss in this section. Unlike many informal reports, most formal reports have common conventional elements and front and back matter (see Figure 14.3). One of the important front-matter elements is the executive summary. Many readers, such as decision makers, will only read the executive summary; some readers will bypass the executive summary and read the body of your report. Because some readers will only read the executive summary, make sure that it gives readers accurate information that they can use to make a decision (see Chapter 11, page 320, for information on executive summaries). This section defines and presents tips for writing the conventional elements of formal reports.

Introduction

The **introduction** sets the stage or prepares readers for the information presented in the report. The introduction

- Identifies the purpose of the report
- Identifies the topic of the report
- Indicates how the report affects or relates to readers
- Presents background information
- Presents an overview or preview of the report

Figure 14.3		
Conventional Elements and Front and Back Matter of Formal Reports	**Front Matter**	**Conventional Elements**	**Back Matter**

Front Matter	**Conventional Elements**	**Back Matter**
Letter of transmittal	Introduction	Works cited
Cover	Methods	Appendixes
Table of contents	Results	Index
List of illustrations	Conclusions	
Executive summary (or abstract)	Recommendations	

Figure 14.4 presents questions that readers may ask as they read the introduction (as well as the other conventional elements of formal reports). As you write introductions, follow these tips:

> **Tips for Writing the Introduction to a Formal Report**

- **State clearly the subject of your report.** If a proposal or progress report has preceded the report, you can most likely "cut and paste" that information directly from one of those documents.

- **State the purpose of your report.** Clearly state the purpose of the report, not the purpose of the project. In the introduction, you are identifying the subject of the report that you are writing. For example, you might write, "In the report that follows, we recommend the most cost-effective option that will allow us to increase our productivity without sacrificing quality and client satisfaction."

- **Identify how the report affects or relates to the readers (optional).** In the introduction to many reports, you want to identify for the readers why they should read the report.

- **Present the background information that the readers need to understand your report.** For some reports, you may want to include a review of current research to demonstrate that you understand relevant research and that you have done your homework. Readers are more likely to accept your conclusions and recommendations if they know that you have looked at other research on your topic; your report will be more credible. For some topics, little, if any, research is available; if that is the case, then tell your readers.

- **Present an overview of the report.** Tell the readers what follows in the report.

Figure 14.5 presents an effective introduction to a formal report from SBC Communications, a telecommunications company. In the first paragraph, the writer introduces the general topic of the report: changing procedures in the proposal centers to improve productivity. The first paragraph also tells how the report affects the reader, who is the division manager who oversees the proposal center. The first and second paragraphs give the reader background about the need to increase productivity without increasing costs. The third paragraph states the specific topic and purpose of the report: to evaluate three options for improving productivity by completing boilerplate text for the proposals and then to recommend one of the options. The introduction doesn't include the conclusions and recommendations because they appear in an executive summary. The introduction also tells the reader what follows in the report.

Figure 14.4

Readers' Questions
About the
Conventional
Elements of Formal
Reports

Element	Readers' Questions
Introduction	What is the topic of the report? What is the purpose of the report? How does the report affect the readers? What is the background of the report? What other research relates to the report (primarily for research reports)? What follows in the report?
Methods	How did you do the research or conduct the study? How did you gather the information that led to your conclusions and recommendations?
Results	What did you find out?
Conclusions	What do the results mean?
Recommendations	Given the results and the conclusions, what should occur?

Methods

The **methods** section of a report answers the question "How did I do the research or conduct the study?" Readers want to learn exactly how you gathered your information. Some readers may be as interested in your methodology as in your results; so use specific, detailed language when describing your methodology. If readers will duplicate your methods, use language specific enough for readers to reproduce your research methods.

▶For more information on specific language, see Chapter 8, "Using Reader-Oriented Language," page 195.

Figure 14.4 lists the questions that readers may ask as they read the methods section of a formal report. As you write the methods section, follow these tips:

> **Tips for Writing the Methods Section of a Formal Report**
>
> - **Tell the readers how you did the research or conducted the study.** By giving readers this information, you add credibility to your results, conclusions, and recommendations.
> - **Use clear, specific language.** If you use vague language, readers may think that you didn't use clearly defined methods and, therefore, that your results or conclusions may not be valid. Without specific language, readers can't duplicate your methods.

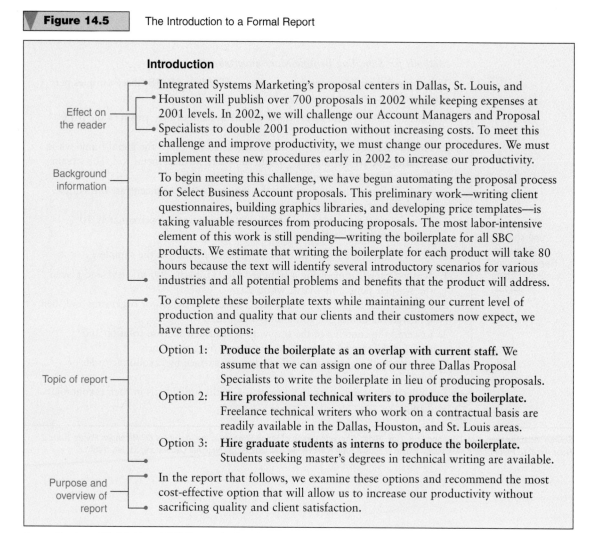

Figure 14.5   The Introduction to a Formal Report

Introduction

Effect on the reader — Integrated Systems Marketing's proposal centers in Dallas, St. Louis, and Houston will publish over 700 proposals in 2002 while keeping expenses at 2001 levels. In 2002, we will challenge our Account Managers and Proposal Specialists to double 2001 production without increasing costs. To meet this challenge and improve productivity, we must change our procedures. We must implement these new procedures early in 2002 to increase our productivity.

Background information — To begin meeting this challenge, we have begun automating the proposal process for Select Business Account proposals. This preliminary work—writing client questionnaires, building graphics libraries, and developing price templates—is taking valuable resources from producing proposals. The most labor-intensive element of this work is still pending—writing the boilerplate for all SBC products. We estimate that writing the boilerplate for each product will take 80 hours because the text will identify several introductory scenarios for various industries and all potential problems and benefits that the product will address.

Topic of report — To complete these boilerplate texts while maintaining our current level of production and quality that our clients and their customers now expect, we have three options:

Option 1: **Produce the boilerplate as an overlap with current staff.** We assume that we can assign one of our three Dallas Proposal Specialists to write the boilerplate in lieu of producing proposals.

Option 2: **Hire professional technical writers to produce the boilerplate.** Freelance technical writers who work on a contractual basis are readily available in the Dallas, Houston, and St. Louis areas.

Option 3: **Hire graduate students as interns to produce the boilerplate.** Students seeking master's degrees in technical writing are available.

Purpose and overview of report — In the report that follows, we examine these options and recommend the most cost-effective option that will allow us to increase our productivity without sacrificing quality and client satisfaction.

Source: Courtesy of Neil Cobb and SBC Communications, Inc.

Figure 14.6 shows an excerpt from the methods section of a report prepared for the U.S. Department of Energy by scientists at the Oak Ridge National Laboratory in Tennessee (the full report appears in Figure 14.14 at the end of this chapter). The report presents the results of a study of macroinvertebrates and fish in streams near two oil retention ponds. This portion of the methods section includes specific references to the procedures used to collect water samples and identify and quantify benthic macroinvertebrates.

| ▼ **Figure 14.6** | The Methods Section of a Formal Report |

Methods for Sampling Benthic Macroinvertebrates

To sample the benthic macroinvertebrates at Stations 1B–4B (three samples per site), we followed these procedures:

1. Placed a 27 × 33 cm metal frame on the bottom of the stream in the riffle area.
2. Held a 363-m mesh drift net at the downstream end of the metal frame while agitating the stream bottom (within the frame) with a metal rod. The stream flow transported suspended materials into the net.
3. Washed the net three times with the stream water to concentrate the sample and remove fine sediments.
4. Transferred the sample to glass jars which contained approximately 10% formalin to preserve the sample.

In the laboratory, we followed these procedures to analyze the samples:

1. Washed each sample using a standard No. 35 mesh (500 m) sieve and placed the washed sample in a large white tray.
2. Examined large pieces of debris (e.g., leaves and twigs) for organisms and then removed the debris not containing organisms.
3. Covered the contents of the tray with a saturated sucrose solution and agitated the tray to separate the organisms from the debris.
4. Identified all organisms that floated to the surface by taxonomic order or family.
5. Collectively weighed (to the nearest 0.1 g) the individuals in each taxonomic group.

The writers use specific language. Readers could duplicate these methods.

Source: Adapted from J. M. Loar and D. K. Cox, *Biotic Characterization of Small Streams in the Vicinity of Oil Retention Ponds 1 and 2 Near the Y-12 Plant Bear Creek Valley Waste Disposal Area* (Oak Ridge, TN: Oak Ridge National Laboratory, 31 Jan. 1984).

Results

Results are the data that you gathered from your research. The results section answers the question "What did you find out?" When writing this section, only present the results; interpret them in the conclusions section. Readers are most likely to understand your logic and your conclusions if you present all the results before you interpret them. If you mix the results with your interpretations, readers may not be able to separate the results from your interpretations.

The arrangement of a results section varies with the topic and the purpose of the report. For some reports, present the results in a series of paragraphs and supporting visual aids, such as tables and graphs. If you used a variety of

TAKING IT INTO THE WORKPLACE

Personal Computers, the Web, and Corporate Information

"In the 1950s, the family car, TV, and supermarkets changed the way we thought about and shopped for daily provisions. In the 1960s and 1970s, the shopping mall replaced Main Street as the place where people gathered. In the 1980s, toll-free phone numbers and database marketing created an explosion in direct-mail commerce and forced mall and department store managers to rethink their strategies. . . . As mass-customization becomes a reality, the opportunity to add value to information-intensive products and services becomes limitless."

—James I. Cash Jr.,
Professor in the MBA Program at Harvard (60)

In the 1990s, the personal computer, technology, and global communication revolutionized how companies conducted daily business—how they distributed information to their employees and to those outside the company. As the use of personal computers and the Web grew, so did the "user's expectation for information availability on or through that machine" and the Web (Foy 24).

Users are increasingly demanding information and services that put information directly into their hands via the computer (Foy 24). While this concept of providing universal access to information seems alluring to you and to organizations, the real issue may be more work and mediocrity (Foy 25). For many organizations, the issue is twofold:

- Deciding how to best create, share, protect, and distribute information
- Making the right information easy to get

Organizations want to "put their best foot forward." Therefore, they want to put out information in the best format for the user and for the information. They want the information to add value to the organization and to avoid the less desirable "data dump"—making all information available regardless of its value. As organizations consider making information available in this new millennium, new formats for the traditional report will evolve—you may help to create these new formats.

Assignment

Using a search engine, locate at least two articles that discuss how technology is changing the way organizations make information available both internally and externally. These articles should relate to information traditionally found in reports, not routine communication. When you have located these articles, write a brief summary of each and e-mail them to your instructor.

methods in your research, you can organize the results section around those methods. You then can structure your discussion of the results in the order in which you present the methods. For example, in the report presented in Figure 14.14, the writers first discuss the methodology for sampling benthic macro invertebrates and then fish. In the results section, they again discuss the results of the benthic macroinvertebrates sampling first. For other reports, use one of the standard patterns of organization to organize the results section (see Chapter 6, pages 139–153).

As you're writing the results section, follow these tips:

> ### ▶ Tips for Writing the Results Section
>
> - **Include only the results.** In the results section, you simply report the results—the data that you gathered. You interpret the results in the conclusions section of the report.
> - **Use a standard pattern of organization to organize the results.** These patterns will help you to present your results in an organized, logical manner.
> - **Use visual aids when appropriate.** If you have numerical data, use visual aids such as tables, line graphs, or bar graphs to present the data. Be sure to introduce and explain any visual aid that you use.

The sample reports presented in Figures 14.13 and 14.14 include results sections. Notice that Figure 14.14 includes visual aids to present some of the results.

Conclusions

The **conclusions** section answers the question "What do the results mean?" In some reports, this section is titled "Discussion of the Results." It interprets and explains the significance of the results. The conclusions and the recommendations sections are often the most important sections of many reports.

State your conclusions clearly and confidently, for you have results and research to support them. Avoid words and phrases that may undermine readers' confidence in what you say. Readers may think that the following conclusion indicates that the writers lack confidence in their conclusion:

Lack of confidence	We believe that Option 1 will maintain current expense levels and may build on current expertise to reduce the time for writing boilerplate text. However, we think that Option 1 fails to appreciably improve the quality of the text and could disrupt the work group.

The grammatical subject of both sentences in this conclusion is "we": "We believe" and "we think." When the sentences focus on the options, not on the writer, the conclusions are more direct and confident:

No lack of confidence	Option 1 maintains current expense levels and builds on current expertise to reduce the time for writing boilerplate text. However, Option 1 fails to appreciably improve the quality of the text and could disrupt the work group.

When writing the conclusions section, you may discover that the results are inconclusive, that none of the options studied meets the criteria, or that the methodology was poor. The conclusions won't always fit into the neat categories that you expected. Nevertheless, you have an ethical responsibility to report clearly what the results mean, even when the conclusions are not what you or your readers expect or want. Figure 14.7 presents the conclusions of the report from SBC Communications. The style of the conclusions is clear, the tone confident.

Recommendations

The **recommendations** section answers the question "Given the results and the conclusions, what should occur?" In this section, the writer recommends a course of action (or perhaps inaction) based on the results and the conclusions. The recommendations section may be shorter than the conclusions section and the results section. Some writers combine the recommendations and conclusions sections.

The recommendations may not be what you or your readers expect. In one report, you might recommend more than one option if the results warrant such a recommendation; or, if none of the options meets the criteria set up in the research, you might be unable to make any recommendations. In another report, you might recommend further research or a revised study because

▼ Figure 14.7

The Conclusions Section of a Formal Report

Each of the three options has definite advantages and disadvantages. Option 1 (produce the work as an overlap with current staff) maintains current expense levels and builds on current expertise to reduce the time for writing boilerplate text. However, Option 1 fails to appreciably improve the quality of the text and could disrupt the work group. Option 2 (hire professional technical writers to do the work) offers the highest quality text at the highest level of productivity, yet could cause the most friction in the workplace. It also carries the highest price tag on a "per-unit" basis. Option 3 (hire graduate students as interns to do the work) delivers improved quality and productivity at minimal cost with the most positive potential effect on the workplace. In fact, the quality of text written by interns and the speed at which they produce it will rival that of the professional writers if we screen the applicants properly.

Based on our evaluation of the options in light of the criteria, productivity and cost are secondary issues. The savings that we realize from automating the proposals will recover the up-front costs of creating the boilerplate text. Therefore, the center is primarily concerned with the quality of the boilerplate and the effect of the option on the workplace.

Source: Courtesy of Neil Cobb and SBC Communications, Inc.

your results are inconclusive. Your readers may not expect such recommendations; but you have a responsibility to give them honest, well-supported recommendations.

Figure 14.8 presents the recommendations section from the report from SBC Communications. The writer simply states the recommendations in one sentence, offering little explanation because he clearly supports the recommendations in the results section. Figure 14.9 presents the recommendations section from the research report prepared for the Department of Energy. The writers recommend more studies and explain the issues the studies should address.

As you write the recommendations section, follow these tips:

 Tips for Writing the Recommendations Section

- **State the recommendations in clear, direct language.** Tell the readers what specific course of action you recommend. Even if your readers may not expect or may resist your recommendations, state them directly.
- **Make sure that your recommendations clearly follow the conclusions and results.** If the readers have closely read your conclusions, they will understand why you are recommending a particular course of action.
- **Eliminate explanations of the recommendations.** If you have drawn well-supported conclusions, the conclusions section will support and explain your recommendations. You don't need to restate the conclusions in the recommendation section.

▶Writing Feasibility Reports

Feasibility reports are a type of recommendation report. Feasibility reports evaluate options based on appropriate criteria and recommend the most feasible or preferable option. These reports answer questions such as: "Should we repair the tower or build another one?" "Which method is best for repairing

Figure 14.8

The Recommendations Section of a Formal Report

> Because Option 3 offers the highest quality for the dollar with potentially no impact on the morale of the work groups, we recommend hiring two technical writing interns in January 2002 to write boilerplate text for Select Business Account (SBA) automated proposals.

Source: Courtesy of Neil Cobb and SBC Communications, Inc.

Figure 14.9

The Recommendations
Section of a Formal
Report

Recommendations

We recommend additional studies to address several important issues:

- More extensive season sampling of the benthic macroinvertebrates and fish communities to obtain a complete inventory of the aquatic biota in the Bear Creek watershed, to investigate the potential recovery of biotic communities downstream of the confluence of Stream 1A, and to identify specific sources of impact to aquatic biota in Bear Creek above the confluence with Stream 1A.
- In situ and acute bioassays to assist with identifying potential sources of impact.
- Chronic bioassays to determine the effects on biota of long-term exposure to various effluent sources.
- Studies of storms and their role in transporting contaminants downstream and in establishing and/or recovering of the biotic communities in Bear Creek.

Source: Adapted from J. M. Loar and D. K. Cox, *Biotic Characterization of Small Streams in the Vicinity of Oil Retention Ponds 1 and 2 Near the Y-12 Plant Bear Creek Valley Waste Disposal Area* (Oak Ridge, TN: Oak Ridge National Laboratory, 31 Jan. 1984).

the tower?" "Should we buy a new computer or update the current one?" To write a feasibility report, follow the basic plan presented in Figure 14.2 with these changes: after you identify the readers and determine your purpose,

- Establish criteria for evaluating the options
- Identify the options
- Evaluate the options based on the criteria and draw conclusions about each option

If you take these steps, you can make effective recommendations that follow from the conclusions.

Establishing Criteria for Evaluating the Options

Criteria are standards or benchmarks that you use to evaluate an option. For example, if you are deciding which personal computer to buy, you will have many choices. How do you decide which one to buy? Do you look only at cost? Do you look only at speed? Do you look only at which one would look best sitting on your desk? In most instances, you will use a combination of these questions to evaluate the options available to you. For example, you might look at cost, speed, accessories, and memory. For cost, speed, and memory, you will probably have minimum requirements or limitations. For example, you can spend no more than $3,000 for your entire personal computing package, both software and hardware. You may also have minimum requirements for speed and memory. For accessories, you will look at what you want, rather than at what you need. You may want a color printer and a scanner to accompany your personal computer. You may also want a flat-screen monitor. Therefore, **minimum requirements** or **limitations** are criteria that define what you must have. **Evaluative criteria** define what you desire, not what you require.

As you set up your feasibility study, you must define the minimum requirements and the evaluative criteria necessary to recommend a course of action. With such criteria established, you can determine the options available to you. If someone has asked you to conduct the feasibility study, the criteria may be established for you. For example, if you are buying the personal computer for your office, your manager probably gave you some minimum requirements, such as the amount of money you can spend and places where you can purchase the computer. If the criteria aren't established for you, you may easily derive the criteria from the research questions that you formulate. However, for some feasibility studies, you may have to derive your criteria by researching your topic. For example, to determine the criteria for purchasing the computer, you might study your software needs for your job.

Identifying the Options

Once you have established the criteria, you can determine the options available. **Options** are possible solutions or courses of action. For example, for the personal computer you are purchasing, your manager has given you a list of the stores where you can purchase the computer. These stores may narrow your options because you can only look at the computers they sell in your price range. You want to look for options that meet your minimum requirements and as many of your evaluative criteria as possible.

As you identify the options, follow these tips:

▶ Tips for Identifying the Options

- **Make sure that you identify all available options.** If you miss an option or simply leave it out, you may eliminate the option that provides the most feasible course of action. Your readers assume that you carefully identified all the options available that meet the criteria, so you have an ethical responsibility to identify every option.

- **Research carefully.** Use a variety of primary and secondary research techniques to ensure that you identify all available options.

- **Avoid the temptation to simplify the study by using fewer options.** Some writers will eliminate options perhaps because they're on a limited time schedule. Remember, you may be eliminating the option that best meets the established criteria.

Evaluating the Options

When you have established criteria and identified options, you're ready to evaluate the options. You may again need to use primary and secondary research techniques to evaluate the options because you will need to gather information about each option. You will want to make sure that you gather the same types of information for each option, so that you can evaluate the options equally. Depending on the criteria, you may gather both subjective and objective information. Objective information might be the cost of a personal computer or the amount of storage space available on the hard drive. Subjective information might be the location of the control switches on the monitor or the comfort associated with the keyboard.

Once you've gathered the information to evaluate your options, you will need some way to weight the criteria. In other words, how do you decide which option most closely meets or exceeds the criteria? You will need a method that will eliminate as much subjectivity as possible. Some writers use a rating system. You might use a simpler rating system for your feasibility study. For example, to evaluate the personal computer that you're buying for your office, you might use a rating system and matrix like that in Figure 14.10. As in Figure 14.10, you might assign a value from 0 to 5, with 5 being the highest and 0 being the lowest. With this rating system, the Dell model scores the highest with 16 points and the Apple model scores the lowest with 11 points. A rating system and matrix will not ensure objectivity, but it will ensure that you are looking at the same criteria for each option.

Figure 14.10   A Table Used to Rank Options Based on Criteria (Five Is the Highest Rating)

Option	Cost	Speed	Amount of Storage on Hard Drive	Warranty	Total
Compaq model	4	4	5	2	15
Dell model	4	4	3	5	16
Hewlett-Packard model	5	3	3	2	13
Apple model	2	4	3	2	11

Organizing the Results Section of a Feasibility Report

▶For information on the comparison/ contrast pattern of organization, see Chapter 6, "Organizing Information for Your Readers," page 147.

In feasibility reports, you can most effectively present the results by using a comparison/contrast organization. Using this basic organization, you have two patterns to choose from:

* Comparing by options
* Comparing by criteria

Comparing by criteria (see Figure 14.11) works best if you are evaluating only a few options. If you are evaluating more than three options, comparing by options (see Figure 14.12) will probably be more effective and accessible. When you compare by criteria, you focus the comparision on the criteria, and the options are subsections of each criterion. When organizing by options, you focus the comparison on the options, and the criteria are the subsections. When you use either organization, you can help readers to understand your results by creating a chart or table that compares each option criterion by criterion.

▼ Figure 14.11

Comparing by Criteria in a Results Section

> Cost of producing the boilerplate text (*criterion*)
>
> * Option 1: Produce the work as an overlap with current staff
> * Option 2: Hire professional technical writers to do the work
> * Option 3: Hire graduate students as interns to do the work
>
> Effect on the productivity of the proposal center (*criterion*)
>
> * Option 1: Produce the work as an overlap with current staff
> * Option 2: Hire professional technical writers to do the work
> * Option 3: Hire graduate students as interns to do the work
>
> Effect on the workplace (*criterion*)
>
> * Option 1: Produce the work as an overlap with current staff
> * Option 2: Hire professional technical writers to do the work
> * Option 3: Hire graduate students as interns to do the work
>
> Quality of the finished product (*criterion*)
>
> * Option 1: Produce the work as an overlap with current staff
> * Option 2: Hire professional technical writers to do the work
> * Option 3: Hire graduate students as interns to do the work

Option 1: Produce the work as an overlap with current staff

- Cost of producing the boilerplate text (*criterion*)
- Effect on the productivity of the proposal center (*criterion*)
- Effect on the workplace (*criterion*)
- Quality of the finished product (*criterion*)

Option 2: Hire professional technical writers to do the work

- Cost of producing the boilerplate text (*criterion*)
- Effect on the productivity of the proposal center (*criterion*)
- Effect on the workplace (*criterion*)
- Quality of the finished product (*criterion*)

Option 3: Hire graduate students as interns to do the work

- Cost of producing the boilerplate text (*criterion*)
- Effect on the productivity of the proposal center (*criterion*)
- Effect on the workplace (*criterion*)
- Quality of the finished product (*criterion*)

▶Two Sample Reports

You will write many formal reports as a professional in your field. Although the topic and purpose of the reports will vary, the principles presented in this chapter will help you to write any informational, analytical, or recommendation report. To create effective reports, think about your readers' needs and expectations and your purpose for writing.

Figures 14.13 and 14.14 present reports that met the readers' needs and expectations as well as the writers' purpose. Figure 14.13 is an internal feasibility report prepared for a division manager at SBC Communications. The writer analyzes three options for writing boilerplate text for Select Business Account proposals. Figure 14.14 includes the conventional elements of a research report prepared for the U.S. Department of Energy by scientists at the Oak Ridge National Laboratory. The report details a study of fish and benthic macroinvertebrates in streams near a landfill.

Figure 14.13   A Sample Feasibility Report

Hiring Technical Writing Interns: A Feasibility Report

Prepared for

Charlie Divine, Division Manager, ISM

Prepared by

Neil Cobb, Account Manager, ISM

November 2001

Figure 14.13 (continued)

Contents

▼ **Figure 14.13**   (continued)

iii

Executive Summary

The writer ——•
summarizes
the report
and states his
recommendation.

I have investigated the feasibility of using current staff, hiring freelance technical writers, and hiring student interns to generate low-cost boilerplate texts for automated proposals. Because interns will work for a low hourly wage with no benefits in exchange for experience, we can produce high-quality, low-cost boilerplate text. By using this boilerplate text, the productivity of Proposal Specialists who serve the Select Business Accounts (SBA) will ultimately increase.

Universities in the Dallas, Houston, and St. Louis areas have programs that can provide these interns. Ninety percent of the students in these programs are looking for internship opportunities to complete their degree requirements. These programs will provide a continuous resource for capable writers to serve as interns.

I recommend hiring two technical writing interns in January 2002 to create boilerplate for SBA automated proposals.

Figure 14.13   (continued)

Introduction

Integrated Systems Marketing's proposal centers in Dallas, St. Louis, and Houston will publish over 700 proposals in 2002 while keeping expenses at 2001 levels. In 2002, we will challenge our Account Managers and Proposal Specialists to double 2001 production without increasing costs. To meet this challenge and improve productivity, we must change our procedures. We must implement these changes early in 2002 to increase our productivity.

The writer explains the background and the purpose of the report.

To begin meeting this challenge, we have begun automating the proposal process for Select Business Accounts. This preliminary work—writing client questionnaires, building graphics libraries, and developing price templates—is taking valuable resources from producing proposals. The most labor-intensive element of this work is still pending—writing the boilerplate for all Southwestern Bell products. We estimate that writing the boilerplate for each product will take 80 hours because the text will identify several introductory scenarios for various industries and all potential problems and benefits that the product will address.

To complete these boilerplate texts while maintaining our current level of production and quality that our clients and their customers now expect, we have three options:

The writer highlights the options in a list.

Option 1: **Produce the boilerplate as an overlap with current staff.** We assume that we can assign one of our three Dallas Proposal Specialists to write the boilerplate in lieu of producing proposals.

Option 2: **Hire professional technical writers to produce the boilerplate.** Freelance technical writers who work on a contractual basis are readily available in the Dallas, Houston, and St. Louis areas.

Option 3: **Hire graduate students as interns to produce the boilerplate.** Students seeking master's degrees are available from area universities.

The writer tells the reader what follows in the report.

In the report that follows, we examine these options and recommend the most cost-effective option that will allow us to increase our productivity without sacrificing quality and client satisfaction.

Methods for Evaluating the Options

To support my recommendation, I evaluate the feasibility of each option using four criteria:

The writer lists the criteria and then explains his methods.

- The cost of producing the boilerplate text
- The effect on the productivity of the proposal center
- The effect on the workplace
- The quality of the finished product

Figure 14.13 (continued)

To gather information for the evaluation, I studied the proposal development process currently used in the proposal center for Select Business Account clients and the proposals for these and major account clients to determine the quality of the proposals, especially the accuracy of the information and the quality of the writing. I interviewed proposal specialists in the proposal center, account representatives who had worked with the proposal center, and an academic specialist in technical communication. The two proposal specialists provided information on the way work flows through our system in the proposal center. The five account representatives gave me their perspective on the proposal center's process and on the quality of the proposals. Finally, the academic specialist provided information on the availability, cost, and abilities of students from technical writing programs and of professional technical writers who work on a freelance basis.

Results of the Evaluation

To determine the feasibility of hiring interns, I evaluated the three options according to the criteria of cost, productivity, quality of the finished proposal, and effect on the workplace.

The writer organizes the results by criteria.

Cost of Producing the Boilerplate Text

Option 1, using the current staff, is least expensive. Option 2, hiring freelance technical writers, is the most expensive.

The writer uses specific figures to clearly explain the cost of each option. He tells the reader how he arrived at the figures.

Option 1: Overlap with Current Staff
Proposal Specialists (SG-22) earn on the average $48,700 per year. Loaded for relief and pension benefits, their total compensation is equivalent to $72,000 per year, or $34.60 per hour. With Option 1, the initial boilerplate for a single product would cost approximately $2,800.[1] Since loaded salaries for the Proposal Specialist are an embedded cost, Option 1 would not affect expenses.

Option 2: Hire Technical Writers on a Contractual Basis
Professional technical writers charge between $35 and $50 per hour, depending on their experience. With this option, the initial boilerplate would cost between $2,800 and $4,000 and would raise our departmental expenses accordingly.

Option 3: Hire Student Interns
Graduate interns will work for $10–$15 per hour in exchange for on-the-job experience. These interns will be classified as part-time employees, so

[1] I am using an 80-hour estimate for development time for determining the cost of producing the boilerplate text.

Figure 14.13   (continued)

the company will not pay them benefits. With Option 3, the initial boilerplate text for a single product would cost between $800 and $1,200 and would raise our expenses accordingly.

Effect on the Productivity of the Proposal Center

Option 2, hiring freelance technical writers, would be most productive. Option 1, using current staff would be the least productive.

Option 1: Overlap with Current Staff

When Account Representatives fill out forms and pricing tables, Proposal Specialists can produce a proposal in eight hours. If we take Proposal Specialists from their regular proposal-writing tasks to write boilerplate text (80 hours of work), we will produce 10 fewer proposals every two weeks until the boilerplate is complete. This option will reduce potential revenues. With this option, the proposal center will not meet the immediate needs of the Account Representatives and thus discourage them from using the center.

This option does have an advantage. Because the proposal specialists are familiar with our products and the proposal-writing process, they may be able to create the boilerplate for a product in less than the estimated 80 hours.

Option 2: Hire Technical Writers on a Contractual Basis

Professional technical writers should be able to produce boilerplate for a single product with the 80-hour benchmark. Some of the writers may require less time, depending on the writers' expertise in telecommunications and how long they work for us. Option 2 may be the most productive scenario overall because it will free Proposal Specialists to continue writing proposals while spending minimal time working with the hired writers to develop and edit the boilerplate.

Option 3: Hire Student Interns

Like the professional technical writers, the interns will lack experience with our products and proposal style. Because they are relatively less experienced writers, we expect their productivity to be less than that of the professional writers. However, student interns are professional writers in training. They will have considerable academic and practical experience from at least 20 hours of technical writing courses. Because much of the course work is "real-world" oriented, the difference in productivity may not be significant. Like Option 2, Option 3 will free Proposal Specialists to continue producing proposals although the specialists may spend more time guiding the process.

▼ Figure 14.13   (continued)

Effect on the Quality of the Finished Product

Options 2 (hiring freelance technical writers) and 3 (hiring student interns) will provide the highest quality in the finished product.

Option 1: Overlap with Current Staff
Account representatives praise the effectiveness of SBA proposals, keying on the "looks" of the documents. However, the quality of the text is presently inferior to that of proposals for major accounts. The content is technically correct—the Proposal Specialists know the products well—but they often write in passive voice and have difficulty writing clear prose. Unfortunately, because the Proposal Specialists know the material so well, they tend to let some difficult concepts and technical descriptions flow unedited into the final document.

Option 2: Hire Technical Writers on a Contractual Basis
Professional technical writers should greatly improve the quality of the written text of SBA proposals. Their writing skills and a fresh perspective on our documents would ensure that the proposals meet the needs of the non-technical readers.

Option 3: Hire Student Interns
Interns would improve the quality of the written text for the same reasons discussed for Option 2. We would see work of higher quality because the interns' graduate advisers would evaluate the text. Their text would have to pass two layers of edits: edits from the advisers and from our Proposal Specialists.

Effect on the Workplace

Option 3, hiring student interns, could positively affect the workplace. Option 1, using current staff, and Option 2, hiring freelance technical writers, could negatively affect the workplace.

Option 1: Overlap with Current Staff
Option 1 will affect the workplace negatively for two reasons. First, taking one Proposal Specialist from the group to write boilerplate will require the others to do additional work or to turn one out of three prospective clients away. Neither result would be acceptable long term, and turning away clients could cripple the automation project before it starts. Second, choosing one Proposal Specialist to write the boilerplate might bruise the egos of the others. This choice could irreparably divide the group.

The writer uses the same order for the options as in the introduction. The writer also uses the same order for the criteria throughout the results and clearly identifies each criterion and option in a heading.

Conclusions   5

Option 2: Hire Technical Writers on a Contractual Basis
Option 2 could help to avoid the negative effects of Option 1, but could also cause problems. The Proposal Specialists might resent management hiring another writer to do "their" work, especially if the freelance writers receive higher wages.

Option 3: Hire Student Interns
Like Option 2, Option 3 should prevent the negative effects of Option 1. Interns could also help us to avoid the problems of Option 2 because the Proposal Specialists would more readily accept the interns as subordinates and take on the responsibility of supervising their work. The interns themselves also will more readily accept the role as subordinates.

The writer presents ——→ **Conclusions**
and justifies the
conclusions.

Each of the three options has definite advantages and disadvantages. Option 1 (produce the work as an overlap with current staff) maintains current expense levels and builds on current expertise to reduce the time for writing boilerplate text. However, Option 1 fails to appreciably improve the quality of the text and could disrupt the work group. Option 2 (hire professional technical writers to do the work) offers the highest quality text at the highest level of productivity, yet could cause the most friction in the workplace. It also carries the highest price tag on a "per-unit" basis. Option 3 (hire graduate students as interns to do the work) delivers improved quality and productivity at minimal cost with the most positive potential effect on the workplace. In fact, the quality of text written by interns and the speed at which they produce it will rival that of the professional writers if we screen the applicants properly.

Based on our evaluation of the options in light of the criteria, productivity and cost are secondary issues. The savings that we realize from automating the proposals will recover the up-front costs of creating the boilerplate text. Therefore, the center is primarily concerned with the quality of the boilerplate and the effect of the option on the workplace.

The writer states ——→ **Recommendations**
and justifies his
recommendations.

Because Option 3 offers the highest quality for the dollar with potentially no impact on the morale of the work groups, we recommend hiring two technical writing interns in January 2002 to write boilerplate text for Select Business Account (SBA) automated proposals.

Source: Courtesy of Neil Cobb and SBC Communications, Inc.

▼ **Figure 14.14**   A Sample Report That Uses the Conventional Elements of a Formal Report

Because the ⎯⎯• **Biotic Characterization of Small Streams in the Vicinity of Oil Retention**
readers are   **Ponds 1 and 2 Near the Y-12 Plant**
biologists, the
writers use
technical   **Introduction**
terminology the
readers will   This report provides data on the aquatic biota in the streams near the oil
understand and   retention ponds west of the Y-12 plant at Oak Ridge National Laboratory.
expect.   Built in 1943, the Y-12 plant originally produced nuclear weapon
                  components and subassemblies and supported the Department of Energy's
                  weapon-design laboratories. In the production of the subassemblies, the
                  plant used materials such as enriched uranium, lithium hydride, and
                  deteride. The plant disposed of both solid and liquid wastes in burial
                  facilities in Bear Creek Valley—approximately one mile west of the plant
                  site. This report fulfills the Department of Energy's commitment to assess
                  the aquatic biota near the man-made oil retention pond in the valley.

                  Methods

The writers list the ⎯⎯• The Environmental Sciences Division conducted quantitative sampling of
specific sites   benthic macroinvertebrates and fish at the following sites:
studied.

- Bear Creek above and below the confluence with Stream 1A, a small
  tributary that drains Oil Retention Pond 1 (Stations 1 and 2,
  respectively)
- Stream 1A just above the confluence with Bear Creek (Station 3)
- Stream 2, a small uncontaminated tributary of Bear Creek that flows
  adjacent to Bear Creek Road (Station 4, the control station)

We also conducted qualitative sampling at the following sites in the
watersheds of Oil Retention Ponds 1 and 2:

- Stream 1A, immediately below Pond 1 (Station 5)
- The diversion ditch that carries surface runoff from portions of Burial
  Grounds B, C, D, and the area north of Burial Ground A to Stream 1A
  just below the pond (Station 6)
- Stream 1A above the diversion ditch (Station 7)
- Oil Retention Pond 2 (Station 8)

We could not sample above or below Pond 2 because of insufficient flows.
We did not sample Oil Retention Pond 1.

The writers use ⎯⎯• *Methods for Sampling Benthic Macroinvertebrates*
lists and
subheadings   To sample the benthic macroinvertebrates at Stations 1B–4B (three samples
to identify the   per site), we followed these procedures:
methods for
sampling benthic 1. Placed a 27 × 33 cm metal frame on the bottom of the stream in the
macroinvertebrates   riffle area.
and fishes.   2. Held a 363-m mesh drift net at the downstream end of the metal frame

Figure 14.14   (continued)

2

while agitating the stream bottom (within the frame) with a metal rod. The stream flow transported suspended materials into the net.

3. Washed the net three times with the stream water to concentrate the sample and remove fine sediments.

4. Transferred the sample to glass jars that contained approximately 10% formalin to preserve the sample.

The writers use specific, detailed language so that readers can duplicate their methods. This language also helps to justify their conclusions and recommendations.

In the laboratory, we followed these procedures to analyze the samples:

1. Washed each sample using a standard No. 35 mesh (500 m) sieve and placed the washed sample in a large white tray

2. Examined large pieces of debris (e.g., leaves and twigs) for organisms and then removed the debris not containing organisms

3. Covered the contents of the tray with a saturated sucrose solution and agitated the tray to separate the organisms from the debris

4. Identified all organisms that floated to the surface by taxonomic order or family

5. Collectively weighed (to the nearest 0.1 g) the individuals in each taxonomic group

Methods for Sampling Fishes

We used a Smith-Root Type XV backpack electroshocker to sample the fish community at Stations 1F–3F. This electroshocker can deliver up to 1200 V of pulsed direct current. We used a pulse frequency of 120 Hz at all times and adjusted the output voltage to the optimal value, based on the water conductivity at the site. We measured the conductivity with a Hydrolab Digital 4041. This instrument also concurrently measured the water temperature and pH.

At each of the sampling stations, we followed these methods to sample the fish community:

1. Made a single pass upstream and downstream using a representative reach. The length of the reach varied among sites (from 22 to 115 m).

2. Held captured fish in a 0.64-cm plastic-mesh cage until we completed the sampling.

3. Anesthetized the fish in the field with MS-222 (tricane methane sulfonate).

4. Counted the fish by species and collectively weighed the individuals of a given species to the nearest 0.5 g on a triple-beam balance.

5. Released the fish to the stream.

In a preliminary sampling we collected representative individuals of each species by seining and preserved the fish in 10% formalin. In the laboratory, we identified the fish using these methods:

3

1. Identified species using unpublished taxonomic keys of Etnier (1976)
2. Compared the mountain redbelly dace (*Phoxinus Oreas*) and the common shiner (*Notropis Cornutus*) with specimens collected from Ish Creek, a small stream on the south slope of West Chestnut Ridge, and identified as *Phoxinus Oreas* and *Notropis Cornutus*

Results

This section presents the results of the sampling and analyzing of the benthic macroinvertebrates and of the fishes in the study sites.

Benthic Macroinvertebrates

Qualitative sampling at the sites near Oil Retention Pond 1 and in Pond 2 resulted in few samples (see Table I). We also found low densities in the quantitative samples taken from Stream 1A, which drains Oil Retention Pond 1, and in Bear Creek near the confluence with Stream 1A (see Tables II and III). Relatively high densities and biomass of benthic organisms appeared in Stream 2, a small uncontaminated tributary of Bear Creek (Station 4). Some of the differences in the composition of the benthic community between this site and the others may have occurred because of substrate differences (e.g., the large amounts of detritus in Stream 2 when compared to the predominately small rubble and gravel at Stations 1 and 2). However, a depauperate benthic fauna existed in Bear Creek and Stream 1A.

The writers summarize the results in tables. The writers use parenthetical notes to refer the readers to tables.

Table I Description of qualitative sampling conducted near Oil Retention Ponds 1 and 2 west of the Y-12 Plant (previous study)

Station	Location	Method	Sampling results
5	Stream 1A just below Oil Retention Pond 1	Kick-seining	No organisms found
6	Diversion ditch just west of Oil Retention Pond 1	Kick-seining	No organisms found
7	Stream 1A above the diversion ditch	Kick-seining	Few Isopoda; unidentified salamander
8	Oil Retention Pond 2	Dip-netting; removal of sediment/litter from margins of ponds	No organisms found

▼ Figure 14.14   (continued)

4

Table II Total number and weight (g, in parentheses) of benthic macro-invertebrates in each of three 27 × 33 cm bottom samples collected from four sampling sites in the vicinity of Y-12 Oil Retention Pond 1

		Sampling station			
Sample no.		1B	2B	3B	4B
1		0	0	0	63(0.8)
2		0	2(0.1)	3(0.1)	46(2.2)
3		0	2(1.8)	0	25(1.0)
Mean no./m² (g/m²)		0	14.9(7.1)	11.2(0.4)	501.3(15.3)
Substrate		Coarse gravel embedded in sand and silt; leaf packs uncommon	Same as Station 1B	Sand, silt, mud, and detritus/ leaves	Deep soft mud covered by leaves and woody debris

The writers use visual aids to present the results.

Table III Density (mean no./m²) of various benthic macroinvertebrate taxa in bottom samples collected from four sampling sites in the vicinity of Y-12 Oil Retention Pond 1. Biomass (wet weight, g/m²) in parentheses. NC = None collected

	Sampling station			
Taxon	1B	2B	3B[a]	4B
Amphipoda	NC	NC	NC	67.3(0.6)
Annelida	NC	7.5(0.4)	NC	NC
Chironomidae	NC	NC	NC	273.1(0.7)
Decapoda	NC	NC	NC	22.4(7.1)
Isopoda	NC	NC	NC	86.1(1.9)
Oligochaeta	NC	NC	11.2(0.4)	NC
Sialidae	NC	3.7(1.5)	NC	NC
Tipulidae	NC	3.7(5.2)	NC	7.5(3.7)
Tricoptera	NC	NC	NC	44.9(1.3)

[a]Damselfly nymph collected by kick-seining.

▼ **Figure 14.14** (continued)

5

Fishes

The four fish species collected at the four sample sites commonly inhabit small streams on the Department of Energy Oak Ridge Reservation. For example, these four species were the most abundant fishes found by electrofishing in Ish Creek, a small, undisturbed tributary of the Clinch River that drains the south slope of Chestnut Ridge. The presence of fish in the lower reaches of Stream 1A is consistent with the results of a bioassay conducted on the water from Oil Retention Pond 1. This bioassay showed no mortality to bluegill sunfish after 96 hours (Giddings). The high density and biomass of fish at Station 3F may relate to the abundant periphyton growth observed in the winter and to the chemistry of the effluent from Oil Retention Pond 1.

We found no aquatic species listed as threatened or endangered by either the U.S. Fish and Wildlife Service or the State of Tennessee. However, the Tennessee Wildlife Resources Agency has identified the mountain redbelly dace (*Phoxinus Oreas*) as a species needing management. The agency assigns this classification to those species which, though not considered threatened within the state, may not currently exist at or near their optimum carrying capacity (see Table IV).

Table IV Species composition, as numbers and biomass (g, in parentheses), of the fish community at four sampling sites near Y-12 Oil Retention Pond 1

	Sampling station		
Species	1F	2F	3F
Blacknose dace	8	1	2
(*Rhynichthys atratulus*)	(21.0)	(1.5)	(2.5)
Common shiner	3	0	1
(*Notropis cornutus*)	(22.5)		(6.5)
Creek chub	42	4	10
(*Semotilus atromaculatus*)	(204.5)	(76.5)	(64.0)
Mountain redbelly dace	39	1	35
(*Phoxinus oreas*)	(64.0)	(3.5)	(51.0)
Total (all species combined)			
Density (no./m^2)	0.30	0.03	1.68
Biomass (g/m^2)	1.00	0.41	4.33

continued on next page

Figure 14.14   (continued)

Table IV (continued)

	Sampling station		
Species	1F	2F	3F
Physical characteristics of sampling site			
Length of stream sampled (m)	115	91	22
Mean width (m)	2.7	2.2	1.3
Mean depth (cm)	19	13	10
Conductivity (S/cm)	260	1005	477
Water temperature (˚C)	8.5	0.5	1.5
pH	7.1	7.6	7.5

Conclusions

The writers interpret the results.

The Y-12 Plant operations have had an adverse impact on the benthic communities of Bear Creek and some of its tributaries. The low benthic densities at Station 2B just above the confluence with Stream 1A suggest that the source of impact is not limited to the effluent from Oil Retention Pond 1. The relatively low fish density at Station 2F also implies an upstream perturbation (such as the S-3 ponds).

Further evidence of upstream impact(s) is available from the results of a similar study conducted 10 years prior to this study. In this study, researchers sampled benthic macroinvertebrates and fish at two sites located 50 m above and 100 m below the Y-12 sanitary landfill site. The west end of the landfill is approximately 1.4 stream kilometers above the confluence of Stream 1A with Bear Creek. No benthic organisms or fish were collected at either of the two sites, and in situ fish bioassays conducted just above and 500 m below the landfill resulted in 100% mortality after 24 hours.

The results of the earlier study differ significantly from those of the present study. The current presence of fish at Station 2F, which is approximately 500 m below the site of the earlier bioassays, may indicate changes in water quality over the past 10 years. However, the occurrence of fish in this region of Bear Creek may only be a temporary phenomenon (such as from a storm), reflecting short-term changes in water quality. The limited sampling in the present study may not have detected such a phenomenon. In view of the information currently available, both explanations of the difference in results seem equally plausible.

| **▼ Figure 14.14** | (continued) |

7

The writers ——→ present only the recommendations here.

Recommendations

We recommend additional studies to address several important issues:

- More extensive season sampling of the benthic macroinvertebrate and fish communities to obtain a complete inventory of the aquatic biota in the Bear Creek watershed, to investigate the potential recovery of biotic communities downstream of the confluence of Stream 1A, and to identify specific sources of impact to aquatic biota in Bear Creek above the confluence with Stream 1A

- In situ and acute bioassays to assist with identifying potential sources of impact

- Chronic bioassays to determine the effects on biota of long-term exposure to effluent sources

- Studies of storms and their role in transporting contaminants downstream and in establishing and/or recovering of the biotic communities in Bear Creek.

Source: Adapted from J. M. Loar and D. K. Cox, *Biotic Characterization of Small Streams in the Vicinity of Oil Retention Ponds 1 and 2 Near the Y-12 Plant Bear Creek Valley Waste Disposal Area* (Oak Ridge, TN: Oak Ridge National Laboratory, 31 Jan. 1984).

<table>
</table>

WORKSHEET ▶ **for Writing Reader-Oriented Formal Reports**

▶ **Principle 1: Identify the Readers and Purpose of Your Reports**

Questions to Ask as You Identify the Readers
- What do your readers know about your field or the topic of your report?
- Why are they reading your report—to gather information? to complete a task? to make a decision?
- How much detail will readers need or expect? Does this need or expectation differ among the various readers? If so, how?
- Do your readers expect an informal or formal report?
- Are the readers internal or external?
- What positions do your readers hold in the organization? If they are internal readers, where are their positions in relation to yours in the organizational hierarchy?
- Will more than one group read the report?
- What do your readers know about you or your organization? Have their previous experiences with you or your organization been positive? If not, why?

Questions to Ask as You Analyze the Purpose
- What is the purpose of your report—to present results? to draw conclusions? or to make recommendations?
- Why are they receiving the report?
- How does the report affect them or their organization?

▶ **Principle 2: Formulate Questions and Research When Needed**
- Have you formulated specific questions?
- Have you conducted research to gather information to answer the questions? Have you used primary and secondary research techniques?

▶ **Principle 3: Make Conclusions and Recommendations Based on Sound Research**
- Did you examine the results of your research and look for cause-and-effect relationships?
- Do any of the results seem to point to the same conclusion?
- Have you used any illogical or unsupported arguments?
- Are your recommendations based on sound research?
- Are the conclusions and recommendations ethical?

▶ **Principle 4: Use the Conventional Elements When Writing Your Report**
- Does the introduction
  - State clearly the subject of your report?
  - State the purpose of your report (not the purpose of your research)?
  - Identify how the report affects or relates to the readers and/or their organization?
  - Present the background information that the readers need to understand your report?

- Present an overview of the report?
- Does the methods section
  - Tell the readers how you did the research or conducted the study?
  - Tell the readers how you gathered the information that led to the results, conclusions, and recommendations?
  - Use clear, specific language?
  - Present adequate detail for readers to duplicate your methods (if the readers might duplicate them)?
- Does the results section
  - Include only the results, not conclusions or interpretations?
  - Use a standard pattern of organization? If you're writing a feasibility study, did you use the comparison/contrast pattern?
  - Use visual aids when appropriate?
- Does the conclusions section
  - Use clear, confident language?
  - Focus on the results, not on what you think or believe?
  - Include conclusions that you can support with thorough, unbiased results?
- Does the recommendations section
  - State recommendations in clear, direct language?
  - Follow clearly from the conclusions?
  - Eliminate explanations of the recommendations?

1. Working with a team, identify a problem at your university, in your community, or at your workplace. Write a feasibility report that examines options for solving this problem. As your team works, follow these guidelines:

   - Make sure that all team members are familiar with the problem and can gather the needed information.
   - Set up reasonable and appropriate criteria for evaluating the options.
   - Decide what methods your team will use to gather the needed information for evaluating the options.
   - Assign each team member an information-gathering task. For example, if your team decides to develop and distribute a questionnaire, decide who will write the questionnaire, who will prepare and distribute the copies, and who will tabulate the returned copies.
   - Use the "Worksheet for Writing Reader-Oriented Formal Reports" as you plan and evaluate your feasibility report, and follow the "Tips for Identifying the Options" on page 438.

2. Working with a team of peers in your major field, identify a problem to research. After identifying the problem, decide how to approach the research. For example, you might identify the methods you would use to research the problem, the means for verifying your results, and so on. Write a memo to your instructor describing the problem and your approach to researching it.

3. Locate a formal report from a federal, state, or city government agency or organization; from a private organization; or from a department or group at your college or university. To find a report, you can ask officials at your university or use a search engine to locate government agencies or organizations. You can also visit with reference librarians; they can help you to locate reports. You can also check your college's or university's Web site because universities routinely place reports on their sites; you can quickly locate these reports by using the site map. When you have located a report, write a memo to your instructor analyzing it. Be sure to

   - Identify the type of report (informational, analytical, or recommendation) and the intended readers
   - Evaluate the use of conventional elements
   - Evaluate the overall effectiveness of the report

▶ **C A S E   S T U D Y**

Deciding Where to Live in the Fall[1]

Background

Each spring, students at your college or university decide where they will live in the fall. Usually they have at least four options:

- Living off campus in an apartment or house and eating off campus
- Living off campus in an apartment or house and using the board plan on campus
- Living on campus in a dorm and using the board plan
- Living on campus in a dorm without using the board plan

These options vary slightly for each college or university. For example, some universities allow students to live only in certain dorms when not using the board plan, and some universities don't offer a board plan to students not living on campus.

Assignment

Your instructor will ask you to prepare either an individual or a team feasibility report recommending the best housing option for undergraduate students at your university.

Individual Reports

If your instructor asks you to prepare an individual feasibility report, follow these steps:

1. Revise the housing options listed in the "Background" section to match those available to students at your college or university.
2. Determine the criteria you will use to evaluate the options.
3. Gather the information necessary to evaluate each option, based on the criteria.
4. Analyze the information about each option according to the criteria.

5. Write a feasibility report for students at your college or university.

Team Reports

If your instructor asks your team to write a feasibility report, follow these instructions.

At the first team meeting . . .

1. List the characteristics of the readers of the report. Use the questions in the "Worksheet for Writing Reader-Oriented Formal Reports."
2. Determine the purpose of your report.
3. Establish the criteria you will use to evaluate the options for deciding the best housing option.
4. Decide how you will identify all available options. You might assign each team member a research task.

At the second team meeting . . .

1. Using the research that you've gathered, determine the options you will evaluate.
2. Set up the methods that you will use to evaluate the options. What rating system will you use? Will you use a chart or matrix?
3. Decide how the team will gather the necessary information for evaluating the options. For example, the team might meet with the director of housing and food services to get costs of food, housing, and parking. The team also might survey different apartments to determine an average cost for rent and utilities.
4. Assign each team member an information-gathering task. (Each member should be ready to report on that information at the third team meeting.)

---

1. Adapted from Brenda R. Sims, *Technical Writing: A Handbook of Examples and Exercises* (Denton: University of North Texas Press, 1995).

At the third team meeting . . .

1. Analyze the information gathered by each member, and determine the best housing option for students.
2. Assign a section or part of a section of the report for each team member to write. (Each team member should complete his or her assignment before the next team meeting.)

At the fourth team meeting . . .

1. Read all sections of each team member's report.
2. Compile one report.
3. Edit and proofread the report.

15

Writing User-Oriented Instructions and Manuals

W e follow instructions at home and in the workplace. Whether we are cooking microwave popcorn or installing new software, we use instructions. Some instructions are short, simple, and informal—perhaps only a few steps or sentences. For example, Figure 15.1 presents simple instructions that accompany a registration form for activities sponsored by a city parks and recreation department. Other instructions may be hundreds of pages long and more complex. Many of these longer instructions are in the form of manuals. Figure 15.2 is an excerpt from a manual for a dishwasher. This brief excerpt tells readers how to change the dishwasher's front panels.

The instructions that you write may be as simple as the list shown in Figure 15.1 or as complex as an entire manual. You might write instructions for tasks that you want your coworkers to complete or for tasks that customers will follow when using your company's products. Regardless of the number and complexity of the tasks, the same principles apply. In this chapter, you will learn five principles to help you write effective, user-oriented instructions.

▶Principle 1: Find Out How Much the Users Know About the Task

Before you can write effective instructions, you must find out how much users know about the task. This information will help you decide how much detail users will need to perform the task correctly and easily. You might also find out about users' background and training by answering these questions:

- Have users performed the task before? Have they performed similar tasks?
- Do users have the same background or knowledge of the task?

▼ Figure 15.1

Simple Instructions

Registering for FunEd Classes

1. Complete the registration form. Please print clearly or type.
2. Determine the appropriate fee for each class on the form. (You can find the fees in the class listings on page 16.)
3. Write your driver's license number and date of birth on the front of the check.
4. Make your check payable to the City of Albany.
5. Write the class number in the lower-left corner of the check.
6. Mail or take your completed registration form and check to Redbud Recreation Center before December 30, 2002. (The mailing address appears on page 18.)

- Will they have different purposes for using the instructions? Will their purposes for using the instructions change?
- How much detail do users need to complete the task? Do they want only minimal instructions?
- What are users' attitudes toward the task and toward the equipment used for the task? (Brockmann 101)

Figure 15.2 An Excerpt from an Instruction Manual

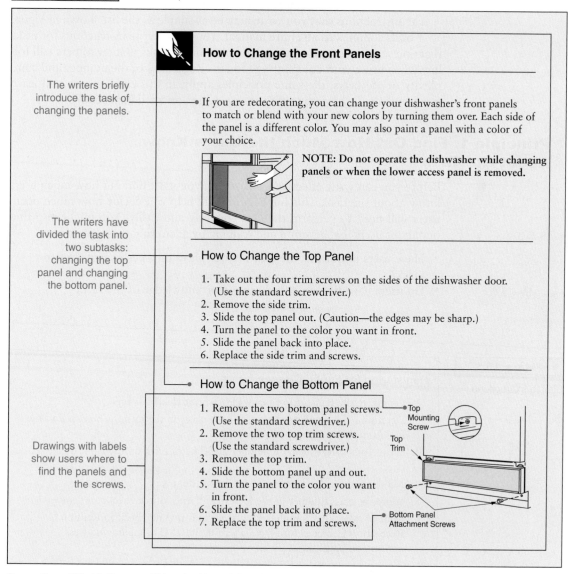

How to Change the Front Panels

The writers briefly introduce the task of changing the panels.

If you are redecorating, you can change your dishwasher's front panels to match or blend with your new colors by turning them over. Each side of the panel is a different color. You may also paint a panel with a color of your choice.

NOTE: Do not operate the dishwasher while changing panels or when the lower access panel is removed.

The writers have divided the task into two subtasks: changing the top panel and changing the bottom panel.

How to Change the Top Panel

1. Take out the four trim screws on the sides of the dishwasher door. (Use the standard screwdriver.)
2. Remove the side trim.
3. Slide the top panel out. (Caution—the edges may be sharp.)
4. Turn the panel to the color you want in front.
5. Slide the panel back into place.
6. Replace the side trim and screws.

How to Change the Bottom Panel

1. Remove the two bottom panel screws. (Use the standard screwdriver.)
2. Remove the two top trim screws. (Use the standard screwdriver.)
3. Remove the top trim.
4. Slide the bottom panel up and out.
5. Turn the panel to the color you want in front.
6. Slide the panel back into place.
7. Replace the top trim and screws.

Drawings with labels show users where to find the panels and the screws.

Top Mounting Screw

Top Trim

Bottom Panel Attachment Screws

Source: General Electric Company, *Dishwasher Use and Care Guide,* 12.

If you know how much users know about the task, you can select the appropriate amount of detail. For example, if you know users have used a Bunsen burner, you won't have to tell them how to work the burner; however, if you know they have never used a Bunsen burner, you will need to include basic instructions for operating one. You can also help your users if you know whether they have performed similar tasks or used similar equipment. You can build on this similarity when giving instructions or introducing equipment. If you know users are familiar with similar tasks, you can compare the familiar tasks with the new task to help users feel comfortable. You also can help users feel comfortable with a task if you know their attitudes toward the task and the equipment (Brockmann 101). For instance, if you know users may resist a change in routine or habits caused by the instructions, frequently reassure them and whenever possible link the new task to what they already know.

Depending on the needs of your users, you may want to include detailed instructions and explanations or perhaps even the theory behind a procedure. For example, novice may need detailed information to perform a task correctly, whereas a more expert user may need—and want—only minimal instructions. Some users may want or need to know the theory underlying a procedure or to understand how the equipment used for the procedure operates; other users want only the basic instructions.

As you decide how much detail and explanatory information to provide, consider users' reasons for reading your instructions or manual. Davida Charney, Lynne Reder, and Gail Wells found that users "with specific tasks in mind need little or no elaboration," but users "without specific goals benefit from explanations of how to apply procedures," not from elaborations that describe general concepts (63). Thus, users who have specific tasks to complete need little if any explanation of the procedure or the concept behind the procedure, and users without specific tasks will benefit from "how-to" statements, not from "why" and "when" statements.

Consider the elaboration in a document on controlling thatch (Koop and Duble).

| General elaboration | Mowers tend to scalp lawns that have excess thatch. |
| **How-to elaboration** | Use vertical mowers specifically designed to remove thatch. When using these mowers, make sure the blades penetrate through the thatch to the soil surface. |

The general elaboration will not help users to control thatch. However, the how-to elaboration gives users specific information about the type of mower to use and how to use that mower to remove thatch.

Find out whether users are likely to have the same background and knowledge of the task and the same purpose for reading. If users don't, find out how they differ in background and knowledge of the task or in their purpose for using the instructions. This information will help you to determine how to organize the instructions to best meet the needs of all users. You also want to consider whether users' needs may change over time. For instance, new users of a software application may first consult the manual to learn how to get started, so they will want basic information. As these users learn more about the software, they may have questions about more advanced commands; they will then want to use the manual as a reference guide, not as a tutorial. The manual thus needs a tutorial-type section for new users and a reference section for users who have become more familiar with the software.

▶Principle 2: Use an Accessible Design

▶ For more information on page design, see Chapter 9, "Designing Documents for Your Readers."

As you plan your instructions and manuals, decide on an appropriate typeface, layout, color, and page size for your purpose and your users (Brockmann 139). As you plan these visual elements, ask yourself how and where users will use the instructions. For example, will they use the instructions at a computer workstation? If so, use a spiral binding so the pages will lie flat, and perhaps use a smaller-than-traditional page size so the instructions fit easily at a computer workstation. Perhaps users will use the instructions not in a typical office environment but in a power plant, a manufacturing plant, or a maintenance facility. To select the design that best suits users needs, consider these questions:

- Will users use the instructions in an environment in which the instructions may become soiled or the pages crumpled?
- What typeface is appropriate for the instructions? Do readers require a particular type size or page size to use the instructions effectively?
- What layout will help users find and follow the instructions?

Design Instructions Suitable for the Users' Environment

If users will use documents outside typical office environments, select paper, a typeface, a type size, and a page size that will make the instructions easy to use. For example, if users will use the instructions in a environment such as a manufacturing or maintenance facility, use laminated paper or card stock that users can easily clean and a hard cover or notebook to protect the pages.

If users must read the instructions from a distance, the type size and page size may need to be larger than usual. For example, the instructions for clearing the air passages of a choking victim in a restaurant might be on a large poster in large type, so users can see the instructions while working with the victim. If users will use the instructions in a small area, the pages must be small enough to fit easily in the work space. For example, quick-reference information for some computer software programs is printed on the front and back of a card that users can lay next to the computer.

Exit

Design Layouts to Help Users Use the Instructions

As you design your instructions, create task-oriented headings and an accessible layout. Consider these headings:

Not task oriented	Deletion, Modification, and Addition
Task oriented	Deleting, Modifying, or Adding a Record

▶ To learn more about using verbs instead of nouns, see Chapter 7, "Writing Reader-Oriented Sentences and Paragraphs."

The first heading uses nouns instead of verbs to identify the tasks described in the section that it introduces. The task-oriented heading uses verbs to identify the tasks. **Task-oriented headings** suggest activities that users may already understand and can find immediately applicable (Brockmann 100). Task-oriented headings also help users who are using instructions as a reference tool to learn how to perform specific tasks.

To display your task-oriented headings, devise a layout that will let users easily search through your document to locate specific instructions. When reading instructions, users generally have a problem to solve or a task to complete. For example, they may need to learn how to install a software program, how to maximize the storage space on a hard drive, or how to install a new airbag in a car. Whatever the task or problem, users want to quickly and easily locate the information they need.

A logical, consistent layout like the one in Figure 15.3 helps users find the information they need. The layout of this page from a user's guide is effective because of the task-oriented wording of the headings, the position of the headings on the page, the use of lists, and the use of color. The headings suggest tasks that users will understand, and the modified hanging format makes the first-level headings easy to see. The second-level headings are also effective because the icon and the color draw attention to each specific task. The numbered lists visually separate each step, so users can easily identify and perform it.

To create an effective visual design for instructions, follow these tips and also review Principles 3 and 4 in Chapter 9:

▶ **Tips for Designing Layouts That Help Users Use Instructions**

- **Use a serif typeface such as Times Roman, Palatino, or Bookman for the text.** Use these conservative typefaces or other similar typefaces because they don't distract the users (Brockman 141–142).
- **Use no more than two typeface families.** If you use two, use a serif typeface for the text and a sans-serif typeface such as Arial or Tahoma for the headings.

(continued on page 469)

▼ **Figure 15.3** An Effective Layout for Instructions

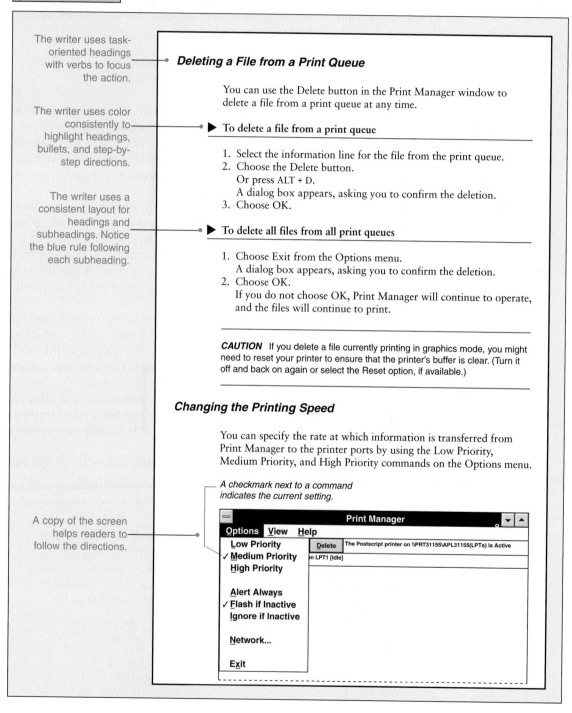

The writer uses task-oriented headings with verbs to focus the action.

The writer uses color consistently to highlight headings, bullets, and step-by-step directions.

The writer uses a consistent layout for headings and subheadings. Notice the blue rule following each subheading.

A copy of the screen helps readers to follow the directions.

Deleting a File from a Print Queue

You can use the Delete button in the Print Manager window to delete a file from a print queue at any time.

▶ **To delete a file from a print queue**

1. Select the information line for the file from the print queue.
2. Choose the Delete button.
   Or press ALT + D.
   A dialog box appears, asking you to confirm the deletion.
3. Choose OK.

▶ **To delete all files from all print queues**

1. Choose Exit from the Options menu.
   A dialog box appears, asking you to confirm the deletion.
2. Choose OK.
   If you do not choose OK, Print Manager will continue to operate, and the files will continue to print.

CAUTION If you delete a file currently printing in graphics mode, you might need to reset your printer to ensure that the printer's buffer is clear. (Turn it off and back on again or select the Reset option, if available.)

Changing the Printing Speed

You can specify the rate at which information is transferred from Print Manager to the printer ports by using the Low Priority, Medium Priority, and High Priority commands on the Options menu.

A checkmark next to a command indicates the current setting.

| — | Print Manager | ▼ ▲ |

Options   **View**   **Help**

| Low Priority | Delete | The Postscript printer on \\PRT31155\APL31155(LPTs) is Active |
| ✓ Medium Priority | on LPT1 [Idle] |
| High Priority |

Alert Always
✓ Flash if Inactive
Ignore if Inactive

Network...

Exit

| **Figure 15.3** | (continued) |

The writer uses typeface and type size consistently for the headings.

▶ **To increase printing speed and slow down applications**

■ Choose High Priority from the Options menu.

This setting uses more of your computer's processor time for Print Manager, causing other applications to run more slowly.

▶ **To print and run applications equally**

■ Choose Medium Priority from the Options menu.

This setting shares your computer's processor time as equally as possible between Print Manager and other applications that are running. This is the standard setting.

▶ **To decrease printing speed and run applications faster**

■ Choose Low Priority from the Options menu.

This setting uses more of the computer's processor time to run applications, causing Print Manager to slow down.

Source: *Microsoft ® Windows 3.0 User's Guide,* 202–203. Reprinted with permission from Microsoft Corporation.

- **Use the modified hanging or left-hanging format for headings (see Figure 9.9, page 236).** The hanging format helps users to locate instructions for specific tasks.
- **When possible, use color consistently to highlight important elements such as first-level headings and lists.** Use the same color throughout so that users won't wonder what different colors mean (Brockmann 161). For example, if you use blue for one first-level heading, use blue for all first-level headings.
- **Use typefaces, type sizes, color, and other design elements consistently.** When you use typeface, type size, and other design elements (such as indenting) consistently, you guide users through your instructions. For example, if you use a left-hanging format and a sans-serif type consistently for first-level headings, you help the users to quickly locate these headings.

TAKING IT INTO THE WORKPLACE

A Note About Paper Versus Online Instructions

"A book's physical appearance is an analog to its conceptual organization and structure. That is, the binding has a front and a back, so we see where we begin and where we end; chapters are differentiated by white space, so readers are kept apprised of their reading progress; progressing three-fourths of the way through a book can be physically verified by the number of pages passed. Online documentation, however, has no inherent physical analog to its organization and structure."
— R. John Brockmann in *Writing Better Computer User Documentation* (70)

As we depend more on computers, more instructions are appearing online instead of on paper. Users access these instructions from their computer and use the keyboard or mouse to move through the instructions. Online instructions, however, aren't just paper instructions displayed on screen. Paper and online instructions differ in several ways:

- Because of the size of most computer screens, writers chunk information presented online in smaller pieces than they do information presented on paper. On-screen line lengths and paragraphs may be shorter.
- Writers use more white space on screen than they do on paper. Otherwise, on-screen text would be hard to read because the ascenders and descenders of letters are often compressed, and the space between lines is less than in most paper documents, making each line blur into the lines immediately above and below it.
- Writers use different typefaces on screen than they might use for paper documents. The screen diminishes the resolution, or sharpness, of letters. On a typeset page, around 17,500 dots create a letter; and on a laser-printed page,

from 600 to 1,200 dots create the same letter; but on a computer screen, about 63 dots create the same letter. Thus many typefaces that are readable on paper are not readable on screen.

- Writers organize effective online instructions differently than they do paper instructions. Effective online instructions may have a tree-type, nonlinear structure, so users can decide how to move through the document. Users are "lost much more easily in the organization" of online documents, especially when confronted with multiple screens and choices (Brockmann 70). Thus writers of online instructions must give users clear navigation tools and offer them different ways of navigating through the documents.

Most of the information presented in this chapter applies to online instructions—except in organization and layout. Therefore, if you are asked to write online instructions, learn more about the software authoring packages that will help you write such instructions and about the differences in the organization and layout of paper and online instructions.

Assignment

- Find online documentation (instructions) for a product or service related to your major.
- Evaluate the online documentation in an e-mail to your instructor. Tell your instructor where to locate the documentation, or bring a copy to class.
- Consider these questions: Could you easily navigate through the instructions? Could you easily find the information that you needed? Did the screen design help you to locate information? How did the writers organize the instructions?

Liability and Instructional Writing: Can You or Your Company Be Liable?

Are companies liable for financial damages when instructions for their products are imprecise or inaccurate? In *Martin v. Hacker*, the New York Court of Appeals unanimously decided that companies are definitely liable. This decision is especially interesting to those who write instructions because the court carefully analyzed the language of instructions in a lawsuit over a drug-induced suicide. Eugene Martin was taking hydrochlorothiazide and reserpine for high blood pressure; although he "had no history of mental illness or depression, [he] shot and killed himself in a drug-induced despondency" (Caher 6). His widow alleged that the written warnings supplied with the drugs were insufficient. The court stated that the case centered on the drug manufacturer's obligation to fully reveal the potential hazards of its products. Therefore, the court specifically examined the accuracy, clarity, and consistency of the warnings. The court scrutinized specific language that the writers used. The court dismissed the lawsuit, stating that the warnings "contained language which, on its face, adequately warned against the precise risk" *(Martin v. Hacker)*.

According to this case and a growing trend, courts will carefully analyze the specific language of technical documents and will hold companies liable for that language (Parson). Companies and writers, then, must be diligent in writing technical instructions—especially in terms of accuracy, clarity, and consistency because the "stakes are substantial" (Caher 10). When a writer's "work is unclear, [and] an operator inadvertently reformats a hard drive, that's unfortunate"; but if a writer's inaccurate or unclear language "claims a life, that's another matter altogether" (Caher 10).

▶Principle 3: Use User-Oriented Language

As you write your step-by-step instructions, you should use user-oriented language. Use a "talker" style: Write as if you were speaking directly to your users (Brockmann; Haramundanis). The following examples contrast *talker style* with *writer style*:

Use Talker Style . . .	Not Writer Style
Press the <return> key for help.	The user should press the <return> key for assistance.
Press the shutter-release button.	The user should press the shutter-release button.
Tighten the knobs on each side of the handle.	The knobs on each side of the handle should be tightened.

Talker style is concise. It uses action verbs, imperative sentences (or commands), and simple and specific language. As you write your instructions, follow these tips that summarize the guidelines presented in this section:

▶ **Tips for Using User-Oriented Language**

- **Use action verbs.** When you use action verbs, you focus the sentence on the task.
- **Use imperative sentences.** Imperative sentences focus the users' attention on the action.
- **Use simple language.** Select words that users can quickly and easily understand.
- **Use specific language.** Without specific language, users may misunderstand the instructions and possibly damage equipment or injure themselves or others.
- **Use language that users will understand.** Use technical terminology only if your users are familiar with this terminology. If you must use terminology that your users won't understand, define those terms.
- **Use technical terminology when your users expect it.** If your users are familiar with the technical terminology, they will expect you to use it.
- **If your users are not native speakers of technical/business English, avoid connotative and ambiguous language and terms.** Such language and terms may have different meanings in other languages.

Use Action Verbs

Action verbs tell users what to do. When writing step-by-step instructions, use verbs such as *run, adjust, press, type,* and *loosen*—not verbs such as *is* or *have.* Notice the action verbs (in boldface type) in these instructions:

> **Replace** the battery with a new one.
>
> **Dial** the phone number that you want to store in memory.
>
> **Press** the power button to turn on the printer.

Each action verb clearly indicates the action that the user should perform. Each action verb is in the active voice (to review the difference between the active and passive voice, see Principle 1 in Chapter 7, page 178).

Use Imperative Sentences

Effective step-by-step instructions consist of talker-style sentences whose grammatical subject is the pronoun *you,* which, however, doesn't appear—as in "Replace the battery." When the grammatical subject is understood to be *you,* the sentence is imperative. An **imperative sentence** is a command. Its main verb tells the user to carry out some action. Imperative sentences focus attention on what the user is to do, not on the user.

Compare these two sentences:

Writer-style sentence	You should locate a wall stud in the area where you want to install your telephone.
Imperative sentence	**Locate** a wall stud in the area where you want to install your telephone.

The writer-style sentence focuses the user's attention on the subject "You," the first word of the sentence. In the imperative sentence, the user understands the subject to be "you" and focuses on the main verb, which expresses the action.

Let's look at two more examples:

Writer-style sentence	Testing of emergency numbers should be performed during off-peak hours, such as in the early morning or late evening.
Imperative sentence	**Test** emergency numbers during off-peak hours, such as in the early morning or late evening.

In the writer-style sentence, the verb is in the passive voice ("should be performed"), and the action that the user is to perform is in the noun *testing*. The imperative sentence expresses the action in the verb *test*. By using imperative sentences, the writer eliminates passive-voice constructions and focuses the user's attention on the action.

Use Simple and Specific Language

Try to resist the temptation to use "fancy" or less familiar words. Figure 15.4 lists alternatives to some less familiar words that you otherwise might use. When writing instructions and manuals, use words that users can quickly and easily understand. If you are unsure whether users will understand a word, choose another word or provide a definition that they will understand.

When writing instructions and manuals, be specific. Otherwise, users might not gather the proper equipment and materials, or they might misunderstand the instructions and injure themselves or damage the equipment. Consider these instructions for changing the oil in an automobile:

> Before changing the oil, run the engine until it reaches normal operating temperature. The engine has reached this temperature when the exhaust pipe is warm to the touch. You should run the engine to mix the dirt and sludge with the oil in the crankcase, so the dirt and sludge drain along with the oil.

Experienced automobile mechanics would know how long to let the engine run before the exhaust pipe became so hot that it burned their hands. Other users might not know how long to let the engine run. Thus the writer should specifically state how long to let the engine run, so that novice users don't risk

Figure 15.4 Simple Words	**Instead of These Less Familiar Words . . .**	**Use These Simple, More Familiar Words**
	assistance	help, aid
	construct	build
	facilitate	help
	indicate	show
	initial	first
	initiate	begin, start
	modify	change
	perform	do
	proceed	go
	subsequent	next, later
	terminate	end, stop
	transmit	send
	utilize	use

burning themselves on a hot exhaust pipe. Specific language is crucial if users are to correctly and safely follow instructions.

Use Language Users Will Understand

Use terminology that users will understand. To determine how "technical" your manual or instructions can be, consider these questions:

- What sort of background and training do your users have? Will they understand technical terminology related to the task?
- Are the users native or expert speakers of technical/business English?

If you know that users have background or training in a field related to the task, use technical terms that they know and will expect. If your users have little relevant background or training, try to avoid technical terms and instead use language that they will understand. If your users are not native or expert speakers of technical/business English, avoid connotative and ambiguous language and terms that may have different meanings in other languages.

Also be sensitive to the tone of your writing. For instance, imperative sentences will make users in some cultures uncomfortable. For some users, you might use labeled drawings, especially when the instructions are relatively simple and require few words (Brockmann 115).

▶ For more information on writing for nonnative speakers of English, see Chapter 8, "Using Reader-Oriented Language," page 211.

►Principle 4: Test Your Instructions

When time and money allow, test your instructions before you release them to your primary users. You want to determine if your instructions or manuals are usable. A **usable document** contains accurate, complete information and is easy to use. **Usability testing** is a process of conducting experiments with people who represent the users of a document. The goal of usability testing is to determine how well the users understand the document and if they can safely and easily use it. You can conduct usability testing on any technical document; however, you will primarily test instructions and manuals. Usability testing can uncover places where users cannot understand what you have written, where you have given too much or too little information, and where users need you to include visual aids. In other words, usability testing tells you whether or not users can

- Locate the information they need to perform the task
- Use the information to perform the task successfully and easily

To perform an effective usability test, you want to put the users in a realistic setting that simulates the actual situations where they will use the document (Zimmerman, Muraski, and Slater 499; Redish and Schell 67). You also want to select real users—users who will actually use the document, not fellow employees who act as users. Most organizations use a setting that simulates the actual situations in which the users will perform the tasks and use the manuals; however, some technical communicators conduct usability testing in the field (Zimmerman, Muraski, and Slater). For example, a group of researchers wanted to test the effectiveness of pesticide-warning labels, so they asked a group of farmers to participate in the usability tests (Zimmerman, Muraski, and Slater 496–97).

You can test instructions several times during the writing process:

- Test the prototype, or first draft, of a chapter or section. Prototype testing occurs early in the writing process before you draft the entire document. Prototype testing helps you to see whether the layout, design, and style you have selected will work for your users.
- Test a complete but preliminary draft of the instructions.
- Test a revised but not yet final draft of the instructions.

Prototype testing provides feedback before you write the entire document. If you wait to test until you are completely satisfied with the instructions, you probably will be near your final deadline and may not have time to revise the document after it is tested.

To conduct an effective usability test, follow these tips:

Tips for Effective Usability Testing

- **Determine the needs of the users.** What do the users already know about the task? Are they advanced users? Are they novice users? In what situations will the users be using the instructions? (See Principle 1 for more information on determining the needs of the users.)

- **Determine the purpose of the test.** What do you want to learn from the test? For example, you might want to test a prototype of the instructions. You can also test an advanced draft of your instructions.

- **Design the test.** For most usability tests, you will work with a team. Each member of the team will be responsible for carrying out one aspect of the test. The team as a whole or one member of the team will develop the test. Make sure that the test asks participants to focus on specific problems such as (Daugherty 17–18):

  - **Content.** Are the instructions missing information? Is the information complete?

  - **Ease.** Can the users easily complete tasks when following the instructions?

  - **Design.** Can the users easily locate information? Is any of the information hard to read or inaccessible?

  - **Sentence structure and language.** Is any of the information confusing?

  - **Visual aids.** Do the visual aids help the users to follow the instructions? Do the instructions need more or fewer visual aids?

- **Select the test participants.** You want to select real users to participate in the test, not your friends or coworkers (unless you're writing a manual for your coworkers). The test participants should mirror your intended users (Brockmann 262).

- **Prepare for the test.** When you have designed a test that has a specific focus, you're ready to prepare for conducting the test:

  - **Reserve the testing facilities.** If you're simulating the situation in which users will perform the task, you will need two rooms: the participants' room with a camera to record the testing, and the observers' room. The observers' room should, if possible, have a one-way mirror, so the observers can see the participants but the participants can't see the observers.

  - **Prepare a schedule of the testing-day events.** Make sure that all the participants and observers know when the testing begins.

(continued on next page)

- **Conduct the test.** To ensure that the test is reliable, consider giving the test twice (Daugherty 19–20) and follow these guidelines:
  - **Explain the purpose of the test, either orally or in writing.**
  - **Tell the participants how they should note problems or make suggestions.** For example, you might give them a survey/questionnaire to complete as they work through the test, or you can give them a notepad.
  - **Observe the participants while they are using the instructions.** Watch for any problems they have while using the instructions.
  - **Conduct an exit interview or debriefing with each participant.** Prepare a brief questionnaire to give each participant at the end of the test. You may ask the participants to complete this questionnaire in writing, or you or another member of your team can simply ask the questions orally, using the written questionnaire as a guide. As part of the debriefing, be flexible. If you or your team members have questions about the participant's actions or answers, ask—even if the question isn't on the questionnaire. If possible, have one team member in charge of the exit interviews to keep the interviews consistent and organized.
- **Interpret the results.** After you have completed the test, you will have much information about your instructions. After you have tabulated and analyzed the data, you will want to write a clear, detailed report (usually an informal report) that includes the results, draws conclusions, and makes recommendations based on those conclusions. For example, you may determine that you need to revise the instructions and conduct more usability testing.

▶Principle 5: Use the Appropriate Conventional Elements of Instructions and Manuals

The structure, length, and formality of instructions varies depending on the procedure and users. If you want to explain to your coworkers how to use the new fax machine, you might first briefly introduce the procedure and then present the step-by-step instructions. You could send these instructions to the users in a memo or by way of e-mail, or you might write the instructions on a card placed next to the fax machine itself. Your coworkers just want to know how to use the fax machine. They probably aren't interested in how a fax machine operates, and they don't need a formal list of materials and equipment. However, suppose you are writing instructions that come in the carton with a fax machine that a customer will buy. These instructions will need to be more formal than the ones for your coworkers and will need to meet the needs of a diverse group of users. These instructions might appear in a manual that has a table of contents and an index. Such a manual will also list the materials, equipment, and instructions for installing and using the fax machine. The manual is likely to have a troubleshooting section for solving common problems.

The conventional elements and format that you use will vary with the procedure and the users. If you're writing simple, less formal instructions to a single group of users, you will include the conventional elements listed in Figure 15.5. If you're writing complex, more formal instructions, you will use a manual format that includes the conventional elements and front and back matter listed in Figure 15.6. To accompany your manual, you might also create a reference guide. In the following sections you will learn about the elements that you might include in either simple instructions or a manual. Note that in a manual, the introduction becomes part of the front matter.

Figure 15.5

The Conventional Elements for Instructions (Elements in Italics Are Optional)

Conventional Elements
Introduction, including safety information
Theory of operation/description of equipment
Step-by-step directions
Troubleshooting guide

Figure 15.6

The Conventional Elements and Front and Back Matter for a Manual (Elements in Italics Are Optional)

Front Matter	Conventional Elements	Back Matter
Letter of transmittal	Step-by-step directions	Glossary
Cover	*Troubleshooting guide*	Works cited
Table of contents		Appendices
List of illustrations		Index
Introduction, including safety information		
Theory of operation/ description of equipment		

Introduction

The introduction gives users the basic information they need to understand how to use the instructions. Introductions for manuals often have titles other than "Introduction." They might have the title "Preface" or "How to Use This Manual." In the manual for Microsoft Money 2000, the title of the introduction is "Welcome to Money 2000." In a manual, the introduction may have some additional elements. For example, the introduction in a manual may explain to the users how the manual is organized; or, if the users may have varied skill levels, the introduction may tell the users where to begin reading the manual based on their level of skill. Figure 15.7 lists the questions that users may ask as they read the introduction (as well as other conventional elements of instructions and manuals).

The introduction for instructions and manuals may include any or all of the information listed in the following tips:

| **Figure 15.7** | Users' Questions About the Conventional Elements of Instructions and Manuals |

Element	Users' Questions
Introduction	• What is the purpose of the instructions? • What should I know before beginning the task or using the equipment? • What materials and equipment do I need? • Is the equipment or the task safe? What do I need to do to protect the equipment from damage? What do I need to do to protect myself from injury? • How is the manual organized? If I am familiar with the tasks, where do I begin reading the manual? • What typographical conventions or terminology, if any, do I need to know to use the instructions?
Theory of operation/ description of equipment	• How does the equipment work? • What is the concept or theory of operation behind the task?
Step-by-step directions	• What do I do first? • What are the specific steps for performing the task? • Can I perform the task in more than one way?
Troubleshooting guide	• How do I solve problem X? What do I do if X happens?

Tips for Writing the Introduction to Instructions and Manuals

- **State the purpose of the instructions.** Tell the users the goal of the instructions.

- **State clearly who should use the instructions and what they should know about the task.** For example, the installation guide for a garbage disposal states that the instructions are "for electricians with a Level 3 or higher certification according to Section 3 of the state electrical code." The writers assume that users know how to install similar equipment and that they understand the electrical code and related ordinances.

- **List all the materials and equipment that users need.** List all the materials and equipment in one place, so users can gather them before beginning the task.

- **Use drawings of some materials and equipment to ensure that users understand what they need.** For example, the parts identification page shown in Figure 15.8 uses drawings and words to make sure users know what tools they need to install a garage door opener. The figure also shows the types of fasteners included in the installation kit. Some writers identify the materials and equipment in a separate section after the introduction.

- **Explain typographical conventions and terminology used in the instructions.** If you use any typographical conventions, icons, or terminology that your users may not understand or recognize, explain them in the introduction. If you use many terms that users may not understand, you can define them in a glossary and introduce the glossary in the introduction. Figure 15.9 shows how the *User's Guide* for Microsoft® Windows explains in its introduction the various typographical conventions, icons, and terminology used throughout the manual.

- **Include any other information necessary to help users use and understand the instructions.** For instance, if you've divided the manual into sections, tell users what information each section includes and perhaps when and how to use each section.

- **Explain any safety information.** See the following section.

Safety Information

You have a legal and ethical responsibility to warn users about possible injury to themselves or others and about possible damage to equipment and materials. In the introduction or in a separate section before or after the introduction,

| Figure 15.8 | Using Drawings to Show the Tools and Equipment Needed for a Procedure |

The writer uses drawings (instead of photographs) to identify the tools and fasteners.

The writer divides the section into tools and fasteners. These subdivisions help users to know what tools they must provide and what fasteners come with the garage door opener. Notice how the writer uses the actual size for each fastener—to help users identify each type of fastener.

Tools and Fasteners

Tools Required to Install Your Genie Operator

Drill and Drill Bits

Ratchet and Sockets

Tape Measure

Hammer

1/4", 5/32", 7/32" Bits

9/16", 7/16", 1/2", 3/8", 1/4" Sockets

Pliers

Standard Tip and Phillips Screwdrivers

Straight Edge

Wire Strippers

Stepladder

Types of Fasteners Included: Fasteners *ARE* actual size.
The required quantity for each fastener appears in parentheses (2).

Shoulder Bolt (2)
1/4-20

Hex Head Limit
Switch Screw (2)
No. 8-32 x 3/8"

Shoulder Bolt (8)
5/16" x 11/16"

Flange Nut (5)
1/4-20

Lag Screw (5)
5/16" x 2"

Source: Adapted from *Genie Automatic Screw Drive Garage Door Operator System* (Alliance, OH: Genie, n.d.) 5. Used by permission of Genie.

you must state the seriousness of the possible injury or damage, using the correct language. The American National Standards Institute suggests specific terms for alerting users to hazards (American National Standards Institute, 1989).

Figure 15.9	Explaining Typographical Conventions, Icons, and Terminology in an Introduction

---

Visual Cues

You will find the following typographic conventions throughout the *User's Guide*.

Type style	Used for
italic	Anything that you must type exactly as it appears. For example, if asked to type *dir\windows*, you would type all the italicized characters exactly as they appear in the guide.
	Italic type also signals a new term. An explanation immediately follows the italicized term.
bold	Placeholders for information you must provide. For instance, if asked to type **filename**, you would type the actual name for a file instead of the word shown in bold print.
ALL CAPITALS	Directory names, filenames, and acronyms.
SMALL CAPITALS	The names of keys on your keyboard. For example, CTRL, ESC, or HOME.
Initial capitals	Menu items, command names, and dialog-box names and options. For example, File menu, Save command, or Line Wrap option.

Symbol	Used for
▶	Signals the beginning of a procedure.
■	Signals a procedure that has only one step.
Mouse	Instructions for mouse users.
Keyboard	Instructions for keyboard users.

Keyboard Formats

Key combinations and key sequences appear in the following format:

Format	Meaning
KEY1 + KEY2	A plus sign (+) between key names means to hold down the first key while you press the second key. For example, Press ALT + ESC means to hold down the ALT key and press the ESC key. Then release both keys.
KEY1, KEY2	A comma (,) between key names means to press and release the keys one after the other. For example, Press ALT, F means to press and release the ALT key. Then press and release the F key.

Terminology

The following terms take on special meanings in the context of Windows.

Term	Meaning
Application	A computer program used for a particular kind of work, such as word processing.
Application icon	A graphical representation of a running application that has been minimized. Application icons appear on the desktop.
Choose	To use a mouse or key combination to pick an item that begins an action in Windows.
Click	To quickly press and release the mouse button.

Source: Adapted from *Microsoft® Windows 3.0 User's Guide*, xxii–xxiii. Reprinted with permission from Microsoft Corporation.

These terms are (emphasis added):

Danger: imminently hazardous situation which, if not avoided, **will result in death or serious injury**

Warning: potentially hazardous situation which, if not avoided, **could result in death or serious injury**

Caution: hazardous situation which, if not avoided, **may** result in **minor or moderate injury**

Use the word *danger* to indicate that death or serious injury will occur. Use *warning* to indicate that death or serious injury could occur. Use *caution* to indicate that a slight injury might occur. Notice these terms in the warning shown in Figure 15.10.

While preparing your instructions, consider these questions:

- Will the procedure or equipment endanger the users, their surroundings, or their equipment?
- Is the safety alert adequate for the circumstances and severity of the hazard (Brockmann 13)?
- Is the safety alert located where users will see it *before* they perform the task that will endanger them?

As you prepare safety information, follow these tips:

▶ **Tips for Writing Safety Information**

- **Place the safety alert before or next to the directions for the hazardous task, not after it.** If the hazard is severe, put the safety alert at the beginning of the instructions or manual and repeat it before or next to the task where the hazard occurs.

- **Use a symbol or an icon to indicate a warning, danger, or caution.** The warning shown in Figure 15.10 uses an exclamation point (!) inside a triangle to indicate a hazard. The writers use this symbol because it is the international symbol for safety alert. They also use simple drawings to illustrate the potential hazard. Graphics are especially important for international users or for users who aren't native or expert speakers of technical/business English.

- **Use a distinct color consistently for the safety alert (or for at least part of it).**

- **Separate the safety alert from the text with white space or a border.**

Theory of Operation/Description of Equipment

The theory of operation/description of equipment section answers the following questions:

▼ **Figure 15.10**   A Warning

⚠ **WARNING**

Overhead doors are large, heavy objects that move with the help of springs under high tension and electric motors. Since moving objects, springs under tension, and electric motors can cause injuries, your safety and the safety of others depend on you reading the information in this manual. If you have questions or do not understand the information presented, call your nearest service representative.

POTENTIAL HAZARD	EFFECT	PREVENTION
MOVING DOOR	Can cause serious injury or death	Keep people clear of opening while the door is moving. **Do not** allow children to play with the door operator. **Do not** operate a door that jams or one that has a broken spring.
ELECTRICAL SHOCK	Can cause serious injury or death	Turn off the power before removing the operator cover. When replacing the cover, make sure wires are not pinched or near moving parts. Properly ground the operator.
HIGH SPRING TENSION	Can cause serious injury or death	**Do not** try to remove, repair, or adjust springs or anything to which door spring parts are fastened, such as wood blocks, steel brackets, or cables. Follow instructions and use proper tools to repair and adjust the spring.

In the following text, the words *danger, warning,* and *caution* are used to emphasize important safety information. The word
⚠ DANGER means that severe injury or death *will* result from failure to follow instructions.
⚠ WARNING means that severe injury or death can result from failure to follow instructions.
⚠ CAUTION means that property damage or injury can result from failure to follow instructions.
The word NOTE indicates important steps or important differences in equipment.

Source: Adapted from *Genie Automatic Screw Drive Garage Door Operator System* (Alliance, OH: Genie, n.d.) 3. Used by permission of Genie.

- What are the concepts or theory of operation behind the task?
- How does the equipment work?

Users often want or need to understand the basic theory of operation or concept governing a procedure. They also may want or need to understand how a piece of equipment operates. For example, in the user's guide for a cordless telephone (see Figure 15.11), the writers explain how cordless telephones work; this information will help users understand how to operate the telephone properly. The writers explain not only how the telephone works but also how this type of operation affects the way users can use the telephone. The writers describe some of the features of the telephone: Automatic Security Coding and AutoSelect. The introduction to these features helps users to know what sections of the manual they will need to read. The brief introduction to the telephone helps them use the manual and the telephone effectively.

| **Figure 15.11** | A Theory of Operation/Description of Equipment Section |

Your AT&T cordless telephone works much like a regular telephone, except that no cord connects the handset to the base unit. Since you're not limited by a cord, you can move freely from room to room, and outside your home, while you're on the phone.

How Far Will It Reach?

Your AT&T cordless telephone operates at the maximum power allowed by the Federal Communications Commission (FCC). Even so, the operating range is limited; the handset can operate only a certain distance from the base unit. Under average conditions, AT&T cordless phones will operate throughout a typical home and immediately outside it. However, the actual operating distance depends on the construction of your home, the weather and other factors. (See "Operating Range," page 21.)

You Should Know . . .

The same features that make a cordless phone convenient create some limitations. Telephone calls are transmitted between the base unit and the handset by radio waves, so radio receiving equipment within range of your cordless handset could intercept your cordless phone conversations. For this reason, you shouldn't think of cordless

phone conversations as being as private as those on corded phones. . . .

Automatic Security Coding

Every time you place the handset in the base, your phone randomly selects one of 65,000 possible security codes—much like an electronic password. With this Automatic Security Coding, your handset and base can recognize each other automatically, minimizing the chance that another cordless phone will use your telephone line.

AutoSelect™

To provide the clearest possible sound quality, your phone has the advanced 10-channel **AutoSelect** feature. A microcomputer in the phone continually monitors the airwaves to determine which of the ten cordless phone channels are used the *least* in your immediate vicinity. When you use the phone, the **AutoSelect** circuit provides the channel that has been vacant the longest, minimizing the chance of interference from nearby cordless phones—such as your neighbor's. Unlike simpler "scanning" systems, the **AutoSelect** feature actually keeps track of channel activity over a long period of time, which greatly improves its accuracy. . . .

Source: Adapted from *AT&T Cordless Telephone 5400 Owner's Manual.*

In sections describing the equipment or the theory of operation, follow these tips:

> **Tips for Writing the Theory of Operation/Description of Equipment Section**
>
> - **Use language users can understand.** If you must use technical terminology, define any terms that the users may not understand. Avoid any jargon that you might understand but that may not be familiar to users outside your field.
> - **Include only the details users need and expect.** Give users only the information they need to understand how a process works or how the equipment works. Additional information may confuse or distract the users.
> - **Place this information near the beginning of the instructions or manual.** You can combine the theory of operation and/or description of equipment with the introduction, as in Figure 15.11, or you can put this information in a separate section soon after the introduction.
> - **Generally, include a theory of operation or description of equipment only for more complex instructions or equipment.** Most users do not need or want you to explain the concepts or theory of operation for simple tasks. Such explanations can be cumbersome and distracting.

Step-by-Step Directions

▶ For more information on classification and division, see Chapter 6, "Organizing Information for Your Readers," page 144.

The step-by-step directions tell users exactly how to carry out a procedure. Before you begin writing these directions, decide how to organize them. To determine how to organize the directions, consider these questions (Brockmann 91–92):

- What action begins each task?
- What are the specific steps for performing the task? Can you group these steps into subtasks?
- What action ends each task?
- Can you perform the task in more than one way? If so, do users need to know both ways?

Once you have considered these questions, categorize the task into major steps and then divide the steps into appropriate substeps. For example, if you are explaining to a novice how to change the oil in a car, you might divide the task into four major steps—(1) drain the old oil, (2) remove the old oil filter, (3) install the new filter, and (4) refill the crankcase with oil—and then subdivide each step into substeps. When you divide the steps into substeps, you will help users to understand the task and to follow your directions. One long list of uncategorized steps will intimidate most users. The simple task of changing the oil could have as many as thirty steps. Most users would prefer four major steps with substeps to a list of thirty steps.

When you write step-by-step directions, list the substeps with each major step. You can tell users what specific materials or equipment they will need for each major step, especially if these materials or equipment vary from step to step. Give step-by-step directions in chronological order, stating any necessary safety alerts. As you write the directions, follow the tips below. The sample instructions shown in Figure 15.14 on page 490 follow these tips.

▶ For more information on chronological order, see Chapter 6, "Organizing Information for Your Readers," page 140.

▶ **Tips for Writing Step-by-Step Directions**

- **Categorize the task into major steps and then divide these steps into substeps.** Such classification and division will help users to understand and follow your directions.

- **Describe only one action in each step or substep.** If you put more than one action in a step, users may not see the second action. The users' eyes will leave the page as they perform the required action. When the users return to the page, they might go to the next numbered step and miss the second action.

- **Number each step.** Without a number, a step may not stand out, and the users may miss it.

- **Use imperative sentences.** See Principle 3 on page 472.

- **Use a list format, so users can follow the directions easily.** If you bury directions in paragraphs or extremely long lines of text, users may skip a step or miss the directions.

- **Use visual aids when appropriate.** Visual aids can help users follow the directions and can clarify the required actions.

Troubleshooting Guide

A **troubleshooting guide** helps users solve commonly encountered problems. It often appears in a table format with the problem in one column and the solution in another column (see Figure 15.12). Alternatively, you can simply use left-hanging headings for the problem and bulleted lists for the solutions. Brief, simple instructions may not need troubleshooting guides.

Troubleshooting guides can save you, your organization, and users time and money by helping users to solve problems without calling customer service. Users who can solve their problems without calling customer service reduce the amount of time and money that organizations must spend on phone support for their products. By anticipating users' problems, troubleshooting guides allow users to solve common problems in less time than a trial-and-error approach would take and without expensive service calls.

▼ Figure 15.12 | A Troubleshooting Guide

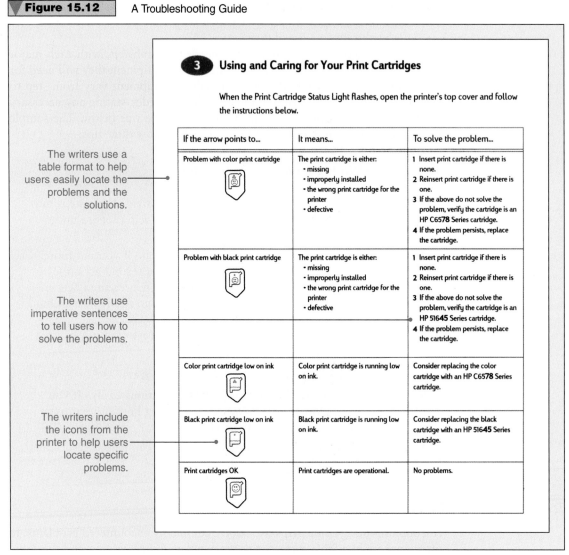

The writers use a table format to help users easily locate the problems and the solutions.

The writers use imperative sentences to tell users how to solve the problems.

The writers include the icons from the printer to help users locate specific problems.

Source: *HP DeskJet Printer User's Guide* (n.p.: Hewlett-Packard, 1999) 30. Used by permission of Hewlett-Packard.

Reference Aids

To help your users find the information they need in your instructions and manuals, you can provide a variety of reference aids, depending on the needs of your users and the length and complexity of the instructions. Common reference aids include the following:

- **Table of contents.** Include a table of contents for all manuals (see Chapter 11, "Preparing Front and Back Matter").

- **Index.** Include an index for all manuals. Indexes help users to find specific information or to solve problems quickly.

- **Headings.** Headings help users locate specific information and provide a road map to the instructions.

- **Quick-reference cards.** Quick-reference cards provide an overview of capabilities or commands. These cards help users who are familiar with the software and hardware and don't need the elaboration of more extensive instructions. Quick-reference cards are usually a separate document from the manual; they may be in the form of a brochure, a small card, or a template. You can also place a quick-reference "card" on the back cover or on the back side of the front or back cover. Figure 15.13 shows a quick-reference card that includes instructions in Spanish and English.

Figure 15.13

A Quick-Reference Card

Función de control remoto	Mandato de operación

Para reproducir los mensajes
    Buzón 1
    Buzón 2
    Buzón 3
	(#) (1)
	(#) (2)
	(#) (3)

Para repetir el mensaje	(#) (4)
Para cesar la operación	(#) (5)
Para saltar el mensaje	(#) (6)
Para grabar un mensaje de contestación	(*) (7)
Para grabar un mensaje de transferencia	(*) (8)
Para activar/desactivar la transferencia	(#) (8)
Para borrar un mensaje	(#) (9)
Para activar (ANSWER ON)	(*) (0)
Para desactivar (ANSWER OFF)	(#) (0)

Remote control function	Command

To play back the message
    Mailbox 1
    Mailbox 2
    Mailbox 3
	(#) (1)
	(#) (2)
	(#) (3)

To repeat the message	(#) (4)
To stop operation	(#) (5)
To skip the message	(#) (6)
To record a greeting	(*) (7)
To record a transfer message	(*) (8)
To turn transferring on/off	(#) (8)
To erase individual message	(#) (9)
To turn on (ANSWER ON)	(*) (0)
To turn off (ANSWER OFF)	(#) (0)

Source: Adapted from *Sony Cordless Telephone with Answering System Operating Instructions* (n.p.: Sony Corporation, 1996). Courtesy of Sony Electronics, Inc.

Sample Instructions

The sample instructions presented in Figure 15.14 accompany a cordless tele-phone that has an internal answering machine. The instructions tell users how to set up the answering machine. The left-hanging headings help users find the steps they want to complete. To help users follow the instructions, the writers included a simple drawing of the telephone and labeled the keys that users will use to set up the answering machine.

▼ **Figure 15.14** | Instructions from a Manual

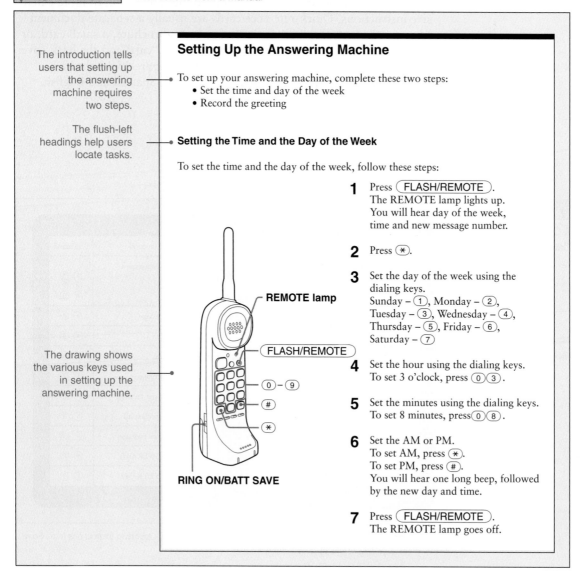

The introduction tells users that setting up the answering machine requires two steps.

The flush-left headings help users locate tasks.

The drawing shows the various keys used in setting up the answering machine.

Setting Up the Answering Machine

To set up your answering machine, complete these two steps:
- Set the time and day of the week
- Record the greeting

Setting the Time and the Day of the Week

To set the time and the day of the week, follow these steps:

1 Press (FLASH/REMOTE).
The REMOTE lamp lights up.
You will hear day of the week, time and new message number.

2 Press ⊛.

3 Set the day of the week using the dialing keys.
Sunday – ①, Monday – ②, Tuesday – ③, Wednesday – ④, Thursday – ⑤, Friday – ⑥, Saturday – ⑦

4 Set the hour using the dialing keys.
To set 3 o'clock, press ⓪③.

5 Set the minutes using the dialing keys.
To set 8 minutes, press ⓪⑧.

6 Set the AM or PM.
To set AM, press ⊛.
To set PM, press #.
You will hear one long beep, followed by the new day and time.

7 Press (FLASH/REMOTE).
The REMOTE lamp goes off.

REMOTE lamp

FLASH/REMOTE

⓪ – ⑨

#

⊛

RING ON/BATT SAVE

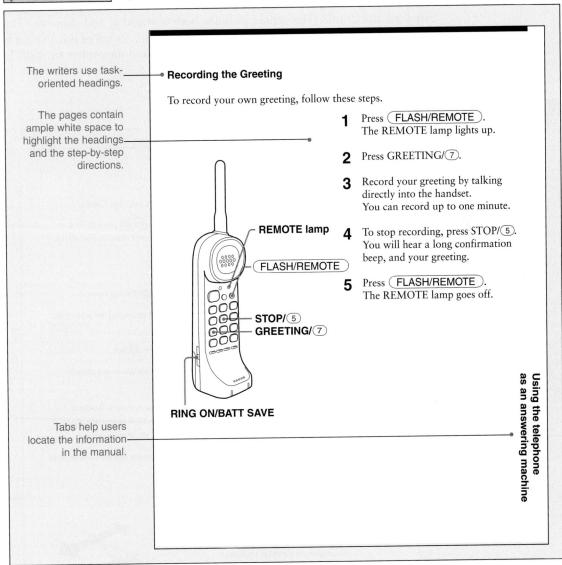

▼ **Figure 15.14**   (continued)

The writers use task-oriented headings.

The pages contain ample white space to highlight the headings and the step-by-step directions.

Recording the Greeting

To record your own greeting, follow these steps.

1 Press FLASH/REMOTE.
The REMOTE lamp lights up.

2 Press GREETING/⑦.

3 Record your greeting by talking directly into the handset.
You can record up to one minute.

4 To stop recording, press STOP/⑤.
You will hear a long confirmation beep, and your greeting.

5 Press FLASH/REMOTE.
The REMOTE lamp goes off.

REMOTE lamp

FLASH/REMOTE

STOP/⑤
GREETING/⑦

RING ON/BATT SAVE

Using the telephone as an answering machine

Tabs help users locate the information in the manual.

Source: Adapted from *Sony Cordless Telephone with Answering System Operating Instructions* (n.p.: Sony Corporation, 1996) 24–25. Courtesy of Sony Electronics, Inc.

Figure 15.15 is an excerpt from a printer manual. The manual writer begins this section by telling the users what materials they will need to clean the print cartridge and cradle. The writer includes both a warning and cautions. The warning alerts users about possible injury, and the cautions tell of possible damage to equipment. Figure 15.16 is another excerpt from the printer manual. In

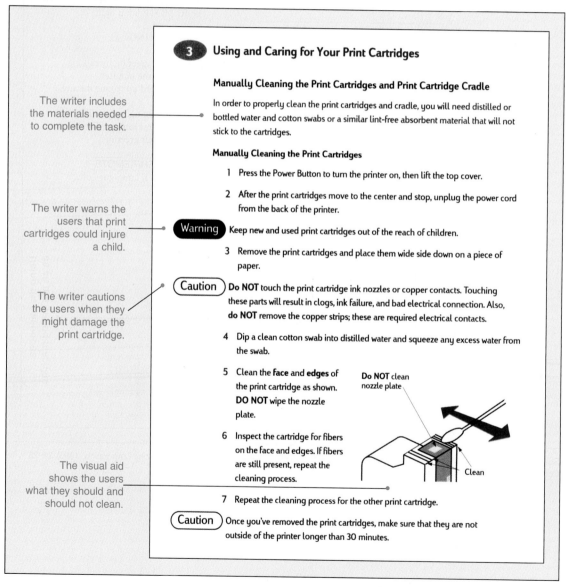

3 Using and Caring for Your Print Cartridges

Manually Cleaning the Print Cartridges and Print Cartridge Cradle

The writer includes the materials needed to complete the task.

In order to properly clean the print cartridges and cradle, you will need distilled or bottled water and cotton swabs or a similar lint-free absorbent material that will not stick to the cartridges.

Manually Cleaning the Print Cartridges

1 Press the Power Button to turn the printer on, then lift the top cover.

2 After the print cartridges move to the center and stop, unplug the power cord from the back of the printer.

The writer warns the users that print cartridges could injure a child.

Warning Keep new and used print cartridges out of the reach of children.

3 Remove the print cartridges and place them wide side down on a piece of paper.

The writer cautions the users when they might damage the print cartridge.

Caution Do **NOT** touch the print cartridge ink nozzles or copper contacts. Touching these parts will result in clogs, ink failure, and bad electrical connection. Also, **do NOT** remove the copper strips; these are required electrical contacts.

4 Dip a clean cotton swab into distilled water and squeeze any excess water from the swab.

5 Clean the **face** and **edges** of the print cartridge as shown. **DO NOT** wipe the nozzle plate.

Do **NOT** clean nozzle plate

6 Inspect the cartridge for fibers on the face and edges. If fibers are still present, repeat the cleaning process.

Clean

The visual aid shows the users what they should and should not clean.

7 Repeat the cleaning process for the other print cartridge.

Caution Once you've removed the print cartridges, make sure that they are not outside of the printer longer than 30 minutes.

Figure 15.16, the writer uses a table format to help users learn how to print on different types of paper and media. These tasks require two types of actions: working with the printer and selecting printer settings. Therefore, the table works well.

▼ Figure 15.15 (continued)

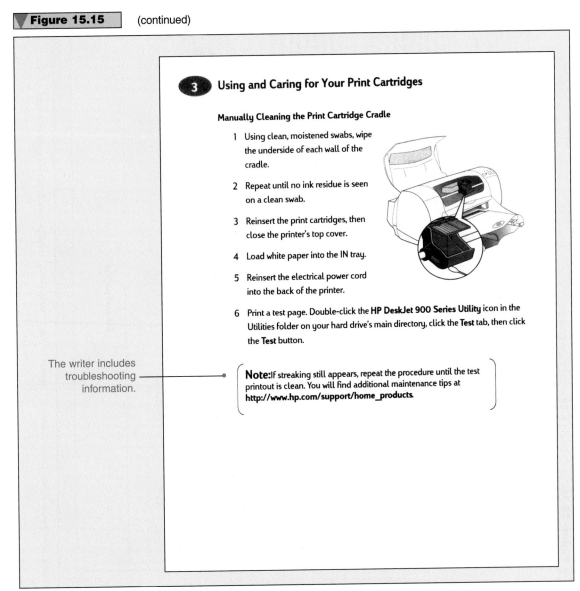

3 Using and Caring for Your Print Cartridges

Manually Cleaning the Print Cartridge Cradle

1 Using clean, moistened swabs, wipe the underside of each wall of the cradle.

2 Repeat until no ink residue is seen on a clean swab.

3 Reinsert the print cartridges, then close the printer's top cover.

4 Load white paper into the IN tray.

5 Reinsert the electrical power cord into the back of the printer.

6 Print a test page. Double-click the **HP DeskJet 900 Series Utility** icon in the Utilities folder on your hard drive's main directory, click the **Test** tab, then click the **Test** button.

The writer includes troubleshooting information.

Note: If streaking still appears, repeat the procedure until the test printout is clean. You will find additional maintenance tips at **http://www.hp.com/support/home_products**.

Source: *HP DeskJet Printer User's Guide* (n.p.: Hewlett-Packard, 1999) 35–36. Used by permission of Hewlett-Packard.

Figure 15.16   Using a Table for Instructions

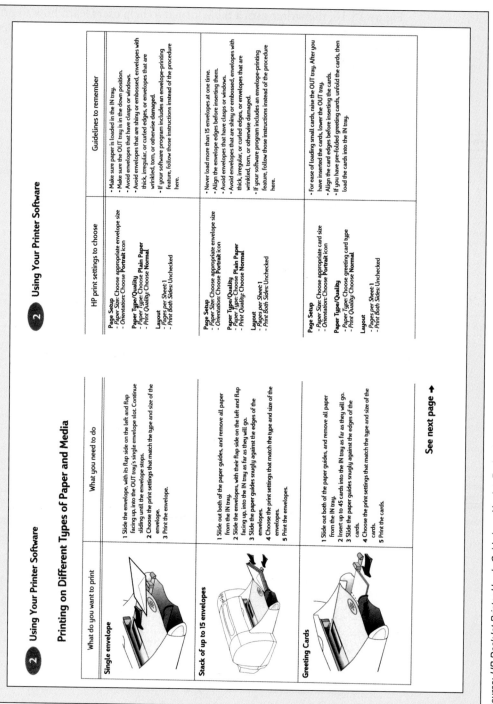

2 Using Your Printer Software

Printing on Different Types of Paper and Media

What do you want to print	What you need to do	HP print settings to choose	Guidelines to remember
Single envelope	1 Slide the envelope, with its flap side on the left and flap facing up, into the OUT tray's single envelope slot. Continue sliding until the envelope stops. 2 Choose the print settings that match the type and size of the envelope. 3 Print the envelope.	**Page Setup** - *Paper Size:* Choose appropriate envelope size - *Orientation:* Choose **Portrait** icon **Paper Type/Quality** - *Paper Type:* Choose **Plain Paper** - *Print Quality:* Choose **Normal** **Layout** - *Pages per Sheet:* 1 - *Print Both Sides:* Unchecked	- Make sure paper is loaded in the IN tray. - Make sure the OUT tray is in the down position. - Avoid envelopes that have clasps or windows. - Avoid envelopes that are shiny or embossed, envelopes with thick, irregular, or curled edges, or envelopes that are wrinkled, torn, or otherwise damaged. - If your software program includes an envelope-printing feature, follow those instructions instead of the procedure here.
Stack of up to 15 envelopes	1 Slide out both of the paper guides, and remove all paper from the IN tray. 2 Slide the envelopes, with their flap side on the left and flap facing up, into the IN tray as far as they will go. 3 Slide the paper guides snugly against the edges of the envelopes. 4 Choose the print settings that match the type and size of the envelopes. 5 Print the envelopes.	**Page Setup** - *Paper Size:* Choose appropriate envelope size - *Orientation:* Choose **Portrait** icon **Paper Type/Quality** - *Paper Type:* Choose **Plain Paper** - *Print Quality:* Choose **Normal** **Layout** - *Pages per Sheet:* 1 - *Print Both Sides:* Unchecked	- Never load more than 15 envelopes at one time. - Align the envelope edges before inserting them. - Avoid envelopes that have clasps or windows. - Avoid envelopes that are shiny or embossed, envelopes with thick, irregular, or curled edges, or envelopes that are wrinkled, torn, or otherwise damaged. - If your software program includes an envelope-printing feature, follow those instructions instead of the procedure here.
Greeting Cards	1 Slide out both of the paper guides, and remove all paper from the IN tray. 2 Insert up to 45 cards into the IN tray as far as they will go. 3 Slide the paper guides snugly against the edges of the cards. 4 Choose the print settings that match the type and size of the cards. 5 Print the cards.	**Page Setup** - *Paper Size:* Choose appropriate card size - *Orientation:* Choose **Portrait** icon **Paper Type/Quality** - *Paper Type:* Choose greeting card type - *Print Quality:* Choose **Normal** **Layout** - *Pages per Sheet:* 1 - *Print Both Sides:* Unchecked	- For ease of loading small cards, raise the OUT tray. After you have inserted the cards, lower the OUT tray. - Align the card edges before inserting the cards. - If you have pre-folded greeting cards, unfold the cards, then load the cards into the IN tray.

See next page →

2 Using Your Printer Software

Source: *HP DeskJet Printer User's Guide* (n.p.: Hewlett-Packard, 1999) 18–19. Used by permission of Hewlett-Packard.

Figure 15.17 is an excerpt from a manual for a television. This excerpt includes a clear diagram that shows the user how to connect the television and the cable box. Many users will only use the visual aid to connect the television and cable box; however, the writers have included text to support the visual aid.

Figure 15.17

Using Visual Aids to Instruct

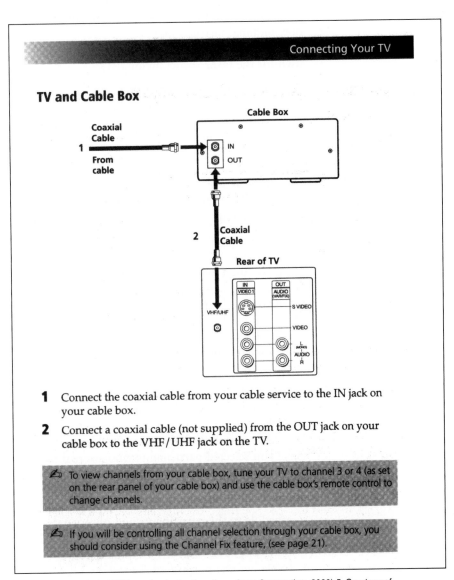

Connecting Your TV

TV and Cable Box

1 Connect the coaxial cable from your cable service to the IN jack on your cable box.

2 Connect a coaxial cable (not supplied) from the OUT jack on your cable box to the VHF/UHF jack on the TV.

✐ To view channels from your cable box, tune your TV to channel 3 or 4 (as set on the rear panel of your cable box) and use the cable box's remote control to change channels.

✐ If you will be controlling all channel selection through your cable box, you should consider using the Channel Fix feature, (see page 21).

Source: *Trinitron Color TV Operating Instructions* (n.p.: Sony Corporation, 2000) 5. Courtesy of Sony Electronics, Inc.

| WORKSHEET | **for Writing User-Oriented Instructions and Manuals** |

▶ **Principle 1: Find Out How Much the Users Know About the Task**
- Have the users performed the task, or similar tasks, before?
- Do the users have the same background or knowledge of the task? Will they have different purposes for using the instructions? Will their purposes for using the instructions change?
- How much detail do the users need to complete the task? Do they want only minimal instructions?
- What are the users' attitudes toward the task and toward the equipment used for the task? (Brockmann 101)

▶ **Principle 2: Use an Accessible Design**
- Is the design appropriate for the users' environment?
- Have you used conservative, easy-to-read typefaces?
- Have you used only two typeface families—serif for text and sans-serif for headings?
- If you have used color, have you used it consistently and appropriately?
- Have you used modified hanging or left-hanging headings?
- Does the layout allow the users to easily use the instructions?
- Are the headings task oriented?

▶ **Principle 3: Use User-Oriented Language**
- Have you used action verbs?
- Have you used imperative sentences?
- Have you used simple and specific language?
- Have you used language users will understand?
- Have you used technical terminology only when your users expect it?
- If your users are not native speakers of technical/business English, have you avoided connotative language and terms?

▶ **Principle 4: Test Your Instructions**
- Have you determined the needs of the users?
- Have you determined the purpose of the test? What do you want to learn from the test?
- Does the test ask the participants to focus on specific problems?
- Have you selected participants who are real users?
- Before the test, have you
  - Reserved the testing room or facility?
  - Prepared a schedule for the testing day? Have you distributed the schedule to the participants and observers?
  - Prepared to observe the participants as they use the instructions?
- For the test, have you
  - Explained the purpose of the test?

- Told the participants how they should note problems or make suggestions?
- After the test, are you ready to conduct an exit interview or debriefing with each participant?
- Have you properly interpreted the results, drawn conclusions, and made recommendations?

▶ **Principle 5: Use the Appropriate Conventional Elements of Instructions and Manuals**

- Does the introduction
  - State the purpose of the instructions?
  - State who should use the instructions and what they should know about the task?
  - List all materials and equipment that users need?
  - Use drawings, where appropriate, to illustrate the materials and equipment?
  - Explain typographical conventions and terminology used in the instructions or manual?
  - Include all the information that users need to use and understand the instructions?
  - Include safety information?
- Does the safety information
  - Appear before or next to the directions for the hazardous task, not after it?
  - Include a symbol or icon to indicate a warning, danger, or caution?
  - Distinguish between dangers, warnings, and cautions?
  - Have ample white space surrounding it?
- Does the theory of operation/description of equipment, if needed,
  - Use language the users can understand?
  - Include only the details that the users need and expect?
  - Appear near the beginning of the instructions or manual?
- For the step-by-step directions, have you
  - Categorized the task into major steps and then divided those steps into substeps?
  - Described only one action in each step or substep?
  - Numbered each step?
  - Used imperative sentences?
  - Used a list format?
  - Used visual aids when appropriate?
- Have you included troubleshooting information?
- Have you included reference aids, if needed?

> **► EXERCISES**

1. Photocopy some instructions that are hard to follow. (Your instructor may specify a length for these instructions.) Then complete these tasks:

   a. Identify the intended users of the instructions. Analyze the content, organization, conventional elements, language, and design to see whether they are appropriate for these users. Using this analysis, determine why the instructions are hard to follow.

   b. Write a memo to your instructor describing the intended users of the instructions and summarizing your analysis. Attach a copy of the instructions to your memo.

   c. Rewrite the instructions (or a portion of the instructions as assigned by your instructor) so the users can follow them easily. When you give the revised instructions to your instructor, attach a copy of the original version.

2. Write instructions for one of the following tasks or for a task related to your major. When you have written the instructions, attach a brief memo to your instructor stating the users and purpose of the instructions. Be sure to include visual aids where appropriate and to follow the principles presented in this chapter.

   - How to create a slide presentation using software such as Microsoft PowerPoint.

   - How to locate, download, and import a graphic from a Web site. Use a search engine to find the site.
   - How to set up voice mail and retrieve messages on a cellular phone.
   - How to transfer the files for a Web site to an Internet service provider.
   - How to use file transfer protocol (FTP) to transport files.
   - How to change the filters for the air conditioning system in your home or apartment.

3. Analyze the language and design of the instructions shown in Figure 15.18. Write a memo presenting your analysis to your instructor.

4. Rewrite the instructions in Figure 15.18, eliminating the problems in language and design that you identified in Exercise 3.

5. Examine the reference aids that accompany a manual. Then write a memo discussing the value of reference aids, using the aids in the manual that you examined to support your discussion. Be prepared to discuss your memo in class.

6. Find some outdated instructions. Update those instructions, correcting any problems with language, design, or organization. Turn in the updated instructions with a copy of the original version to your instructor.

| **Figure 15.18** | The Instructions for Exercises 3 and 4 |

Safe Food Handling for Optimum Nutrition

Shopping
Food safety in the home actually starts at the grocery store.

Plan your purchases so that perishables (meat, poultry, seafood, and dairy products) are selected last. These foods should be refrigerated within 2 hours of purchase (1 hour in hot weather) so that food poisoning bacteria do not multiply.

Bag meat and poultry products to prevent juices from dripping onto other foods and keep them separated from other foods, especially foods that will not be cooked, such as fruits and vegetables.

Buy packaged precooked foods only if packaging is sound, and buy products labeled "keep refrigerated" only if they are stored in a refrigerated case.

Storing Food
Proper storage of food prolongs its shelf-life and preserves nutrients as well as safety. Foods stored too long gradually spoil and also will lose nutritional value.

Make sure your refrigerator is kept clean and maintains a temperature no higher than 40°F.

Your frozen foods will maintain top flavor and nutritional value if the freezer is kept at 0°F or below.

Be sure to keep raw meat and poultry separate from other foods, especially those that will be eaten without further cooking. Poultry and ground meat will keep 1–2 days in the refrigerator; other meat items, 3–4 days.

Canned goods and other shelf-stable items should be stored in a cool, dry place. The temperature should stay above freezing and below 85°F.

Preparing Food
Cleanliness is the first critical step in safe food preparation. Wash hands thoroughly with soap and water before handling food. Wash hands, utensils, cutting boards, and work areas after handling raw meat or poultry products.

Frozen foods should never be thawed at room temperature. Instead, thaw them safely in the refrigerator. Thaw in the microwave only immediately before cooking.

It is essential that raw products of animal origin be cooked to an internal temperature of 160°F (180°F for poultry). Use a meat thermometer to check the temperature of meat and poultry. To check visually, juices should run clear and meat should not be pink.

Do not partially cook food. Have a constant heat source, and don't set the oven temperature under 325°F for cooking meat, poultry, seafood, or dairy-based foods. Microwave food in a covered dish and turn the dish frequently.

Serving Food
Food safety errors can be made during the serving and handling of cooked food.

When serving foods be sure to wash hands thoroughly with hot soapy water. Serve cooked products on clean plates and with clean utensils.

Foods should never sit at room temperature longer than 2 hours, 1 hour in hot weather. During serving, hot foods should be held above 140°F and cold foods should be kept cold.

Leftovers
When handling leftovers, cleanliness and temperature control are critical.

Wash hands before handling leftovers and use clean utensils and surfaces.

Refrigerate or freeze cooked leftovers in small, covered shallow containers within 2 hours after cooking. Leave airspace around containers in the refrigerator to ensure rapid, even cooling.

When reheating leftovers, cover and reheat thoroughly. Sauces, soups, and gravies should be heated to a rolling boil; all other products should be heated to 165°F.

Food spoilage bacteria will grow in the refrigerator, so discard any outdated foods. Most foods will remain safe in the refrigerator for about 4 days, but use highly perishable foods such as stuffing or gravy within 1–2 days.

When in doubt, throw it out!

Source: Dept. of Agriculture, *Nutrition: Eating for Good Health,* Publ. 685 (Washington: GPO, 1994) 184–186.

▶ **C A S E   S T U D Y**

Collaborating on a Manual

Background

Every week, you encounter tasks that require you to follow instructions. These instructions might explain how to use a new software application on a personal computer to complete an assignment or how to conduct a physics experiment to complete a lab report. The instructions might be for tasks as simple as cooking a microwave dinner or changing the oil in your new car. Whatever the task, you frequently need to follow written instructions.

In many organizations, teams collaborate to write instructions and manuals. These teams may write instructions and manuals for a service or product that the organization offers, or these teams may write instructions and manuals that employees will use within the organization.

Assignment

You and your team are to write a manual for a task for which written instructions are not available or adequate for the users to complete the task. To write the manual, you and your team will complete these steps:

1. Select a task. Make sure that all members of your team are familiar with the task. If the task requires equipment, make sure that your team has access to the equipment to prepare and to test the manual. Your instructor may want to approve your topic before you move to step 2.

2. Prepare a detailed outline of the manual. Submit this outline to your instructor to approve.

3. Decide on the reference aids that you will include with the manual.

4. Prepare prototype pages or sample pages showing the language, headings, and design that you plan to use in the manual.

   a. Find sample users. Ask these users to follow the step-by-step directions on the prototype pages. Watch these users as they follow the instructions, noting problems. After these users have completed the instructions, ask them whether the language, headings, and layout helped them to follow the instructions and whether you can improve any of these elements.

   b. Revise the language, headings, and layout as necessary.

5. Write the manual, dividing the writing tasks among team members.

6. Test the manual again. Be sure to follow the guidelines for usability testing in Principle 4, page 475.

7. Revise the manual based on the test.

8. Turn in the final version of the manual to your instructor.

16

Creating User-Oriented Web Sites

▶ **OUTLINE**

Wendy is a technical writer for an engineering company. She will soon begin creating the external Web site for her company's products and services. Wendy feels a little intimidated by the task. Although she uses the Web for researching topics, keeping up with her professional organizations, and querying user groups for answers to computer dilemmas, Wendy has never created a Web site. Her manager thinks a Web site is like a brochure or catalog, except that it's on the computer screen. Because Wendy produces the printed version of these documents, her manager assigned the Web project to Wendy.

Like Wendy, your manager may ask you to develop a Web site. Although you may have already created a personal Web site, you will want to learn a process for creating effective professional Web sites. Before presenting eight principles to help you create user-oriented Web sites, this chapter begins by giving you an overview of the process for creating Web sites. Most anyone can launch a Web site; however, many Web sites contain information that is hard to read, hard to access, and often incomplete or inaccurate. This chapter will help you to avoid these problems.

▶An Overview of the Process of Developing Web Sites

Wendy's manager has the right idea. Wendy can use all the knowledge and skill she has developed creating user-oriented print documents to develop a user-oriented Web site. The process is similiar; it's the medium that's different. Let's focus the process to accommodate the medium of the Web. These are the steps that Wendy or you might take to create an effective Web site (see Figure 16.1):

- **Identify the users and purpose of your site.** As with print documents, all the other decisions about a Web site depend on the users and the purpose. Principle 1 presents information on analyzing the users and determining your purpose.

- **Identify the content for the site.** You might know where to get written material for a brochure, but Web pages can also use sound bites, video clips, and other sources that print documents can't use. You may have to create some content, or you may use content written by others in your organization. Principle 2 presents information and tips to help you select appropriate content for your site.

- **Determine the overall organization of the site.** As with paper documents, you will want to spend some time planning the overall organization of your Web site. The organization of a Web site is different from that of

Some of the information in this chapter is adapted from work by Tonya McKinney, proposal writer and Web designer.

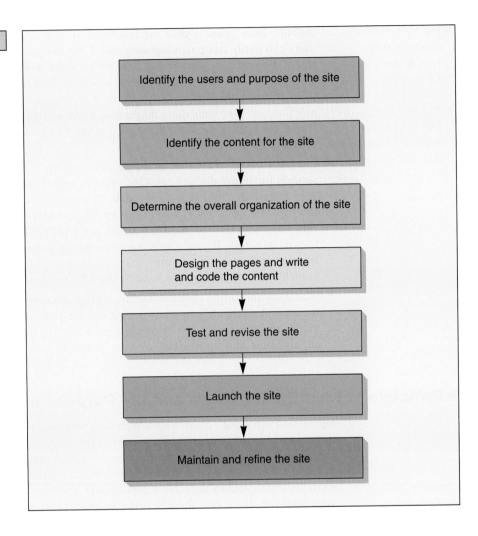

Figure 16.1

The Process of
Creating a Web Site

traditional paper documents. Principle 3 defines organizations that you
might use for Web sites.

- **Design the pages and write and code the content.** Once you have selected
the content and determined the overall organization, you're ready to
design the pages and write and code the content. Principle 4 gives you
some tips for designing effective pages. Principle 5 presents tips for creating a user-oriented style, and Principle 6 suggests ways to help users navigate the site.
- **Test and revise the site.** As with a paper document, you will create a
"rough draft" of your site. You will want to make sure that the site
accomplishes your purpose and that it is usable. You will want to conduct

▶ For more information on usability testing, see Chapter 15, "Writing User-Oriented Instructions and Manuals," page 475.

usability tests to see if your site functions to meet your users' needs, if users can easily navigate your site, and if the navigational instructions are clear. You will also want to know if all the links work. You will want to test the site with various computers, monitors, and browsers to see if the page design, links, and so on work on any computer or monitor or with any browser that your users might use. Then you will want to reuse the site to solve any problems. Principle 7 presents tips on testing and revising your site.

- **Launch the site.** This step of the process corresponds to the printing process for paper documents. Once you've tested and revised your site, you're ready to "publish," or launch, it. If you're posting your site on an Internet service provider's (ISP) server, the provider will have instructions that show you how to use file transfer protocol (FTP) to transport your files to its server. If you're posting your site on your organization's Internet server, you may simply have to remove password protection to launch the site; or you may have to use FTP to transfer your files.

- **Maintain and refine the site.** Unlike a print document, a Web site is a dynamic document. You want people to visit your site more than once, so you must keep it current. Principle 8 presents tips to help you keep your site dynamic and up-to-date.

▶Principle 1: Identify the Users and the Purpose of the Site

Before you can design a successful Web site, you need to define the purpose of the site and identify the users. Do you want the users to buy products and services directly from the Web? to learn how to use or install products on the Web? to use the Web to answer common questions instead of calling customer service representatives? to send for information? You may have several goals for your Web site. If so, rate them in order of importance to help you decide later what to include or emphasize.

Once you have your goals listed, decide how you will measure success. For instance, do you want to attract new customers through the Web and automate the order process through the Web, lessening calls to the order department? You can measure your success by charting the number of sales through the Web while tracking the number of calls the order department receives. If sales increase but the order department has the same number of or fewer calls, you will have succeeded.

Successful Web sites also reflect an intimate knowledge of the users. These Web sites build relationships with the users through the Web, and the users participate in site design. To identify your users, consider conducting some user research. For example, if your Web site is for customers of your organization, survey them. You might include questionnaires with invoices, or you might conduct a focus group with selected customers. In these questionnaires and focus groups, you can find out more than just the demographics of your users. You can discover

- What your users want to learn or expect from a Web site
- How your users want information presented on the Web
- How your users search for information on the Web
- How your users might use the information that you plan to present on your site

As you analyze your users, ask these questions:

- **What do your users know about the subject of your site?** Are you assuming your users have similar backgrounds? For example, if you are creating a site for NASA scientists, you can assume that your users have similar backgrounds and have some understanding of your subject. However, if you are creating a site for anyone interested in NASA, your users might be schoolchildren, teachers, scientists, "amateur" scientists, and so on. Your users may or may not know much about your subject.

- **Why will they visit your site?** What do they want to do—to gather information? to perform a task? to answer a question? to make a decision? to order a product or service? to link to other related sites? to download information to their computers?

- **Are the users internal or external?** Will only people in your organization use your site? Or will people outside your organization use your site? If your users are external, what do they know about your organization? Are their attitudes positive or negative about your organization?

- **What kind of computer equipment do your users have?** You may have been frustrated with a Web site that took a long time to download because you had a slow connection (or because the site had too many visual aids). If you know that your users have a fast Internet connection, you can use more and larger visual aids on the site. If users have a slow connection, however, you will want to use fewer and smaller visual aids so users don't have to wait too long for the visual aids to download. With a slow Internet connection or with a less powerful computer, users may become frustrated if they have to wait. For these users, you will also want to create pages that load quickly.

- **Is your audience global?** Will your organization and your users benefit from putting the content of the site in multiple languages? If your users are not proficient in English, consider publishing your site in your users' language as well as in English. You or your organization may have to hire someone to translate the content into another language; however, you can justify this expense if you have carefully identified your users and know that they will use the site if they can read it in their native language.

▶ Some Web sites will check your site to determine if it meets the needs of visually or hearing impaired users. For example, you might look at the Web site called Bobby (http://www.cast.org/bobby).

- **Are your users visually or hearing impaired?** Visually impaired computer users usually have software that can read text-only sites, but the software may not be able to interpret images. To accommodate this software and these users, provide a text-only version of your Web site. Make sure that the users can link to the text-only version from the homepage. You also want to avoid relying solely on color or sound to emphasize information, especially links. For example, if a user is color blind, he or she may not see the blue link to the homepage. You also want to use type large enough for the visually impaired to read the content on your site.

When you have launched your site, you can use the site itself to gather feedback from your users. You can then refine your site based on that feedback.

▶ Principle 2: Identify the Types of Content for the Site

After you have identified your users and purpose, you need to identify the types of content that the site should include to meet the needs and expectations of the users and to satisfy your purpose. Jan Spyridakis recommends selecting "content that will be interesting and relevant" to the users (361). She explains that "readers comprehend better and retain more information when they are interested in the topic. . . . The more relevant users find content to be," the better they comprehend the information (Spyridakis 361–362). Before you begin designing the site and creating its content, ask yourself: What are the parameters of the site? What do you want the site to do? What is its purpose?

You might think of creating a Web site like building a house. Before you begin drawing the plans, you need to know what you want in the house. For example, how many people will live in the house? Do you need one bedroom or two? Do you want the house to have two stories? If you want two stories, will all members of the household be able to use the stairs? Do you want the master bedroom next to the other bedrooms? Will you need a garage? How many cars should the garage accommodate? What is your budget? How much can you afford? You get the picture; you need to have an idea of your budget and your needs before you can begin to design a house—or, in our case, a Web site.

Before you design your Web site, consider the information and the elements that you want to include and that your users need. For example, you might consider these questions as you decide what to include on your site:

▶ For more information on adapting information for the Web, see Principle 5, page 517.

- **Will you use existing information from paper documents?** If so, you will need to adapt this information for the online format. If the information is copyrighted, make sure that you have permission to use the information (see "The Reader's Corner").

- **Will you have to create new content?** Will you have to gather information before you can create the content? What types of content will you have to

THE READER'S CORNER

Copyright, Intellectual Property, and the Web

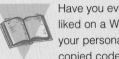 Have you ever found a graphic that you liked on a Web site and then used it on your personal Web site? Have you ever copied code from a Web site and used it for your organization's Web site? Have you ever used a company's logo or trademark from its Web site? If so, you could be guilty of copyright, patent, or trademark infringement. U.S. and international copyright laws protect every element of a Web site—the text, graphics, and HTML code (Le Vie 20). Even if the authors of a site haven't filed a formal copyright application, the law protects their work. Along with copyrights, the law protects an organization's patents, trademarks, and trade secrets. You or your organization can "bruise its reputation by infringing on someone else's copyright" or intellectual property and can face legal penalties (Le Vie 21).

You want to protect your Web site and your products and services. For example, aspirin originally started as a trademarked product, but the manufacturer failed to protect its trademark and *aspirin* became a name used by many manufacturers. To protect your Web site and your intellectual property—or that of your organization—follow these guidelines that will help you maintain the uniqueness of your product or service and keep your customers:

- Place a copyright notice at the bottom of every Web page
- Link from the word *copyright* to another Web page that defines what you "own" on the site (Le Vie 21)

You also want to protect yourself and your company from the legal penalties and bruised reputations that occur when you don't respect the copyrights and intellectual property of others. To protect yourself and your company when designing Web sites,

- Obtain permission for any information, graphic, or HTML code that you use from another site or printed document
- Place the copyright, trademark, and permission information in a conspicuous place (Le Vie 22)

---

create? As you consider the types of content that you will need to create, determine how much time you will need to create the content, how much research, if any, you will need to do, and whether you will create the content alone or with a team.

- **Will you include graphics on the site?** If so, will you use existing graphics? Are these graphics copyrighted? Or will you have to create new graphics?
- **Will you include audio on your site?** If so, will your budget allow for creating the audio? Do you have the tools to create professional audio?
- **Will you link to information on other sites or will you include all information on your site?**
- **What is the budget for creating the site?** How will that budget affect the graphics, audio, design, and so on?

You will want to consider all these questions—and possibly others—before you design your site. The tips below will help you as you identify the content that you will include on your Web site.

▶ **Tips for Identifying Content for Your Web Site**

- **Select content that is relevant and interesting to the users.** Many Web authors fail to filter out irrelevant or uninteresting content because they can easily put the contents of existing paper documents into hypertext markup language (HTML) and place it on the site. These documents may be appropriate for paper, yet they don't serve Web users well. The irrelevant or uninteresting content may be not only text, but also graphics or audio and video.

- **Adapt existing content created for other media.** If you're writing for an organization, you may find that you already have some content for your Web site. For example, you can convert some content— such as text from online presentations—almost directly to Web pages. Or you may have to edit some content for the online medium. Some Web designers simply scan in paper documents and load them onto their sites. These documents may work on paper, but not on the Web. Instead, you will want to decide what information from the document is appropriate for your purpose, your users, and the Web format. Then you can adapt that information for your site.

- **Remember that print may be the best medium for some content.** You may want to leave some documents in print. Print is still a viable medium for some types of information and documents. For example, as Johndan Johnson-Eilola explains, "even though online newspapers provide many useful things (searchability, rapid updating, and wide dissemination), print newspapers are still the medium of choice for most users. Print newspapers are compact, disposable, relatively high resolution, and much larger than most monitors" (18). Like newspapers, your content may best meet readers' needs in a print, rather than online, medium.

- **Make sure that all content helps the site achieve your purpose and meet your users' needs.** The text, graphics, and links should relate directly to the purpose of your site. For example, the former Web site of the IRS began with the title "The Digital Daily" in a newspaper-type layout. This layout and title didn't help the site achieve its purpose because many users might not have recognized the site as the IRS Web site (see Figure 16.2).

Figure 16.2

A Web Page Without
an Informative, Easy-
to-Read Title

Source: Internal Revenue Service. Online. Internet. 31 Dec. 2001.

▶Principle 3: Determine the Overall Organization of the Site

After selecting the content to include on the Web site, you'll need to decide on an overall organization for the site and for individual pages. Use everything you know about your users to structure your site to meet their goals, accommodate their methods for searching, and appeal to their learning styles.

If you have several levels of users, organizing the site becomes complicated. An excellent method to ensure user-oriented design is to role-play each level of user. Approach the site just like a user, and ask questions that a user would ask. For example, on a product and services site, you might initially list products and services alphabetically, but you may realize that users would search in other ways. You might then devise several ways for users to search: keyword search engine, product name and number, product category (such as entertainment, security, sound, and video), and reader lifestyle (such as student, family with children, and home office).

As you consider how your users might approach and use your site, you can also consider how you want to organize your site. In a well-organized site, users can easily find the information that they need. Once you have identified the types of content, you will want to consider how you will balance the amount of information with the ease of navigation. If a site is difficult to navigate, your users may not be able to easily find the information they need. Just as a grocery store should be well organized so that customers can find the items they need, a Web site should be well organized to achieve its purpose and to meet the needs and expectations of the users.

Most Web sites have a basic organization similiar to the one shown in Figure 16.3. As on most Web sites, users enter through a **homepage** (the main page that serves as an entry point) that links to other pages on the site. **Page** refers to a file; the page may fit on one screen or may extend to multiple screens. From the homepage, the users can directly access the pages titled "About the Chamber of Commerce," "Our Mission," "Our Members," "Our Community," and "Links to Small Town, USA, Sites." However, from the homepage the users can't directly access the pages linked to "Our Members."

> **Figure 16.3**   The Organization of a Basic Web Site

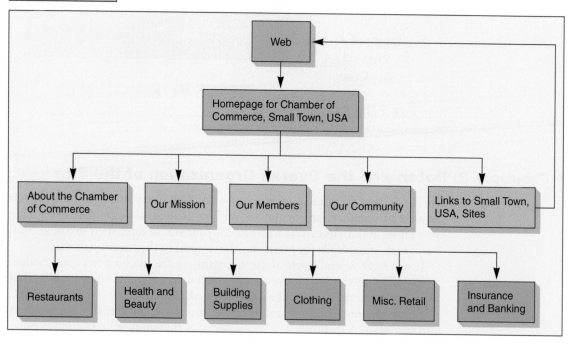

If these links appeared on the homepage, it could have too much information.

If your Web site is relatively simple, you might want to consider an organization with only two levels (see Figure 16.4). In this organization, all the second-level page links appear on the homepage. This two-level organization is easy to implement and easy for users to navigate. However, if your site is complex, this organization can clutter the home page and give users "information overload." For these more complex sites, consider using a multiple-level organization such as the one shown in Figure 16.5. Here, only three links appear on the homepage, yet the site has more than a homepage and three additional pages. This site has four levels. If the Web author had put the links for all the pages on the homepage, the user would have received too much information on one page. However, the users may overlook the pages on the third and fourth levels of the site.

When you have an idea of how you want to organize the site,

▶ To learn more about organizational charts, see Chapter 10, "Creating Effective Visual Aids for Your Readers," page 288.

- **Create an organizational chart** like those in Figures 16.3, 16.4, or 16.5.

- **Use the chart as a guide.** As you write, you may determine that you need more or fewer levels or that a page should appear at a higher or lower level. Make such adjustments as needed.

▶Principle 4: Design User-Oriented Pages

Once you've identified the types of content and created your organizational chart for your Web site, you're ready to consider the design of the individual pages. To a great extent, the kinds of content on your site will drive the design. You want to design a house that meets the needs of the future homeowners.

| **Figure 16.4** | The Organization of a Web Site with Two Levels |

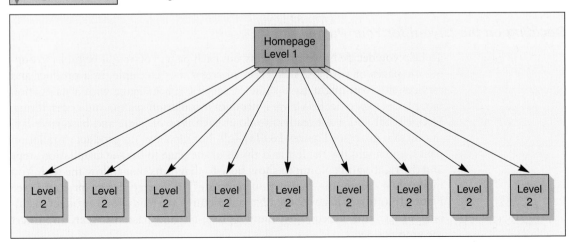

Figure 16.5   The Organization of a Web Site with Multiple Levels

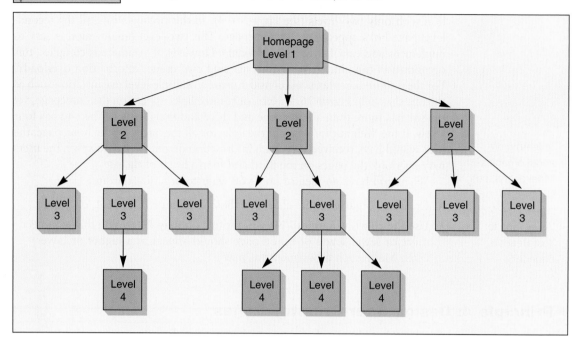

Similarly, if you are building a Web site with a lot of text, you want to select a design that will allow you to include the text without making the pages hard to read. As you design the individual pages, you will want to

- Decide on the layout for the pages
- Select the tool you will use to create the pages

Deciding on the Layout for Your Pages

To help you decide how you will lay out each page, you might begin by grouping the pages of your site into types of pages. For example, in a product and services site, you might have these categories: a homepage with a navigation bar, product specification pages, product installation pages, and order forms. Decide what you want readers to do at each type of page, and base your layout on that goal (see Figures 16.6[a]–[c]). For instance, on product installation pages, you might use the left two-thirds of the page to list the installation steps and the right-hand column to show how-to diagrams that follow the text. You might then create an "instruction template" in a page design program (see Figure 16.6[b]). Whenever the text and pictures are ready for a product installation page, you merely open the template, cut and paste the text, and insert the graphics.

If these links appeared on the homepage, it could have too much information.

If your Web site is relatively simple, you might want to consider an organization with only two levels (see Figure 16.4). In this organization, all the second-level page links appear on the homepage. This two-level organization is easy to implement and easy for users to navigate. However, if your site is complex, this organization can clutter the home page and give users "information overload." For these more complex sites, consider using a multiple-level organization such as the one shown in Figure 16.5. Here, only three links appear on the homepage, yet the site has more than a homepage and three additional pages. This site has four levels. If the Web author had put the links for all the pages on the homepage, the user would have received too much information on one page. However, the users may overlook the pages on the third and fourth levels of the site.

When you have an idea of how you want to organize the site,

- **Create an organizational chart** like those in Figures 16.3, 16.4, or 16.5.

- **Use the chart as a guide.** As you write, you may determine that you need more or fewer levels or that a page should appear at a higher or lower level. Make such adjustments as needed.

▶ To learn more about organizational charts, see Chapter 10, "Creating Effective Visual Aids for Your Readers," page 288.

▶Principle 4: Design User-Oriented Pages

Once you've identified the types of content and created your organizational chart for your Web site, you're ready to consider the design of the individual pages. To a great extent, the kinds of content on your site will drive the design. You want to design a house that meets the needs of the future homeowners.

Figure 16.4   The Organization of a Web Site with Two Levels

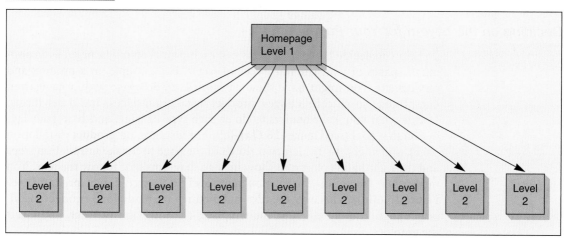

Figure 16.5   The Organization of a Web Site with Multiple Levels

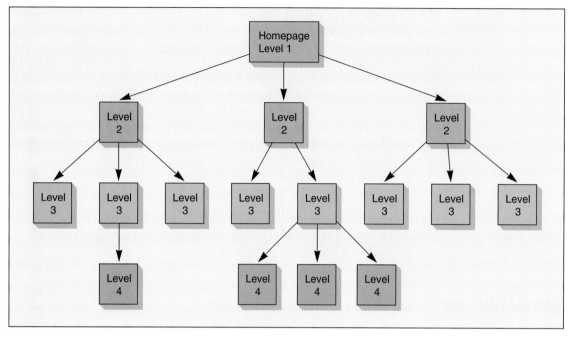

Similarly, if you are building a Web site with a lot of text, you want to select a design that will allow you to include the text without making the pages hard to read. As you design the individual pages, you will want to

- Decide on the layout for the pages
- Select the tool you will use to create the pages

Deciding on the Layout for Your Pages

To help you decide how you will lay out each page, you might begin by grouping the pages of your site into types of pages. For example, in a product and services site, you might have these categories: a homepage with a navigation bar, product specification pages, product installation pages, and order forms. Decide what you want readers to do at each type of page, and base your layout on that goal (see Figures 16.6[a]–[c]). For instance, on product installation pages, you might use the left two-thirds of the page to list the installation steps and the right-hand column to show how-to diagrams that follow the text. You might then create an "instruction template" in a page design program (see Figure 16.6[b]). Whenever the text and pictures are ready for a product installation page, you merely open the template, cut and paste the text, and insert the graphics.

Figure 16.6(a)

A Sample Template for a Homepage

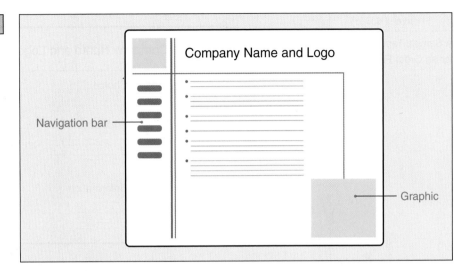

Figure 16.6(b)

A Sample Template for an Instructions Page

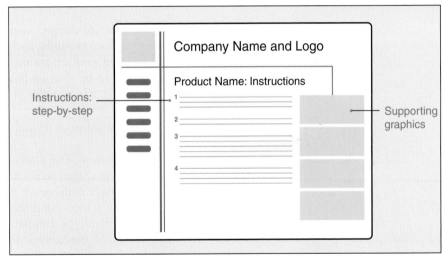

You can also use thumbnail sketches to get an idea of how your pages will look (see Chapter 9, page 224). These sketches can help you to visualize how the text and visual aids will look on the page. If you're working with a team, these sketches can also ensure that everyone on the team understands what you intend.

Along with the thumbnail sketches, you might also consider creating a construction plan for each page or at least each set of pages. This plan should list the type of page, the source of content, the kinds of graphics, any required programming, the edit, and special elements such as sound, video, or animation. In the construction plan include a maintenance schedule: when and what needs to be updated or changed and who will be responsible.

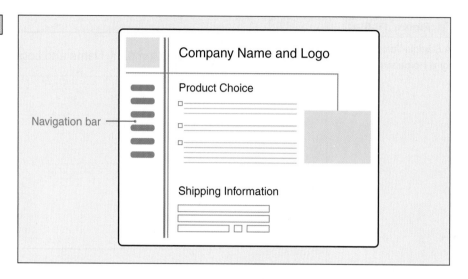

As you design your pages, use a simple design. At your desktop, you have access to colors, sounds, animation, backgrounds, and so on. However, these effects often detract from the message you are trying to send to your users. These effects may also cause the site to be slow to download. The following tips will help you to create a simple yet effective design for your Web pages:

▶ **Tips for Designing User-Oriented Web Pages**

- **Use a consistent design for the pages.** The pages should look like they belong to the same Web site, so you will want to select an appropriate color scheme and use it consistently throughout the site. Use the same color for the same elements and the same background color for every page. For example, if you choose blue for the home icon, use blue every time you show the home icon.

- **Include an informative title at the top of every page** (Farkas and Farkas 356; Spyridakis 361). According to Spyridakis's research, an informative, specific title "helps orient users" (361). When users follow a link to a page, they are looking for information that will confirm that they have arrived at the content they expected. Without a title, they will be confused. For example, Spyridakis points to the former U.S. Internal Revenue Service (IRS) Web site (see Figure 16.2). As Figure 16.2 shows, the title of the page appeared to be "The Digital Daily." Even though the page included several titles, it didn't clearly specify that the user had arrived at the IRS homepage. Users expect to see a

(continued on next page)

straightforward, serious site, not a site that looks like a tabloid or comic book page with words such as "faster than a speeding 1040EZ."

- **Include the site name or logo and an informative header or footer on every page.** The homepage should include the name of the site, its general purpose, and the site's publisher (Farkas and Farkas 356). This information should be the most prominent information on the page, not overshadowed by advertisements or other titles—as in Figure 16.2. If the purpose and publisher are clear, you may omit this information. On all other pages, include the title of the site or a logo. The title or logo should appear in the same place on every page to maintain site identity (Farkas and Farkas 357).

- **Use locating devices to help users access and scan your pages.** You can help users to search, comprehend, and recall the information on your pages by using locating devices such as
  - Headings and subheadings
  - Introductions
  - Overviews and topic sentences at the beginnings of paragraphs and sections
  - Site maps and tables of contents
  - Indexes
  - Hyperlinks within an individual page

  You can find examples of some of these locating devices in Chapters 6 and 11.

- **Use thumbnail graphics when possible and place all images into an image folder to speed download time** (Wilkinson 40). You can tag a thumbnail sketch so users can click on it to link to the larger version of the graphic. You can find examples of thumbnail graphics on sites that give you maps and on weather sites. For example, on the homepage of The Weather Channel (http://www.weather.com), you usually see a thumbnail graphic of a U.S. weather map. You can click to link to a larger version of the map. (For more information on creating faster graphics, see Theresa Wilkinson's article "How to Increase Performance on a Web Site" in *Intercom,* January 2000.)

Selecting the Tool for Creating the Pages

When you have decided on the layout for each type of page, you need to select the tool that you will use to code the content—in other words, how you will put the information into a digital format that you can transmit on the Web. Currently, many Web authors use hypertext markup language (HTML) for

TAKING IT INTO THE WORKPLACE

Making Your Web Site Credible

"Make pages trustworthy. Users are more likely to continue reading and return to a page if they feel the information is credible."

—Jan Spyridakis, "Guidelines for Comprehensible Web Pages" (373)

To encourage people to stop and read your site and to visit it again, you have to establish credibility. You want to gain and maintain the trust of your visitors. According to Jan Spyridakis, "the credibility of a Web page is easily affected by the presence or absence of certain content. For some, the credibility of a company or institution may begin with its Web sites. People may choose a graduate school or a future employer, or purchase a specific brand of product in part because of how credible the company or agency appears to be in its Web site" (373). Spyridakis recommends the following guidelines for making your Web site trustworthy and credible:

- **Include your name and/or the name of the organization that is publishing the site and contact information.** If you're writing for an organization, include the name and purpose of the organization and contact information for the organization. If you are publishing the site, include your credentials—some kind of affiliation, for example, that the user can check.
- **Include the date that you launched the site or the date that you last updated the site.** Users want to know if the information is current. If you launch a site and don't update it frequently, the site will be less credible.
- **Make sure the information on your site is accurate and free of typos, spelling errors, and**

other mistakes. These errors may cause users to assume that the site is not credible. These errors can also "draw the user's attention away from the important information on the page and raise doubts about the author's credibility" (Spyridakis 373).

- **Use a professional tone that is appropriate for your purpose and users.** Avoid hyped-up, unsubstantiated language such as "scientific breakthrough" or "best weather site on the Web." You can find out more about tone and Web site credibility at the U.S. Federal Trade Commission's site (http://www.ftc.gov) and at the Quackwatch Web site (http://www.quackwatch.com).
- **Cite sources.** If you use information from other sources, tell the users where you found the information.
- **Link only to carefully selected Web sites.** These sites should be current and functioning. The sites should have relevant information.

Assignment

For this assignment,

- Locate two Web sites on the same topic: one should be credible and one should be less credible. For example, you might find two Web sites on preventing heart disease.
- Write a memo to your instructor comparing and contrasting the two sites. Be sure to include specific examples from the sites. If you need help with the comparison/contrast pattern of organization, see Chapter 6, "Organizing Information for Your Readers," page 147.

content (text). However, Web authors may also use other standards, such as extensible markup language (XML). To add HTML tags to your text, you have several options:

- **Create text in a word-processing program such as Microsoft Word and save the file as an HTML document.** In Microsoft Word, you can save your files as HTML documents. With this option, you can create a Web page even if you know little, if any, HTML. However, many Web authors don't recommend this option because word-processing programs add unnecessary tags and incorrect tags.

- **Use a Web-authoring program such as Microsoft's FrontPage.** These programs are easy to use and often have predesigned templates. They offer the novice Web author the tools to create Web pages; novice authors, therefore, don't have to be familiar with HTML. These programs offer a better option than saving your word-processing files as HTML documents. However, these programs also introduce unnecessary tags and incorrect tags.

- **Use a text-editing program such as Notepad to code text by hand.** If you learn basic HTML tags, you can code your pages by hand using a text-editing program. With this option, you can avoid the unnecessary tags created by the previous two options and your pages will download much faster (Wilkinson 38). This option also will not limit you with predefined templates that may not allow you to design a page the way you intended.

▶Principle 5: Create User-Oriented Content

When you have a design for your pages, you're ready to create and add the content. You have several options to consider as you create the content:

- **Adapt existing content created for other media.** For example, you might adapt information from a paper document. As we discussed in Principle 2, content designed for other media, especially paper, may not be appropriate for the Web. You will need to analyze the content created for another medium and decide whether you can use it. If you can use it, you will still need to adapt it for the online format. For example, a fifteen-page report may be appropriate for paper media; however, for the Web, you might want to summarize the report and provide a link to a pdf file containing the full text of the report. If users wants to read the report, they can download the file and print the report. If you are creating a Web site as part of your organization's document set, you will want to determine how the Web site fits in with these documents. You may be able to adapt some of the existing documents or to use the content from some of these documents. You will need to select only the relevant, necessary content.

- **Write new content.** If you don't have content to adapt from other media or if the content from other media is not appropriate, you will need to write new content.
- **Select or create appropriate graphics.** As you select or create the graphics that you will include, consider how easily and quickly the users can download the graphics. As we have discussed, if the graphics take too long to download, the users may abandon your site. If you need to include graphics that will take a long time to download, consider using thumbnail graphics.

The principles that you learned in Chapters 7 and 8 apply not only to print documents, but also to Web documents. Follow the principles for writing reader-oriented sentences and paragraphs and using reader-oriented language when writing the text for your Web pages. You will especially want to spend some time carefully selecting words for the headings, links, and pages. When users can easily read and understand the text, they can search the text more effectively and can better comprehend the information. The tips below highlight some of the text features that will especially interest Web authors.

▶ Tips for Making Web Text Easy to Read and Understand

- **Write in small "chunks" and short pages** (Bradbury 24; Spyridakis 363). Web users scan for information rather than stopping and reading an entire paragraph. Small chunks help users to scan. You want to use, in general, short pages instead of long pages, and to put less information on each page. Although you may have more pages, users can "more easily find the information they need and read and retain it" (Spyridakis 363).
- **Use bulleted items and lists** (Bradbury 24 and Nielsen). Bulleted items and lists visually break up the text, make the page easier to read, and guide your users to the information they need.
- **Use simple words and short, concise sentences.** Use words that users can easily read and understand (see Chapter 8, page 205). You want to eliminate any unnecessary detail and use only a few examples of a concept, not provide "exhaustive coverage" (Spyridakis 363).
- **Use active-voice verbs whenever possible and appropriate.** The active voice helps users to move more quickly through Web text. For more information on the active voice, see Chapter 7, page 178.
- **Choose quality over quantity** (Bradbury 24). As we discussed in Principle 1, use only relevant content. Include only the words your users need. Don't be tempted to fill the page just because you can. Remember that white space can enhance a page.

(continued on next page)

> • **Include an introduction or introductory sentence that identifies the purpose of the site and specifies the intended users** (Spyridakis 376). On the homepage, introduce the purpose of the site. If you're writing for an organization, introduce the organization and state what it does.

▶Principle 6: Help Users to Navigate the Site

With a book or magazine, you can see the entire document at once—you can flip from the beginning to the end. However, with a Web document, you can't see the "end" or even the "middle." You can't see the entire site at one time as you can a book or a magazine. Unlike a print document, a Web site does not have a linear organization with pages numbered consecutively from one to whatever. However, a site does have an organization, and you have to tell and show your users how to navigate from the beginning (the homepage) to the middle and to the end. The users also need to know how to navigate between pages and how to get back to the beginning, or the homepage.

As we discussed in Principle 4, your Web site should have a consistent page design. This consistent design helps users to navigate your site. Along with a consistent design, follow these tips to help users navigate your site:

> ▶ **Tips for Helping Users to Navigate Your Web Site**
>
> • **Include a site map.** A site map shows the "global structure" of your site. A site map lists the pages in the site classified into categories. Your site map will be more effective if you include a "You are here" or "Last page visited" marker (Farkas and Farkas 352). Figure 16.7 illustrates a partial site map.
> • **Include an index.** An index is an alphabetical listing of the pages and topics on your Web site. Figure 16.8 illustrates an index. Notice how the users can select a letter near the top of the page rather than have to scroll down the page.
> • **Provide a link to the homepage on every page.** Put the link in the same place on every page. The pages in Figures 16.7 and 16.8 include a clear link to the homepage at the top. You can also use an organization's logo as the link, or you can simply use a link such as "Home."
> • **Include text-only versions of any graphical links.** Some users may use a text-only version of your site because they have slow connections to the Internet and have set their browsers to view text only. Or, more
>
> (continued on next page)

importantly, some of your users may be visually impaired. If you rely solely on a graphic or on color to indicate a link, these users may not find the link.

- **Include a navigation bar on every page of your site.** You will want to put this bar in the same place on each page. For example, the Texas A&M University site has a horizontal navigation bar (see Figure 16.9). This bar has the same design and location on each page, except on the homepage. On the homepage, the navigation bar has a vertical orientation.

▶Principle 7: Test and Revise the Site

Testing a Web site can be expensive and time-consuming, yet invaluable. In print documents, you use many practices based on years of testing and experience. Web sites are a new medium without the research background that print media have, so the value of usability testing is incalculable. If possible, test sections as you complete them. If you test your site in sections, you may save time revising if you catch a problem early enough.

Figure 16.7

A Partial Site Map

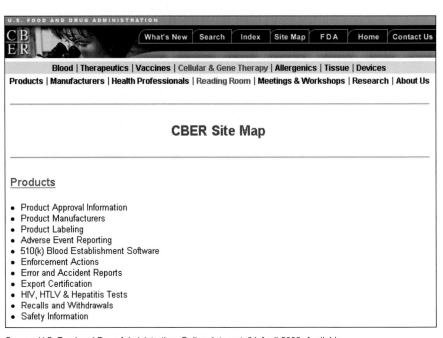

Source: U.S. Food and Drug Administration. Online. Internet. 24 April 2002. Available: http://www.fda.gov/cber/sitemap.htm.

Figure 16.8

A Partial Web Page Index

Source: U.S. Food and Drug Administration. Online. Internet. 31 Dec. 2001. Available: http://www.fda.gov/cber/cberac.htm.

Figure 16.9

A Web Page with a Navigation Bar

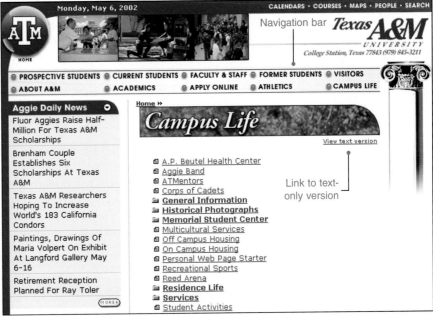

Source: Texas A&M University. Online. Internet. 6 Feb. 2002. Available: http://www.tamu.edu/00/life/index.html. Courtesy of Texas A&M University.

▶ For more information on usability testing, see Chapter 15, "Writing User-Oriented Instructions and Manuals," page 475.

You can conduct a user test of the site. Your organization may already have a department, such as human factors, that can conduct these tests. One of the fastest, most productive tests is a live feedback test. For a live feedback test, follow these steps:

- Set up a computer, video camera, microphone, and, if possible, software to record screen activity
- Select users from the intended audience
- Give the users a list of tasks to complete at your Web site
- Record their screen movements, comments, and actions as they complete the tasks

These tests may indicate that you must revise your site extensively, but revising is better than posting a flawed or ineffective site to the Web.

▶ Principle 8: Edit, Proofread, and Maintain the Site

Unlike a print document, a Web site is a dynamic document that doesn't have the same "sent to the printer" sense of completion. This dynamic nature affects how you edit, proofread, and maintain your site. To effectively edit and proofread your site, you will need to do more than simply read the text and look at the visual aids. Instead, you will need to "put yourself in the user's shoes": go through the site as if you were a user. You might use the site to complete the tasks that a user would complete or to answer a question that a user would ask. The usability testing that you conducted for Principle 7 will help you make sure that the site provides what the users need and that the site is usable. However, you will still want to use the site yourself to ensure that the site is free of problems with text, visual aids, and navigation. As you edit and proofread your site, ask yourself these questions:

- Are you providing the user experience that you set out to provide?
- Is the site achieving its purpose?

Figure 16.10 presents an editing checklist that you can use to edit and proofread your site.

Once you've launched your site, you will need to spend time keeping the site up-to-date. An unmaintained site reflects poorly on you and your organization. It also defeats the purpose and goals of the site. If you don't have the time or budget to maintain the site, don't launch it. To maintain the site, follow these tips:

▶ **Tips for Maintaining Your Web Site**

- **Be sure to regularly check all links to make sure that they still work.** If you have linked to related sites, make sure these links still work; you will also want to make sure that the sites are still relevant and current.

(continued on page 524)

Organization and Navigation

During your first pass, go through the entire site. Ignore the small details and make sure that you have logically organized the site and that the users can navigate easily through the site. Ask these questions:

- Is the organization user oriented?
- Are the navigational methods obvious to the users?
- Will users readily understand where your buttons, icons, or text links take them?
- Are users ever trapped in a page, unable to go to the next logical page or back to the previous pages?
- Does each page have a link to the homepage?
- Are there orientation cues so that users know where they are at all times?
- Do the screens have informative titles and subtitles?
- Do all the links work correctly?

Layout and Design

During your second pass, look at the site's appearance. Ask these questions:

- Is the page layout consistent throughout the site?
- Does any page have too many elements?
- Do the graphics appear at the right quality? Do they download quickly?
- Are the graphics clear?
- Do the graphics repeat and support the information in the text?
- Are page elements—heading sizes, font sizes, and font colors—consistent?

Text Content

During this pass, edit the text for all the problems you look for in print media, plus a few other criteria for online text. Consider these questions:

- Is the text concise?
- Are sentences and paragraphs as short as possible?
- Have you used the active voice?
- Have you used unnecessary nominalizations?

Interactivity and Multimedia

If your site contains special programming for interactivity or multimedia, check that these elements work well within your site. Consider these questions:

- Are your downloadable files actually downloading?
- Are your sound files and video files loading and intelligible?
- Does your multimedia support information already on the screen?

- **Respond to reader mail.** This response is a key to any site that offers the users a feedback or comment feature. *You must respond to user inquiries in a timely manner.* You will anger, frustrate, and alienate users if you don't follow up on their communications. Offer users the option to send you e-mail *only* if you can respond to them in a timely manner.

- **Incorporate user feedback into the site.** If your site does not offer and act on user feedback, you've created one-way communication, much like a printed document. You've eliminated one of the key reasons for having a Web site if you don't allow and encourage two-way interaction.

- **Update the site regularly.** Occasionally you need to review the entire site.

▶Sample Web Pages

Figures 16.11 and 16.12 illustrate effective Web page design. Figure 16.11 is a page from the U.S. Food and Drug Administration's Web site, and Figure 16.12 is a page from the Dallas/Fort Worth International Airport's Web site. These pages illustrate many of the principles and tips discussed in this chapter.

| **Figure 16.11** | The U.S. Food and Drug Administration's Page for the Center for Biologics Evaluation and Research |

The page includes a header that identifies the U.S. Food and Drug Administration and provides a link to the index, site map, and homepage.

The icons and their text labels (blood, therapeutics, etc.) provide links to the areas in which the center conducts research. The text labels help users who use a text-only version of the site, perhaps because they have disabilities.

The page is the opening page for a group of pages for the Center for Biologics Evaluation and Research.

The page has an informative title.

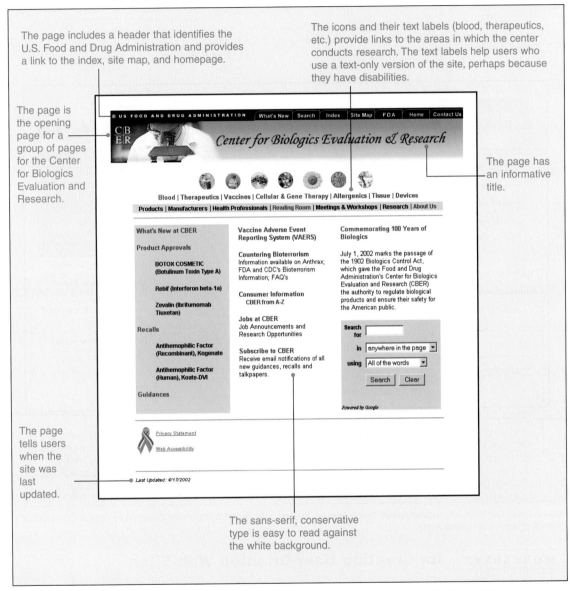

The page tells users when the site was last updated.

The sans-serif, conservative type is easy to read against the white background.

Source: U.S. Food and Drug Administration, Center for Biologics Evaluation and Research. Online. Internet. 15 June 2002. Available: http://www.fda.gov/cber/index.html.

| Figure 16.12 | A Page from the Dallas/Fort Worth International Airport Web Site |

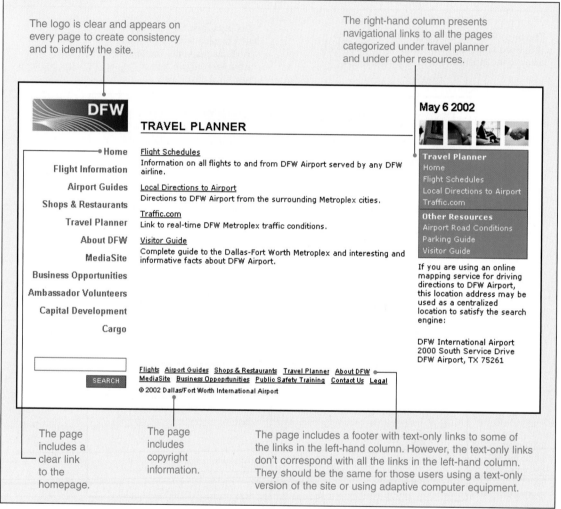

The logo is clear and appears on every page to create consistency and to identify the site.

The right-hand column presents navigational links to all the pages categorized under travel planner and under other resources.

The page includes a clear link to the homepage.

The page includes copyright information.

The page includes a footer with text-only links to some of the links in the left-hand column. However, the text-only links don't correspond with all the links in the left-hand column. They should be the same for those users using a text-only version of the site or using adaptive computer equipment.

Source: Dallas/Fort Worth International Airport. Online. Internet. 15 June 2002. Available: http://www.dfwairport.com/traveler. Courtesy of Dallas/Fort Worth International Airport.

WORKSHEET for Creating User-Oriented Web Sites

▶ **Principle 1: Identify the Users and the Purpose of the Site**
- What is the purpose of your site?
- What do your users know about the subject of your site?
- Why will they visit your site? What do they want to do—to gather information? to perform a task? to answer a question? to make a decision? to order a product or service? to link to other related sites? to download information?

- Are the users internal or external?
- What kind of computer equipment do your users have? How will this equipment affect how you design the site?
- Is your audience global? If so, how will this affect your site?
- Are your users visually or hearing impaired?

▶ **Principle 2: Identify the Types of Content for the Site**
- Is the content relevant and interesting to the users?
- If you're using existing content from print documents, have you appropriately adapted it for the Web?
- Would any of the content be more appropriate for a print medium?
- Does the content help the site to achieve your purpose and meet the users' needs?

▶ **Principle 3: Determine the Overall Organization of the Site**
- Did you create an organizational chart to help you visualize the organization of the site?
- Did you group like pages together?
- Is the organization linear? If so, revise to create a hierarchical organization.

▶ **Principle 4: Design User-Oriented Pages**
- Do the pages have a consistent design? Do the pages look like they belong to the same Web site?
- Is the color scheme appropriate? Have you used the same color for the same elements?
- Have you used the same background color on every page? Does the background color make the text easy to read?
- Does every page have an informative title at the top? Can the users easily locate the title?
- Does the site name or the organization's logo appear in the same place on every page?
- Have you included an informative header and/or footer on every page?
- Have you used locating devices to help users access and scan the pages?
- Have you used thumbnail graphics when possible to speed download time?

▶ **Principle 5: Create User-Oriented Content**
- Have you used small "chunks" and short pages?
- Have you used bulleted items and lists when appropriate to make the page easier to read?
- Have you used simple words and short, concise sentences?
- Have you used the active voice whenever possible and appropriate?
- Have you included only the information that your users need? Have you eliminated unnecessary information?
- Have you included an introduction or an introductory sentence that identifies the purpose of the site and specifies the intended users?

▶ **Principle 6: Help Users to Navigate the Site**
- Have you included a site map?
- Have you included an index?
- Have you provided a link to the homepage on every page?
- Are the links easy to find?
- Have you provided text-only versions of the links for users with disabilities or for users using a text-only version of the site?
- Does each page have a navigation bar?

▶ **Principle 7: Test and Revise the Site**
- Have you selected users from the intended audience to test your site?
- Have you revised your site as necessary based on the usability tests?

▶ **Principle 8: Edit, Proofread, and Maintain the Site**
- Are you providing the user experience that you set out to provide?
- Does the site achieve its purpose?
- Do you have a plan for maintaining and updating the site?

> **EXERCISES**

1. Find three Web sites that have tutorials for coding information for Web pages. When you have located the Web sites, evaluate the credibility of the sites. In your evaluation, consider

   - The author's credentials
   - The reliability of the information (Has the author cited sources? Has the site been updated recently?)
   - The writing style (Is the site free of grammatical errors? Does the writer make unsupported generalizations or use "hyped-up" language?)
   - The links to other sites

   You might also consider the information on the reliability of Internet sources discussed in Chapter 5, "Researching Information Using Primary and Secondary Sources." Write a memo to your instructor summarizing your evaluation.

2. Locate the Web site for a national nonprofit organization, such as the Red Cross or the American Heart Association. Print a copy of the organization's homepage. Then analyze the following aspects of the site:

   - Consistency of page design
   - Use of color (you might want to review the information on color in Chapter 9, "Designing Documents for Your Readers," page 237)
   - Ease of navigation
   - Style of writing
   - Selection of content

   Write an informal report to your instructor citing problems with the site and recommending solutions. You may want to review the problem/solution pattern of organization

   discussed in Chapter 6, "Organizing Information for Your Readers."

3. Working with a team, evaluate your college's or university's Web site and compare it to the sites of two other colleges or universities of similar size and mission. (Your instructor may ask you to work individually rather than with a team.) For example, if you attend a midsized, private university, select Web sites from other midsized, private universities. As part of your evaluation of your school's site, consider

   - The varied users (Who uses the site—just students? faculty? staff? potential students?)
   - Its success in meeting the needs of all users
   - The writing style
   - The visual aids
   - The page design
   - The navigation

   Write an informative informal report to your college or university Webmaster summarizing your evaluation and comparisons.

4. Expand your evaluation of your college's or university's Web site. Determine

   - If the site has appropriately protected its copyright and other intellectual property, such as its logo or seal
   - If the site may have infringed on the copyrighted information or trademarks of others

   Based on your evaluation, write a memo to the Webmaster at your school explaining what you were looking for and whether or not the site adequately protects the school's intellectual property and properly uses copyrighted information and intellectual property.

▶ **CASE STUDY**

Helping a Nonprofit Organization in Your Community

Background

Nonprofit organizations are groups that provide a service without making a profit. Nonprofit organizations include groups such as the Little League association in your community and Habitat for Humanity. They also could be groups that rescue animals or feed the homeless. Some nonprofit organizations don't have the budget or expertise to create a Web site. Even local and regional offices of some larger nonprofit organizations may not have the time, money, or staff to create and maintain a Web site. Sometimes these organizations have Web sites, but they are poorly designed. In your community, you can most likely locate several nonprofit organizations that would benefit from a Web site or from a redesigned Web site.

Assignment[1]

Locate a nonprofit organization in your community. You might go to the Web site for your community; this site may have links to or contacts for local nonprofit organizations. You can also visit with volunteer groups in your community to find names of nonprofit groups. Some universities have volunteer groups that help local nonprofit organizations. If you have trouble locating one, try using a search engine to find nonprofit organizations in your area. When you have located a nonprofit organization,

1. Contact the organization and make an appointment to talk to a representative about creating a Web site.

2. Prepare interview questions before you arrive at the appointment (see Chapter 5, "Researching Information Using Primary and Secondary Sources," for information on interviewing). In your prepared questions, be sure to ask what types of information the organization would like to have on the Web site. You can also ask the representative how the organization and its users would use a Web site.

3. Analyze the users and the purpose for the site using the questions in Principle 1.

4. Select and create the content and visual aids for the site. If you receive printed documents for the site, remember to adapt them for the Web.

5. Create an organizational chart for the site.

6. Design the homepage and the individual pages.

7. Test your Web site and revise as necessary. You might ask the staff at the organization to test your site.

8. Present your Web site to the nonprofit organization and to your instructor. (The organization will launch the site on the Web; you will only create it and test it using the browser on a personal computer.)

---

[1] Your instructor may have you work with a team on this assignment.

17

Creating and Delivering Oral Presentations

▶ **O U T L I N E**

A re you uncomfortable getting up in front of strangers or even your peers and talking? Do you enjoy making oral presentations? Unlike other forms of technical communication, oral presentations offer you the opportunity to interact with your audience. Your job may require that you deliver oral presentations such as the following:

- For your manager, an impromptu status report about a project
- For clients, a 20-minute presentation on a new customized software package
- For upper-level managers, a brief presentation on proposed upgrades to the manufacturing equipment
- For colleagues at a professional meeting, a scripted speech about a research project

These situations vary in the type of preparation they require, in the use of visual aids, and in style of delivery. This chapter presents four principles to help you create and deliver oral presentations.

▶ Understanding the Types of Oral Presentations

Professionals might make any one of the following types of oral presentations:

- **Impromptu.** You do not plan an impromptu presentation. You decide what you will say while you are speaking. You might give an impromptu presentation in a staff meeting when someone asks about your research or about a project. You would talk briefly and then answer questions.

- **Extemporaneous.** You plan an extemporaneous presentation and deliver it (from your notes) in a conversational style. Most audiences prefer this type of presentation to the scripted and memorized types.

- **Scripted.** You write a scripted presentation and read the script to the audience.

- **Memorized.** You write a script, but instead of reading it you memorize it. You don't use notes as you make the oral presentation. Most professionals (except actors) avoid memorized speeches because they make speakers look too stiff and formal (Pfeiffer 6). You also risk losing your place or forgetting an important point.

Figure 17.1 presents advantages, disadvantages, and guidelines for each type of presentation. This chapter will focus on extemporaneous and scripted presentations.

▶ Principle 1: Plan for the Audience and the Occasion

As with any technical communication, an oral presentation requires that you *first* consider your audience's needs. Before you can begin to prepare the text

| **Figure 17.1** | Advantages, Disadvantages, and Guidelines for Four Types of Oral Presentations |

Type of Presentation	Advantages	Disadvantages	Guidelines
Impromptu	• Delivered in a relaxed, conversational manner	• May be disorganized because the speaker can't prepare in advance • May be rambling and unfocused	• Stop and think before speaking • Ask the audience questions to determine what they want you to speak about
Extemporaneous	• Prepared ahead of time • Delivered in a relaxed, conversational manner • Allows the speaker to adjust the presentation in response to the audience's reactions • Takes less time to create than a scripted presentation	• Can easily run over the time limit • May cause the speaker to leave out information	• Rehearse the presentation • Use visual aids to guide you as you give the presentation (these aids will also help the audience) • Define any new information or terminology • Use simple, not fancy, language • Prepare notes or an outline
Scripted	• Prepared ahead of time • Allows the speaker to deliver complete, accurate information • Helps speaker to stay within the time limit	• Often delivered in an unnatural, boring manner • Doesn't allow the speaker to adjust to the audience's reactions • Takes a long time to prepare	• Use for situations where the audience expects precision • Use visual aids and examples • Define any new information or terminology • Use simple, not fancy, language
Memorized	• Prepared ahead of time • Can allow the speaker to deliver complete, accurate information • Helps speaker to stay within the time limit	• Makes the speaker seem stiff and formal • Without notes, the speaker may lose his or her place or forget part of the presentation • Takes a long time to prepare	• Select either the extemporaneous or scripted instead of the memorized presentation

and visual aids for your presentation, consider these questions about your audience:

- **Who is your audience?** Are they colleagues at your workplace or clients outside your organization? What do you know about the demographics of your audience? The more you know about the demographics of your audience, the better you can answer the following questions and prepare an effective oral presentation.

- **What does the audience know about your topic?** You need to determine what your audience already knows about your topic. This information will help you to determine what technical terminology you can use and what the audience will understand. You'll also know how much background, if any, your audience will need to understand your presentation.

- **What is your audience's attitude about your topic?** Do they have a positive, negative, or neutral attitude about your topic? Will the members of the audience have different attitudes about the topic? For example, if you are delivering an oral presentation on new cost-cutting measures for your department, will the audience favorably receive your message, or will they feel threatened by the measures? The answers to these questions will help you to know what types of information to include, what information to emphasize, and so on.

- **What does the audience expect given the presentation occasion?** Is it a formal event or a casual meeting? Be sure that your presentation is appropriate to the occasion.

- **Why is the audience listening to the presentation?** What do they want to do—to gather information? to make a decision? to learn how to do something? What is their purpose for listening?

- **What are the audience's attitudes about you or your organization?** Will your audience be hostile? Will they be enthusiastic? Do they not yet have an attitude about you or your organization?

Once you have identified your audience, you'll need to spend some time considering your purpose:

- **Why are you giving the presentation?**

- **What do you want to accomplish?** What are your goals for the presentation?

- **Is your goal to inform or to persuade, or both?** For example, if you are delivering a presentation on how to use a new product that the audience has just bought from your organization, your purpose is to inform. However, if you are delivering a presentation on the benefits of this new product to an audience that might purchase it, your purpose is to persuade.

When you have identified your audience and purpose, you are ready to prepare your presentation. To help you prepare an effective presentation, this section presents two guidelines:

- Give the audience only the information they need.
- Anticipate the audience's needs and questions.

Give the Audience Only the Information They Need

Keep your presentation short and simple. Audiences want to hear only the information they need and no more. As you prepare your presentation, consider the following:

- **Listening to information takes twice as long as reading that same information.** Thus, if you can read 10 pages in 8 minutes, your listeners can comprehend the same information in about 16 minutes.
- **Condense your presentation into a few key points.** Don't try to give the audience every bit of information you have about a topic or all the tiny details. Instead, select the key points and present those. If necessary, you can refer the audience to your written research, to published articles, or to handouts that you have prepared.
- **Stay within your allotted time and speak to the requirements of the occasion.** For example, if you are speaking at a professional conference, the conference organizers will tell you how long to speak. They expect you to speak for no more than the allotted time—if they give you 30 minutes, they expect you to make your presentation and answer questions during that 30 minutes. If you take more than your allotted time, another speaker may not have his or her full 30 minutes. When you speak longer than your allowed time, you are being inconsiderate and most audiences will begin to "tune you out."
- **Plan the presentation to take slightly less than the allowed time.** Look for ways to tighten your presentation, so you have time for the audience's questions. Most audiences prefer a presentation that is a few minutes short over one that is a few minutes long.

Anticipate the Audience's Needs and Questions

As you prepare your presentation, think about what the audience already knows and what they will want to know about the topic:

- Define any terminology the audience may not know. If your audience members aren't experts in your field, avoid technical terminology when possible.
- Explain any information that may be new to the audience.
- Clarify and support unfamiliar information, especially if the audience may disagree with or try to reject it.

▶Principle 2: Plan Your Presentation

After you have planned for the audience and the occasion, you're prepared to determine the information you will include in and the overall organization of your presentation. As with a written document, begin by selecting the information that you want to include. Remember that for most presentations you will have a specified time period, so you should prioritize the information according to the needs and expectations of the audience and to your purpose. For example, imagine you are studying the effects of mercury emissions on health. At the end of the study, you will present your results to a group of chemists. In a written document, you would give the background of the research, the methods, the results, the conclusions, and possible recommendations. However, the audience of chemists will be interested primarily in your conclusions; so if you have only 20 minutes for your presentation, you will want to spend the majority of your presentation on the conclusions. You would briefly state the purpose of your research and how you conducted the research. You would only summarize the methods, if you mention them at all. Instead, you might refer the readers to a handout that describes, in detail, your methods.

▶ For more information on how to prepare an outline, see Chapter 6, "Organizing Information for Your Readers," page 153.

Once you have prioritized the information that you will present, you will want to prepare an outline of your presentation—as you would for a written document. Some speakers use a storyboard approach for their outline. A **storyboard** is a "sketch" of the document or presentation; it maps out each section or module of your document or presentation along with the accompanying visual aids. For an oral presentation, the storyboard includes an outline on the left side of the page and a list of the corresponding visual aids on the right side. You could include a description of the visual aids, or you could include small printouts or thumbnail sketches of the visual aids. Figure 17.2 illustrates a storyboard for part of a presentation on creating user-oriented Web sites for an audience that has never created a Web site. On the left side of the storyboard the writer includes the outline, and on the right side the Microsoft PowerPoint slides that will accompany the information in the outline.

When you have prepared your outline and/or storyboard, you can prepare your notes for the presentation. To prepare the notes, you might

- Prepare note cards.
- Prepare speaker notes if you're using presentation-graphics software such as PowerPoint. Figures 17.3(a) and 17.3(b) illustrate two ways that you might prepare your speaker notes. In Figure 17.3(a), the speaker has used the notes view to create notes for the slide. If you prefer to put more slides on a page, you can print three slides per page and write your notes on the right in the lines provided, as in Figure 17.3(b). You can print the slide in color or in black and white.

| **Figure 17.2** | An Excerpt from a Storyboard for an Oral Presentation |

Creating User-Oriented Web Sites

Introduction

- To create user-oriented Web sites, follow three principles: consider the users and the purpose, select the right tools, and design the Web site and its individual pages.

Slide: List of the three principles in reverse type on blue background with yellow bullets (all lists will appear in this format)

Consider the users and the purpose

- Think about the users and their purpose for visiting the site.

Slide: List of subordinate points
Slide: Excerpts from two Web sites that meet the users' needs

- Think about the purpose of your site.

- Gather the information to write the pages.

Slide: Sample list of information from a Web site designed by our team

Select the right tools

- Hardware you'll need

Slide: List of the hardware items needed

- Software you'll need: a text editor and possibly a graphics program

- Web design software available

Slide: Chart listing types of Web design software, their capabilities, and their advantages

---

▶Principle 3: Use Audience-Oriented Visual Aids

Visual aids give the audience something to focus on while you're speaking. Audiences often have difficulty staying focused on an oral presentation—even when the topic is interesting. However, guard against using too many visual aids or simply reading your visual aids to your audience. If you use too many visual aids, the audience may focus on the visual aids instead of on your message. Visual aids enhance your presentation when they

- Keep the audience focused on what you are saying
- Help the audience to remember key points and follow the organization of your presentation
- Help you to stay with your planned organization, to remember what you planned to talk about, and to stay within the allotted time (especially with an extemporaneous presentation)
- Help you to explain ideas, concepts, products, or technical information concisely and briefly

▼ **Figure 17.3(a)**

Speaker Notes

What Substances Cause Air Pollution?

- Ozone
- Nitrogen Oxides
- Sulfur Dioxides
- Volatile Organic Compounds

- Define ozone and give examples
- Introduce next slide that defines nitrogen oxides

▼ **Figure 17.3(b)**   Speaker Notes

What Substances Cause Air Pollution?

- Ozone
- Nitrogen Oxides
- Sulfur Dioxides
- Volatile Organic Compounds

THE READER'S CORNER

Overcoming Those Nervous Jitters

 Even speakers with years of experience making oral presentations will occasionally feel nervous before a presentation. You might be nervous because you're speaking to a group of managers at your company, and you might be nervous because you've never formally presented the topic or because the idea is new. Or perhaps you're nervous because you don't like to speak in front of a group. Whatever the reason, we all have been or will be nervous before speaking. You can overcome this speaker anxiety or nervousness by following these "no-nerves" guidelines developed by William S. Pfeiffer:[1]

No-Nerves Guideline 1: Prepare Well. If you identify your readers, plan your presentation, and create an outline and notes, you will help to eliminate much speaker anxiety. The more prepared you feel, the better you will be able to overcome those nervous jitters.

No-Nerves Guideline 2: Prepare Yourself Physically. Get a good night's sleep before you speak. Avoid too much caffeine for several hours before you speak. Drink several glasses of water in the hours before your presentation.

No-Nerves Guideline 3: Arrange the Room the Way You Want. If possible, arrange the chairs, lectern, lights, and equipment in the way that makes you most comfortable.

No-Nerves Guideline 4: Be Prepared for Emergencies. Principle 4 suggests ways for being prepared. When you are prepared for emergencies, you will feel more confident and, therefore, less nervous.

No-Nerves Guideline 5: Remember That You Are the Expert. When you make an oral presentation, remember that you are providing information that the audience does not have. Your audience wants "to hear what you have to say. Tell yourself, 'I'm the expert here!' " (Pfeiffer 123).

No-Nerves Guideline 6: Slow Down. When nervous, many speakers tend to speak too fast. Rehearse your speech, so you will be more confident. You might write on your notes to speak slowly or to slow down. Some speakers will videotape a rehearsal to help them speak more slowly.

[1] I have adapted these "no-nerves" guidelines from William S. Pfeiffer, *Pocket Guide to Public Speaking*, 119–124.

Visual aids can be as simple as handouts, or they can be charts, tables, photographs, or drawings presented by means of computer slides, overhead transparencies, posters, blackboards, or television. Many types of media are available to help you visually enhance your presentation and to help the audience understand it. For example, you can use presentation-graphics software such as PowerPoint to create professional visual aids and displays. This software allows you to use your laptop computer, computer disk, or CD-ROM to project slides directly from the computer to a screen. Figure 17.4 describes the media that you can use and presents guidelines for using each medium.

Before you decide the type of visual aids you will use, find out about the room where you will give your presentation. If you plan to use computer slides

▼ **Figure 17.4**	Types of Media for Visual Aids

Medium	Advantages	Disadvantages	Guidelines
Computer Presentations	• Professional appearance. • Versatile: You can use charts, graphs, screen shots, etc., and you can include video clips and animation. You can use presentation-graphics software. • Legible: If prepared with the audience in mind, you can use them in a variety of settings—both large rooms and small rooms.	• You may have to bring your own computer and projector as some rooms may not have the equipment you need. • If you prepare the presentations with one software program, you most likely must use that software to project the presentations. • You must prepare them ahead of time. • The room must be somewhat dark. • The equipment might fail.	• Prepare the computer presentation several days before you plan to speak. • Use a consistent design throughout the presentation. • View the presentation before you speak. • Practice setting up and speaking while using your equipment. • Print copies of your computer presentation so you will have a copy as you're speaking or in case of emergencies. • Have a backup plan in case the equipment fails.
Overhead Projector	• Inexpensive: Transparencies are relatively inexpensive. • Easy to create. • Flexible: You can draw transparencies during the presentation, prepare them ahead of time, or use a combination. • You can show them with the lights on. • Most organizations will have the equipment needed for showing transparencies.	• The appearance isn't as professional as slides. • You have to place each transparency on the projector—this process can take time and can be awkward.	• If you prepare the transparencies during your presentation, write neatly and legibly. • Look at the audience—not at the screen. • Put each prepared transparency in an acetate sleeve or mount it on a cardboard frame so you can easily handle the transparency. • Put the transparencies in sequence before you begin speaking.

(continued on next page)

▼ **Figure 17.4**   (continued)

Medium	Advantages	Disadvantages	Guidelines
			• Turn the projector off when you don't want the audience to look at a transparency.
Slide Projector	• Professional appearance. • Flexibility: You can use charts, tables, photographs, and diagrams. • Ease: You can easily operate the slide projector and manipulate the slides.	• Slides are one of the more expensive visual aids. • The room must be mostly dark. • The equipment might fail (so have a backup plan).	• Put the slides in sequence before you begin speaking. • Practice setting up and speaking while using your equipment. • Plan for a light source so you can see your notes.
Opaque Projector	• You can display paper documents, so you can display documents from your audience. • Requires little if any preparation or expense.	• Less professional quality. • Image quality is poor with some projectors. • You have to place each page on the projector. • The room must be dark. • Appropriate only for small rooms and audiences.	• Allow time for the projector to warm up. • Leave the projector on until you are finished. • Plan for a light source so you can see your notes. • Make sure that your audience is close enough to see the images.
VCR or DVD Player	• You can play video clips, movies, and recordings. • Professional quality is possible. • Versatile: You can show professionally made videos and movies or amateur videos showing research, observations, and so on.	• Video and DVD recordings are time-consuming and expensive to create. • You need high-quality equipment to create professional quality video or DVD recordings.	• View the presentation before you speak. • Practice setting up and speaking while using your equipment. • Have a backup plan in case the equipment fails.

(continued on next page)

Figure 17.4   (continued)

Medium	Advantages	Disadvantages	Guidelines
	• Easy to advance and reverse.	• You may have to bring your own equipment, as some rooms may not have the equipment you need. • You can't prepare handouts from the recordings.	• Make sure the recordings are relevant and interesting to the audience. • Combine recordings with other media or the audience may "tune out" the recordings, especially if the recordings are too long for the audience and the occasion.
Poster	• Flexible: You can write or draw on the posters during the presentation, prepare them ahead of time, or use a combination of these methods. • You can show them with the lights on. • You don't need equipment to show posters. • Inexpensive to prepare.	• Hard to transport. • Can have an unprofessional appearance. • Appropriate only for small rooms and audiences.	• Use at least 20- by 30-inch sturdy poster board. • Use a simple, uncluttered design. • Make sure that every person in the audience can read the posters. • Use intense colors to create contrast between the poster color and the type. • For a more professional appearance, put a premade border on the posters.
Flip Chart[1]	• Flexible: You can write or draw on the flip chart during the presentation, prepare the posters ahead of time, or use a combination of these methods.	• Appropriate only for small rooms and audiences. • Can have an unprofessional appearance.	• Use bright colors that the audience can easily see. • Keep the flip chart simple—don't write too much on one poster. (continued on next page)

[1] A flip chart is a series of posters bound together at the top in a loose-leaf fashion—often called an easel pad. The flip chart is usually placed on an easel. The flip chart can also be large sheets of blank paper bound together.

▼ **Figure 17.4**   (continued)

Medium	Advantages	Disadvantages	Guidelines
	• You can easily flip backward and forward in the chart. • Relatively inexpensive. • Requires little if any equipment.		• Use only in rooms with good lighting. • Make sure that every person in the audience can read the chart.
Chalkboard or Dry-Erase Board	• Flexible: You can write or draw on the board during the presentation. • Excellent for informal presentations and for incorporating the audience's ideas into the presentation. • Available in many settings or rooms.	• Inappropriate for complex visual aids. • Appropriate only for small rooms and audiences. • Can have an unprofessional appearance, especially in formal presentations.	• Write legibly. • Make sure that every person in the audience can see what you put on the board (and understand it). • Maintain eye contact with the audience.
Props[2]	• Add visual interest to the presentation. • A prop, such as a model or prototype, may be the only way to convey some ideas or concepts.	• Can distract the audience. They may look at the prop rather than listen to your presentation. • Can take awhile to pass around the room. • Can become damaged. • Appropriate only for small rooms and audiences.	• If the prop is large or hard to handle, simply show the prop or have the audience come up and look at it. • If the prop is extremely valuable or irreplaceable, don't pass it around the room.
Handouts	• Present complex information and additional information that you may only refer to in the presentation. • Help the audience to remember the information that you present to them.	• The audience may read the handouts rather than listen to your presentation. • The audience may read ahead and interrupt you with questions about information that you've not yet presented.	• Give the readers the handouts at the end of the presentation. • Make sure the handouts are free of errors and have a professional appearance.

[2] Props are objects, samples of materials, models, and so on that you can pass around the room or hold up for the audience to see.

such as those created by Microsoft PowerPoint, make sure the room has a screen on which to project the slides and appropriate electrical outlets. If you plan to use a dry-erase board or blackboard, make sure the room has these boards and adequate lighting. As you plan your visual aids, follow these tips:

 Tips for Creating Effective Visual Aids for Oral Presentations

- **Use only the visual aids your audience will need to understand your presentation.** Give your audience only the visual aids they need to understand your key points. Don't complicate your presentation with unnecessary visual aids or overly complex visual aids.

- **Make sure that each visual aid has a specific purpose.** Each visual aid should have a specific purpose and should relate directly to the key points of your presentation. Avoid using visual aids to entertain.

- **Make sure that everyone in the audience can read the visual aids, not just those sitting up front.** Remember that less is more, especially with slides created with presentation-graphics software such as PowerPoint. For example, instead of trying to fit all the information about a specific point on one slide or overhead by using a smaller type size or margins, use two or more slides. Let's look at some examples. Figure 17.5 has too many words and the type is too small. Figure 17.6 has ample margins and uses an appropriate type size. You also want to use legible typefaces and to avoid shadowing, underlining, or outlined type. For transparencies and slides, use a boldfaced sans-serif typeface such as Ariel, Tahoma, or Helvetica and a type that is black on a white background. If you use a colored background, select a typeface color that is legible (for example, white on dark blue or yellow on dark blue).

- **Use backgrounds that are appropriate for the presentation occasion and that don't distract or make reading difficult.** Some of the backgrounds available for PowerPoint and other presentation-graphics software distract—with some of these backgrounds, the audience can't easily read the words. Select backgrounds without images behind the words and with appropriate colors and tone for your presentation. Let's look at some examples. The background in Figure 17.7 makes reading difficult, whereas the background in Figure 17.8 enhances the reading.

- **Select simple visual aids.** Each visual aid should present only one main idea. The audience should be able to easily and quickly comprehend the information that the visual aid is presenting.

- **Use brief phrases rather than sentences.** In a document, you generally use sentences. In a visual aid for an oral presentation, sentences

(continued on page 547)

What Substances Cause Air Pollution?

- Ozone, a highly reactive form of oxygen
- Nitrogen Oxides (NOx), a form of nitrogen and oxygen that combine at high temperatures during the combustion of fossil fuels
- Sulfur Dioxides (SO2), a combination of sulfur and oxygen that occurs during combustion
- Volatile Organic Compounds (VOCs), forms of hydrocarbon that are emitted from substances such as paints, solvents and gasoline, as well as natural vegetation.

The type is too small for reading on a screen.

The slide has too much information for one visual aid.

What Substances Cause Air Pollution?

- **Ozone**
- **Nitrogen Oxides**
- **Sulfur Dioxides**
- **Volatile Organic Compounds**

The type is easy to read.

The slide has ample white space.

Figure 17.7

A Slide with a
Background That
Distracts

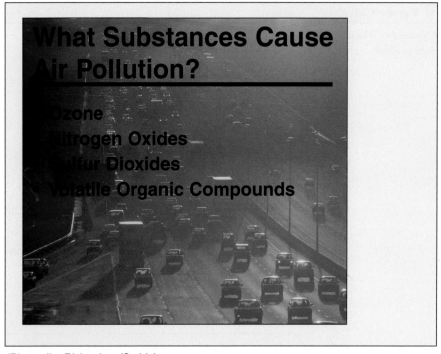

(Photo: Jim Richardson/Corbis)

Figure 17.8

A Slide with a
Background That Does
Not Distract

What Substances Cause Air Pollution?

- Ozone
- Nitrogen Oxides
- Sulfur Dioxides
- Volatile Organic Compounds

can clutter the visual aid and make it illegible. Instead, use phrases. For example:

Document Text	Hydroelectric power has these disadvantages:
	• It causes the loss of wildlife habitats.
	• It takes significant amounts of land for constructing the reservoir.
Visual Aid Text	Disadvantages of hydroelectric power
	• Loss of wildlife habitats
	• Loss of land

- **Make sure that visual aids are free of errors in style or grammar and contain correct information.** Your visual aids represent you and/or your organization. If they contain errors in grammar and style, or if they contain incorrect information, you will lose credibility. Your audience may not trust you or the information that you are presenting because they may believe that if the visual aids are sloppy or incorrect, your information, research, service, or product is not trustworthy.

▶Principle 4: Use Effective Strategies for Delivering the Presentation

To deliver smooth presentations and to put yourself and your audience at ease, spend time getting ready and use effective strategies:

- Rehearse your talk and prepare visual aids and the room ahead of time.
- Be prepared for emergencies.
- Help your audience enjoy your presentation.
- Provide previews, transitions, examples, and reviews to help the audience follow your presentation.

Rehearse Your Presentation and Prepare Ahead of Time

Spend time rehearsing and timing your presentation, putting your visual aids in the order you will present them, and checking out the room and its equipment. As you rehearse and prepare, follow these tips:

 Tips for Rehearsing and Preparing Your Presentation

- **Make your rehearsal realistic.** If possible, rehearse your presentation with the actual equipment you will use and in the room where you will speak. As you rehearse, practice with any visual aids that you will use.

(continued on next page)

- **Time your presentation.** Most oral presentations have an allotted time; so as you rehearse, time your presentation. If the presentation is too long, cut some of the text or some of the visual aids. Allow time for questions from your audience, and stay within your allotted time.

- **Put your visual aids in order.** Before your presentation, put your visual aids in the order in which you will present them. Also, note in your outline or on your note cards where to present each visual aid. That way, you won't have to shuffle through your visual aids while your audience sits and waits.

- **Check out the room and its equipment.** If you are speaking in an unfamiliar setting, check it out before you speak. Find the electrical outlets (if needed), look at the lighting, and determine whether you will need a microphone or a pointer.

- **Practice setting up the computer and projection equipment.** If you will use media that requires a computer or a projector, practice setting up the equipment. The setup can take more time than you think, so you will want to know how much time to allow.

Be Prepared for Emergencies

In case your presentation doesn't go as planned, be prepared for emergencies and be flexible. You can lessen the likelihood of some emergencies by doing the following:

- Put transparencies in a three-ring binder. (Put the transparencies in plastic sleeves made for three-ring binders.)
- Take an extra light bulb for the overhead projector or slide projector.
- Take a backup disk or CD-ROM if you're using computer projection.
- Have a backup plan in case the computer, projector, VCR, or DVD player doesn't work.

▶ See Principle 2 for information on preparing notes.

- Prepare notes. If you use note cards, number the cards. If you use speaker notes from presentation-graphics software, the pages should automatically be numbered. If you have rehearsed, you may only occasionally refer to your notes. However, your notes will help you if you lose your place during the presentation.

Help the Audience Enjoy Your Presentation

Use these simple guidelines to help the audience enjoy and focus on your presentation. These guidelines will become increasingly easy to follow the more you rehearse and the more presentations you give. If you are well prepared, these guidelines will be easy to follow because you will feel comfortable and confident.

- Talk slowly and distinctly, making sure the audience can understand your words.
- Look the audience in the eye. Audiences tend to be suspicious of speakers who don't maintain eye contact.
- Speak with enthusiasm and confidence. The audience doesn't want to listen to someone who seems uninterested or who lacks confidence.
- Avoid verbal tics ("um," "ah," "uh"). Rehearsing will help you to eliminate them.

Provide Previews, Transitions, Examples, and Reviews

To help the audience follow your presentation, give them a road map and some examples. The following tips will help you guide your audience through your presentation:

▶ Tips for Guiding Your Audience Through Your Oral Presentation

- **Preview your presentation.** Tell (and possibly show) the audience how you have organized the presentation. State what you will be telling them. In this preview, describe the organization of the presentation. Introduce the key points you will discuss (in the order in which you will discuss them). For example, you might say, "This morning, I will talk about X, Y, and Z," and support this preview with a visual aid that lists X, Y, and Z. Then you would discuss X, Y, and Z in the order in which you mentioned them.

- **Use clear transitions between topics.** Transitions tell the audience that you are changing the subject. Without transitions, the audience may misunderstand your words, get confused, or lose their focus. To alert the audience to a change, use transitions such as "My second point is" and "Next, I will discuss." You can also use visual aids to signal a change.

- **Use specific, unambiguous examples.** Examples help the audience to understand complicated or abstract concepts. You can use oral examples, or you can present examples in visual aids.

- **Summarize your presentation at the end.** In the conclusion, summarize your key points. Tell the audience what you've told them. You can use a visual aid to emphasize this summary.

- **Field questions from the audience.** Ask the audience if they have any questions. If appropriate for the situation, you can encourage the audience to ask you questions during your presentation—for example, you can give the audience the opportunity to ask questions

(continued on page 551)

TAKING IT INTO THE WORKPLACE

Taking Your Cues from the Audience

"Read the audience's eyes, watch what they do as you are presenting, and check their engagement factor."
—Karl Walinskas, Professional Engineer and Speaker (24)

Your audience can give you cues about whether you are meeting their expectations. Karl Walinskas suggests that you take those cues and adjust how you are delivering your presentation. He identifies three cues the audience will give you:

- **"The eyes have it."** Your first clue to audience interest is the eyes of each person. (If the room and the audience are large, you can use the people in the first few rows.) Walinskas suggests making sure "their eyes are *open!* . . . Shut eyelids mean a bored crowd" (24). Is the audience looking around the room or at their laps rather than at you and your visual aids? If so, change the pace or volume of your speech (24).
- **"Actions speak louder than words."** The audience's body language can also give you cues. For example, if people in the audience are lean-

ing back in their chairs getting comfortable (perhaps for a nap), you might want to change the pace of your presentation or get the audience involved. You might ask them to look at something on a screen or in a handout.
- **"The engagement factor."** Walinskas explains that "the level to which your audience participates is a critical factor in determining how well they are receiving" your presentation (24). For example, even if you have asked them to hold questions until the end, someone in the audience may be so engaged that he or she can't wait. This signal tells you and the rest of the audience that your presentation is engaging.

Walinskas summarizes audience cues and possible adjustments based on those cues in the table below.

Assignment

Attend an oral presentation and evaluate how well the speaker delivers the presentation based on the audience cues. Write a memo to your instructor including the name of the speaker, the title and date of the presentation, and your evaluation.

AUDIENCE CUE	WHAT IT MEANS	HOW TO ADJUST
Shut eyelids	Boredom, fatigue	Change pace, volume, and subject matter; use humor to get them laughing
Wandering eyes	Distraction	Use dramatic action; call attention to an important point and ask for audience focus; use humor
Mass exodus	Boredom, they've heard it before	Change tactics; use pointed humor (not shtick); do something dramatic to reconnect; add controversy; move on to the next point; work on content for next time
Leaning back in seats	Apathy, waiting for something better	Use dramatic action; insert an exercise to involve them; use humor
Shaking heads	Disagreement	Confront a select head-shaker ("You disagree? Tell us why."); offer an alternative viewpoint that others embrace (even though you may not)
No questions during Q&A	Disinterest, confusion, hesitation	Plant seed questions with several people in the audience ahead of time to get the ball rolling; call on people who you read as being most engaged during the presentation

Source: Reprinted by permission of Karl Walinskas, The Speaking Connection, www.speakingconnection.com.

if they don't understand something. As you field questions, do the following:

- Repeat the question, so you can make sure that you heard it correctly and that everyone in the audience knows the question that you will be answering.
- Take a few seconds to think before you answer, so you can respond in an organized, clear manner.
- If you don't know the answer to a question, say so. Your audience will sense if you are "making up" an answer. You will gain the respect of your audience if you are honest and ethical.
- If someone disagrees with you or criticizes your presentation, be respectful.

▶Conclusion

As a professional, you are likely to give oral presentations in a variety of situations. You might give a presentation informally to your coworkers, or you might present your research or product to hundreds of people attending a professional meeting. In either case, the principles presented here will help you to prepare the text and visual aids and deliver the presentation. Oral presentations may often begin and end your work, so be prepared to use them to your advantage. Use the "Worksheet for Creating and Delivering Oral Presentations" as you prepare.

 WORKSHEET ▶ **for Creating and Delivering Oral Presentations**

▶ **Principle 1: Plan for the Audience and the Occasion**
- Who is your audience? Are they colleagues at your workplace or clients outside your organization? What do you know about the demographics of your audience?
- What does the audience know about your topic?
- What is your audience's attitude about your topic? Do they have a positive, negative, or neutral attitude about the topic?
- What does the audience expect from the presentation occasion? Is it a formal event or a casual meeting?
- Why is the audience listening to the presentation? What do they want to do—to gather information? to make a decision? to learn how to do something?
- What is the audience's attitude about you or your organization?
- Why are you giving the presentation?
- What do you want to accomplish?
- Is your goal to inform or to persuade?

▶ **Principle 2: Plan Your Presentation**
- Have you selected information relevant and appropriate for your audience?
- Have you selected information that you can present in the allotted time for the presentation?
- Have you prepared an outline?
- Have you prepared notecards or speaker notes?

▶ **Principle 3: Use Audience-Oriented Visual Aids**
- Have you selected the appropriate media for your presentation, your audience, and the room?
- Does each visual aid have a specific purpose?
- Have you selected visual aids your audience can understand?
- Does each visual aid contain information relevant to your audience and to your key points?
- Are the visual aids legible? Can everyone in the audience read the visual aids—even those seated at the back of the room?
- Have you used backgrounds that enhance reading? Do any of the backgrounds make the visual aids hard to read?
- Does each visual aid present only one idea?
- Have you used brief phrases rather than sentences?
- Is each visual aid free of errors in style and grammar?
- Does each visual aid contain accurate, correct information?
- Does each visual aid have the appropriate professional appearance? Does it represent you and your organization in a positive, professional manner?

▶ **Principle 4: Use Effective Strategies for Delivering the Presentation**
- Have you practiced delivering the presentation?
  - Have you rehearsed your presentation using the visual aids and equipment?
  - Have you timed the presentation? Did it fit in the allotted time? If not, have you decided what to delete from the presentation?
  - Have you put your visual aids in the order that you will present them?
  - Have you checked out the room and its equipment?
  - Have you practiced setting up the equipment?
- Are you prepared for emergencies?
  - If you're using transparencies, have you put them in acetate sleeves and placed them in the correct order in a three-ring binder?
  - Do you have an extra light bulb for the projector?
  - Do you have a backup disk or CD-ROM if you're using computer projection?
  - Have you prepared notes? Are the notes numbered?
- Are you prepared to help your audience enjoy your presentation?
  - Will you talk slowly and distinctly?

- Will you look the audience in the eye?
- Will you speak with enthusiasm and confidence?
- Have you rehearsed enough to avoid verbal tics?
- Have you included an introduction that previews the organization of your presentation?
- Have you planned clear transitions between topics?
- Have you included specific and unambiguous examples?
- Have you included a summary to end your presentation?
- Are you prepared to field questions from the audience?

1. Find out what presentation-graphics software you have available at your college or university or at your workplace. Practice creating a slide presentation with the software. When you are comfortable using the software, write instructions for creating a slide presentation with the software. The readers of your instructions are your classmates. If you need help writing instructions, refer to Chapter 15, "Writing User-Oriented Instructions and Manuals."

2. Using the presentation-graphics software that you learned in Exercise 1, create a design that you can use as a master slide for an oral presentation. Make sure that your slide follows the tips presented in Principle 3.

3. Create an oral presentation on one of the following topics. The audience of your presentation is your classmates. Your presentation should include visual aids. Your instructor will tell you the time allotted for the presentation.

- Define a concept in your major.
- Explain a procedure you commonly follow at your workplace or will use as a professional in your field.
- Explain how to use a piece of equipment used on campus, at home, in your major, or at your workplace (your instructor may want to approve this topic before you begin creating the presentation).
- Explain a procedure that students follow at your college or university.
- Present the conclusions and/or results of a report that you prepared for your technical communication class.

4. Using the evaluation sheet in Figure 17.9, evaluate the presentations of your classmates. Be sure to consider the tips presented in Principles 3 and 4 as you evaluate. Your instructor may ask you to complete this evaluation online and e-mail it to him or her. The sheet is available on the Web site for this book.

Figure 17.9

Evaluation Sheet for Oral Presentations

Name of Speaker: _____

Topic of Presentation: _____

In the box to the left of the requirement, place a check to indicate the presentation met the requirement.

Content

❑ The speaker introduced the topic and purpose of the presentation at the beginning.

❑ The speaker introduced the key points at the beginning.

❑ The speaker introduced the organization of the presentation at the beginning.

❑ The speaker used clear transitions and previews to indicate he or she was changing topics.

❑ The speaker summarized the key points at the end of the presentation.

Visual Aids

❑ The speaker used visual aids to reinforce and/or explain key points.

❑ The visual aids helped me to understand how the presentation was organized.

❑ The visual aids were uncluttered and professional in appearance.

❑ I could read the visual aids.

❑ The speaker selected the right medium/media for the visual aids. If not, what medium/media should the speaker have selected? _____

Delivery

❑ The speaker enunciated clearly and distinctly.

❑ The speaker was appropriately enthusiastic and confident.

❑ The speaker spoke at the appropriate volume and delivery rate (the speaker didn't speak too soft or too loud and didn't speak too fast or too slow).

❑ The speaker avoided distracting verbal tics.

❑ The speaker maintained eye contact with the audience.

❑ The speaker answered questions politely and confidently.

Comments

_____

_____

Evaluator's Signature: _____

▶ **C A S E   S T U D Y**

Working With a Team to Prepare an Oral Presentation

Background

You and your team have developed a product or service that community groups might use for fund-raising. You want to get people to buy your product or service, so you have decided to prepare an oral presentation introducing your product or service to groups in your community. You and your team will work together to prepare and deliver the presentation. The purpose of your presentation is to

- Introduce your product or service
- Explain the advantages of your product or service
- Persuade the group to use your product or service for its next fund-raising project

Assignment

Your team will complete the following steps to meet the requirements of this case study:

1. Create a product or service that you can use for your presentation. (You don't have to actually create a product—you can simply describe it.)
2. Decide what community group would likely use your product or service for fund-raising.
3. Using the questions in Principle 1, analyze the audience of your presentation. (This audience would be the group that you identified in step 2.)
4. Plan your presentation. Be sure to make notes.
5. Create appropriate visual aids for the presentation.
6. Rehearse the presentation. Be sure to assign roles to each member of the team. Every member should have a part in the presentation.
7. Deliver the presentation to your instructor and/or your classmates. They will use the evaluation sheet in Figure 17.9 as they listen to your presentation.

IV

Using the Writer's Tools to Correspond with Your Readers

18

Writing Reader-Oriented Letters, Memos, and E-Mail

▶ OUTLINE

Principle 1: Determine the Objectives of Your Letter, Memo, or E-Mail

Principle 2: Find Out About Your Readers and How They Will Perceive Your Message

Principle 3: Use a Reader-Oriented Tone

Principle 4: Determine the Most Effective Approach for Your Readers

Principle 5: Use an Appropriate Format

The Reader's Corner: Early Snail Mail

Taking It into the Workplace: E-Mail and Netiquette

Conclusion

Worksheet for Writing Reader-Oriented Letters, Memos, and E-Mail

Exercises

Case Study: A "Mixed-Up" Situation

Like most professionals in the workplace, you will use letters, memos, and e-mail to correspond with coworkers and with people outside your organization. Memos, letters, and e-mail are the everyday communication tools of the workplace. You will write **letters** primarily to communicate with people outside your organization. You might also use them inside your organization to handle confidential matters such as personnel and salary issues. A letter is often more formal than a memo or e-mail. The standard elements of letters are the date, the address of the sender, the address of the reader, a subject line, a salutation, a closing, and the letter writer's signature. Figure 18.1 illustrates these standard elements.

You will write **memos** to communicate with people within your organization. You might use a memo for routine correspondence about an organizational picnic or for an informal report. Memos have a format that includes the date, a "to" line, a "from" line, and a "subject" line. Your organization may have a preprinted form or preferred format for memos. If it does not, you can use the format illustrated in Figure 18.2.

Regardless of the format you use, create a template for that format with your word-processing program. In some word-processing programs, you can select the auto-format function and the program will format a letter or memo for you. By using a template, you can call up the letter or memo format, fill in the required information, and write the text of your letter or memo. Templates can save you time and create a consistent look for your letters and memos.

You can use **e-mail** to correspond with people inside or outside your organization. E-mail offers several advantages:

- **E-mail is faster than traditional paper letters and memos.** You can send an e-mail message to a coworker across the globe in seconds instead of the days required for traditional mail, and the coworker can respond within seconds.
- **E-mail is often faster and more convenient than telephone communication.** When you use e-mail, you can send messages anytime. You don't have to wait for your receiver to be available by phone. With e-mail you need not leave messages and wait for someone to return your call.
- **E-mail saves organizations money.** E-mail communication is cheaper than most paper and telephone communication.
- **E-mail gives organizations flexibility and increases productivity.** E-mail lets organizations put together research and development teams by tapping the best people for a project without worrying about geographic location—eliminating stressful transfers and expensive temporary assignments (Perry 24). Team members can work in different locations, using inexpensive e-mail as their communication link.

Even though e-mail is quick, inexpensive, and convenient, you will still want to consider using paper letters and memos for these reasons:

| **Figure 18.1** | The Standard Elements of Letters |

POWER ENGINEERING, INC. •————Address of the sender

400 North Zang ▪ Shreveport, LA 75201 ▪ (318) 555-4578

June 10, 2002 •————————————————————————Date

Mr. John Smithson •————————————————Address of the reader
Robinson Creek Medical Center
P.O. Box 3547
Franklin, North Dakota 57890

Subject: Unit No. 3 Boiler Thermocouple Installation—P.I.D. No. 567-4678 •————Subject line

Dear John: •————————————————————————Salutation

This letter reports the current status of project 567-4678, the boiler thermocouple installation on Unit No. 3. We have ordered a Pyrosonic 2000 temperature detector that will include bent tube openings for the transmitter and receiver and a remote digital display. We will install the transmitter and receiver at elevation 526' $9^1/_4$" above the superheated tube section.

The company has approved thermocouple specification 567-4678-S401, so I have submitted a requisition to purchase the thermocouples. The contractor will install 61 thermocouples.

As we discussed, I have outlined our respective project responsibilities in the following paragraphs.

Responsibilities of Power Engineering
Power Engineering will provide the following:

- instructions for installing the equipment, the wiring diagrams, the bills of materials, and construction drawings needed for installing all thermocouples up to and including the junction boxes
- the same support for installing the Pyrosonic 2000 temperature detector up to and including the processor cabinet

The contractor will provide all the hardware to complete the installation, except the Pyrosonic 2000, the thermocouples, and the thermocouple junction boxes.

Responsibilities of Robinson Creek Engineering Support
You and your group will be responsible for all the equipment and labor from the end devices named above up to and including the recorder located in the control room. You will also be responsible for locating and installing the remote digital display supplied with the Pyrosonic 2000.

If you have questions, please call me at (318) 555-5555 or e-mail me at mcm@pe.com.

Sincerely, •————————————————————— Closing

Mathew R. McCarroll

Mathew R. McCarroll •——————————————— Signature of the sender

Figure 18.2	A Standard Memo Format

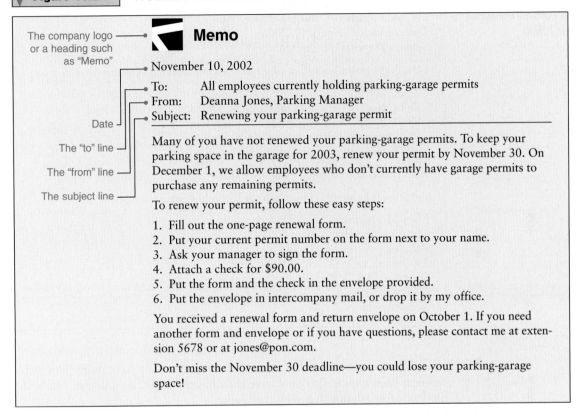

The company logo or a heading such as "Memo"

Memo

November 10, 2002

To: All employees currently holding parking-garage permits
From: Deanna Jones, Parking Manager
Subject: Renewing your parking-garage permit

Date

The "to" line

The "from" line

The subject line

Many of you have not renewed your parking-garage permits. To keep your parking space in the garage for 2003, renew your permit by November 30. On December 1, we allow employees who don't currently have garage permits to purchase any remaining permits.

To renew your permit, follow these easy steps:

1. Fill out the one-page renewal form.
2. Put your current permit number on the form next to your name.
3. Ask your manager to sign the form.
4. Attach a check for $90.00.
5. Put the form and the check in the envelope provided.
6. Put the envelope in intercompany mail, or drop it by my office.

You received a renewal form and return envelope on October 1. If you need another form and envelope or if you have questions, please contact me at extension 5678 or at jones@pon.com.

Don't miss the November 30 deadline—you could lose your parking-garage space!

- Your readers may not have access to e-mail.
- For some documents, you, your reader, or your organization may need a paper copy of a correspondence with original signatures. A paper copy may be needed for legal purposes.

The format for e-mail varies from writer to writer and organization to organization. Many e-mail messages have the same general format as a memo, even when written to readers outside a company; however, many e-mail messages include a signature line at the end of the message (see Figure 18.3).

▶ Principle 1: Determine the Objectives of Your Letter, Memo, or E-Mail

Before writing a letter, memo, or e-mail, decide what you want it to accomplish. Do you want readers to take a particular action after reading your correspondence? Do you want readers to give you information? Do you want to inform readers about good or perhaps bad news? As you think about writing

Figure 18.3

A Possible Format for an E-Mail

From: "Mary Gonzalez" <mmg@sw.com>
To: "Bob Cosgrove" <cosgrove@pbe.com>
Date: Sunday, February 10, 2002
Subject: Proposal for Chemco

I have attached a revised outline based on our meeting yesterday. In this meeting, we agreed to the following schedule:

3/7   rough draft due to me (you can send me the draft via e-mail)
3/10 revised draft from me for you to review
3/11 suggested changes to the draft due to me
3/12 deliver final copies of proposal to you

Please verify this schedule by return e-mail.

I appreciate your help. Please call me if you have questions.

Mary M. Gonzalez
Computer Specialist
PBE, Inc.
2600 South Valley Creek Parkway
Scranton, PA 17854
(717) 678-7890
mmg@sw.com

your message, remember that your correspondence may have more than just a business objective; it also may have the objective of maintaining or establishing a positive relationship with the reader.

These questions will help you determine both the business and the human-relations objectives of your letters, memos, and e-mail:

- **What is the purpose of the correspondence? What do you expect it to accomplish?** Your correspondence frequently will have more than one objective. For example, the primary objective of the letter shown in Figure 18.4 is to inform the reader of the new customer comment cards. The secondary objective is to mend a damaged relationship with the reader and ensure the continued business and good will of that reader.
- **What action, if any, do you expect readers to take after reading the correspondence?** Determine what—if anything—you want readers to do after reading your correspondence. If you decide that you want readers to do something, clearly and directly state what you want them to do. Much correspondence is ineffective because the writer doesn't clearly and directly state what the writer expects the reader to do after reading the correspondence. The writer assumes that the reader will know what to do. If the writer has assumed incorrectly, the readers will not do what the writer expects.

| **Figure 18.4** | A Message with a Primary and Secondary Objective |

Computers on Wheels

February 6, 2002

Mrs. Wanda Perrill
902 Indian Creek
St. Paul, Minnesota 57904

Dear Mrs. Perrill:

After our conversation last month about the quality of service in your home, we created a yellow "Customer Comment Card." To improve our service to you, your computer team will now leave this card on each visit. The purpose of the card is to solicit your comments about our service on a regular basis. These cards resulted directly from our conversation—thanks for the suggestion.

The comment cards will help us to maintain and monitor the quality of service that we provide in your home. They also are part of a new incentive program for our employees, so please take a moment after each maintenance visit to fill out the postage-paid card and drop it in the mail. Your comments will help us to provide the service you need and expect.

Thank you, Mrs. Perrill, for your comments that led to these new cards. We appreciate the confidence that you have placed in Computers on Wheels.

Sincerely,

Bob Congrove
Owner

"Serving you so you can work at home"

**302 Macarthur, Suite 204
St. Paul, Minnesota 57904**

- **What do you expect readers to know after reading the correspondence?** What, exactly, do you want your readers to know after reading your correspondence? If *you* don't know, neither will your readers. Try informally listing what you want your readers to know. This list can also help you to spot information that is irrelevant or that your readers won't understand.

▶Principle 2: Find Out About Your Readers and How They Will Perceive Your Message

Effective letters, memos, and e-mail are

- **Reader oriented.** Correspondence oriented toward readers contains all of the information that readers need to understand the message. It doesn't contain more than they need, and it doesn't leave them guessing about the writer's intended message.
- **Helpful.** Correspondence that is helpful anticipates and provides answers to readers' questions.
- **Tactful.** Correspondence that is tactful is courteous and, when possible, positive. It maintains or gains the reader's good will by using an appropriate tone.

What can you do to ensure that your correspondence is reader oriented, helpful, and tactful? Find out as much as possible about your readers. For much of the correspondence that you will write, this task will be relatively simple because you will know the readers personally. However, sometimes you will be writing to readers whom you don't know. These questions will help you gather information, especially about readers you don't know:

- **Who will read the correspondence? Will more than one person read it?** If you will have more than one reader, prepare to meet the needs and expectations of all readers. If their needs and expectations vary substantially, consider writing separately to each person or group.
- **What are the readers' positions and responsibilities? How might their positions and responsibilities affect how they perceive your message?** If you know readers' positions and responsibilities in the organization, you can better determine what they know about you, your responsibilities, and possibly the subject of your message. This information about your readers can also help you to anticipate how they will perceive and react to your message. Suppose the purpose of your letter is to inform readers about the organization's new travel policy. Under this new policy, your readers will no longer receive a corporate credit card to pay for their travel expenses. Instead, they will use their own credit cards or cash, and the organization will reimburse them. Because your readers travel extensively, you know that this information may not please them.

- **If the readers are external, what is their relationship to you and your organization? How will this relationship affect how they perceive your message?** Find out as much as possible about past interactions between the readers, their organization, and your organization. This information will help you understand how the readers may perceive you and your organization; and it will help guide you in selecting the information, language, and structure for the correspondence.
- **What do the readers know about the subject of the correspondence?** If you can find out what readers know about the subject of your correspondence, you'll be more likely to include the appropriate amount of background and detail.

After you have specifically answered these questions for several letters, memos, or e-mail messages, use them to guide you as you gather information about your readers and how they might perceive your messages.

▶Principle 3: Use a Reader-Oriented Tone

Create a tactful and, when possible, positive tone for your letters, memos, and e-mail. Many writers have the most difficulty achieving a reader-oriented tone when writing e-mail. Recipients of e-mail often complain about the bluntness or unintentional rudeness of the messages. A blunt or rude tone may be common because writers write e-mail quickly—rarely taking time to proofread or to consider how readers will perceive their words. This problem may also stem from the informality of e-mail. E-mail is less formal and less inhibited in style than traditional letters and memos (Stein and Yates 101). Because of this informality, many e-mail users write what they think or feel, often without considering how their words will affect their readers.

To create a reader-oriented tone, ask yourself how readers will respond to your message. Compare the letters shown in Figures 18.5 and 18.6. The writer of the letter in Figure 18.5 didn't carefully consider the tone of his letter. He uses language focused on himself and on his company. This writer-oriented tone is evident in the pronouns that refer to him and his company (*we* and *our*). It also is evident in the way he focuses on company actions and policy instead of on the reader and her problem. In the final paragraph of his letter, he seems to be saying that the reader was negligent—not the company.

In the letter shown in Figure 18.6, the writer achieves a reader-oriented, positive tone. He focuses on the reader and her interests instead of on the company. He uses a positive tone and refers to the reader frequently by name and with second-person pronouns (*you* and *your*).

Readers want to know how a message will affect them, not how it will affect the writer or his or her organization, and they want to know how a message will benefit them. When reading correspondence, many readers ask themselves, "How will this message affect me?" or "How will this message benefit me?"

▼ **Figure 18.5**   A Letter with a Writer-Oriented Tone

colorado outfitters
1212 canyon drive
boulder, co 67899
(303) 555-4986
d r r @ c o . c o m

May 18, 2002

Mrs. Annie Shepard
1244 Fork Road
Socorro, NM 54233

Dear Mrs. Shepard:

We here at Colorado Outfitters are always pleased to hear from our customers. We try to please our customers with quality recreational gear and equipment. Our newest feature for customers is our Colorado Outfitters Catalog, a way to shop by telephone, e-mail, or the Web. However, this feature does have one drawback—our mailing list for the catalog is incomplete.

Recently, we received your letter about a problem with our service: Your neighbor purchased a Flashmagic 2-person tent for $250 during our spring catalog sale, but you bought the same tent at the full price of $350 during January.

It is a shame that you weren't on our mailing list, so we could have offered you the Flashmagic 2-person tent for $250. We will put you on our mailing list today, so you won't miss any more of our sales. If we can serve you in any way, please call, write, or e-mail us—Colorado Outfitters is here to make your recreational activities fun and easy.

Happy camping,

David R. Rowland
Manager

Figure 18.6   A Letter with a Reader-Oriented Tone

colorado outfitters
1212 canyon drive
boulder, co 67899
(303) 555-4986
d r r @ c o . c o m

May 18, 2002

Mrs. Annie Shepard
1244 Fork Road
Socorro, NM 54233

Dear Mrs. Shepard:

Your recent letter about your purchase of a Flashmagic 2-person tent in January concerned us. You explained that a neighbor had purchased the same tent during the spring catalog sale; however, you paid $100 more than your neighbor. We understand your concern, so we have enclosed a 50% discount coupon good on your next purchase from Colorado Outfitters.

Undoubtedly, you must wonder why you didn't receive a catalog. The spring catalog is the first one that we sent to our customers as part of our new shop-at-home service. Because this service is new, we are still adding long-standing customers on the mailing list. We have now entered your name and address on the mailing list. You will receive all future catalogs and sales notices. In the future, you—like your neighbor—can shop at home and take advantage of sales available exclusively to customers on our mailing list.

Mrs. Shepard, please let us know if we can serve you further. You are a valued customer.

Happy camping,

David R. Rowland
Manager

encl.: discount coupon

Readers resist messages that point out their mistakes or messages that carry bad news. Just as you prefer to receive positive news, so will your readers. They will respond more favorably if a message concentrates on the positive, deemphasizes their mistakes, and, when possible, focuses on ways of doing better in the future. Even when you can't focus on the positive or deemphasize mistakes, try to use a tone that will create good will for yourself and your organization.

Compare the impression made by a positive and a negative tone:

Negative tone	You failed to read the instructions at the top of the form. If you had read them, you would have signed the back of the form on the appropriate line. Without this signature, your application for a patent cannot be processed.
Positive tone	We will gladly process your patent application. Please sign the back of the enclosed form on line 28 and return it to us.

The negative example does not create good will; it points out the reader's mistake instead of offering a way to remedy that mistake. Careless, writer-oriented language may lead readers to make incorrect assumptions. Figure 18.7 gives you some tips for choosing words and phrases that will help readers to perceive your messages as you intend them.

▶Principle 4: Determine the Most Effective Approach for Your Readers

Letters, memos, and e-mail present a message directly or indirectly (Dragga).

The Direct Approach

In most of your letters, memos, and e-mail, you will use the direct approach. This approach helps readers to find the purpose of your correspondence quickly:

In the First Paragraph: Present the Main Message
- Tell readers why you are writing.

In the Middle Paragraph(s): Explain the Main Message
- Explain the main message presented in the first paragraph.
- Present necessary details about the main message.

In the Final Paragraph: Close the Correspondence
- Tell readers if and when they or you will act next.
- Tell readers, if necessary, what to do.
- State where readers can call, write, or e-mail to ask questions, send information, and so on.

Figure 18.7

Tips for Choosing
Reader-Oriented
Words and Phrases in
Correspondence

Avoid words and phrases that point out readers' mistakes in a negative tone or a tone that makes readers feel inferior or ignorant.
• You neglected to read . . . • We cannot believe that you did not observe . . . • You failed to notify . . . • You ignored the instructions . . . • We fail to see how you could possibly . . . • We cannot understand how . . . • We are at a loss to know how you . . .
Avoid phrases that demand or insist that readers act. (Demanding or insisting that readers act often backfires, causing readers to resist or ignore your demand.)
• You should . . . • You ought to . . . • We must insist that you . . . • We must request that you . . .
Avoid implying that your readers are lying.
• You claim that . . . • Your letter (memo, e-mail) implies that . . . • You insist that . . .
Avoid ambiguous words and phrases that may sound fine to you but may make readers feel inferior.
• No doubt . . . • Obviously . . . • You will of course . . . • Of course, you understand . . .
Avoid impersonal and inflated words and phrases and "business-ese" that your readers may perceive as pompous, insincere, or overused.
• Your cooperation in this matter will be greatly appreciated. (Instead, use "I appreciate your help.") • We are cognizant of the fact that . . . (Instead, use "We know that . . .") • Please endeavor to ascertain . . . (Instead, use "Please try to find out . . .")
Avoid negative words when possible, especially when referring to readers, their actions, or their requests.

impossible	unfortunate	unable
will not	inferior	regret
misfortune	fail	neglect
wrong	overlook	deny
difficulty	complaint	inconvenient

Source: Adapted from the work of Elizabeth Tebeaux.

You can adapt the direct approach for most correspondence situations. The letter shown in Figure 18.8 incorporates it in the following ways:

- A subject line specifically states the subject of the letter.
- The first paragraph states the main message or purpose of the letter.
- The middle paragraphs explain the main message by including specific, researched facts to support the writer's request.

The Indirect Approach

When you use the indirect approach, you delay or buffer the main message until you have graciously opened the letter and explained the message:

In the First Paragraph: Buffer the Message
- Begin with a buffer—a positive or neutral statement. A buffer may help readers to better receive to the message, especially if the message is negative.

In the Middle Paragraph(s): Explain and Then State the Message
- Explain the message. For instance, state the reason for a refusal or rejection. By properly explaining the message, you prepare readers for the negative news.
- State the message.
- Suggest an alternative or remedy if possible when the message is negative. By suggesting an alternative or remedy, you may be able to keep the good will of your readers and show that you want to meet their needs.

In the Final Paragraph: Close the Correspondence
- End the correspondence with a gracious statement.

Most writers rarely use this approach, but it can be appropriate when the news is not urgent or doesn't require readers to respond or act. This approach may also be appropriate in correspondence with international readers who may be accustomed to a less direct approach than is common in American business (Sims and Guice).

Before you use the indirect approach, consider whether it is an ethically appropriate choice for the situation. The indirect approach can inappropriately obscure information. It also can mislead some readers into thinking that the message is good because the gracious, usually positive opening delays the bad news. Readers who read no further than the opening may misinterpret the purpose of the correspondence. Thus, before using the indirect approach, carefully consider your readers and how they are likely to read the message.

The letter shown in Figure 18.9 illustrates the indirect approach:

- The first paragraph makes a positive statement.
- The second paragraph explains the main message before directly stating that message, and it offers an alternative (reapplying for the intern position next year).
- The final paragraph makes a gracious closing statement.

| **Figure 18.8** | A Letter Incorporating the Direct Approach |

402 Summer Court
Carrollton, TX 75007
June 11, 2002

Mrs. Norma Rowland
Denton County Appraisal District
3911 Morse Street
Denton, TX 76202-3816

Subject: Appraisal of block 5, lot 15, in Villages of Indian Creek phase 1

Dear Mrs. Rowland:

The writer tells the reader why he is writing. → I am requesting that you reconsider the 2002 appraisal of my home, 402 Summer Court in Carrollton. I have included information from the 2002 Dallas County appraisal and a market analysis by a local realtor. Based on this information, I request that you consider appraising the home between $101,300 and $105,352.

The Dallas County Appraisal

The writer explains the main message presented in the first paragraph. He also presents details about the message. → Dallas County appraised my home as follows in 2001 and 2002.

	Total Value	Improvements	Land	Sq. ft.	$ per sq. ft.
2001	$103,220	$86,220	$17,000	2,030	51
2002	$99,820	$84,820	$15,000	2,030	49

Denton County appraised my home as follows in 2001 and 2002.

	Total Value	Improvements	Land	Sq. ft.	$ per sq. ft.
2001	$106,896	$72,896	$34,000	2,170	49
2002	$122,931	$83,831	$39,100	2,170	56

As the above tables show, Denton County increased the appraisal by $16,035 while Dallas decreased the appraisal by $3,400. This increase in the appraised value is especially puzzling since similar homes in our neighborhood have not sold for more than $98,000.

The Market Analysis

A local realtor with Providence Reality, Ms. Ellen Babcock, reports that the price per square foot should be between $48.59 and $52.00 for our home. Ms. Babcock reports that similar homes in this neighborhood have not sold for more than $52.00 per square foot. As the tables in the above section show, the 2002 Denton County appraisal is $4.00 more per square foot than the upper end of the range reported by Ms. Babcock.

The writer closes the letter by offering to supply documents or to answer questions. The writer tells the reader how to contact him. → I will be happy to supply documents from the Dallas appraisal or the realtor. If you would like these documents or have questions, please contact me at (972) 555-4302 or at the above address.

Sincerely,

William W. Sims

William W. Sims

Figure 18.9 A Letter Incorporating the Indirect Approach

Independent's Research, Incorporated
1010 West Main • Los Alamos, New Mexico 87890 • (505) 565-3000

May 16, 2002

Ms. Lisa Jackson
402A Summer Court
Edwardsville, IL 67843

Dear Ms. Jackson:

The first paragraph includes a positive statement about the reader.

Last week, we told you that we were recommending you for a summer intern position with our Research and Development Department. Your excellent background and education would allow you and us to benefit from your interning.

The writer explains the main message in the first sentence and then presents the message in the second and third sentences. The final sentence suggests an alternative.

Last week, the board of directors announced a hiring freeze for all positions until the end of the year. We hoped this freeze would not include the internship positions, but sadly it does. Therefore, we will not be able to offer you an internship this summer. The board feels certain that these intern positions will once again be available next summer. Since you are currently a sophomore, please reapply next year.

The letter concludes with a gracious statement.

We appreciate your interest in our company and look forward to your application next year.

Sincerely,

Peggy Fagner

Peggy Fagner
Manager, Recruitment

The following tips will help you decide whether the direct or indirect approach is the appropriate choice:

> ### Tips for Selecting the Direct or Indirect Approach
>
> - **If your readers expect the bad news, use the direct approach.** Since your readers expect the bad news, put it in the first paragraph. The readers may assume that the news is now good if you move it to the second paragraph.
> - **If your readers may read only the first paragraph or skim the correspondence, use the direct approach (Locker 229).** The indirect approach may mislead readers—they may not see the main message and may misinterpret the purpose of the correspondence.
> - **If you know that your readers will resist the news or "won't take no for an answer," use the direct approach (Locker 230).** In these situations, the indirect approach may mislead readers into thinking that they can persuade you or your organization to change the news or the "answer."
> - **If the news is urgent or if you have sent the message repeatedly, use the direct approach.** If you have repeatedly sent a message to readers and they have not responded or if they have not responded as you intended, put the main message in the first paragraph. With the indirect approach, the readers may again ignore your message or may not respond as you intend.

▶Principle 5: Use an Appropriate Format

Letters, memos, and most e-mail have basic formats that are appropriate in any business setting. If your organization has its own formats for letters, memos, and e-mail, use those formats.

Letters

The three basic formats for letters are *block style* (see Figures 18.10 and 18.11), *modified block style* (see Figures 18.12 and 18.13), and *AMS Simplified style* (see Figure 18.14; "AMS" stands for Administrative Management Society). In letters in each of these formats, most of these elements are standard:

- **Inside address.** The address of the writer or the writer's organization, usually preprinted on the letterhead.
- **Date.** The date the writer completes and/or mails the letter.
- **Outside address.** The reader's address.

THE READER'S CORNER

Early Snail Mail

 Postal systems developed independently around the ancient world—Egypt, China, Rome, Inca, Maya—as a means of governing extensive empires. The Romans learned about the Chinese post-house relay system from Greek historians and refined this system to the point where couriers could cover 170 miles a day—a speed not duplicated until the 1800s. The uncertain political climate of the Middle Ages made extensive postal systems impossible in Western Europe. Instead, independent kings, city-states, religious orders, and universities all maintained their own private corps of messengers. The rise of international commerce during the late Middle Ages, however, spurred the growth of business correspondence. The great Italian commercial centers of Florence, Genoa, and Siena developed regular postal exchanges among themselves; Venice sent mail to Constantinople, a city considered beyond the European frontier at the time. Gutenberg's printing press (c. 1450) greatly increased the volume of this mail, the carrying of which became a profitable business, and also led eventually to standardized rates and increasingly speedy and frequent deliveries. By the late nineteenth century, messengers delivered mail several times a day in some European and American cities. The increasingly commercial use of e-mail may soon transform postal systems around the world once more.

- **Subject or reference line.** A subject line tells readers what the letter is about. A reference line refers readers to the date of previous correspondence or to the project, order, or account mentioned in the letter. Subject lines are often preceded by "subject" and reference lines by "re." These lines are optional in the block and modified block styles; a subject line is required for the AMS Simplified style.

- **Salutation or greeting.** "Dear" followed by the reader's name (or official title if you don't know the reader's name) and a colon—for example,

  Dear Mr. Sampson:
  Dear Personnel Director:

  Always use a nonsexist salutation. When you don't know the reader's name, using "Dear Sir" or "Dear Madam" is inappropriate. If you don't know the gender of your reader, use the AMS Simplified style and omit the salutation (see Figure 18.14), or use the reader's title in the salutation. Also, avoid "To whom it may concern"; this salutation is unprofessional.

- **Body.** The text of the letter.

- **Complimentary closing.** Expressions such as "Sincerely" or "Best regards."

- **Signature of the writer.**

- **Signature block.** The writer's name and title.

| Figure 18.10 | A Letter in Block Style on Letterhead |

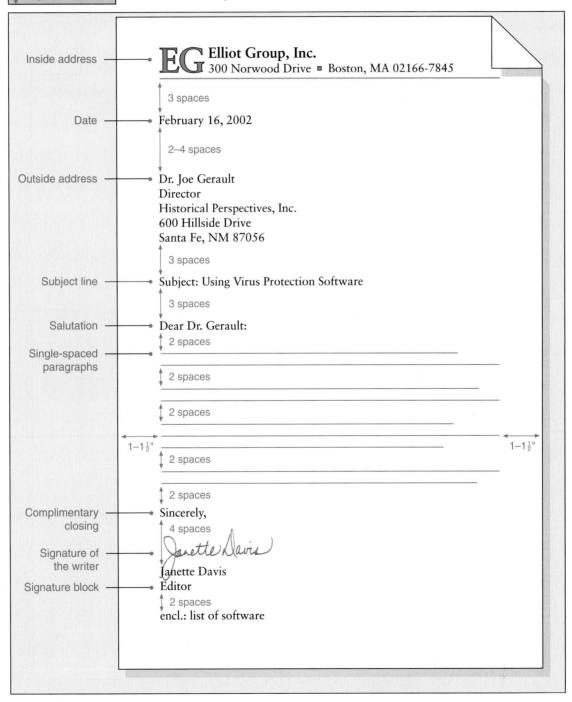

Inside address

EG **Elliot Group, Inc.**
300 Norwood Drive ▪ Boston, MA 02166-7845

3 spaces

Date — February 16, 2002

2–4 spaces

Outside address — Dr. Joe Gerault
Director
Historical Perspectives, Inc.
600 Hillside Drive
Santa Fe, NM 87056

3 spaces

Subject line — Subject: Using Virus Protection Software

3 spaces

Salutation — Dear Dr. Gerault:

2 spaces

Single-spaced
paragraphs

2 spaces

2 spaces

1–1½" _____ 1–1½"

2 spaces

2 spaces

Complimentary
closing — Sincerely,

4 spaces

Signature of
the writer — *Janette Davis*
Janette Davis

Signature block — Editor

2 spaces

encl.: list of software

| ▼ **Figure 18.11** | A Letter in Block Style Without Letterhead |

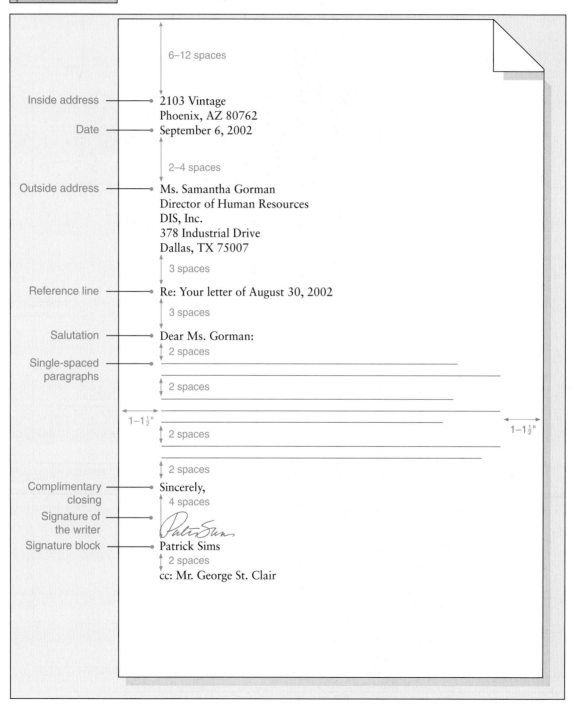

| **Figure 18.12** | A Letter in Modified Block Style on Letterhead |

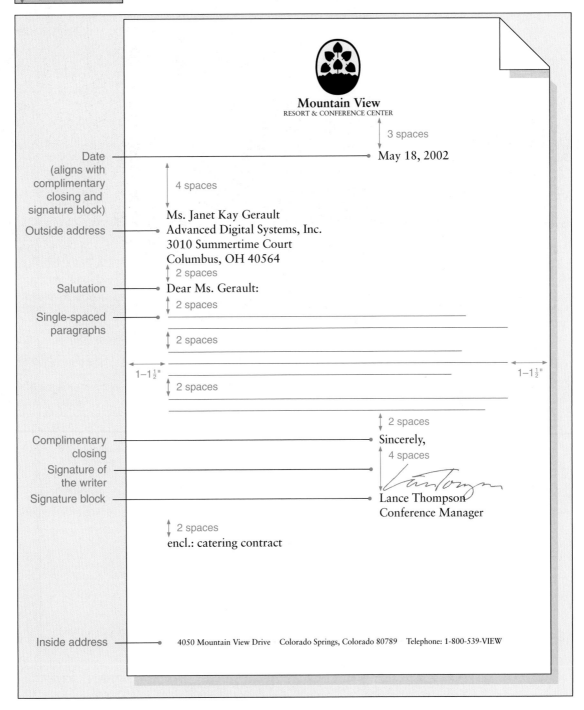

Mountain View
RESORT & CONFERENCE CENTER

3 spaces

Date
(aligns with
complimentary
closing and
signature block) — May 18, 2002

4 spaces

Outside address —
Ms. Janet Kay Gerault
Advanced Digital Systems, Inc.
3010 Summertime Court
Columbus, OH 40564

2 spaces

Salutation — Dear Ms. Gerault:

2 spaces

Single-spaced
paragraphs

2 spaces

1–1½"   1–1½"

2 spaces

2 spaces

Complimentary
closing — Sincerely,

4 spaces

Signature of
the writer

Signature block — Lance Thompson
Conference Manager

2 spaces

encl.: catering contract

Inside address — 4050 Mountain View Drive   Colorado Springs, Colorado 80789   Telephone: 1-800-539-VIEW

Figure 18.13   A Letter in Modified Block Style Without Letterhead

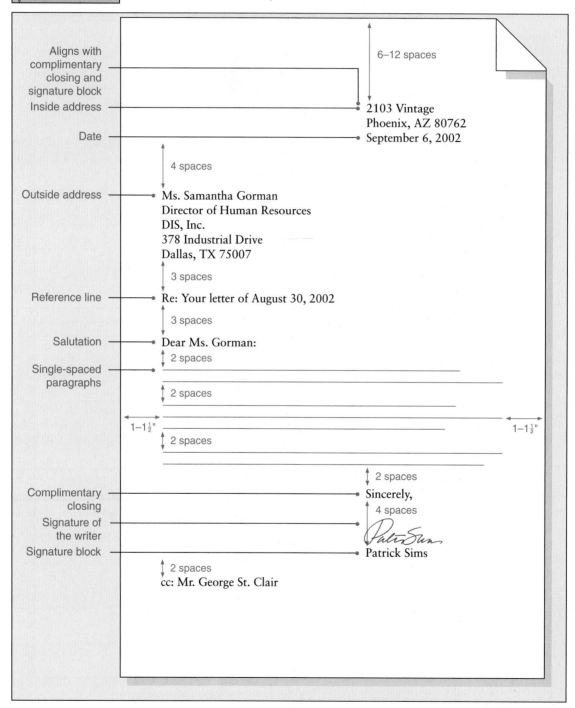

Figure 18.14   A Letter in AMS Simplified Style Without Letterhead

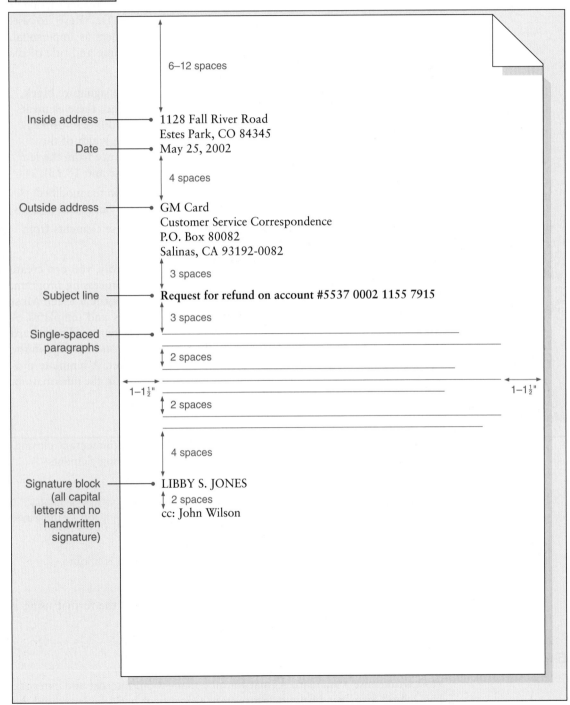

The AMS Simplified style omits the salutation, the complimentary closing, and the signature. This format is useful when you don't know the reader's name or you don't know which courtesy title (Ms., Mrs., Mr., Dr., Rev.) to use. However, the AMS Simplified style may strike some readers as impersonal. Therefore, whenever possible, take the time to find the name and title of the reader. The three formats differ in the following ways:

- **Position of the date, the complimentary closing, and the signature block.** In letters set up in block or AMS Simplified formats, place these elements flush against the left margin. In letters set up in modified block format, indent these elements from one-half to two-thirds of the width of the page. Be sure to indent all three elements the same distance from the left margin, so that they align on the page (see Figures 18.12 and 18.13).
- **Paragraph indentation.** Indenting paragraphs is optional in the modified block format. Do not indent paragraphs in block or AMS Simplified formats.
- **Use of salutation and complimentary closing.** Omit these elements from letters in AMS Simplified format.

Once you decide which formats you will use most frequently, you can create templates or use wizards for these formats in your word-processing program, so you won't have to re-create the format each time you write a letter. Most word-processing programs have letter and memo wizards and templates. A **wizard** creates a letter or memo according to your preferences. The wizard guides you through the process by asking you questions; you then type in the information that you want to appear in the memo or letter. A **template** provides the format for the letter or memo, and you simply fill in the information.

Memos

Unlike a letter, a memo does not include a salutation, complimentary closing, and writer's signature. Instead, a memo includes the following elements:

- **Date on which the memo is written.**
- **"To" line.** The name and possibly the title or department of the reader.
- **"From" line.** The name, possibly the title or department of the writer, and the writer's handwritten initials.
- **Subject line.** A phrase that tells readers what the memo is about.
- **Body.** The text of the memo.

Figure 18.15 presents a typical memo. The writer created the format using a template in a word-processing program.

E-Mail

Most writers use a standard format for all e-mail—both internal and external. This hybrid format is likely to incorporate elements of both the letter and the

Figure 18.15   A Standard Memo Format

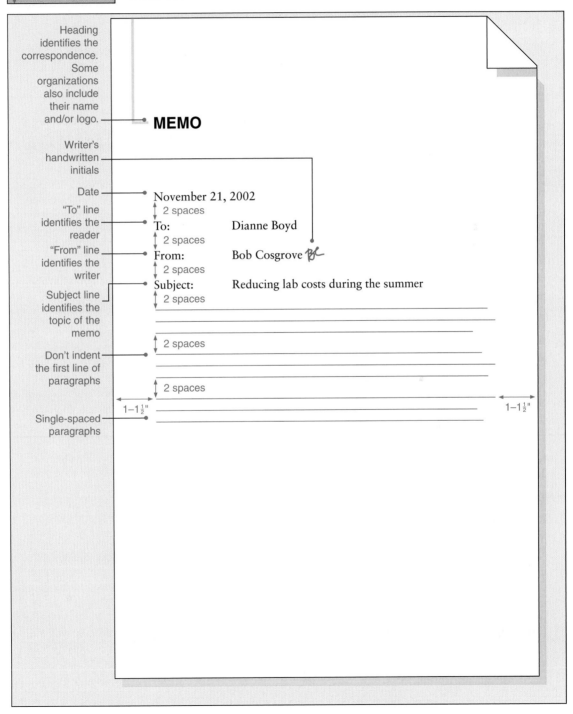

Heading identifies the correspondence. Some organizations also include their name and/or logo. —

MEMO

Writer's handwritten initials

Date — November 21, 2002
‡ 2 spaces

"To" line identifies the reader — To: Dianne Boyd
‡ 2 spaces

"From" line identifies the writer — From: Bob Cosgrove
‡ 2 spaces

Subject line identifies the topic of the memo — Subject: Reducing lab costs during the summer
‡ 2 spaces

‡ 2 spaces

Don't indent the first line of paragraphs

‡ 2 spaces

1–1½″

Single-spaced paragraphs

1–1½″

TAKING IT INTO THE WORKPLACE

E-Mail and Netiquette

"Many of us regard our e-mail merely as a modernization of lunchroom gab and not as formal business communication. Lawyers, however, have a different opinion, and they now have access to an abundance of people's own words that they can use against them. Just ask Bill Gates—during his recent anti-monopoly woes, the United States Department of Justice used Microsoft's own internal e-mails against the company."

—David J. Rogers, MIS Manager, and Monica C. Perri, Senior Technical Editor (11)

Like face-to-face conversations, e-mail allows for spontaneous responses and feedback (Lakoff; Ong). E-mail writers who misuse this spontaneity often misspell words and inappropriately use lowercase or capital letters; they may also use emoticons (faces created with type such as :-) to indicate emotions or facial expressions). When you begin working for an organization, read the e-mail of others before you send your own e-mail. Determine the level of formality expected. Does the e-mail read like a letter or memo? If it does, then use a more formal tone. If the writers use a less formal tone, then use a less formal tone. Regardless of the tone, follow these guidelines of netiquette (etiquette on a network):

- **Include an informative, specific subject line.** Most readers use the subject line to decide if or when to read e-mail. If the subject line is not informative or specific, your readers may simply ignore your e-mail.
- **Make messages easy to read and paragraphs short.** Use upper- and lowercase letters. Skip lines between paragraphs, and keep them short.
- **Make your messages brief and put the main message in the first paragraph.** Include only the information readers need, so they don't have to scroll through irrelevant or unnecessary information to find the main message.

- **Use a polite tone—don't flame.** Flaming is sending rude or angry e-mail messages. If an e-mail message angers you or if you are angry, wait awhile before responding or writing.
- **Send messages only when you have something to say—don't send "junk mail."** Unnecessary or uninformative e-mail wastes readers' time.
- **Remember that e-mail is permanent.** Most organizations archive all e-mail written by their employees. Organizations back up the e-mail and store it on tape; so don't write anything in e-mail that you wouldn't put in print or want others to read.
- **Copy and send e-mail only when you have the writer's permission.** Before you copy and send another person's e-mail, get the writer's permission. The writer may want the message to remain private.
- **Proofread your messages.** Even when e-mail is informal, it shouldn't be sloppy. Proofread to eliminate spelling, grammar, and style errors.
- **Remember that your e-mail represents you and your organization.** Incorrect punctuation, spelling errors, and grammatical errors make you and your organization look sloppy. If your e-mail includes these types of errors, readers may think you don't pay attention to details.

Assignment

Many organizations prohibit employees from using e-mail at work for nonbusiness issues. Interview representatives from at least two organizations and ask them the following questions. Report your findings in an e-mail to your instructor.

- Does your organization have a policy governing e-mail? If so, would you share a copy with me?
- Does the policy allow employees to send and receive personal e-mail? Why or why not?

memo (see Figure 18.16). Many formal e-mails include these elements:

- **Name and e-mail address of the writer.** Most e-mail software automatically includes the e-mail address of the writer. This element usually follows "From."
- **Date on which the e-mail is sent.** E-mail software automatically includes the date and usually the time that the writer sends a message.
- **Name and e-mail address of the reader.** This element usually follows "To."
- **Subject.** A phrase that tells readers what the e-mail is about.
- **Optional greeting.** Many writers will include an optional greeting such as "Dear Jim," "Jim," or even "Dear Mr. Jackson."
- **Body.** The text of the e-mail message.
- **Signature block.** Sometimes called a "signature" in e-mail software, this element includes the writer's name and possibly the writer's title, company or organization, mailing address, telephone number, fax number, and e-mail address. With most e-mail software, you can create an electronic signature that you can easily insert into your messages. The software allows you to customize the signature. For example, some e-mail software will allow you to insert your business card into your e-mail.

▶**Conclusion**   Letters, memos, and e-mail are tools to get work done. Before you send correspondence to your reader, ask yourself these questions:

1. Is it reader oriented? Have you considered the reader's interests?
2. Is it tactful? Are you courteous? Have you put yourself in the reader's place?
3. Is it clear and concise? Do your sentences generally contain no more than one main idea? Are these ideas linked with strong transitions? Do you avoid technical terms that may not be clear to your reader?
4. Is it forceful and friendly? Do you generally use a "personal" subject ("I" or "we" as opposed to "the Company") and the active voice? Have you eliminated "negative" words?
5. Is it conversational? Do you avoid "commercialese" and "business English" and use words and phrases from your everyday speaking vocabulary?
6. Is it helpful? Have you anticipated and met the reader's needs? Have you given the reader useful information he or she may not have expected?
7. Have you affected your reader agreeably? Have you created good will for your company?

If you can answer "yes" to each of these questions, you have written an effective letter.[1]

Although these questions first appeared in 1961 and applied to letters, you can apply them to any correspondence.

---

[1] Adapted from Effective Letters Program (n.p.: New York Life Insurance Company, 1961). Copyright 1961 New York Life Insurance Company. Used by permission.

Figure 18.16

A Formal E-Mail
Format with Signature
Block and Optional
Greeting

From: "Debbie Botsford" <dbots@txi.com>
To: "Don Price" <don_price@txi.com>
Sent: Wednesday, February 15, 2002 1:12 PM
Subject: Problem with the eaton.menu program

Optional → Don,
greeting

I found a "bug" in our program. Some users found that they
Main message → had documents that had been created in Qoffice, but the program did not select them. Evidently, the program didn't select
them because the documents failed the file test.

2 spaces →

While talking with Jeff Seagraves, I learned that Jeff had used
these files in an environment other than Qoffice. When a document is altered in another environment, it loses its document
characteristics and becomes a "hybrid document" that no
longer tests out as "data."

2 spaces →

This problem could just be an isolated one, but I wanted you to
be aware of it. If you would like me to investigate the problem,
please let me know.

Signature → Debbie Botsford
block   Computer Specialist III
TXI, Inc.
2600 West Olive
Phoenix, AZ 84902
(302) 555-5409
dbots@txi.com

WORKSHEET | ## for Writing Reader-Oriented Letters, Memos, and E-Mail

▶ **Principle 1: Determine the Objectives of Your Letter, Memo, or E-Mail**
- What is the purpose of the correspondence? What do you want or expect it to accomplish?
- What action, if any, do you expect your readers to take after reading the correspondence?
- What do you expect readers to know after reading the correspondence?

▶ **Principle 2: Find Out About Your Readers and How They Will Perceive Your Message**
- Who will read the correspondence? Will more than one person read it?
- What are the readers' positions and responsibilities? How might their positions and responsibilities affect how they perceive your message?

- If the readers are external, what is their relationship to you and your organization? How will this relationship affect how they perceive your message?
- What do the readers know about the subject of the correspondence?

▶ **Principle 3: Use a Reader-Oriented Tone**
- Have you avoided words that point out readers' mistakes in a negative tone and words that may make readers feel inferior or ignorant?
- Have you avoided phrases that demand or insist that readers act?
- Have you avoided words that imply that readers are lying and impersonal, inflated words that readers may perceive as pompous or insincere?
- Have you avoided ambiguous words and phrases that sound fine to you but may make readers feel inferior?
- Have you avoided negative words, especially when referring to readers or to their actions or requests?
- Have you used a tactful tone?

▶ **Principle 4: Determine the Most Effective Approach for Your Readers**
- Is the approach that you have selected appropriate?
- If you have selected the indirect approach, is the choice ethical? Is this approach likely to mislead readers?

▶ **Principle 5: Use an Appropriate Format**
- For a letter, have you
  - Included all the appropriate standard elements for the readers and for the chosen format?
  - Included a complete inside and outside address and a date?
  - Used an appropriate salutation (greeting) for the block or modified block format?
  - Included an informative subject line for the AMS Simplified format? If you've used the AMS Simplified format, is that format appropriate for your readers?
- For a memo, have you
  - Included the date?
  - Identified the reader?
  - Included your name?
  - Used an informative, specific subject line?
- For e-mail, have you
  - Included an informative, specific subject line?
  - Included a signature block to identify you and/or your organization?
  - Identified (in the signature block) the information that readers need to contact you by telephone, e-mail, fax, and traditional mail?

► **E X E R C I S E S**

1. Revise these sentences to improve their tone. Improve the clarity and conciseness of the sentences when necessary.

   a. We are sorry that we cannot fill your order for our product. We get so many orders for our product that we find it impossible to fill them all.

   b. You understand, of course, that we cannot credit your account for the price of the unused plane ticket.

   c. We are searching for the faulty parts that you claim to have mailed to us on April 26.

   d. Your cooperation in this matter will be appreciated. Thank you.

   e. We cannot understand how you could have omitted your quarterly check when you mailed your copy of the statement.

   f. Since your company has defaulted on several loan payments in the past two years, we must deny you a loan for the addition to your Seattle plant.

   g. In filling out your warranty information, you failed to fill in the serial number of the new turbine.

   h. On the mechanical drawings, you do not indicate the size of the doors—as the drawings should. Please specify a size for the doors.

   i. Understand me. The research proposal is VERY important—we don't want to just "stick in" some thoughtless, unsubstantiated budget estimates because the company will have to LIVE WITH the budget for the next three years.

   j. After reviewing the dimensions for the elevator lobbies, it seems you made an error.

2. Write an e-mail message or a memo to your instructor explaining how the direct and indirect approaches differ. Then suggest three specific writing situations where you would use the direct approach and three where you would use the indirect approach. Justify your suggestions.

3. You manage a large group of employees at a ring-manufacturing plant. One of your responsibilities is to evaluate the performance of your employees. Recently, Timothy Elam, your most senior employee, has been performing poorly. He reported to work late twelve times in the past month—on four days he was more than two hours late. His work has severely decreased in quality and quantity. Timothy doesn't seem at all interested in his work. In recent years, he was a model employee. Just two years ago, he won the award for "Most Productive Employee." Because Timothy is popular, his coworkers picked up his share of the work for several weeks; but they are no longer willing to carry his share. They are tired of Timothy's lateness and inadequate performance.

   As you prepare to evaluate Timothy, you wonder what has caused his performance to decline. You realize that his fellow employees have legitimate complaints about having to carry his share of the work, but you also realize that until recently Timothy was a valuable employee. You decide to let your manager know about the problem. Your manager will be concerned because he likes Timothy but wants the group to be productive.

   Assignment: Write a memo to your manager describing Timothy's performance and the morale problem that his performance is creating in your group. Suggest a course of action, or ask your manager for suggestions. Remember to keep the good will and respect of your manager while specifically explaining the problems that Timothy's performance is causing.

4. Write a memo to your instructor explaining why you used the direct or indirect approach in the memo in Exercise 3.

5. You are the regional manager of a large chain of retail electronics stores. Today, you received a letter from a customer, Ms. Amy Dula (3567 Rockcreek, Tampa, FL 10067). Ms. Dula writes that she purchased a new computer and color ACR monitor from the Tampa store a month ago. Two days after she purchased the computer and monitor, the monitor quit working—it showed no images. She immediately returned the monitor to the Tampa store and asked for a replacement. The manager of the store refused to replace the monitor and instead offered to repair it. Your company doesn't offer replacements— only repairs. Ms. Dula doesn't want the monitor repaired because a clerk at the Tampa store told her that several customers had returned "repaired" ACR monitors.

Assignment: Write a letter to Ms. Dula explaining the company's policy but ensuring her good will and future business.

6. You manage several project teams for an environmental engineering firm. Recently, many members of the project teams have been charging personal expenses to their corporate charge cards. Several team members have been unable to pay for these expenses when the statements are due. When the members pick up their charge cards each year, they receive a copy of the company policy for using corporate charge cards for personal expenses. The policy reads as follows: "You may use your corporate charge card for travel and other business-related expenses during the year. You may not use your card for personal expenses such as meals, gifts, and personal travel."

Assignment: Write a memo to your project teams restating the policy and explaining that the firm will take the card away from any employees who misuse it.

7. Think of a service, procedure, or policy that your college or university should change. Write a memo or e-mail message to the appropriate official at your college or university suggesting the change.

8. Think of a service or product with which you have recently experienced problems. Write a letter to the appropriate person about the problems, and ask for an appropriate remedy. If you cannot find the name of the appropriate person, use the AMS Simplified style (see Figure 18.14).

9. Log on to the Web. Find the address of a company or government agency that may have sample materials or information that you need for a class project. Write an e-mail to this company or agency requesting such information or materials. Print a copy of your e-mail for your instructor.

10. You are the network manager of the computer network for your company.[2] Over the past few weeks, many users have tied up the network by failing to log off; by using the Web to download graphics for personal use during peak business hours; and by surfing the Web for personal business during regular business hours. When users fail to log off, other users can't log on during peak hours while an open network account sits idle. The downloaded graphics and surfing consume enormous amounts of

---

[2] The idea for this exercise came from John Pollard, one of my graduate students.

memory on the network server, slowing the speed of the network responses.

You have sent several e-mails to all network users about this problem; but the number of users failing to log off has not lessened. Yesterday, you confiscated a downloaded and printed graphic of Mickey and Minnie Mouse and of the president's dog from the White House. Today, two top-level managers could not log on to the Web between 11 A.M. and 1 P.M. because employees were downloading graphics and surfing the Web for personal business.

You are unusually frustrated and angry. You write the following e-mail to all network users:

Today, two top-level mangers could not take care of company business between 11:00 and 1:00 because the network was saturated with users surfing the Web and downloading and printing graphics for personal use. During the past week during regular business hours, I have confiscated printouts—in color—of the President's dog, Mickey and Minnie Mouse, and the Baywatch crew. I will say it again: IT IS AGAINST COMPANY POLICY TO SURF THE WEB OR TO DOWNLOAD AND PRINT GRAPHICS FOR PERSONAL USE DURING REGULAR BUSINESS HOURS. In the future, I will permanently log off all users who fail to log off when they leave the office or who download and print graphics for personal use.

The message is direct, abrupt, and writer oriented. You mean the threat humorously; however, your message offends several employees.

Assignment: This assignment has two parts:

a. Write an e-mail to all employees retracting your "humorous" threat and explaining the company's Web policies. Make the message reader oriented and, when possible, positive. (If you don't have access to e-mail, write a memo.)

b. Write a memo to your manager explaining the problems the network users are creating and the "threatening" e-mail message that you sent to all network users. Explain to your manager how you are smoothing out the situation, and ask your manager for suggestions for solving these network problems.

> **CASE STUDY**

A "Mixed-Up" Situation[3]

Background

You are the customer service manager for Kitchen Wizard, Inc. Your company manufactures small kitchen appliances such as blenders, food processors, and mixers. Yesterday you received a letter and package from Joanna Logan. The text of her letter appears in Figure 18.17. Ms. Logan evidently has not read her warranty or the owner's manual that she received with her mixer. The manual clearly states that users should not allow food to get into the motor housing. The company expects that some dust from flour and powdered sugar and dried dough on occasion will creep into the housing. However, allowing bread dough to rise in the mixer is clearly not a normal or appropriate use for the mixer. The manual also clearly tells the users not to immerse the motor in water. This warning also appears on the mixer. By immersing the mixer in water, users not only damage the motor, they could also electrocute themselves if the mixer is plugged into an electrical outlet.

You want to keep Ms. Logan's business—after all, she sent you cookies (and the cookies were really quite tasty!). However, her warranty is no longer valid because she has immersed the mixer in water and she has used the mixer for letting bread dough rise. You now must write Ms. Logan explaining that you will not repair the mixer—it can't be repaired—and that you can't give her a new mixer. However, you have decided to give her a coupon for 40 percent off a new mixer.

Assignment

Write a letter to Ms. Logan explaining why you cannot repair or replace her mixer. Remember to tell her about the coupon and to use an appropriate tone.

---

[3]Adapted from Brenda R. Sims, *Technical Writing: Examples and Exercises* (Denton: U of North Texas P, 1995).

May 15, 2002

Customer Service Manager
Kitchen Wizard, Inc.
36789 Industrial Blvd.
Houston, Texas 77843

Dear Customer Service Manager:

I have enclosed my Kitchen Wizard mixer, model 69B. I bought the mixer 3 years ago at
Smith Hardware in Ennis, Texas. I have enclosed the registration card and warranty for the
mixer. Last week, the mixer stopped working. I took the cover off the motor to see if it was
clogged from flour, powdered sugar, or bread dough. (When I make bread, I let the bread
dough rise in the mixing bowl on the mixer stand. When the bread rises to the motor
casing, I know that it has doubled. Sometimes I get to talking on the telephone and let the
bread rise too high and a little bread dough gets into the motor.) The motor had a lot of
dried bread dough and powdered sugar in it. (I also make a lot of cookies that call for
powdered sugar. Sometimes when I dump 6 cups of powdered sugar into the mixing bowl
and turn on the mixer at high speed, the powdered sugar gets into the motor and on the
ceiling and walls. It makes a big mess, but the cookies are great. I have also enclosed some
of these cookies for you to sample.)

I cleaned the motor well. I soaked it in hot soapy water for several hours and then dried the
motor with my shop vac. However, now the mixer won't turn on. Please repair the mixer
since it is still under warranty and return it to me in the same box. If you can't repair it, I
will happily accept a new mixer. Enjoy the cookies.

Best regards,

Joanna Logan
Expert Baker

P.S.: If you like the cookies, let me know and I'll send you the recipe.

Enclosure

19

Writing Reader-Oriented Job Correspondence

Nicole will graduate from college in three months. She is excited about finding a job in her chosen field and beginning her career, but first she has to find that job. Nicole realizes that all the jobs she applies for will require a résumé—even those that she learns about at her university career placement center. For jobs that she discovers for herself, she will also need to write a letter of application, or cover letter, to accompany her résumé.

Like Nicole, you soon will graduate and look for a job. This chapter presents five principles to help you locate job opportunities and then to write appropriate job correspondence before and after the interview process.

▶Principle 1: Consider Various Methods for Locating Job Opportunities

To locate job opportunities in your field, you can use several methods:

- **Contact your college or university placement center.** Most colleges and universities have career-planning and placement centers that help graduating seniors and recent graduates find jobs. These placement centers link companies, organizations, and their recruitment officers with qualified prospective employees. Most placement centers require that you register with them before you can interview. As part of the registration procedure, you probably will need to create a dossier (or file) that includes an information sheet about you and your job interests, your résumé, and your college or university transcripts. In your dossier, you also may include samples of your work and other information that may interest potential employers. After receiving your dossier, the placement center will give copies of it to the recruitment officers. The recruitment officers will use the placement center to set up interviews on campus. You will want to consider using your college's or university's placement center because it is free, simple, and convenient.

▶ To learn more about writing a letter of application, see Principle 4, page 612.

- **Respond to job advertisements in print publications.** You may find job advertisements in the following print publications: newspapers (especially the Sunday classified sections in large city newspapers), technical journals, and public-relations catalogs (such as *College Placement Annual*). When responding to these job advertisements, you will want to send a letter of application with your résumé.

- **Respond to job advertisements published on an organization's Web site.** You may find job advertisements on an organization's Web site. These advertisements will probably tell you how to apply. They may instruct you to fill out an electronic form, to e-mail your application, to send a paper letter of application and résumé, or to apply in person.

- **Respond to advertisements and/or post your résumé on online job boards.** Job boards are Web sites sponsored by Internet service providers, federal agencies, professional organizations, and private organizations. Job boards function in two ways:

▶ To learn more about preparing and sending an electronic résumé, see Principle 3, page 609.

- Some job boards only list positions. You then can apply for those positions by mailing or e-mailing your résumé and letter of application.
- Some job boards allow you to submit your résumé electronically so employers can search for qualified candidates and contact them directly.

- **Network with others in your field, with people who know you personally, and with your professors.** Tell people in your field that you are looking for a job. Also, tell personal and family friends that you are looking for a job, and perhaps send them a copy of your résumé. These friends may have contacts to help you locate job opportunities.

- **Send out unsolicited letters of application.** If you are interested in working for a specific organization, send an unsolicited letter of application to that organization. Many organizations do not advertise job opportunities, so unsolicited letters can be effective. Unsolicited letters do have an obvious disadvantage: the organization may not have any openings when it receives your letter. However, if you are truly interested in working for a particular organization, an unsolicited letter of application may be worth your time.

- **Use professional employment agencies.** Professional employment agencies present your résumé to potential employers. They work much like a college placement center but charge a fee paid either by potential employers or by you. The fee often is a percentage of your first-year salary once you accept a job.

If you plan on using an online job board, follow these tips:

▶ **Tips for Using an Online Job Board**

- **Determine if an online job board meets your needs.** Before you post your résumé or any information on a job board, you might ask yourself these questions:
  - Who will be able to access your résumé and/or information? You might want to leave out your home address and telephone number from your information, especially if it is accessible to the general public.
  - Will the job board charge you a fee to post or to update your résumé? Some job boards charge a fee for posting your résumé, and some will charge you each time you update your résumé. Make sure that you know about the charges ahead of time. If a

(continued on next page)

job board will charge you for updating your résumé, you might consider using a free site.

- **Find out how you will know if an employer has requested your résumé.** Some job boards will notify you while others will not. If you know an employer has requested your résumé, you should follow up to find out about potential job opportunities.

- **Find out whether your current employer or manager will see your résumé.** Depending on your employer or manager, you may jeopardize your current job if he or she finds out you are searching for another position. If he or she knows you're looking for another position, use the job board. If not, you might consider using other methods for finding job opportunities.

▶ For information on search engines, see Chapter 5, "Researching Information Using Primary and Secondary Sources," page 112.

- **Use more than one online job board.** A potential employer may not see your résumé or personal information if you use only one job board. To find job boards, use a search engine; enter keywords such as "jobs" and "employment." You might also narrow your search by combining one of these general keywords with a word related to your field. For example, you might enter "jobs and engineering." Some of the more popular and larger job boards are:
  - Monster: http://www.monster.com
  - America's Job Bank: http://www.ajb.dni.us (the U.S. Department of Labor sponsors this board)
  - Career Builder: http://www.careerbuilder.com
  - After College: http://www.aftercollege.com
  - HotJobs: http://www.hotjobs.com

▶Principle 2: Determine What Information You Want Employers to Know About You

Before you put together a résumé or send out any letters of application, think specifically about what information you want employers to know about you, and think generally about what information employers want to know about potential employees. The information you provide should give potential employers a positive, accurate picture of you and what you can offer their organization.

You might begin by determining what information is likely to interest prospective employers. You might concentrate on these categories: education, work experience, activities, goals, and skills. After selecting your categories, brainstorm to create lists of information about yourself in each category (to learn about brainstorming, refer to the Web site for this book). For instance, under education, list the degree you will receive when you graduate, the date when you will receive the degree, your grade-point average, and significant projects that you completed in your major field of study.

Figure 19.1 shows the brainstorming list that Nicole created. Although she may not use all the information on her list, it gives her information to work with when she begins preparing her résumé and letter of application. To create your brainstorming list, write down any information that you think will help an employer understand you and your qualifications—information that will impress an employer.

| ▼ **Figure 19.1** | Nicole's Brainstorming List |

Education
B.S. in mechanical engineering from University of Oklahoma
  expect to graduate in August 2002
Dean's list three semesters, Fall 2000, Spring 2001, and Spring 2002
GPA—3.2

Work Experience
Internship in robotics research lab (two semesters)
  helped design robotics machinery for automated assembly lines
  used CAD in refining designs
  learned to work in a dust-free environment and to work as a team member
Trinity Pharmacy—pharmacy technician since October 1999
  began as cashier and did general cleanup of store
  operate the cash register
  enter prescription information into the computer system
  help customers needing information about over-the-counter drugs and other items in the pharmacy
Lifeguard and swimming instructor—summers since high school
  know CPR
  certified Red Cross lifeguard at YMCA pool at home
  received lifeguard of the month award four times (find out years and months)
  certified Red Cross swimming instructor
  taught private, semiprivate, and group swimming to children and adults through the YMCA
  worked frequently with children with disabilities to help them learn to swim and to be comfortable in water

Skills
  programming in C++ and Java
  have designed Web pages for YMCA; however, not very experienced here
  know computers, including statistics packages, spreadsheets, and CAD
  people skills—have learned to interact with customers and to be a team player
  work well with children

Activities
  Mortar Board, senior year
  American Society of Mechanical Engineers
  Swim team all four years—won district and national honors in platform diving

My Career Goals
  to find an engineering position in robotics

You can also consider the information that specific employers may want to know about you. If you are applying for several jobs at the same time, you may not be able to pull together this information for each potential employer. Therefore, you probably will want to prepare a résumé first, concentrating on information that will demonstrate what you offer to employers. Later, you can customize your letter of application and your résumé for each employer, including information that will particularly interest each employer or that relates directly to a specific job opportunity.

▶Principle 3: Prepare an Effective Résumé

Robert Greenly of Lockheed Martin writes that "your résumé is the first impression you make. It should be eye-catching, clearly written, and easy to read" (47). Your résumé and letter of application generally are the first information that an employer sees about you, so you want these documents to persuade employers to interview you. To write an effective résumé,

- Organize your résumé to highlight your qualifications.
- Include specific, appropriate information about your qualifications.
- Use dynamic, persuasive language that demonstrates what you can do.
- Create an eye-catching, accessible design for paper résumés.
- Use a simpler design for effective electronic or scannable résumés.

Organize Your Résumé to Highlight Your Qualifications

Once you have decided what major categories of information to include, you can determine how to organize your résumé. Think about two levels of organization:

- The overall organization of the major categories of information (education, work experience, skills, and so on)
- The local organization within these categories

For the overall organization, decide what category of information you want the employer to see first. Many recent college graduates begin with their education—possibly including college-related activities or honors—and move to work experience or skills.

After determining the overall organization, think about how you will organize the information within each category. For example, work experience is often the longest category in the résumé and, for experienced job-seekers, the most important. For this category, you can use one of two methods of organization:

- Chronological organization
- Functional organization

If you organize your résumé chronologically, you will present the information in both the work experience and the education categories in *reverse* chronological order: you will begin with your most recent or your current job or degree and end with the least recent. The résumé shown in Figure 19.2 has a chronological organization. In the education category, the writer begins with her most recent college work and ends with her least recent work. In the work experience category, she begins with her current work at the University of North Texas and Twin Eagles Restaurant and ends with her least recent work as a checker at Tom Thumb.

Most job-seekers "prefer the logical progression of a chronological résumé" (Greenly 44); and for recent college graduates or for job-seekers looking for their first career job, functional résumés generally are less effective than chronological résumés. Some job-seekers, however, need a functional résumé—one that focuses the reader's attention on the writer's marketable job skills and accomplishments rather than on a chronological listing of his or her work experience. A functional organization is especially effective in two situations:

- When you want to present your most important accomplishments or skills early in the résumé—or at least in a lead-off position within categories (Greenly 44).
- If you want to change careers and a chronological organization might undermine your search (Greenly 44).

The résumé in Figure 19.3 illustrates a functional organization. The major accomplishments category focuses on the job-seeker's skills and accomplishments in two areas—financial planning and financial analysis.

Include Specific, Appropriate Information About Your Qualifications

As you plan your résumé, select information that highlights your qualifications and will prompt employers to interview you. Include appropriate and effective information in these categories: career objective, education, work experience, skills and specialized training, and personal information. You may choose not to include all of these categories in your résumé.

Career Objective

A career objective states the kind of work you are seeking in the form of a brief phrase. For example, you might write, "Objective: Entry-level corporate marketing position." Many hiring managers consider these statements important because they indicate that the writer has goals. However, other managers find these statements limiting, especially if the statements are general or don't relate directly to the advertised job. For example, the following career objective could cause a manager to pass over a qualified job applicant: "An entry-level

> ▼ **Figure 19.2**   A Résumé with a Chronological Organization

---

Leigh Andrea Thomas

204 Oak Street
Denton, TX 76205
(817) 555-2858
lthomas@twlab.unt.edu

Objective	An entry-level corporate position in technical communication

---

Education	**University of North Texas, Denton, TX** Bachelor of Science in English August 2002 Grade Point Average: 3.5/4.0 **Advanced Courses** Online Documentation Designing Technical Documents Writing Technical Proposals Software Documentation **Baylor University, Waco, TX** Foundation Courses

---

Work Experience

The writer puts the information in reverse chronological order.

University of North Texas, Denton, TX
Assistant to the Director of Technical Communication
October 1999 to present
• Assisted director in writing proposal that resulted in a new Master's in Technical Communication and the potential of 50 new graduate students each year.
• Designed a new brochure for the Technical Communication Program.

SWB Telecommunications, Dallas, TX
Technical Writing Intern
May 2000 to September 2000, May 2001 to September 2001
• Developed a Web site describing wireless services offered by SWB.
• Assisted senior technical writer in designing and testing online documentation for switching equipment.
• Edited and proofread customer documentation for wireless telephones.

Twin Eagles Restaurant, Denton, TX
Cashier/Server
December 1999 to May 2000
• Awarded the Silver Eagle for service in February and April 1999.

Tom Thumb, Lewisville, TX
Checker
June 1998 to December 1999

Organizations	Society for Technical Communication The Freshman Council (a leadership organization) Baylor President's Council (a leadership and service organization)

| ▼ **Figure 19.3** | A Résumé with a Functional Organization |

Katherine Diane Spence
1126 Baldpate
Chicago, IL 60637
(217) 555-4678
kdspence@aol.com

Major Accomplishments ●————————————————————— The writer highlights her
major accomplishments.

Financial Planning
- Researched funding options that enabled company to achieve a 34% return on its investment.
- Developed long-range funding requirements to respond to government contracts that totaled more than $1.6 billion.
- Developed and implemented computer software for long- and short-term financial planning that saved the company 70% in labor.

Financial Analysis and Information System Design
- Worked as a research analyst for 14 years in two different industries.
- Received three awards for innovations in information system design from the Association of Financial Planners.
- Developed computer software that applies current research to practical problems of corporate finance.

Education
University of Washington—Seattle, Washington
Master of Business Administration
May 2000

University of Colorado—Boulder, Colorado
Bachelor of Science (summa cum laude)
May 1998
Major: Computer Science
Minor: Finance

Work Experience ●————————————————————— The writer includes a brief
listing of her work
experience (in reverse
chronological order) to
show employers how she
has advanced in the
company and spent her
time since earning her
MBA.

Arthur Andersen (June 2000 to present)
Chicago, Illinois
- Senior Analyst (July 2002 to present)
- System Analyst (July 2000 to July 2002)

Activities and Interests
Member, Association of Corporate Financial Planners
Amateur soccer player and coach

References available upon request

position in computer programming with the opportunity to advance into management." A broad statement like that can have unintended consequences. Reading such a statement, a potential employer might decide not to consider the applicant for a job that will not quickly lead to a management position. Résumés that omit the objective can give employers "greater flexibility in considering you for any number of peripheral positions that your experience and training qualify you for, perhaps even future openings that do not yet exist" (Greenly 43). If you decide to include a career objective, follow these guidelines:

- Use brief, specific statements directly related to the specific job for which you are applying.
- State only the position, goals, or tasks specifically stated in the job advertisement.
- Avoid general, broad statements such as "a position where I can use my programming skills."

Education

Identify your college or university degrees, naming the institution awarding the degree, its location, and the date you received or will receive the degree. If you haven't yet graduated, list the colleges or universities that you have attended beyond high school, their location, and the anticipated date of your degree. For example, a senior at San Diego State University might write

San Diego State University, San Diego, California
Bachelor of Science in Mechanical Engineering
Anticipated May 2003

In addition to listing your degree (or degrees), you can include information such as

- Major and minor courses that qualify you for the type of job you are seeking
- Academic scholarships or fellowships that you received
- A high grade-point average (above 3.0 on a 4-point scale)
- Academic honors or awards that you received as a college or university student
- Any outstanding accomplishments, such as special projects or research that you did as a student

If you list courses related to the work you are seeking, include primarily upper-level courses in your major. List courses by title, not by number. For example, if you want to mention a course in advanced automated systems, write "Advanced Automated Systems," not "MECH 4302."

THE READER'S CORNER

Ethically Challenged Résumés

Jobs in almost every profession have become very competitive. One particularly gloomy estimate is that only 1 out of 1,470 résumés put into circulation ever actually results in a job offer. Given such odds, young professionals are often tempted to tamper with the truth on their résumés. According to one survey, fully one-third of people between the ages of 15 and 30 were willing to lie on their résumés, and experts predict that the percentage of job-hunters who actually do so may make up one-third of applicants or more.[1] Such deception occurs at the most elite levels. Jean Houston, the now infamous psychologist who counseled Hillary Rodham Clinton to imagine herself in dialogue with deceased luminaries like Eleanor Roosevelt, reported on her résumé having received a doctorate in the philosophy of religion from Columbia University. Investigations,

reported in the *New York Times,* brought to light that Houston had never completed her dissertation, a requirement for the doctorate.[2] In her defense, Houston claimed that an aide had selected a résumé from the "bottom of the barrel" of résumés she kept on file. Houston's ethical lapse on her résumé, inflating her credentials, is one that résumé writers often make. Other common résumé deceits include inflating one's title or responsibilities and omitting firings or failings. Hiring managers have become more alert to the probable areas of deception and are double-checking advanced degrees, unexplained periods in employment history, and job titles. So the bottom line is—your résumé must be honest and accurate.

[1] *Working Woman* March 1996:18.
[2] *New York Times* 26 June 1996: B9.

The education category shown in Figure 19.4 includes several of the optional items along with the writer's degree information. The writer lists his grade-point average (3.7) along with a reference point (4.0). He also mentions his academic honors. Notice that he states in this section that he worked part-time to help pay for his schooling. With this format, he is highlighting his impressive achievement of earning a high grade-point average and receiving honors while holding down a job.

Work Experience

In the work experience category, use reverse chronological order, beginning with your most recent experience. Include this information:

- Name and location of the company or organization where you worked
- The years (or months if less than a year) of your work with that company or organization
- Your job title
- Verb phrases describing what you did (your job responsibilities)

As you describe your responsibilities, demonstrate that you can produce results. "The most qualified people don't always get the job. It goes to the

Education

University of New Mexico
Albuquerque, New Mexico

Degree	Bachelor of Science
Major	Mechanical Engineering
	Expected in May 2003
GPA	3.7/4.0
Honors	Dean's List (Fall 2001, Spring 2002, Fall 2002)
	Alpha Lambda Delta (Freshman Honor Society)
	Tau Beta Pi (General Engineering Society)
	Outstanding College Students of America

Worked part-time to pay for my education

person who presents himself [or herself] most persuasively in person and on paper. So don't just list where you were and what you did . . . tell *how well you did*. Were you the best salesperson? Did you cut operating costs? Give numbers, statistics, percentages, increases in sales or profits" (Simon). Describe how well you did your job.

Figures 19.5 and 19.6 illustrate how two writers approached the work experience category. In Figure 19.5, instead of using vague, unimpressive language, the writer, an experienced job-seeker, uses specific information to demonstrate how well he did his job:

Vague and unimpressive	Facilitated work teams
	Improved production
Specific and impressive	Facilitated two self-directed work teams of 26 total team members
	Reduced cycle time from 5 days to 2 days
	Saved $250,000 annually

The writer doesn't just tell prospective employers that he saved the company money or reduced the cycle time. He states the specific reduction in days and the amount saved in dollars.

The experience section in Figure 19.6 is an excerpt from a college student's résumé. This student is looking for her first job in her field. She doesn't have the extensive work experience of the writer in Figure 19.5. However, she can demonstrate how well she did the jobs she held as a student at the University of Washington. She lists her award for service at Shoreside Restaurant along with the year she received the award. She also lists her Tutor of the Semester Award. These awards and her promotion demonstrate that she did her jobs well.

Figure 19.5	A Work Experience Section Written by a Job-Seeker with Experience

Texas Instruments, Inc. Dallas, Texas

Manufacturing Facilitator (2000–present)
- Facilitated two self-directed work teams of 26 total team members performing screen printing and painting operations.
- Led screen printing team to win Gold Teaming for Excellence Award.
- Converted coating system to low VOC formulations that comply with existing air-quality standards.

Reengineering Team Leader (1996–2000)
- Reengineered screen printing work flow to eliminate non-value added effort and reduce task handoffs from one person to another. Reduced cycle time from 5 days to 2 days, increased productivity by 25%, and saved $250,000 annually.
- Received Site Quality Improvement Award two consecutive years (1999 and 2000) for reducing cycle time and improving quality.

Process Improvement Engineer of Finish and Assembly Areas (1994–1996)
- Designed and installed custom equipment and machine upgrades that reduced manual labor required by $100,000 per year.
- Improved part racking on plating line, reducing scrap by $20,000 annually.

Figure 19.6

A Work Experience Section Written by a Job-Seeker Without Experience

University of Washington   Seattle, Washington
Computer Lab Tutor   2000–present

- Received Tutor of the Semester Award (Fall and Spring 2001).
- Promoted to senior tutor. Taught new tutors the software used in the lab.
- Answered students' questions about word-processing, desktop-publishing, and statistics-software packages.
- Helped students with computer-related problems.

Shoreside Restaurant   Seattle, Washington
Server   1999–present

- Received the Outstanding Service Award (2000).

Like the writer in Figure 19.6, you may not have work experience in your field. However, you can list your summer or part-time jobs. If you were promoted or received any awards as a part of these jobs, include this information to help potential employers see that you are reliable and hardworking.

Skills and Specialized Training

Some writers include a category listing their skills or a category listing any specialized training or education they have received. These sections are most common in functional résumés. If used in a functional résumé, the skills section usually appears prominently near the beginning of the résumé and can have various headings such as "Major Accomplishments" or "Skills." Figure 19.7 shows the skills section from the résumé of a job-seeker wanting to change careers. Figure 19.8 shows a specialized training section. If you decide to use one of these categories in your résumé, include only information relevant to the type of job you are seeking.

Personal Information

You may want to include some personal information that gives readers "a glimpse of the personal you" and furthers "the image you've worked to project in the preceding sections" of the résumé (Simon). You can list any of the following information if it will enhance a prospective employers' picture of you:

- Community activities (such as volunteer work for charitable organizations, membership in community service organizations, or leadership or work with community youth organizations)
- College activities (such as membership on teams and in organizations, offices held, and awards won)
- Professional memberships—perhaps in organizations in your field, including any leadership positions you've held with the organization
- Personal interests and hobbies, especially if they relate to your qualifications
- Sports or recreational activities that you enjoy

Perhaps you've been a Girl Scout or Boy Scout leader in your community, or you've organized a blood drive for your college or university campus, or

Figure 19.7
The Skills Section of a Résumé

Skills

Management Skills
- Hired and supervised 14 employees in a $2.3 million catering business.

Communication Skills
- Trained new employees in a catering business.
- Wrote performance evaluations, designed marketing brochures, and designed the Web site for a catering business.

Teaching Skills
- Coached youth soccer, baseball, and basketball.
- Tutored math in the McKinney Independent School District and for the Collin County Boys' and Girls' Clubs.

| Figure 19.8 | The Specialized Training Section of a Résumé |

Special Training	• Business Process Engineering (Reengineering)
	• Statistical Process Control (Design of Experiments and Six Sigma Quality)
	• Structural Steel Design

you've won awards for your leadership abilities. These activities and awards show that you are a team player, that you care about your community, and that you are disciplined.

As you prepare the personal section, do not include information that might invite employers to discriminate—for example, information about your marital status, age, or health.

Use Dynamic, Persuasive Language That Demonstrates What You Can Do

The guideline for word choice in your résumé is simple: keep your writing style clear and uncluttered. Exclude extraneous information, and use dynamic, persuasive language. Follow these tips:

> ### Tips for Using Dynamic, Persuasive Language in a Résumé
>
> • **Keep the information and language simple and direct.** The employer reading your résumé may be reading hundreds of other résumés for the same job.
>
> • **State your information or qualifications directly; omit any unnecessary information.** Be brief. Give employers the information they need to know about your abilities and background—and then stop!
>
> • **Use dynamic action verbs.** Use verbs such as *saved, created, supervised, directed,* and *designed.* Avoid words and phrases that don't describe action and don't demonstrate what you have achieved and can achieve. Avoid phrases such as "My responsibilities included" or "Tasks or duties were."
>
> • **Use specific language that emphasizes your accomplishments and what you can do.** Use specific language that demonstrates what you have accomplished and what you can do. When possible, use figures as part of your specific language. Figures can effectively demonstrate your abilities.
>
> • **Use verb phrases, not sentences.** Because you want to focus on what you have accomplished and to present your information briefly, use verb phrases, not full sentences.

TAKING IT INTO THE WORKPLACE

The Electronic Job Search

"Electronic résumés are simple, fast, and efficient. With an electronic résumé we can scan the résumé into a database, so the candidate's information is available to more people and the candidate has more opportunities for securing a job. When the candidate's information is in a database, I can send it to managers throughout the company."

—Shannon Reid, Centex Construction Group

The Web offers a wealth of information for the job-seeker—information about job fairs, employers, job openings, and job hunting. Some sites, such as Monster.com, will even help you write and post your electronic résumé. An electronic résumé has several forms:

- **A résumé sent as an attachment to an e-mail.** You may attach your résumé as a word-processing file, such as a Microsoft Word file, to an e-mail message. Most employers will be able to open and read a Microsoft Word file. However, some employers may use another word-processing software program, or their e-mail software may not be able to read attached files. Look in the job advertisement; if it requests a plain-text document sent in the body of the message, don't send an attached file. Instead, put your résumé in the e-mail message.
- **A Web-based résumé.** You can post your résumé on an online job board (see page 592),

or you might post your résumé on your personal Web site—and hope that an employer sees your site. Avoid using your personal Web site as the sole means of distributing your résumé.

- **A printed résumé that an employer will scan into a database.** Even when you send employers a printed résumé, they may scan it into a database. If you send a printed résumé,
  - Use white paper
  - Don't fold or staple the résumé
  - Use a laser printer with high resolution

How do you know which form to use for your résumé? How do you know if an employer prefers an electronic or a traditional résumé? Most job ads will tell you how to submit your résumé. Some job-seekers will tell potential employers that a paper copy of their résumé is available and then send a paper copy as a backup. However, some employers may discourage sending the paper copy.

Assignment

Many job boards, Web sites, and Usenet groups provide information on preparing electronic and scannable résumés.

1. Using a search engine, gather information on writing electronic and/or scannable résumés.
2. Write an e-mail to your instructor summarizing what you learned.
3. Be sure to include complete bibliographic information about the job boards, Web sites, or Usenet groups that you used to gather information.

The following examples illustrate phrases that use dynamic, persuasive language (the action verbs appear in bold type):

Not Dynamic/Persuasive   Created a computer program for students logging into the lab.

Dynamic/Persuasive	**Designed** and **programmed** software that **reduced** the number of employees needed in the student computer labs and saved the university $16,640 annually.
Not Dynamic/Persuasive	Regional sales manager for 4 years.
Dynamic/Persuasive	Regional sales manager for 4 years with a telecommunications company. **Led** my region to **win** the top sales award for 3 consecutive years.
Not Dynamic/Persuasive	Was responsible for designing and installing custom equipment and upgrading machines.
Dynamic/Persuasive	**Designed** and **installed** custom equipment and machine upgrades that **reduced** the manual labor required by $100,000 annually.

The language—along with the design—of your résumé gives employers their first impression of you. You want that impression to be positive.

Create an Eye-Catching, Accessible Design for Paper Résumés

Design your résumé so an employer can quickly get a good idea of your important qualifications (Greenly 42). In other words, "design résumés so that employers don't have to hunt for your qualifications"; employers should be able to quickly locate your qualifications without "playing detective" (Parker 318). If they have to play detective, they may overlook or ignore your résumé. To help employers find information, create visual categories with white space, headings, type sizes, and bulleted lists.

In the résumé shown in Figure 19.9, employers can easily spot the categories of information because of the headings and the white space surrounding those headings. These headings allow employers to quickly locate information about the writer's qualifications. The writer uses boldface type and different type sizes within the categories to highlight and prioritize information. The writer also uses bulleted lists to help employers easily read about his work.

As you design your paper résumé, follow these tips:

▶ **Tips for Designing Effective Paper Résumés**

- **Use headings and subheadings to create visual categories.** Use type size to differentiate among the headings, subheadings, and text of the résumé. If you want to further differentiate the headings and subheadings from the text, use boldface type.

- **Surround the headings with enough white space for employers to easily see the headings.** Highlight the headings with white space. (See Chapter 9, "Designing Documents for Your Readers," for

(continued on page 609)

▼ **Figure 19.9**   A Well-Designed Résumé

C. Randall Harrison

310 North Edna
Lewisville, Texas 75057
(972) 555-7893

Objective	An engineering position requiring creativity, equipment design expertise, and knowledge of manufacturing methods.

Experience   **Texas Instruments, Inc.** Dallas, Texas
Manufacturing Facilitator (2000–present)
- Facilitated two self-directed work teams of 26 total team members performing screen printing and painting operations.
- Led screen printing team to win Gold Teaming for Excellence Award.
- Converted coating system to low VOC formulations that comply with existing air-quality standards.

Reengineering Team Leader (1996–2000)
- Reengineered screen printing work flow to eliminate non-value added effort and reduce task handoffs from one person to another. Reduced cycle time from 5 days to 2 days, increased productivity by 25%, and saved $250,000 annually.
- Received Site Quality Improvement Award two consecutive years (1999 and 2000) for reducing cycle time and improving quality.

Process Improvement Engineer of Finish and Assembly Areas (1994–1996)
- Designed and installed custom equipment and machine upgrades that reduced manual labor required by $100,000 per year.
- Improved part racking on plating line, reducing scrap by $20,000 annually.

Amco Manufacturing Yazoo City, Mississippi
Project Engineer (1993–1994)
- Developed agricultural tillage implements using design skills in structural steel weldments and hydraulics.

Education
- Master of Science in Agricultural Engineering (1993), Texas A&M University, College Station, Texas
- Bachelor of Science in Agricultural Engineering—Magna Cum Laude (1989), Texas A&M University, College Station, Texas

Special Training
- Business Process Engineering (Reengineering)
- Statistical Process Control (Design of Experiments and Six Sigma Quality)
- Structural Steel Design

Personal
- Work with local chapter of Habitat for Humanity to build homes.
- Avid "do-it-yourselfer" with my own woodworking and metalworking shop.

Source: Courtesy of C. Randall Harrison.

information on white space.)

- **Use bulleted lists instead of paragraphs.** You can help employers to locate information by using bulleted lists instead of paragraphs, especially in the work experience section. The paragraph and bulleted list shown in Figure 19.10 present the same information. A prospective employer glancing at the paragraph might miss the information about the Gold Teaming for Excellence Award. The bulleted list highlights the award.

- **Use only one typeface.** Many writers use a serif typeface such as Times Roman, but traditional sans-serif typefaces such as Helvetica or Tahoma are also appropriate for résumés. Whether you choose a serif or sans-serif typeface, select a typeface that is easily readable and looks professional.

- **Use 8$\frac{1}{2}$-by-11-inch white bond paper.** Use good-quality bond paper. Because some employers will scan or copy your résumé, you may want to use white paper because even off-white paper will darken the scanned image.

- **Proofread; then proofread again!** Make sure your résumé is free of grammatical, spelling, and punctuation errors. Even the smallest of punctuation errors can cost you an interview.

Use a Simpler Design for Effective Electronic or Scannable Résumés

You will organize an electronic or scannable résumé much like a printed or paper résumé. You will also include the same information. However, you will

---

▼ Figure 19.10

Comparison of Paragraph and Bulleted List Formats in a Paper Résumé

Manufacturing Facilitator
2000–present

- Facilitated two self-directed work teams of 26 total team members performing screen printing and painting operations.
- Led screen printing team to win Gold Teaming for Excellence Award.
- Converted coating system to low VOC formulations that comply with existing air-quality standards.

- -

Manufacturing Facilitator
2000–present

Facilitated two self-directed work teams of 26 total team members performing screen printing and painting operations. Led screen printing team to win Gold Teaming for Excellence Award. Converted coating system to low VOC formulations that comply with existing air-quality standards.

want to use a simpler design and to focus on nouns rather than verbs to accommodate the electronic format. Figure 19.11 is an electronic version of the résumé in Figure 19.2. The writer has used ASCII text (which includes only letters, numbers, and basic punctuation marks) and eliminated all boldface, bullets, and horizontal lines. The writer has also included a list of keywords. As you prepare your electronic or scannable résumé, follow these tips:

▶ **Tips for Preparing Effective Electronic or Scannable Résumés**

- **Include keywords an employer might use to search for qualified job candidates.** For example, if an employer is looking for a candidate with excellent oral and written communication skills, include keywords such as "communication skills" and "writing skills." If an employer is looking for someone who has experience designing Web sites, you might include keywords such as "Web site," "Web pages," "Java," or "HTML." You might even include industry-specific jargon that an employer might search for in a résumé database. Include keywords only if they refer to skills you actually have—never lie or mislead on a résumé.

- **Include nouns as keywords.** Traditional résumés focus on verbs while electronic, especially scannable, résumés focus on nouns. You will want to make sure that your résumé includes the keywords that will help employers to locate your information in a database.

- **Use a 10- to 12-point sans-serif typeface for a scannable résumé, and use ASCII text for an electronic résumé.** You might select Ariel or Tahoma. Avoid boldface, italics, underlining, special characters, and formatting such as horizontal or vertical lines and visual aids. When you save your résumé file for the electronic résumé, save it as text only.

- **Align all information on the left margin.** Don't indent or use double columns.

- **Use a line length of no more than 70 characters.** If you use a line no longer than 70 characters, the lines will appear as you intend regardless of the readers' computer equipment.

- **Use spaces instead of tabs.** The readers may have their default tabs set differently than yours.

- **Open your résumé in a text editor, such as Notepad, or e-mail your résumé to yourself before you send it to an employer.** Make sure the résumé contains only ASCII characters and verify that the formatting is correct.

| **▼ Figure 19.11** | An Electronic and Scannable Résumé |

ASCII text with no boldface or special formatting

● Leigh Andrea Thomas
204 Oak Street
Denton, TX 76205
(817) 555-2858
lthomas@twlab.unt.edu

● Objective
An entry-level corporate position in technical communication

Education
University of North Texas, Denton, TX
Bachelor of Science in English
August 2002
Grade Point Average: 3.5/4.0

Advanced Courses
Online Documentation
Designing Technical Documents
Sans-serif type ──● Writing Technical Proposals
Software Documentation

Baylor University, Waco, TX
Foundation Courses

Work Experience
University of North Texas, Denton, TX
Assistant to the Director of Technical Communication
● October 2001 to present
Assisted Director in writing proposal that resulted in a new Master's in
Text aligned at the ─● Technical Communication and the potential of 50 new graduate students
left margin each year.
● Designed a new brochure for the Technical Communication Program.

SWB Telecommunications, Dallas, TX
Technical Communication Intern
May 2000 to September 2000, May 2001 to September 2001
Developed a Web site describing wireless services offered by SWB.
Assisted senior technical writer in designing and testing online
documentation for switching equipment.
Lines have no more ─● Edited and proofread customer documentation for SWB 2000 and SWB 2020
than 70 characters wireless telephones.

(continued on next page)

▼ **Figure 19.11**   (continued)

Twin Eagles Restaurant, Denton, TX
Cashier/Server
December 1999 to May 2000

No bullets ——• Awarded the Silver Eagle for service in February and April 2000.

Tom Thumb, Lewisville, TX
Checker
June 1998 to December 1999

Organizations
Society for Technical Communication
The Freshman Council (a leadership organization)
Baylor President's Council (a leadership and service organization)

List of keywords ——• Keywords: technical communication, writing, communication skills, technical writing, online documentation, proposal writing, software documentation

Source: Courtesy of Leigh Thomas.

►Principle 4: Write a Reader-Oriented Letter of Application

▶ To learn more about writing letters and e-mail, see Chapter 18, "Writing Reader-Oriented Letters, Memos, and E-Mail."

You will need a letter of application, or cover letter, to send with your résumé. If you send an electronic résumé, you might also include a letter of application—as an e-mail. A letter of application introduces your résumé and gives the employer additional information about you and your experience. Address the letter personally to the executive or manager most likely to make the hiring decision (Greenly 42; Simon). Address your letter to a specific person and spell the addressee's name correctly. If you don't know who should receive your letter, don't address it to "Dear Sir or Madam," "To Whom It May Concern," a department, or a person's job title—unless the advertisement says to address the letter to a department or a person's job title. Instead, call the organization to find out who will receive you résumé. If you can't find out by telephone, address the letter to an executive such as the president or chief executive officer—and use the person's name.

Once you have found out who will read your letter of application, customize your letter for that reader and appeal directly to his or her needs (Greenly 42). For example, if you have experience or classwork especially relevant to the job you are applying for or to that employer, discuss that experience or classwork in the body of your letter.

Your customized, generally one-page letter will have three sections:

• Your purpose for writing: the introductory paragraph
• Your qualifications: the education and experience paragraphs
• Your goal (what you want from the employer): the concluding paragraph

Your Purpose for Writing: The Introductory Paragraph

In the introductory paragraph, tell your readers why you're writing. As you write, follow these guidelines:

- **Identify the position you are applying for.** Employers often receive many letters of application for several jobs at the same time, so identify the specific job you are seeking.

- **Tell the employer where you found out about the job.** Because employers may be soliciting résumés in more than one place, they often want to know where you found out about the job. This information is especially important if you learned of the job from an employee, coworker, or acquaintance of the employer. This information may lead the employer to show more interest in your résumé. If you are writing an unsolicited letter, "quickly explain why you are approaching the company," and then ask whether a job is available (Simon).

Figure 19.12 presents three sample introductory paragraphs. Each specifically identifies the job and the writer's purpose for writing. The first writer uses a personal contact (Dr. Maggy Smith) to open the paragraph and get the employer's attention. The second writer mentions a specific job advertisement. The third writer is sending an unsolicited letter. That writer is not responding to a specific job advertisement and doesn't know whether the company currently has job openings.

As these introductions illustrate, the tone of a letter of application must be positive and confident—not tentative or boastful. State your qualifications in a positive manner without focusing on your weaknesses, but be careful not to

---

▼ Figure 19.12

Sample Introductions for Three Letters of Application

Dr. Maggy Smith suggested that I contact you about the project engineer position you currently have open. My experience as an intern in the energy conservation lab at FSN, Inc., provides me with the qualifications you are seeking. Please consider me for the project engineer position.

- -

My extensive course work in computer science and my experience as an intern for Image Software qualify me for the software designer position that you advertised in the May 16 issue of the *Atlanta Gazette*. Please consider me for that position.

- -

My experience as a manager for Good Eats Grill and my degree in hotel and restaurant management give me a solid foundation in the restaurant business. Please consider me for a position in your management training program.

sound arrogant. You want to appear confident about your education, experience, and abilities while indicating that you know you have much to learn—and are eager to learn—about your profession.

Your Qualifications: The Education and Experience Paragraphs

After you have told the employer why you are writing, present information about your education and experience. As you write the education and experience paragraphs, follow these guidelines:

- **Follow the order of your résumé when discussing your education and work experience.** If your résumé gives information about your education first, then discuss your education first in the letter of application. If your résumé gives information about your work experience first, then discuss your experience first. When you have many years of work experience, you can eliminate the education paragraph and include two or more experience paragraphs.

- **Highlight, add to, or expand on the information in your résumé.** Don't simply repeat the information in your résumé or give the details of your education and experience in chronological order. Instead, highlight or add to information that may especially interest the employer or that is particularly relevant to the job for which you are applying.

- **Create a unified theme in these paragraphs.** Avoid the temptation to simply list (often unrelated) information about your education or work experience. Instead, begin each paragraph with a topic sentence and then develop that topic in the sentences that follow. As you discuss your education, consider how it uniquely qualifies you for the job that you seek. For instance, if the job advertisement says that applicants should write well, you might discuss projects where writing was a significant component.

- **Consider how your experience uniquely qualifies you for the job.** This task is especially difficult if your experience does not directly relate to the job you seek. For example, Rodney is a new college graduate looking for an engineering job. He has never worked in the field of engineering, but he worked as a tutor in a computer lab for three years and was promoted to student manager of the lab. He has several skills that will impress employers. He was promoted because of his ability to work well with others and his ability to supervise his peers. In addition, his university implemented several of his ideas, such as putting a monitor with the weekly schedule of classes outside the lab so that students would know when their classes will meet in the lab and when the lab is open for general access. This idea saved the lab $1,000 a year on paper costs. Although Rodney's experience is not directly related to engineering, he can write a paragraph focusing on his abilities to work with others and to be a team player by suggesting money-saving ideas.

Figures 19.13 and 19.14 illustrate how two writers approached the experience and education paragraphs for a letter of application. The writer of the paragraphs shown in Figure 19.13 has no work experience in her field. The writer of the paragraphs shown in Figure 19.14 has work experience. The writer with work experience begins with this experience and moves to education because his résumé follows that order. This writer also includes his major, degrees received, and school in the education category. The tone of both writers is

Education and Experience Paragraphs Written by a Job-Seeker Without Experience

At Chambers University, I have taken many courses requiring writing. In an advanced technical communication course, I used FrameMaker to produce a 40-page user's manual for inventory software used by Minyards, Inc. (a regional grocery-store chain). Currently, all Minyards stores use the manual to train new employees on the inventory system and as a reference guide for employees after initial training.

For the past three years, I have worked in the Technical Communication Computer Lab at Chambers University. I began as a lab tutor, assisting students with software questions, especially related to Microsoft Word, FrameMaker, and Microsoft PowerPoint. After eighteen months, I was promoted to student lab manager. As manager, I work with the faculty to schedule classes in the lab, work with the lab tutors to set up their schedules, and conduct meetings each week with the lab tutors. Most recently, I set up a scheduling system that uses e-mail instead of paper. This system saved $400 in paper costs annually. As manager and tutor in the lab, I have developed interpersonal skills that would benefit Writers, Inc.

Education and Experience Paragraphs Written by a Job-Seeker with Experience

While at Texas Instruments, I worked as an innovative design engineer. I have more than 15 years of research, production, and manufacturing experience, especially in the areas of machine design, power transmission, and structural analysis. I began as a process improvement engineer and was promoted to reengineering team leader and finally to manufacturing facilitator. As manufacturing facilitator, I supervised two self-directed work teams of 26 total team members. I led one of these teams, the screen printing team, to win the Gold Teaming for Excellence Award. I also received the Site Quality Improvement Award in 1999 and 2000 for increasing productivity by 25% annually.

Along with my experience as a design engineer for Texas Instruments, I have a Bachelor of Science and a Master of Science degree in agricultural engineering from Texas A&M University. As part of my academic experience, I worked as a research assistant in the agricultural engineering department. I designed and constructed custom equipment and instrumentation used in energy conservation research.

confident as they mention facts about their education and experience and state qualities and experiences that are relevant to potential employers.

Your Goal: The Concluding Paragraph

In the concluding paragraph, directly state what you want from the reader: an opportunity to meet the employer and discuss your qualifications. In the paragraphs preceding the conclusion, you have provided specific, detailed information about yourself—information to convince the employer to invite you for an interview. In the concluding paragraph, do the following:

- **Refer the employer to your résumé.**
- **Request an interview.**
- **Tell the employer how to contact you by telephone and e-mail.** Give the employer your phone number, and mention the best time to call. You can encourage the employer to act by including this specific information in the concluding paragraph.

Use specific language in the concluding paragraph. Avoid vague language as in the following examples, in which the writers don't confidently state the goal of meeting the employer or encourage the employer to contact them:

Vague	I look forward to hearing from you soon. Thank you for considering my résumé.
Vague	If possible, may I meet with you or someone in your company to discuss my résumé and my qualifications?

▶ For more information on tone, see Chapter 18, "Writing Reader-Oriented Letters, Memos, and E-Mail," page 565.

Instead, use specific language. The writers of the following paragraphs refer the employer to their résumés and directly ask the employer to contact them for an interview. These writers also use a polite, respectful, confident tone:

Specific	My résumé provides additional information about my education and work experience. I would enjoy discussing my application with you. Please write me at raign@aol.com, or call me anytime at (307) 555-9061.
Specific	You can find more information about my education and experience on the enclosed résumé. I would appreciate the opportunity to discuss my résumé with you at your convenience. Please e-mail me at jscott@attbi.com or call me at (505) 555-9033 weekdays or at (505) 555-0034 evenings and weekends.

Figures 19.15 and 19.16 illustrate effective letters of application. The writers use a respectful yet confident tone and include specific information to persuade the employer to invite them for an interview.

| ▼ **Figure 19.15** | A Letter of Application Written by a Graduating Senior |

204 Oak Street
Denton, TX 76205
April 16, 2002

Dr. Brandon McCarroll
Nortel Technology
2221 Lakeside Boulevard
Richardson, TX 75082

Dear Dr. McCarroll:

I am writing in response to your advertisement in the April 12 *Dallas Morning News*.
Would you please consider me for the entry-level position in technical documentation? I
believe that my experience as an intern with SWB Telecommunications, along with my
education in technical communication from the University of North Texas, uniquely
qualify me for the position.

My education at the University of North Texas has given me a strong background in
technical communication. I have concentrated on paper and online documentation and on
Web design. For a senior-level course, I, along with two students in computer science,
designed an intranet site for Texas Instruments employees; the site describes corporate
history and culture at Texas Instruments. For my senior project, I designed a Web site for
the technical communication program at the University of North Texas. You can view the
site at www.twlab.unt.edu.

While working as an intern for SWB Telecommunications, I applied my academic training
in a workplace environment. For one of my projects, I used my experience in designing
documents for the Internet to develop a Web site describing the wireless services offered by
SWB. More than 2,000 employees and customers use this site each week. During my
second summer with SWB, I updated this Web site. I also edited and proofread customer
documentation for wireless telephones. Customers now receive this documentation when
they buy these telephones.

My résumé provides further information about my education and work experience. Dr.
McCarroll, I would enjoy the opportunity of meeting with you personally to discuss my
qualifications and résumé. You can reach me at (817) 555-2858 or lthomas@twlab.unt.edu.

Sincerely,

Leigh Thomas

Leigh Thomas

Enclosure

▼ **Figure 19.16**   A Letter of Application Written by a Job-Seeker with Extensive Work Experience

310 North Edna
Lewisville, Texas 75057
February 16, 2002

Mr. Barry Boswell
AMC Engineering, Inc.
26789 Westfall Road
Portland, Oregon 97501

Dear Mr. Boswell:

Mr. John Botsford of your research and development department suggested that I contact you. He believes that my experience as a design engineer for Texas Instruments qualifies me for the manufacturing engineer position that you currently have open in your production division. My experience and education in reengineering and in supervising work teams provide me with the qualifications that you are seeking.

While at Texas Instruments, I worked as an innovative design engineer. I have more than 15 years of research, production, and manufacturing experience, especially in the areas of machine design, power transmission, and structural analysis. I began as a process improvement engineer and was promoted to reengineering team leader and finally to manufacturing facilitator. As manufacturing facilitator, I supervised two self-directed work teams of 26 total team members. I led one of these teams, the screen printing team, to win the Gold Teaming for Excellence Award. I also received the Site Quality Improvement Award in 1999 and 2000 for increasing productivity by 25% annually.

Along with my experience as a design engineer for Texas Instruments, I have a Bachelor of Science and a Master of Science degree in agricultural engineering from Texas A&M University. As part of my academic experience, I worked as a research assistant in the agricultural engineering department. I designed and constructed custom equipment and instrumentation used in energy conservation research.

The enclosed résumé provides further information about my experience and my education. Mr. Boswell, I would like to meet with you to discuss my qualifications for this position. Please call me at (972) 555-7893. I look forward to visiting with you.

Sincerely,

C. Randall Harrison

C. Randall Harrison

Encl.: résumé

▶ Principle 5: Use Letters to Follow Up

Follow-up letters are important to your job search. You can write a follow-up letter in several situations:

- **When you have sent a letter of application and résumé and have not received a response within three or four weeks.** If you have not received a response, write a brief, polite letter. Mention your previous letter and its date, and include another copy of your résumé. To know when to write such letters, keep copies of all the letters of application that you send, and keep a file of the responses you receive from employers. Without these copies and a detailed file, you may not know when to send follow-up letters.

- **After an interview.** Within two days of an interview, write a brief thank-you letter addressed to the manager who will decide whether to hire you. If you had extensive interviews with more than one person, write to all the people who interviewed you. In your letters, state your interest in the job and the organization. Use these letters to reinforce what you offer the organization—what you can bring to the job. Mention the organization by name, and mention the names of people in the organization with whom you talked.

- **When you accept a job.** When you accept a job, write a brief letter confirming your acceptance. In this letter, you can confirm details such as when you will begin work.

- **When you reject a job offer or no longer want an employer to consider you for a job.** When you accept a job, don't forget to write the other organizations that seriously considered you for a job. You may want to work for or with one of those organizations in the future, so do them the courtesy of writing a brief letter. Thank the organization and the person who interviewed you for their interest in you. State that you have taken a job with another organization. You don't have to identify the specific job offer that you accepted; instead, you can simply write: "I have decided to accept another offer." Include only positive comments about the organization and your experiences with the interviewer. End your letter with a brief statement of good will, such as "Thank you for the interest you showed in my application."

Remember to write follow-up letters, especially after an interview. Post-interview letters offer an excellent opportunity to restate your qualifications and to add any information about your application that you didn't have the opportunity to discuss during the interview (Simon). Figure 19.17 illustrates a post-interview follow-up letter.

▶ Conclusion

Use the "Worksheet for Writing Reader-Oriented Job Correspondence" for writing résumés, letters of application, and follow-up letters. Although the job correspondence itself will not get you a job, it can be the first step toward that job.

Figure 19.17	A Post-Interview Follow-Up Letter

402 Spring Avenue, Apt. 6C
Alexandria, VA 23097
(703) 555-0922
cdempsey@aol.com
May 4, 2002

Mr. Dwight Wilson
Senior Production Engineer
I-2 Technology, Inc.
San Diego, CA 92093

Dear Mr. Wilson:

Thank you for taking time from your busy schedule yesterday to show me I-2 Technology's facilities and to discuss the quality control job. I especially enjoyed meeting many of your coworkers. Please thank Ms. Johnson in the quality control division.

As a result of our visit, I have a good understanding of I-2 Technology and appreciate its progressive approach to maximizing production without sacrificing quality control. I feel confident that my experience as a quality control engineer can benefit your division.

I-2 Technology's place in the semiconductor industry and your colleagues in the quality control division confirm my impression that I-2 Technology would be an exciting place to work. If I can answer further questions, please call me at (703) 555-0922.

Best regards,

Cynthia Demsey

Cynthia Demsey

| WORKSHEET | **for Writing Reader-Oriented Job Correspondence** |

▶ **Principle 1: Consider Various Methods for Locating Job Opportunities**
- Have you checked for job opportunities available through your college or university placement center?
- Have you looked for job advertisements in publications such as newspapers?
- Have you looked for job advertisements published on organizations' Web sites?
- Have you looked for advertisements posted on online job boards?
- Have you considered sending out unsolicited letters of application?
- Have you considered posting your résumé on an online job board? If so,
  - Does the board meet your needs?
  - Can you update your résumé free of charge? Or will the job board charge you a fee?
  - Do you need to delete your home address and telephone number from your résumé?
  - Will you know if an employer has requested your résumé?
  - Will your current employer or manager see your résumé? If so, will that jeopardize your current job?
  - Should you post your résumé to more than one job board?
  - Have you networked with others in your field, with friends and acquaintances, and with your professors?

▶ **Principle 2: Determine What Information You Want Employers to Know About You**
- Did you brainstorm about your education, work experience, activities, goals, and skills?
- Did you include information that will help employers understand you and your qualifications?
- Does the brainstorming list contain information that will impress employers?

▶ **Principle 3: Prepare an Effective Résumé**
- Does your résumé include enough specific information to distinguish you from others applying for the job?
- For any chronological information, have you used reverse chronological order?
- Is your résumé free of grammatical, spelling, and punctuation errors?
- For a paper résumé, have you
  - Used dynamic, action verbs?
  - Used specific, persuasive language?
  - Used headings and subheadings to create visual categories? Will readers be able to find the categories in your résumé easily? Are the headings set off with enough white space?
  - Used only one typeface?
  - Used bulleted lists when appropriate?

- For an electronic or scannable résumé, have you
  - Included keywords an employer might use to search for qualified job candidates?
  - Used nouns as keywords?
  - Used a 10- to 12- point sans-serif typeface?
  - Used ASCII text for the electronic résumé?
  - Eliminated boldface, italics, underlining, and special characters such as bullets?
  - Aligned all information on the left margin?
  - Used a line length of no more than 70 characters?
  - Used spaces instead of tabs?
  - Opened your résumé in a text editor to check for non-ASCII characters?

▶ **Principle 4: Write a Reader-Oriented Letter of Application**
- Is the letter addressed to a specific person?
- Does the introductory paragraph
  - Identify the job you are applying for?
  - Identify where you found out about the job or the organization?
  - State your interest in the job or a specific type of job?
- Do the education and experience paragraphs
  - Have a unified focus and clear topic sentences?
  - Show how your education and experience uniquely qualify you for the job?
  - Follow the order of your résumé?
- Does the concluding paragraph
  - Refer the employer to your résumé?
  - Confidently and respectfully request an interview?
  - Tell the employer how to contact you?
- Does the letter have a polite yet confident tone?
- Is the letter free of grammatical, spelling, style, and punctuation errors?

▶ **Principle 5: Use Letters to Follow Up**
- Is the letter addressed to a specific person?
- Does the letter thank the addressee for the interview?
- Does the letter state your interest in the job and the organization (if appropriate)?
- Does the letter reinforce what you have to offer the organization—what you can bring to the job?
- Have you used the organization's name and the names of people with whom you talked?
- Is the letter brief?
- Does the letter have a controlled, professional tone?
- Is the letter free of grammatical, spelling, style, and punctuation errors?

1. Find a job opportunity in your field that you are qualified for or will be qualified for when you graduate. You can look for these opportunities on online job boards, at your college placement center, or on the Web. You also can locate job opportunities by talking to acquaintances, family, and friends in business and industry. After you have located a job opportunity, complete one of these steps:

   • If you located the job through a printed advertisement, copy or cut out the advertisement.

   • If you located the job on an online job board or the Web, print out a copy of the advertisement.

   • If you talked to someone about the job, ask for a business card from that person or a copy of the job announcement.

2. Decide on the categories of information that you might include in your résumé for the job you located in Exercise 1. Then create a list of the information that you could include in each of these categories. Your list might look like Nicole's brainstorming list in Figure 19.1. Include specific, detailed information in your list.

3. Using some or all of the information from the list that you created in Exercise 2, prepare a paper résumé. Use the questions in the "Worksheet for Writing Reader-Oriented Job Correspondence" as you write your résumé.

4. Create an electronic version of the résumé that you created for Exercise 3. Remember to follow the tips for creating electronic and scannable résumés on page 610. E-mail your résumé to your instructor.

5. Write a letter of application for the job you located in Exercise 1. Use the "Worksheet for Writing Reader-Oriented Job Correspondence" as you write your letter.

6. Evaluate the résumé shown in Figure 19.18 for organization, effectiveness, design, clarity, and correctness as both a paper and electronic résumé. Use the questions for résumés in the "Worksheet for Writing Reader-Oriented Job Correspondence." Then write a memo to your instructor explaining your evaluation.

7. Using the questions in the "Worksheet for Writing Reader-Oriented Job Correspondence," evaluate your paper résumé, electronic résumé, and letter of application. Your instructor may also ask you to use these questions to evaluate the résumés and letters of application of two of your classmates.

8. Write a paragraph evaluating the following excerpt from a follow-up letter. Use the questions for follow-up letters in the "Worksheet for Writing Reader-Oriented Job Correspondence" to guide you as you evaluate the letter.

   Dear Penny:

   Meeting you and all your coworkers was great fun. The company seems to be a wonderful place to work. Thanks for showing me the facilities and for taking me to lunch. I would love to become one of your coworkers.

   Again, I would enjoy working with you and your coworkers. And I believe that I have a lot to offer your company. Have a great week.

9. Rewrite the follow-up letter from Exercise 8.

Figure 19.18   The Résumé for Exercise 6

Maureen Peterson
1713 Canadian Trail
Harrison, Arkansas 72601
(972) 555-9873

Education
University Arkansas, Fayetteville, Arkansas
B.S. in Horticulture, 2002
3.5 G.P.A.

Johnson High School
Johnson, Kansas
Graduate June 1998

Experience
Earthcare Landscaping, Johnson, Kansas
Assistant manager. Responsible for keeping record of daily sales, deposits, inventory, and purchasing. Fill in for manager when necessary. Supervise sales clerks. Summers only 1999, 2000.

White Dove Nursery, Fayetteville, Arkansas
Manager. In charge of nursery maintenance and customer service. I also ordered all plants and set up landscaping appointments with customers. In charge of six other employees. Assistance to customers looking for the right plants for their landscapes. Full responsibility for the smooth running of the nursery. 2000 to present.

A Taste of Italy, Fayetteville, Arkansas
Server. August 1998 to May 1999.

Personal
Currently active in a national sorority at University of Arkansas at Fayetteville, holding a position on the pledge committee. Certified Nurseryman 1999. Volunteer as a landscaper for the city of Fayetteville Parks and Recreation Department. Awarded Harrison Mother's Club scholarship in 2000.

References available upon request.

Appendixes

A

Documenting Your Sources[1]

___
[1]Written with Susan C. Audrain.

Your organization and your instructor may have a preferred style for documenting sources. Find out what style they expect and use that style. Many will expect you to use one of the following styles, which appear in this appendix:

- *MLA Handbook for Writers of Research Papers,* 5th ed. (New York: MLA, 1999). This style is used in the humanities.
- *Publication Manual of the American Psychological Association,* 4th ed. (Washington: APA, 1994). This style is used in the social sciences and other fields.

▶APA Style

When you document information using APA style, you should consider two areas: citing the information in the text and preparing the references at the end of the document.

Citing Information Using APA Style

When using APA style to cite information in a document, you typically will include the following information:

- The author's last name
- The year the source was published
- The page number(s) if you are giving a specific fact, idea, or quotation

For example, a citation might read as follows:

Thomas (2002) identified the reaction times while working in Alaska.

Documents with an illogical structure make readers' tasks more difficult (Cobb 2002).

The textual citations may vary depending on the type of information and context. If the models above don't fit your information, consult the *Publication Manual of the American Psychological Association.*

Preparing the Reference List Using APA Style

A reference list gives readers the information they need to find each source that you have cited in your document. Each entry in the reference list normally includes the following:

- The author's name
- The year of publication
- The title of the publication
- The publishing information

In your reference list, include only those sources that you have actually used and cited in your document. You should not include sources that you used for background reading. When you prepare your reference list in APA style, follow these guidelines:

- **Put the sources in alphabetical order by the author's last name.** If you have more than one source from the same author, arrange the sources by date—beginning with the earliest source and moving to the latest (or most recent) source. If the sources are from the same year, use lowercase letters to distinguish the articles (for example, *Johnson 2002a, Johnson 2002b,* and so on).
- **Use only initials for the author's first and/or middle name (for example,** *Smith, E.,* **not** *Smith, Ellen*).
- **Capitalize only the first word of each title (and the first word of the subtitle, if necessary).** This rule applies to book and article titles.
- **Italicize or underline the names of journals, magazines, newspapers, and books.** Also italicize or underline journal volume and issue numbers. Use the underlining or italics consistently.
- **End each reference with a period.**
- **Use a hanging indent of five to seven spaces to indicate the second (and subsequent) lines of a reference.** You can see this indent in the examples throughout this section.
- **Give the complete page numbers when citing a range of page numbers.** For example, write *345–352,* not *345–52.*

The following sections present examples of references in APA style.

Journals, Magazine Articles, and Newspaper Articles

Journal Article, One Author

The elements of an APA-style journal reference include the author's last name and initials, followed by the article's publication year, the title of the article, the title and volume number of the publication, and the page number(s) of the article.

Smith, E. O. (2000). Points of reference in technical communication scholarship. *Technical Communication Quarterly, 9,* 427–453.

Journal Article, Two Authors

The elements of an APA-style journal article reference with two authors follow the same format as a single-author journal article reference. Separate the author's names with a comma and an ampersand (&). Use the same format for each author's name: last name first.

Winn, W., & Beck, K. (2000). The persuasive power of design elements on an e-commerce Web site. *Technical Communication, 49 (1),* 17–35.

Journal Article, Three to Five Authors

The elements of an APA-style journal article reference with three to five authors follow the same format as a single-author journal article reference.

Separate the authors' names with commas, and include an ampersand (&) between the final two authors' names.

Constantinides, H., St. Amant, K., & Kampf, C. (2001). Organizational and intercultural communication: An annotated bibliography. *Technical Communication Quarterly, 10,* 31–58.

Journal Article, Six or More Authors

When a journal article references six or more authors, list the first three authors' names, then finish the author reference with *et al.* The remaining elements are the same as the other journal article references.

Smith, E. O., Audrain, S., Bowie, J., et al. (2001). 2000 ATTW bibliography. *Technical Communication Quarterly, 10,* 447–479.

Magazine Article

When referencing a magazine article, list the author's last name and initials (if an author is referenced), the article title, the date of the publication (include as much detail as you have), the publication name and volume number, and the page number(s) of the article. If the article does not have an author, alphabetize the reference by the title of the article, ignoring all articles (*a, an,* and *the*).

Learning online storytelling. (2000, October 13). *Computing Canada, 26,* 40.

Newspaper Article

When referencing a newspaper article, list the author's last name and initials, the publication date (include as much detail as you have), the title of the article, the title of the publication, and the page numbers of the article. Use *p.* for a single-page article and *pp.* for a multipage article. If the article runs on continuous pages, separate the page numbers with an en dash (pp. 1–2). If the article runs on discontinuous pages, separate the page numbers with a comma (pp. 1, 3).

Young, J. R. (2000, November 9). Going to class in a 3-D lecture hall. *New York Times* (Late ed.). p. G8.

Article or Chapter in an Edited Book

When referencing an article or a chapter within an edited book, list the last name and initials of the author, the publication year of the book, and the title of the article or chapter. Use the word *In,* and then reference the editor of the book with initials and last name, the abbreviation *Ed.* in parentheses, the title of the book, and the inclusive page numbers of the article or chapter. At the end of the reference, list the book's publication information (city and publisher).

Ornatowski, C. M. (2000). Ethics in technical/professional communication: From telling the truth to making better decisions in a complex world. In M. A. Pemberton (Ed.). *The ethics of writing instruction: Issues in theory and practice* (pp. 139–166). Stamford, CT: Ablex.

Article from a Volume of Proceedings

When referencing an article from a volume of conference proceedings, list the author's last name and initials, the publication date of the proceedings, and the title of the article. At the end of the reference, list the title of the published proceedings and the volume's publication information (city and publisher).

DeLoach, S. (2001). An overview of HTML-based help. *Proceedings of the 48th International Technical Communication Conference.* Fairfax, VA: Society for Technical Communication.

Journal, Magazine, or Newspaper Article with No Author Cited

For articles with no author cited, follow the same format as articles with authors cited. Use the correct format for journal, magazine, or newspaper entries, then alphabetize the reference by the article title.

Vista's Edge, Inc., wins technical writing award (2001, September 3). *San Diego Business Journal, 36,* 10.

Books and Brochures

Book by One Author

When referencing a book, list the author's last name and initials, followed by the publication year, the title of the book, and the publication information (city and publisher).

Beaufort, A. (2000). *Writing in the real world: Making the transition from school to work.* New York: Teachers College Press.

Book by Multiple Authors

When referencing a book with more than one author, separate the authors' names with commas and use an ampersand (&) between the final two authors' names. Follow the same rules for multiple authors as with journal authors (see page 628).

Miller, J. D., & Kimmel, L. G. (2001). *Biomedical communication: Purposes, audiences, and strategies.* San Diego: Academic.

Book in Edition Other Than First

When a book is in a later edition, list the book's authors and the publication year. Then, list the title of the book, the edition of the book in parentheses, and the publication information (city and publisher).

Williams, J. (2000) *Style: Ten lessons in clarity and grace.* (6th ed.) Boston: Longman.

Book Issued by an Organization

When referencing a book "authored" by an organization, list the name of the authoring organization, the publication date, the name of the publication, the edition number (if any), and the publication information (city and publisher).

American Psychological Association. (2001). *Publication manual of the American Psychological Association* (5th ed.). Washington, DC: American Psychological Association.

An Edited Book

When referencing an edited book, list the name(s) of the editor(s), following the same rules for multiple editors as for multiple authors. Next, list the publication year, the title of the book, and the publication information (city and publisher).

Kynell, T. C., & Moran, M. G. (Eds.). (1998). *Three keys to the past: The history of technical communication.* Stamford, CT: Ablex.

Book, No Author or Editor

When a book lists no author or editor, begin the reference with the title of the book. Then, list the edition number (if any), the publication year, and the publication information (city and publisher).

Webster's New Explorer Medical Dictionary. (1999). New York: Federal Street Press.

Brochure, Corporate Author

When referencing a brochure with a corporate author, begin with the corporation and the publication year. Then, list the title of the brochure with the word *Brochure* in brackets following the title. At the end of the reference, list the publication information (city and corporate publisher).

IBM. (2001). *IBM Annual Report 2000.* [Brochure]. White Plains, NY: IBM.

Technical Reports and Government Documents

Technical Report

When referencing a technical report, list the author's last name and initials, the publication year, the title of the report, the series name and number of the report, and the publication information (city and publisher).

Scott, D. D. (2000). *Archeological overview and assessment for Wilson's Creek National Battlefield, Greene and Christian Counties, Missouri.* (Midwest Archeological Center technical report No. 66). Lincoln, NE: U.S. Department of the Interior, National Park Service, Midwest Archeological Center.

Government Document

When referencing a government document published by the Government Printing Office (GPO), list the government agency that released the document followed by the publication year. At the end of the reference, list the title of the document and the publication information (city and publisher).

U.S. Department of Justice. (2000). *Bellows report: Final report of the attorney general's review team on the handling of the Los Alamos National Laboratory investigation.* Washington, DC: U.S. Government Printing Office.

Electronic Documents

Reference from a Web Site

When referencing an electronic document from a Web site, list the author of the reference (or the organization if an organization has issued the reference). Then, list the date of the reference (or *n.d.* if the reference doesn't have a publication date), the title of the document, the retrieval date, and the URL. If necessary, you may break a URL to a new line after a slash or before a period, but do not insert a hyphen at the break. Omit the period following the URL.

Society for Technical Communication (2001 October). *2001 Technical Communicator Salary Survey.* Retrieved from http://www.stc.org/pdf_files/2001_salary_survey.pdf

Electronic Copy of an Article Retrieved from a Database

When referencing an electronic article that you retrieved from a database, list the author's name and initials, the date, the title of the article, and the title of the publication. Next, list the retrieval date, the source of the information, and the URL or location. Omit the period following the URL.

> Webster, John. (2001, October 15). Professional edge: Staffed for analytics. *InfoWorld*. Retrieved December 15, 2001, from Electric Library database (magazines) via http://www.elibrary.com

E-Mail Message

When referencing an e-mail message in the body of a document, cite the author of the message in the same way you would cite the source of a personal communication. Do not include the e-mail in the reference list.

Message Posted to Online Forums, Discussion Groups, or Electronic Mailing Lists

When referencing a message posted to an online forum, discussion group, or electronic mailing list, cite the author's name, the date (as exact as you can), and the subject of the message. Finally, cite the posting information. Omit the period following the URL. Because messages posted to online forums, discussion groups, and electronic mailing lists are informal, take care when using these messages as references. Make sure that any electronic message you cite has relevant scholarly value and that your readers can retreive it.

> Chiaviello, A. (2001, November 16). XML = XHTML? Message posted to http://lyris.acs.ttu.edu/cgi-bin/lyris.pl?enter=attw-l

▶MLA Style

When you document information using MLA style, you should consider two areas: citing the information in the text and preparing the references at the end of the document. In MLA style, the reference list is called "Works Cited."

Citing Information Using MLA Style

When using MLA style to cite information in a document, you typically will include the following information:

- The author's last name
- The page number being referred to

For example, a citation might read as follows:

> Thomas identified the reaction times while working in Alaska during the 1950s (14–28).

> Documents with an illogical structure make readers' tasks more difficult (Cobb 18).

If you're citing an entire source, you would include only the author's last name. The textual citations may vary depending on the type of information and context. If the models above don't fit your information, consult the *MLA Handbook for Writers of Research Papers.*

Preparing the List of Works Cited Using MLA Style

A list of works cited gives readers the information they need to find each source that you have cited in your document. Each entry in the reference list normally includes the following:

- The author's name
- The year of publication
- The title of the publication
- Publishing information

In your reference list, you should include only those works that you have actually used and cited in your document. You should not include works that you used for background reading. When you prepare your list of works cited in MLA style, follow these guidelines:

- **Put the sources in alphabetical order by the author's last name.** If you are citing two or more works by the same author, arrange the sources by title. If you are citing works by an organization, alphabetize the work by the first important word in the name of the organization. For example, if the American Heart Association wrote the work, you would alphabetize by the word *American.*
- **Use title-case capitalization—capitalize each important word in the titles and subtitles.**
- **Italicize or underline the names of journals, magazines, newspapers, and books.** Use the italics or underlining consistently.
- **Put the titles of articles and other short works in quotation marks.**
- **End each reference with a period.**
- **Use a hanging indent of one-half inch to indicate the second (and subsequent) lines of a reference.** You can see this indent in the examples throughout this section.
- **Give only the last two digits of the page number when citing a range of page numbers.** For example, write *345–52,* not *345–352.* Don't include *p.* or *pp.* to indicate page(s).
- **Follow this format for dates:** day, month, year, without commas (29 June 2002).

The following sections present examples of references in MLA style.

Journals, Magazine Articles, and Newspaper Articles

Journal Article, One Author
When referencing a journal article with one author, list the author's full name (last name first), the title of the article inside quotation marks, the title of the journal, the volume number, publication date, and page numbers.

Smith, Elizabeth Overman. "Points of Reference in Technical Communication Scholarship." *Technical Communication Quarterly* 9 (2000): 427–53.

Journal Article, Two or Three Authors

When referencing a journal article with two or three authors, list the authors' names in the order they appear in the publication (which is not necessarily in alphabetical order). List the first author's name with last name first followed by a comma, and the next author's name in normal order. Separate the last two authors with the word *and*. Then, list the article title, the journal title and volume number, the publication date, and page numbers.

Constantinides, Helen, Kirk St. Amant, and Connie Kampf. "Organizational and Intercultural Communication: An Annotated Bibliography." Technical *Communication Quarterly* 10 (2001): 31–58.

Journal Article, More Than Three Authors

When referencing a journal article with more than three authors, you may cite the first author's name in full and add *et al.*, or you may give all of the names in full. After the authors' names, list the article title, the journal title and volume number, the publication date, and page numbers.

Smith, Elizabeth Overman, et al. "2000 ATTW Bibliography." *Technical Communication Quarterly* 10 (2001): 447–79.

Magazine Article

When referencing a magazine article, list the author's name (if an author is referenced), the article title, the title of the article in quotation marks, the name of the magazine, the publication date, and the page numbers. Do not list the magazine's volume and issue numbers. If the article is on more than one page, list the first page followed by a plus sign (+) with no intervening space. If the article does not have an author, alphabetize the reference by the title of the article, ignoring all articles (*a, an,* and *the*).

"Learning Online Storytelling." *Computing Canada* 13 Oct. 2000: 40+.

Newspaper Article

When referencing a newspaper article, list the author's last name and initials, the title of the article in quotation marks, and the name of the publication. If the city of publication is not included in the name of a locally published newspaper, add the city in square brackets following the newspaper title. Next, list the complete newspaper name, the date, the edition, and the page numbers. If the article is on more than one page, list the first page followed by a plus sign (+) with no intervening space.

Young, Jeffrey R. "Going to Class in a 3–D Lecture Hall." *New York Times* 9 Nov. 2000, late ed.: G8.

Article or Chapter in an Edited Book

When referencing an article or chapter in an edited book, list the name of the article's author, the title of the article or chapter, and the title of the edited book. Include the abbreviation *Ed.* for editor, the editor's name, and the book's publication information. Be sure to include the page numbers of the article or chapter at the end of the citation.

Ornatowski, Cezar J. "Ethics in Technical/Professional Communication: From Telling the Truth to Making Better Decisions in a Complex World." Ed. M. A. Pemberton. *The Ethics of Writing Instruction: Issues in Theory and Practice.* Stamford, CT: Ablex, 2000. 139–66.

Article from a Volume of Proceedings

When referencing an article from a volume of conference proceedings, list the author's name, the title of the article, the title of the proceedings, and the publication information.

DeLoach, Scott S. "An Overview of HTML-Based Help." *Proceedings of the 48th International Technical Communication Conference.* Fairfax, VA: Society for Technical Communication, 2001.

Journal, Magazine, or Newspaper Article with No Author Cited

For articles with no author cited, follow the same format as articles with authors cited. Use the correct format for journal, magazine, or newspaper entries, then alphabetize the reference by the article title.

Vista's Edge, Inc., Wins Technical Writing Award. *San Diego Business Journal* 3 Sep. 2001: 10.

Books and Brochures

Book by One Author

When referencing a book by one author, list the author's name, the title of the book, and the publication information.

Beaufort, Anne. *Writing in the Real World: Making the Transition from School to Work.* New York: Teachers College Press, 2000.

Book by Multiple Authors

When referencing a book with multiple authors, list the authors' names in the order they appear on the title page (which is not necessarily in alphabetical order). List the first author's name with the last name first followed by a comma, and then the next author's name in normal order. Separate the last two authors with the word *and*. If a book has more than three authors, you may list the first author's name only followed by *et al.*

Miller, Jon D., and Linda G. Kimmel. (2001). *Biomedical Communication: Purposes, Audiences, and Strategies.* San Diego: Academic, 2001.

Book in Edition Other Than First

When referencing a book in a second or subsequent edition, list the author(s), the title of the book, the edition information, and the publication information.

Williams, Joseph. *Style: Ten Lessons in Clarity and Grace.* 6th ed. Boston: Longman, 2000.

Book Issued by an Organization
When referencing a book issued by an organization, cite the name of the organization, the title of the book, and the publication information. The organization and the publisher may be the same.

American Psychological Association. *Publication Manual of the American Psychological Association*. 5th ed. Washington: American Psychological Association, 2001.

Book Compiled by an Editor or Issued Under an Editor's Name
When referencing an edited book, list the editor(s) names, followed by the abbreviation *ed.* or *eds.* Then list the title of the book and the publication information.

Kynell, Teresa C., and Michael G. Moran, eds. *Three Keys to the Past: The History of Technical Communication*. Stamford, CT: Ablex, 1998.

Book, No Author or Editor
When a book lists no author or editor, begin the reference with the title of the book. Next, list the edition number (if any) and the publication information.

Webster's New Explorer Medical Dictionary. New York: Federal Street Press, 1999.

Brochure, Corporate Author
Treat a brochure or pamphlet the same way you would treat a book.

IBM. *IBM Annual Report 2000*. White Plains, NY: IBM, 2001.

Government Documents

Government Document
When referencing a government document, list the government agency that released the document, the title of the document, and the publication information.

U.S. Department of Justice. *Bellows Report: Final Report of the Attorney General's Review Team on the Handling of the Los Alamos National Laboratory Investigation*. Washington: U.S. Government Printing Office, 2000.

Electronic Documents

Document from a Web site or Database
When referencing an electronic document from a Web site, list the author (if one is given), the document title, the title of the Web site, and the publication date (if one is given). Next, list the name of the publishing organization, the date you accessed the document, and the URL inside angled brackets. Close the reference with a period.

"2001 Technical Communicator Salary Survey." *STC*. October 2001. Society for Technical Communication. 15 December 2001. <http://www.stc.org/PDF_Files/2001_Salary_Survey.pdf>.

E-Mail Message

When referencing an e–mail message, list the name of the writer, the title of the message taken from the subject line, the name of the recipient, and the date of the message.

Sims, Patrick. "Re: Graduate Program Questions." E-mail to Susan Audrain.
14 Nov. 2001.

Message Posted to Online Forums, Discussion Groups, or Electronic Mailing Lists

When referencing a message posted to an online forum, list the author's name and the subject of the message followed by the description *Online posting*. Next, list the message posting date, the name of the online forum, and the URL in angled brackets. Close the reference with a period.

Chiaviello, Anthony. "XML = XHTML?" Online posting. ATTW-L Discussion List.
16 Nov. 2001. <http://lyris.acs.ttu.edu/cgi-bin/lyris.pl?enter=ATTW-L>.

B

Review of Common Sentence Errors, Punctuation, and Mechanics

Grammar, punctuation, and mechanics help a reader to understand your writing. They are like road signs that help you to get to your destination. Without them, readers may become confused or may not get to the meaning you intend.

This appendix presents information about common sentence errors, punctuation, and mechanics. The topics within each section appear in alphabetical order, and an abbreviation (such as *cs* for comma splice) accompanies each topic. You can use these abbreviations as you edit your own papers or those of your team members. A complete list of these abbreviations appears at the end of this appendix on page 660. This appendix only briefly reviews grammar, usage, and mechanics; if you want complete information on these topics, consult a handbook for grammar and style.

►Common Sentence Errors

This section presents common sentence errors and suggests ways to eliminate these errors.

Agreement Error—Pronoun and Referent

A pronoun should refer clearly to a specific noun or pronoun—its referent (also called its *antecedent*)—and should agree in number and in gender with that referent.

Correct	**Gwen** paid cash for **her** new **car** although **it** cost more than **she** was hoping to pay.
Correct	The **students** received a trophy for **their** class project.

When you use a pronoun, make sure that its referent is clear.

Vague	Douglas told Bill that he should move his car.
Clear	Douglas told Bill, "I should move my car." Douglas told Bill, "You should move your car." Douglas told Bill, "I should move your car."

Pronoun-referent agreement becomes especially tricky with indefinite pronouns (such as *each, everyone, anybody, someone,* and *none*) and collective nouns. When an indefinite pronoun is the referent, the pronoun is singular, as in this example:

Incorrect	**Each** student will receive **their** diploma through the mail.
Correct	**Each** student will receive **his or her** diploma through the mail.

When a collective noun is the referent, determine whether the noun is singular or plural in its context. A collective noun may take a singular or a plural pronoun as its referent. Let's look at an example:

| Incorrect | The **university** will begin a new e-mail service for **their** students. |
| Correct | The **university** will begin a new e-mail service for **its** students. |

In this sentence, *university* refers to a single unit, not to individual members of the university community. In this context, it is singular, and the pronoun referring to it must also be singular.

A collective noun can also be plural, as in this example:

| Incorrect | The **faculty** can pick up **its** paychecks on Friday. |
| Correct | The **faculty** can pick up **their** paychecks on Friday. |

Here, *faculty* is a collective noun referring to the faculty in a context that emphasizes the individuals who comprise the group. The faculty wouldn't pick up their checks as a group, but individually.

Agreement Error—Subject and Verb

The subject and verb should agree in number. Often writers commit subject-verb agreement errors when the verb follows a prepositional phrase:

| Incorrect | The **consequence** of the accidents **trouble** several board members. |
| Correct | The **consequence** of the accidents **troubles** several board members. |

The noun *accidents* in the prepositional phrase *of the accidents* does not affect the number of the verb; only the subject of the sentence affects the number of the verb.

Comma Splice

A comma splice occurs when writers incorrectly use a comma to link two independent clauses, as in this example:

| Comma splice | We baked 10,000 pretzels, we dipped them in dark chocolate. |

To correct a comma splice:

• Change the comma to a period followed by a capital letter:

  We baked 10,000 pretzels. We dipped them in dark chocolate.

- Change the comma to a semicolon:

  We baked 10,000 pretzels; we dipped them in dark chocolate.

- Leave the comma and add after it an appropriate coordinating conjunction (*and, or, nor, so, for, yet, but*):

  We baked 10,000 pretzels, and we dipped them in dark chocolate.

- Add a subordinating conjunction to create a sentence consisting of one dependent and one independent clause. A *dependent clause* has a subject and a verb but can't stand alone; an *independent clause* has a subject and a verb and can stand alone. In the following example, the dependent clause begins with *after:*

  After we baked 10,000 pretzels, we dipped them in dark chocolate.

Modification Error—Dangling Modifiers

See Chapter 8, page 197.

Modification Error—Misplaced Modifiers

See Chapter 8, page 197.

Lack of Parallelism

Use parallel structure when you put items in a series or in a list. All the items in a series or list must have the same grammatical structure. If the first item is a verb, the remaining items must be verbs. If the first item is a noun, the remaining items must be nouns.

Not parallel   To complete the course, you will **write a research paper, take four exams, two collaborative projects,** and **participation.**

The first two items in the series are verb phrases, the third item is a noun phrase, and the fourth item is an unmodified noun. To make items in this series parallel in structure, the writer needs to make the third and fourth items verb phrases:

Parallel   To complete the course, you will **write a research paper, take four exams, complete two collaborative projects,** and **participate in class discussions.**

For more information on parallelism, see the discussion of parallelism and headings in Chapter 6, page 165.

Run-On Sentences

A run-on sentence (sometimes called a *fused sentence*) occurs when two or more independent clauses appear together without any punctuation (independent clauses have a subject and a verb and can stand alone). To correct a run-on sentence, you can use the same techniques you would use to correct a comma splice.

Run-on	We baked 10,000 pretzels we dipped them in dark chocolate.
Correct	We baked 10,000 pretzels. **We** dipped them in dark chocolate.
Correct	We baked 10,000 pretzels; **we** dipped them in dark chocolate.
Correct	We baked 10,000 pretzels, **and we** dipped them in dark chocolate.
Correct	**After** we baked 10,000 pretzels, we dipped them in dark chocolate.

Sentence Fragment

A sentence fragment is an incomplete sentence. Sentence fragments usually appear because the writer has left out the subject or the verb or failed to write an independent clause, which can stand alone.

Fragments Resulting from Missing Subjects

Fragment	Detached the coupon from the statement.
Complete sentence	Norma detached the coupon from the statement.
Complete sentence	Detach the coupon from the statement.

The fragment lacks a subject—no actor is doing the detaching. The first complete sentence has a subject—*Norma*. The second complete sentence has an understood *you* as its subject.

Fragments Resulting from Missing Verbs

Fragment	Norma detaching the coupon from the statement.
Complete sentence	Norma is detaching the coupon from the statement.

The fragment lacks a verb; the *-ing* form requires *is, was,* or *will be* to function as a verb in a complete sentence. Let's look at another fragment:

Fragment	The power surge caused by the thunderstorm.
Complete sentence	The power surge caused by the thunderstorm damaged my computer.

In the fragment, *caused* functions as an adjective, not as a verb.

Fragments Resulting from Failure to Write an Independent Clause

Fragment	You can use the cellular telephone. **If you charge the battery.**
Complete sentence	You can use the cellular telephone if you charge the battery.

If you charge the battery cannot stand alone as a sentence because it begins with the subordinating word *if*. An independent clause has a subject and a verb, can stand alone, and does not begin with a subordinating word.

Verb Tense Errors

Writers of technical material often misuse the present and the past perfect tenses and shift tense unnecessarily.

Present Tense

Use the present tense to describe timeless principles and recurring events.

Incorrect	In 1997, the Mars *Pathfinder* scientists discovered that the climate of Mars **was** extremely cold.
Correct	In 1997, the Mars *Pathfinder* scientists discovered that the climate of Mars **is** extremely cold.

The scientists made their discovery in the past—in 1997—but the climate of Mars continues to be cold.

Past Perfect Tense

Use the past perfect tense (indicated by *had*) to indicate which of two past events occurred first.

Correct	The presentation **had started** when we found the overhead projector.

The writer uses the past perfect tense to make clear that when the presentation started, they had not found the overhead projector.

Unnecessary Shifts in Tense

Within a sentence, do not change tense unnecessarily.

Unnecessary	He **tested** the new hardware, **loaded** the software, **adjusts** the computer settings, and **waited** for the network to respond.

Needless shifts in tense distract readers. In this example, the tense of the four verbs should be the same:

Correct   He **tested** the new hardware, **loaded** the software, **adjusted** the computer settings, and **waited** for the network to respond.

Correct   He **tests** the new hardware, **loads** the software, **adjusts** the computer settings, and **waits** for the network to respond.

▶Punctuation

Apostrophe

Use the apostrophe to indicate possession, to create some plural forms, and to form contractions.

Apostrophes to Indicate Possession

You can use apostrophes to indicate possession in the following situations:

- To create the possessive form of *most* singular nouns, including proper nouns, use an apostrophe and *s,* as in these examples:

  gas's odor

  Charles's calculator

  student's book

If adding an apostrophe and *s* would create an *s* or *z* sound that is hard to pronounce, then add only an apostrophe, as in *Moses'.* (Try pronouncing *Moses's* and then *Charles's* to see the difference.)

When a plural noun does not end in *s,* add an apostrophe and *s.* When a plural noun does end in *s,* add only an apostrophe.

men's   students'

children's   members'

- To indicate joint possession, add an apostrophe and *s* to the last noun. To indicate separate possession, add an apostrophe and *s* to each noun.

  Joint possession   John and Stephanie's multimedia presentation
  Separate possession   John's and Stephanie's multimedia presentations

- To create the possessive form of pronouns, add an apostrophe and *s* only to indefinite pronouns. Personal pronouns and the relative pronoun *who* have special forms that indicate possession.

Possessives of Indefinite Pronouns	Possessives of Other Pronouns
anyone's	mine (my)
everybody's	his, hers (her), its
everyone's	yours (your)
nobody's	ours (our)
no one's	theirs (their)
other's (*also* others')	whose

Notice that the possessive form of *it* does not have an apostrophe. When you add an apostrophe and *s* to *it*, you create *it's*, the contraction for *it is.*

Incorrect	The city does not believe the pollution is **it's** problem.
Correct	The city does not believe the pollution is **its** problem.

Apostrophes to Create Plural Forms

Use an apostrophe to create the plural form of letters and numbers:

a's and b's

8's and 5's (*or* 8s and 5s)

Some organizations prefer omitting the apostrophe in plural numbers. Check your organization's style guidelines to determine what your organization prefers.

Apostrophes to Form Contractions

Use an apostrophe to indicate the omission of a letter or letters in a contraction.

cannot	can't	who is	who's
you are	you're	let us	let's
it is	it's	they are	they're
does not	doesn't	she will	she'll

Brackets

Use brackets in the following situations:

- To indicate that you've added words to a quotation:

Correct	The press release said, "They [Thompson and Congrove] voted against the amendment."

- To identify parenthetical information within parentheses:

Correct	(For more information, see *Publication Manual of the American Psychological Association* [Washington, D.C.: APA, 1999].)

Colon

Use a colon to introduce some quotations and lists; to introduce some words, phrases, and clauses; and to observe other stylistic conventions.

Colons to Introduce Quotations

Use a colon to introduce a long or formal quotation:

Correct	In the Gettysburg Address, Lincoln began: "Four score and seven years ago our fathers brought forth on this continent, a new nation, conceived in Liberty, and dedicated to the proposition that all men are created equal."

Colons to Introduce Lists

Use a colon to introduce a list when the introductory text would be incomplete without the list:

Correct	For the user testing, you will need the following items: the beta version of the software, a CD-ROM, and a notepad.

Colons to Introduce Words, Phrases, and Clauses

Use a colon to introduce a word, phrase, or clause that illustrates or explains a statement:

Correct	Our manager asked the following people to attend the meeting: production editor, art editor, and copy editor.
Correct	He suggested this solution: balancing the turbine to eliminate the vibration.

The text before a colon must have a subject and verb and must be able to stand alone.

Incorrect	We discovered problems in: the piping system and the turbine.
Correct	We discovered problems in the piping system and the turbine.

In the incorrect example, *We discovered problems in* cannot stand alone; therefore, the colon is incorrect.

Other Conventional Uses of Colons

- **Salutations.** Use a colon after the salutation (with a title such as Dr., Mr., or Ms.) in a letter:

  Dear Mr. Johnson:

- **Time.** Use a colon to separate hours and minutes:

  8:30 A.M.

- **Subtitles.** Use a colon to separate the main title from a subtitle:

  Creating Web Pages: A Handbook for Beginners

Comma

You will use the comma more often than you use any other punctuation. These guidelines will help you to use commas correctly.

Commas to Separate the Clauses of a Compound Sentence

A *compound sentence* has two or more independent clauses (independent clauses have a subject and verb and can stand alone). Use a comma to separate the clauses of a compound sentence when a coordinating conjunction (*and, or, for, nor, but, so, yet*) links those clauses.

Correct   We distributed 500 surveys to the shoppers, but we expect only 20 percent to return the surveys.

Often, the comma between the clauses of a compound sentence prevents readers from at first thinking that the subject of the second clause is an object of the verb of the first clause:

Incorrect   Bob will use the test results and the survey results will help him to prepare a prototype of the software.

Correct   Bob will use the test results, and the survey results will help him to prepare a prototype of the software.

Without the comma before *and*, readers at first may think that Bob will use both the test results and the survey results. The comma signals that an independent clause, not the object of the verb *use*, follows *and*.

Commas to Separate Items in a Series

Use commas to separate items in a series composed of three or more items:

Correct   The assistant will deliver, collect, and tally the questionnaires.

The comma before the coordinating conjunction *and* is optional; however, many style manuals encourage writers to use the comma to distinguish items, to prevent ambiguity, and to prevent misreading.

Commas to Set Off Introductory Words, Phrases, or Dependent Clauses

Generally, use a comma to set off an introductory word, phrase, or dependent clause from the main clause:

Correct	Therefore, NASA launched the shuttle two hours later. (introductory word)
Correct	To localize documents, some companies hire translation agencies. (introductory phrase)
Correct	Because the team lost the debate, the school will not receive the prize money. (introductory dependent clause)

A comma after an introductory clause can prevent misreading:

Incorrect	After we completed bathing the cat jumped into the tub.
Correct	After we completed bathing, the cat jumped into the tub.

Without the comma, readers at first might think that the cat were being bathed.
  If the introductory text is short and readers can't misunderstand what you mean, you can omit the comma.

Commas to Set Off Nonrestrictive Modifiers

A nonrestrictive modifier is not essential to the meaning of a sentence. Writers can omit a nonrestrictive modifier and readers will still understand the sentence. In contrast, when writers omit a restrictive modifier, they change the meaning of the sentence. Consider these examples:

Restrictive	Homeowners **who don't pay their property taxes** risk severe penalties and interest.
Nonrestrictive	Homeowners, **whether novice or experienced,** can benefit from the seminar on home equity.

The restrictive modifier makes clear that not all homeowners, only those who don't pay their property taxes, risk severe penalties and interest. The writer restricts, or limits, the homeowners to those who don't pay their property taxes. The restrictive modifier is essential, and commas should not be used. The nonrestrictive modifier is not essential, and commas should be used.

Commas to Separate Coordinate Adjectives

Use a comma to separate *coordinate adjectives*—adjectives that modify the same noun equally.

Correct	The company will test this fast, powerful computer next week.
Correct	The new design incorporates a bright, rectangular screen.

When adjectives are coordinate, the sentence would still make sense if you replaced the comma with the coordinating conjunction *and*. When adjectives are not coordinate, do not separate the adjectives with a comma. Adjectives are not coordinate when the noun and the adjective closest to the noun are closely associated in meaning.

Incorrect	We will begin the test after the second, special session.
Correct	We will begin the test after the second special session.

In this example, the adjective *second* modifies the combination of the adjective *special* and the noun *session*.

Other Conventional Uses of Commas

- **Dates.** Use commas to separate the parts of a date.

Correct	After Friday, January 1, 2003, you may use your corporate card to charge your tickets and meals.

Notice the comma after 2003. If you do not mention the day (January 2003), then omit the comma between the month and year. If you mention the day before the month (1 January 2003), then don't use a comma.

- **Towns, states, and countries.** Use commas to separate the parts of an address.

Correct	The senator from Madison, Wisconsin, asked the first question.

Notice the comma after *Wisconsin*.

- **Titles of persons.** Use commas before and after a title that follows a person's name.

Correct	Joseph Gerault, Ph.D., will address the faculty on Tuesday.

- **Direct address.** Use a comma or commas to set off nouns used in direct address.

Correct	My friends, I am happy to report the results of the second test.
Correct	If you are willing to talk, Thomas, we will select a time convenient for you.

- **Quotations.** Use a comma to introduce most quotations.

Correct	According to John Keyes, "Color grabs a reader's attention before the reader understands the surrounding informational context."
Correct	They asked, "How long will the network be down?"

- **Interjections and transitional adverbs.** Use a comma or commas to separate interjections and transitional adverbs from the other words in a sentence:

Correct	Well, we did not budget any money for the new generator.
Correct	Therefore, we must wait until the next budget period to purchase the generator.
Correct	The old generator, however, is still fairly reliable.

Dash

Use a dash or dashes to emphasize a parenthetical statement or to indicate a sharp change in thought or tone.

Correct	The United States is a locale, China is a locale, and India is a locale—each has its own set of rules and cultural experiences.
Correct	The judge found the company guilty of deceptive advertising—as I remember.

Exclamation Point

Place an exclamation point at the end of an *exclamatory sentence*—a sentence that expresses strong emotion.

Correct	The new physics building, originally budgeted for $1.5 million, cost more than $5.5 million!

Since technical communication strives for objectivity, you will rarely use exclamation points in technical documents.

Hyphen

Use hyphens to form compound words, adjectives, fractions, and numbers and to divide words at the end of a line.

Hyphens in Compound Words

A *compound word* is a word made up of two or more words. Not all compound words are hyphenated. If you are unsure about whether to hyphenate a compound word, check your dictionary.

Hyphenated	**Not Hyphenated**
up-to-date	workplace
editor-in-chief	proofread
self-image	bulletin board

Hyphens to Form Compound Adjectives

A *compound adjective* is two or more words that serve as a single adjective before a noun.

twenty-one-inch monitor	**up-to-the-minute** news
self-induced attack	**reader-oriented** sentences
black-spotted kitten	**general-to-specific** pattern

Hyphens in Fractions and Compound Numbers

Use hyphens to connect the numerator and denominator of fractions and to hyphenate compound numbers from twenty-one to ninety-nine when spelling out numbers is appropriate.

three-fourths	twenty-three
one-third	seventy-seven

For more information on number conventions, see page 658.

Hyphens for End-of-Line Word Breaks

Use a hyphen to divide a word at the end of one line and continue it on the next line. Divide words only between syllables. Consult a dictionary to identify correct syllable breaks. Your word-processing software should automatically divide the words between syllables.

Correct   Documents can change across cultures just as body language, everyday expressions, and greetings change.

Whenever possible, avoid breaking a word at the end of a sentence. You can avoid end-of-line hyphens by using an unjustified right margin. You also can set your word-processing software not to hyphenate any words at the ends of lines.

Parentheses

Use parentheses—always in pairs—in the following situations:

- To enclose supplementary or incidental information:

Correct	Please e-mail me (jsmith@aol.com) when you complete your section of the report.
Correct	To readers in the United States, *EPA* (for Environmental Protection Agency) and *IRS* (for Internal Revenue Service) are common acronyms.

- To enclose numbers and letters used to identify items listed within a sentence:

Correct	To log on to the network, (1) type your login name, (2) press the tab key, and (3) type your password.

Parentheses are unnecessary when you display a list vertically:

Correct	To log on to the network, complete these steps:

         1. Type your login name.
         2. Press the tab key.
         3. Type your password.

Period

Use a period at the end of most sentences, after most abbreviations, and as a decimal point.

Periods to Create an End Stop

Put a period at the end of any sentence that does not ask a direct question or express strong emotion (an exclamation):

Correct	The Web has changed the way companies communicate with their employees.
Correct	Families living near the landfill are asking why the city is hauling in trash from other states.

Periods After Abbreviations

- Use a period after most abbreviations:

Ph.D.   etc.
J.D.   U.S.

- Omit periods from abbreviations for the names of organizations such as corporations and government and international agencies:

GM (for General Motors)
NCAA (for National Collegiate Athletic Association)
FBI (for the Federal Bureau of Investigation)
UN (for the United Nations)

- Omit periods from *acronyms*—pronounceable words formed from the initial letters of the words in a name—such as:

NASA
WHO
DARE

Periods as Decimal Points

Use a period in decimal fractions and as a decimal point between dollars and cents:

6.079   69.8%
.05 $789.40

Question Mark

- Put a question mark at the end of a sentence that asks a direct question:

Correct   How many volunteers participated in the survey?

- Don't put a question mark at the end of an indirect question:

Incorrect The director asked how many volunteers participated in the survey?
Correct   The director asked how many volunteers participated in the survey.

- When a question mark appears within quotation marks, don't include any other end punctuation:

Correct   The director asked, "How many volunteers participated in the survey?"

Quotation Marks

Enclose short quotations and the titles of some published works in quotation marks. Most writers know when to use quotation marks but have trouble knowing how to use other marks of punctuation with them; therefore, this section presents conventions for punctuation that accompanies quotation marks.

Quotation Marks to Enclose Short Quotations

Enclose a quotation within quotation marks when it is short enough to fit within a sentence and takes up no more than three lines of text:

Correct   According to Thompson, "Monarch butterflies have reddish-brown, black-edged wings."

When a quotation is longer than three lines, follow these guidelines:

- Indent the quotation ten spaces from the left-hand margin.
- Omit the quotation marks. The indentation serves the same purpose as the quotation marks enclosing a short quotation.
- Introduce the quotation with a complete sentence followed by a colon.

Correct   Thompson (2000) writes the following about monarch butterflies:

> Monarch butterflies have reddish-brown, black-edged wings. The larvae of these butterflies feed on milkweed. These butterflies migrate hundreds of miles through North America. They have been sighted as far south as Mexico and as far north as Canada. (261)

Quotation Marks Around the Titles of Some Works

Place quotation marks around titles of articles from journals, newspapers, and other periodicals:

Correct   Tumminello and Carlshamre's article "An International Internet Collaboration" . . .

Conventional Punctuation with Quotation Marks

Follow the conventions presented below when using quotation marks with other punctuation.

- **Commas and periods.** Put commas and periods inside the quotation marks.

Correct	Joanna Tumminello and Pär Carlshamre wrote "An International Internet Collaboration."
Correct	He cited "An International Internet Collaboration," an article by Joanna Tumminello and Pär Carlshamre.

- **Semicolons and colons.** Put semicolons and colons outside the quotation marks.

Correct	Joanna Tumminello and Pär Carlshamre wrote "An International Internet Collaboration"; this article includes valuable information about collaborating to complete a research project.

- **Question marks, dashes, and exclamation points.** Put question marks, dashes, and exclamation points inside the quotation marks when they apply to the quoted material only and outside the quotation marks when they apply to the entire sentence.

Correct	She asked, "Have you completed the audit?" (inside)
Correct	Did she ask, "Have you completed the audit"? (outside)

Semicolon

Use semicolons in the following situations.

Semicolons to Link Independent Clauses

Place a semicolon between two independent clauses not linked by a coordinating conjunction (*and, or, nor, so, for, but, yet*):

Incorrect	The newest version of the software has more options; but it requires more memory and a faster processor.
Correct	The newest version of the software has more options; however, it requires more memory and a faster processor.

Semicolons to Separate Items in a Series

Use a semicolon to separate the items in a series when any one of the items already has internal punctuation:

Correct   The production team consists of the following people: Patrick Sims, managing editor; Norma Rowland, production editor; Gwen Chavez, copy editor; and Thomas Thompson, art editor.

▶Mechanics

Abbreviations

Use abbreviations judiciously because your readers may not be familiar with them. If your readers include people who are not experts in your field, avoid using abbreviations. If you must use abbreviations, attach a list explaining what each one means. Whenever you are uncertain about whether or how to use an abbreviation, spell out the term.

When you use abbreviations, follow these guidelines:

- Use the singular form for most units of measure even when the word would be plural if spelled out:

  psi   means either "pound per square inch" or "pounds per square inch"

  oz   means either "ounce" or "ounces"

- Use a period after the abbreviation for clarity if readers might confuse an abbreviation for some other word. Otherwise, generally omit the period from technical abbreviations. These abbreviations, for example, might require a period:

  in.   fig.   bar.

- Spell out short or common terms:

  ton

  acre

- Abbreviate units of measurement only when a number precedes them:

Incorrect	How many sq ft?
Correct	How many square feet?
Incorrect	10 square feet
Correct	10 sq ft

Capitalization

In technical communication, follow standard capitalization conventions. The conventions listed here are the most important ones; for a more complete list, consult your dictionary. Most dictionaries put the list in the end matter—after the list of words. You can also consult the style guides mentioned in Appendix A.

- Capitalize proper nouns, such as personal names, formal titles, place-names, languages, religions, organizations, days of the week, and months:

  Kathryn Sullivan (personal name)

  Chief Counsel (formal title)

  Europe (place-name)

  Chinese (language)

  Catholicism (religion)

  American Association of Mechanical Engineers (organization)

  Monday, Tuesday (days of the week)

  January, February (months)

- Don't capitalize seasons, compass directions (unless the reference is to a geographic region), and areas of study (unless the area already is a proper noun):

  winter, spring, summer, fall (seasons)

  We traveled north through Wyoming. (direction)

  The storm hit the Pacific Northwest. (geographic region)

  the study of language (area of study)

  the study of the French language (area of study)

- Capitalize the first word, the last word, and every important word in titles and headings:

  Technical Communication for Readers and Writers (title)

  Research on Electronic Mail and Other Media (heading)

  If you are using the titles in a list of references, follow the guidelines for that style—such as APA or MLA.

Italics

Instead of italics, you can use underlining, although most organizations and publishers prefer italics. Use italics or underlining in the following instances:

- For Latin scientific names:

  Lagerstroemia indica (crepe myrtle)

  Tryngites subruficollis (buff-breasted sandpiper)

- For the titles of books, plays, pamphlets, periodicals, manuals, radio and television programs, movies, newspapers, lengthy musical works, trains, airplanes, ships, and spacecraft:

  War and Peace (book)   *Madame Butterfly* (musical work)

  Hamlet (play)   *Titanic* (ship)

  60 Minutes (television program)   *Apollo V* (spacecraft)

  New York Times (newspaper)

- For foreign words that are not widely considered to be part of the English language:

  The county levied an *ad valorem* tax.

  Your dictionary may help you decide whether italics are necessary.

- For words, letters, and numbers referred to as such:

  Use the coordinating conjuctions *and, so, nor, but, yet, for, or.*

  The students should work on writing lowercase *a* and *d* and the number *8.*

Numbers

Rules for using numbers vary widely and in many instances differ from one field to another. Follow the standard practices of your field or organization, and use numbers consistently throughout each document. These guidelines will apply to most technical documents:

- When a number is the first word of a sentence, do not use numerals. Either spell out the number or, if you can't express it in two words, rewrite the sentence.

Incorrect	25 years ago, we began offering this degree.
Correct	Twenty-five years ago, we began offering this degree.
Incorrect	One thousand seventy-five of the 6,500 people we contacted returned the questionnaire.
Correct	Of the 6,500 people we contacted, 1,075 returned the questionnaire.

- Use numerals for days and years in dates, exact sums of money, exact times, addresses, percentages, statistics, scores, and units of measurement:

  March 31, 1999 or 31 March 1999 (dates)

  $6,432.58 (money)

  6:34 P.M. (time)

2600 St. Edwards Court (address)
67 percent or 67% (percentage)
a mean of 13 (statistic)
a total score of 98.7 (score)
37°F (unit of measurement)

- When mentioning rounded-off figures, use words:

  about five million dollars
  approximately nine o'clock

- When mentioning two different numbers back to back, use numerals for one and spell out the other:

  nine 2-inch screws

Correction Symbols

Common Sentence Errors

agr p	agreement error—pronoun and referent
agr sv	agreement error—subject and verb
cs	comma splice
dgl	dangling modifier
mm	misplaced modifier
ll	lack of parallelism
ro	run-on sentences
frag	sentence fragment
t	verb tense error

Punctuation

ap	apostrophe
[ ]/	brackets
:/	colon
,/	comma
—/	dash
!/	exclamation point
-/	hyphen
( )/	parentheses
./	period
?/	question mark
" "/	quotation marks
;/	semicolon

Mechanics

ab	abbreviation
cap	capitalization
ital	italics
num	numbers

WORKS CITED

"AECMA Simplified English Description." *AECMA.* 9 May 2002. <http://www.aecma.org/publications/senglish/sengbrc.htm>.

American National Standards Institute. "American National Standards for Product Safety Signs and Labels." American National Standards Institute, 1989.

Anderson, Paul. "What Survey Research Tells Us About Writing at Work." *Writing in Nonacademic Settings.* Ed. Lee Odell and Dixie Goswami. New York: Guilford, 1985. 3–84.

Baker, William H. "How to Produce and Communicate Structured Text." *Technical Communication* 41 (1994): 456–66.

Barabas, Christine. *Technical Writing in a Corporate Culture: A Study of the Nature of Information.* Norwood: Ablex, 1990.

Barnum, C., and R. Fischer. "Engineering Technology as Writers: Results of a Survey." *Technical Communication* 31.2 (1984): 9–11.

Beason, Gary. "Redefining Written Products with WWW Documentation: A Study of the Publication Process at a Computer Company." *Technical Communication* 43 (1996): 339–48.

Beauchamp, Tom L., and Norman E. Bowie. *Ethical Theory and Business.* 2nd ed. Englewood Cliffs: Prentice Hall, 1983.

Bellis, Jack. "Information: What Should Go Online and What Should Go in Print?" *Intercom* (Nov. 1996): 20–21.

Benson, Philippa J. "Writing Visually: Design Considerations in Technical Publications." *Technical Communication* 32.4 (1985): 35–39.

Blain, Jennifer, and Taylor Lincoln. "Make Yourself Essential." *Intercom* (April 1999): 9–11.

Bosley, Deborah S. "International Graphics: A Search for Neutral Territory." *Intercom* (Aug./Sept. 1996): 4–7.

Bradbury, S. Gayle. "Writing for the Web." *Intercom* (Nov. 2000): 24.

Braffman-Miller, Judith. "When Medicine Went Wrong: How Americans Were Used Illegally as Guinea Pigs.," *USA Today* March 1995: 84.

Brockmann, R. John. *Writing Better Computer User Documentation: From Paper to Hypertext Version* 2.0. New York: Wiley, 1990.

Caher, John M. "Technical Documentation and Legal Liability." *The Journal of Technical Writing and Communication* 25 (1995): 5–10.

Cash, J. I., Jr. "A New Farmers' Market." *InformationWeek* 26 Dec. 1994: 60.

Charney, Davida, Lynee Reder, and Gail Wells. "Studies of Elaboration in Instructional Texts." *Effective Documentation: What We Have Learned from Research.* Ed. Stephen Doheny-Farina. Cambridge: MIT, 1988. 47–72.

Cobb, Neil. E-mail interview. 8 Dec. 2001.

- - -. Telephone interview. 30 Aug. 1997.

Coleman. *Gas Barbecue Use, Care and Installation Manual.* Neosho: Coleman, 1999.

Daugherty, Shannon. "The Usability Evaluation: A Discount Approach to Usability Testing." *Intercom* (Dec. 1997): 16–20.

Dautermann, Jennie. "Writing with Electronic Tools in Midwestern Businesses." *Electronic Literacies in the Workplace: Technologies of Writing.* Ed. Patricia Sullivan and Jennie Dautermann. Urbana: NCTE, 1996.

Digital Equipment Co. *The Personal Computer Documenter's Guide.* Maynard: Digital Equipment, 1983.

Dombrowski, Paul. *Ethics in Technical Communication.* Needham Heights: Allyn & Bacon, 2000.

Dragga, Sam. "Classifications of Correspondence: Complexity Versus Simplicity." *The Technical Writing Teacher.* 18.1 (1991): 1–14.

Duin, Ann Hill. "How People Read: Implications for Writers." *The Technical Writing Teacher* 15 (1988): 185–93.

- - -. "Reading to Learn and Do." *Proceedings of the 35th International Technical Communication Conference, May 10–13, 1988, Philadelphia.* Washington: Society for Technical Communication, 1988.

Ede, Lisa, and Andrea Lunsford. *Singular Texts/Plural Authors: Perspectives on Collaborative Writing.* Carbondale: Southern Illinois UP, 1990.

Elbow, Peter. *Writing with Power: Techniques for Mastering the Writing Process.* Oxford: Oxford UP, 1981.

Farkas, David K., and Jean B. Farkas. "Guidelines for Designing Web Navigation." *Technical Communication* 47.3 (2000): 341–358.

Felker, Daniel B., et al. *Guidelines for Document Designers.* Washington: American Institutes for Research, 1981.

Foy, Patricia S. "The Reinvention of the Corporate Information Model." *IEEE Transactions on Professional Communication* 39 (1996): 23–29.

Fry, Pamela S. Informal interview. Oct. 1996.

Fugate, Alice E. "Writing for Your Web Site: What Works, and What Doesn't." *Intercom* (May 2001): 39–40.

Golen, Steven, Celeste Powers, and M. Agnes Titkemeyer. "How to Teach Ethics in a Basic Business Communication Class—Committee Report of the 1983 Teaching Methodology and Concepts Committee, Subcommittee 1." *Journal of Business Communication* 22.1 (1985): 75–83.

Gomes, Lee. "Advanced Computer Screens Have Age-Old Rival." *San Jose Mercury News* 21 Feb. 1994.

Greenly, Robert. "How to Write a Résumé." *Technical Communication* (1993): 42–48.

Hahn, Harley. "What Is Usenet?" 9 Nov. 2001. <http://www.harley.com/usenet/whatis-usenet.html>.

Halpern, J. W. "An Electronic Odyssey." *Writing in Nonacademic Settings.* Ed. Lee Odell and Dixie Goswami. New York: Guilford, 1985. 157–201.

Hansen, Amy. "Whatever Happened to the Traditional Résumé: Preparing Students for an Electronic Job Search." *ATTW Bulletin*.

Hansen, James B. "Editing Your Own Writing." *Intercom* (Feb. 1997): 14–16.

Hansen, Randall S., and Katherine Hansen. "The Importance of Good Writing Skills." 31 Aug. 2001. <http://www.quintcareers.co/writing/skills.html>.

Haramundanis, Katherine. *The Art of Technical Documentation*. Maynard: Digital Press, 1992.

Harris, Irene. "The 'Seven Commandments' of Keyboard Ergonomics." *Intercom* 43.10 (1996): 16–17.

Hayes, John R., and Linda S. Flower. "On the Structure of the Writing Process." *Topics in Language Disorders* 7 (1987): 19–30.

Helyar, Pamela S. "Product Liability: Meeting Legal Standards for Adequate Instructions." *Journal of Technical Writing and Communication* 22.2 (1992): 125–47.

Holland, V. Melissa, Veda R. Charrow, and William W. Wright. "How Can Technical Writers Write Effectively for Several Audiences at Once?" *Solving Problems in Technical Writing*. Ed. Lynn Beene and Peter White. New York: Oxford UP, 1988. 27–54.

Horton, William. "The Almost Universal Language: Graphics for International Documents." *Technical Communication* 40 (1993): 682–93.

Horton, William. *Illustrating Computer Documentation*. New York: Wiley, 1991.

- - -. "Overcoming Chromophobia: A Guide to the Confident and Appropriate Use of Color." *IEEE Transactions on Professional Communication* 34 (1991): 160–71.

Johnson-Eilola, Johndan. *Designing Effective Web Sites: A Concise Guide*. Boston: Houghton Mifflin, 2002.

- - -. "Relocating the Value of Work: Technical Communication in a Post-Industrial Age." *Technical Communication Quarterly* 5.3 (1996): 245–70.

Johnson, Melissa Ewey. "Managing for the Ages." *Cooking Light* (April 2001): 72–79.

Kellogg, Ronald T. "Attentional Overload and Writing Performance: Effects of Rough Draft and Outline Strategies." *Journal of Experimental Psychology: Learning, Memory, and Cognition* 14 (1988): 355–65.

Keyes, Elizabeth. "Typography, Color, and Information Structure." *Technical Communication* 40 (1993): 638–54.

Kintsch, Eileen. "Macroprocesses and Microprocesses in the Development of Summarization Skill." ERIC Document ED305613. Washington: Educational Research Information Center, 1989.

Kleimann, Susan. "The Reciprocal Relationship of Workplace Culture and Review." *Writing in the Workplace: New Research Perspectives*. Ed. Rachel Spilka. Carbondale: Southern Illinois UP, 1993. 56–70.

Klein, Fred. "Beyond Technical Translation: Localization." *Intercom* (May 1997): 32–33.

Koop, W. E., and R. L. Duble. *Thatch Control in Home Lawns.* College Station: Texas Agricultural Extension Service, 1982.

Kratts, Aimee. "Running a Successful International Teleconference." *Intercom* (May 2001): 18–19.

Krull, Robert, and Jeanne M. Hurford. "Can Computers Increase Writing Productivity?" *Technical Communication* 34 (1987): 243–49.

Krull, Robert, and Philip Rubens. "Effects of Color Highlighting on User Performance with Online Information." 33 (1986): 268–69.

Lakoff, R. T. "Some of My Favorite Writers Are Literate: The Mingling of Oral and Literate Strategies in Written Communication." *Spoken and Written Language.* Ed. D. Tannen. Advances in Discourse Processes, Series 9. Norwood: Ablex, 1982: 239–60.

LaQuey, Tracy. *The Internet Companion: A Beginner's Guide to Global Networking.* Reading, MA: Addison, 1994.

Lawrence, Steve and Lee Giles. "Accessibility of Information on the Web." *Nature.* 400 (1999): 107–09.

Lay, Mary M. "Nonrhetorical Elements of Layout and Design." *Technical Writing: Theory and Practice.* Ed. Bertie E. Fearing and W. Keats Sparrow. (New York: MLA, 1989): 72–89.

Le Vie, Donald S., Jr. "Internet Technology and Intellectual Property." *Intercom* (Jan. 2000): 20–23.

Li-Ron, Yael. "Office Assistant: Dog or Genius?" *PC World Online Edition* (April 1998).

Locker, Kitty O. *Business and Administrative Communication.* Homewood: Irwin, 1989.

Lorch, Robert F., and Elizabeth Pugzles Lorch. "Online Processing of Text Organization." ERIC Document ED245210. Washington: Educational Research Information Center, 1984.

Mannix, Margaret. "Writing a Computer-Friendly Résumé: The Old Rules of Presenting Yourself Might Now Hurt." *U.S. News and World Report* 26 Oct. 1992: 90–93.

"Marketers Should Target Online Seniors." 29 Aug. 2001. <http://www.nua.ie/surveys/index.cgi>.

Martin, Cynthia J. "Individually and as Executrix of Eugene J. Martin, Deceased, v. Arthur Hacker, et al., and Chelsea Laboratories, Inc., et al." *83 NY2nd I* 23 Nov. 1993.

Martinez, Benjamin, and Jacqueline Block. *Visual Forces.* Englewood Cliffs: Prentice Hall, 1988.

Mirshafiei, Mohsen. "Culture as an Element in Teaching Technical Writing." *Technical Communication* 41.2 (1994): 276–82.

National Council of Teachers of English. *Guidelines for Nonsexist Use of Language in NCTE Publications.* Rev. ed. Urbana: NCTE, 1985.

Neilsen, Jakob. "The Web Backlash of 1996." 18 Sept. 1997. <http://www.useit.com/alertbox/9604.html>.

Ong, W. J. "Literacy and Orality in Our Times." *The Writing Teacher's Sourcebook.* Ed. G. Tate and Edward P. J. Corbett. New York: Oxford UP, 1981. 36–48.

Parker, Roger, and Patrick Berry. *Looking Good in Print.* 4th ed. Scottsdale: The Coriolis Group, 1998.

Parson, Gerald M. "A Cautionary Legal Tale: The Bose v. Consumers Union Case." *The Journal of Technical Writing and Communication* 22 (1992): 377–86.

Perl, Sondra. "The Composing Processes of Unskilled College Writers." *Research in the Teaching of English* 13 (1979): 317–36.

Perry, T. S. "E-Mail at Work." *IEEE Spectrum* (Oct. 1992): 24–28.

Perry, T. S., and J. A. Adam. "E-Mail Pervasive and Persuasive." *IEEE Spectrum* Oct. 1992: 22–23.

Pfeiffer, William S. *Pocket Guide to Public Speaking.* Upper Saddle River: Prentice Hall, 2002.

Pugh, A. "The Development of Silent Reading." *The Road to Effective Reading.* Ed. W. Latham. London: Ward Lock, 1975.

Raign, Kathryn, and Brenda Sims. "Gender, Persuasion Techniques, and Collaboration." *Technical Communication Quarterly* 2.1 (1993): 89–104.

Raytheon. "Decision-Making Model." 1 Dec. 2001. <http://www.raytheon.com/ethics/decmod.htm>.

Raytheon. "Ethics Quick Test." 1 Dec. 2001. <http://www.raytheon.com/ethics/qtest.htm>.

Redish, Janice C., and David A. Schell. "Writing and Testing Instructions for Usability." In *Technical Writing Theory and Practice.* Eds. Bertie E. Fearing and W. Keats Sparrow. New York: Modern Language Association, 1987: 61–71.

Redish, Janice (Ginny). "Adding Value as a Professional Technical Communicator." *Technical Communication* 42.1 (1995): 26–39.

Reich, Robert B. *The Work of Nations: Preparing Ourselves for 21st-Century Capitalism.* New York: Knopf, 1991.

Reid, Shannon. Interview. 6 Nov. 2001.

Rogers, David J., and Monica C. Perri. "E-Mail and Tattoos: A Primer on Netiquette." *Intercom* (Dec. 2000): 10–11.

Rubens, Philip M. "Reinventing the Wheel? Ethics for Technical Communicators." *Journal of Technical Writing and Communication* 11 (1981): 329–39.

Samuels, Marilyn Schauer. "Scientific Logic: A Reader-Oriented Approach to Technical Writing." *Journal of Technical Writing and Communication* 12.4 (1982): 307–28.

Selzer, Jack. "Arranging Business Prose." *Writing in the Business Professions.* Ed. Myra Kogen. Urbana: NCTE, 1989.

Shimberg, H. Lee. "Technical Communicators and Moral Ethics." *Technical Communication* 27 (1980): 10–12.

Shroyer, Roberta. "Actual Readers Versus Implied Readers: Role Conflicts in Office 97." *Technical Communication* 47.2 (2000): 238–40.

Simon, Jerold. "How to Write a Résumé." N.p.: International Paper Company, 1981.

Sims, Brenda R. "Electronic Mail in Two Corporate Workplaces." *Electronic Literacies in the Workplace: Technologies of Writing.* Eds. Patricia Sullivan and Jennie Dautermann. Urbana: NCTE, 1996. 41–64.

- - -. "Linking Ethics and Language in the Technical Communication Classroom." *Technical Communication Quarterly* 2.3 (1993): 285–99.

Sims, Brenda R., and Stephen Guice. "Differences between Business Letters from Native and Non-Native Speakers of English." 29.1 (1992): 23–39.

Sims, William W. Personal interview. 12 Feb. 1997.

Spivey, Nancy Nelson, and James R. King. "Readers as Writers Composing from Sources." *Reading Research Quarterly* 24.1 (1989): 7–26.

Spyridakis, Jan H. "Guidelines for Authoring Comprehensible Web Pages and Evaluating Their Success." *Technical Communication* 47.3 (2000): 359–382.

Stein, Judith, and JoAnne Yates. "Electronic Mail: How Will It Change Office Communication? How Can Managers Use It Effectively?" *Information Systems and Business Communication.* Eds. Raymond W. Beswick and Alfred B. Williams. Urbana: American Business Communication Assn., 1983. 99–105.

Sticht, T. "Understanding Readers and Their Uses of Text." *Designing Usable Texts.* Orlando: Academic Press, 1985.

Sticht, T., L. Fox, R. Hauke, and D. Welty-Zapf. *The Role of Reading in the Navy.* San Diego: Navy Personnel R and D Center, 1977.

Taylor, Barbara M., and Richard W. Beach. "The Effects of Text Structure Instruction on Middle-Grade Students' Comprehension and Production of Expository Text." *Reading Research Quarterly* 19.2 (1984): 134–46.

Thomas, L. *The Self-Organized Learner and the Printed Page.* Cambridge: Brunel University Centre for the Study of Human Learning, 1976.

Tumminello, Joanna, and Pär Carlshamre. "An International Internet Collaboration." *Technical Communication* 43.4 (1996): 413–18.

University of Maryland Baltimore County. "A Survey of the Frequency, Types, and Importance of Writing Tasks in Four Career Areas." 29 Aug. 2001. <http://userpages.umbc.edu/~rachd1/oral.html>.

Walinskas, Karl. "Reading Your Audience." *Intercom* (Dec. 2001): 23–24.

Wambeam, Cynthia A., and Robert Kramer. "Design Teams and the Web: A Collaborative Model for the Workplace." *Technical Communication* 43.4 (1996): 349–56.

Weber, Jean H. "Taming a Telecommuting Team." *Intercom* (Aug./Sept. 1996): 22–23.

White, Jan. *Visual Design for the Electronic Age.* New York: Watson-Guptill, 1988.

Wicclair, Mark R., and David K. Farkas. "Ethical Reasoning in Technical Communication: A Practical Framework." *Technical Communication* 31 (1984): 15–19.

Wilkinson, Theresa A. "How to Increase Performance on a Web Site." *Intercom* 47.1 (2000): 38, 40.

Williams, Joseph M. *Style: Ten Lessons in Clarity and Grace.* 6 ed. New York: Longman, 2000.

Wilson, Gina. E-mail interview. 20 Nov. 2001.

Winsor, Dorothy A. "The Construction of Knowledge in Organizations: Asking the Right Questions about the *Challenger*." *Journal of Business and Technical Communication* 4.2 (1990): 7–20.

Yeo, Sarah C. "Designing Web Pages That Bring Them Back." *Intercom* 43.3 (1996): 12–14.

Zemke, Ron, Claire Raines, and Bob Filipczak. *Generations at Work: Managing the Clash of Veterans, Boomers, Xers, and Nexters in Your Workplace.* Minneapolis: Performance Research Associates, 2000.

Zimmerman, Donald E., Michel Lynn Muraski, and Michael D. Slater. "Taking Usability Testing to the Field." *Technical Communication* 46.4 (1999): 495–500.